LAW AND LAW ENFORCEMENT ISSUES

LAW AND LAW ENFORCEMENT ISSUES

GERALD M. KESSLER
EDITOR

Nova Science Publishers, Inc.
New York

For permission to use material from this book please contact us:
Telephone 631-231-7269; Fax 631-231-8175
Web Site: http://www.novapublishers.com

LIBRARY OF CONGRESS CATALOGING-IN-PUBLICATION DATA

Law and law enforcement issues / Gerald M. Kessler, editor.
p. cm.
ISBN 978-1-60456-044-2 (hardcover)
1. Criminal justice. Administration of–United States. I. Kessler, Gerald M.
KF9223.A75L377 2007
345.73'052--dc22
2007038574

Published by Nova Science Publishers, Inc. ✦ New York

CONTENTS

PREFACE

This new book presents important issues and developments in the law and law enforcement field including both federal and international laws and law enforcement.

Chapter 1 - This article provides a brief overview of Federal statutes and where to find them, both in hard copy and on the Internet. When Congress passes a law, it may be amending or repealing earlier enactments or it may be writing on a clean slate. Newly enacted laws are published chronologically, first as separate statutes (in "slip law" form) and, later, cumulatively in a series of volumes known as the Statutes At Large. Statutes are numbered by order of enactment either as Public Laws or, far less frequently, Private Laws, depending on their scope. Additionally, most statutes are also incorporated separately into the United States Code. The United States Code (and its commercial counterparts) takes those Federal statutes that are of a general and permanent nature and arranges them by subject into separate titles. As the statutes that underlay the Code are revised, superceded, or repealed, the provisions of the Code are updated to reflect these changes.

Slip law versions of Public Laws are not widely available in hard copy form outside Capitol Hill except at university libraries, law school libraries, or similar depositories (though these often have slip laws in microfiche format only). They are more readily available on the Internet. Statutes At Large is used primarily to research the original language of statutes and laws that are not codified in the Code, appropriations statutes and private laws, for example. The Statutes At Large series often is available at large libraries. The United States Code (and its commercial counterparts) are usually available at local libraries. The Code also is readily available on the Internet, though not always in user-friendly form.

Most significant statutes – the Social SecurityAct, the Elementary and Secondary Education Act, and the Clean Air Act, for example – are published and updated both in a stand alone version, as amended, and as they appear in the Code. Only some, but not all, titles of the Code are the authoritative version of the "law." For other titles, the authoritative version of the statutes codified therein is the underlying public law, as amended – *e.g.*, the Immigration and Nationality Act of 1952, as amended, is the authoritative version, not title 8 of the Code.

After providing an overview on the basics of Federal statutes, this article gives guidance on where Federal statutes, in their various forms, may be located on the Internet, where they are most readily accessible.

Chapter 2 - Declaring it necessary to bring to justice those responsible for the terrorist attacks on the United States of September 11, 2001, President Bush signed a Military Order

(M.O.) authorizing the trial by military commission of certain non-citizens. The order directs the Secretary of Defense to establish the procedural rules for the operation of the military commissions convened pursuant to the M.O. The Department of Defense prepared regulations providing for procedures of military commissions, but these were invalidated by the Supreme Court in *Hamdan v. Rumsfeld*. The Bush Administration has proposed legislation to reinstate military commissions for the trials of suspected terrorists.

This article provides a brief overview of procedural rules applicable in selected historical and contemporary tribunals for the trials of war crimes suspects.

Chapter 3 - On April 11, 2002, the Rome Statute of the International Criminal Court received its sixtieth ratification, meaning it will come into effect July 1, 2002, establishing the first global permanent international court with jurisdiction to prosecute individuals for "the most serious crimes of concern to the international community." The United Nations, many human rights organizations, and most democratic nations have expressed support for the new court. The Bush Administration firmly opposes it and has formally renounced the U.S. obligations under the treaty. At the same time, however, the Administration has stressed that the United States shares the goal of the ICC's supporters – promotion of the rule of law – and does not intend to take any action to undermine the ICC.

The primary objection given by the United States in opposition to the treaty is the ICC's possible assertion of jurisdiction over U.S. soldiers charged with "war crimes" resulting from legitimate uses of force. The main issue faced by the current Congress is whether to adopt a policy aimed at preventing the ICC from becoming effective or whether to continue contributing to the development of the ICC in order to improve it.

This article provides an historical background of the negotiations for the Rome Statute, outlines the structure of the ICC as contained in the final Statute, and describes the jurisdiction of the ICC. The report identifies the specific crimes enumerated in the Rome Statute as supplemented by the draft elements of crime. A discussion of procedural safeguards follows, including reference to the draft procedural rules. The report then discusses the implications for the United States as a non-ratifying country when the ICC comes into being, and outlines some legislation enacted and proposed to regulate U.S. relations with the ICC, including versions of the American Servicemembers' Protection Act (ASPA) contained in H.R. 1646 and H.R. 4775, the American Servicemember and Citizen Protection Act, H.R. 4169, and the American Citizens' Protection and War Criminal Prosecution Act of 2001, S. 1296/H.R. 2699.

Chapter 4 - One month after the International Criminal Court (ICC) officially came into existence on July 1, 2002, the President signed legislation that limits U.S. government support and assistance to the ICC; curtails certain military assistance to many countries that have ratified the Rome Statute establishing the ICC; regulates U.S. participation in United Nations (U.N.) peacekeeping missions commenced after July 1, 2003; and, most controversially among European allies, authorizes the President to use "all means necessary and appropriate to bring about the release" of certain U.S. and allied persons who may be detained or tried by the ICC. The provision withholding military assistance under the programs for Foreign Military Financing (FMF) and International Military Education and Training (IMET) from certain States Parties to the Rome Statute came into effect on July 1, 2003. The 109th Congress reauthorized the Nethercutt Amendment as part of the FY2006 Consolidated Appropriations Act (H.R. 3057/P.L. 109-102). Unless waived by the President, it bars Economic Support Funds (ESF) assistance to countries that have not agreed to protect U.S.

citizens from being turned over to the ICC for prosecution. H.R. 5522 would continue the prohibitions for FY2007.

The ICC is the first permanent world court with nearly universal jurisdiction to try individuals accused of war crimes, crimes against humanity, genocide, and possibly aggression. While most U.S. allies support the ICC, the Bush Administration firmly opposes it and has renounced any U.S. obligations under the treaty. After the Bush Administration threatened to veto a United Nations Security Council resolution to extend the peacekeeping mission in Bosnia on the ground that it did not contain sufficient guarantees that U.S. participants would be immune to prosecution by the ICC, the Security Council adopted a resolution that would defer for one year any prosecution of participants in missions established or authorized by the U.N. whose home countries have not ratified the Rome Statute. That resolution was renewed through July 1, 2004, but was not subsequently renewed. In addition, the United States is pursuing bilateral "Article 98"agreements to preclude extradition by other countries of U.S. citizens to the ICC. However, in what some view as a sign that the Administration is softening its stance with respect to the ICC, the United States did not exercise its veto power at the Security Council to prevent the referral of a case against Sudan's leaders for the alleged genocide in Darfur.

This article outlines the main objections the United States has raised with respect to the ICC and analyzes the American Servicemembers' Protection Act (ASPA), enacted to regulate the U.S. cooperation with the ICC. The report concludes with a discussion of the implications for the United States, as a non-ratifying country, as the ICC begins to take shape, as well as the Administration's efforts to win immunity from the ICC's jurisdiction for Americans. A description of the ICC's background and a more detailed analysis of the ICC organization, jurisdiction, and procedural rules may be found in CRS Report RL31437, *International Criminal Court: Overview and Selected Legal Issues*, by Jennifer K. Elsea.

Chapter 5 - November 13, 2001, President Bush issued a Military Order (M.O.) pertaining to the detention, treatment, and trial of certain non-citizens in the war against terrorism. Military commissions pursuant to the M.O. began in November, 2004, against four persons declared eligible for trial, but proceedings were suspended after a federal district court found one of the defendants could not be tried under the rules established by the Department of Defense. The D.C. Circuit Court of Appeals reversed that decision, *Rumsfeld v. Hamdan*, but the Supreme Court granted review and reversed the decision of the Court of Appeals. Military commissions will not be able to go forward until the Department of Defense revises its rules to conform with the Supreme Court's *Hamdan* opinion or Congress approves legislation conferring authority to promulgate rules that depart from the strictures of the Uniform Code of Military Justice (UCMJ) and U.S. international obligations.

The M.O. has been the focus of intense debate both at home and abroad. Critics argued that the tribunals could violate the rights of the accused under the Constitution as well as international law, thereby undercutting the legitimacy of any verdicts rendered by the tribunals. The Administration responded by publishing a series of military orders and instructions clarifying some of the details. The procedural aspects of the trials were published in Military Commission Order No. 1 ("M.C.O. No. 1"). The Department of Defense also released two more orders and nine "Military Commission Instructions," which set forth the elements of some crimes that may be tried, establish guidelines for civilian attorneys, and provide other administrative guidance. These rules were praised as a significant improvement over what might have been permitted under the M.O., but some argued that the enhancements do not go far enough, and the Supreme Court held that the amended rules did not comply with the UCMJ.

This article provides a background and analysis comparing military commissions as envisioned under M.C.O. No. 1 to general military courts-martial conducted under the UCMJ. A summary of the *Hamdan* case follows, in particular the shortcomings identified by the Supreme Court. The report provides an overview of relevant legislation (H.R. 3044, H.R. 3038, and S. 3614). Finally, the report provides two charts to compare the regulations issued by the Department of Defense to standard procedures for general courts-martial under the Manual for Courts-Martial and to proposed legislation. The second chart, which compares procedural safeguards incorporated in the regulations with established procedures in courts-martial, follows the same order and format used in CRS Report RL31262, *Selected Procedural Safeguards in Federal, Military, and International Courts*, in order to facilitate comparison with safeguards provided in federal court and international criminal tribunals.

Chapter 6 - Federal court denial of British extradition requests in the cases of four fugitives from Northern Ireland led to the Supplementary Extradition Treaty. The Treaty proved controversial, and before the Senate would give its consent, it insisted upon modifications, some quite unusual. Those modifications have been eliminated in a newly negotiated treaty to which the Senate has recently given its advice and consent and which incorporates features often more characteristic of contemporary extradition treaties with other countries.

There was initial criticism of the new Treaty's

- exemptions to the political offense bar to extradition;
- elimination of judicial inquiry into politically motivated extradition request;
- treatment of probable cause;
- clause relating to extradition for crimes committed overseas;
- dropping the statute of limitations defense;
- discretionary authority for provisional arrest and detention;
- language relating to the seizure of assets;
- exceptions to the rule of speciality (permitting prosecution for crimes other than those for which extradition was granted); and retroactive application.

The Treaty also contains articles relating to capital punishment, waiver of extradition, extradition involving third countries, double jeopardy, the elimination of nationality as a bar to extradition, translations, and deferred prosecution.

The Senate conditioned its approval of the Treaty upon an understanding, two declarations and three provisos which relate to the Treaty's treatment of the exception for politically motivated requests and the role of the courts, its changes in the double jeopardy clause, assurances that the Treaty is not designed to accomplish the extradition of fugitives from Northern Ireland covered by the Belfast/Good Friday Agreement, and reporting requirements concerning the disposition of requests under the Treaty.

Chapter 7 - Almost all assessments of the attacks of September 11, 2001, have concluded that U.S. intelligence and law enforcement agencies had failed to share information that might have provided advance warning of the plot. This realization led Congress to approve provisions in the USA PATRIOT Act (P.L. 107-56) and subsequent legislation that removed barriers to information sharing between intelligence and law enforcement agencies, and mandated exchanges of information relating to terrorist threats. Most experts agreed that statutory changes, albeit difficult to enact, were essential to change the approaches taken by executive branch agencies.

The barriers that existed prior to September 2001 had a long history based on a determination to prevent government spying on U.S. persons. This had led to the establishment of high statutory barriers to the sharing of law enforcement and intelligence information. The statutes laid the foundation of the so-called "wall" between intelligence and law enforcement that was buttressed by regulations, Justice Department policies, and guidance from the judicial branch.

Despite the widespread acceptance of a barrier between law enforcement and intelligence, by the early 1990s it had become apparent to some that the two communities could mutually support efforts to combat international criminal activities including narcotics smuggling. Later in the decade dangerous threats to the U.S. posed by international terrorists came into sharper focus. Nevertheless, efforts to adjust laws, regulations, and practices did not succeed, drawing strong opposition from civil libertarians. Only the tragedy of the 9/11 attacks overcame earlier concerns and led Congress and the executive branch to remove most statutory barriers to information sharing.

Laws and regulations have changed significantly since September 2001 and an Information Sharing Executive (ISE) has been established within the Office of the Director of National Intelligence to design and implement information sharing procedures. It is clear, however, that sustaining the exchange of law enforcement and intelligence information remains a challenge. In particular, there is continued concern about sharing of information that might in some way jeopardize the rights of free speech or association of U.S. persons. This opposition has contributed to the difficulty Congress has had in addressing legislation in this area and can be expected to continue. Some argue that, given the extent of legislation enacted in recent years, extensive oversight of information sharing efforts may be an appropriate way to ensure that the balance between ensuring domestic security and protecting civil liberties can be maintained.

Chapter 8 - This article discusses the federal statutory protections contained within the Whistleblower Protection Act (WPA) for federal employees who engage in "whistleblowing," that is, making a disclosure evidencing illegal or improper government activities. The protections of the WPA apply to most federal executive branch employees and become applicable where a "personnel action" is taken "because of" a "protected disclosure" made by a "covered employee." Generally, whistleblower protections may be raised within four forums or proceedings: (1) employee appeals to the Merit Systems Protection Board of an agency's adverse action against an employee, known as "Chapter 77" appeals; (2) actions instituted by the Office of Special Counsel; (3) individually maintained rights of action before the Merit Systems Protection Board (known as an individual right of action, or IRA); and (4) grievances brought by the employee under negotiated grievance procedures.

On March 9, 2007, the House Committee on Oversight and Government Reform reported H.R. 985 (110th Cong.) H.Rept. 110-42, the Whistleblower Protection Enhancement Act of 2007, which would amend the WPA by providing protections for certain national security, government contractor, and science-based agency whistleblowers, and by enhancing the existing whistleblower protections for all federal employees.

Chapter 9 - This article tracks nominations made by President George W. Bush to judgeships on the U.S. courts of appeals, the U.S. district courts, and the U.S. Court of

International Trade — the lower courts on which, pursuant to Article III of the Constitution, judges serve "during good Behaviour." It lists and keeps count of all nominations made to these courts during the 110th Congress, including pertinent actions taken by the Senate Judiciary Committee and the full Senate. It also tracks the number of judicial vacancies on the courts (including vacancies classified by the federal judiciary as "judicial emergencies"), the number of nominations pending to fill the vacancies, and the names of the pending nominees. Last, the report presents the total number of persons nominated by President Bush to each category of lower Article III court during his entire presidency (breaking down each total to show the number confirmed, pending, returned and not re-nominated, and withdrawn).

As of April 9, 2007:

- President Bush had nominated eight individuals to judgeships on the U.S. courts of appeals during the 110th Congress, with the Senate having confirmed two of them.
- President Bush had nominated 36 individuals to U.S. district court judgeships during the 110th Congress, with the Senate having confirmed 13 of them.
- There were 14 judicial vacancies on the U.S. courts of appeals, with six nominations pending to fill these vacancies.
- There were 33 U.S. district court vacancies, with 21 nominations pending to fill these judgeships, and an additional two nominations pending to fill future district court vacancies.
- No vacancies had occurred on the U.S. Court of International Trade during the 110th Congress (and thus no nominations have been made to the court during the Congress).
- During his entire presidency (from January 20, 2001 to the present), President Bush had made 315 nominations to Article III lower court judgeships. Of the 315 total, 271 had received Senate confirmation, 29 were pending in the 110th Congress, nine had been returned to the President in a previous Congress and not resubmitted, and six had been withdrawn by the President.

For corresponding information about President Bush's appeals and district court nominations during earlier Congresses, see CRS Report RL31868, *U.S. Circuit and District Court Nominations by President George W. Bush During the 107th-109th Congresses*, by Denis Steven Rutkus, Kevin M. Scott, and Maureen Bearden.

Chapter 10 - United States attorneys, who prosecute violations of federal law and defend the federal government in civil suits, are nominated by the President and confirmed by the Senate, and, once confirmed, serve four-year terms. The President may terminate the appointment of a U.S. attorney at any time. Recent controversy over the termination of seven U.S. attorneys, and the method by which the interim appointments were made to replace them, has focused attention on reasons for departure of U.S. attorneys.

This article provides data on U.S. attorneys who did not complete their full four-year term after confirmation by the Senate and whose terms did not carry over a change in presidential administration. The data collected employ records of presidential appointment and Senate confirmation of U.S. attorneys, and rely on secondary sources to provide information on reasons U.S. attorneys left office before completion of their four-year terms.

At least 54 U.S. attorneys appointed by the President and confirmed by the Senate left office before completion of a four-year term between 1981 and 2006 (not counting those whose tenure was interrupted by a change in presidential administration). Of those 54, 17 left to become Article III federal judges, one left to become a federal magistrate judge, six left to serve in other positions in the executive branch, four sought elective office, two left to serve in state government, one died, and 15 left to enter or return to private practice.

Of the remaining eight U.S. attorneys who left before completing a four-year term without a change in presidential administration, two were apparently dismissed by the President, and three apparently resigned after news reports indicated they had engaged in questionable personal actions. No information was available on the three remaining U.S. attorneys who resigned.

Interim U.S. attorneys are appointed by the Attorney General and serve until the President nominates, and the Senate confirms, a successor. Legislation has been introduced in the 110th Congress (H.R. 580; S. 214) to revert the system of appointment of interim U.S. attorneys to the system in place from 1986 to 2006. Under that system, the appointment of an interim U.S. attorney by the Attorney General expired after 120 days. After that appointment expired, district courts could appoint interim U.S. attorneys who could serve until the President nominated, and the Senate confirmed, a permanent replacement.

Chapter 11 - In the United States, the general rule, which derives from common law, is that each side in a legal proceeding pays for its own attorney. There are many exceptions, however, in which federal courts, and occasionally federal agencies, may order the losing party to pay the attorneys' fees of the prevailing party. The major common law exception authorizes federal courts (not agencies) to order a losing party that acts in bad faith to pay the prevailing party's fees.

There are also roughly two hundred statutory exceptions, which were generally enacted to encourage private litigation to implement public policy. Awards of attorneys' fees are often designed to help to equalize contests between private individual plaintiffs and corporate or governmental defendants. Thus, attorneys' fees provisions are most often found in civil rights, environmental protection, and consumer protection statutes.

In addition, the Equal Access to Justice Act (EAJA) makes the United States liable for attorneys' fees of up to $125 per hour in many court cases and administrative proceedings that it loses (and some that it wins) and fails to prove that its position was substantially justified. EAJA does not apply in tax cases, but a similar statute, 26 U.S.C. § 7430, does.

Most Supreme Court decisions involving attorneys' fees have interpreted civil rights statutes, and this article focuses on these statutes. It also discusses awards of costs other than attorneys' fees in federal courts, how courts compute the amount of attorneys' fees to be awarded, statutory limitations on attorneys' fees, and other subjects. In addition, it sets forth the language of all federal attorneys' fees provisions, and includes a bibliography of congressional committee reports and hearings concerning attorneys' fees.

In 1997, Congress enacted a statute allowing awards of attorneys' fees to some prevailing criminal defendants.

Chapter 12 - As more attention is being focused on juvenile offenders, some question whether the justice system is dealing with this population appropriately. Since the late 1960s, the juvenile justice system has undergone significant modifications resulting from U.S. Supreme Court decisions, changes in federal and state law, and the growing belief that juveniles were increasingly involved in more serious and violent crimes. Consequently, at both the federal and states levels, the juvenile justice system has shifted from a mostly rehabilitative system to a more punitive one, with serious ramifications for juvenile offenders. Despite this shift, juveniles are generally not afforded the panoply of rights afforded to adult criminal defendants. The U.S. Constitution requires that juveniles receive many of the features of an adult criminal trial, including notice of charges, right to counsel, privilege against self-incrimination, right to confrontation and cross-examination, proof beyond a reasonable doubt, and double jeopardy. However, in *McKeiver v. Pennsylvania*, the Court held that juveniles do not have a fundamental right to a jury trial during adjudicatory proceedings.

The Sixth Amendment explicitly guarantees the right to an impartial jury trial in criminal prosecutions. In *Duncan v. Louisiana*, the U.S. Supreme Court held that this right is fundamental and guaranteed by the Due Process Clause of the Fourteenth Amendment. However, the Court has since limited its holding in *Duncan* to adult defendants by stating that the right to a jury trial is not constitutionally required for juveniles in juvenile court proceedings. Some argue that because the Court has determined that jury trials are not constitutionally required for juvenile adjudications, courts should not treat or consider juvenile adjudications in subsequent criminal proceedings. In addition, some argue that the use of non-jury juvenile adjudications in subsequent criminal proceedings violates due process guarantees, because juvenile justice and adult criminal proceedings are fundamentally different.

Has the juvenile justice system changed in such a manner that the Supreme Court should revisit the question of jury trials in juvenile adjudications? Are the procedural safeguards in the juvenile justice system sufficient to ensure their reliable use for sentence enhancement purposes in adult criminal proceedings? To help address these questions, this article provides a brief background on the purpose of the juvenile system and discusses procedural due process protections provided by the Court for juveniles during adjudicatory hearings. It also discusses the Court's emphasis on the jury's role in criminal.

Chapter 13 - With recent U.S. Supreme Court decisions regarding the role of judges and juries in making factual determinations upon which sentences are made, there has been increased congressional interest in federal sentencing. One aspect of federal sentencing includes recidivism statutes that provide longer sentences for repeat offenders. One such statute, the Armed Career Criminal Act (ACCA), requires imposition of a 15-year prison sentence for an individual with prior serious drug or violent felony convictions. Under the ACCA, non-jury juvenile adjudications qualify as prior convictions. The use of these non-jury juvenile adjudications raises several constitutional due process questions and continues to spark debate among courts at the federal and state levels. Opinions vary, in part, because of conflicting interpretations of the U.S. Supreme Court's jury trial jurisprudence stressing the constitutional requirement of juries, rather than judges, making factual determinations upon which sentences are based. This article summarizes the competing views on the constitutionality of the use of non-jury juvenile adjudications in subsequent criminal proceedings.

The Armed Career Criminal Act (ACCA) requires imposition of a minimum 15-year term of imprisonment for unlawful possession of a firearm in violation of 18 U.S.C. § 922(g) by an individual with three prior serious drug or violent felony convictions. The ACCA defines "conviction" to include "a finding that a person has committed an act of juvenile delinquency involving a violent felony." Defendants have begun to challenge, with mixed results, the courts' ability to use non-jury juvenile adjudications as a prior conviction under the ACCA. Opinions vary, in part, because of conflicting interpretations of the U.S. Supreme Court's recent jury trial jurisprudence, as well as the the nature of juvenile court proceedings.

In a series of cases, the U.S. Supreme Court has held that given the Sixth Amendment right to trial by jury, judges cannot impose sentences beyond the prescribed statutory maximum unless the facts supporting such an increase are found by a jury beyond a reasonable doubt. In *Jones v. United States*, the Court struck down the federal carjacking statute that enhanced the maximum prison sentence that Nathaniel Jones could receive depending upon the amount of bodily injury that accompanied the carjacking. In *Jones*, it was the sentencing judge, not a jury, who found the victims incurred serious bodily injury and imposed a prison sentence of 25 years. The *Jones* majority held that

> under the Due Process Clause of the Fifth Amendment and the notice and jury trial guarantees of the Sixth Amendment, any fact (other than a prior conviction) that increases the maximum penalty for a crime must be charged in an indictment, submitted to a jury, and proven beyond a reasonable doubt.

Apprendi v. New Jersey (*Apprendi*) reaffirmed *Jones* by holding that "other than the fact of a prior conviction, any fact that increases the penalty for a crime beyond the prescribed statutory maximum must be submitted to a jury, and proved beyond a reasonable doubt." In *Apprendi*, the Court struck down New Jersey's hate crime law, which allowed a judge to increase a sentence to double the statutory maximum if he or she found, by a preponderance of the evidence, that the defendant acted with a purpose to intimidate an individual or group of individuals because of race. In reversing the lower court's decision, the Court declared that the jury trial and notification clauses of the Sixth Amendment and the due process clauses of the Fifth and Fourteenth Amendments embody a principle that insists that, except in the case of recidivists, a judge could not on his own findings sentence a criminal defendant to a term of imprisonment greater than the statutory maximum assigned for which he had been convicted by the jury. The *Apprendi* Court specifically held that its "prior conviction" exception was a narrow one.

In: Law and Law Enforcement Issues
Editor: Gerald M. Kessler, pp. 1-9
ISBN: 978-1-60456-044-2

Chapter 1

FEDERAL STATUTES: WHAT THEY ARE AND WHERE TO FIND THEM*

Mark Gurevitz

ABSTRACT

This article provides a brief overview of Federal statutes and where to find them, both in hard copy and on the Internet. When Congress passes a law, it may be amending or repealing earlier enactments or it may be writing on a clean slate. Newly enacted laws are published chronologically, first as separate statutes (in "slip law" form) and, later, cumulatively in a series of volumes known as the Statutes At Large. Statutes are numbered by order of enactment either as Public Laws or, far less frequently, Private Laws, depending on their scope. Additionally, most statutes are also incorporated separately into the United States Code. The United States Code (and its commercial counterparts) takes those Federal statutes that are of a general and permanent nature and arranges them by subject into separate titles. As the statutes that underlay the Code are revised, superceded, or repealed, the provisions of the Code are updated to reflect these changes.

Slip law versions of Public Laws are not widely available in hard copy form outside Capitol Hill except at university libraries, law school libraries, or similar depositories (though these often have slip laws in microfiche format only). They are more readily available on the Internet. Statutes At Large is used primarily to research the original language of statutes and laws that are not codified in the Code, appropriations statutes and private laws, for example. The Statutes At Large series often is available at large libraries. The United States Code (and its commercial counterparts) are usually available at local libraries. The Code also is readily available on the Internet, though not always in user-friendly form.

Most significant statutes – the Social Security Act, the Elementary and Secondary Education Act, and the Clean Air Act, for example – are published and updated both in a stand alone version, as amended, and as they appear in the Code. Only some, but not all, titles of the Code are the authoritative version of the "law." For other titles, the authoritative version of the statutes codified therein is the underlying public law, as

* Excerpted from CRS Report RL30812, dated January 16, 2001.

amended – *e.g.*, the Immigration and Nationality Act of 1952, as amended, is the authoritative version, not title 8 of the Code.

After providing an overview on the basics of Federal statutes, this article gives guidance on where Federal statutes, in their various forms, may be located on the Internet, where they are most readily accessible.

PUBLIC LAWS AND PRIVATE LAWS

When a piece of legislation is enacted – that is, when it becomes law under the procedures set forth in Article 1, section 7 of the Constitution – it is characterized as a "public law" or a "private law." Each new statute is also assigned a number chronologically according to its order of enactment within a particular Congress (*e.g.*, the tenth public law enacted in the 106th Congress was numbered as Public Law 106-10; the tenth private law as Private Law 106-10). Private laws are enacted for the benefit of a named individual or entity – *e.g.*, laws in which Congress, due to exceptional individual circumstances, provides an immigration status or government reimbursement to a named person who would not be eligible under generally applicable law. By contrast, public laws are of general applicability. It is the latter category which is of most frequent concern and which forms the basis for the United States Code. Some general laws that are not permanent and continuing in nature, such as appropriations, are not included in the Code and must be researched in the Public Laws/Statutes At Large format.

Each new law is first published in pamphlet form (the "slip law" version) by the Government Printing Office (GPO). Individual "slip laws" often are difficult to find outside Capitol Hill, though some libraries may compile them in looseleaf binders or in microfiche collections. Recently enacted laws, especially public laws, are often easier to find in the hardcopy compilations discussed presently, or from Internet resources, as discussed below.

Alternative Sources of Public Laws (Hardcopy Version)

The United States Code Congressional and Administrative News (U.S.C.C.A.N.) is a commercial service that, among other information, publishes Public Laws chronologically in slip law version. In addition to its annual bound volumes, U.S.C.C.A.N. issues monthly paperbound supplements that include the texts of new enactments and selected portions of the accompanying Senate, House, and/or conference reports. As noted in our discussion of the annotated versions of the Code below, both the United States Code Service and the United States Code Annotated publish new public laws chronologically as supplements.

THE UNITED STATES STATUTES AT LARGE

Slip laws (both public laws and private laws) are accumulated at the end of each session of Congress and published in a series of bound volumes entitled Statutes At Large. These laws are cited by volume and page; *e.g.*, 96 Stat. 1259 refers to page 1259 of volume 96 of Statutes At Large. Researchers are most likely to resort to this publication when they are interested in the original language of a statute or in statutes that are not codified, such as appropriations and other temporary laws or private laws.

PUBLIC LAWS, AS AMENDED

Most statutes do not initiate new programs. Rather, most statutes revise, repeal, or add to existing statutes. Consider the following sequence of enactments:

- In 1952, Congress passed the Immigration and Nationality Act of 1952 (Pub. L. 82-414, 66 Stat. 163). This law generally consolidated and amended Federal statutory law on the admission and stay of aliens in the U.S. and how they may become citizens. The Immigration and Nationality Act of 1952 was codified in title 8 of the U.S. Code and comprises almost all of its contents.
- In 1986, Congress passed the Immigration Reform and Control Act of 1986 (Pub. L. 99-603, 100 Stat. 3359). Section 101 of this law, in part, contained provisions that for the first time made it illegal to hire aliens illegally in the U.S. The 1986 Act added these new employer sanctions to the Immigration and Nationality Act of 1952 as a new section 274A. The new employer sanctions, as added to the Immigration and Nationality Act of 1952, were codified in title 8 of the U.S. Code as a new section 1324a (8 U.S.C. § 1324a).
- In 1996, Congress passed the Illegal Immigration Reform and Immigrant Responsibility Act of 1996 (Pub. L. 104-208 (Division C), 110 Stat. 3009). Section 412 of the 1996 Act amended the employer sanctions process an employer must undergo to verify that a new employee is not an illegal alien. As with the 1986 Act, the 1996 Act makes its changes by expressly amending the Immigration and Nationality Act of 1952 – section 274A in this case – with the corresponding section being changed in title 8 of the U.S. Code (section 1324a) noted parenthetically.

As the above sequence illustrates, the canvass upon which Congress works is often an updated, stand-alone version of an earlier public law (*e.g.* the Immigration and Nationality Act of 1952, as amended), and not the U.S. Code. The reason for this is evidenced by the list of the titles of the U.S. Code contained after the title page in each Code volume. An asterisk appears next to some, but not all, of the titles. The asterisks refer to a note that states: "This title has been enacted as law." In other words, unless a title is asterisked, the authoritative version of the statutory material codified therein – the "positive law" – is represented in the freestanding public laws, as amended. The provisions of the Code in these titles are technically only evidence of the "law." For example, there is no asterisk beside Title 42 of the U.S. Code in the title list; thus the provisions codified in Title 42 are not authoritative. Rather, the many public laws, as amended, that are codified there are – *e.g.,* the Social Security Act (as amended), the Public Health Service Act (as amended), the Head Start Act (as amended), the Clean Air Act (as amended), etc.

The legislative sequence above also indicates that current versions of law represented in the titles without asterisks may be found in one of two places: the codified version in the current U.S. Code and the *amended* version of the underlying public laws. For instance, current law on employer sanctions, illustrated above, cannot be found in the Immigration and Nationality Act as first enacted (in either slip law or Statutes At Large form) or in any single public law that subsequently amended it.

Of the two places where current law may be found in these cases, legal and policy experts most commonly refer to the public law, as amended, version – *e.g.*, the Social Security Act, as amended – and not to the codified counterparts of its provisions. However, it is often difficult to find current, updated versions of frequently amended public laws. Many congressional committees periodically issue committee prints containing the major public laws within their respective jurisdictions. However, the frequency of these prints varies and they are often difficult to obtain. Alternatively, various commercial publishers print updated versions of major public laws. Also, the amended versions of major public laws can sometimes be found via the Internet, as is discussed further below.

United States Code

The first edition of the United States Code [U.S.C.] appeared in 1926. It is now published every 6 years and supplemented during the intervals by annual cumulative bound volumes. The latest edition is the 1994 edition. The U.S.C. is printed by the United States Government Printing Office.

Those statutes that are included in the Code are grouped by subject into fifty titles. Each title is further organized into chapters, sections and subsections, again by subject matter.

The Code is cited by title and section, *e.g.*, 28 U.S.C. Sec. (Or §) 534 refers to section 534 of Title 28 of the United States Code.

Each volume of the U.S.C. contains a listing of its titles, whose names provide general guidance as to their contents. For example, Title 7 deals with agriculture, and Title 45 with railroads. However, this is only general guidance, since legislation on broad topics is frequently scattered throughout several titles of the Code.

Notes at the end of each section provide additional information, including statutory origin of the code provision (both by public law number and Statutes At Large citation), the effective date(s), a brief citation and discussion of any amendments, and cross references to related provisions.

Annotated Editions of the United States Code

The United States Code Annotated (U.S.C.A.) and the United States Code Service (U.S.C.S.) are unofficial, privately published editions of the United States Code, published by West Publishing Company and Lawyer's Co-operative Publishing Company, respectively. The major additional features of these publications include annotations to judicial decisions interpreting the Code sections and references to pertinent sections in the Code of Federal Regulations (C.F.R.). The main distinction is that the U.S.C.A. purports to include all annotations, so that a single volume may encompass only two or three Code sections, while the U.S.C.S. provides more selective but more detailed annotations, and also includes references to some law review articles.

Bound volumes of the U.S.C.A. and the U.S.C.S. are brought up to date through use of annual inserts, known as "pocket parts," and more frequent paperbound supplements. These updates include newly codified laws and new annotations. Both U.S.C.A. and U.S.C.S. also issue pamphlets containing copies of recently enacted laws arranged in chronological order. Since there is frequently a time lag in publishing the United States Code, codified versions of new enactments usually appear first in U.S.C.A. and U.S.C.S. supplements.

Additionally, versions of the finding aids discussed below are also available in the U.S.C.A. and U.S.C.S.

General Subject Index

Each edition of the United States Code has a comprehensive subject matter index, under which it is possible to research laws by subject matter. Assuming one wished to locate the provision of law establishing a review committee for farm marketing quotas. Using the index under the term "farm marketing quotas," one is referred to several other subject headings, including the Agricultural Adjustment Assistance Act of 1938. Turning to that heading and looking under the subheading "farm marketing quotas," there is a reference to a "committee for review" codified at 7 U.S.C. § 1363.

Popular Name Table

Each edition of the Code also has a Popular Name Table, "Acts Cited by Popular Name," through which it is possible to obtain information (Public Law number, location in the Statutes At Large, location in the United States Code) on laws by checking the names by which they are commonly known. If the original laws have been amended, the same information is provided for each amendment. To illustrate, assume we are interested in locating the "Special Drawing Rights Act" in the United States Code. Looking at the Popular Names Table, we find that it has been codified at 22 U.S.C. § 286q.

Statutes at Large Table

By showing the relationship between public laws, the Statutes At Large, and the United States Code, the Statutes at Large table for the Code is one of the most useful statutory research tools. Thus a researcher who has either a public law number or a Statutes at Large citation can use this table to ascertain where that law is or was codified, as well as its present status.

It is particularly useful when the researcher is interested in one section of a law that contains many sections, since it is possible to use this table to find where individual sections of a public law have been codified. For purposes of illustration suppose that we were interested in finding where § 1403 of Public law No. 99-661 has been placed in the U.S. Code. Through the Statutes At Large table, we can determine that it can be found at 20 U.S.C. § 4702.

FEDERAL STATUTES ON THE INTERNET

The Internet has made legal resources, including Federal statutes, more widely available to both scholars and the general public. Still, one must use care in obtaining Internet materials:

- Materials on Internet sites may not be up-to-date, and it may be difficult to discern how current the material is or whether it has been revised.
- However extensive Internet materials may be, it still may be difficult to find current federal statutes, especially in the case of "popular name" statutes that are amended frequently. Not all Federal agencies include current versions of the statutes they administer on their websites. At the same time, many agencies that do not include the full text of the statutes that govern their programs do provide useful summaries and discussions of them.
- As is the case with other Internet materials, the inclusiveness and location of statutory materials on a given website may change frequently. Also, websites clearly vary in the ease of finding materials through them.

Selected Sites

With the foregoing caveats in mind, we include the sites below as possible public sources for the selected statutory materials noted. The absence of a particular statute on the list does not imply that it is unavailable electronically. Nor does the inclusion of a site guarantee its continuing location or currency.

Public Laws

Thomas Public Laws [http://thomas.loc.gov/bss/d106/d106laws.html]

GPO Public Laws [http://www.access.gpo.gov/nara/publaw/106publ.html]

U.S.C.

Office of Law Revision Counsel U.S.C. page [http://uscode.house.gov/uscode.htm] Cornell Law School U.S.C. page http://www4.law.cornell.edu/uscode/] GPO U.S.C. [http://www.access.gpo.gov/congress/cong013.html]

Popular Name

General

Cornell Law School Popular Name Index [http://www4.law.cornell.edu/uscode/topn/]

Chronological list of laws and regulations regarding Reclamation Activities [http://www.usbr.gov/laws/chronol.html]

FedLaw - Federal Laws and Regulations [http://www.legal.gsa.gov/intro2.htm]

Selected specific statutes

Abandoned Shipwreck Act of 1987 [http://www2.cr.nps.gov/laws/ship.htm]

American Antiquities Act of 1906 [http://www.cr.nps.gov/local-law/anti1906.htm]

American Indian Religious Freedom Act of 1978 [http://www2.cr.nps.gov/laws/religious.htm]
Americans with Disabilities Act
[http://www.usdoj.gov/crt/ada/pubs/ada.txt]
Archaeological and Historic Preservation Act of 1974 [http://www2.cr.nps.gov/laws/archpreserv.htm]
Archaeological Protection Act of 1979
[http://www2.cr.nps.gov/laws/archprotect.htm]
Antiquities Act of 1906
[http://www4.law.cornell.edu/uscode/16/431.html]
Bankruptcy Code
[http://www.alltheweb.com/go/01/H/www.law.cornell.edu/uscode/11/]
Civil Rights Act of 1964, Title 7 [http://www.eeoc.gov/laws/vii.html]
Clean Air Act
[http://www.epa.gov/oar/caa/contents.html]
Clean Water Act (CWA)
[http://www4.law.cornell.edu/uscode/33/ch26.html]
CERCLA or Superfund Act
[http://www4.law.cornell.edu/uscode/42/ch116.html]
Clayton Act
[http://www.usdoj.gov/atr/foia/divisionmanual/ch2.htm#a1]
[http://www.law.cornell.edu/uscode/15/12.shtml]
Controlled Substances Act
[http://www.deadiversion.usdoj.gov/21cfr/21usc/index.html]
Davis-Bacon Act
[http://www.dol.gov/dol/esa/public/regs/statutes/whd/dbra.htm]
Endangered Species Act (ESA)
[http://www4.law.cornell.edu/uscode/16/ch35.html]
Energy Policy and Conservation Act
[http://www.law.cornell.edu:80/uscode/42/ch77.html]
Equal Access to Justice Act
[http://www.law.cornell.edu/uscode/5/504.html]
Fair Labor Standards Act (FLSA) and Amendments
[http://www.dol.gov/dol/esa/public/regs/statutes/whd/allfair.htm]
Fair Packaging and Labeling Act
[http://www.law.cornell.edu/uscode/15/ch39.html]
Family and Medical Leave Act (FMLA)
[http://www.dol.gov/dol/esa/public/regs/statutes/whd/fmla.htm]
Federal Communications Act 1934
[http://www.fcc.gov/Reports/1934new.pdf]
Federal Food, Drug, and Cosmetic Act (FFDCA) [http://www4.law.cornell.edu/uscode/21/ch9.html]
Federal Insecticide, Fungicide and Rodenticide Act(FIFRA) [http://www4.law.cornell.edu/uscode/21/ch9.html]
Federal Trade Commission Act
[http://www.law.cornell.edu:80/uscode/15/41.shtml]

Freedom of Information Act
[http://www.nara.gov/fedreg/legal/apa/552.html]
Historic Sites Act of 1935
[http://www.cr.nps.gov/local-law/hsact35.htm]
Immigration and Nationality Act
[http://www.ins.usdoj.gov/graphics/lawsregs/INA.htm]
Individuals with Disabilities Education Act
[http://www.ed.gov/offices/OSERS/IDEA/the_law.html]
Intermodal Surface Transportation Efficiency Act of 1991 [http://www.bts.gov/smart/cat/istea.html]
Job Training Partnership Act
[http://www.doleta.gov/regs/statutes/jtpalaw.asp]
Labor-Management Reporting and Disclosure Act
[http://www.dol.gov/dol/esa/public/regs/statutes/olms/lmrda.htm]
Lanham Trademark Act
[http://www.law.cornell.edu:80/uscode/15/ch22.html] Longshore and Harbor Workers' Compensation Act [http://www.oalj.dol.gov/public/lgshore/refrnc/lhwca.htm]
National Environmental Policy Act of 1969 (NEPA) [http://es.epa.gov/oeca/ofa/nepa.html]
National Labor Relations Act [http://www.nlrb.gov/publicat.html]
National Park Service Organic Act
[http://www.nps.gov/legacy/organic-act.htm]
Occupational Safety and Health Act (OSHA) [http://www.nps.gov/legacy/organic-act.htm]
Oil Pollution Act of 1990 (OPA)
[http://www4.law.cornell.edu/uscode/33/ch40.html]
Pollution Prevention Act (PPA)
[http://www.epa.gov/opptintr/p2home/uscode.htm]
Rehabilitation Act Amendments of 1973
[http://www.access-board.gov/enforcement/rehabact-text.htm]
Resource Conservation and Recovery Act (RCRA) [http://www.epa.gov/opptintr/p2home/uscode.htm]
Safe Drinking Water Act (SDWA)
[http://www4.law.cornell.edu/uscode/42/300f.html]
Securities Act of 1933
[http://www.law.uc.edu/CCL/33Act/index.html]
Securities and Exchange Act of 1934
[http://www.law.uc.edu/CCL/34Act/index.html]
Sherman Antitrust Act
[http://www.usdoj.gov/atr/foia/divisionmanual/ch2.htm#a1]
Small Business Act
[http://www.sbaonline.sba.gov/regulations/sbaact/sbactdec99.html]
Small Business Investment Act of 1958
[http://www.sbaonline.sba.gov/INV/act/sbicactaug99.html]
Small Business Regulatory Enforcement Fairness Act of 1996 [http://www.sbaonline.sba.gov/regfair/regfairreg.html]

Social Security Act
[http://www.ssa.gov/OP_Home/ssact/comp-toc.htm]
Toxic Substances Control Act (TSCA)
[http://www.ssa.gov/OP_Home/ssact/comp-toc.htm]
War Powers Resolution
[http://www.law.cornell.edu/uscode/50/1541.html]

In: Law and Law Enforcement Issues
Editor: Gerald M. Kessler, pp. 11-35

ISBN: 978-1-60456-044-2

Chapter 2

SELECTED PROCEDURAL SAFEGUARDS IN FEDERAL, MILITARY, AND INTERNATIONAL COURTS*

Jennifer K. Elsea

ABSTRACT

Declaring it necessary to bring to justice those responsible for the terrorist attacks on the United States of September 11, 2001, President Bush signed a Military Order (M.O.) authorizing the trial by military commission of certain non-citizens. The order directs the Secretary of Defense to establish the procedural rules for the operation of the military commissions convened pursuant to the M.O. The Department of Defense prepared regulations providing for procedures of military commissions, but these were invalidated by the Supreme Court in *Hamdan v. Rumsfeld*. The Bush Administration has proposed legislation to reinstate military commissions for the trials of suspected terrorists.

This article provides a brief overview of procedural rules applicable in selected historical and contemporary tribunals for the trials of war crimes suspects. The chart in this chapter compares selected procedural safeguards employed in criminal trials in federal criminal court with parallel protective measures in military general courts-martial, international military tribunals used after World War II, including the International Military Tribunal (IMT or "Nuremberg Tribunal"), and the International Criminal Courts for the former Yugoslavia (ICTY) and Rwanda (ICTR). The chart identifies a selection of basic rights in rough order of the stage in the criminal justice process where they might become most important. The text of the chart indicates some of the procedural safeguards designed to protect these rights in different tribunals. Recognizing that fundamental fairness relies on the *system* of procedural safeguards as a whole rather than individual rules, the chart is intended only as an outline to compare some of the rules different courts and tribunals might use to safeguard certain rights.

For comparison of the Department of Defense rules for military commissions that were struck down in *Hamdan* to recent legislative proposals, see CRS Report RL31600, *The Department of Defense Rules for Military Commissions: Analysis of Procedural*

---

* Excerpted from CRS Report RL31262, dated September 18, 2006.

Rules and Comparison with Proposed Legislation and the Uniform Code of Military Justice.

Declaring it necessary to bring to justice those responsible for the terrorist attacks on the United States of September 11, 2001, President Bush signed a Military Order (M.O.) authorizing the trial by military commission of certain non-citizens.[1] The order directed the Secretary of Defense to establish the procedural rules for the operation of the military commissions convened pursuant to the M.O. The Department of Defense implemented regulations and convened commissions; however, one of the accused petitioned for *habeas corpus* in federal district court and the Supreme Court invalidated the regulations as inconsistent with the Uniform Code of Military Justice (UCMJ[2]) and the Geneva Conventions.[3]

U.S. COURTS AND MILITARY TRIBUNALS

The Constitution imposes on the government a system of restraints to provide that no unfair law is enforced and that no law is enforced unfairly. What is fundamentally fair in a given situation depends in part on the objectives of a given system of law weighed alongside the possible infringement of individual liberties that system might impose. In the criminal law system, some basic objectives are to discover the truth, punish the guilty proportionately with their crimes, acquit the innocent without unnecessary delay or expense, and prevent and deter further crime, thereby providing for the public order. Military justice shares these objectives in part, but also serves to enhance discipline throughout the armed forces, serving the overall objective of providing an effective national defense. The equation for international criminal law may also consider foreign policy elements as well as international law and treaty obligations.

The Fifth Amendment to the Constitution provides that "no person shall be ... deprived of life, liberty, or property, without due process of law." Due process includes the opportunity to be heard whenever the government places any of these fundamental liberties at stake. The Constitution contains other explicit rights applicable to various stages of a criminal prosecution. Criminal proceedings provide both the opportunity to contest guilt and to challenge the government's conduct that may have violated the rights of the accused. The system of procedural rules used to conduct a criminal hearing, therefore, serves as a safeguard against violations of constitutional rights that take place outside the courtroom.

The Bill of Rights applies to all citizens of the United States and all aliens within the United States.[4] However, the methods of application of constitutional rights, in particular the remedies available to those whose rights might have been violated, may differ depending on the severity of the punitive measure the government seeks to take and the entity deciding the case. The jurisdiction of various entities to try a person accused of a crime could have a profound effect on the procedural rights of the accused. The type of judicial review available also varies and may be crucial to the outcome.

International law also contains some basic guarantees of human rights, including rights of criminal defendants and prisoners. Treaties to which the United States is a party are expressly made a part of the law of the land by the Supremacy Clause of the Constitution,[5] and may be codified through implementing legislation.[6] International law is incorporated into U.S. law.[7] The law of war, a subset of international law, applies to cases arising from armed conflicts (i.e., war crimes).[8] It is unclear exactly how the law of war applies to the current hostilities involving non-state terrorists, and the nature of the rights due to accused terrorist/war criminals may depend in part on their status under the Geneva Conventions. The Supreme Court has ruled that Al Qaeda fighters are entitled at least to the baseline protections applicable under Common Article 3 of the Geneva Conventions,[9] which includes protection from the "passing of sentences and the carrying out of executions without previous judgment pronounced by a regularly constituted court, affording all the judicial guarantees which are recognized as indispensable by civilized peoples."

Federal Court

The federal judiciary is established by Article III of the Constitution and consists of the Supreme Court and "inferior tribunals" established by Congress. It is a separate and co-equal branch of the federal government, independent of the executive and legislative branches, designed to be insulated from the public passions. Its function is not to make law but to interpret law and decide disputes arising under it. Federal criminal law and procedures are enacted by Congress and housed primarily in title 18 of the U.S. Code. The Supreme Court promulgates procedural rules for criminal trials at the federal district courts, subject to Congress's approval. These rules, namely the Federal Rules of Criminal Procedure (Fed. R. Crim. P.) and the Federal Rules of Evidence (Fed. R. Evid.), incorporate procedural rights that the Constitution and various statutes demand. The chart cites relevant rules or court decisions, but makes no effort to provide an exhaustive list of authorities.

General Courts-Martial

The Constitution, in order to provide for the common defense,[10] gives Congress the power to raise, support, and regulate the armed forces,[11] but makes the President Commander-in-Chief of the armed forces.[12] Article III does not give the judiciary any explicit role in the military, and the Supreme Court has taken the view that Congress' power "[t]o Make Rules for the Government and Regulation of the land and naval Forces"[13] is entirely separate from Article III.[14] Therefore, courts-martial are not considered to be Article III courts and are not subject to all of the rules that apply in federal courts.[15]

Although military personnel are "persons" to whom the Bill of Rights applies, in the military context it might be said that discipline is as important as liberty as objectives of military justice. Also, the Constitution specifically exempts military members accused of a crime from the Fifth Amendment right to a grand jury indictment, from which the Supreme Court has inferred there is no right to a civil jury in courts-martial.[16] However, in part because of the different standards provided in courts-martial, their jurisdiction is limited to those persons and offenses the military has a legitimate interest in regulating.[17] Courts-martial jurisdiction extends mainly to service members on active duty, prisoners of war, and persons accompanying the armed forces in time of declared war,[18] as well as certain violators of the law of war.[19]

Selected Procedural Safeguards in Federal, Military, and International Courts

Constitutional Safeguards	Federal Court	General Courts-Martial	Nuremberg/Tokyo	ICTY/ICTR
Presumption of Innocence "The principle that there is a presumption of innocence in favour of the accused is the undoubted law, axiomatic and elementary, and its enforcement lies at the foundation of the administration of our criminal law." Coffin v. United States, 156 U.S. 432, 453 (1895).	If the defendant fails to enter a proper plea, a plea of not guilty will be entered. Fed. R. Crim. P. 11(a). Defendant is entitled to jury instructions explaining that guilt must be proved on the evidence beyond a reasonable doubt. Taylor v. Kentucky, 436 U.S. 478 (1978). Defendant is entitled to appear in court without unnecessary physical restraints or other indicia of guilt, such as appearing in prison uniform, that may be prejudicial to jury. *See* Holbrook v. Flynn, 475 U.S. 560 (1986).	If the defendant fails to enter a proper plea, a plea of not guilty will be entered. R.C.M. 910(b). Members of court martial must be instructed that the "accused must be presumed to be innocent until the accused's guilt is established by legal and competent evidence beyond a reasonable doubt." R.C.M. 920(e). The accused shall be properly attired in uniform with grade insignia and any decorations to which entitled. Physical restraint shall not be imposed unless prescribed by the military judge. R.C.M. 804.	No written rule addressing presumption of innocence, although U.S. negotiators were able to win a concession from Soviet negotiators to the effect that the rule would apply. *See* Henry T. King, Jr., *Robert Jackson's Transcendent Influence Over Today's World*, 68 ALB. L. REV. 23, 25 (2006).	"The accused shall be presumed innocent until proved guilty according to the provisions of the present Statute." ICTY Stat. art. 21(3); ICTR Stat. art. 20. If the accused fails to enter a plea, the court must enter a plea of not guilty on the accused's behalf. ICTY Rule 62(a)(iv); ICTR Rule 62(a)(iii). Instruments of restraint may not be used during court proceedings. ICTY Rule 83; ICTR Rule 83. Guilty pleas may be accepted only if the trial chamber determines it is voluntary, informed, unequivocal, and supported by evidence. ICTY Rule 63 *bis*; ICTR Rule 62(B).

Constitutional Safeguards	Federal Court	General Courts-Martial	Nuremberg/Tokyo	ICTY/ICTR
Right to Remain Silent "No person…shall be compelled in any criminal case to be a witness against himself …." Amendment V.	Incriminating statements made by defendant under duress or without prior *Miranda* warning are inadmissible as evidence of guilt in a criminal trial. Miranda v. Arizona, 384 U.S. 436 (1966). Before a jury is allowed to hear evidence of a defendant's confession, the court must determine that it was voluntarily given. 18 U.S.C. § 3501.	Coerced confessions or confessions made without statutory equivalent of Miranda warning are not admissible as evidence. Art. 31, UCMJ, 10 U.S.C. § 831. The prosecutor must notify the defense of any incriminating statements made by the accused that are relevant to the case prior to the arraignment. Motions to suppress such statements must be made prior to pleading. Mil. R. Evid. 304.	No right to remain silent. The Tokyo rules specifically provided that "all purported admissions or statements of the accused are admissible." IMTFE Charter art 13.	A suspect to be questioned by the prosecutor during an investigation must be informed of his right to remain silent. ICTY Rule 42; ICTR Rule 42. Persons are to be informed of the right to remain silent upon their arrest. ICTY Rule 55; ICTR Rule 55. "No evidence shall be admissible if obtained by methods which cast substantial doubt on its reliability or if its admission is antithetical to, and would seriously damage, the integrity of the proceedings." ICTY Rule 95; ICTR Rule 95.
Freedom from UnreasonableSearches & Seizures "The right of the people to be secure … against unreasonable searches and seizures, shall not be violated; no Warrants shall issue, but upon probable cause…" Amendment IV.	Evidence, including derivativeevidence, gained through unreasonable searches and seizures may be excluded in court. Boyd v. United States, 116 U.S. 616 (1886); Nardone v. United States, 308 U.S. 338 (1938); Fed. R. Crim. P. 41. A search warrant issued by a magistrate on a showing of probable cause is generally required for law enforcement agents to conduct a search of an area where the subject has a reasonable expectation of privacy, including searches and seizures of telephone or	"Evidence obtained as a result of an unlawful search or seizure … is inadmissible against the accused …" unless certain exceptions apply. Mil. R. Evid. 311. "Authorization to search" may be oral or written, and may be issued by a military judge or an officer in command of the area to be searched, or if the area is not under military control, with authority over persons subject to military law or the law of war. It must be based on probable cause. Mil. R. Evid. 315.	Not provided.	"No evidence shall be admissible if … its admission is antithetical to, and would seriously damage, the integrity of the proceedings." ICTY Rule 95; ICTR Rule 95.

Constitutional Safeguards	Federal Court	General Courts-Martial	Nuremberg/Tokyo	ICTY/ICTR
	other communications and emissions of heat and other phenomena detectable with means other than human senses. Katz v. United States, 389 U.S. 347 (1967). Evidence resulting from overseas searches of American property by foreign officials is admissible unless foreign police conduct shocks judicial conscience or participation by U.S. agents is so substantial as to render the action that of the United States. United States v. Barona, 56 F.3d 1087 (9th Cir. 1995).	Interception of wire and oral communications within the United States requires judicial application in accordance with 18 U.S.C. §§ 2516 *et seq.* Mil. R. Evid. 317. A search conducted by foreign officials is unlawful only if the accused is subject to "gross and brutal treatment." Mil. R. Evid. 311(c).		
Assistance of Effective Counsel "In all criminal prosecutions, the accused shall enjoy the right ... to have the Assistance of Counsel for his defense." Amendment VI.	Defendants in criminal cases have the right to representation by an attorney at all stages of prosecution. The defendant may hire an attorney or, if indigent, have counsel appointed at the government's expense. If two or more codefendants are represented by one attorney, the court must inquire as to whether a conflict of interest exists. Fed. R. Crim. P. 44. Conversations between attorneys and clients are privileged. Fed. R. Evid. 501. Procedures for ensuring adequate representation of	The defendant has a right to military counsel at government expense. The defendant may choose counsel, if that attorney is reasonably available, and may hire a civilian attorney in addition to military counsel. Art 38, UCMJ, 10 U.S.C. § 838. Appointed counsel must be certified as qualified and may not be someone who has taken any part in the investigation or prosecution, unless explicitly requested by the defendant. Art. 27, UCMJ, 10 U.S.C. § 827. The attorney-client privilege is	"Each defendant has the right to conduct his own defense or to have the assistance of counsel," and was required to be told of that right. Only one counsel was permitted to appear at the trial for any defendant, unless the IMT granted special permission. The IMT was to designate counsel for any defendant who failed to apply for particular counsel or if the counsel requested was not available, unless the defendant elected in writing to conduct his own defense. IMT Rule 2. The IMTFE Charter provided	Prior to being charged, "[i]f questioned, the suspect shall be entitled to be assisted by counsel of his own choice, including the right to have legal assistance assigned to him without payment by him in any such case if he does not have sufficient means to pay for it, as well as to necessary translation into and from a language he speaks and understands." ICTY Stat. art. 18; ICTR Stat. art. 17. The accused has the right "to communicate with counsel of his own choosing ... and to defend himself in person or through legal assistance of his own choosing; to be informed, if he

Constitutional Safeguards	Federal Court	General Courts-Martial	Nuremberg/Tokyo	ICTY/ICTR
	defendants are outlined at 18 U.S.C. §§ 3005 (capital cases) and 3006A.	honored. Mil. R. Evid. 502.	that "[e]ach accused shall have the right to be represented by counsel of his own selection, subject to the disapproval of such counsel at any time by the Tribunal. ... If an accused is not represented by counsel and in open court requests the appointment of counsel, the Tribunal shall designate counsel for him. In the absence of such request the Tribunal may appoint counsel for an accused if in its judgment such appointment is necessary to provide for a fair trial." IMTFE Charter art. 9(c).	does not have legal assistance, of this right; and to have legal assistance assigned to him, in any case where the interests of justice so require, and without payment by him in any such case if he does not have sufficient means to pay for it." ICTY Stat. art. 21; ICTR Stat. art. 20. All communications between lawyer and client are privileged, and disclosure cannot be ordered unless the client or has waived the privilege by voluntarily disclosing the content of the communication to a third party. ICTY Rule 97; ICTR Rule 97. Qualifications for counsel and assignment of counsel to indigent defendants are set forth in ICTY Rules 44-45 and ICTR Rules 44-45.
Right to Indictment and Presentment "No person shall be held to answer for a capital, or otherwise infamous crime, unless on a presentment or indictment of a Grand Jury, except in cases arising in the land or naval forces, or in the Militia, when in actual service in time of War or public danger	Where the accused is in danger of being subjected to an infamous punishment if convicted, he has the right to insist that he shall not be tried except on the accusation of a grand jury. *Ex parte* Wilson, 114 U.S. 417 (1885); Fed. R. Crim. P. 7. Jurors must be selected from a fair cross section of the community; otherwise, an	The right to indictment by grand jury is explicitly excluded in "cases arising in the land or naval forces." Amendment V. Whenever an offense is alleged, the commander is responsible for initiating a preliminary inquiry and deciding how to dispose of the offense. R.C.M. 303-06.	"Each individual defendant in custody shall receive not less than 30 days before trial a copy, translated into a language which he understands, (1) of the Indictment, (2) of the Charter, (3) of any other documents lodged with the Indictment...." IMT Rule 2. The Tokyo Tribunal required the same documents to be provided not less than 14 days	The prosecutor, if satisfied that there is sufficient evidence to provide reasonable grounds for believing that a suspect has committed a crime within the jurisdiction of the ICTY (or ICTR), prepares an indictment for confirmation by a Judge, setting forth the name and particulars of the suspect, and a concise statement of the facts of the case and of the crime with which the suspect is charged.

Constitutional Safeguards	Federal Court	General Courts-Martial	Nuremberg/Tokyo	ICTY/ICTR
" Amendment V.	accused can challenge the indictment. 28 U.S.C. §§ 1861 *et seq.* Once an indictment is given, its scope may not be increased. *Ex parte* Bain, 121 U.S. 1 (1887). (Amendments to an indictment must undergo further grand jury process.)		before trial. IMTFE Rule 1.	ICTY Stat. arts. 18-19 and ICTY Rule 47; ICTR Stat. arts. 17-18; ICTR Rule 47. A person against whom an indictment has been confirmed is to be taken into custody and immediately informed of the charges in a language he understands. ICTY Stat. arts. 20-21 and Rule 47; ICTR Stat. arts. 19-20 and ICTR Rule 47. The prosecutor may amend the indictment as prescribed in ICTY Rule 50 or ICTR Rule 50.
Right to Written Statement of Charges "In all criminal prosecutions, the accused shall enjoy the right…to be informed of the nature and cause of the accusation; …" Amendment VI.	Defendant is entitled to be informed of the nature of the charge with sufficiently reasonable certainty to allow for preparation of defense. Cook v. United States, 138 U.S. 157 (1891).	Charges and specifications must be signed under oath and made known to the accused as soon as practicable. Art. 30, UCMJ, 10 U.S.C. § 830.	See above.	An arrested person must be completely informed of charges, which may be satisfied by presentation to the accused of a copy of the written charges, translated, if necessary. ICTY Rule 59 *bis*. At the ICTR, the registrar is required to prepare certified copies of the indictment in a language the accused understands, but there does not appear to be a requirement that the accused be furnished with a written copy. ICTR Rule 47.
Right to be Present at Trial The Confrontation Clause of Amendment VI guarantees the accused's right to be present in the	The language, history, and logic of Rule 43 support a straightforward interpretation that prohibits the trial in absentia of a defendant who is	The presence of the accused is required during arraignment, at the plea, and at every stage of the court-martial unless the accused waives the right by	Not provided. "The Tribunal shall have the right to take proceedings against a person charged … in his absence, if he has not been found or if the	The accused has the right "to be tried in his presence." ICTY Stat. art. 21; ICTR Stat. art. 20. *In absentia* trials are permitted

Constitutional Safeguards	Federal Court	General Courts-Martial	Nuremberg/Tokyo	ICTY/ICTR
courtroom at every stage of his trial. Illinois v. Allen, 397 U.S. 337 (1970).	not present at the beginning of trial. Crosby v. United States, 506 U.S. 255, 262 (1993); Fed. R. Crim. P. 43. When defendant knowingly absents himself from court during trial, court may "proceed with trial in like manner and with like effect as if he were present." Diaz v. United States, 223 U.S. 442, 455 (1912).	voluntarily absenting him or herself from the proceedings after the arraignment or by persisting in conduct that justifies the trial judge in ordering the removal of the accused from the proceedings. R.C.M. 801.	Tribunal, for any reason, finds it necessary, in the interests of justice, to conduct the hearing in his absence." IMT Charter art. 12. (Martin Bormann, who was never located and was rumoured to be dead, was convicted in absentia and sentenced to death.) The Tokyo rules provided that "Any accused or any other person may be excluded from open session of the Tribunal for failure to observe and respect the directives or dignity of the Tribunal." IMTFE Rule 3.	only in cases of exceptional contempt of court, where the accused voluntarily absents himself from the proceeding. *Prosecutor v. Blaskic*, Case No. IT-95-14-AR 108 *bis*, Decision on Subpoena, ICTY App. Ch. 59 (1997).
Prohibition against Ex Post Facto Crimes "No ... ex post facto law shall be passed." Art. I, § 9, cl. 3.	Congress may not pass a law punishing conduct that was not a crime when perpetrated, increasing the possible sentence for a crime, or reducing the government's evidentiary burden. Calder v. Bull, 3 Dall. (3 U.S.) 386 (1798); Ex Parte Garland, 4 Wall (71 U.S.) 1867.	Courts-martial will not enforce an ex post facto law, including increasing amount of pay to be forfeited for specific crimes. U.S. v. Gorki, 47 M.J. 370 (1997).	Not provided. Article 6 of the IMT Charter provided for jurisdiction to try not only war crimes, but also "crimes against peace" and "crimes against humanity," which had never before been defined as international crimes. The IMT rejected defenses based on the ex post facto nature of the charges, remarking that the rule against such charges "is not a limitation of sovereignty, but is in general a principle of justice." The IMT went on to conclude that justice does not prohibit, but rather requires the punishment of "those who in defiance of treaties and	Jurisdiction is limited to specified crimes. ICTY Stat. arts. 2-5 (grave breaches of the Geneva Conventions, violations of the laws or customs of war, genocide, and crimes against humanity). ICTR jurisdiction is limited to genocide, crimes against humanity, and violations of Article 3 Common to the Geneva Conventions and of Additional Protocol II. ICTR Stat. arts. 1-4.

Constitutional Safeguards	Federal Court	General Courts-Martial	Nuremberg/Tokyo	ICTY/ICTR
			assurances have attacked neighbouring states without warning." IMT Opinion and Judgment: The Law of the Charter. The statute for the Tokyo Tribunal provided it jurisdiction over the specific violations "whether or not in violation of the domestic law of the country where perpetrated." IMTFE Charter art. 5.	
Protection against Double Jeopardy "… nor shall any person be subject for the same offence to be twice put in jeopardy of life or limb; …" Amendment V. Subject to "dual sovereign" doctrine, that is, federal and state courts may prosecute an individual for the same conduct without violating the clause.	Jeopardy attaches once the jury is sworn or where there is no jury, when the first evidence is presented. If the trial is terminated after jeopardy has attached, a second trial may be barred in a court under the same sovereign, particularly where it is prosecutorial conduct that brings about the termination of the trial. Illinois v. Somerville, 410 U.S. 458 (1973).	Double jeopardy clause applies. *See* Wade v. Hunter, 336 US 684, 688-89 (1949). Art. 44, UCMJ prohibits double jeopardy, provides for jeopardy to attach after introduction of evidence. 10 U.S.C. § 844. General court-martial proceeding is considered to be a federal trial for double jeopardy purposes. Double jeopardy does not result from charges brought in state or foreign courts, although courtmartial in such cases is disfavored. United States v. Stokes, 12 M.J. 229 (C.M.A. 1982).	Not provided. Jurisdiction was concurrent with national courts, but the IMT could only try serious crimes not limited to a specific geographical location.	"No person shall be tried before a national court for acts constituting serious violations of international humanitarian law under the present Statute, for which he or she has already been tried by the International Tribunal…" A person who has been tried by a national court for acts constituting serious violations of international humanitarian law may be subsequently tried by the ad hoc tribunal, but only if: (a) the act for which he or she was tried was characterized as an ordinary crime; or (b) the national court proceedings were not impartial or independent, were designed to shield the accused from

Constitutional Safeguards	Federal Court	General Courts-Martial	Nuremberg/Tokyo	ICTY/ICTR
		Once military authorities have turned service member over to civil authorities for trial, military may have waived jurisdiction for that crime, although it may be possible to charge the individual for another crime arising from the same conduct. *See* 54 AM. JUR. 2D, Military and Civil Defense §§ 227-28.		international criminal responsibility, or the case was not diligently prosecuted. ICTY Stat. art. 10; ICTR Stat. art. 9. "When...criminal proceedings have been instituted against a person before a court of any State for a crime for which that person has already been tried by the Tribunal, a Trial Chamber shall…issue a reasoned order requesting that court permanently to discontinue its proceedings. If that court fails to do so, the ICTY President may report the matter to the Security Council." ICTY Rule 13; ICTR Rule 13. However, the prosecution can seek to appeal an acquittal, including based on the discovery a new fact that was unknown at the time of the proceedings but that could have been decisive. ICTY Stat. art. 26.; ICTR Stat. art. 25.
Speedy & Public Trial "In all criminal prosecutions, the accused shall enjoy the right to a speedy and public trial, ..." Amendment VI.	Trial is to commence within seventy days of indictment or original appearance before court. 18 U.S.C. § 3161. Closure of the courtroom during trial proceedings is justified only if 1) the proponent of closure advances an overriding interest likely to	In general, accused must be brought to trial within 120 days of the preferral of char ges or the imposition of restraint, whichever date is earliest. R.C.M. 707(a). The right to a public trial applies in courts-martial but is not absolute. R.C.M. 806.	The IMT was to ensure expeditious proceedings, although this principle was not framed in terms of the rights of the accused. The IMT was to "take strict measures to prevent any action which will cause unreasonable delay, and rule out irrelevant issues and statements of any kind	The accused has the right "to be tried without undue delay." ICTY Stat. art. 21; ICTR Stat. art. 20. Proceedings are to be public unless otherwise provided. ICTY Rule 78; ICTR Rule 78. "The press and the public [may]

Constitutional Safeguards	Federal Court	General Courts-Martial	Nuremberg/Tokyo	ICTY/ICTR
	be prejudiced; 2) the closure is no broader than necessary; 3) the trial court considers reasonable alternatives to closure; and 4) the trial court makes findings adequate to support closure. *See* Waller v. Georgia, 467 U.S. 39, 48 (1984).	The military trial judge may exclude the public from portions of a proceeding for the purpose of protecting classified information if the prosecution demonstrates an overriding need to do so and the closure is no broader than necessary. United States v. Grunden, 2 M.J. 116 (CMA 1977).	whatsoever," and to "deal summarily with any contumacy, imposing appropriate punishment, including exclusion of any Defendant or his Counsel from some or all further proceedings, but without prejudice to the determination of the charges." IMT Charter art. 18; IMTFE Charter art. 12. The IMT was to rule in open court upon all questions arising during the trial, although it could deliberate certain matters in closed proceedings. IMT Rule 8. The IMTFE rules permitted the tribunal, "when necessary, [to] order the closing or clearing of the court and take any other steps which to the Tribunal seem just." IMTFE Rule 5. Provision was made for the publication of all proceedings in multiple languages. IMT Charter art. 25. At the Tokyo Tribunal, "[s]o much of the record and of the proceedings may be translated into Japanese as the Tribunal considers desirable in the interest of justice and for the information of the public." IMTFE Rule 6.	be excluded from all or part of the proceedings for reasons of: (i) public order or morality; (ii) safety, security or nondisclosure of the identity of a victim or witness...; or (iii) the protection of the interests of justice." ICTY Rule 79; ICTY Rule 79.

Constitutional Safeguards	Federal Court	General Courts-Martial	Nuremberg/Tokyo	ICTY/ICTR
Burden & Standard of Proof Due Process requires the prosecution to prove the defendant guilty of each element of a crime beyond a reasonable doubt. *In re* Winship, 397 U.S. 358 (1970).	Defendant is entitled to jury instructions clarifying that the prosecution has the burden of presenting evidence sufficient to prove guilt beyond a reasonable doubt. Cool v. United States, 409 U.S. 100 (1978).	Members of court martial must be instructed that the burden of proof to establish guilt is upon the government and that any reasonable doubt must be resolved in favor of the defendant. R.C.M. 920(e).	The IMT could "admit any evidence which it deem[ed] to be of probative value." IMT Charter art. 19; IMTFE Rule 13. Guilty verdicts and sentences required a majority vote, that is, three out of four votes. IMT Charter art. 4.	"A finding of guilt may be reached only when a majority of the Trial Chamber is satisfied that guilt has been proved beyond reasonable doubt." ICTY Rule 87; ICTR Rule 87. "A Chamber may admit any relevant evidence which it deems to have probative value," and "… shall apply rules of evidence which will best favour a fair determination of the matter before it and are consonant with the spirit of the Statute and the general principles of law." ICTY Rule 89; ICTR Rule 89. At the ICTY, "A Chamber may receive the evidence of a witness orally or, where the interests of justice allow, in written form." ICTY Rule 90. At the ICTR, "Witnesses shall … be heard directly by the Chambers unless [it] has ordered that the witness be heard by means of a deposition as provided for in Rule 71." ICTR Rule 90.
Privilege Against Self-Incrimination "No person … shall be compelled in any criminal case to be a witness	Defendant may not be compelled to testify. Jury may not be instructed that guilt may be inferred from the defendant's refusal to testify. Griffin v. California, 380 U.S.	No person subject to the UCMJ may compel any person to answer incriminating questions. Art. 31(a) UCMJ, 10 U.S.C. § 831(a).	Not provided.	The accused may not to be compelled to testify against himself or to confess guilt. ICTY Stat. art. 21; ICTR Stat. art. 20. "A witness may object to making

Constitutional Safeguards	Federal Court	General Courts-Martial	Nuremberg/Tokyo	ICTY/ICTR
against himself…" Amendment V.	609 (1965). Witnesses may not be compelled to give testimony that may be incriminating unless given immunity for that testimony. 18 U.S.C. § 6002.	Defendant may not be compelled to give testimony that is immaterial or potentially degrading. Art. 31(c), UCMJ, 10 U.S.C. § 831(c). No adverse inference is to be drawn from a defendant's refusal to answer any questions or testify at court-martial. Mil. R. Evid. 301(f). Witnesses may not be compelled to give testimony that may be incriminating unless granted immunity for that testimony by a general court-martial convening authority, as authorized by the Attorney General, if required. 18 U.S.C. § 6002; R.C.M. 704.		any statement which might tend to incriminate the witness. The Chamber may ...compel the witness to answer the question [but such testimony] shall not be used as evidence in a subsequent prosecution against the witness for any offence other than false testimony." ICTY Rule 90; ICTR Rule 90.
Right to Examine or Have Examined Adverse Witnesses "In all criminal prosecutions, the accused shall enjoy the right … to be confronted with the witnesses against him; …." Amendment VI.	Rules of Evidence prohibit generally the introduction at trial of statements made out of court to prove the truth of the matter stated unless the declarant is available for crossexamination at trial (hearsay rule). Fed. R. Evid. 801 *et seq*. The government is required to disclose to defendant any relevant evidence in its possession or that may become known through due diligence. Fed. R. Crim. P. 16.	Hearsay rules apply as in federal court. Mil. R. Evid. 801 *et seq*. In capital cases, sworn depositions may not be used in lieu of witness, unless courtmartial is treated as non-capital or it is introduced by the defense. Art. 49, UCMJ, 10 U.S.C. § 849.	Defendants had the right "to present evidence at the Trial in support of [their] defense, and to cross-examine any witness called by the Prosecution." IMT Charter art. 16(d), IMTFE Charter art. 15. Hearsay was not strictly prohibited. The judges were empowered to inquire into the nature of evidence and determine its reliability. IMT Charter art. 20; IMTFE Charter art. 15 (tribunal to determine "admissibility" and	The accused has the right "to examine, or have examined, the witnesses against him…." ICTY Stat. art. 21; ICTR Stat. art. 20. Hearsay evidence may be admissible. "A Chamber may admit any relevant evidence which it deems to have probative value. ... A Chamber may exclude evidence if its probative value is substantially outweighed by the need to ensure a fair trial." ICTY Rule 89. "A Trial Chamber may admit, in

Constitutional Safeguards	Federal Court	General Courts-Martial	Nuremberg/Tokyo	ICTY/ICTR
			"relevance"of evidence). "A document [was admissible before the Tokyo Tribunal], regardless of its security classification and without proof of its issuance or signature, which appears to the Tribunal to have been signed or issued by any officer, department, agency or member of the armed forces of any government." IMTFE Charter art. 13.	whole or in part, the evidence of a witness in the form of a written statement in lieu of oral testimony which goes to proof of a matter other than the acts and conduct of the accused as charged in the indictment." ICTY Rule 92 *bis*. Unsworn written testimony and transcripts are admissible only under certain circumstances, including where the declarant is unavailable but there are sufficient indicia of reliability to satisfy the court. *Id*. The ICTY has held that out-of court statements that are relevant and found to have probative value are admissible but that judges may be guided by "hearsay exceptions generally recognised by some national legal systems, as well as the truthfulness, voluntariness and trustworthiness of the evidence, as appropriate." Prosecutor v. Tadic, Case No.IT-94-1-T, Decision on Defense Motion on Hearsay, 5 August 1996, 7-19.
Right to Compulsory Process to Obtain Witnesses "In all criminal prosecutions, the accused	Defendants have the right to subpoena witnesses to testify in their defense. The court may punish witnesses who fail to appear. Fed. R. Crim. Pro. Rule 17.	Defendants before courtmartial have the right to compel appearance of witnesses necessary to their defense. R.C.M. 703.	The defense had an opportunity to apply to the Tribunal for the production of witnesses or of documents by written application stating where the witness or	The accused has the right "to examine, or have examined, the witnesses against him and to obtain the attendance and examination of witnesses on his behalf under the same conditions

Constitutional Safeguards	Federal Court	General Courts-Martial	Nuremberg/Tokyo	ICTY/ICTR
shall enjoy the right … to have compulsory process for obtaining witnesses in his favor, ….” Amendment VI.		Process to compel witnesses in court-martial cases is to be similar to the process used in federal courts. Art. 46, UCMJ, 10 U.S.C. § 846.	document was thought to be located and the facts proposed to be proved. The Tribunal had the discretion to grant applications and seek to have evidence made available by cooperating states. IMT Rule 4; IMTFE Charter art. 9.	as witnesses against him.” ICTY Stat. art. 21; ICTR Stat. art. 20.
Right to Trial by Impartial Judge “The Judicial Power of the United States, shall be vested in one supreme Court, and in ... inferior courts .... The Judges ... shall hold their Offices during good Behaviour, and shall receive ... a Compensation, which shall not be diminished during their Continuance in Office.” Article III § 1.	The independence of the judiciary from the other branches was established to ensure trials are decided impartially, without the “potential domination by other branches of government.” United States v. Will, 449 U.S. 200, 217-18 (1980). Judges with a pecuniary interest in the outcome of a case or other conflicts of interest are disqualified and must recuse themselves. 28 U.S.C. § 455.	A qualified military judge is detailed to preside over the court-martial. The convening authority may not prepare or review any report concerning the performance or effectiveness of the military judge. Art. 26, UCMJ, 10 U.S.C. § 826. Article 37, UCMJ, prohibits unlawful influence of courtsmartial through admonishment, censure, or reprimand of its members by the convening authority or commanding officer, or any unlawful attempt by a person subject to the UCMJ to coerce or influence the action of a courtmartial or convening authority. Art. 37, UCMJ, 10 U.S.C. § 837.	Each state party to the London Agreement establishing the IMT nominated one judge, whom they could replace “for reasons of health or for other good reasons,” except that no replacement was permitted to take place during a trial, other than by an alternate. IMT Charter art. 3.	The judges are to be “persons of high moral character, impartiality and integrity....” ICTY Stat. art. 13; ICTR Stat. art. 12. “A Judge may not sit on a trial or appeal in any case in which the Judge has a personal interest or concerning which the Judge has or has had any association which might affect his or her impartiality. ” ICTY Rule 15; ICTR Rule 15.
Right to Trial By Impartial Jury “The Trial of all Crimes, except in Cases of Impeachment, shall be by	The pool from which juries are drawn must represent a fair cross section of the community. Taylor v. Louisiana, 419 U.S. 522 (1975).	A military accused has no Sixth Amendment right to a trial by petit jury. *Ex Parte* Quirin, 317 U.S. 1, 39-40 (1942) (*dicta*). However, “Congress has provided for	There was no provision for a jury trial.	The ICTY and ICTR follow the civil law tradition of employing a panel of judges to decide questions of both fact and law. There is no provision for trial by jury.

Constitutional Safeguards	Federal Court	General Courts-Martial	Nuremberg/Tokyo	ICTY/ICTR
Jury; ....” Art III § 2 cl. 3. “In all criminal prosecutions, the accused shall enjoy the right to a ... trial, by an impartial jury of the state ....” Amendment VI.	There must further be measures to ensure individual jurors selected are not biased (i.e., the *voir dire* process). Lewis v. United States, 146 U.S. 370 (1892); *see* Fed. R. Crim. P. 24 (peremptory challenges). The trial must be conducted in a manner designed to avoid exposure of the jury to prejudicial material or undue influence. If the locality of the trial has been so saturated with publicity about a case that it is impossible to assure jurors will not be affected by prejudice, the defendant is entitled to a change of venue. Irvin v. Dowd, 366 U.S. 717 (1961).	trial by members at a court-martial.” United States v. Witham, 47 MJ 297, 301 (1997); Art. 25, UCMJ, 10 U.S.C. § 825. The Sixth Amendment requirement that the jury be impartial applies to courtmartial members and covers not only the selection of individual jurors, but also their conduct during the trial proceedings and the subsequent deliberations. United States v. Lambert, 55 M.J. 293 (2001). The absence of a right to trial by jury precludes criminal trial of civilians by court-martial. Reid v. Covert, 354 U.S. 1 (1957); Kinsella v. United States *ex rel.* Singleton, 361 U.S. 234 (1960).		
Right to Appeal to Independent Reviewing Authority “The Privilege of the Writ of Habeas Corpus shall not be suspended, unless when in Cases of Rebellion or Invasion the public Safety may require it” Article I § 9 cl. 2.	Originally, the writ of *habeas corpus* permitted collateral attack upon a prisoner's conviction only if the sentencing court lacked subject matter jurisdiction. It later evolved into an avenue for the challenge of federal and state convictions on other due process grounds, to determine whether a prisoner's detention is	The writ of *habeas corpus* provides the primary means by which those sentenced by military court, having exhausted military appeals, can challenge a conviction or sentence in a civilian court. The scope of matters that a court will address is more narrow than in challenges of federal or state convictions. Burns v. Wilson, 346 U.S. 137	None. “The judgment of the Tribunal as to the guilt or the innocence of any Defendant shall give the reasons on which it is based, and shall be final and not subject to review.” IMT Charter art. 26. The Control Council for Germany was empowered to reduce or otherwise alter the sentences, but could not	The ICTY Statute creates an Appeals Chamber, which may hear appeals from convicted persons or from the prosecutor on the grounds of “an error on a question of law invalidating the decision,” or “an error of fact which has occasioned a miscarriage of justice.” ICTY Stat. art. 25; ICTY Stat. art. 24.

Constitutional Safeguards	Federal Court	General Courts-Martial	Nuremberg/Tokyo	ICTY/ICTR
	"contrary to the Constitution or laws or treaties of the United States." 28 U.S.C. §§ 2241 *et seq.*	(1953). However, Congress created a civilian court, the Court of Appeals for the Armed Forces, to review military cases.	increase its severity. IMT Charter art. 29. General MacArthur had similar authority with respect to decisions of the IMTFE. IMTFE Charter art. 17.	
Protection against Excessive Penalties "Excessive bail shall not be required, nor excessive fines imposed, nor cruel and unusual punishments inflicted." Amendment VIII.	The death penalty is not *per se* unconstitutional, but its discriminatory and arbitrary imposition may be, and the death penalty may not be automatic. *See* Gregg v. Georgia, 428 U.S. 153 (1976); 18 U.S.C.§ 3592 (mitigating /aggravating circumstances). When the death penalty may be imposed, the defendant shall be provided a list of potential jurors and witnesses, unless the court finds that such action might jeopardize the life or safety of any person. 18 U.S.C. § 3432. A special hearing is held to determine whether the death sentence is warranted. 18 U.S.C. § 3593.	Death may only be adjudged for certain crimes where the defendant is found guilty by unanimous vote of courtmartial members present at the time of the vote. Prior to arraignment, the trial counsel must give the defense written notice of aggravating factors the prosecution intends to prove. R.C.M. 1004. A conviction of spying during time of war under article 106, UCMJ, carries a mandatory death penalty. 10 U.S.C. § 906.	Penalties included "death or such other punishment as shall be determined by [the IMT] to be just." IMT Charter art. 27; IMTFE Charter art. 16. The IMT at Nuremberg could also order the convicted person to deliver any stolen property to the Control Council for Germany. IMT Charter art. 28.	Penalties are limited to imprisonment; there is no death penalty. The ICTY may also order the return of any property and proceeds acquired by criminal conduct to their rightful owners. ICTY Stat. art. 24; ICTR Stat. art. 23. Sentences are to be imposed consistently with the general practice regarding prison sentences in the courts of the former Yugoslavia or Rwanda, taking into account such factors as the gravity of the offence and the individual circumstances of the convicted person. ICTY Stat. art. 24; ICTR Stat. art. 23.

Congress regulates the armed forces largely through title 10 of the U.S. Code, which contains as Chapter 47 the Uniform Code of Military Justice (UCMJ) regulating the system of military courts-martial. The Supreme Court has found the procedures Congress set through the UCMJ to provide adequate procedural safeguards to satisfy constitutional requirements and the interest in maintaining a strong national defense.

Congress has delegated to the President the authority to make procedural rules for the military justice system.[20] The President created the Rules for Courts-Martial (R.C.M.) and the Military Rules of Evidence (Mil. R. Evid.) pursuant to that delegation.[21] The comparison chart will cite provisions of the UCMJ and the applicable rules, as well as military appellate court opinions as applicable.

Defendants are not able to appeal their courts-martial directly to federal courts, but may seek relief in the form of a writ of habeas corpus, although review may be limited. However, Congress has provided for a separate system of reviewing convictions by court-martial, which includes a civilian appellate court. In cases in which the convening authority approves a sentence of death, or, unless the defendant waives review, approves a bad-conduct discharge, a dishonorable discharge, dismissal of an officer, or confinement for one year or more, the Court of Criminal Appeals for the appropriate service[22] must review the case for legal error, factual sufficiency, and appropriateness of the sentence.

The Court of Appeals for the Armed Forces (CAAF) exercises appellate jurisdiction over the services' Courts of Criminal Appeals, with respect to issues of law. The CAAF is an Article I court composed of five civilian judges appointed for 15-year terms by the President with the advice and consent of the Senate. Its jurisdiction is established in Article 67 of the UCMJ (10 U.S.C. § 867), and is discretionary except in death penalty cases.

Military Commissions

The Constitution empowers the Congress to declare war and "make rules concerning captures on land and water,"[23] to define and punish violations of the "Law of Nations,"[24] and to make regulations to govern the armed forces.[25] The power of the President to convene military commissions flows from his authority as Commander in Chief of the Armed Forces and his responsibility to execute the laws of the nation.[26] Under the Articles of War and subsequent statute[27] the President has at least implicit authority to convene military commissions to try offenses against the law of war.[28] There is, therefore, somewhat of a distinction between the authority and objectives behind convening military courts-martial and commissions.[29] Rather than serving the internally directed purpose of maintaining discipline and order of the troops, the military commission is externally directed at the enemy as a means of waging successful war by punishing and deterring offenses against the law of war.

Jurisdiction of military commissions is limited to time of war and to trying offenses recognized under the law of war or as designated by statute.[30] While case law suggests that military commissions could try U.S. citizens as enemy belligerents,[31] the Military Order of November 13, 2001 limits their jurisdiction to non-citizens.

As non-Article III courts, military commissions are not subject to the same constitutional requirements that are applied in Article III courts.[32] Congress has delegated to the President the authority to set the rules of procedure and evidence for military tribunals, applying "the principles of law and the rules of evidence generally recognized in the trial of criminal cases in the United States district court" insofar as he considers it practicable.[33] The rules "may not be contrary to or inconsistent with the UCMJ"[34] and must be uniform insofar as practicable with courts-martial.[35]

The United States first used military commissions to try enemy belligerents accused of war crimes during the occupation of Mexico in 1847, and made heavy use of them in the Civil War.[36] However, prior to the President's Military Order, no military commissions had been convened since the aftermath of World War II. Because of the lack of standards of procedure used by military commissions, it is difficult to draw a meaningful comparison with the other types of tribunals. For a comparison of the Department of Defense rules for military commissions that were struck down in *Hamdan* to recent legislative proposals, see CRS Report RL31600, *The Department of Defense Rules for Military Commissions: Analysis of Procedural Rules and Comparison with Proposed Legislation and the Uniform Code of Military Justice*.

International War Crimes Tribunals

Prior to the twentieth century, war crimes were generally tried, if tried at all, by belligerent States in their own national courts or special military tribunals. After World War I, the Allies appointed a 15-member commission to inquire into the legal liability of those responsible for the war and the numerous breaches of the law of war that it occasioned. It recommended the establishment of an international military tribunal to prosecute those accused of war crimes and crimes against humanity. After Germany refused to comply with the locally unpopular provision of the peace treaty requiring it to turn over accused war criminals to the Allied forces for trial, a compromise was reached in which Germany agreed to prosecute those persons in its national courts.[37] Of 901 cases referred to the German Supreme Court for trial at Leipzig, only 13 were convicted.[38] Because German nationalism appeared to have hindered the earnest prosecution of war criminals, the results were largely seen as a failure.[39]

International Military Tribunals

In the aftermath of World War II, the Allies applied lessons learned at Leipzig and formed special international tribunals for the European and Asian theaters. In an agreement concluded in London on August 8, 1945, the United States, France, Great Britain and the Soviet Union together established the International Military Tribunal (IMT) at Nuremberg for the trial of war criminals[40] The four occupying powers also established Control Council Law No. 10, authorizing military tribunals at the national level to try the less high-profile war crimes and crimes against humanity.[41]

The evidentiary rules used at Nuremberg and adopted by the Tokyo tribunals were designed to be non-technical, allowing the expeditious admission of "all evidence [the Tribunal] deems to have probative value."[42] This evidence included hearsay, coerced confessions, and the findings of prior mass trials.[43] It has also been argued that the tribunals violated the principles of legality by establishing *ex post facto* crimes and dispensing victor's justice.[44] However, while the historical consensus seems to have accepted that the Nuremberg Trials were conducted fairly[45] some observers argue that the malleability of the rules of procedure and evidence could and did have some unjust results, in particular as they were applied by the national military tribunals.[46] The Tokyo tribunal decisions were subject to criticism by dissenters on the Supreme Court in the *Yamashita* case.[47] Some argue that procedural safeguards considered sufficient for the World War II tribunals would not likely meet today's standards of justice[48]

Nuremberg

The jurisdiction of the Nuremberg Tribunal was based on universally applicable international law regulating armed conflict, and its authority was based on the combined sovereignty of the Allies and Germany's unconditional surrender.[49] The Tribunal rejected the defendants' contention that the tribunal violated fundamental legal principles by trying them for conduct that was not prohibited by criminal law at the time it was committed.[50] The Nuremberg Tribunal also adopted the doctrine of individual responsibility for war crimes, rejecting the idea that state sovereignty could protect those responsible from punishment for their misdeeds.

Twenty-four Nazi leaders were indicted and tried as war criminals by the International Military Tribunal (IMT). The indictments contained four counts: (1) crimes against the peace, (2) crimes against humanity, (3) war crimes, and (4) a common plan or conspiracy to commit the aforementioned acts. Nineteen of the defendants were found guilty, three were acquitted, one committed suicide before the sentence, and one was physically and mentally unfit for trial. Sentences ranged from death by hanging (twelve), life imprisonment (three), and imprisonment for ten to twenty years (four).

Tokyo

The International Military Tribunal for the Far East (IMTFE) in Tokyo was established by a Special Proclamation of General Douglas MacArthur as the Supreme Commander in the Far East for the Allied Powers.[51] Many provisions of the IMTFE were adapted from the London Agreement. The Tokyo tribunal tried only the most serious crimes, crimes against peace. General MacArthur appointed eleven judges, one from each of the victorious Allied nations who signed the instrument of surrender and one each from India and the Philippines, to sit on the tribunal. General MacArthur also appointed the prosecutor. Of the twenty-five people indicted for crimes against peace, all were convicted, with seven executed, sixteen given life imprisonment, and two others serving lesser terms. Some 300,000 Japanese nationals were tried for conventional war crimes (primarily prisoner abuse) and crimes against humanity in national military tribunals.

Ad Hoc International Courts

The U.N. Security Council (UNSC), acting under its Chapter VII authority of the U.N. Charter, established two ad hoc criminal courts, the International Criminal Tribunal for the former Yugoslavia (ICTY)[52] and the International Criminal Tribunal for Rwanda (ICTR).[53] Both tribunals are still operating, and employ virtually identical procedural rules.

Their jurisdiction is coexistent with that of national courts, but they also may assert primacy over national courts to prevent trials of the same individuals in more than one forum. Their jurisprudence may provide important precedent for the interpretation of Common Article 3.

Yugoslavia

Based in the Hague, Netherlands, the ICTY has jurisdiction to try crimes conducted within the territory of the former Yugoslavia, including the crime of "ethnic cleansing," whether committed in the context of an international war or a war of non-international character. It tries violations of the Geneva Conventions of 1949, violations of the laws or customs of war, genocide, and crimes against humanity when committed in the context of an armed conflict. It is composed of sixteen permanent independent judges, who are elected by the UN General Assembly from a list of nominations provided by the Security Council. It has an Appeals Chamber consisting of seven judges, five of whom sit on a panel in any given case.

The Prosecutor, an independent organ of the court appointed by the UN Security Council on the recommendation of the UN Secretary-General, investigates and prosecutes those responsible for covered offenses. When the Prosecutor finds that sufficient evidence exists to try an individual, he issues an indictment, subject to the approval of a judge from the Trial Chamber.

Rwanda

The ICTR, based in Arusha, Tanzania, was established by the UN Security Council in response to genocide and other systematic, widespread, and flagrant violations of humanitarian law applicable in the context of a non-international armed conflict, that is, Common Article 3 of the Geneva Conventions and Additional Protocol II, genocide, and crimes against humanity. Its structure and composition are similar to those of the ICTY. As of June 2006, the ICTR has tried 28 accused, convicting 25 and acquitting three.[54] Twenty-seven defendants are undergoing trial, and another fourteen await trial.[55]

REFERENCES

[1] Military Order, November 13, 2001 Detention, Treatment, and Trial of Certain NonCitizens in the War Against Terrorism §1(a), 66 Fed. Reg. 57,833 (Nov. 16, 2001).

[2] 10 U.S.C. § 801 *et seq.*

[3] Hamdan v. Rumsfeld, 548 U.S. __ (2006), *rev'g* 415 F.3d 33 (D.C. Cir. 2005). The Geneva Conventions were held to be incorporated by implication into the UCMJ. For an analysis of the decision, see CRS Report RS22466, *Hamdan v. Rumsfeld: Military Commissions in the 'Global War on Terrorism,'* by Jennifer K. Elsea.

[4] Wong Wing v. United States, 163 U.S. 228 (1896)(aliens are entitled to due process of law).

[5] U.S. CONST. Art. VI ("[A]ll Treaties ... shall be the Supreme Law of the Land; ...").

[6] *See, e.g.* 18 U.S.C. § 2441 (War Crimes Act).

[7] *See* RESTATEMENT (THIRD) OF FOREIGN RELATIONS § 111 (1987).

[8] For a brief explanation of the sources of the law of war, see generally CRS Report RL31191, *Terrorism and the Law of War: Trying Terrorists as War Criminals before Military Commissions*, by Jennifer Elsea.

[9] *Hamdan*, slip op. at 67 (citing art. 3 § 1(d) of The Geneva Convention Relative to the Treatment of Prisoners of War, August 12, 1949, 6 U.S.T. 3317). The identical provision is included in each of the four Geneva Conventions and applies to any "conflict not of an international character." The majority declined to accept the President's interpretation of Common Article 3 as inapplicable to the conflict with al Qaeda and interpreted the phrase "in contradistinction to a conflict between nations," which the Geneva Conventions designate a "conflict of international character."

[10] U.S. CONST. Preamble.

[11] *Id.* art. I § 8, cls. 11-14 (War Power).

[12] *Id.* art. II § 2, cl. 1.

[13] *Id.* art. I § 8, cl. 14.

[14] *See* Dynes v. Hoover, 61 U.S. (How.) 65 (1857).

[15] *See* WILLIAM WINTHROP, WINTHROP'S MILITARY LAW AND PRECEDENTS 48-49 (2d. ed. 1920)(describing courts-martial as *instrumentalities of the executive power*, provided by Congress for the President as Commander-in-chief, to aid him in properly commanding the army and navy and enforcing discipline therein) (emphasis in original).

[16] *See Ex parte* Milligan, 71 U.S. (4 Wall.) 2 (1866). Congress has, in article 32, UCMJ, provided for a pre-trial hearing that performs the same basic function as a grand jury. Court-martial panels consist of a military judge and several panel members, who function similarly to a jury.

[17] For an overview of the court-martial process, see CRS Report RS21850, *Military Courts-Martial: An Overview*, by Jennifer K. Elsea.

[18] *See* 10 U.S.C. § 802. "In time of war" refers to war declared by Congress. United States v. Averette, 17 USCMA 363 (1968).

[19] *See* 10 U.S.C. § 818.

[20] 10 U.S.C. § 836. Article 36 authorizes the President to prescribe rules for "pretrial, trial, and post-trial procedures, including modes of proof, for cases arising under this chapter triable in courts-martial, military commissions and other military tribunals." Such rules are to "apply the principles of law and the rules of evidence generally recognized in the trial of criminal cases in the United States district courts" insofar as the President "considers practicable" but that "may not be contrary to or inconsistent" with the UCMJ.

[21] The rules are set forth in the Manual for Courts-Martial (M.C.M.), established as Exec. Order No. 12473, Manual for Courts-Martial, United States, 49 Fed. Reg 17,152, (Apr. 23, 1984), as amended.

[22] There are four such courts — the Army Court of Criminal Appeals, the Navy-Marine Corps Court of Criminal Appeals, the Air Force Court of Criminal Appeals, and the Coast Guard Court of Criminal Appeals. These courts are established by the Judge Advocate General of the respective service. 10 U.S.C. § 866.

[23] U.S. CONST. art. I, § 8, cl. 11.

[24] *Id.* art. I, § 8, cl. 10.

[25] *Id.* art. I, § 8, cl. 14.

[26] *Id.* art. II.

[27] The Articles of War were re-enacted at 10 U.S.C. § 801 *et seq.* as part of the UCMJ. Although there is no case law interpreting the UCMJ as authorizing military commissions, the relevant sections of the UCMJ, which recognize the concurrent jurisdiction of military commissions to deal with "offenders or offenses designated by statute or the law of war," are essentially identical to the corresponding language in the Articles of War. *See* 10 U.S.C. § 821.

[28] *Ex parte* Quirin, 317 U.S. 1 (1942).

[29] *See* WINTHROP, *supra* note 15, at 831 (describing distinction between courts-martial and military tribunals).

[30] 10 U.S.C. § 821. Statutory offenses for which military commissions may be convened are limited to aiding the enemy, 10 U.S.C. § 904, and spying, 10 U.S.C. § 906.

[31] *See Ex parte* Quirin, 317 U.S. 1 (1942).

[32] *See Ex parte* Quirin, 317 U.S. at 38; *Ex parte* Milligan, 71 U.S. (4 Wall.) 2, 123 (1866) (noting a servicemember "surrenders his right to be tried by the civil courts").

[33] 10 U.S.C. § 836. The Supreme Court has held that the President's discretion to determine whether the application of procedural rules that apply in federal courts is not without limitation. Hamdan v. Rumsfeld, 548 U.S. __ (2006).

[34] Id.

[35] *Id.*

[36] For more information about the history of military commissions in the United States, see CRS Report RL31191, *Terrorism and the Law of War: Trying Terrorists as War Criminals before Military Commissions*, by Jennifer K. Elsea; CRS Report RL32458, *Military Tribunals: Historical Patterns and Lessons*, by Louis Fisher; CRS Report RL31340: *Military Tribunals: The Quirin Precedent*, by Louis Fisher.

[37] *See id.* at 46.

[38] *See id.* at 49.

[39] *See id.* at 51-52.

[40] *See* Agreement for the Prosecution and Punishment of the Major War Criminals of the European Axis Powers and Charter of the International Military Tribunal, Aug. 8, 1945, 82 U.N.T.S. 279 [hereinafter "London Charter"], *available at* [http://www.yale.edu/lawweb/ avalon/imt/proc/imtconst.htm]. The Rules of Procedure (IMT Rules) are available at [http://www.yale.edu/lawweb/avalon/imt/proc/imtrules.htm].

[41] Approximately 185 people were indicted. Thirty people were sentenced to death, one hundred twenty were given prison sentences, and thirty-five were acquitted.

[42] *See* Evan J. Wallach, *The Procedural And Evidentiary Rules of the Post-World War II War Crimes Trials: Did They Provide An Outline For International Legal Procedure?*, 37 COLUM. J. TRANSNAT'L L. 851, 860 (1999).

[43] *See id.* at 871-72.

[44] *See* KRIANGSAK KITTICHAISAREE, INTERNATIONAL CRIMINAL LAW 20 (2001).

[45] *See*, Wallach, *supra* note 42, at 852 (citing VIRGINIA MORRIS and MICHAEL SCHARF, 1 AN INSIDER'S GUIDE TO THE INTERNATIONAL CRIMINAL TRIBUNAL FOR THE FORMER YUGOSLAVIA 9-10 (1995)).

[46] *See id.* at 869; Application of Homma, 327 U.S. 759, 760 (1946) (Murphy, J. dissenting). *But see* Jonathan A. Bush, *Lex Americana: Constitutional Due Process and*

the Nuremberg Defendants, 45 ST. LOUIS U. L.J. 515, 526 (2001)(arguing that in many ways, "the new [Tokyo and Nuremberg] tribunals' charters gave defendants many rights that went beyond anything allowed in the American system" at the time of the trials).

[47] Justice Murphy wrote: [The rules], as will be noted, permit[] reception of documents, reports, affidavits, depositions, diaries, letters, copies of documents or other secondary evidence of their contents, hearsay, opinion evidence and conclusions, in fact of anything which in the commission's opinion "would be of assistance in proving or disproving the charge," without any of the usual modes of authentication. A more complete abrogation of customary safeguards relating to the proof, whether in the usual rules of evidence or any reasonable substitute and whether for use in the trial of crime in the civil courts or military tribunals, hardly could have been made. So far as the admissibility and probative value of evidence was concerned, the directive made the commission a law unto itself. *In re Yamashita*, 327 U.S. at 49 (Murphy, J. dissenting).

[48] *See* Wallach, *supra* note 42.

[49] *See* Matthew Lippman, *Crimes Against Humanity*, 17 B.C. THIRD WORLD L.J. 171, 238 (1997).

[50] *See* KITTICHAISAREE,*supra* note 44, at 18 (citing the judgment of the tribunal in the context of "crimes against peace" to the effect that justice required, rather than prohibited, the punishment of those responsible for unprovoked attacks against neighboring states "in defiance of treaties and assurances").

[51] Charter of the International Military Tribunal For The Far East, Apr. 26, 1946 ("IMTFE Charter"), T.I.A.S. No. 1589, *available at* [http://www.yale.edu/lawweb/ avalon/ imtfech. htm].

[52] UN Doc. S/Res/808 (1993; UN Doc. S/Res/827 (1993). Its statute (ICTY Stat.) and procedural rules (ICTY Rule) are available at [http://www.un.org/icty/legaldoc-e/ index.htm]. For more information, see CRS Report RL30864, *Yugoslavia War Crimes Tribunal: Current Issues for Congress*, by Julie Kim.

[53] UN Doc. S/Res/955 (1994). Its statute (ICTR Stat.) and procedural rules (ICTR Rule) are available at [http://69.94.11.53/default.htm].

[54] *See* [http://69.94.11.53/ENGLISH/factsheets/achievements.htm].

[55] *See* [http://69.94.11.53/ENGLISH/factsheets/detainee.htm]. More information is available at the ICTY website, [http://www.un.org/icty/].

In: Law and Law Enforcement Issues
Editor: Gerald M. Kessler, pp. 37-82
ISBN: 978-1-60456-044-2

Chapter 3

INTERNATIONAL CRIMINAL COURT: OVERVIEW AND SELECTED LEGAL ISSUES*

Jennifer K. Elsea

ABSTRACT

On April 11, 2002, the Rome Statute of the International Criminal Court received its sixtieth ratification, meaning it will come into effect July 1, 2002, establishing the first global permanent international court with jurisdiction to prosecute individuals for "the most serious crimes of concern to the international community." The United Nations, many human rights organizations, and most democratic nations have expressed support for the new court. The Bush Administration firmly opposes it and has formally renounced the U.S. obligations under the treaty. At the same time, however, the Administration has stressed that the United States shares the goal of the ICC's supporters – promotion of the rule of law – and does not intend to take any action to undermine the ICC.

The primary objection given by the United States in opposition to the treaty is the ICC's possible assertion of jurisdiction over U.S. soldiers charged with "war crimes" resulting from legitimate uses of force. The main issue faced by the current Congress is whether to adopt a policy aimed at preventing the ICC from becoming effective or whether to continue contributing to the development of the ICC in order to improve it.

This article provides an historical background of the negotiations for the Rome Statute, outlines the structure of the ICC as contained in the final Statute, and describes the jurisdiction of the ICC. The report identifies the specific crimes enumerated in the Rome Statute as supplemented by the draft elements of crime. A discussion of procedural safeguards follows, including reference to the draft procedural rules. The report then discusses the implications for the United States as a non-ratifying country when the ICC comes into being, and outlines some legislation enacted and proposed to regulate U.S. relations with the ICC, including versions of the American Servicemembers' Protection Act (ASPA) contained in H.R. 1646 and H.R. 4775, the American Servicemember and Citizen Protection Act, H.R. 4169, and the American Citizens' Protection and War Criminal Prosecution Act of 2001, S. 1296/H.R. 2699.

---

* Excerpted from CRS Report RL31437, dated June 5, 2002.

INTRODUCTION AND NEGOTIATING HISTORY

On April 11, 2002, the Rome Statute of the International Criminal Court[1] received its sixtieth ratification, meaning it will come into effect July 1, 2002, years earlier than had been predicted. The ICC will be the first global permanent international court with jurisdiction to prosecute individuals for "the most serious crimes of concern to the international community;"[2] the United Nations, many human rights organizations, and most democratic nations have expressed support for the new court.[3] The Bush Administration, however, firmly opposes it and has taken the measure of formally renouncing any U.S. obligations under the treaty.[4] Some critics have remarked that the issue is causing a rift between the United States and its allies in the war against terrorism.[5] At the same time, the Administration has stressed that the United States shares the goal of the ICC's supporters – promotion of the rule of law – and does not intend to take any action to undermine the ICC.[6] In a move that may foreshadow the Administration's strategy, the United States is also reportedly seeking assurances from the United Nations that no U.N. personnel taking part in the peacekeeping mission in East Timor will be subject to prosecution by any local or international court for war crimes – a move that has met with resistance from U.S. allies because they say it could undermine the principles of the ICC.[7]

While the United States initially supported the idea of creating an international criminal court[8] and was a major participant at the Rome Conference,[9] in the end, the United States — joined by Iran, Iraq, China, Israel, Sudan, and Libya — voted against the Statute.[10] Nevertheless, President Clinton signed the treaty December 31, 2000 – the last day it was open for signature without simultaneous ratification, at the same time declaring that the treaty contained "significant flaws" and that he would not submit it to the Senate for its advice and consent "until our fundamental concerns are satisfied."[11] The Bush Administration has likewise declined to submit the Rome Statute to the Senate for ratification, and has notified the depositary of the United Nations of the U.S. intent not to ratify the treaty.[12] The primary objection given by the United States in opposition to the treaty is the ICC's possible assertion of jurisdiction over U.S. soldiers charged with "war crimes" resulting from legitimate uses of force, even if the United States does not ratify the Rome Statute. The United States sought to exempt U.S. soldiers and employees from the jurisdiction of the ICC based on the unique position the United States occupies with regard to international peacekeeping.[13] The main issue faced by the Congress is the level of cooperation to allow between the United States and the ICC: to withhold all cooperation from the ICC and its member nations in order to prevent the ICC from becoming effective, to continue contributing to the development of the ICC in order to improve it, or to adopt a pragmatic approach based solely on U.S. interests.[14]

This article provides an historical background of the negotiations for the Rome Statute, outlines the structure of the ICC as contained in the final Statute, and describes the jurisdiction of the ICC. The report identifies the specific crimes enumerated in the Rome Statute as supplemented by the draft elements of crime drawn up by the Preparatory Commission established by the Rome Conference. A discussion of procedural safeguards follows, including reference to the draft procedural rules. The report then discusses the implications for the United States, as a non-ratifying country as the ICC comes into being, and outlines some legislation enacted and proposed to regulate U.S. relations with the ICC.

The creation of the ICC is the culmination of a decades-long effort to establish an international court with the jurisdiction to try individuals for the commission of crimes against humanity.[15] The post-World War II tribunals to try Nazi and Japanese war criminals established precedent for the ICC. The later International Criminal Tribunal for Yugoslavia (ICTY) and the International Criminal Tribunal for Rwanda (ICTR) built upon the Nuremberg legacy. However, all of these courts were created *ad hoc* with limited jurisdiction. An international court with jurisdiction over all crimes of the worst nature affecting mankind was urged in order to end impunity for *any and all* perpetrators of large-scale atrocities. The U.N. General Assembly voted to establish an Ad Hoc Committee on the Establishment of an International Criminal Court[16] and created a Preparatory Committee charged with "preparing a widely acceptable consolidated text of a convention for an International Criminal Court as a next step towards consideration by a conference of plenipotentiaries."[17]

The Preparatory Committee held six sessions between March 1996 and April 1998 to prepare a text for consideration at the Rome Conference.[18] The most contentious issue at the Conference revolved around the level of independence the ICC would have vis-à-vis national courts and the U.N. Security Council. The Preparatory Commission considered two basic options for defining the jurisdiction of the ICC: The ICC might assert jurisdiction over all relevant crimes, exercising primacy over national courts, without regard to the nationality of the victims or perpetrators. Under this option, "rogue" regimes would be unable to insulate themselves from responsibility for crimes committed against opposing forces or ethnic minorities, even during internal armed conflicts. Many countries, including the United States, objected to the idea as an intrusion into the sovereignty of nations. Second, the ICC's power to try cases could be "complementary" to that of national courts, where the ICC would exercise jurisdiction only when national courts of the country in which the crime took place, or whose national was accused, were unable or unwilling to prosecute. The second model, which the United States had supported, was adopted in principle.[19]

The adoption of the complementarity model of jurisdiction led to the even more intractable question of how and when the ICC would take a case. Possible options included a recommendation by the U.N. Security Council, a recommendation by a country with personal or subject matter jurisdiction over the crime or the accused, or upon the initiative of the ICC itself. Taking the position that treaty regimes should apply only to those states that choose to become parties and not to those that choose to remain outside, the United States delegation offered amendments at Rome to require the consent of both the State in which the crime was allegedly committed and of the state of nationality of the alleged perpetrator, or, failing that, at least of the state of nationality, to the jurisdiction of the Court.[20] Under the U.S. proposals, the ICC would have jurisdiction over citizens of non-consenting non-parties only in cases referred or authorized by the U.N. Security Council, which would have allowed the United States and other permanent members of the Council to veto any attempt to prosecute their citizens, but would allow for the prosecution of state architects of genocidal policies, for example, as long as the political support could be generated in the Security Council.

The conferees rejected this proposal on the grounds that it would essentially mirror the present application of *ad hoc* tribunals, bringing some perpetrators of crimes against humanity to justice while allowing others to escape with impunity.[21] Additionally, in their view, a treaty that subjects citizens of non-parties to an international court's jurisdiction does not bind the non-party state to *do* anything and thus does not infringe on its sovereignty.[22]

Aliens who commit crimes are subject to the jurisdiction of local courts in any event. Under this view, assuming that the referring state would have the jurisdiction to try or extradite an alien accused of a crime on its territory, the referring state could just as legitimately cede its jurisdiction over the accused to an international court.[23]

The U.S. delegation also proposed to exempt from the Court's jurisdiction conduct that arises from the official actions of a non-party state acknowledged as such by the non-party. The United States, it was argued, would willingly acknowledge the official nature of conduct related to peacekeeping missions or other foreign affairs activity and thus gain an exemption from the Court's jurisdiction for alleged crimes arising from such missions.[24] This, it proposed, would eliminate the disincentive for non-party States to participate in peacekeeping missions. Dictators, it said, would be reluctant to admit responsibility for conduct that could be viewed as criminal under the Rome Statute. The conference voted to take no action on the proposal.[25] The final rule allows the ICC to take a case on the recommendation of one of the countries with the appropriate jurisdiction, the U.N. Security Council, or the ICC Prosecutor.

The U.S. delegation to Rome, led by David Scheffer, then Ambassador-at-Large for War Crimes Issues, argued that allowing the Prosecutor to initiate cases would potentially put U.S. military personnel in jeopardy of being summoned in front of the ICC on groundless charges. The United States is in a unique position in the world, Scheffer argued, in which it is frequently called upon to respond to international crises, often by deploying U.S. troops and government officials to hostile countries. If those countries could retaliate by accusing the United States and its officials or military personnel of war crimes, for example, the United States could find itself hamstrung in its peacekeeping efforts. The Rome delegates adopted four methods to accommodate U.S. concerns regarding abuse of prosecutorial discretion: limiting the power of the ICC Prosecutor, requiring the consent of a country which would have jurisdiction over an alleged crime before initiating a prosecution, narrowly defining the crimes for which a person may be prosecuted, and creating a role for the U.N. Security Council,[26] though not adopting the U.S. suggestion which would have allowed any permanent member of the Security Council to veto any proposed prosecution.

Instead, the Rome Conference adopted the so-called Singapore Proposal, which, rather than requiring unanimity of the permanent members of the Security Council to initiate a prosecution, would require unanimity in order to block prosecution temporarily.[27] Because the Permanent Five would have to cooperate in order to authorize a peace-keeping mission in the first place, it was reasoned, all five could be expected to agree to block any unwarranted ICC prosecutions that might arise.[28] This proposal would not guarantee immunity in the case of a unilateral action on the part of the United States, however, and failed to gain the support of the U.S. delegation.

Although the United States voted against the Rome Statute to establish an ICC, it did sign the Final Act of the Conference.[29] As a consequence, it was able to participate as a voting member of the Preparatory Commission created by the Rome conference. The Preparatory Commission has developed draft rules of procedure and evidence, the elements of crimes, a relationship agreement between the ICC and the U.N., financial regulations, an agreement on privileges and immunities, a budget, and the rules of procedure to govern the Assembly of States Parties.[30] It has not yet completed its work on the definition of the crime of aggression.

STRUCTURE OF THE ICC

The Rome Statute establishes the Court's structure and provides rules for its limited governance by the states parties to the Statute. The ICC will consist of the Presidency, three Trial Divisions, the Office of the Prosecutor, and the Registry.[31] It will have international legal personality to carry out its functions,[32] and its relationship to the United Nations will be established by agreement between the ICC president and the U.N.[33]

The Rome Statute is designed to provide for the independence of the prosecutor and judges. However, it also provides a system of checks and balances designed to rein in overzealous prosecutors and prevent the ICC from falling under the control of biased judges or states with an interest in the outcome. For example, for a prosecutor to initiate a case, he must first get independent authorization from the ICC's Pre-Trial Chamber to continue an investigation.[34] The statute's requirements for election of judges are designed to diminish the possibility that the pre-trial chamber would be politicized, thereby increasing its ability to prevent prosecutors from bringing unwarranted charges. The candidates for judge are required to be competent in either criminal law or in relevant areas of international law,[35] and no two judges are permitted to be from the same state.[36] The person being investigated may request the disqualification of any judge when the judge's "impartiality might reasonably be doubted."[37] The trial and appellate chambers are kept separate to enable parties to challenge both interlocutory and final decisions before different judges. Finally, it provides mechanisms for checks by majority vote of the Assembly of States Parties, a representative body of the member states.

The Judges of the ICC: The Presidency and Trial Divisions

A total of eighteen judges will be elected to serve staggered nine-year terms on the ICC, subject to a possible increase in the number of judges upon recommendation by the President and its approval by the Assembly of States Parties. States parties to the ICC may nominate one qualified candidate for each election. Judicial candidates must be nationals of states parties to the Rome Statute, although not necessarily of the nominating state.[38] The Assembly of States Parties may establish an advisory committee on nominations as it deems appropriate.[39] Judges will be selected by vote of the Assembly of States Parties to be representative of the world's population in terms of legal systems, geography, legal specialties, and gender.[40] Judges will not be permitted to pursue outside occupations, and may be removed from office by a vote of two-thirds majority of the Assembly of States Parties to affirm a recommendation by two-thirds of the other judges that the judge be removed for serious misconduct or inability to carry out the functions of the position.[41]

The Presidency consists of a President and two Vice-Presidents, who are to be elected from the judge corps by an absolute majority of its members.[42] The President and Vice Presidents serve for three-year terms, unless their terms as judges expire earlier, with one opportunity for re-election. The President will have overall responsibility for the administration of the Court (with the exception of the Office of the Prosecutor) and for other functions, such as deciding which judges will hear which cases and whether to excuse a particular judge or prosecutor from any particular case for reasons of possible conflict of interest.

The eighteen judges will be divided among the Pre-Trial Division, Trial Division, and Appeals Division. Judges assigned to the Appeals Division remain there throughout their tenure, while judges initially assigned to the Trial or Pre-Trial Divisions serve three-year terms plus any time necessary to complete ongoing hearings. Judges assigned to the Trial or Pre-Trial Divisions may be temporarily shifted between the two divisions to accommodate the workload of the ICC, but judges assigned to the Appeals Division, which will include the President, may not be temporarily assigned to another division.[43]

The Pre-Trial Division, by majority vote of a three-judge chamber, decides issues regarding admissibility of evidence and jurisdiction of the Court to hear a case, authorizes the prosecutor to pursue self-initiated investigations, determines whether sufficient evidence exists to support an indictment, and issues rulings regarding the withholding of material held by a state that deems the disclosure of such information to be prejudicial to the national security of that state.[44] Other issues may be decided by individual judges, including rulings necessary to ensure privacy and security of witnesses and actions to seek the cooperation of a state in executing one of the majority-issued orders.

The Trial Division consists of two chambers of three judges each and is responsible for the fair and expeditious conduct of trials with proper regard for the rights of the accused and security of witnesses. The Trial Chambers have the authority to decide intermediary issues by majority decision or to refer such issues to the Pre-Trial Division. They are responsible for confirming that the accused understands the nature of the charges and that pleas are voluntary, and for providing an accurate transcript of the proceedings. The Trial Division also sentences the accused upon conviction, based on all relevant evidence supplemented by means of additional hearings, when necessary.[45]

The Appeals Division consists of a single chamber of five judges, including the ICC President, that hears appeals of convictions, sentences, and acquittals, as well as interlocutory rulings on admissibility of evidence, jurisdiction, and the like. The Appeals Chamber has powers comparable to those of the Trial Division, and may reverse or amend a decision or sentence, or it may order a new trial before a different chamber.[46] A convicted person or his survivors or designee may bring an appeal any time new evidence becomes available that could have changed the outcome of a case. The Appeals Division may reject such an application it determines to be unfounded, or it may order new proceedings before the original or a new Trial Chamber, or retain jurisdiction over the matter.[47] In cases of grave and manifest miscarriages of justice, it may award compensation to an arrested or convicted person.[48]

Prosecutor

The Prosecutor is selected by an absolute majority of the Assembly of States Parties via secret ballot.[49] The Assembly then votes, again in secret, to select Deputy Prosecutors from a list of candidates provided by the Prosecutor. The Prosecutor and Deputy Prosecutors are each eligible to hold office for one nine-year term, without the possibility of re-election. During their terms in office, they may not engage in any activities that might place their impartiality in doubt, and any of them may be disqualified from a particular case by the

Appeals Chamber if the person being investigated or prosecuted so requests. If it is found that the Prosecutor has committed serious misconduct, breached his or her duties, or is no longer able to carry out his or her functions under the Statute, an absolute majority of the Assembly may decide by secret ballot to disqualify him or her. A Deputy Prosecutor may be removed for like reasons by an absolute majority of the Assembly upon the recommendation of the Prosecutor. In either proceeding, the Prosecutor or Deputy Prosecutor is allowed to present and receive evidence in order to dispute the charges.

The Office of the Prosecutor receives referrals from the U.N. Security Council and member states on possible crimes within the jurisdiction of the Court for investigation to determine whether prosecution is warranted. The Rome Statute also allows investigations to be initiated by the Prosecutor, subject to approval by the majority of a Pre-Trial Chamber. The Prosecutor determines whether the information available establishes a reasonable basis to conduct an investigation.[50] If there is such a basis, the Prosecutor shall "extend the investigation to cover all facts and evidence relevant to an assessment of whether there is criminal responsibility under [the Rome] Statute," giving equal consideration to exonerating evidence as is given to incriminating information, and taking care to respect the interests of victims and witnesses, as well as the rights of the accused.[51] The Prosecutor may conduct investigations on the territory of a state that is a party to the Statute or agrees to cooperate.[52]

The role of the ICC Prosecutor remains a point of contention for the United States, which sought more limits on the power of the Prosecutor to launch cases on his own initiative. The U.S. opposed granting this discretion to the Prosecutor on the grounds it would "encourage overwhelming the Court with complaints and risk diversion of its resources, as well as embroil the Court in controversy, political decision making, and confusion."[53]

Registry

The Office of the Registry is responsible under the Rome Statute for the nonjudicial administration of the Court,[54] including providing for witness protection and assistance, as well as for receiving prisoners, arranging for the defense of indigents, and surrendering convicted persons to the state of incarceration. The Registrar, who will head the Registry as the chief administrative officer of the Court, is elected by an absolute majority of the judges by secret ballot after considering the Assembly's recommendations. The Registrar serves on a full-time basis for up to two five-year terms. Deputy registrars may serve shorter terms and need not serve full-time.

As part of its duties with regard to witnesses, the Registrar is responsible for the creation of the Victims and Witnesses Unit (VWU), which will be charged with recommending and providing protection, counseling, and assistance to witnesses and victims who appear before the Court, as well as others who may be placed at risk due to testimony given by other witnesses, in order to prevent their suffering mental or physical violence.[55] VWU staff must have expertise in treating trauma victims, including children and victims of sex crimes and violence.

The Rome Statute does not provide for a separate unit within the Registry to provide its mandated support to the defense.[56] However, draft Rules of Procedure and Evidence, Rule 20[57] requires the Registrar to organize the staff of the Registry "in a manner that promotes the rights of the defense, consistent with the principle of fair trial," and to perform certain duties in order to ensure the independence of defense counsel, providing the defense with support, facilities, and information; helping the accused to obtain the assistance of competent legal counsel;[58] and cooperating with state defense and bar associations. The Registrar is responsible for drafting a list of criteria for assigning defense counsel[59] and a code of professional responsibility for all counsel.[60]

Assembly of States Parties

The Assembly of States Parties is not an organ of the ICC, but is comprised of a representative of each ratifying state, with each state having one vote.[61] Non-party states who have signed the Rome Statute or its Final Act may participate as observers but may not vote. The Assembly provides management and oversight to the Presidency, the Prosecutor, and the Registrar regarding the administration of the ICC, including the budget, the number of judges, and rules of procedure and evidence. The Assembly also makes determinations in the event a state party fails to comply with a request to cooperate, or refers the matter to the U.N. Security Council if the case was referred to the ICC by that body. The Assembly also elects 21 persons to serve three-year terms as members of the Bureau, and it may establish other subsidiary bodies to carry out oversight functions.

The Assembly of States Parties may amend the Rome Statute in accordance with art. 121. After seven years have passed since the Statute has entered into force, any state party may propose an amendment, which will be adopted if a two-thirds majority of the Assembly of States Parties votes in its favor. Amendments enter into force for all states parties one year after seven-eighths of the states parties have deposited their instruments of ratification or acceptance with the U.N. Secretary-General. Any state party which has not accepted the amendment may withdraw from the Statute with immediate effect by giving notice within one year after its entry into force.

Critics of the Rome Statute question the future ability of the Assembly of States Parties to exercise any real accountability over the operations of the ICC.[62] They predict that the one-vote-per-state rule could lend lopsided sway to tiny countries,[63] and complain that the Statute does not provide for the democratic accountability of a state's representative at the Assembly to the citizens of the state. Critics also note that representatives will be able to vote at the Assembly and influence the development of the ICC even though they may represent non-democratic countries with poor human rights records or who are proclaimed adversaries of the United States.[64]

JURISDICTION

Subject Matter Jurisdiction

Article 5 of the final Statute limits the jurisdiction of the ICC to the "most serious crimes of concern to the international community as a whole," namely, genocide, crimes against humanity, war crimes and, potentially, aggression and terrorism.[65] Article 8 of the final

Statute limits the ICC's jurisdiction over "war crimes" primarily to those committed as "part of a plan or policy or as part of a large-scale commission of such crimes."[66]

The ICC's jurisdiction will extend only to crimes committed after its inception. However, the Statute allows states parties to the Statute to opt out of the ICC's jurisdiction over war crimes for a period of seven years after becoming a party, as well as its jurisdiction over any new crimes that may be added to the Statute in the future.[67] The United States had wanted an initial opt-out provision that would have allowed states parties to assess the effectiveness and impartiality of the Court for a longer period of time with respect to *all* of the covered crimes before deciding whether to submit to the full jurisdiction of the Court. However, the proposal was rejected, as was a U.S. proposal allowing non-states parties to opt out (or in) for the ICC's jurisdiction over specific crimes. Thus, the ICC appears initially to have broader jurisdiction over war crimes allegedly committed by citizens of non-member states than it will have over war crimes allegedly committed by citizens of states that ratify the treaty.[68]

The elements of each of the crimes, drafted largely at the insistence of the U.S. negotiating team,[69] will likely be adopted once the ICC comes into existence and should serve to check the discretion of the ICC judges and prosecutor.[70] The draft elements may also help to resolve any possible problems caused by vagueness, inherent in international treaties due to the perceived elevated importance of compromise over clarity, but seen as detrimental to fairness in enforcing criminal law, which requires specificity.[71] The Rome Statute provides for amendment of the elements of crimes by two-thirds vote of the Assembly of State Parties. The crimes and their draft elements are summarized below.

Genocide

The Preparatory Committee borrowed the language regarding the crime of genocide used in the 1948 Genocide Convention,[72] which prohibits a number of acts when carried out "with intent to destroy, in whole or in part, a national, ethnical, racial or religious group, as such,"[73] whether carried out in war or during peacetime. The definition is virtually identical to that adopted by Congress in the Genocide Convention Implementation Act of 1987, except that the U.S. Code covers only conduct committed by a U.S. national or conduct committed within the United States.[74]

The victim of genocide is not the individual but the group itself, membership in which is determined automatically by birth rather than by individual choice.[75] The aim must be physical destruction and not merely "cultural genocide," or eliminating the cultural attributes of specific groups, for example, through forced assimilation.[76] To make out a case for genocide, the prosecutor must show that the victim or victims were members of a particular national, ethnic, racial or religious group; the perpetrator intended to destroy that group in whole or in part; and that the perpetrator's conduct (which might include failure to take certain actions[77]) took place in the context of a manifest pattern of similar conduct directed against that group or was conduct that could itself effect such destruction.[78] It is the *mens rea* element that separates genocide from other crimes against humanity: the intent to destroy a group of people as a whole or in significant part.[79]

Crimes Against Humanity

The London Charter creating the Nuremberg tribunal was the first codification of the prohibition using the term "crimes against humanity," although the drafters did not treat it as a new concept.[80] There exists no treaty requiring states to prosecute crimes against humanity, but there is universal jurisdiction under customary international law to punish as *hostis humani generis* – enemies of mankind – without regard to territorial jurisdiction over a crime or criminal.[81] These crimes include universally condemned acts such as murder, extermination, enslavement, deportation, or religious or political persecution, when carried out as part of a widespread or systematic attack against a civilian population.[82] The distinction between these crimes and war crimes is that they may occur during war or peace and may be perpetrated against stateless victims and persons of the perpetrator's own nationality or that of an allied state.[83] Random crimes would not amount to crimes against humanity; "widespread or systematic" plan or policy does not necessarily connote an intent to destroy a group of people in whole or in part.

The last two elements for each of the crimes against humanity clarify the requisite participation in and knowledge of the systematic plan or attack, but are not intended to be interpreted as requiring proof that the perpetrator had knowledge of all characteristics of the attack or the precise details of the plan or policy of the state or organization.[84] The mental element is satisfied in the case of an emerging attack if the perpetrator intended to further such an attack by any means. The acts need not constitute a military attack. An act perpetrated without constructive or actual knowledge of the existence of the widespread policy or plan would lack the *mens rea* for a crime against humanity. Motive is not relevant.[85]

Although there is no U.S. statute codifying crimes against humanity as such, U.S. criminal law prohibits most of the crimes enumerated under the Rome Statute as possible crimes against humanity, as long as they are committed within the United States or by military personnel.[86] Under current law, acts that could constitute crimes against humanity committed by U.S. civilians overseas generally are not triable in U.S. civil or military courts unless they involve torture or certain acts of international terrorism.[87]

War Crimes

War crimes are violations of the international law of war committed during an armed conflict or military occupation,[88] whenever a belligerent "crosses the line" with respect to acceptable combat practices.[89] The Rome statute defines war crimes in art. 8, reiterating war crimes as they are defined in detail in the Geneva[90] and Hague Conventions,[91] with emphasis on those crimes committed as part of a plan or policy or as part of a large-scale commission of such crimes.[92] States that are parties to the treaty have the right under Article 124 to opt out of the ICC's jurisdiction with respect to war crimes for a period of seven years.

The prosecutor must show that the crimes took place in the context of an armed conflict, that the perpetrator was aware of those circumstances, and that the perpetrator was aware that the victim had protected status under the Geneva Conventions or Protocols.[93] There is no need to show that the act was committed as part of a widespread series of violations.[94]

The War Crimes Act of 1996[95] establishes U.S. federal jurisdiction to punish war crimes, as defined in international treaties to which the United States is a party, when perpetrated by or against U.S. nationals. U.S. service members and others may also be tried by courts-martial or military commission for acts in violation of the law of war;[96] ordinarily, U.S. practice is to try U.S. service members by court-martial rather than in federal court for offenses against the law of war.[97]

Aggression

The Rome Conference Delegates included "aggression" among the crimes over which the ICC would have jurisdiction, but were unable to reach an agreement to adopt a definition.[98] Instead, the Conferees agreed to work toward establishing a definition after the Rome Statute enters into force. The ICC will be able to exercise jurisdiction over the crime of aggression only after such a provision has been adopted and entered into force for the relevant state party.

Although there were trials for aggression at Nuremberg,[99] an acceptable definition for its elements has long eluded the international community, impeding earlier attempts to establish an international criminal court.[100] Article 39 of the U.N. Charter leaves it to the Security Council to determine the existence of and take action with respect to "any threat to the peace, breach of the peace, or act of aggression."[101] Aggression is not defined in the U.N. Charter, however, because it was reportedly feared that advances in weapons and techniques of modern warfare would make the definition impractical and subject to manipulation, and might cause the Security Council to take premature action.[102] The U.N. General Assembly adopted a resolution in 1974[103][3] addressing the definition of aggression, but it has only been invoked once by the Security Council, to declare South Africa guilty of aggression against Angola.[104] The definition contains an enumeration of offenses included as possible aggression, but leaves the determination to the Security Council.[105]

Any definition of aggression adopted for the ICC must "be consistent with the relevant provisions of the Charter of the United Nations."[106] If this provision is interpreted to include a determination by the Security Council that an act of aggression has been committed in the definition for aggression under the Rome Statute, then the United States and NATO likely need not fear prosecution for acts of aggression.[107] On the other hand, some observers have expressed concern that the Rome Statute can be used to divest the Security Council of its prerogative in determining whether an act of aggression has occurred, allowing legitimate acts of self-defense to be punished as aggression.[108] Such a result could, they argue, curtail the U.S.' options for using military force for valid reasons.

Jurisdiction over Persons

It is widely accepted that the above crimes enumerated in the Statute are subject to universal jurisdiction under international law;[109] that is, any nation may lawfully try any individual accused of such crimes in its domestic court system without regard to the nationality of the alleged perpetrator or the territory where the crime is alleged to have taken place.[110] In practice, however, political realities appear often to have precluded nations from asserting jurisdiction over suspected war criminals,[111] allowing many of them to enjoy impunity for their alleged crimes. The ICC is intended to resolve the problem of impunity for perpetrators of atrocities,[112] but has led to a different concern, namely, that the ICC may be used by some countries to make trumped-up allegations accusing other states' policymakers, or even implementors of disfavored policies, of engaging in criminal conduct. Probably the most divisive issue at the Rome Conference was the effort to reach a balance between the two extremes – how to bring perpetrators of atrocities to justice while protecting innocent persons from frivolous prosecution and unjust punishment. The conferees finally adopted a somewhat complex system of triggering mechanisms to control how cases were to be referred to the ICC for possible prosecution.

Although the ICC's jurisdiction over the class of suspected criminals is based on the concept of universal jurisdiction for the covered crimes,[113] the ICC may not establish jurisdiction over accused persons unless certain pre-conditions are met. First, unless a case has been referred to the ICC by the U.N. Security Council, the ICC's jurisdiction is complementary to that of national courts: the ICC will try cases only when the state with custody of the accused is unable or unwilling genuinely to prosecute.[114] Where that is determined to be the case, the ICC may take jurisdiction if either the state on whose territory the conduct occurred or the state of nationality of the person accused is a party to the Rome Statute or consents to the jurisdiction of the ICC.

Triggering Mechanisms

There are three avenues through which cases may be referred to the ICC. Either a state party to the Statute, the ICC prosecutor, or the U.N. Security Council[115] may refer cases to the ICC, in accordance with corresponding articles of the Statute. The Security Council may also defer an investigation referred by a state or the prosecutor for a renewable period of 12 months by adopting a resolution under Chapter VII of the U.N. Charter to that effect.[116] During the negotiations, the United States sought a more powerful role for the Security Council, in which any permanent member would be able to veto a referral. The conferees ultimately rejected this proposal because it was seen to re-introduce political considerations to the prosecutions that are perceived to be responsible for the phenomenon of impunity the ICC is intended to avoid. The Statute as finally adopted allows a single permanent member of the Security Council to veto a *deferral*, allowing the Prosecutor to move forward with a case. With the support of the Permanent Five and four other members of the Security Council, the provision could allow the ICC's exercise of jurisdiction to be forestalled indefinitely.

Referral by a State Party

A state party to the ICC may refer a "situation" to the Prosecutor for investigation where it appears that one or more crimes under the jurisdiction of the ICC have been committed.[117] The referral must be made in writing,[118] and as far as possible, must specify the relevant circumstances and be accompanied by all of the supporting documentation available to the referring state.[119] There is no requirement that the referring state have territorial jurisdiction to prosecute the crime or custody of the alleged perpetrators. If the Prosecutor determines there is sufficient cause to commence an investigation, he or she must notify all states parties and any other state that would normally be able to assert jurisdiction over the crime, possibly on a confidential basis and taking measures to preserve evidence or prevent the absconding of persons.[120]

If a state with conventional jurisdiction notifies the Prosecutor within one month of its intent to investigate the crime, the Prosecutor must defer to that state, but may make an application to the Trial Chamber to commence an investigation on the basis that the state's investigation is not "genuine."[121] The Prosecutor may request the state to provide periodic status reports on the investigation. The decision as to whether a state is "unwilling or unable genuinely" to carry out its investigation is determined by the Pre-Trial Chamber. The state must be informed that the Prosecutor intends to challenge a state's intent or ability to investigate, allowing sufficient time for the state to prepare to present evidence on its behalf. The state may challenge the determination to the Appeals Chamber, and if that challenge is unsuccessful, may later bring a challenge to the admissibility of the case under article 19, providing there are additional facts or a significant change of circumstances.

In the event the Prosecutor decides not to initiate an investigation, the referring state may request a review before the Pre-Trial Chamber,[122] which may request the Prosecutor to reconsider the decision within ninety days following notification.[123] The Pre-Trial Chamber may conduct a review of the Prosecutor's decision on its own motion if the decision is based on the Prosecutor's determination that a prosecution is not in the interest of justice as specified in paragraphs 1(c) or 2(c) of article 53. The decision of the Pre-Trial Chamber in this case is controlling. If new information or evidence becomes available after the Prosecutor has decided not to investigate or if the Pre-Trial Chamber does not authorize an investigation, the Prosecutor may initiate a new investigation.[124]

Initiation by Prosecutor

If the Prosecutor becomes aware of possible crimes within the jurisdiction of the ICC, he or she may commence self-initiated investigation. There does not appear to be any limitation on how the Prosecutor receives the information or who can submit it. The Prosecutor may request information from states, non-governmental organizations (NGO), or any other reliable source as deemed appropriate, and must protect the confidentiality of all such information in accordance with the Rome Statute and Rules of Procedure and Evidence.[125] If the Prosecutor concludes that there is a "reasonable basis" for an investigation in a given situation, he or she must first submit a request to the PreTrial Chamber for authorization to proceed. The Chamber, in turn, must determine both that there is a "reasonable basis" to proceed with an investigation and that "the case appears to fall within the jurisdiction of the Court." Victims may make presentations to the Pre-Trial Chamber, but there does not appear to be an opportunity for a state with jurisdiction to intercede at this juncture. Once the investigation is authorized, the Prosecutor must notify relevant parties as in the case of a referral by a state party.[126] At that time, a state with jurisdiction over the crime may submit its request for deferral.

If the Prosecutor determines that sufficient basis for an investigation does not exist, he or she must inform those who provided the information,[127] but there is no opportunity for the referring persons or entities to challenge the decision. However, the Pre-Trial Chamber may initiate its own review, giving the Prosecutor a deadline for the submission of observations.[128]

As noted above, the U.N. Security Council may issue a stay preventing the Prosecutor from proceeding in cases submitted by states parties or initiated by the Prosecutor. There does not appear to be a provision in the Rome Statute or Draft RPE stating when, if ever, any organ of the ICC is required to inform the Security Council of an investigation under consideration. Moreover, before the Security Council can act under Chapter VII of the U.N. Charter, as required to defer an investigation under art. 16 of the Rome Statute, the Council must first determine there is "a threat to the peace, breach of the peace or act of aggression . . . ."[129]

Referral by the U.N. Security Council

One of the reasons for initiating an international criminal court was to give the Security Council a permanent forum for war crimes trials, without necessitating the intense effort required to set up an *ad hoc* tribunal. The Security Council may thus, pursuant to its mandate under Chapter VII of the U.N. Charter, refer a case to the Prosecutor for investigation.[130] Presumably, however, the U.N. Security Council is not precluded from initiating a separate *ad hoc* tribunal if for some reason it were to determine that the ICC would be unable to conduct a fair and effective trial, although some predict that the ICC will bring an end to the use of such tribunals.[131]

Once the Prosecutor receives a referral by the U.N. Security Council, he or she determines whether or not an investigation is warranted using the same procedure as in the case of any other type of referral. The Security Council may request that the Pre-Trial Chamber review a decision of the Prosecutor not to initiate an investigation, but may not *require* the Prosecutor to proceed. The most important difference between a referral by the Security Council and the other types of referrals is that the consent of neither the state of nationality of the accused nor the state on whose territory the crime was committed is necessary for the ICC to assert its jurisdiction. The Prosecutor need not inform states with jurisdiction in accordance with art.18, in order to give such states the opportunity to request deferral; however, it appears that those states retain the right to contest the jurisdiction of the ICC based on complementarity.

ICC Jurisdiction over Citizens of Non-Parties

The above-outlined triggering mechanisms for jurisdiction of the ICC make it possible for the ICC to investigate and try citizens of states that have not signed or ratified the Rome Statute. Thus, under certain circumstances the ICC could exercise jurisdiction over a U.S. citizen accused of one or more of the crimes specified in the treaty, even if the United States does not ratify it. If the United States voluntarily consents to the exercise of ICC jurisdiction, or if the state on whose territory an American citizen has allegedly committed the crime consents, the ICC could try a case despite the fact that neither state has ratified the treaty.[132] If an American citizen is accused of committing one of the covered crimes on the territory of a state party, consent is automatic on the part of the territorial state, but either state can supercede the ICC's jurisdiction by undertaking to prosecute the crime in its domestic courts.

Thus, U.S. nationals could be subject to investigation and trial by the ICC if the country in which the alleged crime occurred is either a party to the Rome Statute or consents to the ICC's jurisdiction, and has or is able to gain custody of the alleged U.S. offender. This possibility appears to exist mainly with respect to U.S. military personnel stationed or found in such a country. It also appears to exist with respect to U.S. public officials whose actions are alleged to have caused one of the crimes designated in the Rome Statute, should that official be found in (or extradited to) the country where the crime allegedly occurred.[133] Such exercises of jurisdiction over U.S. nationals could occur pursuant to the initiative of the state where the crime allegedly occurred or of the Prosecutor.[134]

Given the nature of acts covered as crimes that can be prosecuted by the ICC, it is thought to be a rare situation in which an American citizen acting in his or her own capacity could commit such a crime. Americans who are not servicemembers or government officials could, at present, presumably fall under the jurisdiction of the ICC only if they participate in insurgencies abroad or commit any of the covered acts on behalf of a foreign government or entity. If the United States is able to and does assert jurisdiction over the crime and the accused, the ICC could not proceed with prosecution unless it were to find the United States unwilling or unable genuinely to investigate or prosecute the crime. If another country has jurisdiction and decides to surrender a U.S. person accused of a covered crime to the ICC, the United States could appeal the jurisdiction of the ICC.[135]

If the jurisdiction of the ICC eventually is expanded to include terrorism and drug trafficking, there is arguably a greater probability that Americans abroad could be tried by the ICC, as those crimes may not require as a prerequisite a showing that they are part of a greater scheme. However, it has been noted, Americans abroad who are accused of perpetrating a terrorist act or engaging in illicit drug trade are subject to the laws and legal system of the country where the crime took place, without regard to whether the United States consents to such jurisdiction. Some observers have raised the possibility, therefore, that in such cases accused Americans could conceivably enjoy more comprehensive procedural due process rights before the ICC than they would receive in the domestic courts of some foreign states.

Complementarity and other Challenges to Jurisdiction

According to Article 17 of the Rome Statute, the ICC must find it has no jurisdiction where a state with jurisdiction is investigating or prosecuting the crime, or has investigated the case and genuinely determined that prosecution of the person is unwarranted.[136] The ICC shall determine a case is inadmissible if the accused has already stood trial for the conduct unless it determines the trial was conducted solely for the purpose of shielding the individual from prosecution by the ICC or if it was otherwise conducted in a manner "inconsistent with an intent to bring the person concerned to justice."[137] In order to give the appropriate states the opportunity to take charge of a given situation, the Prosecutor is required to inform all states parties and other interested states when there is a "reasonable basis to commence an investigation" (except in cases referred by the Security Council).[138]

The United States may thus challenge the ICC's jurisdiction over its national in a preliminary proceeding on the basis that it is willing and able to undertake investigation itself. The Statute also provides that a state "from which acceptance of jurisdiction is required under article 12" may challenge the court's jurisdiction.[139] Presumably, the United States could challenge the ICC's jurisdiction over a crime allegedly committed by its national even if no U.S. court has jurisdiction over the crime, by challenging one of the other prerequisites for admissibility of the case. For example, the United States could argue the gravity of the crime of which its national is accused is not sufficiently severe to warrant a trial at the ICC, or that the crime is merely an isolated incident and not part of a larger campaign as required for covered crimes.[140]

Thus, many supporters of the Rome Statute believe that the principle of complementarity, properly applied, is sufficient to insulate U.S. servicemembers and civilians from prosecution at the ICC. After all, they argue, it is virtually inconceivable that the American judicial system will suffer such a massive breakdown as one that would render it "unable to obtain the accused or the necessary evidence and testimony or otherwise unable to carry out its proceedings."[141] Neither is it likely that the United States would be unwilling to investigate alleged atrocities committed by its own troops or officials abroad.[142] Some have suggested that changes in U.S. statutes to broaden the jurisdiction of federal courts to cover all crimes over which the ICC might assert jurisdiction could enhance the implementation of complementarity by precluding a finding by the ICC that the United States is "unable" to prosecute one of its citizens.[143] Opponents of the ICC, however, question whether complementarity will operate as promised, or whether the ICC judges will focus on a perceived deficiency in U.S. trial or court-martial practice to declare that a particular U.S. prosecution or investigation was not conducted in a manner consistent with "the intent to bring the person concerned to justice."[144]

Thus, the primary issue regarding complementarity is the extent to which the ICC will defer to national decisions regarding the handling of purported crimes under the jurisdiction of the ICC. It is unclear, for example, whether the ICC would defer to a decision by a nation to constitute a truth and reconciliation commission, where such a commission could grant amnesty to the perpetrators of genocide in exchange for a full accounting of the events underlying the charge. The granting of amnesty is arguably contrary to the intent to bring criminals to justice, but a nation recovering from the effects of genocide might find it in its interest to form such a commission rather than try to prosecute the alleged perpetrators.[145]

Rules of Procedure and Evidence

The Rome Statute contains a comprehensive set of procedural safeguards for the rights of the accused. While some legal experts agree that the Rome Statute contains "the most comprehensive list of due process protections which has so far been promulgated,"[146] some of the ICC's detractors maintain that the procedures nevertheless fall short of U.S. constitutional standards of due process.[147] Some observers caution that the attempt to create a hybrid set of rules, mixing ideas from the common law and civil law traditions, may lead to unpredictable and possibly unjust results.[148]

The Preparatory Commission completed its draft of the Rules of Procedure and Evidence[149] at its Fifth Session in June of 2000. These rules implement and embellish the procedural aspects of the Rome Statute, and are subject to approval by the Assembly of States Parties at its first meeting. A summary comparison of some procedural safeguards in the Rome Statute and those mandated by the U.S. Constitution is set out below.[150]

The Right to a Jury Trial

The Rome Statute does not provide for trial by jury; instead, it follows the civil law tradition of employing a panel of judges to decide questions of both fact and law. This issue does not appear to have been a major point of contention for U.S. participants during the negotiations of the Rome Statute. This may be true because the Americans considered most at risk, U.S. service members, are subject to court martial under the Uniform Code of Military Justice (UCMJ) and are not entitled to trial by civil jury.[151] American civilians who are accused of crimes overseas are subject to the jurisdiction of the country where the crime took place, and may be tried under that country's laws, which in many cases do not include the right to a trial by jury.

Some opponents of the Rome Treaty argue that it would be unconstitutional for the United States to ratify the Rome Statute because U.S. participation in any court that does not provide for a jury trial in cases where the Constitution requires one would be unlawful.[152] The counter position to this argument is that the Constitution does not bar trial by military commission without a jury under certain circumstances,[153] even the trial of American citizens not members of the armed forces.[154] They also note that the United States has participated in international courts previously, even where American citizens could be tried before them.[155] Finally, the Supreme Court has ruled that persons may be extradited to stand trial in a foreign country despite the lack of jury trial and other procedural safeguards that would be available to that same person if tried in U.S. courts.[156]

The Presumption of Innocence

The Rome Statute provides that "[e]veryone shall be presumed to be innocent until proven guilty before the Court ...."[157] It also places the burden of proof on the Prosecutor and sets the standard for a conviction to proof beyond a reasonable doubt.[158] The Prosecutor must first have confirmed by the Pre-Trial Chamber that there are sufficient grounds to believe the accused committed the crime as charged.[159] The accused may object to the charges, challenge the evidence against him, or present his own evidence.[160] Once the Pre-Trial Chamber has confirmed the charges, the case will come before a Trial Chamber, which must ensure the accused understands the nature of the charges and then allow the accused to enter a plea of innocence or make an admission of guilt.[161] If the accused has admitted guilt, the Trial Chamber must review the evidence to ensure it is sufficient to support the admission.[162] If the Trial Chamber is not satisfied that the evidence is sufficient, it will proceed with the trial as if the accused entered a plea of innocence.[163] The Trial Chamber is not bound by any plea agreements the Prosecutor may have made with the accused.[164]

In U.S. courts, the accused is entitled to appear in court "without unnecessary physical restraints or other indicia of guilt, such as appearing in prison uniform, that may be prejudicial to the jury."[165] The ICC rules provide that any instruments of restraint "shall be removed when the person appears before a Chamber."[166] The rules do not specify whether military personnel are entitled to appear in uniform before the court.

The Privilege Against Compelled Self-Incrimination

During an investigation, if there is reason to believe a person has committed a crime under the jurisdiction of the ICC, that person has the right "[t]o remain silent, without such silence being a consideration in the determination of guilt or innocence."[167] Any individual questioned during an investigation "[s]hall not be compelled to incriminate himself or herself or to confess guilt; [and s]hall not be subjected to any form of coercion, duress or threat, to torture or to any other form of cruel, inhuman or degrading treatment or punishment;

...."[168] At the initial stages of an investigation or prosecution, in fact, the Rome Statute may provide broader protection than does the U.S. Constitution: the Miranda Rule requires oral notice of rights only when a defendant is interrogated in police custody;[169] the ICC statute requires such a warning *whenever* the prosecution has grounds to believe that the person being questioned has committed a crime.

The defendant also has a right not to testify before the ICC or to refuse to make incriminating statements.[170] A defendant's invocation of the right to remain silent may not be used by the judges in determining the guilt or innocence of the defendant.[171] This safeguard appears to be analogous to the Fifth Amendment to the Constitution.

Witnesses may refuse to give testimony that might incriminate them. The ICC has the authority to give assurances to the witness that he or she will not be prosecuted or detained by the ICC for conduct prior to departure from the requested state or for incriminating testimony.[172] The ICC may also allow *in camera* testimony by the witness, giving assurances that the content of the testimony will not be disclosed to the public or any state.[173] Unless the ICC grants such assurances, the witness may not be compelled to answer.[174] Presumably, the right to avoid self-incrimination would extend beyond the crimes triable by the ICC to evidence which could credibly lead to prosecution by a state. It is not clear whether the ICC would respect the immunity of witnesses or accused persons granted by states, or whether it would exclude compelled testimony taken by officials of a state.

The Right to Confront Witnesses

The Rome Statute provides that "the accused shall be entitled ... to examine, or to have examined ... the witnesses against him or her ...[and] to obtain the attendance and examination of witnesses on his or her behalf..."[175] There is an exception, however, in cases where the alleged crime involves sexual violence or violence against children.[176] The ICC may invoke procedures to protect the identities of victims if such protection is deemed necessary.[177] Such procedures include live testimony by means of audio-visual broadcast "provided that such technology permits the witness to be examined by the Prosecutor, the defense, and by the Chamber itself, at the time that the witness so testifies," and "is conducive to the giving of truthful and open testimony and to the safety, physical and psychological well-being, dignity and privacy of the witness."[178]

U.S. law prohibits (with exceptions) the use of out-of-court statements to prove the truth of the matter stated, otherwise known as "hearsay" evidence.[179] The Rome Statute and Draft RPE do not explicitly provide for a similar rule. If the practice of the International Criminal Tribunal for the Former Yugoslavia (ICTY) is followed, hearsay evidence will likely be admissible on a more frequent basis than in U.S. courts. In civil law courts, hearsay evidence is not considered to be unduly prejudicial in most cases because the judges, unlike lay jurors, are presumed to be capable of accurately assessing the credibility of hearsay evidence and discounting any prejudicial content.

The United States Supreme Court has recognized the need for special measures for the protection of witnesses in some criminal trials, notwithstanding the defendant's right to face his accusers.[180] Measures such as one-way closed circuit television system may be employed to protect a child witness who might suffer emotional trauma at the sight of the accused, as long as sufficient safeguards were in place to preserve rigorous adversarial testing of the testimony.[181] Similar to the procedure approved by the Supreme Court, the Rome Statute provisions for protective measures must be ordered by the ICC taking into consideration all the relevant circumstances,[182] and such measures "shall not be prejudicial to or inconsistent with the rights of the accused and a fair and impartial trial."[183]

The Protection Against Double Jeopardy

The Statute bars the ICC from trying any person who has been tried and convicted or acquitted by another court, unless that trial was for the purpose of "shielding the person concerned from criminal responsibility" or was otherwise "inconsistent with an intent to bring the person concerned to justice."[184] The *ne bis in idem* rule in the Rome Statute is in some ways more protective of the accused than the United States Constitution, which allows a person to be tried by more than one sovereign (federal or state court) or in some cases, for a separate crime arising out of the same conduct.[185] In contrast, the Rome Statute specifies the ICC may not try a person who has been tried by any other court for the same conduct, unless it finds the trial or investigation to be improper for one of the enumerated reasons. Thus, the danger of the ICC trying a person who has already been tried by a national court will ultimately depend on the ICC's deference to national judicial decisions.[186]

The Rome Statute further provides that "no person shall be tried by another court for a crime" for which the ICC has already convicted or acquitted the person.[187] Non-parties would not be bound by this rule, however, so a person tried by the ICC could conceivably be tried again by the court of a non-party state, or possibly even by a party to the Statute that seeks to punish the same conduct under another criminal charge.

Another issue that raises possible double jeopardy implications is the prosecutorial appeal of an acquittal.[188] Under U.S. law, prosecutors may appeal only on questions of law, but may not appeal a final acquittal.[189] The Rome Statute allows the Prosecutor to appeal any decision based on procedural error, error of fact, or error of law. The defendant may also appeal on these grounds, as well as "any other ground that affects the fairness or reliability of the proceedings."[190]

The Freedom from Unreasonable Searches and Seizures

Although the Rome Statute does not contain an express reference to the right to be free from unreasonable searches and seizures, it does provide for an exclusionary rule to prevent evidence tainted by a violation of "internationally recognized human rights"[191] The ICC will not apply national law to determine the admissibility of evidence unless it is consistent with the Rome Statute as well as treaties, principles, and rules of international law.[192] Consequently, accused persons are protected from unreasonable searches and seizures to the extent that international law forbids them. The right to privacy against such intrusion is protected under a number of international documents and treaties, including the Universal Declaration of Human Rights (UDHR)[193] and the International Covenant on Civil and Political Rights (ICCPR),[194] both of which have been ratified by a majority of nations participating at the Rome Conference.[195]

Such a standard may turn out to be higher than that applied by U.S. courts in certain cases, inasmuch as U.S. courts apply a lower standard in the event that evidence was gathered outside the territorial jurisdiction of the United States.[196] However, the ICC need not necessarily consider, for example, whether a search warrant should have been necessary. Because evidence is likely to be collected either by or with the cooperation of national law enforcement authorities, investigators will probably find it necessary to rely on national laws rather than try to discern international norms to guide the conduct of the investigation. It may therefore emerge from the ICC's practice that national laws carry more weight than the Rome Statute would suggest. At any rate, any comparison between the ICC and U.S. courts' practice with regard to tainted evidence must await the ICC's development of relevant practice. In particular, the extent to which the exclusionary rule of the ICC will apply to evidence *derived* from unlawfully seized evidence remains to be seen.

The Right to Be Present at Trial

The Rome Statute provides that "[t]he accused shall be present during the trial."[197] The Trial Chamber may order the accused removed from the courtroom in exceptional circumstances when the accused causes continuous disruption, but only for such duration as is necessary, and may make provision for the accused to observe the trial and direct counsel from outside the courtroom through applicable communications technology.[198]

In U.S. jurisprudence, the Confrontation Clause of Amendment VI guarantees the accused's right to be present in the courtroom at every stage of his trial.[199] However, as long as the defendant is present at the beginning of the trial, the trial will not be rendered invalid if the defendant voluntarily absents himself during later stages of the trial.[200] The Rome Statute does not address the voluntary absence of the accused once the trial begins.

The Right to Effective Assistance of Counsel

Article 67 of the Rome Statute provides that "the accused shall be entitled ... to have legal assistance assigned by the Court where the interests of justice so require, and without payment if the accused lacks sufficient means to pay for it...."[201] Defense counsel must also be well-qualified[202] according to criteria to be established.[203] The Registrar has a duty to provide adequate administrative support to the defense.[204] The Statute also guarantees that "the accused shall be entitled ... to communicate freely with counsel of accused's choosing ...."[205] Similar to the attorney-client privilege practiced in the U.S. judicial system,[206] Draft RPE 73 provides that such communications are privileged and need not be disclosed at trial.

The Right to a Speedy and Public Trial

The U.S. Constitution guarantees the right to a speedy and public trial.[207] Similarly, the Rome Statute provides that the accused is entitled to be tried "without undue delay" by means of a public hearing.[208]

Speedy Trial

In U.S. federal courts, criminal trials generally must commence within seventy days after an indictment or original appearance before the court.[209] In courts-martial, the time limit is 120 days from the preferral of charges or the imposition of restraint, whichever date is earliest.[210] Statutes of limitations for crimes also guard against undue delay between the government's discovery of evidence and its prosecution of an accused person. A denial of the right to a speedy trial results in a dismissal of the indictment.[211] However, if the accused is found to have waived the right, or the circumstances and justice otherwise require it, a delay may not be fatal to the prosecution.[212] In determining whether the right has been denied, a court may consider such factors as the length of the delay, the reason for the delay, whether the defendant asserted his right to a speedy trial, and the prejudice to the defendant caused by the delay.[213]

The Rome Statute does not define "undue delay." The Draft RPE instruct the Trial Chamber to impose "strict time limits" for orders relating to discovery.[214] Draft RPE 101 provides:

> In making any order setting time limits regarding the conduct of any proceedings, the Court shall have regard to the need to facilitate fair and expeditious proceedings, bearing in mind in particular the rights of the defence and the victims.

The Rome Statute does not provide a statute of limitation for any of the crimes under its jurisdiction.[215] Under U.S. law, there is no statute of limitation for the crime of genocide[216] or for any crime for which the death penalty may be imposed,[217] which includes any war crime that causes the death of its victim,[218] or any terrorism-related offense that involves the risk of death or serious injury.[219] For non-capital crimes, however, the statute of limitation is generally five years.[220]

Public Trial

In U.S. courts, closure of the courtroom during trial proceedings is justified only if 1) the proponent of closure advances an overriding interest likely to be prejudiced; 2) the closure is no broader than necessary; 3) the trial court considers reasonable alternatives to closure; and 4) the trial court makes findings adequate to support closure.[221] The right to a public trial in courts-martial is also guaranteed, but not absolute.[222] A defendant may request a closed trial, but must meet the same stringent standards applied to a request by the prosecution. Additionally, the press and public have a First Amendment right to have access to trials,[223] which must sometimes be considered in addition to the other factors.

The Rome Statute provides for public hearing unless "special circumstances require that certain proceedings be in closed session for the purposes set forth in article 68 [to protect witnesses or victims], or to protect confidential or sensitive information to be given in evidence."[224] The Trial Chamber must first give all parties notice and the opportunity to respond to any proposed special protective procedures.[225] Possible protective measures include the use of a pseudonym or technological disguise measures for witnesses, gag orders for certain information as well as its removal from the public record, or the closure of part of the hearing.[226] Additionally, any state may make an application to the ICC for necessary measures to protect its agents or sensitive national security information.[227]

Right to Appeal

Either the defendant or the prosecutor can appeal a decision of the Trial Chamber to the Appeals Chamber based on "procedural error, error of fact or law, or disproportion between the crime and the sentence." The accused or his heirs may bring an appeal at any time based on new evidence or information that the conviction is based on false evidence, or that any of the judges or prosecutors committed any misdeeds.[228]

The ICC's opponents criticize the appeal process as inadequate because it does not provide for review outside the ICC.[229] As discussed above, the conferees sought to implement checks and balances as well as create a separation between the Appeals Division and the other trial divisions. It might also be noted that prior to 1993, international criminal courts did not include an appellate body,[230] nor did national courts review the decisions of such tribunals.[231] Practice in the International Criminal Tribunal for Yugoslavia (ICTY) and the International Criminal Tribunal for Rwanda (ICTR) suggests that an appellate body within an international court may not always necessarily affirm the decisions of trial chambers.[232]

Freedom from Indefinite or Arbitrary Detention

The Fourth Amendment to the U.S. Constitution protects persons from unreasonable seizures, including the arrest of a person without probable cause,[233] and sometimes, without a warrant. A person unlawfully arrested is not automatically released from custody,[234] however, although evidence derived through the unlawful arrest may be excludable from evidence.[235] The Fifth Amendment protects individuals from deprivation of liberty without due process of law. The Rome Statute contains corresponding safeguards to prevent the arbitrary arrest and detention of persons,[236] and includes provisions for interim release of the accused prior to trial.[237] Because the ICC has no law enforcement arm, relying instead largely on states to provide for the arrest and detention of accused persons using national police resources, however, the procedures may vary depending on the state of custody.

The Prosecutor must seek an arrest warrant or a summons from the Pre-Trial Chamber when necessary to ensure an accused's appearance at trial.[238] The application must identify the person and the crime of which the person is accused, including a concise statement of facts supporting the allegation and a summary of evidence. On the basis of the warrant, the ICC may request the provisional arrest or arrest and surrender under part 9 of the Rome Statute. The ICC is required to establish procedures for ensuring it is notified once a person is detained by a custodial state on the request of the ICC, and must provide a copy of the warrant to the accused in a language he or she understands.[239]

The Pre-Trial Chamber is to receive notification whenever a detainee has requested interim release in accordance with the laws of the custodial state, and makes recommendations to the national court as to the suitability of release.[240] The custodial state is not permitted to consider whether the warrant was properly issued under the Rome Statute,[241] but the accused may challenge the warrant before the PreTrial Chamber.[242] If the accused is in the custody of the ICC, the accused may apply for interim release pending trial, which the Pre-Trial Chamber may grant with or without conditions.[243] If the person is detained for an unreasonable period prior to trial due to inexcusable delay by the Prosecutor, the ICC may release the person, with or without conditions.[244] A person wrongfully arrested, detained, or convicted *may* be awarded compensation by the ICC.[245]

Once a person is convicted, the ICC will select from states willing to serve as "state of enforcement" to incarcerate the convicted person subject to any ICC conditions. The prisoner may not be tried, punished, or extradited to a third state for conduct engaged in prior to the person's incarceration without the approval of the ICC.[246] In designating a state of enforcement, the ICC must consider:

> (a) The principle that states parties should share the responsibility for enforcing sentences of imprisonment, in accordance with principles of equitable distribution, as provided in the Rules of Procedure and Evidence; (b) The application of widely accepted international treaty standards governing the treatment of prisoners; (c) The views of the sentenced person; (d) The nationality of the sentenced person; and (e) Such other factors regarding the circumstances of the crime or the person sentenced, or the effective enforcement of the sentence, as may be appropriate in designating the state of enforcement.[247]

Additionally, the ICC will monitor the treatment of the prisoner, and the prisoner may petition to be moved to another state of enforcement at any time.[248]

Implications for the United States as Non-Member

The U.S. initially used the proceedings of the Preparatory Commission in part as a means of trying to rectify what it saw as the faults of the Rome Statute, and it participated as an equal during the initial conferences.[249] However, the current Administration has reduced the level of the U.S. participation,[250] and in any event, the Preparatory Commission will cease to exist after the first meeting of the Assembly of States Parties; U.S. eligibility to participate on an equal basis with other states in setting some of the ground rules for the ICC will then have ended. The Assembly of States Parties will take over as the governing body to oversee the implementation and possible amendment of the Rome Statute. Review Conferences are an alternative forum for considering amendments to the Statute; an initial Review Conference will be convened seven years after the Statute enters into effect, now expected to be July 2002. Thereafter, Review Conferences may be convened from time to time by the U.N. Secretary-General upon request by a majority of the states parties.[251] As a non-party, the United States will have no vote in either body. However, it will remain eligible to participate in both the Assembly and in Review Conferences as an observer.[252]

Observer Role

The role of observers ultimately will be defined by the rules of procedure adopted for the two bodies.[253] If the current finalized draft rules are adopted, observers will be entitled to participate in the deliberations of the Assembly and any subsidiary bodies that might be established. Observer states will receive notifications of all meetings and records of Assembly proceedings on the same basis as states parties. They will not, however, be permitted to suggest items for the agenda or to make motions during debate, such as points of order or motions for adjournment. Thus, the United States may be able to participate substantially in Assembly debates as well as proffer and respond to proposals, even if it does not become a party to the Statute. The United States may also use its influence at the United Nations as a way to be heard by the Assembly of States Parties.[254]

As noted, the United States will not be able to vote in these bodies if it does not ratify the Rome Statute. It could not nominate U.S. nationals to serve as judges or cast a vote in elections for judges or the Prosecutor (or for their removal). It could not vote on the ICC's budget. It could not vote on the definition of the crime of aggression or its inclusion within the jurisdiction of the ICC, when the matter is considered at first Review Conference, or on any other amendment to the Rome Statute.

The United States, as a non-party, will have no right itself to refer situations to the Prosecutor for investigation; as a Permanent Member of the Security Council, however, it could participate as part of a Security Council referral.[255] Similarly, it could still participate in Security Council requests to the Prosecutor to defer an investigation or prosecution[256] and to the Pre-Trial Chamber to review a decision of the Prosecutor not to investigate or prosecute.[257] As a non-party to the treaty, the United States could, but would not be obligated to, cooperate with the ICC in its investigation and prosecution of crimes within its jurisdiction;[258] and under the Statute, it could, but would not be obligated to, arrest a person named in a request for provisional arrest or for arrest and surrender from the ICC.[259] The U.S. would also retain the right not to provide information or documents the disclosure of which would prejudice its national security interests[260] and to refuse to consent to the disclosure by a state party of information or documents provided to that state in confidence.[261] Finally, as a non-party, the U.S. would not be under any obligation to contribute to the budget for the ICC, except, perhaps indirectly, to the extent that the U.N. General Assembly contributes to its support.[262]

Political Implications

Perspectives differ on the impact of the ICC on U.S. interests, once it begins operation. Some see the ICC as a fundamental threat to the U.S. armed forces, its political leaders, and U.S. defense and foreign policy.[263] Others see it as a valuable foreign policy tool for defining and deterring crimes against humanity, a step forward in the decades-long U.S. effort to end impunity for egregious mass crimes. Debate over the ICC has brought out a tension between enhancing the international legal justice system and encroaching on what some countries perceive as their legitimate use of force. The review by the International Criminal Tribunal for the Former Yugoslavia (ICTY) of allegations that NATO bombing in Kosovo might be deemed a war crime is illustrative of this tension. Many opponents of the ICC and members of the U.S. military were outraged that the issue was even considered. They questioned the legitimacy of the tribunal's actions, and their anger was not assuaged by the Tribunal's ultimate decision that there was "no basis for opening an investigation into any of those allegations or into other incidents relating to NATO bombing."[264] While opponents of the ICC interpret this event as an indication that the ICC is likely to pursue spurious and politically motivated cases against U.S. citizens, proponents of the ICC see it as illustrating that similar unfounded allegations would be dismissed by the ICC Prosecutor.

The United States has often been a leader in the struggle against impunity and the quest for peace, justice and human rights. The United States led the world community in calling for establishment of the ad hoc tribunals for the former Yugoslavia and Rwanda. Supporters of the ICC argue that it could be the ultimate symbol of enforcement of basic human rights norms. Such countries, which include a number of U.S. allies, might view the true test of the U.S. commitment to international and universal concepts of justice and human rights to be its willingness to be bound by the rules established for others. From this perspective, despite the Administration's asserted intent to continue U.S. leadership in supporting human rights through means other than the ICC,[265] the U.S. refusal to ratify the Rome Statute could undermine the status of, and others' regard for, the United States as a proponent of human rights.

Others, however argue that despots like Cambodia's Pol Pot or Iraq's Saddam Hussein have not weighed possible future legal ramifications before committing massive crimes.[266] In their view, establishment of the ICC might have the effect of hardening the resolve of ruthless tyrants who may feel they have nothing to gain by giving up their power to more democratic or less ruthless regimes – as General Pinochet did in Chile or Duvalier in Haiti. The critical element from this perspective is simply the treaty's entry into force, not whether the U.S. ratifies it, other than perhaps to provide support to an argument challenging the legitimacy of the ICC.

U.S. allies, such as France and Canada, which also deploy forces abroad in peacekeeping and other interventions, initially shared U.S. concerns about the ICC's ability to judge the actions of their nationals particularly with regard to use of force. During negotiations, these countries concluded that the ICC's larger value outweighed any potential risk posed to their nationals or foreign policy. While some Americans fear the ICC could be used for political purposes, many U.S. allies see the ICC as more limited. In their view, the ICC would intervene to prosecute crimes of genocide, crimes against humanity, and war crimes only when a country fails to try its own citizens for committing such acts. Some countries are adopting war crimes provisions as part of their own domestic laws with the thought that the ICC would never be called on to intervene. For example, France amended its constitution before ratifying the Rome Statute.[267]

For the U.S. government, the situation appears to be more complicated. With several hundred thousand persons stationed abroad, often involved in undertakings that might be subject to allegations of war crimes, the United States is particularly cautious. U.S. military leaders are especially concerned that countries that do not ratify the ICC treaty could consent to the ICC's jurisdiction over foreign peacekeeping troops for crimes committed on their territory, while declining to allow the ICC to try the persons responsible for whatever atrocities brought peacekeepers there in the first place.[268] Concern about U.S. citizens being tried by the ICC stem from an underlying fear that a politicized court could be used by hostile states as a vehicle for challenging U.S. foreign policy. Given that the ICC could exercise jurisdiction over U.S. citizens in some situations even if the U.S. does not ratify the treaty, these concerns seem likely to persist even if the U.S. remains a non-party.

CONGRESSIONAL ACTION

Congress has passed several riders effectively precluding the use of funds to support the ICC.[269] The fundamental issue for Congress is whether to pass legislation to actively oppose the ICC, or whether to adopt a more benign approach aimed at encouraging the ICC to develop in a manner conducive to U.S. policy aims. There are currently two bills in Congress adopting the first approach, and one taking the second tack. The House of Representative added a rider to the Bob Stump National Defense Authorization Act for Fiscal Year 2003, H.R. 4546, expressing the sense of the Congress that "none of the funds appropriated pursuant to authorizations of appropriations in this Act should be used for any assistance to, or to cooperate with or to provide any support for, the International Criminal Court."[270] Additionally, the Administration may ask Congress to pass legislation to close jurisdictional gaps in U.S. criminal law in order to ensure U.S. territory does not become a safe haven for those accused of genocide, war crimes, and crimes against humanity.[271]

American Servicemembers' Protection Act of 2001

The American Servicemembers' Protection Act (ASPA) was originally introduced in the 106th Congress as S. 2726. The proposed legislation is intended to shield members of the United States Armed Forces and other covered persons from the jurisdiction of the ICC. The Senate Committee on Foreign Relations held hearings[272] the same day the bill was introduced but did not report it. The ASPA was reintroduced in the 107th Congress as S. 857 on May 9, 2001. An amended version was introduced as S. 1610 on November 1, 2001.

Two versions of the ASPA have been passed by the House of Representatives. The first is contained in the Foreign Relations Authorization Act, Fiscal Years 2002 and 2003, H.R.1646, Title VI, subtitle B. The Senate amended version of H.R. 1646 does not include the ASPA. H.R. 1646 is in conference at the time of this writing. The second version was passed as Title II of the supplemental appropriations bill for the fiscal year ending September 30, 2002, H.R. 4775.

The Senate also passed a version of the ASPA, as part of the Departments of Commerce, Justice, and State, the Judiciary, and Related Agencies Appropriations Act, 2002, HR 3338, but it was replaced in the enacted law with language prohibiting spending to support the ICC.[273] Title II of H.R. 4775 is substantially similar to S. 857 (H.R. 1794), and would repeal the provision passed as part of H.R. 3338. Title VI, subtitle B of H.R. 1646 is summarized below, followed by a description of the additional language contained in Title II of H.R. 4775.

The ASPA would prohibit cooperation with the ICC on the part of any agency or entity of the federal government, or any state or local government. (Sec. 634) Covered entities are prohibited from responding to a request for cooperation by the ICC or providing specific assistance, including arrest, extradition, seizure of property, asset forfeiture, service of warrants, searches, taking of evidence, and similar matters. It prohibits agents of the ICC from conducting any investigative activity on U.S. soil related to matters of the ICC. Sec. 634(d) states that the United States "shall exercise its rights to limit the use of assistance provided under all treaties and executive agreements for mutual legal assistance in criminal matters ... to prevent ... use by the [ICC of such assistance]." It does not ban the communication to the ICC of U.S. policy or assistance to defendants. Sec. 636 requires the President to put "appropriate procedures" in place to prevent the direct or indirect transfer of certain classified national security information to the ICC.

The ASPA would further restrict U.S. participation in U.N. peacekeeping operations to missions where the President certifies U.S. troops may participate without risk of prosecution by the ICC because the Security Council permanently exempted U.S. personnel for prosecution for activity conducted as participants, or because each other country participating in the mission is either not a party to the ICC and does not consent to its jurisdiction, or has entered into an agreement "in accordance with article 98" of the Rome Statute.[274] It also prohibits military assistance to any non-NATO country that is member of the ICC, unless the President waives the restriction (Sec. 637).

Sec. 638 authorizes the President to use "all means necessary and appropriate" to bring about the release of covered United States and allied persons,[275] upon the request of the detainee's government, who are being detained or imprisoned by or on behalf of the ICC. The Act does not provide a definition of "necessary and appropriate means" to bring about the release of covered persons, other than to exclude bribes and the provision of other such incentives. The language could arguably be interpreted to authorize the use of armed force to conduct rescue operations to free some prisoners charged with war crimes, genocide, or crimes against humanity.

The President may waive the restrictions on participation in peacekeeping operations and providing military assistance for a renewable period of one year after notifying appropriate congressional committees of his intent to do so and reporting that the ICC has entered into a binding agreement that prohibits it from exercising jurisdiction over covered U.S. and allied persons (from certain countries for so long as those countries have not ratified the treaty). (Sec. 633) The President may also waive some requirements with respect to a specific "named individual," if there is reason to believe the named individual is guilty of the charge, it is in the national interest of the United States for the ICC to prosecute the person, and that during the investigation, no covered U.S. or allied person will be arrested, detained, prosecuted, or imprisoned by or on behalf of the ICC with regard actions taken in their official capacities.

H.R. 4775

The version of the ASPA included in H.R. 4775 (which is substantially similar to the Senate amended version of HR 3338) contains an additional exception at section 2011, stating that the restrictions on cooperation with the ICC (sec. 2004 of H.R. 4775) and protecting classified information (sec. 2006) do not apply to "any action or actions with respect to a specific matter taken or directed by the President on a case-by-case basis in the exercise of the President's authority as Commander in Chief of the Armed Forces of the United States under article II, section 2 of the United States Constitution or in the exercise of the executive power under article II, section 1 of the United States Constitution."[276] The section would require the President to notify Congress within 15 days of the action, unless such notification would jeopardize national security. It further clarifies that "nothing in [the] section shall be construed as a grant of statutory authority to the President to take any action." Sec. 2012 prohibits delegation of the authorities vested in the President by secs. 2003 (waiver provision) and 2011(a) (constitutional exception).

Inasmuch as sections 2004 and 2006 are already subject to presidential waiver under section 2003(c) in the case of the investigation or prosecution of a "named individual," it appears that this section is drafted to avoid possible conflicts of the separation of powers between the President and Congress. In the event that the President takes the position that the prohibitions of sections 2004 and 2006 infringe upon his constitutional authority in certain cases, he might assert that Congress has no power even to require a waiver under section 2003. Section 2011 appears to ensure notification of Congress, at least at some point after the action has been taken, regardless of whether the President believes that sections 2004 and 2006 impinge his constitutional authority.

The effect of sec. 2011 is not entirely clear, depending as it does on the interpretation of the President's executive powers under article II, section 1 of the Constitution and his authority as Commander in Chief of the Armed Forces. Interpreted broadly, the constitutional executive power includes the power to execute the law, meaning the execution of *any* law, whether statutory or constitutional, or even international law. Such an interpretation would seem to render the waiver provision of sec. 2003(c) superfluous. Interpreted narrowly, the executive authorities cited above could refer to those powers which the President does not share with Congress. Under a narrow interpretation, Congress would be deemed to be without authority to regulate such actions in any event, in which case it would appear to make little sense to restrict its application to sections 2004 and 2006. The language could be construed by a court to imply a waiver authority apart from the restrictions outlined in section 2003.

The American Servicemember and Citizen Protection Act of 2002

The American Servicemember and Citizen Protection Act of 2002, H.R.4169, introduced April 11, 2002, issues findings that under the U.S. Constitution and international law, the President's signature on a treaty without ratification by the Senate is not binding on the United States, and that therefore the ICC Statute has no validity with respect to U.S. The bill proclaims the Rome Statute to be "ultra vires" (sec. 2(9)) and in violation of international law, the American Declaration of Independence, and the Constitution (sec. 2(12)). It also urges the President to rescind the U.S. signature and take steps (sec. 3) to prevent the establishment of the ICC. Sec. 4 prohibits the expenditure of funds for use in any manner for the "establishment or operation of the [ICC]" (with a penalty of 5 years or $50,000 for violations, sec. 6). Sec. 5 provides that actions against U.S. soldiers shall be considered to be an act of aggression, and actions against other U.S. persons shall be considered "to be an offense against the law of nations."

The American Citizens' Protection and War Criminal Prosecution Act of 2001

This bill, S.1296 (H.R. 2699), seeks a more conciliatory approach to the ICC, providing that the President should certify that the ICC "has established a demonstrated record of fair and impartial prosecution of genocide, war crimes, and crimes against humanity" before the Rome Statute is submitted to the Senate for its advice and consent. (Sec. 10). Sec. 4 provides a sense of the Congress that the United States should "maintain a policy of fully supporting the due process rights of all United States citizens before foreign tribunals, including the [ICC]". It recommends the U.S. government participate as an observer in the Assembly of States Parties in order to protect and further U.S. interests. Sec. 8 requires the President to ensure appropriate procedures are in place to protect national security information.

Sec. 5 prohibits the United States from taking any action to extradite U.S. citizens and servicemembers to the ICC if the accused is investigated or prosecuted in a U.S. court, and urges the United States to exercise its right to assert jurisdiction over such persons (to invoke complementarity), unless the President determines it is not in the national interest. If a U.S. citizen is prosecuted by the ICC, the President "shall use appropriate diplomatic and legal resources to ensure that such person receives due process ..." and provide whatever exculpatory evidence may be available to assist the accused. Sec. 7 authorizes support to the ICC on a case-by-case basis if such support would serve important U.S. interests, particularly if the victims of the crimes alleged are citizens of the United States or friendly countries.

The bill contains a number of reporting requirements for assessments of the operation of the ICC and its effects on U.S. interests. Sec. 6 outlines reporting procedures, requiring the President to compare due process protections afforded to persons before the ICC to those afforded U.S. servicemembers under status of forces agreements, and to bilateral or multilateral extradition treaties. Sec. 5 requires the Administration to conduct a study to determine what statutory amendments may be necessary to close jurisdictional gaps in the criminal code or Uniform Code of Military Justice. Sec. 9 requires a report on command arrangements that could place U.S. servicemembers at risk of prosecution by the ICC and measures taken to mitigate the risks.

REFERENCES

[1] U.N. Doc. A/CONF.183/9 (1988)("Rome Statute").

[2] These include genocide, crimes against humanity, war crimes, and potentially the crime of aggression, if the Assembly of States Parties is able to reach an agreement defining it. Rome Statute art. 5(1). *See infra* text accompanying note 98.

[3] *See* Barbara Crossette, *World Criminal Court is Ratified – Praised by U.N., Opposed by U.S.*, N.Y. TIMES Apr. 12, 2002, *available at* 2002 WL-NYT 0210200003. For the current status of signatures, ratifications and reservations, visit http://untreaty.un.org/ENGLISH/bible/englishinternetbible/ partI/chapterXVIII/treaty10.asp.

[4] *See* Jonathon Wright, *U.S. Renounces Obligations to International Court*, REUTERS, May 6, 2002. Although some in the media have described the act as an "unsigning" of the treaty, it may be more accurately described as a notification of intent not to ratify. The letter from Under Secretary of State for Arms Control and International Security John R. Bolton to the U.N. Secretary General stated: This is to inform you, in connection with the Rome Statute of the International Criminal Court adopted on July 17, 1998, that the United States does not intend to become a party to the treaty. Accordingly, the United States has no legal obligations arising from its signature on December 31, 2000. The United States requests that its intention not to become a party, as expressed in this letter, be reflected in the depositary's status lists relating to this treaty. *Reprinted at* http://www.state.gov/r/pa/prs/ps/2002/9968.htm.

[5] See Give it a Welcome - The Coming World Criminal Court, ECONOMIST (London), Apr. 13, 2002, available at 2002 WL 7245784; James Bone, War Crimes Court Pits United States Against the World, TIMES OF LONDON, Apr. 11, 2002, available at 2002 WL 4198476; Stuart Taylor Jr., Be Wary of the War Crimes Court, but Not Too Wary, NAT'L J., Apr. 6, 2002, available at 2002 WL 7094917.

[6] *See* Marc Grossman, Under Secretary for Political Affairs, Remarks to the Center for Strategic and International Studies, Washington, D.C., (May 6, 2002) (prepared remarks available at http://www.state.gov/p/9949pf.htm). Secretary Grossman promised that: Notwithstanding our disagreements with the Rome Treaty, the United States respects the decision of those nations who have chosen to join the ICC; but they in turn must respect our decision not to join the ICC or place our citizens under the jurisdiction of the court. So, despite this difference, we must work together to promote real justice after July 1, when the Rome Statute enters into force. The existence of a functioning ICC will not cause the United States to retreat from its leadership role in the promotion of international justice and the rule of law.

[7] *See* Colum Lynch, *U.S. Seeks Court Immunity for E. Timor Peacekeepers*, WASH. POST May 16, 2002 at A22, *available at* 2002 WL 20709611 (reporting there are currently no U.S. troops serving in U.N. missions); Edith M. Lederer, *U.S. Makes Int'l Court Demands*, AP May 20, 2002, *available at* 2002 WL 21234979 (reporting that France, Britain, Ireland, Norway, and Colombia oppose the U.S. request).

[8] *See* Ruth Wedgwood, Harold K. Jacobson and Monroe Leigh, *The United States and the Statute of Rome,* 95 AM. J. INT'L L. 124 (2001) (commenting that the United States has "repeatedly and publicly declared its support in principle" for an international criminal court). Congress expressed its support for such a court, providing the rights of U.S. citizens were recognized. *See, e.g.,*Foreign Operations Appropriations Act § 599E, P.L. 101-513, 104 Stat. 2066-2067 (1990)(expressing the sense of the Congress that "the United States should explore the need for the establishment of an International Criminal Court" and that "the establishment of such a court or courts for the more effective prosecution of international criminals should not derogate from established standards of due process, the rights of the accused to a fair trial and the sovereignty of individual nations"); Anti-Drug Abuse Act of 1988 § 4108, P.L. 100-690, 102 Stat. 4181, 4266 (1988)(encouraging the President to initiate discussions with foreign governments about the possibility of creating an international court to try persons accused of having engaged in international drug trafficking or having committed international crimes, providing constitutional guarantees of U.S. citizens are recognized); P.L. 99-399, Sec. 1201 (1986) .

[9] See U.N. International Criminal Court: Hearings before the Subcomm. on International Operations of the Senate Foreign Relations Committee 105th Cong. (1998) (testimony of David J. Scheffer, Ambassador-at-Large for War Crimes Issues).

[10] *See* Wedgwood, *et al., supra* note 8, at 124 (noting that the final vote for the Statute was 120 in favor to seven against).

[11] *See* Statement on the Rome Treaty on the International Criminal Court, Dec. 31, 2000, 37(1) Weekly Compilation of Presidential Documents 4 (2001).

[12] Because the United States signed the Rome Statute, it had been obligated under international law to refrain from conducting activity in contravention of the object and purpose of the treaty. *See* Vienna Convention on the Law of Treaties, *opened for*

signature May 23, 1969, art. 18, 1155 U.N.T.S. 335. However, this obligation ends once a signatory state has indicated an intent *not* to ratify the treaty. *Id.* Some press reports initially indicated the Administration was also planning to renounce the Vienna Convention. *See* Neil A. Lewis, *U.S. to 'Unsign' Treaty, Disavow World Tribunal*, SAN DIEGO UNION and TRIB., May 5, 2002 at A1. The report was apparently based on a misunderstanding of the Administration's statement explaining the intent behind its action, which was reportedly to avoid any obligations on the part of the United States that may have been incurred through its signature of the Rome Statute, in accordance with article 18 of the Vienna Convention.

[13] *See* Grossman, *supra* note 6.

[14] *See* David J. Scheffer, *Staying the Course with the International Criminal Court,* 35 CORNELL INT'L L.J. 47 (2000) (arguing the United States could most effectively influence the shape of the ICC through cooperating with it rather than impeding it).

[15] For a general background and discussion of the ICC, see The Rome Statute of the International Criminal Court: Selected Legal and Constitutional Issues, CRS Report RL30091, Feb. 22, 1999; The International Criminal Court Treaty: Description, Policy Issues, and Congressional Concerns, CRS Report RL30020, Jan. 5, 1999.

[16] GA Res. 49/53, U.N. GAOR, 49th Sess.,U.N. Doc. A/RES/49/53 (1994).

[17] GA Res. 50/46, U.N. GAOR, 50th Sess.,U.N. Doc. A/RES/50/46 (1995).

[18] *See* United Nations, "The Draft Statute of the International Criminal Court: Background Information," *available at* http://www.un.org/icc/statute.htm.

[19] Rome Statute arts. 12-14.

[20] See Johan D. van der Vyver, Personal and Territorial Jurisdiction of the International Criminal Court, 14 EMORY INT'L L. REV. 1, 32 (2000).

[21] *See* Wedgwood, *et al.*, *supra* note 8, at 126 (commenting that the U.S. proposal would "exempt not only U.S. nationals, but also the nationals of rogue states, which are most likely to produce or to harbor war criminals in the future and which are the least likely to consent to having their nationals tried by the ICC").

[22] *See id.* at 127 (arguing that "while a non-party state is not itself bound to accept an assertion of jurisdiction over itself unless it has consented, the same is not true of its nationals if they commit offenses in the territory of a state that is a party").

[23] This was the operational theory providing jurisdiction at the Nuremberg tribunals. *See* M. Cherif Bassiouni, *Universal Jurisdiction for International Crimes: Historical Perspectives and Contemporary Practice*, 42 VA. J. INT'L L. 81, 91-92 (2001)(positing that sovereignty does not limit the exercise of criminal jurisdiction to single states)(citing IMT Judgment, Sept. 30, 1946, that signatory states to the London Charter "have done together what any one of them might have done singly; for it is not to be doubted that any nation has the right thus to set up special courts to administer law.").

[24] *See* van der Vyver, *supra* note 20, at 18 (describing U.S. position with regard to acceptable regimes as an attempt to secure immunity for U.S. citizens).

[25] See id.

[26] Rome Statute art. 16 (allowing the Security Council to delay any investigation or prosecution indefinitely). The Security Council can also initiate prosecution under Article 13(b).

[27] *See* Lawrence Weschler, *The United States and the ICC*, *in* THE UNITED STATES AND THE INTERNATIONAL CRIMINAL COURT 85, 93 (Sarah B. Sewall and Carl Kaysen, eds. 2000) [hereinafter "THE U.S. AND THE ICC"].

[28] See id.

[29] U.N. Doc. A/CONF.183/10. The Final Act is separate from the Rome Statute and consists largely of a recitation of the events that led to the convening of the Conference and of the proceedings and decisions at the Conference.

[30] These documents may be found at http://www.un.org/law/icc.

[31] Rome Statute art. 34.

[32] *Id.* art. 4.

[33] *d.* art. 2. The Preparatory Commission adopted a draft proposed agreement in the fall of 2000, which will require further action by the Assembly of States Parties once the treaty enters into force in July 2002, in order to become finalized. *See* Draft Relationship Agreement between the United Nations and the International Criminal Court, U.N. Doc. PCNICC/2000/WGICC-UN/L.1 (2000), *available at* http://www.un.org/law/icc /prepcomm/ nov2000/english/ wgiccl1e.pdf.

[34] Rome Statute art.15.

[35] *Id.* art. 36(3)(b)(i)-(ii).

[36] *Id.* art. 36(7).

[37] *See* Matthew A. Barrett, Note, *Ratify or Reject: Examining the United States' Opposition to the International Criminal Court*, 28 GA. J. INT'L and COMP. L. 83, 97 (1999) (citing the Rome Statute, art. 41(2)(a)-(b)).

[38] Rome Statute art. 36.

[39] *Id.* art. 36(5).

[40] *Id.* art. 36(8).

[41] *Id.* art. 46.

[42] *Id.* art. 38.

[43] *Id.* art. 39.

[44] *Id.* art. 57.

[45] *Id.* art. 76.

[46] *Id.* art. 83.

[47] *Id.* art. 84.

[48] *Id.* art. 85.

[49] *Id.* art. 42.

[50] *Id.* art. 53

[51] *Id.* art. 54.

[52] *Id.* arts. 54 and 87(5).

[53] *Developments at the Rome Treaty Conference: Hearings before the Senate Comm. on Foreign Relations*, 105th Cong. (1998) (statement of David Scheffer, Ambassador-at-Large for War Crimes Issues). For more detail about the procedure for Prosecutor-initiated investigations, see *infra* text accompanying notes 125 *et seq.*

[54] Rome Statute art. 43.

[55] *Id.* art. 43(6).

[56] *See* Christopher Keith Hall, *The First Five Sessions of the U.N. Preparatory Commission for the International Criminal Court*, 94 AM. J. INT'L L. 773, 783

(2000)(describing initiative on the part of Canada, France, Germany, and the Netherlands to address the issue).

[57] Draft Rule of Procedure and Evidence (RPE) Report of the Preparatory Commission for the International Criminal Court; Addendum: Finalized Draft Text of the Rules of Procedure and Evidence, U.N. Doc. PCNICC/2000/INF/3/Add.1 (2000), *available at* http:// www.iccnow.org/html/un.html [hereinafter Draft RPE].

[58] Draft RPE 22 requires that counsel have "established competence in international or criminal law and procedure, as well as the necessary relevant experience, whether as judge, prosecutor, advocate or in other similar capacity, in criminal proceedings."

[59] *See* Draft RPE 21.

[60] *See* Draft RPE 8.

[61] *See* Rome Statute art. 112. The right to vote may be suspended if a state party falls in arrears of its payments for more than two full years. *Id.* art. 112(8).

[62] *See* Lee A. Casey, *The Case Against the International Criminal Court*, 25 FORDHAM INT'L L.J. 840, 845-46(2002) (arguing that the Assembly of States Parties will be a "congress of ambassadors from different and hostile interests" that can claim "no democratic legitimacy even on a theory of virtual representation").

[63] *See id.* at 844.

[64] *See id.* at 845.

[65] Rome Statute art. 5. The preparatory committee was unable to reach a consensus on a definition for the crime of "aggression."

[66] *Id.* art. 8.

[67] *Id.* arts. 124 and 121.

[68] The ICC's jurisdiction may operate in a similar manner with respect to new crimes added by the Assembly of States Parties under the amendment procedures of the Rome Statute. Amendments to add new crimes or change the definitions of those already covered enter into force only for those states parties which have accepted an amendment one year after the deposit of their instruments of ratification or acceptance. The ICC may not exercise its jurisdiction regarding such a crime when committed by nationals of or on the territory of a state party which has not accepted the amendment. The ICC may assert jurisdiction over such crimes committed on the territory of non-party states (or by their nationals) as soon as the amendment enters into force, providing all of the preconditions for jurisdiction are met. *See* Scheffer, *supra* note 14, at 87.

[69] *See* Didier Pfirter, *The Position of Switzerland with Respect to the ICC Statute and in Particular the Elements of Crimes*, 32 CORNELL INT'L L.J. 499, 502 (1999) (describing U.S. proposal and initial resistence to the detailed definition of crimes, which is not standard practice in most legal systems).

[70] *See generally* William K. Lietzau, *Checks and Balances and Elements of Proof: Structural Pillars for the International Criminal Court*, 32 CORNELL INT'L L.J. 477 (1999) (exploring issues surrounding establishment of well-defined elements of crimes).

[71] *See id.* at 487 (noting that the need for effective mechanisms to enforce criminal law against individuals requires precision and specificity rather than ambiguity and nuance).

[72] Convention on the Prevention and Punishment of Genocide, Dec. 9, 1948, 78 U.N.T.S. 277.

[73] *Id.* art. II. Rome Statute art. 6 lists the following acts: (a) Killing members of the group; (b) Causing serious bodily or mental harm to members of the group; (c) Deliberately inflicting on the group conditions of life calculated to bring about its physical destruction in whole or in part; (d) Imposing measures intended to prevent births within the group; (e) Forcibly transferring children of the group to another group.

[74] Genocide Convention Implementation Act of 1987, Pub. L. No. 100-606, 102 Stat. 3045 (codified at 18 U.S.C. §§ 1091-93).

[75] *See* KRIANGSAK KITTICHAISAREE, INTERNATIONAL CRIMINAL LAW 69 (2001) (noting that "mobile" groups, such as professions and political groups, are not covered, despite attempts by some delegates at the Rome Conference to include them).

[76] *See id.* at 70 (noting forcible transfer of children as a possible exception because the ultimate result is the physical destruction of a named type of group).

[77] Prosecutor v. Jean Kambanda, Case No. ICTR-97-23-S, ICTR T. Ch., Sep. 4, 1998 (former Prime Minister of Rwanda guilty of genocide for failing to take action to halt ongoing massacres).

[78] Report of the Preparatory Commission for the International Criminal Court, Part II, Finalized draft text of the Elements of Crimes, U.N. Doc. PCNICC/2000/1/Add.2, Nov. 2, 2000 (hereinafter "Draft Elements").

[79] *See* KITTICHAISAREE, *supra* note 75, at 72-73.

[80] *See id.* at 86.

[81] *See* Michael P. Scharf, *Justice Versus Peace, in* THE U.S. AND THE ICC, *supra* note 27, at 179, 185.

[82] Rome Statute art. 7 lists: (a) Murder; (b) Extermination; (c) Enslavement; (d) Deportation or forcible transfer of population; (e) Imprisonment or other severe deprivation of physical liberty in violation of fundamental rules of international law; (f) Torture; (g) Rape, sexual slavery, enforced prostitution, forced pregnancy, enforced sterilization, or any other form of sexual violence of comparable gravity; (h) Persecution against any identifiable group or collectivity on political, racial, national, ethnic, cultural, religious, gender as defined in paragraph 3, or other grounds that are universally recognized as impermissible under international law, in connection with any act referred to in this paragraph or any crime within the jurisdiction of the Court; (i) Enforced disappearance of persons; (j) The crime of apartheid; (k) Other inhumane acts of a similar character intentionally causing great suffering, or serious injury to body or to mental or physical health.

[83] *See* Scharf, *supra* note 81, at 87.

[84] *See* Draft Elements, *supra* note 78, at 9.

[85] *See* KITTICHAISAREE, *supra* note 75, at 92.

[86] See Douglass Cassel, Empowering United States Courts to Hear Crimes Within the Jurisdiction of the International Court, 35 NEW ENG. L. REV. 421, 429 (2001).

[87] *See id.* n.39 (listing relevant crimes over which U.S. courts have extraterritorial jurisdiction). Additionally, U.S. courts have jurisdiction to try criminal offenses committed by persons employed by or accompanying the armed forces overseas, or ex-servicemembers who committed a crime overseas, if such crime would be punishable by imprisonment for more than one year if it had committed within the territorial jurisdiction of the United States. 18 U.S.C. § 3261.

[88] *See* Terrorism and the Law of War: Trying Terrorists as War Criminals before Military Commissions, CRS Report RL31191(summary description of sources and contents of the international law of war).

[89] *See* JEAN PICTET, HUMANITARIAN LAW AND THE PROTECTION OF WAR VICTIMS 31 (1975) (describing the principle that "belligerents shall not inflict on their adversaries harm out of proportion to the object of warfare, which is to destroy or weaken the military strength of the enemy").

[90] Geneva Convention for the Amelioration of the Condition of the Wounded and Sick in Armed Forces in the Field, opened for signature Aug. 12, 1949, 6 U.S.T. 3114, T.I.A.S. No. 3362, 75 U.N.T.S. 31 (entered into force Oct. 21, 1950); Geneva Convention for the Amelioration of the Condition of Wounded, Sick and Shipwrecked Members of Armed Forces at Sea, opened for signature Aug. 12, 1949, 6 U.S.T. 3217, T.I.A.S. No. 3363, 75 U.N.T.S. 85 (entered into force Oct. 21, 1950); Geneva Convention Relative to the Treatment of Prisoners of War, opened for signature Aug. 12, 1949, 6 U.S.T. 3316, T.I.A.S. No. 3364, 75 U.N.T.S. 135 (entered into force Oct. 21, 1950)[hereinafter "GPW"]; Geneva Convention Relative to the Protection of Civilian Persons in Time of War, opened for signature Aug. 12, 1949, 6 U.S.T. 3516, T.I.A.S. No. 3365, 75 U.N.T.S. 287 (entered into force Oct. 21, 1950) [hereinafter referred to collectively as the "1949 (Conventions" or "Conventions"].

[91] Hague Convention No. IV Respecting the Laws and Customs of War on Land, Oct. 18, 1907, 36 Stat. 2277, 205 Consol. T.S. 277.

[92] Rome Statute art. 8(1). Art. 8(2). enumerates the following as war crimes: (a)...(i) Wilful killing; (ii) Torture or inhuman treatment, including biological experiments; (iii) Wilfully causing great suffering, or serious injury to body or health; (iv) Extensive destruction and appropriation of property, not justified by military necessity and carried out unlawfully and wantonly; (v) Compelling a prisoner of war or other protected person to serve in the forces of a hostile Power;(vi) Wilfully depriving a prisoner of war or other protected person of the rights of fair and regular trial; (vii) Unlawful deportation or transfer or unlawful confinement; (viii) Taking of hostages. (b) Other serious violations of the laws and customs applicable in international armed conflict, within the established framework of international law, namely, any of the following acts: (i) Intentionally directing attacks against the civilian population as such or against individual civilians not taking direct part in hostilities; (ii) Intentionally directing attacks against civilian objects, that is, objects which are not military objectives; (iii) Intentionally directing attacks against personnel, installations, material, units or vehicles involved in a humanitarian assistance or peacekeeping mission in accordance with the Charter of the United Nations, as long as they are entitled to the protection given to civilians or civilian objects under the international law of armed conflict; (iv) Intentionally launching an attack in the knowledge that such attack will cause incidental loss of life or injury to civilians or damage to civilian objects or widespread, long-term and severe damage to the natural environment which would be clearly excessive in relation to the concrete and direct overall military advantage anticipated; (v) Attacking or bombarding, by whatever means, towns, villages, dwellings or buildings which are undefended and which are not military objectives; (vi) Killing or wounding a combatant who, having laid down his arms or having no longer means of defense, has surrendered at discretion; (vii) Making improper use of a flag of truce, of the flag or of the military

insignia and uniform of the enemy or of the United Nations, as well as of the distinctive emblems of the Geneva Conventions, resulting in death or serious personal injury; (viii) The transfer, directly or indirectly, by the Occupying Power of parts of its own civilian population into the territory it occupies, or the deportation or transfer of all or parts of the population of the occupied territory within or outside this territory; (ix) Intentionally directing attacks against buildings dedicated to religion, education, art, science or charitable purposes, historic monuments, hospitals and places where the sick and wounded are collected, provided they are not military objectives; (x) Subjecting persons who are in the power of an adverse party to physical mutilation or to medical or scientific experiments of any kind which are neither justified by the medical, dental or hospital treatment of the person concerned nor carried out in his or her interest, and which cause death to or seriously endanger the health of such person or persons; (xi) Killing or wounding treacherously individuals belonging to the hostile nation or army; (xii) Declaring that no quarter will be given; (xiii) Destroying or seizing the enemy's property unless such destruction or seizure be imperatively demanded by the necessities of war; (xiv) Declaring abolished, suspended or inadmissible in a court of law the rights and actions of the nationals of the hostile party; (xv) Compelling the nationals of the hostile party to take part in the operations of war directed against their own country, even if they were in the belligerent's service before the commencement of the war; (xvi) Pillaging a town or place, even when taken by assault; (xvii) Employing poison or poisoned weapons; (xviii) Employing asphyxiating, poisonous or other gases, and all analogous liquids, materials or devices; (xix) Employing bullets which expand or flatten easily in the human body, such as bullets with a hard envelope which does not entirely cover the core or is pierced with incisions; (xx) Employing weapons, projectiles and material and methods of warfare which are of a nature to cause superfluous injury or unnecessary suffering or which are inherently indiscriminate in violation of the international law of armed conflict, provided that such weapons, projectiles and material and methods of warfare are the subject of a comprehensive prohibition and are included in an annex to this Statute, by an amendment in accordance with the relevant provisions set forth in articles 121 and 123; (xxi) Committing outrages upon personal dignity, in particular humiliating and degrading treatment; (xxii) Committing rape, sexual slavery, enforced prostitution, forced pregnancy, as defined in article 7, paragraph 2 (f), enforced sterilization, or any other form of sexual violence also constituting a grave breach of the Geneva Conventions; (xxiii) Utilizing the presence of a civilian or other protected person to render certain points, areas or military forces immune from military operations; (xxiv) Intentionally directing attacks against buildings, material, medical units and transport, and personnel using the distinctive emblems of the Geneva Conventions in conformity with international law; (xxv) Intentionally using starvation of civilians as a method of warfare by depriving them of objects indispensable to their survival, including wilfully impeding relief supplies as provided for under the Geneva Conventions; (xxvi) Conscripting or enlisting children under the age of fifteen years into the national armed forces or using them to participate actively in hostilities. (c) In the case of an armed conflict not of an international character, serious violations of article 3 common to the four Geneva Conventions of 12 August 1949, namely, any of the following acts committed against persons taking no active part in the hostilities, including members of armed forces who have laid down their arms and those placed hors de combat by sickness, wounds, detention or any other cause: (i) Violence to life and person, in particular murder of all kinds, mutilation, cruel treatment and torture; (ii) Committing outrages upon personal dignity, in particular humiliating and degrading treatment; (iii) Taking of hostages; (iv) The passing of sentences and the carrying out of executions without previous judgement pronounced by a regularly constituted court, affording all judicial guarantees which are generally recognized as indispensable. (d) Paragraph 2 (c) applies to armed conflicts not of an international character and thus does not apply to situations of internal disturbances and tensions, such as riots, isolated and sporadic acts of violence or other acts of a similar nature. (e) Other serious violations of the laws and customs applicable in armed conflicts not of an international character, within the established framework of international law, namely, any of the following acts: (i) Intentionally directing attacks against the civilian population as such or against individual civilians not taking direct part in hostilities; (ii) Intentionally directing attacks against buildings, material, medical units and transport, and personnel using the distinctive emblems of the Geneva Conventions in conformity with international law; (iii) Intentionally directing attacks against personnel, installations, material, units or vehicles involved in a humanitarian assistance or peacekeeping mission in accordance with the Charter of the United Nations, as long as they are entitled to the protection given to civilians or civilian objects under the law of armed conflict; (iv) Intentionally directing attacks against buildings dedicated to religion, education, art, science or charitable purposes, historic monuments, hospitals and places where the sick and wounded are collected, provided they are not military objectives; (v) Pillaging a town or place, even when taken by assault; (vi) Committing rape, sexual slavery, enforced prostitution, forced pregnancy, as defined in article 7, paragraph 2 (f), enforced sterilization, and any other form of sexual violence also constituting a serious violation of article 3 common to the four Geneva Conventions; (vii) Conscripting or enlisting children under the age of fifteen years into armed or groups or using them to participate actively in hostilities; (viii) Ordering the displacement of the civilian population for reasons related to the conflict, unless the security of the civilians involved or imperative military reasons so demand; (ix) Killing or wounding treacherously a combatant adversary; (x) Declaring that no quarter will be given; (xi) Subjecting persons who are in the power of another party to the conflict to physical mutilation or to medical or scientific experiments of any kind which are neither justified by the medical, dental or hospital treatment of the person concerned nor carried out in his or her interest, and which cause death to or seriously endanger the health of such person or persons; (xii) Destroying or seizing the property of an adversary unless such destruction or seizure be imperatively demanded by the necessities of the conflict; (f) Paragraph 2 (e) applies to armed conflicts not of an international character and thus does not apply to situations of internal disturbances and tensions, such as riots, isolated and sporadic acts of violence or other acts of a similar nature. It applies to armed conflicts that take place in the territory of a State when there is protracted armed conflict between governmental authorities and organized armed groups or between such groups.

[93] *See* Draft Elements, *supra* note 78, at 18.

[94] Rome Statute art. 8(1)([The ICC has jurisdiction over war crimes] "*in particular* when committed as a part of a plan or policy or as part of a large-scale commission of such

crimes."(emphasis added)). According to the Draft Elements, "elements for war crimes under ... [the Rome] Statute shall be interpreted within the established framework of the international law of armed conflict...." *See* Draft Elements, *supra* note 78, at 18. International law does not appear to require proof of the existence of any policy, official or unofficial, to commit a war crime. *See* Kriangsak Kittichaisaree, *The NATO Military Action and the Potential Impact of the International Criminal Court*, 4 SING. J. INT'L and COMP. L. 498, 517 (2000). The "in particular" language is meant to serve as a jurisdictional threshold to prevent the ICC from taking up relatively insignificant cases. *See id.* Critics have argued, however, that this threshold is still too low, increasing the likelihood of prosecution of members of the armed forces. *See* Jimmy Gurulé, *United States Opposition to the 1998 Rome Statute Establishing an International Criminal Court: Is the Court's Jurisdiction Truly Complementary to National Criminal Jurisdictions?*, 35 CORNELL INT'L L.J. 1, 30-31 (2002).

[95] 18 U.S.C. § 2441.

[96] Article 18 of the UCMJ, 10 U.S.C. § 818, provides general court martial jurisdiction over "any person who by the law of war is subject to trial by a military tribunal and may adjudge any punishment permitted by the law of war." UCMJ art. 21, 10 U.S.C. § 821, provides that court-martial jurisdiction does not deprive military commissions of jurisdiction to try any person for such crimes.

[97] *See* Department of the Army, FM 27-10, THE LAW OF LAND WARFARE para. 507 (1956).

[98] See generally Silvia A. Fernandez de Gurmendi, The Working Group on Aggression at the Preparatory Commission for the International Criminal Court, 25 FORDHAM INT'L L.J. 589 (2002).

[99] *See id.* at 592 (discussing World War II precedents for charging persons with aggression).

[100] *See* Gurulé, *supra* note 94, at 2.

[101] U.N. Charter art. 39.

[102] *See* Kittichaisaree, *supra* note 94, at 504.

[103] U.N. GAOR, Supp. No. 19, U.N. Doc A/9615 (1974).

[104] *See* Kittichaisaree, *supra* note 94, at 505 (citing U.N. Security Council Resolution 418 of 4 Nov. 1977).

[105] *See id.* at 504-05.

[106] Rome Statute art. 5(2).

[107] *See* Kittichaisaree, *supra* note 94, at 506 (predicting that "NATO members who are also Permanent Members of the Security Council would certainly veto any draft Security Council resolution determining that an act of aggression has been committed by NATO").

[108] *See* Scheffer, *supra* note 14, at 83 (advocating U.S. involvement in the ICC to avoid a definition of "aggression" that does not include a determination by the U.N. Security Council).

[109] The Geneva Conventions require signatory nations to enact domestic legislation to punish perpetrators of grave breaches of the Conventions, and to actively investigate such crimes, and prosecute or extradite the alleged perpetrators. *See* GPW, *supra* note 90, art. 129. Other treaties with similar clauses include the Conventions on Hijacking and Aircraft Sabotage, as well as most other conventions against terrorism. *See* Michael

P. Scharf, *Universal Jurisdiction: Myths, Realities, and Prospects: Application of Treaty-based Universal Jurisdiction to Nationals of Non-Party States,* 35 NEW ENG.L. REV. 363 (2001). *But see* Casey, *supra* note 62, at 855 (disputing the validity of universal jurisdiction). For an in-depth analysis on the applicability of universal jurisdiction to various crimes under international law, see generally Bassiouni, *supra* note 23.

[110] This concept is distinct from domestic jurisdiction. For example, although there is universal jurisdiction over grave breaches of the Geneva Conventions, U.S. law only allows prosecution of such crimes in its federal courts where the victim or perpetrator is a U.S. national. *See generally* Cassel, *supra* note 86 (recommending changes in U.S. law to fully encompass crimes over which the ICC will have jurisdiction); 18 U.S.C. § 2441 (War Crimes Act).

[111] *See* Bassiouni, *supra* note 23, at 136 (concluding that state practice does not support the assertion that universal jurisdiction has reached the level of customary international law in all cases where it has been claimed).

[112] Rome Statute preamble (declaring signatory states are "[d]etermined to put an end to impunity for the perpetrators of these crimes and thus to contribute to the prevention of such crimes").

[113] *Id.* ("Recalling that it is the duty of every State to exercise its criminal jurisdiction over those responsible for international crimes"); *see* Jordan Paust, *The Reach of ICC Jurisdiction Over Non-Signatory Nationals*, 33 VAND. J. TRANSNAT'L L. 1, 7 (2000) (describing ICC jurisdiction as a "form of limited universal jurisdiction").

[114] Rome Statute art. 17. *See* van der Vyver, *supra* note 20, at 2-3 (describing principle of complementarity and the possible questions it raises regarding state sovereignty in any determination of "unwillingness to prosecute").

[115] Rome Statute art. 13 states that the U.N. Security Council may recommend investigation of alleged crimes using its authority under chapter VII of the U.N. Charter.

[116] *Id.* art.16.

[117] *Id.* art. 14.

[118] Draft RPE 45.

[119] Rome Statute art. 14(2).

[120] *Id.* art. 18(1).

[121] *Id.* art. 18(2-5).

[122] *Id.* art. 53.

[123] Draft RPE 107.

[124] Rome Statute arts. 15 and 53(4).

[125] Draft RPE 46.

[126] Rome Statute art. 18(1).

[127] *Id.* art. 15(6).

[128] Draft RPE 109.

[129] U.N. Charter art. 39. *See* Gurulé, *supra* note 94, at 22 (criticizing Rome Statute art. 16 for perceived weaknesses).

[130] Rome Statute art. 13(b).

[131] See Mark A. Summers, A Fresh Look at the Jurisdictional Provisions of the Statute of the International Criminal Court: the Case for Scrapping the Treaty, 20 WIS. INT'L L.J.

57, 75 (2001); Michael P. Scharf, The United States and the International Criminal Court: A Recommendation for the Bush Administration 7 ILSA J INT'L and COMP. L. 385, 387 (2001).

[132] Rome Statute art. 13.

[133] The Rome Statute makes military commanders criminally responsible for the acts of forces under "his or her effective command and control." It also eliminates all immunities "based on official capacity." *Id.* arts. 28 and 27, respectively.

[134] *Id.* art. 13. The concurrence of the state in which the crime took place would be necessary for the ICC to maintain its jurisdiction. The ICC can also exercise its jurisdiction pursuant to a referral from the Security Council, whether or not the state of nationality or territoriality concurs. Because the U.S. possesses a veto in the Security Council, such a referral could only occur if the U.S. consented.

[135] Such country would also have the option of trying the case in its own courts or extraditing the prisoner to the United States. The Rome Statute provides that states parties who receive a request for surrender from the ICC and a request for extradition from a non-party state, with which it has an extradition treaty or the like, shall decide which course to take based on the dates of the requests, the interest of the requesting state in prosecuting the crime, and the possibility of subsequent surrender of the person between the ICC and the non-party state. Rome Statute art. 19. If there is no obligation to extradite, the requested state should give priority to the ICC. *Id.* Under Article 98 of the Rome Statute, the ICC may not proceed with a request for surrender or assistance which would require the requested state to act inconsistently with its obligations under international law regarding state or diplomatic immunity or an agreement not to surrender the country's national to the ICC unless the ICC gains the cooperation of that third state. It is unclear whether a treaty violation that results in the ICC's custody of an accused is grounds for challenging the ICC's jurisdiction, either by the accused or the state of nationality of the accused.

[136] *See* Rome Statute art. 17. Paragraph 1 provides the ICC shall determine a case is inadmissible where: (a) The case is being investigated or prosecuted by a State which has jurisdiction over it, unless the State is unwilling or unable genuinely to carry out the investigation or prosecution; (b) The case has been investigated by a State which has jurisdiction over it and the State has decided not to prosecute the person concerned, unless the decision resulted from the unwillingness or inability of the State genuinely to prosecute; (c) The person concerned has already been tried for conduct which is the subject of the complaint, and a trial by the Court is not permitted under article 20, paragraph 3; (d) The case is not of sufficient gravity to justify further action by the Court.

[137] *Id.* art. 20.

[138] *Id.* art. 18. A state has one month after receipt of the notification to advise the ICC that it is investigating (or has investigated) the situation. The Prosecutor must then defer, unless he or she obtains an authorization to investigate from a Pre-Trial Chamber.

[139] Presumably this language refers to both the state where a crime allegedly occurred and the state whose national allegedly perpetrated it, even though the acceptance of only one of them is *required* for the ICC to find jurisdiction.

[140] *See* Finalized Draft Text of the Elements of Crimes, Report of the Preparatory Commission for the International Criminal Court, PCNICC/2000/1 (2000), *available at*

http://www.un.org /law/icc/statute/elements/elemfra.htm. As currently defined, genocide crimes have as an element that the "conduct took place in the context of a manifest pattern of similar conduct directed against [the target] group or was conduct that could itself effect such destruction." Crimes against humanity include the elements that the conduct was committed with knowledge or intent that it contribute to a "widespread or systematic attack directed against a civilian population." *See id.* at 9. War crimes listed under paragraphs (a) and (b) of Article 8 of the Rome Statute apply to situations of international armed conflict and incorporate the Geneva Conventions of 1949. Paragraph 2(e) applies to armed conflicts not of an international character and explicitly excludes "internal disturbances and tensions, such as riots, isolated and sporadic acts of violence or other acts of a similar nature." There must be "protracted armed conflict between governmental authorities and organized armed groups or between such groups" before any conduct can be considered a war crime under that paragraph.

[141] Rome Statute art. 12. *See* Ruth Wedgwood, *The Constitution and the ICC*, *in* THE U.S. AND THE ICC, *supra* note 27, at 119, 127.

[142] *See id.* at 127.

[143] *See* Cassel, *supra* note 86, at 437; Robinson O. Everett, American Servicemembers and the ICC, *in* THE US AND THE ICC, *supra* note 27, at 137, 142.

[144] Rome Statute art. 12(2(c)). *See* Gurulé, *supra* note 94, at 27-28 (arguing that the ICC's jurisdiction is not truly complementary because the Rome Statute allows the ICC to second-guess the decisions of national courts).

[145] *See generally* Michael P. Scharf, *Justice versus Peace*, *in* THE U S. AND THE ICC, *supra* note 27, at 179.

[146] *See, e.g., The International Criminal Court: Hearing before the House Comm. on International Relations*, 106th Cong. 92-101, 96 (2000) (statement of Monroe Leigh on behalf of the American Bar Association); Scheffer, *supra* note 14, at 94; Wedgwood, *supra* note 141, at 123.

[147] *See, e.g.* Casey, *supra* note 62.

[148] See generally Robert Christensen, Getting to Peace by Reconciling Notions of Justice: The Importance of Considering Discrepancies Between Civil and Common Legal Systems in the Formation of the International Criminal Court, 6 UCLA J. INT'L L. and FOREIGN AFF. 391 (2001).

[149] Draft RPE, *supra* note 57.

[150] For a brief comparison of ICC procedural safeguards to federal and military rules of procedure and evidence in chart form, see Selected Procedural Safeguards in Federal, Military, and International Courts, CRS Report RL31262. Of course, just as the U.S. Constitution is interpreted in large measure through caselaw, the Rome Statute may be expected to acquire some new contours in the light of the ICC's interpretation of the Statute as well as caselaw interpretation.

[151] *See id*; Wedgwood, *et al.*, *supra* note 8, at 130.

[152] *See* Casey, *supra* note 62, at 861-62.

[153] *See* Wedgwood, *supra* note 141, at 126 (citing *Ex parte* Quirin, 317 U.S. 1 (1942)).

[154] *See* Madsen v. Kinsella, 343 U.S. 341 (1952)(upholding jurisdiction of military commission to try civilians in occupied foreign territory).

[155] *See* Wedgwood, *supra* note 141, at 122 (giving as an example the International Criminal Tribunal for the Former Yugoslavia).

[156] *See id.* at 124 (citing Charleton v. Kelly, 229 U.S. 447 (1913)).

[157] Rome Statute art. 66.

[158] Id.

[159] *Id* art. 61.

[160] *Id* art. 61(6).

[161] *Id* art. 64(8).

[162] *Id.* art. 65.

[163] *Id.* art. 65(3).

[164] *Id.* art. 65(5).

[165] *See* Holbrook v. Flynn, 475 U.S. 560 (1986). A similar rule applies to courts-martial. *See* Manual for Courts Martial (M.C.M.), established as Exec. Order No. 12473, 49 Fed. Reg 17,152, (Apr. 23, 1984). Rules for Courts-Martial (R.C.M.) Rule. 804 provides that "[t]he accused shall be properly attired in uniform with grade insignia and any decorations to which entitled. Physical restraint shall not be imposed unless prescribed by the military judge."

[166] Draft RPE 121.

[167] Rome Statute art. 54.

[168] *Id.* art. 55.

[169] *See* Wedgwood, *supra* note 141, at 123.

[170] Rome Statute art. 67(1)(g).

[171] Id.

[172] *Id.* art. 93(2); Draft RPE 74.

[173] Draft RPE 74.

[174] Id.

[175] Rome Statute art. 67(1)(e).

[176] *Id.* art. 68.

[177] Measures to protect national security could also conflict with the accused's right to confront witnesses. *See infra* section addressing the right to a public trial.

[178] Draft RPE 67.

[179] *See* Fed. R. Evid. chapter. VIII.

[180] *See* Maryland v. Craig, 497 U.S. 836 (1990).

[181] See id.

[182] *See id.* at 855 (distinguishing Coy v. Iowa, 487 U.S. 1012 (1988), in which similar measures were invalidated because they were imposed statutorily without requiring a case-specific inquiry into the need for protective measures).

[183] Rome Statute art. 68.

[184] Rome Statute art. 20 (*Ne bis in idem*). "No person who has been tried by another court ... shall be tried by the Court with respect to the same conduct unless the proceedings in the other court [were not properly conducted]."

[185] *See* United States v. Lanza, 260 U.S. 377 (1922).

[186] *See* Christensen, *supra* note 148, at 420.

[187] *Id.* art. 20(2).

[188] See Mark C. Fleming, Appellate Review in the International Criminal Tribunals, 37 TEX. INT'L L.J. 111, 117 (2002).

[189] United States v. Martin Linen Supply Co., 430 U.S. 564 (1977).

[190] Rome Statute art. 81(1).

[191] *See id.* art. 69(7): Evidence obtained by means of a violation of this Statute or internationally recognized human rights shall not be admissible if: (a) The violation casts substantial doubt on the reliability of the evidence; or (b) The admission of the evidence would be antithetical to and would seriously damage the integrity of the proceedings. *See generally* George E. Edwards, *International Human Rights Law Challenges to the New International Criminal Court: The Search and Seizure Right to Privacy* 26 YALE J. INT'L L. 323 (2001).

[192] Rome Statute art. 21; Draft RPE 63(5).

[193] G.A. Res. 217A (III), art. 12, U.N. Doc. A/810 (1948).

[194] International Covenant on Civil and Political Rights, Dec. 16, 1966, art. 17, 999 U.N.T.S. 171, 6 I.L.M. 368 (entered into force Mar. 23, 1976).

[195] *See* Edwards, *supra* note 191, at 330.

[196] For example, evidence resulting from overseas searches of American property by foreign officials may be admissible unless foreign police conduct shocks judicial conscience or participation by U.S. agents is so substantial as to render the action that of the United States. *See* United States v. Barona, 56 F.3d 1087 (9th Cir. 1995).

[197] Rome Statute arts. 63, 67(1)(d).

[198] Rome Statute art. 63(2).

[199] Illinois v. Allen, 397 U.S. 337 (1970).

[200] Diaz v. United States, 223 U.S. 442, 455 (1912).

[201] Rome Statute art. 67(1)(d).

[202] Rule 22 provides:counsel for the defence shall have established competence in international or criminal law and procedure, as well as the necessary relevant experience, whether as judge, prosecutor, advocate or in other similar capacity, in criminal proceedings. A counsel for the defence shall have an excellent knowledge of and be fluent in at least one of the working languages of the Court. Counsel for the defence may be assisted by other persons, including professors of law, with relevant expertise.

[203] Rule 21.

[204] Rule 20 provides that the Registrar "shall organize the staff of the Registry in a manner that promotes the rights of the defence, consistent with the principle of fair trial as defined in the Statute."

[205] Rome Statute art. 67(1)(b).

[206] Fed. R. Evid. 501.

[207] U.S. CONST. Amend. VI.

[208] Rome Statute art. 67(1).

[209] 18 U.S.C. § 3161.

[210] Rules for Courts-Martial (R.C.M.) §707(a).

[211] Strunk v. United States, 412 U.S. 434 (1973).

[212] *See* Barker v. Wingo, 407 U.S. 514, 532 (1972).

[213] *See id.*; United States v. Baker, 63 F.3d 1478, 1497 (9th Cir. 1995).

[214] Draft RPE 84.

[215] Rome Statute art. 29.

[216] 18 U.S.C. §1091(e).

[217] 18 U.S.C. §3281.
[218] 18 U.S.C. §2441.
[219] 18 U.S.C. §3286(b).
[220] 18 U.S.C. §3282.
[221] *See* Waller v. Georgia, 467 U.S. 39, 48 (1984).
[222] R.C.M. §806.
[223] *See* Richmond Newspapers v. Virginia, 448 U.S. 555 (1980).
[224] Rome Statute art. 67(7).
[225] Draft RPE 87.
[226] Id.
[227] Rome Statute art. 68(6).
[228] Rome Statute art. 87.
[229] *See* Casey, *supra* note 62, at 87 (arguing that the Appeals Division will have identical institutional interests to those of the trial chambers and would not be capable of providing truly independent review).
[230] *See* Fleming, *supra* note 188, at 112.
[231] *See, e.g.,* Hirota v. MacArthur, 338 U.S. 197 (1948) (declining to review decision of internationally composed military commission).
[232] *See generally* Fleming, *supra* note 188.
[233] *See Ex parte* Burford, 7 U.S. (3 Cr.) 448 (1806).
[234] *See* Ker v. Illinois, 119 U.S. 436 (1886).
[235] *See* Wong Sun v. United States, 371 U.S. 471 (1963).
[236] Rome Statute arts. 55(1b), 55(1d).
[237] *Id.* arts. 59(3), 60(2).
[238] *Id.* art. 58.
[239] Draft RPE 117.
[240] *Id.* art. 59.
[241] *Id.* art. 59(4).
[242] Draft RPE 117.
[243] Draft RPE 119. Such conditions may include: (a) The person must not travel beyond territorial limits set by the Pre-Trial Chamber without the explicit agreement of the Chamber; (b) The person must not go to certain places or associate with certain persons as specified by the Pre-Trial Chamber; (c) The person must not contact directly or indirectly victims or witnesses; (d) The person must not engage in certain professional activities; (e) The person must reside at a particular address as specified by the Pre-Trial Chamber; (f) The person must respond when summoned by an authority or qualified person designated by the Pre-Trial Chamber; (g) The person must post bond or provide real or personal security or surety, for which the amount and the schedule and mode of payment shall be determined by the Pre-Trial Chamber; (h) The person must supply the Registrar with all identity documents, particularly his or her passport.
[244] Rome Statute art. 60.
[245] *Id.* art. 85; Draft RPE 173-75.
[246] Rome Statute art. 108.
[247] *Id.* art. 103.
[248] *Id.* arts. 104 and 106.
[249] *See* Scheffer, *supra* note 14, at 74.

[250] *See id.* at 63.

[251] Rome Statute art. 123.

[252] *Id.* arts. 112 and 123. States which have signed the Statute or the Final Act are eligible to participate as observers in both bodies. The Administration's notification of intent not to ratify the Statute should have no effect on eligibility, although it may signal an intent not to participate.

[253] U.N. Doc., PCNICC/2001/1/Add.4, Draft Rules of Procedure of the Assembly of States Parties Jan. 8 (2002) (hereinafter "Draft Assembly Rules").

[254] The United Nations has a standing invitation to participate as an observer. Draft Assembly Rule 35. It may also propose items for the agenda. Draft Assembly Rule 11.

[255] Rome Statute art. 13. Non-parties might also be able to provide information to enable the Prosecutor to initiate a self-referred investigation, but would have no *official* role in advocating prosecution.

[256] *Id.* art. 16.

[257] *Id.* art. 53.

[258] *Id.* arts. 86, 87, and 93.

[259] *Id.* arts. 59 and 89.

[260] *Id.* art. 72.

[261] *Id.* art. 73.

[262] *Id.* art. 115.

[263] *See* Casey, *supra* note 62, at 849-50.

[264] *See* Final Report to the Prosecutor by the Committee Established to Review the NATO Bombing Campaign Against the Federal Republic of Yugoslavia, *available at* http://www.un.org/icty/pressreal/nato061300.html.

[265] *See* Grossman, *supra* note 6. However, some predict that once the ICC begins to operate, future *ad hoc* tribunals are not likely to be created, which may effectively limit the means available to support such an effort.

[266] *The International Criminal Court: Hearing Before the House Committee on International Relations*, 106th Cong. 4 (2000) (prepared testimony of John Bolton, Senior Vice President, American Enterprise Institute).

[267] See Appendix I – the French Solution to Constitutional Issues in *the International Criminal Court: Manual for the Ratification and Implementation of the Rome Statute* at the Canadian government's website on the ICC (http://209.217.98.79/ english/ 10_guide_e /10_guide_e.htm).

[268] *See* Scheffer, *supra* note 14, at 73 n.94.

[269] *See* Department of Defense Appropriations for 2002, P.L. 107-117. § 8173. None of the funds made available in division A of this Act may be used to provide support or other assistance to the International Criminal Court or to any criminal investigation or other prosecutorial activity of the International Criminal Court. *See also* Departments of Commerce, Justice, and State, the Judiciary, and Related Agencies Appropriations Act, 2002 § 630, P.L.107-77.

[270] H.R. 4546 § 1034.

[271] *See* Grossman, *supra* note 6.

[272] The International Criminal Court: Protecting American Servicemen and Officials from the Threat of International Prosecution, Hearing before the Senate Comm. on Foreign Relations, 106th Cong. (2000).

[273] P.L. 107-117 § 8173. *See supra* note 269.

[274] Rome Statute art. 98 prohibits the ICC from pursuing requests for assistance or surrender that would require the requested state to act inconsistently with its international obligations.

[275] "Covered allied persons" includes military personnel, elected or appointed officials, and other persons working for a NATO country or a major non-NATO ally, which includes Australia, Egypt, Israel, Japan, Jordan, Argentina, the Republic of Korea, and New Zealand, or Taiwan, "so long as that government is not a party to the International Criminal Court and wishes its officials and other persons working on its behalf to be exempted from the jurisdiction of the [ICC]." Sec. 642(3). Covered allies currently could include persons from the Czech Republic, Turkey, Australia, Egypt, Israel, Japan, the Republic of Korea, and Taiwan. (Of these countries, only Turkey, Taiwan, and Japan have not signed the Rome Statute.)

[276] H.R. 4775 § 2011; *see also* S. 1610 § 11.

In: Law and Law Enforcement Issues
Editor: Gerald M. Kessler, pp. 83-110

ISBN: 978-1-60456-044-2

Chapter 4

U.S. POLICY REGARDING THE INTERNATIONAL CRIMINAL COURT*

Jennifer K. Elsea

ABSTRACT

One month after the International Criminal Court (ICC) officially came into existence on July 1, 2002, the President signed legislation that limits U.S. government support and assistance to the ICC; curtails certain military assistance to many countries that have ratified the Rome Statute establishing the ICC; regulates U.S. participation in United Nations (U.N.) peacekeeping missions commenced after July 1, 2003; and, most controversially among European allies, authorizes the President to use "all means necessary and appropriate to bring about the release" of certain U.S. and allied persons who may be detained or tried by the ICC. The provision withholding military assistance under the programs for Foreign Military Financing (FMF) and International Military Education and Training (IMET) from certain States Parties to the Rome Statute came into effect on July 1, 2003. The 109th Congress reauthorized the Nethercutt Amendment as part of the FY2006 Consolidated Appropriations Act (H.R. 3057/P.L. 109-102). Unless waived by the President, it bars Economic Support Funds (ESF) assistance to countries that have not agreed to protect U.S. citizens from being turned over to the ICC for prosecution. H.R. 5522 would continue the prohibitions for FY2007.

The ICC is the first permanent world court with nearly universal jurisdiction to try individuals accused of war crimes, crimes against humanity, genocide, and possibly aggression. While most U.S. allies support the ICC, the Bush Administration firmly opposes it and has renounced any U.S. obligations under the treaty. After the Bush Administration threatened to veto a United Nations Security Council resolution to extend the peacekeeping mission in Bosnia on the ground that it did not contain sufficient guarantees that U.S. participants would be immune to prosecution by the ICC, the Security Council adopted a resolution that would defer for one year any prosecution of participants in missions established or authorized by the U.N. whose home countries have not ratified the Rome Statute. That resolution was renewed through July 1, 2004, but was not subsequently renewed. In addition, the United States is pursuing bilateral "Article 98"agreements to preclude extradition by other countries of U.S. citizens to the ICC.

* Excerpted from CRS Report RL31495, dated June 14, 2006.

However, in what some view as a sign that the Administration is softening its stance with respect to the ICC, the United States did not exercise its veto power at the Security Council to prevent the referral of a case against Sudan's leaders for the alleged genocide in Darfur.

This article outlines the main objections the United States has raised with respect to the ICC and analyzes the American Servicemembers' Protection Act (ASPA), enacted to regulate the U.S. cooperation with the ICC. The report concludes with a discussion of the implications for the United States, as a non-ratifying country, as the ICC begins to take shape, as well as the Administration's efforts to win immunity from the ICC's jurisdiction for Americans.

INTRODUCTION[1]

July 1, 2002, marked the birth of the International Criminal Court (ICC), meaning that crimes of the appropriate caliber committed after that date could fall under the jurisdiction of the ICC. The ICC is the first global permanent international court with jurisdiction to prosecute individuals for "the most serious crimes of concern to the international community."[2] Since its creation, the ICC has received three referrals by States Parties, which involved allegations of war crimes in the Republic of Uganda, the Democratic Republic of Congo, and the Central African Republic.[3]

The United Nations Security Council has also referred a situation to the Prosecutor — allegations of atrocities occurring in Darfur, Sudan.[4] The Chief Prosecutor subsequently decided to open investigations into three of the referred cases: Democratic Republic of the Congo,[5] Republic of Uganda,[6] and Darfur, Sudan.[7] Currently, five arrest warrants have been issued by the Court, all in connection to the situation in Northern Uganda.[8]

The United Nations, many human rights organizations, and most democratic nations have expressed support for the ICC.[9] The Bush Administration, however, opposes it and in May, 2002, formally renounced any U.S. obligations under the treaty,[10] to the dismay of the European Union.[11] On August 2, 2002, President Bush signed into law the American Servicemembers' Protection Act (ASPA) to restrict government cooperation with the ICC. The Administration had earlier stressed that the United States shares the goal of the ICC's supporters — promotion of the rule of law — and does not intend to take any action to undermine the ICC.[12]

While the United States initially supported the idea of creating an international criminal court[13] and was a major participant at the Rome Conference,[14] in the end, the United States voted against the Statute.[15] Nevertheless, President Clinton signed the treaty December 31, 2000, at the same time declaring that the treaty contained "significant flaws" and that he would not submit it to the Senate for its advice and consent "until our fundamental concerns are satisfied."[16] The Bush Administration has likewise declined to submit the Rome Statute to the Senate for ratification, and has notified the U.N. Secretary General, as depositary, of the U.S. intent not to ratify the treaty.[17] The primary objection given by the United States in opposition to the treaty is the ICC's possible assertion of jurisdiction over U.S. soldiers charged with "war crimes" resulting from legitimate uses of force, and perhaps over civilian policymakers, even if the United States does not ratify the Rome Statute. The United States sought to exempt U.S. soldiers and employees from the jurisdiction of the ICC based on the unique position the United States occupies with regard to international peacekeeping.[18]

On June 30, 2002, the United States threatened to veto a draft U.N. resolution to extend the peacekeeping mission in Bosnia because the members of the Security Council refused to add a guarantee of full immunity for U.S. personnel from the jurisdiction of the ICC, a move that provoked strong opposition from ICC supporters concerned with the viability of that institution, and that also raised some concerns about the future of United Nations peacekeeping.[19] Ultimately, however, the Security Council and the U.S. delegation were able to reach a compromise and adopted unanimously a resolution requesting the ICC defer, for an initial period of one year, any prosecution of persons participating in U.N. peacekeeping efforts who are nationals of states not parties to the ICC.[20] The compromise reached by the Security Council did not provide permanent immunity for U.S. soldiers and officials from prosecution by the ICC; rather, it invoked article 16 of the Rome Statute[21] to defer potential prosecutions for one year. Some States Parties to the Rome Statute and other supporters have argued that article 16 was meant only to apply to specific cases and was not intended to permit a blanket waiver for citizens of a specific country. The U.N. Security Council adopted another resolution extending the deferral to July 1, 2004.[22] However, during the summer of 2004, opposition to extending the deferral through 2005 eventually led the Administration to drop its pursuit. The United States continues to pursue bilateral agreements to preclude extradition by other countries of U.S. citizens to the ICC.

This article outlines the main objections the United States has raised with respect to the ICC and analyzes the American Servicemembers' Protection Act (ASPA)[23] enacted to regulate U.S. cooperation with the ICC. The report discusses the implications for the United States, as a non-ratifying country, as the ICC begins to take shape, as well as the Administration's efforts to win immunity from ICC jurisdiction for Americans. A description of the ICC's background and a more detailed analysis of the ICC's organization, jurisdiction, and procedural rules may be found in CRS Report RL31437, *International Criminal Court: Overview and Selected Legal Issues*.

U.S. Objections to the Rome Statute

The primary objection given by the United States in opposition to the treaty is the ICC's possible assertion of jurisdiction over U.S. soldiers charged with "war crimes" resulting from legitimate uses of force, or its assertion of jurisdiction over other American officials charged for conduct related to foreign policy initiatives. The threat of prosecution by the ICC, it is argued, could impede the United States in carrying out military operations and foreign policy programs, impinging on the sovereignty of the United States. Detractors of the U.S. position depict the objection as a reluctance on the part of the United States to be held accountable for gross human rights violations or to the standard established for the rest of the world.

Below, in bold type, are summarized some of the main objections voiced by U.S. officials and other critics of the Rome Statute. Each objection is followed by the counterpositions likely to be voiced by representatives of U.S. foreign allies that support the ICC, as well as a very brief discussion of the issue. This section is intended to familiarize the reader with the basic issues that comprise the current debate, and not to provide an exhaustive analysis of the issues.[24] None of the statements in the section below should be interpreted to represent the view of CRS, since CRS does not take positions on policy issues.

Issue #1 Jurisdiction over Nationals of Non-Parties

Only nations that ratify treaties are bound to observe them. The ICC purports to subject to its jurisdiction citizens of non-party nations, thus binding non-party nations.[25] ICC supporters may argue that the ICC has jurisdiction over persons, not nations. Non-party states are not obligated to *do* anything under the treaty. Therefore, the Rome Statute does not purport to bind non-parties, although non-party states may cooperate or defend their own interests that may be affected by a pending case. ICC opponents, however, may point out that if individuals are charged for conduct related to carrying out official policy, the difference between asserting jurisdiction over individuals and over the nation itself becomes less clear.[26]

After all, it is arguably the policy decision and not the individual conduct that is actually at issue. The threat of prosecution, however, could inhibit the conduct of U.S. officials in implementing U.S. foreign policy. In this way, it is argued, the ICC may be seen to infringe U.S. sovereignty.

Some ICC supporters have asserted that the crimes covered by the Rome Statute are already prohibited under international law either by treaty or under the concept of "universal jurisdiction" or both; therefore, all nations may assert jurisdiction to try persons for these crimes. The ICC, they argue, would merely be exercising the collective jurisdiction of its members, any of which could independently assert jurisdiction over the accused persons under a theory of "universal jurisdiction"; the Nuremberg trials serve as an example of such collective jurisdiction.[27] ICC opponents may note that the existence of "universal jurisdiction" has been disputed by some academics, who argue that actual state practice does not provide as much support for the concept as many ICC supporters may claim.[28] However, ICC supporters note, the Rome Statute does not rely entirely on universal jurisdiction; certain pre-conditions to jurisdiction must be met, including the consent of either the State on whose territory the crime occurred or the State of nationality of the accused.[29] The United States is already party to most of the treaties that form the basis for the definitions of crimes in the Rome Statute, meaning U.S. citizens are already subject to the prohibitions for which the ICC will have jurisdiction.

ICC supporters may further argue that if the ICC could not assert jurisdiction over non-party States, so-called "rogue regimes" could insulate themselves from the reach of the ICC simply by not ratifying the Rome Statute. The purpose for creating the ICC would be subverted. The United States had proposed to resolve this problem by creating a mandatory role for the U.N. Security Council in deciding when the ICC should assert jurisdiction, but the majority of other countries refused to adopt such a rule on the stated grounds that it would mirror the uneven prosecution of war crimes and crimes against humanity under the present system of *ad hoc* tribunals.

Issue #2 Politicized Prosecution

The ICC's flaws may allow it to be used by some countries to bring trumped-up charges against American citizens, who, due to the prominent role played by the United States in world affairs, may have greater exposure to such charges than citizens of other nations.[30] ICC supporters argue that the principle of "complementarity" will ensure that the ICC does not take jurisdiction over a case involving an American citizen, unless the United States is unwilling or unable genuinely to investigate the allegations itself, a scenario some argue is virtually unthinkable. Some also take exception to the notion that Americans are more likely to be targeted for prosecution although many other countries that participate in peacekeeping operations, for example, are willing to subject their soldiers and officials to the jurisdiction of the ICC. Many U.S. opponents of the ICC express concern that the ICC will be able to second-guess a valid determination by U.S. prosecutors to terminate an investigation or decline to prosecute a person. It is not uncommon for unfriendly countries to characterize U.S. foreign policy decisions as "criminal." The ICC could provide a forum for such charges. Some ICC supporters dispute the likelihood of such an occurrence, and express confidence that unfounded charges would be dismissed.

A recent determination by the ICC's Chief Prosecutor seems to demonstrate a reluctance to launch an investigation against the United States based on allegations regarding its conduct in Iraq. On February 9, 2006, the Chief Prosecutor issued a letter explaining his reasons for declining to launch an investigation despite multiple submissions by private groups urging action against the United States.[31] In addition to acknowledging the limits of the Court's jurisdiction, which he noted precluded pursuing charges based on the legality of the decision to invade,[32] the Prosecutor noted that the allegations about U.S. nationals' behavior during the Iraq occupation were "of a different order than the number of victims found in other situations under investigation," and concluded that the allegations were of insufficient gravity to warrant an investigation.[33]

Issue #3 the Unaccountable Prosecutor

The Office of the Prosecutor, an organ of the ICC that is not controlled by any separate political authority, has unchecked discretion to initiate cases, which could lead to "politicized prosecutions."[34] ICC supporters may counter that the ICC statute does contain some restraints on the Prosecutor, including a provision that the Prosecutor must seek permission from a pre-trial chamber to carry out a self-initiated prosecution, and a provision for removal of the Prosecutor by vote of the Assembly of States Parties.[35] The independence of the prosecutor, it is argued, is vital in order to ensure just results, free from political control. U.S. negotiators at the Rome Conference had pressed for a role for the U.N. Security Council to check possible "overzealous" prosecutors and prevent politicized prosecutions. The majority of nations represented at the Rome Conference took the view that the U.N. Security Council, with its structure and permanent members, would pose an even greater danger of "politicizing" ICC prosecutions, thereby guaranteeing impunity for some crimes while prosecuting others based on the national interests of powerful nations.

Issue #4 Usurpation of the Role of the U.N. Security Council

The ICC Statute gives the ICC the authority to define and punish the crime of "aggression," which is solely the prerogative of the Security Council of the United Nations under the U.N. Charter.[36] ICC supporters may argue that all States Parties will have the opportunity to vote on a definition of aggression after the treaty has been in effect for seven years, which definition must comport with the U.N. Charter, thereby preserving the role of the U.N. Security Council.[37] The ICC, under this view, is merely providing a forum for trying persons accused of committing "aggression" under international law. Opponents of the ICC, however, may argue that the lack of agreement among nations as to the definition of aggression suggests that any definition adopted only by a majority of member states of the ICC may not be sufficiently grounded in international law to be binding as *jus cogens*.[38] The U.N. General Assembly adopted a resolution in 1974[39] addressing the definition of aggression, but it has only been invoked once by the Security Council.[40] The definition contains an enumeration of offenses included as possible aggression,[41] but leaves the determination to the Security Council.

Issue #5 Lack of due Process Guarantees

The ICC will not offer accused Americans the due process rights guaranteed them under the U.S. Constitution, such as the right to a jury trial. Supporters of the Rome Statute contend it contains a comprehensive set of procedural safeguards that offers substantially similar protections to the U.S. constitution.[42] Some also note that the U.S. Constitution does not always afford American citizens the same procedural rights. For example, Americans may be tried overseas, where foreign governments are not bound to observe the Constitution. Moreover, cases arising in the armed services are tried by court-martial, which is exempt from the requirement for a jury trial. The current U.S. policy about the use of military tribunals in the war against terrorism could lead to suggestions of a double standard on the part of the United States with respect to procedural safeguards in war crimes trials.

Congressional Action

Congress has passed several riders effectively precluding the use of funds to support the ICC.[43] The 107th Congress passed the American Servicemembers' Protection Act of 2002 (ASPA) as title II of the supplemental appropriations bill for 2002, which was signed by the President on August 2, 2002.[44] The 108th Congress included a provision in the Consolidated Appropriations Act, P.L. 108-447, to prohibit the use of funds made available under the Economic Support Fund heading to provide assistance to countries who are members of the ICC and who have not entered into a so-called "Article 98" agreement with the United States. This provision, known as the Nethercutt Amendment, was reauthorized by the 109th Congress as part of the FY2006 Consolidated Appropriations Act (H.R. 3057/P.L. 109-102). A substantially identical provision is included in H.R. 5522, The Foreign

Operations, Export Financing, and Related Programs Appropriations Act, 2007, as passed by the House of Representatives (§ 572).

American Servicemembers' Protection Act of 2002

Both the House of Representatives and the Senate added the American Servicemembers' Protection Act (ASPA) to the supplemental appropriations bill for the fiscal year ending September 30, 2002, H.R. 4775, 107th Congress. The conferees adopted the Senate version of the bill, which included a new provision that the ASPA will not prevent the United States from cooperating with the ICC if it prosecutes persons such as Saddam Hussein or Osama bin Laden.[45]

Legislative History

Originally introduced in the 106th Congress as S. 2726, the ASPA is intended to shield members of the United States Armed Forces and other covered persons from the jurisdiction of the ICC. The Senate Committee on Foreign Relations held hearings[46] the same day the bill was introduced but did not report it.

Prohibitions and Requirements

The ASPA prohibits cooperation with the ICC by any agency or entity of the federal government, or any state or local government. (Section 2004) Covered entities are prohibited from responding to a request for cooperation by the ICC or providing specific assistance, including arrest, extradition,[47] seizure of property, asset forfeiture, service of warrants, searches, taking of evidence, and similar matters.[48] It prohibits agents of the ICC from conducting any investigative activity on U.S. soil related to matters of the ICC. Section 2004(d) states that the United States "shall exercise its rights to limit the use of assistance provided under all treaties and executive agreements for mutual legal assistance in criminal matters ... to prevent ... use by the [ICC of such assistance]." It does not ban the communication to the ICC of U.S. policy, or U.S. government assistance to defendants. It does not prevent private citizens from providing testimony or evidence to the ICC. Section 2006 requires the President to put "appropriate procedures" in place to prevent the direct or indirect transfer of certain classified national security information to the ICC.[49]

Restrictions on Participation in Peacekeeping Missions

Unless subject to a blanket waiver under section 2003,[50] section 2005 of the ASPA restricts U.S. participation in U.N. peacekeeping operations to missions where the President certifies U.S. troops may participate without risk of prosecution by the ICC because the Security Council has permanently exempted U.S. personnel from prosecution for activity conducted as participants,[51] or because each other country in which U.S. personnel will participate in the mission is either not a party to the ICC and does not consent to its jurisdiction, or has entered into an agreement "in accordance with Article 98" of the Rome Statute.[52] The latter option may not provide as much assurance as the first; an Article 98 agreement would prevent the surrender of certain persons to the ICC by parties to the Article 98 agreement,[53] but would not bind the ICC if it were to obtain custody of the accused through other means. If the alleged crime is committed on the territory of a state party to the

Rome Statute, the consent requirement for the jurisdiction of the ICC would be met, despite the existence of the Article 98 agreement. That country could, however, carry out its own investigation and invoke complementarity to preclude the ICC's jurisdiction. Additionally, the country that is the object of the peacekeeping mission may consent to the ICC's jurisdiction over U.S. participants for alleged crimes committed on its territory, whether or not it is a member of the ICC.

The restriction may also be waived for peacekeeping missions where the President certifies that U.S. participation is in the national interest of the United States. The national interest qualification would appear to be the most easily met of the three waiver options; whenever the United States uses its vote in the Security Council to approve a peacekeeping operation, the mission presumably is deemed to serve the national interest.[54] This section could conceivably be interpreted to suggest the President has the authority to commit U.S. troops to participate in U.N. peacekeeping missions without the prior approval of Congress. The restriction does not apply to peacekeeping missions established prior to July 1, 2003.[55]

Restriction on Provision of Military Assistance

Effective 1 July 2003, the ASPA also prohibits military assistance to any country that is a member of the ICC, except for NATO countries and major non-NATO allies,[56] unless the President waives the restriction (section 2007) or a blanket waiver is in effect under section 2003. Military assistance, as defined in the ASPA, includes foreign assistance under chapters 2 and 5 of Part II of the Foreign Assistance Act of 1961, as amended,[57] and defense articles and services financed by the government, including loans and guarantees, under section 23 of the Arms Export Control Act.[58] The President may waive the prohibition without prior notice to Congress if he determines and reports to the appropriate committees that such assistance is important to the national interest or the recipient country has entered into a formal Article 98 agreement to prevent the ICC's proceeding against U.S. personnel present in such country.

The restriction does not appear to apply to any regional organizations that may receive military assistance. The restrictions on military assistance will no longer apply to these countries if they agree to sign Article 98 agreements with the United States, or if the President waives the restrictions as he deems justified with respect to a particular country in accordance with national interests.

One hundred countries are reported to have signed Article 98 agreements with the United States as of May 3, 2005.[59] It is not clear whether all of the agreements have been ratified by their respective governments so as to be effective at present.

Authority to Free Persons from ICC

Section 2008 authorizes the President to use "all means necessary and appropriate" to bring about the release of covered United States and allied persons,[60] upon the request of the detainee's government, who are being detained or imprisoned by or on behalf of the ICC. The Act does not provide a definition of "necessary and appropriate means" to bring about the release of covered persons, other than to exclude bribes and the provision of other such incentives. Section 2008 also authorizes the President to direct any federal agency to provide legal representation and other legal assistance, as well as any exculpatory evidence on behalf of covered U.S. or allied persons who are arrested, detained, investigated, prosecuted or imprisoned by, or on the behalf of the ICC. Section 2008 further permits the government to appear before the ICC in defense of the interests of the United States.

Waivers and Exceptions

The ASPA contains multiple waiver provisions and exceptions. Section 2003(a)-(b) provides for presidential waivers of sections 2005 and 2007 (restriction on U.S. participation in U.N. peacekeeping missions and prohibition on military assistance) if the President certifies to Congress that the ICC has agreed not to seek to assert jurisdiction over any covered U.S. or allied person with respect to actions undertaken by such person in an official capacity. This blanket waiver may be extended for successive periods of one year if the ICC abides by the agreement. As described above, section 2005 may be waived under its own terms with respect to specific peacekeeping missions if satisfactory protection can be achieved through U.N. Security Council measures or by agreement with other participants, or if the national interests of the United States justify participation in the mission.[61] Section 2007 also contains its own waiver provision, allowing the President to provide military assistance to a particular country if he determines and reports to Congress that it is in the national interest or that the country in question has entered into an agreement with the United States "pursuant to Article 98 of the Rome Statute preventing the International Criminal Court from proceeding against United States personnel present in such country."[62] NATO and major non-NATO allies are excepted from the prohibition in section 2007.[63]

If the ICC enters into and abides by an agreement under sections 2003(a) or (b), section 2003(c) permits the President to waive sections 2004 and 2006 (prohibiting cooperation with the ICC and directing the President to implement measures to prohibit the transfer of classified information) with respect to specific cases before the ICC. To waive the prohibitions and allow cooperation with the ICC, the President must first certify to Congress that there is reason to believe the accused is guilty as charged, it is in the national interest to waive the prohibitions, and that the investigation and prosecution by the ICC will not result in the investigation or arrest of any covered U.S. or allied persons with respect to any actions undertaken by them in an official capacity. It is somewhat unclear what a waiver of section 2006 would entail, in that the section does not directly prohibit any action. Instead, it directs the President to implement rules to prevent transfer of classified national security information and law enforcement information to the ICC, and to prevent indirect transfer of material related to matters under investigation or prosecution by the ICC to the United Nations and ICC member countries unless assurances are received from the recipient that such information will not be made available to the ICC. A waiver of section 2006 could be interpreted to mean that the President's requirement to implement the rules is waived, or that the requirement to obtain assurances from recipients other than the ICC is waived, or that the rules themselves may be waived with respect to a particular case.

Section 2011 provides an exception for certain presidential authorities, stating that the restrictions on cooperation with the ICC (section 2004) and the requirement for procedures to protect certain sensitive information (section 2006) do not apply to "any action or actions with respect to a specific matter taken or directed by the President on a case-by-case basis in the exercise of the President's authority as Commander in Chief of the Armed Forces of the United States under article II, section 2 of the United States Constitution or in the exercise of the executive power under article II, section 1 of the United States Constitution."[64] The section would require the President to notify Congress within 15 days of the action, unless such notification would jeopardize national security. It further clarifies that "nothing in [the] section shall be construed as a grant of statutory authority to the President to take any action."[65] Section 2012 prohibits delegation of the authorities vested in the President by sections 2003 (waiver provision) and 2011(a) (constitutional exception).[66]

Inasmuch as sections 2004 and 2006 are already subject to presidential waiver under section 2003(c) in the case of the investigation or prosecution of a "named individual," it appears that this section is drafted to avoid possible conflicts of the separation of powers between the President and Congress. In the event that the President takes the position that the prohibitions of sections 2004 and 2006 infringe upon his constitutional authority in certain cases, he might assert that Congress has no power even to require a waiver under section 2003. Section 2011 appears to ensure notification of Congress, at least at some point after the action has been taken, regardless of whether the President believes that sections 2004 and 2006 impinge his constitutional authority.

The effect of section 2011 is not entirely clear, depending as it does on the interpretation of the President's executive powers under article II, section 1 of the Constitution and his authority as Commander in Chief of the Armed Forces. Interpreted broadly, the constitutional executive power includes the power to execute the law, meaning the execution of *any* law, whether statutory or constitutional, or even international law. Such an interpretation would seem to render sections 2004 and 2006, as well as the waiver provision of section 2003(c), largely superfluous.[67]

Interpreted narrowly, the executive authorities cited above could refer to those powers which the President does not share with Congress. Under a narrow interpretation, Congress would be deemed to be without authority to regulate such actions in any event, in which case it would appear to make little sense to restrict its application to sections 2004 and 2006. The language could be construed by a court to imply a waiver authority apart from the restrictions outlined in section 2003.

Section 2015 provides clarification with respect to assistance to international efforts. It states:

> Nothing in this title shall prohibit the United States from rendering assistance to international efforts to bring to justice Saddam Hussein, Slobodan Milosovic, Osama bin Laden, other members of Al Qaeda, leaders of Islamic Jihad, and other foreign nationals accused of genocide, war crimes or crimes against humanity.[68]

This language would appear to have the effect of limiting the prohibitions in section 2004 to cases in which the ICC prosecutes non-U.S. citizens for the crimes currently under the jurisdiction of the ICC, although the United States may be obligated to deny such assistance in the case of an accused foreign national who is a national of a country with which the United States has entered into a reciprocal Article 98 agreement. The provision could also eliminate the restrictions on participation in peacekeeping missions or provision of military assistance where such participation or aid could be interpreted to further an international effort to prosecute the named crimes. There is no definition of "foreign national" in the ASPA; its use in section 2015 could lead to a conflict with sub-sections (d) and (f) of section 2004 (22 U.S.C. § 7423) as they apply to permanent resident aliens.

Reporting Requirements

In addition to the congressional notifications required by some of the waiver authorities described above, the ASPA encourages the President to submit, by February 2, 2003, a report for each military alliance to which the United States is a party assessing the command arrangements they entail and the degree to which such arrangements may place U.S. servicemembers under the command or control of foreign officers subject to the jurisdiction of the ICC.[69] No later than August 2, 2003, the President was encouraged to submit a report describing possible modifications to such alliance command arrangements that would reduce the risks to U.S. servicemembers identified in the first report.[70]

The Nethercutt Amendment

Section 574 of the FY2005 Consolidated Appropriations Act (H.R. 4818/P.L. 108-447) prohibited Economic Support Funds (ESF) assistance to the government of any country that is a party to the ICC that has not entered into an Article 98 agreement with the United States, except for countries eligible for assistance under the Millennium Challenge Act of 2003. It authorized the President to waive the prohibition with respect to NATO members and major non-NATO allies without prior notice to Congress, if he determined and reported to the appropriate committees that a waiver was in the U.S. national security interest. The President could also waive the prohibition on economic assistance for countries that entered into Article 98 agreements with the United States. (Presumably, this provision would have applied to countries that later agreed to enter into such an Article 98 agreement, to ensure congressional notification).

The Nethercutt Amendment was re-enacted by the 109th Congress as part of the FY2006 Consolidated Appropriations Act (H.R. 3057/P.L. 109-102). The FY2006 measure, however, requires that the President give Congress notice before he invokes a waiver, but he may grant a waiver not only with respect to any NATO or major non-NATO ally, but also to "such other country as he may determine if he determines and reports to the appropriate congressional committees that it is important to the national interests of the United States to waive such prohibition." The Foreign Operations Appropriations bill for FY2007,[71] recently passed by the House of Representatives and referred to the Senate Appropriations Committee, would continue these prohibitions. As with prior years' legislation, the bill does not affect the funding for the Millennium Challenge Corporation.

Prospective Legislation

Some observers have suggested that Congress should pass legislation to close jurisdictional gaps in U.S. criminal law in order to ensure U.S. territory does not become a safe haven for those accused of genocide, war crimes, and crimes against humanity.[72] The War Crimes Act of 1996,[73] for example, establishes U.S. federal jurisdiction to punish war crimes, as defined in international treaties to which the United States is a party, but only when perpetrated by or against U.S. nationals. Likewise, the Genocide Convention Implementation Act of 1987 prohibits acts that would constitute genocide under the Rome Statute, except that the U.S. Code covers only conduct committed by a U.S. national or conduct committed within the United States.[74] Some observers have expressed concern that war criminals or perpetrators of genocide from other countries could seek refuge in the United States from extradition to and prosecution by the ICC. However, the exception in section 2013 of the ASPA, which allows U.S. entities to cooperate with the ICC in the case of foreign nationals accused of war crimes, may obviate the need for such legislation.

Some have suggested that changes in U.S. statutes to broaden the jurisdiction of federal courts to cover all crimes over which the ICC might assert jurisdiction could enhance the implementation of complementarity by precluding a finding by the ICC that the United States is "unable" to prosecute one of its citizens.[75] For the most part, war crimes committed by U.S. persons are covered by the War Crimes Act, although there may be some acts covered by the Rome Treaty that are not explicitly prohibited by U.S. law. Also, there is no U.S. statute codifying crimes against humanity as such. U.S. criminal law prohibits most of the crimes enumerated under the Rome Statute as possible crimes against humanity, as long as they are committed within the United States or by military personnel.[76] Under current law, acts that could constitute crimes against humanity committed by U.S. civilians overseas generally are not triable in U.S. civil or military courts unless they involve torture or certain acts of international terrorism.[77] In the event a U.S. citizen is alleged to have committed such an act, the United States may not be deemed able to investigate and prosecute the alleged crime, a prerequisite for asserting complementarity.

Implications of the ICC for the United States as a Non-Member

As a member of the Preparatory Commission established by the Rome Statute, the United States played a significant role during the drafting of rules of procedure, elements of crimes, and other documents detailing how the ICC will operate. Now that the Rome Statute has entered into force, the Preparatory Commission has been replaced by the Assembly of States Parties ("Assembly") as the governing body to oversee the implementation of the Rome Statute. The Assembly held its first conference September 3 - 10, 2002, during which it adopted rules of evidence and procedure and a host of other regulations, including the methods for nominating and electing its officials. During its subsequent session in February, the Assembly elected 18 judges, who later elected Canadian jurist Philippe Kirsch to be their president. In April of 2003, the Assembly elected Argentinian lawyer Luis Moreno Ocampo to be the ICC's first prosecutor.

The first Review Conference, an alternative forum for considering amendments to the Statute, is to be convened in July of 2009, seven years after the Statute has entered into effect.[78] Thereafter, Review Conferences may be convened from time to time by the U.N. Secretary-General upon request by a majority of the States Parties.[79] As a non-party, the United States has no vote in either body. However, it will remain eligible to participate in both the Assembly and in Review Conferences as an observer.[80]

Observer Role

The Assembly of States Parties adopted procedural rules for its activities at its first conference, including rules setting forth the role of observers and other participants.[81] Observers are entitled to participate in the deliberations of the Assembly and any subsidiary bodies that might be established. Observer States will receive notifications of all meetings and records of Assembly proceedings on the same basis as States Parties. They will not, however, be permitted to suggest items for the agenda or to make motions during debate, such as points of order or motions for adjournment. Thus, the United States may be able to participate substantially in Assembly debates as well as proffer and respond to proposals, even if it never becomes a party to the Statute.[82] The United States may also use its position at the United Nations to communicate to the Assembly of States Parties.[83]

As noted, the United States is not able to vote in these bodies so long as it does not ratify the Rome Statute. It may not nominate U.S. nationals to serve as judges or cast a vote in elections for judges or the Prosecutor (or for their removal), or vote on the ICC's budget. It will not be able to vote on the definition of the crime of aggression or its inclusion within the jurisdiction of the ICC, when the matter is considered at first Review Conference, or on any other amendment to the Rome Statute, unless it ratifies the Rome Statute.

The United States, as a non-party, will have no right itself to refer situations to the Prosecutor for investigation; as a Permanent Member of the Security Council, however, it could seek to influence referrals by the Security Council.[84] Similarly, it may participate in Security Council requests to the Prosecutor to defer an investigation or prosecution[85] and to the Pre-Trial Chamber to review a decision of the Prosecutor not to investigate or prosecute.[86] As a non-party to the treaty, the United States is eligible, but not obligated, to cooperate with any ICC investigation and prosecution;[87] and under the Statute, the United States could, but would not be obligated to, arrest a person named in a request for provisional arrest or for arrest and surrender from the ICC.[88] The United States also retains the right not to provide information or documents the disclosure of which would prejudice its national security interests[89] and to refuse to consent to the disclosure by a state party of information or documents provided to that state in confidence.[90] Finally, as a non-party, the United States is not under any obligation to contribute to the budget for the ICC, except, perhaps indirectly, to the extent that the U.N. General Assembly regular budget might include ICC support.[91]

Foreign Policy Implications

Perspectives differ on the impact of the ICC on U.S. interests, as it begins to operate. Some see the ICC as a fundamental threat to the U.S. armed forces, civilian policy makers, and U.S. defense and foreign policy.[92] Others see it as a valuable foreign policy tool for defining and deterring crimes against humanity, a step forward in the decades-long U.S. effort to end impunity for egregious mass crimes. Debate over the ICC has created a tension between enhancing the international legal justice system and encroaching on what some countries perceive as their legitimate use of force. The review by the International Criminal Tribunal for the Former Yugoslavia (ICTY) of allegations that NATO bombing in Kosovo might be deemed a war crime is illustrative of this tension. Many opponents of the ICC were outraged that the issue was even considered. They questioned the legitimacy of the tribunal's actions, and their anger was not assuaged by the Tribunal's ultimate decision that there was "no basis for opening an investigation into any of those allegations or into other incidents relating to NATO bombing."[93] While opponents of the ICC interpret this event as an indication that the ICC is likely to pursue spurious and politically motivated cases against U.S. citizens, proponents of the ICC see it as illustrating that similar allegations would be dismissed by the ICC Prosecutor.

Another consideration is the practical effect that the U.S. position will have on the ICC itself. Because the ICC relies largely on States Parties to provide mechanisms and manpower for arresting suspects and enforcing verdicts of the ICC, it has been argued that the lack of U.S. participation in the ICC may seriously impair the ICC's ability to function.[94] Those who believe the ICC is a fundamental threat to U.S. foreign and defense policy may welcome this outcome; while ICC supporters may argue that an ineffective court could serve the interests of human rights abusers, ensuring impunity and decreasing the likelihood of future *ad hoc* tribunals.

The United States has enjoyed a long reputation for leadership in the struggle against impunity and the quest for universal human rights and the rule of law. Human rights organizations have expressed concern that U.S. refusal to ratify the Rome Statute, coupled with any actions that might undermine the ICC, could cause the United States to lose the moral high ground and damage its influence world-wide, including its ability to influence the development of the law of war.[95] The perceived U.S. willingness to hold U.N. peacekeeping missions hostage to U.S. demands for immunity from the ICC may deepen the rift between the United States and allies that support the ICC. The withholding of military assistance and other economic aid to members of the ICC may also be seen as an effort to coerce countries to refuse to ratify the Rome Statute or to sign an Article 98 agreement, which could appear to some as undermining the ICC and negating the Administration's stated intent to respect the decisions of other countries to join the ICC. By seemingly demanding special treatment in the form of immunity from the ICC, the United States may bolster the perception of its unilateral approach to world affairs and its unwillingness to abide by the same laws that apply to other nations. This perception could undermine U.S. efforts at coalition-building to gain international support for the present war against terrorism and operations in Iraq, as well as future international endeavors.[96]

Others argue that the perception of U.S. commitment to the rule of law has little effect on countries where human rights abuses are most rampant. Despots like Cambodia's Pol Pot or Iraq's Saddam Hussein have not weighed possible future legal ramifications before committing massive crimes.[97] Under this view, the establishment of the ICC might have the unintended effect of hardening the resolve of ruthless tyrants who may feel they have nothing to gain by giving up their power to more democratic regimes if they fear prosecution for the crimes they committed while in power. From this perspective, in terms of curbing human rights abuses, it does not matter whether the U.S. ratifies the Rome Statute, other than perhaps to provide support to an accused dictator's argument challenging the legitimacy of the ICC. According to this viewpoint, the costs to the United States appear to outweigh the benefits.

Strategy for Precluding ICC Prosecution of U.S. Troops and Officials

ASPA § 2005 prohibits U.S. participation in peacekeeping and peace-enforcing missions established by the Security Council unless the President certifies and reports to the appropriate committees of Congress that U.S. personnel are not placed at risk of prosecution by the ICC because they are guaranteed immunity by the U.N. Resolution or because of arrangements with the host government.[98] The Bush Administration has pursued efforts in the U.N. Security Council and with individual States to prevent the possibility that American citizens could be prosecuted before the ICC. This effort has met with some success but also some resistance.

Agreement with the U.N. Security Council

On July 12, 2002, in response to the U.S. veto of the extension of peacekeeping operations in Bosnia, the U.N. Security Council adopted a resolution requesting a blanket deferral of prosecutions by the ICC of peacekeepers from states not parties to the Rome Statute for a period of one year. Resolution 1422 provides, in pertinent part:

Acting under Chapter VII of the Charter of the United Nations,

1. *Requests*, consistent with the provisions of Article 16 of the Rome Statute, that the ICC, if a case arises involving current or former officials or personnel from a contributing State not a Party to the Rome Statute over acts or omissions relating to a United Nations established or authorized operation, shall for a twelve-month period starting 1 July 2002 not commence or proceed with investigation or prosecution of any such case, unless the Security Council decides otherwise;
2. *Expresses* the intention to renew the request in paragraph 1 under the same conditions each 1 July for further 12-month periods for as long as may be necessary;
3. *Decides* that Member States shall take no action inconsistent with paragraph 1 and with their international obligations;
4. *Decides* to remain seized of the matter.[99]

The resolution, which was renewed for another year under Security Council Resolution 1487, appeared to fall short of the President's original proposal, which would have provided permanent immunity for U.S. troops and officials from the jurisdiction of the ICC. Opponents of the original proposal objected that the U.N. Security Council does not have the authority to "rewrite" international treaties. The compromise invoked article 16 of the Rome Statute, which provides:

> No investigation or prosecution may be commenced or proceeded with under this Statute for a period of 12 months after the Security Council, in a resolution adopted under Chapter VII of the Charter of the United Nations, has requested the Court to that effect; that request may be renewed by the Council under the same conditions.

Although some opponents of the U.S. position had argued that article 16 was intended to be invoked only on a case-by-case basis, the language of the article does not expressly state such a requirement. Therefore, Resolutions 1422 and 1487 appear to be consistent with the Rome Statute. The language deferred ICC action for one year; it does not provide absolute immunity for actions occurring during the deferral period. Because the Security Council did not extend the deferral past July 2004, it appears that the ICC may investigate and prosecute any purported crimes under its subject matter jurisdiction that occurred at any time after the Rome Statute's entry into force, subject to other provisions of the Rome Statute.

Other U.N. Missions

U.S. military personnel were able to participate in the United Nations Mission in Liberia (UNMIL) because, in authorizing the multinational force to enforce the cease-fire, the Security Council decided that

> current or former officials or personnel from a contributing State, which is not a party to the Rome Statute of the International Criminal Court, shall be subject to the exclusive jurisdiction of that contributing State for all alleged acts or omissions arising out of or related to the Multinational Force or United Nations stabilization force in Liberia, unless such exclusive jurisdiction has been expressly waived by that contributing State.[100]

Unlike the previous arrangement with respect to the U.N. mission in Bosnia, the authorization for operations in Liberia appears to provide permanent immunity to U.S. participants from the jurisdiction of the ICC with respect to conduct linked to the U.N. mission. Accordingly, President Bush made the appropriate certification to Congress under ASPA § 2005 (22 U.S.C. § 7424).[101] Liberia had signed the Rome Statute in 1998 but did not ratify it until September of 2004.

The United States also sent troops to participate in the U.N. mission to establish peace in Haiti in 2004.[102] In April of 2004, the U.N. Security Council established the United Nations Stabilization Mission in Haiti (MINUSTAH).[103] In June of that year, President Bush certified that U.S. servicemembers could safely participate because Haiti had signed an Article 98 agreement.[104]

U.N. Action Regarding the Situation in Darfur

On March 31, 2005, the U.N. Security Council, acting under Chapter VII of the U.N. Charter, adopted Resolution 1593 (2005) which refers reports about the situation in Darfur, Sudan (dating back to July 1, 2002), to the ICC Prosecutor, Luis Moreno-Ocampo.[105] This is the first time such a referral from the U.N. Security Council has been made. As Sudan is not a party to the ICC, and has not consented to its jurisdiction, the ICC jurisdiction over the case could only be established by means of a U.N.S.C. referral. Under the ICC Statute, the ICC is authorized, but not required, to take such a case.[106] The Resolution, which is binding on all U.N. member states, was adopted by a vote of 11 in favor, none against and with 4 abstentions — the United States, China, Algeria, and Brazil.[107]

U.S. foreign policy respecting action to address the situation in Darfur was complicated by its position regarding the ICC and its jurisdiction over non-member states. In September 2004, the United States concluded that genocide had taken place in Darfur. According to the State Department, it supported the formation of the International Commission of Inquiry[108] but preferred a tribunal in Africa to be the mechanism of accountability for those who committed crimes in Darfur. After these proposals failed to garner sufficient support, the United States agreed to abstain from voting on the Resolution (which is not equivalent to a veto in the U.N. Security Council) once language was introduced into the Resolution that dealt with the sovereignty questions of concern and essentially protected U.S. nationals and other persons of non-party States outside Sudan from prosecution.[109]

The abstention did not change the fundamental objections of the United States to the ICC. Although some view the decision as a sign that the Administration is softening its stance with respect to the ICC,[110] it may also be seen as consistent with the U.S. support of a version of the Rome Statute that would have allowed the U.N. Security Council to refer cases involving non-States Parties to the ICC, but would not have allowed other states to refer cases. At the same time, the compromise allowed the United States to show support for the need for the international community to come together and take action on the atrocities occurring in Darfur.[111]

Article 98 Agreements

The United States is also pursuing bilateral options for achieving protection for U.S. troops, within or outside U.N. peacekeeping arrangements, by concluding agreements similar to the status-of-forces agreements (SOFA) routinely negotiated where U.S. troops are stationed abroad. The United States has so far concluded 100 bilateral agreements whereby each signatory promises that it will not surrender citizens of the other signatory to the ICC, unless both parties consent in advance to the surrender.[112] The Department of State is seeking to conclude these agreements with as many states as possible, even those who are not parties to the ICC and others who would not be subject to the sanctions under ASPA.

The agreements are intended to make use of Article 98 of the Rome Statute, which states:

Cooperation with respect to waiver of immunity and consent to surrender

1. The Court may not proceed with a request for surrender or assistance which would require the requested State to act inconsistently with its obligations under international law with respect to the State or diplomatic immunity of a person or property of a third State, unless the Court can first obtain the cooperation of that third State for the waiver of the immunity.
2. The Court may not proceed with a request for surrender which would require the requested State to act inconsistently with its obligations under international agreements pursuant to which the consent of a sending State is required to surrender a person of that State to the Court, unless the Court can first obtain the cooperation of the sending State for the giving of consent for the surrender.[113]

Paragraph 1 of Article 98 appears intended to retain diplomatic immunity and immunity for heads of state, while paragraph 2 seems to contemplate typical SOFA arrangements, in which countries hosting members or units of the armed forces of allies agree to forego certain types of jurisdiction over the soldiers and other government officers stationed there. The use of the term "sending state" in the second paragraph appears to indicate that it is meant to cover only persons who are sent to accomplish government business, and not citizens present in the country for personal or business reasons. The State Department reportedly sought broader application for the bilateral agreements. In 2002, the European Council argued that parties to the ICC who signed such agreements with the United States would be acting inconsistently with their obligations under the Rome Statute.[114] The European Union (EU), all of whose members are parties to the Rome Statute, initially opposed the agreements altogether, but its members reached a compromise to allow member countries to sign.[115]

The EU issued guidelines for member countries for the acceptable terms of Article 98 agreements, specifying that coverage would be limited to government representatives on official business, the United States would expressly pledge to prosecute any war crimes committed by Americans, and the agreements would not contain a reciprocal promise to prevent the surrender of European citizens to the ICC.[116] In response to the Nethercutt Amendment, the European Council released a statement calling on President Bush to make "full use of his waiver authority" and reiterated the EU stand with respect to Article 98 agreements, referring to the 2002 guidelines.[117]

Despite the EU compromise, the U.S. pursuit of "immunity" has been criticized by some as unnecessary or as an outright effort to undermine the ICC.[118] Supporters of the policy note that agreements, such as SOFAs, that provide immunity for soldiers from prosecution in foreign courts are not unusual. For example, the 19-member International Security Assistance Force (ISAF), a joint force authorized by the U.N. Security Council to provide assistance to the interim government in Afghanistan,[119] included a clause providing immunity for participants in its Military Technical Agreement with the interim government.[120] Furthermore, supporters point out, the agreements are based on and consistent with Article 98 of the Rome Statute, and therefore cannot be said to undermine the ICC.

The practical effect of the Article 98 agreements is as of yet uncertain. The use of such agreements with host countries does not provide absolute immunity from the ICC. They would bind only countries that choose to sign, and would have the effect only of preventing the host nation from surrendering an accused to the ICC for prosecution. While the Rome Statute gives some discretion to States Parties to honor their international obligations applicable to extradition of persons who are identified in an ICC request for surrender,[121] there does not appear to be a provision for accused persons or their states of nationality to challenge the jurisdiction of the ICC based on the violation of a bilateral agreement. Therefore, States Parties to the Rome Statute are not precluded from entering into Article 98 agreements that provide for immunity of foreign troops from surrender, but if the ICC were nevertheless to gain custody over the accused through other means, its jurisdiction may not be affected by the agreement.

Options

Though the Administration continues to seek to conclude Article 98 agreements with relevant countries, it is not clear how many more such agreements are likely to be forthcoming. To strengthen the Administration's pursuit of these agreements, Congress could make more forms of aid contingent on the recipient country's agreement to protect U.S. troops from surrender to the ICC, or it could enact legislation to restrict the President's discretion to grant waivers. If further negotiations fail to garner necessary support, or in case the agreements should turn out to less effective than desired, policymakers may seek alternative avenues. One option might be to implement a policy of investigating, and if warranted, prosecuting, all crimes under the ICC jurisdiction alleged to be committed by a U.S. person, thus preempting the ICC through application of the complementarity principle. Such a policy, coupled with changes in U.S. statutes to broaden the jurisdiction of federal courts to cover all relevant crimes, could further insulate U.S. citizens from the reach of the ICC. The United States could seek to further enhance its reputation for conducting fair and credible investigations and trials of suspected war criminals, as well as perpetrators of crimes against humanity or genocide, through the use of consistent procedures that are as open as security considerations permit. Such a practice may help to overcome any charges that a U.S. investigation or prosecution of an accused is not "genuine" for the purposes of complementarity.

Finally, some have argued that a policy of cooperation with the ICC in the prosecution of persons accused of crimes that the United States agrees amount to "the most serious crimes of concern to the international community"[122] would enhance the reputation of the United States as a promoter of human rights and the rule of law. Such a policy could take the form of passive non-interference with the ICC to active assistance, including working from within the U.N. Security Council to refer cases to the ICC. By actively keeping the Security Council involved in the referral of cases, some of the predicted problems with referrals by States Parties or by the prosecutor could be minimized. On the other hand, some argue a cooperative posture with respect to the ICC in the case of foreigners while pursuing immunity for U.S. citizens would be perceived as a double standard.

REFERENCES

[1] Emily Cowley, Law Clerk, contributed research assistance to this report.

[2] *See* Rome Statute of the International Criminal Court, Preamble, U.N. Doc. A/CONF.183/9 (1998)("Rome Statute"). These include genocide, crimes against humanity, war crimes, and potentially the crime of aggression, if the Assembly of States Parties is able to reach an agreement defining it. *Id.* art. 5(1). *See generally* International Criminal Court, *How Does the Court Work?* [http://www.icc-cpi.int/ataglance/whatistheicc/howdoesthecourtwork. html], (hereinafter *How the ICC Works*) (last visited June 8, 2006), explaining the two ways investigations are initiated in the ICC: (1) a situation may be referred to the Prosecutor by States Parties or the United Nations Security Council or (2) the Prosecutor may independently initiate investigations on the basis of information received from reliable sources, if, after examining the information, he determines that there is a reasonable basis to proceed with an investigation.

[3] *See* International Criminal Court, Situations and Cases, [http://www.icc-cpi.int/cases.html] (last visited June 9, 2006); *see also* American University War Crimes Research Office, International Criminal Court Status Update, [http://www.wcl.american.edu/warcrimes/ icc.status.cfm] (June 9, 2006) (providing a time line of significant events at the ICC).

[4] SC Res. 1593, U.N. Doc S/RES/1593 (2005); *see infra* note 105 and accompanying text; *How the ICC Works*, *supra* note 2.

[5] Press Release, International Criminal Court, The Office of the Prosecutor of the International Criminal Court Opens its First Investigation (June 23, 2004) *available at* [http://www.icc-cpi.int/pressrelease_details and id=26 and l=en.html](last visited June 14, 2006).

[6] *See* Press Release, International Criminal Court, The Prosecutor of the International Criminal Court Opens an Investigation into Northern Uganda (July 29, 2004) *available at* [http://www.icc-cpi.int/pressrelease_details and id=33 and l=en.html](last visited June 14, 2006).

[7] *See* Press Release, International Criminal Court, The Prosecutor of the ICC Opens Investigation in Darfur (June 6, 2006) *available at* [http://www.icc-cpi.int/pressrelease_details and id=107 and 1=en.html](last visited June 14, 2006).

[8] *See* Situation in Uganda, Case No. ICC-02/04-01-05, Warrant of Arrest for Joseph Kony Issued on July 2005 as Amended on 27 September 2005, 42 (Sept. 27, 2005) *available at* [http://www.icc-cpi.int/library/cases/ICC-02-04-01-05-53_English.pdf](last visited June 14, 2006) (charging Joseph Kony, the founder and leader of the Lord's Resistance Army (LRA), with 33 counts of war crimes and crimes against humanity); *see also Court Seeks Arrests of Ugandan Rebels*, N.Y. TIMES, Oct. 15, 2005, at A10 (reporting that warrants were issued for the arrest of four other senior leaders in addition to Joseph Kony).

[9] *See* Barbara Crossette, *World Criminal Court is Ratified — Praised by U.N., Opposed by U.S.*, N.Y. TIMES Apr. 12, 2002, *available at* 2002 WL-NYT 0210200003. As of Nov. 15, 2005, 100 nations have ratified the Rome Statute. For the current status of signatures, ratifications and reservations, visit [http://www.icc-cpi.int/asp/statesparties.html](last visited June 14, 2006).

[10] *See* Jonathon Wright, *U.S. Renounces Obligations to International Court*, REUTERS, May 6, 2002. Although some in the media described the act as an "unsigning" of the treaty, it may be more accurately described as a notification of intent not to ratify. The U.S. letter to the U.N. Secretary General stated: This is to inform you, in connection with the Rome Statute of the International Criminal Court adopted on July 17, 1998, that the United States does not intend to become a party to the treaty. Accordingly, the United States has no legal obligations arising from its signature on December 31, 2000. The United States requests that its intention not to become a party, as expressed in this letter, be reflected in the depositary's status lists relating to this treaty. *See* U.N. Treaty Database, Rome Statute of the International Criminal Court, *available at* [http://untreaty.un.org/].

[11] The EU issued a statement at the Preparatory Commission for the International Criminal Court expressing "disappointment and regret," noting the "potentially negative effect that this particular action by the United States may have on the development and reinforcement of recent trends towards Individual accountability for the most serious crimes of concern to the international community and to which the United States shows itself strongly committed." *See* Statement of the European Union on the position of the United States of America towards the International Criminal Court, U.N. Doc. PCNICC/2002/INF/7, May 20, 2002.

[12] *See* Marc Grossman, Under Secretary for Political Affairs, Remarks to the Center for Strategic and International Studies, Washington, D.C., (May 6, 2002), prepared remarks available at [http://www.state.gov/p/9949.htm](last visited June 13, 2006). Secretary Grossman promised that: Notwithstanding our disagreements with the Rome Treaty, the United States respects the decision of those nations who have chosen to join the ICC; but they in turn must respect our decision not to join the ICC or place our citizens under the jurisdiction of the court. So, despite this difference, we must work together to promote real justice after July 1, when the Rome Statute enters into force. The existence of a functioning ICC will not cause the United States to retreat from its leadership role in the promotion of international justice and the rule of law.

[13] *See* Ruth Wedgwood, Harold K. Jacobson and Monroe Leigh, *The United States and the Statute of Rome,* 95 AM. J. INT'L L. 124 (2001) (commenting that the United States has "repeatedly and publicly declared its support in principle" for an international criminal court). Congress expressed its support for such a court, providing the rights of U.S. citizens were recognized. *See, e.g.,* Foreign Operations Appropriations Act § 599E, P.L. 101-513, 104 Stat. 2066-2067 (1990)(expressing the sense of the Congress that "the United States should explore the need for the establishment of an International Criminal Court" and that "the establishment of such a court or courts for the more effective prosecution of international criminals should not derogate from established standards of due process, the rights of the accused to a fair trial and the sovereignty of individual nations"); Anti-Drug Abuse Act of 1988, § 4108, P.L. 100-690, 102 Stat. 4181, 4266 (1988)(encouraging the President to initiate discussions with foreign governments about the possibility of creating an international court to try persons accused of having engaged in international drug trafficking or having committed international crimes, providing constitutional guarantees of U.S. citizens are recognized); P.L. 99-399, § 1201 (1986) .

[14] See U.N. International Criminal Court: Hearings before the Subcomm. on International Operations of the Senate Foreign Relations Committee, 105th Cong. (1998) (testimony of David J. Scheffer, Ambassador-at-Large for War Crimes Issues).

[15] *See* Wedgwood *et al., supra* note 13, at 124 (noting that the final vote for the Statute was 120 in favor to seven against).

[16] *See* Statement on the Rome Treaty on the International Criminal Court, 37 WEEKLY COMP. PRES DOC 4 (Dec. 31, 2000).

[17] Because the United States signed the Rome Statute, it had been obligated under international law to refrain from conducting activity in contravention of the object and purpose of the treaty. *See* Vienna Convention on the Law of Treaties, *opened for signature* May 23, 1969, art. 18, 1155 U.N.T.S. 335. However, this obligation ends once a signatory state has indicated an intent *not* to ratify the treaty. *Id.*

[18] *See* Grossman, *supra* note 12.

[19] See Colum Lynch, Dispute Threatens U.N. Role in Bosnia; U.S. Wields Veto in Clash over War Crimes Court, WASH. POST, Jul. 1, 2002, at A1.

[20] SC Res. 1422, U.N. Doc. S/RES/1422 (2002).

[21] *See infra* note 99, and accompanying text.

[22] SC Res. 1487, U.N. Doc. S/RES/1487 (2003). The vote was 12-0, with France, Germany and Syria abstaining.

[23] P.L. 107-206, title II, 116 Stat. 889 (2002), *codified at* 22 U.S.C. §§ 7421 *et seq.*

[24] For a more in-depth analysis of these issues, see CRS Report RL31437, *International Criminal Court: Overview and Selected Legal Issues*, by Jennifer K. Elsea.

[25] *See* Fact Sheet: The International Criminal Court, U.S. Department of State Office of War Crimes Issues, May 6, 2002; Grossman, *supra* note 12 (asserting "the United States has never recognized the right of an international organization to [detain and try American citizens] absent consent or a U.N. Security Council mandate").

[26] *See* Ruth Wedgwood, *The United States and the International Criminal Court: TheIrresolution of Rome*, 64 LAW and CONTEMP. PROBS. 193, 199 (2001) (arguing the state whose national is charged remains a "party in interest"to the prosecution).

[27] See Jordan J. Paust, The Reach of ICC Jurisdiction over Non-Signatory Nationals, 33 VAND. J. TRANSNAT'L L. 1, 3-4 (2000).

[28] *See* Wedgwood, *supra* note 26, at 199 (pointing out there is "no ordinary precedent for delegating national criminal jurisdiction to another tribunal, international or national, without consent of the affected states, except in the aftermath of international belligerency"). Some observers, however, note that one of the reasons for constituting an international criminal court was to do away with the need for military conquest prior to prosecuting war crimes, in the hope of eliminating the perception of "victor's justice."

[29] Rome Statute, *supra* note 2, art. 12. *See generally* CRS Report RL31437, *International Criminal Court: Overview and Selected Legal Issues*, by Jennifer Elsea, at 21-26, (summarizing jurisdictional requirements). There is no consent requirement in cases referred by the Security Council.

[30] *See* Grossman, *supra* note 12.

[31] Letter from Luis Moreno-Ocampo, Chief Prosecutor, International Criminal Court, (Feb. 9, 2006) *available at* [http://www.icc-cpi.int/library/organs/otp/OTP_letter_to_senders_ re_Iraq_9_February_2006.pdf]

[32] *See id.* at 3-4 (explaining that the ICC does not have personal jurisdiction over non-State Party nationals who performed the alleged crimes in a non-State Party territory).

[33] *See id.* at 9. The Prosecutor also seemed satisfied with U.S. efforts to investigate and prosecute possible war crimes: In light of the conclusion reached on gravity, it was unnecessary to reach a conclusion on complementarity. It may be observed, however, that the Office also collected information on national proceedings, including commentaries from various sources, and that national proceedings had been initiated with respect to each of the relevant incidents. *Id.*

[34] *See* Grossman, *supra* note 12.

[35] Rome Statute, *supra* note 2, art. 46, provides procedures for removing a Prosecutor who: (a) Is found to have committed serious misconduct or a serious breach of his or her duties under [the Rome] Statute, as provided for in the Rules of Procedure and Evidence; or (b) Is unable to exercise the functions required by this Statute.

[36] *See* Grossman, *supra* note 12.

[37] See CRS Report RL31437, *International Criminal Court: Overview and Selected Legal Issues*, by Jennifer Elsea, at 20-21 (summarizing issues relevant to the definition of "aggression").

[38] A mutually acceptable definition for the elements of the crime of aggression has long eluded the international community, impeding earlier attempts to establish an international criminal court. *See* Jimmy Gurulé, *United States Opposition to the 1998 Rome Statute Establishing an International Criminal Court: Is the Court's Jurisdiction Truly Complementary to National Criminal Jurisdictions?*, 35 CORNELL INT'L L.J. 1, 2 (2002). Article 39 of the U.N. Charter leaves it to the Security Council to determine the existence of and take action with respect to any act of aggression, but does not provide a definition.

[39] G.A. Res. 3314, U.N. GAOR, 29th Sess., Supp. No. 19, U.N. Doc A/9615 (1974).

[40] *See* Kriangsak Kittichaisaree, *The NATO Military Action and the Potential Impact of the International Criminal Court*, 4 SING. J. INT'L and COMP. L. 498, 505 (2000)

(citing U.N. Security Council Resolution 418 of 4 Nov. 1977, declaring South Africa guilty of aggression against Angola).

[41] G.A. Res. 3314, art. 3, lists the following examples of possible acts of aggression: (a) The invasion or attack by the armed forces of a State of the territory of another State, or any military occupation, however temporary, resulting from such invasion or attack, or any annexation by the use of force of the territory of another State or part thereof; (b) Bombardment by the armed forces of a State against the territory of another State or the use of any weapons by a State against the territory of another State; (c) The blockade of the ports or coasts of a State by the armed forces of another State; (d) An attack by the armed forces of a State on the land, sea or air forces, or marine and air fleets of another State; (e) The use of armed forces of one State which are within the territory of another State with the agreement of the receiving State, in contravention of the conditions provided for in the agreement or any extension of their presence in such territory beyond the termination of the agreement; (f) The action of a State in allowing its territory, which it has placed at the disposal of another State, to be used by that other State for perpetrating an act of aggression against a third State; (g) The sending by or on behalf of a State of armed bands, groups, irregulars or mercenaries, which carry out acts of armed force against another State of such gravity as to amount to the acts listed above, or its substantial involvement therein.

[42] *See id.* at 29-38 (describing procedural safeguards in the Rome Statute); *see also* Selected Procedural Safeguards in Federal, Military, and International Courts, CRS Report RL31262 (providing brief comparison of ICC procedural safeguards to federal and military rules of procedure and evidence).

[43] *See* Department of Defense Appropriations for 2002, P.L. 107-117. § 8173. None of the funds made available in division A of this Act may be used to provide support or other assistance to the International Criminal Court or to any criminal investigation or other prosecutorial activity of the International Criminal Court. *See also* Departments of Commerce, Justice, and State, the Judiciary, and Related Agencies Appropriations Act, 2002, § 630, P.L.107-77; 22 U.S.C. § 7401 (prohibiting appropriated funds from obligation for use by the ICC or to assist the ICC unless the United States becomes a party to the Rome Statute).

[44] P.L. 107-206, title II, 16 Stat. 899 (2002), *codified at* 22 U.S.C. §§ 7421 *et seq.*

[45] *See* H.R. REP. NO. 107-593 (2002).

[46] The International Criminal Court: Protecting American Servicemen and Officials from the Threat of International Prosecution, Hearing before the Senate Comm. on Foreign Relations, 106th Cong. (2000).

[47] The expenditure of funds for the extradition or transfer of U.S. citizens to countries that are obligated to surrender persons to the ICC is prohibited by 22 U.S.C. § 7402 unless the receiving country provides assurances that such citizen will not be surrendered to the ICC. The same prohibition applies with respect to giving consent to other countries to transfer or extradite U.S. citizens to States Parties of the ICC.

[48] 22 U.S.C. § 7423.

[49] 22 U.S.C. § 7425.

[50] 22 U.S.C. § 7422; *see infra* page 14.

[51] The compromise reached by the U.N. Security Council in Resolution 1422 (2002) provided for a one-year deferral, thus providing neither immunity nor permanent protection, which would not appear to meet this criterion. *See infra* note 99.

[52] 22 U.S.C. § 7424. The Rome Statute, *supra* note 2, art. 98, prohibits the ICC from pursuing requests for assistance or surrender that would require the requested state to act inconsistently with certain international obligations. This provision, as well as other provisions that refer to articles of the Rome Statute, may be seen as somewhat inconsistent with finding (11) of section 2, which states that the United States "will not be bound by any of [the terms of the Rome Statute]."

[53] Article 98 appears to cover only persons sent by the government to the requested state on official business, such as officials and military personnel, and would not cover private citizens who are present in the requested state for reasons unrelated to official duty. An agreement signed by a state party to the ICC that promises not to surrender any other citizens of another state to the ICC would appear to be covered by art. 97 of the Rome Statute, which requires the requested state to consult with the ICC if honoring a request for surrender to the ICC would cause the requested state to breach its international obligations. *See infra* note 112.

[54] *See, e.g.,* 22 U.S.C. § 287b(e)(2)(B) (requiring as part of an annual report to Congress on U.N. activities information about possible authorization for peacekeeping missions, including the "vital national interest to be served").

[55] 22 U.S.C. § 7424(b).

[56] Major non-NATO allies include Australia, Egypt, Israel, Japan, Jordan, Argentina, the Republic of Korea, and New Zealand. (§ 2007(d)). Taiwan is also exempt under § 2007. The President may designate other nations as major non-NATO allies under 22 U.S.C. § 2321k, by notifying Congress 30 days in advance.

[57] 22 U.S.C. § 2151 *et seq.* Chapter 2 is codified at 22 U.S.C. §§ 2311 - 2321k (provision of defense articles and services). Chapter 5 is codified at 22 U.S.C. §§ 2347 - 2347d (international military education and training of foreign personnel in furtherance of the goals of international peace and security, to improve the recipient's self-defense capabilities, and to increase awareness of human rights).

[58] 22 U.S.C. § 2763 (authorizing President to provide credit to friendly foreign countries and international organizations for the purchase of defense articles and services).

[59] See Press Release, U.S. Department of State, U.S. Signs 100th Article 98 Agreement , May 3, 2005, *available at* [http://www.state.gov/r/pa/prs/ps/2005/45573.htm](last visited June 14, 2006). For an unofficial list of signators, see Coalition for the ICC, Status of Bilateral Immunity Agreements (April 14, 2006), *available at* [http://www.iccnow.org/documents/ CICCFS_BIAstatusCurrent.pdf] (last visited June 14, 2006).

[60] 22 U.S.C. § 7427. "Covered allied persons" include military personnel, elected or appointed officials, and other persons working for a NATO country or a major non-NATO ally, "so long as that government is not a party to the International Criminal Court and wishes its officials and other persons working on its behalf to be exempted from the jurisdiction of the [ICC]." 22 U.S.C. § 7432(3). Covered allies currently could include persons from the Czech Republic, Turkey, Egypt, Israel, Japan, the Republic of Korea, and Taiwan. All of these exempted countries are members of the ICC except the Czech Republic, Israel, Egypt, Turkey, Taiwan, and Japan. The Czech Republic, Egypt,

and Israel signed the Rome Statute but have not ratified it. In August of 2002, Israel notified the U.N. Secretary General that it does not intend to ratify the Rome Statute.

[61] 22 U.S.C. § 7424.

[62] 22 U.S.C. § 7426(c). "United States personnel" is not defined. Presumably it is limited to officials representing the government in some capacity, similar to "covered U.S. persons" as defined in §7432(4).

[63] 22 U.S.C. § 7426(e).

[64] 22 U.S.C. § 7430.

[65] 22 U.S.C. § 7430(a).

[66] 22 U.S.C. § 7431. It is unclear what authority is meant with respect to section 2011(a) (22 U.S.C. § 7430(a)), since section 2011 does not vest any authority in the President. *See* 22 U.S.C. § 7430(c). Perhaps section 2012 should be interpreted to prohibit delegation of the authorities to which sections 2004 and 2006 do not apply under section 2011.

[67] Section 2004 (22 U.S.C. § 7423) restricts the conduct of federal and state agencies and courts. Therefore, the exception in section 2011 could not be invoked with respect to state courts and other non-federal entities. Section 2006 (22 U.S.C. § 7425) applies only to the President, directing him to implement procedures to safeguard certain information from the ICC; a broad interpretation of section 2011 would appear to render section 2006 a nullity. Perhaps section 2011 is meant to provide the President authority to suspend regulations promulgated under section 2006 with respect to certain cases under the jurisdiction of the ICC.

[68] 22 U.S.C. § 7433(a).

[69] 22 U.S.C. § 7428. No such report was made public, but the report may have been submitted in classified form pursuant to subsection (c).

[70] Id.

[71] Foreign Operations, Export Financing, and Related Programs Appropriations Act, H.R. 5522, 109th Cong. § 572 (2006).

[72] *See* Grossman, *supra* note 12.

[73] 18 U.S.C. § 2441.

[74] Genocide Convention Implementation Act of 1987, P.L. 100-606, 102 Stat. 3045 (codified at 18 U.S.C. §§ 1091-93).

[75] See Douglass Cassel, Empowering United States Courts to Hear Crimes Within the Jurisdiction of the International Court, 35 NEW ENG. L. REV. 421, 437 (2001); Robinson O. Everett, American Servicemembers and the ICC, in THE UNITED STATES AND THE INTERNATIONAL CRIMINAL COURT 137, 142 (Sarah B. Sewall and Carl Kaysen, eds. 2000).

[76] See Douglass Cassel, Empowering United States Courts to Hear Crimes Within the Jurisdiction of the International Court, 35 NEW ENG. L. REV. 421, 429 (2001).

[77] *See id.* n.39 (listing relevant crimes over which U.S. courts have extraterritorial jurisdiction). Additionally, U.S. courts have jurisdiction to try criminal offenses committed by persons employed by or accompanying the armed forces overseas, or ex-servicemembers who committed a crime overseas, if such crime would be punishable by imprisonment for more than one year if it had committed within the territorial jurisdiction of the United States. 18 U.S.C. § 3261.

[78] Rome Statute, *supra* note 2, art. 123.

[79] *Id.* art. 23.

[80] *Id.* arts. 112 and 123. States that have signed the Statute or the Final Act are eligible to participate as observers in both bodies. The Administration's notification of intent not to ratify the Statute should have no effect on eligibility, although it may signal an intent not to participate. The United States did not participate at the final meeting of the Preparatory Commission in early July, possibly signaling the intent of the Administration to forego participation as an observer.

[81] *See* Assembly of States Parties to the Rome Statute of the International Criminal Court, First Session, Official Records, U.N. Doc ICC ASP/1/3 (2003). The Rules of Procedure of the Assembly of States Parties ["Assembly Rules"] are reprinted in part IIC of the conference report.

[82] Unlike the previous administration, the Bush Administration did not participate actively in Preparatory Commission meetings, suggesting that the Administration does not envision playing an active role as observer at the Assembly of States Parties.

[83] The United Nations has a standing invitation to participate as an observer. Assembly Rule 35. It may also propose items for the agenda. Assembly Rule 11. Finally, the U.N. may provide funding for the ICC, in particular with respect to cases referred by the Security Council. Rome Statute, *supra* note 2, art. 115; *see also* U.N. Doc., PCNICC/2001/1/Add. 1, Draft Relationship Agreement between the Court and the United Nations.

[84] Rome Statute, *supra* note 2, art. 13. Non-parties might also be able to provide information to enable the Prosecutor to initiate a self-referred investigation, but would have no *official* role in advocating prosecution.

[85] *Id.* art. 16.

[86] *Id.* art. 53.

[87] *Id.* arts. 86, 87, and 93.

[88] *Id.* arts. 59 and 89.

[89] *Id.* art. 72.

[90] *Id.* art. 73.

[91] *Id.* art. 115.

[92] *See* Lee A. Casey, *The Case Against the International Criminal Court*, 25 FORDHAM INT'L L.J. 840, 849-50 (2002).

[93] *See* Final Report to the Prosecutor by the Committee Established to Review the NATO Bombing Campaign Against the Federal Republic of Yugoslavia, *available at* [http://www.un.org/icty/pressreal/nato061300.htm](last visited June 14, 2006).

[94] *See, e.g.*, Leila Nadya Sadat and S. Richard Carden, *The New International Criminal Court: An Uneasy Revolution,* 88 GEO. L.J. 381, 392 (2000) (suggesting that the refusal of the United States to participate in the ICC could bring about its demise, just as the U.S.' failure to join the League of Nations contributed to the failure of that institution).

[95] *See* Major Eric S. Kraus and Major Mike O. Lacy, *Utilitarian vs. Humanitarian: The Battle over the Law of War*, PARAMETERS, Jul. 1, 2002, *available at* 2002 WL 18222339. (commenting that U.S. refusal to ratify Protocol I to the Geneva Conventions, the treaty banning antipersonnel landmines, and the Rome Statute appear to be diminishing U.S. influence on the development of customary international law).

[96] An example might be the impact the U.S. policy has had on U.S. relations with Europe. *See* CRS Report RS21612, *East Central Europe: Status of International Criminal Court (ICC) Exemption Agreements and U.S. Military Assistance*, by Julie Kim.

[97] *The International Criminal Court: Hearing Before the House Committee on International Relations*, 106th Cong. 4 (2000) (prepared testimony of John Bolton, Senior Vice President, American Enterprise Institute).

[98] *See supra* note 50. For information about U.S. participation in U.N. peacekeeping missions, see CRS Issue Brief IB90103, *United Nations Peacekeeping: Issues for Congress*, by Marjorie Ann Browne.

[99] SC Res. 1422, U.N. Doc. S/Res/1422 (2002), *available at* [http://daccessdds.un.org].

[100] SC Res. 1497, U.N. Doc. S/RES/1497, Para. 7 (Aug. 1, 2003).

[101] Certification Concerning U.S. Participation in the U.N. Mission in Liberia Consistent With Section 2005 of the American Servicemembers' Protection Act, 68 Fed. Reg. 63,975 (2003).

[102] SC Res. 1529, U.N. Doc. S/RES/1529 (2004) (authorizing multinational interim force to deploy to Haiti).

[103] SC Res. 1542, U.N. Doc. S/RES/1542 (2004).

[104] 69 Fed. Reg. 34,043 (June 14, 2004).

[105] *See* "Security Council Refers Situation in Darfur, Sudan, to Prosecutor of International Criminal Court," Press Release, SC/8351; "Secretary-General Welcomes Adoption of Security Council Resolution Referring Situation in Darfur, Sudan to International Criminal Court Prosecutor," March 31, 2005, Press Release SG/SM/9797 AFR/1132. For background, see "Report of the International Commission of Inquiry on Darfur to the United Nations Secretary-General," S/2005/60, January 25, 2005

[106] *See* "U.N. Commission's Report on Violations of International Humanitarian Law in Darfur: Security Council Referral to the International Criminal Court," Frederic L. Kirgis, Am. Soc'y Int'l L Insight (Addendum), April 5, 2005.

[107] United Nations Security Council Resolution 1593 was adopted by the Security Council at its 518th meeting on 31 March 2005, U.N. Doc. S/RES/1593 (2005).

[108] *See* SC Res. 1564, U.N. Doc. S.RES/1564(2004) (requesting the establishment of an International Commission of Inquiry).

[109] *See* SC Res. 1593, Para. 6; *see also* Kirgis, *supra* note 106.

[110] *See* Jess Bravin, *U.S. Warms To Hague Tribunal*, WALL ST. J., June 14, 2006, at A4.

[111] United States Mission to the United Nations, "Statement on the Sudan Accountability Resolution," Ambassador Anne W. Patterson, March 31, 2005. *See* CRS Issue Brief IB98043, *Sudan: Humanitarian Crisis, Peace Talks, Terrorism, and U.S. Policy*, by Ted Dagne.

[112] *See* DOS Press Release, *supra* note 59. For the text of one such agreement, see Agreement Between the Government of the United States of America and the Republic of Uzbekistan Regarding the Surrender of Persons to the International Criminal Court, September 18, 2002, T.I.A.S. No. _____, *reprinted in* 42 I.L.M. 39 (2003).

[113] Rome Statute, *supra* note 2, art. 98.

[114] Risks for the Integrity of the Statute of the International Criminal Court, Resolution 1300 of the Parliamentary Assembly of the Council of Europe (September 25, 2002).

[115] *See* Phillip Shiskin and Jesse Bravin, *EU Offers Deal on U.S. Immunity from Tribunal*, WALL ST. J., Sep. 13, 2002, at A8.

[116] *See* Council of the European Union: Council Conclusions and EU Guiding Principles, 42 I.L.M. 240 (2003); *see also* Council of the European Union, Threats to the International Criminal Court, Resolution 1336 (2003).

[117] Press Release, Council of the European Union, 15864/1/04 REV 1 (Presse 353) P 136/04, Dec. 10, 2004.

[118] *See, e.g.* Coalition for the International Criminal Court, Overview of the United States' Opposition to the International Criminal Court (Nov. 1, 2005), *available at* [http://www.iccnow.org/documents/CICCFS_US%20Opposition%20toICC_FINAL_en g% 20_2_.pdf] (last visited June 14, 2006); Human Rights Watch, United States Efforts to Undermine the International Criminal Court, (Sep. 4, 2002), *available at* [http://hrw.org/ campaigns/icc/docs/art98analysis.htm](last visited June 14, 2006).

[119] Relevant U.N. Security Council Resolutions are S/RES/1386 (2001), S/RES/1413 (2002), S/RES/1444 (2002, S/RES/1510 (2003), S/RES/1563 (2004), and S/RES/1623 (2005). None of these resolutions makes provisions regarding immunity for participating troops.

[120] *See* Colum Lynch, *Deal Gave Europe's Troops Immunity*, INT'L HERALD TRIB., June 20, 2002, at A1. Section 1.4 of Annex A to the MTA provides: The ISAF and supporting personnel, including associated liaison personnel, will be immune from personal arrest or detention. ISAF and supporting personnel, including associated liaison personnel, mistakenly arrested or detained will be immediately handed over to ISAF authorities. The Interim Administration agree that ISAF and supporting personnel, including associated liaison personnel, may not be surrendered to, or otherwise transferred to the custody of, an international tribunal or any other entity or State without the express consent of the contributing nation. ISAF Forces will respect the laws and culture of Afghanistan. The text of the agreement may be downloaded from the U.K. ISAF website at [http://www.operations.mod.uk/isafmta.doc](last visited June 14, 2006).

[121] *See* Rome Statute, *supra* note 2, arts. 97 and 98.

[122] *Id.* art. 5(1).

In: Law and Law Enforcement Issues
Editor: Gerald M. Kessler, pp. 111-161

ISBN: 978-1-60456-044-2

Chapter 5

THE DEPARTMENT OF DEFENSE RULES FOR MILITARY COMMISSIONS: ANALYSIS OF PROCEDURAL RULES AND COMPARISON WITH PROPOSED LEGISLATION AND THE UNIFORM CODE OF MILITARY JUSTICE*

Jennifer K. Elsea

ABSTRACT

November 13, 2001, President Bush issued a Military Order (M.O.) pertaining to the detention, treatment, and trial of certain non-citizens in the war against terrorism. Military commissions pursuant to the M.O. began in November, 2004, against four persons declared eligible for trial, but proceedings were suspended after a federal district court found one of the defendants could not be tried under the rules established by the Department of Defense. The D.C. Circuit Court of Appeals reversed that decision, *Rumsfeld v. Hamdan*, but the Supreme Court granted review and reversed the decision of the Court of Appeals. Military commissions will not be able to go forward until the Department of Defense revises its rules to conform with the Supreme Court's *Hamdan* opinion or Congress approves legislation conferring authority to promulgate rules that depart from the strictures of the Uniform Code of Military Justice (UCMJ) and U.S. international obligations.

The M.O. has been the focus of intense debate both at home and abroad. Critics argued that the tribunals could violate the rights of the accused under the Constitution as well as international law, thereby undercutting the legitimacy of any verdicts rendered by the tribunals. The Administration responded by publishing a series of military orders and instructions clarifying some of the details. The procedural aspects of the trials were published in Military Commission Order No. 1 ("M.C.O. No. 1"). The Department of Defense also released two more orders and nine "Military Commission Instructions," which set forth the elements of some crimes that may be tried, establish guidelines for civilian attorneys, and provide other administrative guidance. These rules were praised as

* Excerpted from CRS Report RL31600, dated July 25, 2006.

a significant improvement over what might have been permitted under the M.O., but some argued that the enhancements do not go far enough, and the Supreme Court held that the amended rules did not comply with the UCMJ.

This article provides a background and analysis comparing military commissions as envisioned under M.C.O. No. 1 to general military courts-martial conducted under the UCMJ. A summary of the *Hamdan* case follows, in particular the shortcomings identified by the Supreme Court. The report provides an overview of relevant legislation (H.R. 3044, H.R. 3038, and S. 3614). Finally, the report provides two charts to compare the regulations issued by the Department of Defense to standard procedures for general courts-martial under the Manual for Courts-Martial and to proposed legislation. The second chart, which compares procedural safeguards incorporated in the regulations with established procedures in courts-martial, follows the same order and format used in CRS Report RL31262, *Selected Procedural Safeguards in Federal, Military, and International Courts*, in order to facilitate comparison with safeguards provided in federal court and international criminal tribunals.

Introduction

Rasul v. Bush, issued by the U.S. Supreme Court at the end of its 2003 - 2004 term, clarified that U.S. courts do have jurisdiction to hear petitions for habeas corpus on behalf of the approximately 550 persons detained at the U.S. Naval Station in Guantanamo Bay, Cuba, in connection with the war against terrorism,[1] establishing a role for federal courts to play in determining the validity of the military commissions convened pursuant to President Bush's Military Order (M.O.) of November 13, 2001.[2] After dozens of petitions for habeas corpus were filed in the federal District Court for the District of Columbia, Congress passed the Detainee Treatment Act of 2005 (DTA),[3] revoking federal court jurisdiction over habeas claims, at least with respect to those not already pending, and created jurisdiction in the Court of Appeals for the District of Columbia Circuit to hear appeals of final decisions of military commissions. The Supreme Court overturned a decision by the D.C. Circuit that had upheld the military commissions, *Hamdan v. Rumsfeld*,[4] holding instead that although Congress has authorized the use of military commissions, such commissions must follow procedural rules as similar as possible to courts-martial proceedings, in compliance with the Uniform Code of Military Justice (UCMJ).[5]

Military Commissions: General Background

Military commissions are courts usually set up by military commanders in the field to try persons accused of certain offenses during war.[6] They are distinct from military courts-martial, which are panels set up to try U.S. service members (and during declared wars, civilians accompanying the armed forces) under procedures prescribed by Congress in the UCMJ. U.S. service members charged with a war crime are normally tried before courts-martial but may also be tried by military commission or in federal court, depending on the nature of the crime charged.[7] All three options are also available to try certain other persons for war crimes. Federal and state criminal statutes and courts are available to prosecute specific criminal acts related to terrorism that may or may not be triable by military commission.

Military commissions trying enemy belligerents for war crimes directly apply the international law of war, without recourse to domestic criminal statutes, unless such statutes are declaratory of international law.[8] Historically, military commissions have applied the same set of procedural rules that applied in courts-martial.[9]

Military Commissions at Guantánamo Bay

The President's Military Order establishing military commissions to try suspected terrorists has been the focus of intense debate both at home and abroad. Critics argued that the tribunals could violate any rights the accused may have under the Constitution as well as their rights under international law, thereby undercutting the legitimacy of any verdicts rendered by the tribunals. The Administration initially responded that the M.O. provided only the minimum requirements for a full and fair trial, and that the Secretary of Defense intended to establish rules prescribing detailed procedural safeguards for tribunals established pursuant to the M.O. The procedural rules released in March 2002 were praised as a significant improvement over what might have been permitted under the language of the M.O., but some continued to argue that the enhancements do not go far enough and that the checks and balances of a separate rule-making authority and an independent appellate process are necessary.[10] The release of the Military Commission Instructions sparked renewed debate, especially concerning the restrictions on civilian attorneys,[11] resulting in further modifications to the rules. Critics noted that the rules do not address the issue of indefinite detention without charge, as appears to be possible under the original M.O.,[12] or that the Department of Defense may continue to detain persons who have been cleared by a military commission.[13] The Pentagon has stated that its Inspector General (IG) looked into allegations, made by military lawyers assigned as prosecutors to the military commissions, that the proceedings are rigged to obtain convictions, but the IG did not substantiate the charges.[14]

The Department of Defense (DoD) in 2003 released eight "Military Commission Instructions" ("M.C.I. No. 1-8")[15] to elaborate on the set of procedural rules to govern military tribunals. Those rules are set forth in Military Commission Order No. 1 ("M.C.O. No. 1"), issued in March 2002 and amended several times since.[16] The instructions set forth the elements of some crimes that may be tried by military commission, establish guidelines for civilian attorneys, and provide other administrative guidance and procedures for military commissions. Additionally, Major General John D. Altenburg, Jr. (retired), the Appointing Authority for the commissions, issued several Appointing Authority Regulations, governing disclosure of communications, interlocutory motions, and professional responsibility.

In August 2005, DoD amended M.C.O. No. 1 to make the presiding officer function more like a judge and to have other panel members function more like a jury. Under the new rules, the presiding officer was assigned the responsibility of determining most questions of law while the other panel members were to make factual findings and decide any sentence, similar to courts-martial proceedings. Other provisions were modified to clarify the accused's privilege to be present except when necessary to protect classified information and only in instances where the presiding officer concludes that the admission of such evidence would not prejudice a fair trial and to require that the presiding officer exclude any evidence that would result in the denial of a full and fair trial from lack of access to the information.[17]

President Bush determined that twenty of the detainees at the U.S. Naval Station in Guantánamo Bay are subject to the M.O. and may consequently be charged and tried before military commissions.[18] Six detainees declared eligible in 2003 included two citizens of the U.K. and one Australian citizen.[19] After holding discussions with the British and Australian governments regarding the trial of their citizens, the Administration agreed that none of those three detainees will be subject to the death penalty.[20] The Administration agreed to modify some of the rules with respect to trials of Australian detainees[21] and agreed to return the U.K. citizens, including the two who had been declared eligible for trial by military commission, to Great Britain.[22] The Administration agreed to return one Australian citizen, but another, David Hicks has been charged with conspiracy to commit war crimes; attempted murder by an unprivileged belligerent and aiding the enemy.[23] One citizen from Yemen and one from the Sudan were formally charged with conspiracy to commit certain violations of the law of war (and other crimes triable by military commission).[24] Salim Ahmed Hamdan of Yemen, accused of providing physical security for Osama bin Laden and other high ranking Al Qaeda members and charged with conspiracy to attack civilians, commit murder by an unprivileged belligerent and terrorism,[25] provided the Supreme Court its first opportunity to address the validity of the military commissions.

HAMDAN V. RUMSFELD

Salim Ahmed Hamdan, who was captured in Afghanistan and is alleged to have worked for Osama Bin Laden as a body guard and driver, brought this challenge to the lawfulness of the Secretary of Defense's plan to try him for alleged war crimes before a military commission,[26] arguing that the military commission rules and procedures were inconsistent with the UCMJ[27] and that he had the right to be treated as a prisoner of war under the Geneva Conventions.[28] U.S. District Judge Robertson agreed, finding no inherent authority in the President as Commander-in-Chief of the Armed Forces to create such tribunals outside of the existing statutory authority, with which the military commission rules did not comply. He also concluded that the Geneva Conventions apply to the whole of the conflict in Afghanistan, including under their protections all persons detained in connection with the hostilities there,[29] and that Hamdan was thus entitled to be treated as a prisoner of war until his status was determined to be otherwise by a competent tribunal, in accordance with article 5 of the Third Geneva Convention (prisoners of war).

Interpreting the UCMJ in light of the Geneva Conventions, which permits the punishment of prisoners of war "only if the sentence has been pronounced by the same courts according to the same procedure as in the case of members of the armed forces of the Detaining Power,"[30] Judge Robertson found no congressional authority for Hamdan's trial under the DoD's rules for military commissions. Hamdan, he ruled, was not "an offender triable by military tribunal under the law of war" within the meaning of UCMJ art 21.[31] Further, he found the rules established by DoD to be fatally inconsistent with the UCMJ, contrary to UCMJ art. 36[32] because they give military authorities the power to exclude the accused from hearings and deny him access to evidence presented against him.[33]

The government appealed, arguing that the district court should not have interfered in the military commission prior to its completion, that Hamdan is not entitled to protection from the Geneva Conventions, and that the President has inherent authority to establish military commissions, which need not conform to statutes regulating military courts-martial.[34] The D.C. Circuit Court of Appeals rejected the government's argument that the federal courts had no jurisdiction to interfere in ongoing commission proceedings, but otherwise agreed with the government. Writing for a unanimous court, Judge Randolph reversed the lower court's finding, ruling that the Geneva Conventions are not judicially enforceable,[35] that even if they were, Hamdan is not entitled to their protections, and that in any event, the military commission would qualify as a "competent tribunal" where Hamdan may challenge his non-POW status, within the meaning of U.S. Army regulations implementing the Conventions.[36]

The appellate court did not accept the government's argument that the President has inherent authority to create military commissions without any authorization from Congress, but found such authority in the Authorization to Use Military Force(AUMF),[37] read together with UCMJ arts. 21 and 36.[38] The court interpreted art. 36 to mean that military commission rules have only to be consistent with those articles of the UCMJ that refer specifically to military commissions, and not that Congress meant to incorporate procedural rules for courts-martial into those applicable to military commissions. However, because the procedural rules to be used by the military commissions did not, in its view, affect jurisdiction, the court found it unnecessary to resolve the issue at the interlocutory stage of the case.

With respect to the Geneva Conventions, the D.C. Circuit cited to a footnote from the World War II *Eisentrager[39]* opinion that expresses doubt that the Court could grant relief based directly on the 1929 Geneva Convention:

> We are not holding that these prisoners have no right which the military authorities are bound to respect. The United States, by the Geneva Convention of July 27, 1929, 47 Stat. 2021, concluded ... an agreement upon the treatment to be accorded captives. These prisoners claim to be and are entitled to its protection. It is, however, the obvious scheme of the Agreement that responsibility for observance and enforcement of these rights is upon political and military authorities. Rights of alien enemies are vindicated under it only through protests and intervention of protecting powers as the rights of our citizens against foreign governments are vindicated only by Presidential intervention.[40]

Judge Williams wrote a concurring opinion, agreeing with the government's conception of the conflict with Al Qaeda as separate from the conflict with the Taliban but construing Common Article 3 to apply to any conflict with a non-state actor, without regard to the geographical confinement of such a conflict within the borders of a signatory state. Supreme Court nominee John G. Roberts concurred in the opinion without writing separately.

The Supreme Court granted review and reversed.

Before reaching the merits of the case, the Supreme Court dispensed with the government's argument that Congress had, by passing the Detainee Treatment Act of 2005 (DTA),[41] stripped the Court of its jurisdiction to review habeas corpus challenges by or on behalf of Guantanamo detainees whose petitions had already been filed.[42] The government's argument that the petitioner had no rights conferred by the Geneva Conventions that could be adjudicated in federal court likewise did not persuade the Court to dismiss the case. Regardless of whether the Geneva Conventions provide rights that are enforceable in Article III courts, the Court found that Congress, by incorporating the "law of war" into UCMJ art. 21,[43] brought the Geneva Conventions within the scope of law to be applied by courts. The Court disagreed that the *Eisentrager* case requires another result, noting that the Court there had decided the treaty question on the merits based on its interpretation of the Geneva Convention of 1929 and that the 1949 Conventions were drafted to reject that interpretation.[44] Justice Scalia, joined by Justices Thomas and Alito, dissented, arguing that the DTA should be interpreted to preclude the Court's review.

In response to the holding by the court below that Hamdan, as a putative member of al Qaeda, was not entitled to any of the protections accorded by the Geneva Conventions, the Court concluded that at the very least, Common Article 3 of the Geneva Conventions applies, even to members of al Qaeda, according to them a minimum baseline of protections, including protection from the "passing of sentences and the carrying out of executions without previous judgment pronounced by a regularly constituted court, affording all the judicial guarantees which are recognized as indispensable by civilized peoples."[45] Although recognizing that Common Article 3 "obviously tolerates a great degree of flexibility in trying individuals captured during armed conflict" and that "its requirements are general ones, crafted to accommodate a wide variety of legal systems," the Court found that the military commissions under M.C.O. No. 1 do not meet these criteria. In particular, the military commissions are not "regularly constituted" because they deviate too far, in the Court's view, from the rules that apply to courts-martial, without a satisfactory explanation of the need for such deviation.[46]

With respect to the authority to create the military commissions, the Court held that any power to create them must flow from the Constitution and must be among those "powers granted jointly to the President and Congress in time of war."[47] It disagreed with the government's position that Congress had authorized the commissions either when it passed the Authorization to Use Military Force (AUMF)[48] or the DTA. Although the Court assumed that the AUMF activated the President's war powers, it did not view the AUMF as expanding the President's powers beyond the authorization set forth in the UCMJ. The Court also noted that the DTA, while recognizing the existence of military commissions, does not specifically authorize them. At most, these statutes "acknowledge a general Presidential authority to convene military commissions in circumstances where justified under the 'Constitution and laws,' including the law of war."[49]

In addition to limiting military commissions to trials of offenders and offenses that are by statute or by the law of war consigned to such tribunals, the UCMJ provides limitations with respect to the procedural rules that may be employed. Article 36 (10 U.S.C. § 836) authorizes the President to prescribe rules for "pretrial, trial, and post-trial procedures, including modes of proof, for cases arising under this chapter triable in courts-martial, military commissions and other military tribunals." Such rules are to "apply the principles of law and the rules of evidence generally recognized in the trial of criminal cases in the United States district courts" insofar as the President "considers practicable" but that "may not be contrary to or inconsistent" with the UCMJ. In addition, rules made pursuant to this authority "shall be uniform insofar as practicable." The President had determined with respect to the military commissions that "it is impracticable to apply the rules and principles of law that govern 'the trial of criminal cases in the United States district courts'" but made no determination with respect to the practicability of applying rules different from those that apply in courts-martial.[50]

The Court interpreted article 36 to provide the President discretion to determine which federal court rules need not be applied by various military tribunals[51] due to their impracticability. However, the Court read the uniformity requirement as according less discretion to the President to determine what is practicable when providing different rules for courts-martial, military commissions, and other military tribunals.[52] Unlike the requirement for rules to track closely with federal court rules, which the President need follow only insofar as *he deems* practicable, the Court reasoned, the uniformity requirement applies unless its application is demonstrably impracticable. Thus, less deference was found owing, and the Court found that the government had failed to demonstrate that circumstances make any courts-martial rules impracticable for use in military commissions. Further, the Court found that some of the rules provided in the Defense Department rules set forth in Military Commission Order No. 1 ("M.C.O. No. 1"), in particular the provision allowing the exclusion of the defendant from attending portions of his trial or hearing some of the evidence against him, deviated substantially from the procedures that apply in courts-martial in violation of UCMJ article 36.[53]

Department of Defense Rules for Military Commissions

M.C.O. No. 1 sets forth procedural rules for the establishment and operation of military commissions convened pursuant to the November 13, 2001, M.O. It addresses the jurisdiction and structure of the commissions, prescribes trial procedures, including standards for admissibility of evidence and procedural safeguards for the accused, and establishes a review process. The *Hamdan* Court found the rules insufficient to meet UCMJ standards and noted that the review process was not sufficiently independent of the armed services to warrant the Court's abstention until the petitioner's case was finally decided. M.C.O. No. 1 also contains various mechanisms for safeguarding sensitive government information, which the Court found problematic in that they could have permitted evidence to be withheld from the accused but nevertheless considered by the military commission. The *Hamdan* Court left open the possibility that the rules established by M.C.O. No. 1 would be valid if Congress were to explicitly approve them.

Other orders and instructions may also call for specific congressional approval to remain valid. M.C.O. No. 3, "Special Administrative Measures for Certain Communications Subject to Monitoring," establishes procedures for authorizing and controlling the monitoring of communications between detainees and their defense counsel for security or intelligence-gathering purposes. M.C.O. No. 2 and 4 designate appointing officials.

M.C.I. No. 1 provides guidance for interpretation of the instructions as well as for issuing new instructions. It states that the eight M.C.I. apply to all DoD personnel as well as prosecuting attorneys assigned by the Justice Department and all civilian attorneys who have been qualified as members of the pool. Failure on the part of any of these participants to comply with any instructions or other regulations "may be subject to the appropriate action by the Appointing Authority, the General Counsel of the Department of Defense, or the Presiding Officer of a military commission."[54] "Appropriate action" is not further defined, nor is any statutory authority cited for the power.[55] M.C.I. No. 1 also reiterates that none of the instructions is to be construed as creating any enforceable right or privilege.

Jurisdiction

The President's M.O. has been criticized as overly broad in its assertion of jurisdiction, because it could be interpreted to cover non-citizens who have no connection with Al Qaeda or the terrorist attacks of September 11, 2001. It has been argued that the constitutional and statutory authority of the President to establish military tribunals does not extend any further than Congress' authorization to use armed force in response to the attacks.[56] Under a literal interpretation of the M.O., however, the President may designate as subject to the order any non-citizen he believes has ever engaged in any activity related to international terrorism, no matter when or where these acts took place. A person subject to the M.O. may be detained and possibly tried by military tribunal for violations of the law of war and "other applicable law."[57]

M.C.O. No. 1 does not explicitly limit its coverage to the scope of the authorization of force, but it clarifies somewhat the ambiguity with respect to the offenses covered. M.C.O. No. 1 establishes that commissions may be convened to try aliens who are designated by the President as subject to the M.O., whether captured overseas or on U.S. territory, for violations of the law of war and "all other offenses triable by military commissions." Although this language is somewhat narrower than "other applicable law," it remains vague. However, the statutory language recognizing the jurisdiction of military commissions is similarly vague, such that the M.C.O. does not appear on its face to exceed the statute with respect to jurisdiction over offenses. Justice Stevens, joined in that portion of the *Hamdan* opinion by only three other Justices, undertook an inquiry of military commission precedents to determine that "conspiracy" is not a valid charge. M.C.O. No. 1 does not resolve the issue of whether the President may, consistent with the Constitution, direct that criminal statutes defined by Congress to be dealt with in federal court be redefined as "war crimes" to be tried by the military, but the *Hamdan* decision may be interpreted to counsel against such an interpretation.

By statute, military tribunals may be used to try "offenders or offenses designated by statute or the law of war."[58] There are only two statutory offenses for which convening a military commission is explicitly recognized: aiding the enemy and spying (in time of war).[59] It appears that "offenses designated by the law of war" are not necessarily synonymous with "offenses *against* the law of war." Military tribunals may also be used to try civilians in occupied territory for ordinary crimes.[60] During a war, they may also be used to try civilians for committing belligerent acts, even those for which lawful belligerents would be entitled to immunity under the law of war, but only where martial law or military government may legally be exercised or on the battlefield,[61] where civilian courts are closed.[62] Such acts are not necessarily offenses against the law of war (that is, they do not amount to an international war crime), but are merely *unprivileged* under it, although courts and commentators have tended to use the terms interchangeably. Justice Stevens opined for the plurality that military commissions in the present circumstances have jurisdiction only for belligerent offenses and that martial law and military occupation courts will not serve as precedent for jurisdiction purposes.[63]

Some argue that civilians, including unprivileged combatants unaffiliated with a state (or other entity with "international personality" necessary for hostilities to amount to an "armed conflict"), are not directly subject to the international law of war and thus may not be prosecuted for violating it.[64] They may, however, be prosecuted for most belligerent acts under ordinary domestic law, irrespective of whether such an act would violate the international law of war if committed by a soldier. Under international law, those offenders who are entitled to prisoner of war (POW) status under the Third Geneva Convention ["GPW"] are entitled to be tried by court-martial and may not be tried by a military commission offering fewer safeguards than a general court-martial, even if those prisoners are charged with war crimes.[65] In the case of a non-international conflict, Common Article 3 of the Geneva Conventions protects even non-POWs from the "passing of sentences and the carrying out of executions without previous judgment pronounced by a regularly constituted court, affording all the judicial guarantees which are recognized as indispensable by civilized peoples."[66]

Subject-Matter Jurisdiction

M.C.I. No. 2, Crimes and Elements for Trials by Military Commission, details some of the crimes that might be subject to the jurisdiction of the commissions. Unlike the rest of the M.C.I. issued so far, this instruction was published in draft form by DoD for outside comment. The final version appears to have incorporated some of the revisions, though not all, suggested by those who offered comments.[67] The revision clarifies that the burden of proof is on the prosecution, precludes liability for *ex post facto* crimes,[68] adds two new war crimes, and clearly delineates between war crimes and "other offenses triable by military commission."

M.C.I. No. 2 clarifies that the crimes and elements derive from the law of war, but does not provide any references to international treaties or other sources that comprise the law of war. The instruction does not purport to be an exhaustive list; it is intended as an illustration of acts punishable under the law of war[69] or triable by military commissions.[70] "Aiding the enemy" and "spying" are included under the latter group, but are not defined with reference to the statutory authority in UCMJ articles 104 and 106 (though the language is very similar).[71] Terrorism is also defined without reference to the statutory definition in title 18, U.S. Code.[72] Although the Supreme Court long ago stated that charges of violations of the law of war tried before military commissions need not be as exact as those brought before regular courts,[73] it appears that the current Court will look more favorably on prosecutions where charges are fully supported by precedent.

It appears that "offenses triable by military commissions" in both the M.O. and M.C.O. No. 1 could cover ordinary belligerent acts carried out by unlawful combatants, regardless of whether they are technically war crimes. The draft version of M.C.I. No. 2 made explicit that

> Even an attack against a military objective that normally would be permitted under the law of armed conflict could serve as the basis for th[e] offense [of terrorism] if the attack itself constituted an unlawful belligerency (that is, if the attack was committed by an accused who did not enjoy combatant immunity).

Thus, under the earlier draft language, it appeared that a Taliban fighter who attacked a U.S. or coalition soldier, or perhaps even a soldier of the Northern Alliance prior to the arrival of U.S. forces, for example, could be charged with "terrorism" and tried by a military tribunal.[74]

However, the final version of M.C.I. No.2 substituted the following language:

> The requirement that the conduct be wrongful for this crime necessitates that the conduct establishing the offense not constitute an attack against a lawful military objective undertaken by military forces of a State in the exercise of their official duties.

The change appears to have eliminated the possibility that Taliban fighters could be charged with "terrorism" in connection with combat activities; however, under the DoD rules, such a fighter could still be charged with murder or destruction of property "by an unprivileged belligerent"[75] for participating in combat, as long as the commission finds that the accused "did not enjoy combatant immunity," which, according the to the instruction, is enjoyed only by "lawful combatants."[76] "Lawful combatant" is not further defined. Inasmuch as the President had declared that all of the detainees incarcerated at Guantánamo Bay, whether members of the Taliban or members of Al Qaeda, are unlawful combatants, it appears unlikely that the defense of combat immunity would be available.[77] It is unclear whether other defenses, such as self-defense or duress, would be available to the accused. M.C.I. No. 2 states that such defenses *may* be available, but that "[i]n the absence of evidence to the contrary, defenses in individual cases are presumed not to apply."[78]

Temporal and Spatial Jurisdiction

The law of war has traditionally applied within the territorial and temporal boundaries of an armed conflict between at least two belligerents.[79] It has not traditionally been applied to conduct occurring on the territory of neutral states or on the territory of a belligerent that lies outside the zone of battle, to conduct that preceded the outbreak of hostilities, or to conduct during hostilities that do not amount to an armed conflict. With respect to the international conflict in Afghanistan, in which coalition forces ousted the Taliban government, it appears relatively clear when and where the law of war would apply. The war on terrorism, however, does not have clear boundaries in time or space,[80] nor is it entirely clear who the belligerents are. The broad reach of the M.O. to encompass conduct and persons customarily subject to ordinary criminal law evoked criticism that the claimed jurisdiction of the military commissions exceeds the customary law of armed conflict, which M.C.I. No. 2 purports to restate.[81] Any military commissions established to comply with *Hamdan* will likely have a better chance of withstanding court scrutiny if they are supported by ample precedent or explicit statutory definition.

A common element among the crimes enumerated in M.C.I. No.2 is that the conduct "took place in the context of and was associated with armed conflict." The instruction explains that the phrase requires a "nexus between the conduct and armed hostilities,"[82] which has traditionally been a necessary element of any war crime. However, the definition of "armed hostilities" is broader than the customary definition of war or "armed conflict." "Armed hostilities" need not be a declared war or "ongoing mutual hostilities."[83] Instead, any hostile act or attempted hostile act might have sufficient nexus if its severity rises to the level of an "armed attack," or if it is intended to contribute to such acts. Some commentators have argued that the expansion of "armed conflict" beyond its customary bounds improperly expands the jurisdiction of military commissions beyond those that by statute or under the law of war are triable by military commissions.[84] The Supreme Court has not clarified the scope of the "Global War on Terrorism" but seems to have demonstrated a willingness to address the issue rather than deferring to the President's interpretation.

The definition for "Enemy" provided in M.C.I. No. 2 raises similar issues. According to § 5(B), "Enemy" includes

> any entity with which the United States or allied forces may be engaged in armed conflicts or which is preparing to attack the United States. It is not limited to foreign nations, or foreign military organizations or members thereof. "Enemy" specifically includes any organization of terrorists with international reach.

Some observers argue that this impermissibly subjects suspected international criminals to the jurisdiction of military commissions in circumstances in which the law of armed conflict has never applied.[85] The distinction between a "war crime," traditionally subject to the jurisdiction of military commissions, and a common crime, traditionally the province of criminal courts, may prove to be a matter of some contention during some of the proceedings.[86]

Composition and Powers

Under M.C.O. No. 1, the planned military commissions consist of a panel of three to seven military officers as well as one or more alternate members who had been "determined to be competent to perform the duties involved" by the Secretary of Defense or his designee,[87] and could include reserve personnel on active duty, National Guard personnel in active federal service, and retired personnel recalled to active duty. The rules also permit the appointment of persons temporarily commissioned by the President to serve as officers in the armed services during a national emergency.[88] The presiding officer is required to be a judge advocate in any of the U.S. armed forces, but not necessarily a military judge.[89]

The presiding officer is vested with the authority to decide evidentiary matters and interlocutory motions, or to refer them to the commission or certify them to Appointing Authority for decision. The presiding officer has the power to close any portion of the proceedings in accordance with M.C.O. No. 1, and "to act upon any contempt or breach of Commission rules and procedures," including disciplining any individual who violates any "laws, rules, regulations, or other orders" applicable to the commission, as the presiding officer saw fit. Presumably this power was to include not only military and civilian attorneys but also any witnesses who had been summoned under order of the Secretary of Defense pursuant to M.C.O. No. 1 § 5(A)(5).[90] The UCMJ authorizes military commissions to punish contempt with a fine of $100, confinement for up to 30 days, or both[91] Under the UCMJ, a duly subpoenaed witness who is not subject to the UCMJ and who refuses to appear before a military commission may be prosecuted in federal court.[92] To the extent that M.C.O. No. 1 would allow disciplinary measures against civilian witnesses who refuse to testify or produce other evidence as ordered by the commission, M.C.O. No. 1 would appear to be inconsistent with the UCMJ.

One of the perceived shortcomings of the M.O. has to do with the problem of command influence over commission personnel. M.C.O. No. 1 provides for a "full and fair trial," but contains few specific safeguards to address the issue of impartiality. Under the rules as presently written, the President would have complete control over the proceedings. He or his designee decide which charges to press, select the members of the panel, the prosecution and the defense counsel, select the members of the review panel, and approve and implement the final outcome. The procedural rules remain entirely under the control of the President or his designees, who are vested with authority to write them, interpret them, enforce them, and amend them at any time. All commission personnel other than the commission members themselves are under the supervision of the Secretary of Defense, directly or through the DoD General Counsel.[93] The Secretary of Defense acted as the direct supervisor of Review Panel members.[94] Originally, both the Chief Prosecutor and the Chief Defense Counsel were to report ultimately to the DoD General Counsel, which led some critics to warn that defense counsel were insufficiently independent from the prosecution.[95] DoD subsequently amended the instructions so that the Chief Prosecutor reports to the Legal Advisor to the Appointing Authority, but as Justice Kennedy noted in his concurring opinion, the concentration of authority in the Appointing Authority remains a significant departure from the structural safeguards Congress has built into the military justice system.[96]

The following sections summarize provisions of the procedural rules meant to provide appropriate procedural safeguards.

Procedures Accorded the Accused

The military commissions established pursuant to M.C.O. No. 1 have procedural safeguards similar to many of those that apply in general courts-martial, but the M.C.O. does not specifically adopt any procedures from the UCMJ, even those that explicitly apply to military commissions.[97] The M.C.O. provides that only the procedures it prescribes or any supplemental regulations that may be established pursuant to the M.O., *and no others* shall govern the trials,[98] perhaps precluding commissions from looking to the UCMJ or other law to fill in any gaps. The M.C.O. does not explicitly recognize that accused persons have rights under the law. The procedures that are accorded to the accused do not give rise to any enforceable right, benefit or privilege, and are not to be construed as requirements of the U.S. Constitution.[99] The accused has no opportunity to challenge the interpretation of the rules or seek redress in case of a breach.[100]

The procedural safeguards are for the most part listed in section 5. The accused is entitled to be informed of the charges sufficiently in advance of trial to prepare a defense,[101] shall be presumed innocent until determined to be guilty beyond a reasonable doubt by two thirds of the commission members,[102] shall have the right not to testify at trial unless he so chooses, shall have the opportunity to present evidence and cross-examine witnesses for the prosecution, and may be present at every stage of proceeding unless it is closed for security concerns or other reasons.[103] The presumption of innocence and the right against self-incrimination will result in an entered plea of "Not Guilty" if the accused refuses to enter a plea or enters a "Guilty" plea that is determined to be involuntary or ill informed.[104]

Open Hearing

The trials themselves are to be conducted openly except to the extent the Appointing Authority or presiding officer closes proceedings to protect classified or classifiable information or information protected by law from unauthorized disclosure, the physical safety of participants, intelligence or law enforcement sources and methods, other national security interests, or "for any other reason necessary for the conduct of a full and fair trial."[105] DoD invited members of the press to apply for permission to attend the trials,[106] although it initially informed Human Rights Watch and other groups that logistical issues would likely preclude their attendance.[107] However, at the discretion of the Appointing Authority, "open proceedings" need not necessarily be open to the public and the press.[108] Proceedings may be closed to the accused or the accused's civilian attorney, but not to detailed defense counsel. Furthermore, counsel for either side must obtain permission from the Appointing Authority or the DoD General Counsel in order to make a statement to the press.[109]

Because the public, and not just the accused, has a constitutionally protected interest in public trials, the extent to which trials by military commission are open to the press and public may be subject to challenge by media representatives.[110] The First Amendment right of public access extends to trials by court-martial,[111] but is not absolute. Trials may be closed only where the following test is met: the party seeking closure demonstrates an overriding interest that is likely to be prejudiced; the closure is narrowly tailored to protect that interest; the trial court has considered reasonable alternatives to closure; and the trial court makes adequate findings to support the closure.[112] Because procedures established under M.C.O. No. 1 appear to allow the exclusion of the press and public based on the discretion of the Appointing Authority without any consideration of the above requirements with respect to the specific exigencies of the case at trial, the procedures may implicate the First Amendment rights of the press and public.

Although the First Amendment bars government interference with the free press, it does not impose on the government a duty "to accord the press special access to information not shared by members of the public generally."[113] The reporters' right to gather information does not include an absolute right to gain access to areas not open to the public. Thus, if the military commissions were to sit in areas off-limits to the public for other valid reasons, media access may be restricted for reasons of operational necessity.[114] Access of the press to the proceedings of military commissions may be an issue of contention for the courts ultimately to decide, even if those tried by military commission are determined to lack the protection of the Sixth Amendment right to an open trial or means to challenge the trial.[115]

Right to Counsel

Once charges are referred,[116] the defendant will have military defense counsel assigned free of cost, but may request another JAG officer, who will be provided as a replacement if available in accordance with any applicable instructions or supplementary regulations that might later be issued.[117] The accused does not have the right to refuse counsel in favor of self-representation.[118] M.C.I. No. 4 requires detailed defense counsel to "defend the accused zealously within the bounds of the law ... notwithstanding any intention expressed by the accused to represent himself."[119]

The accused may also hire a civilian attorney at his own expense, but must be represented by assigned defense counsel at all relevant times, even if he retains the services of a civilian attorney. Civilian attorneys may apply to qualify as members of the pool of eligible attorneys, or may seek to qualify *ad hoc* at the request of an accused. Some critics argue the rules provide disincentives for the participation of civilian lawyers.[120] Civilian attorneys must agree that the military commission representation will be his or her primary duty, and are not permitted to bring any assistants, such as co-counsel or paralegal support personnel, with them to the defense team. Originally, all defense and case preparation was to be done on site, and civilian attorneys were not to share documents or discuss the case with anyone but the detailed counsel or the defendant. These restrictions, read literally, might have prevented civilian defense counsel from conducting witness interviews or seeking advice from experts in humanitarian law, for example.[121] However, the Pentagon later released a new version of M.C.I. No. 5 that loosened the restrictions to allow communications with "individuals with particularized knowledge that may assist in discovering relevant evidence."[122]

Civilian attorneys must meet strict qualifications to be admitted before a military commission. The civilian attorney must be a U.S. citizen (except for those representing Australian detainees[123]) with at least a SECRET clearance,[124] who is admitted to the bar of any state or territory. Furthermore, the civilian attorney may not have any disciplinary record, and must agree in writing to comply with all rules of court.[125] The civilian attorney is not guaranteed access to closed hearings or information deemed protected under the rules, which may or may not include classified information.[126]

The requirement that civilian counsel must agree that communications with the client may be monitored has been modified to require prior notification and to permit the attorney to notify the client when monitoring is to occur.[127] Although the government will not be permitted to use information against the accused at trial, some argue the absence of the normal attorney-client privilege could impede communications between them, possibly decreasing the effectiveness of counsel. Civilian attorneys are bound to inform the military counsel if they learn of information about a pending crime that could lead to "death, substantial bodily harm, or a significant impairment of national security."[128] M.C.I. No. 5 provides no criteria to assist defense counsel in identifying what might constitute a "significant impairment of national security."

All defense counsel are under the overall supervision of the Office of the Chief Defense Counsel, which is entrusted with the proper management of personnel and resources the duty to preclude conflicts of interest.[129] The M.C.O. further provides that "in no circumstance shall accommodation of counsel be allowed to delay proceedings unreasonably."[130] The Appointing Authority may revoke any attorney's eligibility to appear before any commission.[131]

Some attorneys' groups have voiced opposition to the restrictions and requirements placed on civilian defense counsel, arguing the rules would not allow a defense attorney ethically to represent any client. The board of directors for the National Association of Criminal Defense Lawyers issued an ethics statement saying that it is unethical for a lawyer to represent a client before a military tribunal under the current rules and that lawyers who choose to do so are bound to contest the unethical conditions."[132] The House of Delegates of the American Bar Association (ABA) took no position on whether civilian lawyers should participate in the tribunals, but urged the Pentagon to relax some of the rules, especially with respect to the monitoring of communications between clients and civilian attorneys.[133] The National Institute of Military Justice, while echoing concerns about the commission rules, has stated that lawyers who participate will be performing an important public service.[134]

Discovery

The accused has the right to view evidence the Prosecution intends to present as well as any exculpatory evidence known, as long as it is not deemed to be protected under Sec.

6(D)(5).[135] In courts-martial, by contrast, the accused has the right to view any documents in the possession of the Prosecution related to the charges, and evidence that reasonably tends to negate the guilt of the accused, reduce the degree of guilt or reduce the punishment.[136]

The accused may also obtain witnesses and documents "to the extent necessary and reasonably available as determined by the Presiding Officer" and subject to secrecy determinations. The Appointing Authority shall make available to the accused "such investigative or other resources" deemed necessary for a full and fair trial.[137] Access to other detainees who might be able to provide mitigating or exculpatory testimony may be impeded by the prohibition on defense counsel from entering into agreements with "other Accused or Defense Counsel that might cause them or the Accused they represent to incur an obligation of confidentiality with such other Accused or Defense Counsel or to effect some other impediment to representation."[138] In other words, communications with potential witnesses would not be privileged and could be used against the witness at his own trial.

The overriding consideration with regard to whether the accused or defense counsel (including detailed defense counsel) may gain access to information appears to be the need for secrecy. The presiding officer may delete specific items from any information to be made available to the accused or defense counsel, or may direct that unclassified summaries of protected information be prepared.[139] However, no evidence may be admitted for consideration by the rest of the commission members unless it has been made available to at least the detailed defense counsel.[140] Information that was reviewed by the presiding officer *ex parte* and *in camera* but withheld from the defense over defense objection will be sealed and annexed to the record of the proceedings for review by the various reviewing authorities.[141] Nothing in the M.C.O. limits the purposes for which the reviewing authorities may use such material.

Right to Face One's Accuser

The presiding officer may authorize any methods appropriate to protect witnesses, including telephone or other electronic means, closure of all or part of the proceedings and the use of pseudonyms.[142] The commission may consider sworn or unsworn statements, and these apparently may be read into evidence without meeting the requirements for authentication of depositions and without regard to the availability of the witness under the UCMJ, as these provisions expressly apply to military commissions.[143] UCMJ articles 49 and 50 could be read to apply to military commissions the same rules against hearsay used at courts-martial; however, the Supreme Court has declined to apply similar provisions to military commissions trying enemy combatants.[144]

It was the provision for the use of secret evidence and for the exclusion of the accused from portions of the hearings that the district court found most troubling in *Hamdan.[145]* The court declared "[i]t is obvious beyond the need for citation that such a dramatic deviation from the confrontation clause could not be countenanced in any American court ..." and found it apparent that "the right to trial 'in one's presence' is established as a matter of international humanitarian and human rights law."[146] Under UCMJ art. 39,[147] the accused at a court-martial has the right to be present at all proceedings other than the deliberation of the members.

Admissibility of Evidence

The standard for the admissibility of evidence remains as it was stated in the M.O.; evidence is admissible if it is deemed to have "probative value to a reasonable person."[148] This is a significant departure from the Military Rules of Evidence (Mil. R. Evid.), which provide that "[a]ll relevant evidence is admissible, except as otherwise provided by the Constitution of the United States [and other applicable statutes, regulations and rules]."[149] In a court-martial, relevant evidence may be excluded if its probative value is substantially outweighed by other factors.[150]

"Probative value to a reasonable man" is a seemingly lax standard for application to criminal trials.[151] A reasonable person could find plausible sounding rumors or hearsay to be at least somewhat probative, despite inherent questions of reliability and fairness that both federal and military rules of evidence are designed to address. Furthermore, defendants before military commissions do not appear to have the right to move that evidence be excluded because of its propensity to create confusion or unfair prejudice, or because it was unlawfully obtained or coerced through the use of measures less severe than torture. In March 2006, DoD released M.C.I. No. 10 prohibiting prosecutors from introducing, and military commissions from admitting, statements established to have been made as a result of torture.

Sentencing

The prosecution must provide in advance to the accused any evidence to be used for sentencing, unless good cause is shown. The accused may present evidence and make a statement during sentencing proceedings; however, this right does not appear to mirror the right to make an unsworn statement that military defendants may exercise in regular courts-martial.[152] Statements made by the accused during the sentencing phase appear to be subject to cross-examination.

Possible penalties include execution,[153] imprisonment for life or any lesser term, payment of a fine or restitution (which may be enforced by confiscation of property subject to the rights of third parties), or "such other lawful punishment or condition of punishment" determined to be proper. Detention associated with the accused's status as an "enemy combatant" will not count toward serving any sentence imposed.[154] If the sentence includes confinement, it is unclear whether or how the conditions of imprisonment will differ from that of detention as an "enemy combatant." Sentences agreed in plea agreements are binding on the commission, unlike regular courts-martial, in which the agreement is treated as the maximum sentence. Similar to the practice in military courts-martial, the death penalty may only be imposed upon a unanimous vote of the Commission.[155] In courts-martial, however, both conviction for any crime punishable by death and any death sentence must be by unanimous vote.[156] None of the rules specify which offenses might be eligible for the death penalty, but the Pentagon announced the death penalty will not be sought in the cases brought so far.

Post-Trial Procedure

One criticism leveled at the language of the M.O. was that it does not include an opportunity for the accused to appeal a conviction, and appears to bar habeas corpus relief. Another was that it appears to allow the Secretary of Defense (or the President) the discretion to change the verdict, and does not protect persons from double jeopardy.[157] M.C.O. No.1 addresses these issues in part.

Review and Appeal

The rules provide for the administrative review of the trial record by the Appointing Authority, who forwards the record, if found satisfactory, to a review panel consisting of three military officers, one of whom must have experience as a judge. The Bush Administration has announced its intent to commission four individuals to active duty to serve on the Military Commission Review Panels.[158] They are Griffin Bell, a former U.S. attorney general and judge of the U.S. Court of Appeals for the 5th Circuit; Edward Biester, a former Member of the U.S. House of Representatives and current judge of the Court of Common Pleas of Bucks County, Pennsylvania; the Honorable William T. Coleman Jr., a former Secretary of Transportation; and Chief Justice Frank Williams of the Rhode Island Supreme Court.

There is no opportunity for the accused to appeal a conviction in the ordinary sense. The review panel may, however, at its discretion, review any written submissions from the prosecution and the defense, who do not appear to have an opportunity to view or rebut the submission from the opposing party.[159] If the review panel forms a "firm and definite conviction that a material error of law occurred," it returns the case to the Appointing Authority for further proceedings. If the review panel determines that one or more charges should be dismissed, the Appointing Authority is bound to do so.[160] For other cases involving errors, the Appointing Authority is required to return the case to the military commission. Otherwise, the case is forwarded to the Secretary of Defense with a written recommendation. (Under the UCMJ, the trial record of a military commission would be forwarded to the appropriate JAG first.)[161]

After reviewing the record, the Secretary of Defense may forward the case to the President or return it for further proceedings for any reason, not explicitly limited to material errors of law. The M.C.O. does not indicate what "further proceedings" may entail. If the Secretary of Defense is delegated final approving authority, he can approve or disapprove the finding, or mitigate or commute the sentence. The rules do not clarify what happens to a case that has been "disapproved." It is unclear whether a disapproved finding is effectively vacated and remanded to the military commission for a rehearing.

The UCMJ forbids rehearings or appeal by the government of verdicts amounting to a finding of Not Guilty, and prohibits the invalidation of a verdict or sentence due to an error of law unless the error materially prejudices the substantial rights of the accused.[162] The M.C.O. does not contain any such explicit prohibitions, but M.C.I. No. 9 defines "Material Error of Law" to exclude variances from the M.O. or any of the military orders or instructions promulgated under it that would not have had a material effect on the outcome of the military commission.[163] M.C.I. No. 9 allows the review panel to recommend the disapproval of a finding of Guilty on a basis other than a material error of law.[164] It does not indicate what options the review panel would have with respect to findings of Not Guilty.

M.C.O. No. 1 does not provide a route for a convicted person to appeal to any independent authority. Persons subject to the M.O. are described as not privileged to "seek any remedy or maintain any proceeding, directly or indirectly" in federal or state court, the court of any foreign nation, or any international tribunal.[165] However, a defendant may petition a federal court for a writ of habeas corpus to challenge the jurisdiction of the military commission.[166]

Protection Against Double Jeopardy

The M.C.O. provides that the accused may not be tried for the same charge twice by any military commission once the commission's finding on that charge becomes final (meaning once the verdict and sentence have been approved).[167] Therefore, apparently, jeopardy does not attach —there has not been a "trial" — until the final verdict has been approved by the President or the Secretary of Defense. In contrast, at general courts-martial, jeopardy attaches after the first introduction of evidence by the prosecution. If a charge is dismissed or is terminated by the convening authority after the introduction of evidence but prior to a finding, through no fault of the accused, or if there is a finding of Not Guilty, the trial is considered complete for purposes of jeopardy, and the accused may not be tried again for the same charge by any U.S. military or federal court without the consent of the accused.[168] Although M.C.O. No. 1 provides that an authenticated verdict[169] of Not Guilty by the commission may not be changed to Guilty,[170] either the Secretary of Defense or the President may disapprove the finding and return the case for "further proceedings" prior to the findings' becoming final, regardless of the verdict. If a finding of Not Guilty is referred back to the commission for rehearing, double jeopardy may be implicated.[171]

Another double jeopardy issue that might arise is related to the requirements for the specification of charges.[172] M.C.O. No. 1 does not provide a specific form for the charges, and does not require an oath or signature.[173] If the charge does not adequately describe the offense, another trial for the same offense under a new description is not as easily prevented. M.C.I. No. 2, setting forth elements of crimes triable by the commissions, may provide an effective safeguard; however, new crimes may be added to its list at any time.

The M.O. also left open the possibility that a person subject to the order might be transferred at any time to some other governmental authority for trial.[174] A federal criminal trial, as a trial conducted under the same sovereign as a military commission, could have double jeopardy implications if the accused had already been tried by military commission for the same crime or crimes, even if the commission proceedings did not result in a final verdict. The federal court would face the issue of whether jeopardy had already attached prior to the transfer of the individual from military control to other federal authorities.

Conversely, the M.O. provides the President may determine at any time that an individual is subject to the M.O., at which point any state or federal authorities holding the individual would be required to turn the accused over to military authorities. If the accused were already the subject of a federal criminal trial under charges for the same conduct that resulted in the President's determination that the accused is subject to the M.O., and if jeopardy had already attached in the federal trial, double jeopardy could be implicated by a new trial before a military commission. M.C.O. No. 1 does not explicitly provide for a double jeopardy defense under such circumstances.

ROLE OF CONGRESS

The President's order appears to be broader than the authority exercised by previous Presidents and may cover aliens in the United States legally who are citizens of countries with which the nation is at peace. M.C.O. No. 1 clarifies that the commissions will have jurisdiction only over violations of the law of war but does not expressly limit jurisdiction to coincide with Congress' authorization for the use of force. It does not limit the provisions appearing to allow for the indefinite detention of non-citizens, whether or not they are accused of having committed a violation of the law of war, based solely on the President's determination that there is reason to believe the individual is a member of the class of persons subject to the order, in possible contradiction to the USA PATRIOT Act.[175] It does not clarify whether the President intends to use the statutory definitions of "acts of international terrorism" to determine who is subject to the order.

Congress has the authority to regulate the operation of military commissions, but has not in the past prescribed procedural regulations.[176] Congress may also draft legislation defining offenses against the law of war triable by military commissions. Because the draft regulations appear to provide some of the safeguards critics argued were missing from the original M.O., supporters of the Administration's policy will likely urge Congress not to interfere. Notably, M.C.O. No. 1 is subject to amendment without notification to Congress, and the Secretary of Defense has the authority to direct that some other procedures be used.[177] M.C.O. No. 1 also states that no "other rules" will govern, which could mean that the rules are not to be construed with reference to the UCMJ or any other statute. Indeed, M.C.O. No. 1 § 10 states that "[n]o provision in [the] Order shall be construed to be a requirement of the United States Constitution." Finally, an act of Congress would appear necessary to enable the federal courts to take appellate jurisdiction over the military commissions.[178]

Several bills were introduced in the 108th Congress to address military commissions. The Military Tribunal Authorization Act of 2003, introduced in the Senate as Title I, subtitle C of S. 22 (Justice Enhancement and Domestic Security Act of 2003), and in the House of Representatives as H.R. 1290, would have authorized the establishment of extraordinary tribunals for offenses arising from the September 11, 2001 attacks. The bill would have narrowed the field of potential defendants from that stated in the M.O., expanded the minimum procedural requirements to be established by the Secretary of Defense, and provided for appeal to the Court of Appeals for the Armed Forces and review by the Supreme Court on writ of certiorari. H.R. 2428 would have provided for congressional review and possible disapproval of regulations relating to military tribunals. None of these bills advanced beyond referral to committee.

Three bills in the 109th Congress would provide for military commissions. The Guantanamo Detainees Procedures Act of 2005, H.R. 3038, affirms the President's authority to detain certain foreign nationals and prescribes procedural rules with respect to their detention and possible trial by military commission, apparently irrespective of where a covered person is captured or detained. Convictions would be subject to administrative review by the Defense Department and appeal to the United States Court of Appeals for the Armed Forces, with the possibility of review by the Supreme Court on a writ of certiorari.

The Military Commissions Act of 2005, H.R. 3044, would amend the UCMJ to include a new article 135a, entitled "Military commissions for offenses against the law of war or in furtherance of terrorism." The bill would authorize the President to appoint military commissions to try law-of-war violations or "any offense defined in United States law when such offense is committed in furtherance of international terrorism as defined in section 2331 of title 18."[179] The bill does not contain geographical limitations as to jurisdiction; the use of military commissions to try aliens for terrorism-related crimes not cognizable under the law of war, at least for offenses committed within the United States, could raise constitutional questions.[180]

The bill would authorize the President to promulgate procedural rules for trials under UCMJ art. 36 (10 U.S.C. § 836), but would expressly require such rules to contain certain minimum due process guarantees, including the right to a fair trial. Unlike the military commissions established under M.C.O. No. 1, the proposed military commissions under H.R. 3044 would have a judge advocate appointed as the presiding officer, who would act in a role similar to that of military judge. The presiding officer would instruct the members of the commission on all matters of law and procedure, including interlocutory questions that arise during the proceedings. Other commission members would vote to decide the factual issues. The Court of Appeals of the Armed Forces (CAAF) would review sentences of death or imprisonment for five or more years, or other cases as prescribed by the President. The bill would also require DoD to submit an annual report on its use of military commissions, applicable procedural rules, and an accounting of funds.

The Unprivileged Combatant Act of 2006, S. 3614, would authorize the President to establish military commissions to try crimes involving international terrorism defined in chapter 113B of title 18, U.S. Code, violations of the law of war committed by unprivileged combatants, and other offenses triable by military commissions or pursuant to M.C.I. No. 2. The U.S. Court of Military Appeals, probably meaning the CAAF, would have jurisdiction to hear appeals, with the possibility of Supreme Court review on writ of certiorari. The bill would also require DoD to submit a report identifying all detainees at the Guantanamo Bay detention facility whom the Department wishes to continue detaining as unprivileged combatants and a summary of the evidence supporting the continuation of custody. It would direct the Secretary of Defense to appoint a commission to review the policy, procedures, and practice of the classification system for national security information.

The following charts provide a comparison of the proposed military tribunals under the regulations issued by the Department of Defense, standard procedures for general courts-martial under the Manual for Courts-Martial, and military tribunals as proposed H.R. 3038, H.R. 3044, and S. 3614. Table 1 compares the legal authorities for establishing military tribunals, the jurisdiction over persons and offenses, and the different structures of the tribunals. Table 2, which compares procedural safeguards incorporated in the DoD regulations and the UCMJ, follows the same order and format used in CRS Report RL31262, *Selected Procedural Safeguards in Federal, Military, and International Courts*, in order to facilitate comparison of the proposed legislation to safeguards provided in federal court and the International Criminal Court.

Table 1. Comparison of Courts-Martial and Military Commission Rules

	General Courts Martial	Military Commission Order No. 1 (M.C.O.)	Military Commissions Act of 2005 H.R. 3044	Guantanamo Detainees Procedures Act of 2005 H.R. 3038	Unprivileged Combatant Act of 2006 S. 3614
Authority	U.S. Constitution, Article I, § 8.	U.S. Constitution, Article II; Presidential Military Order of Nov. 13, 2001 (M.O).	U.S. Constitution, Article I, § 8.	U.S. Constitution, Article I, § 8.	U.S. Constitution, Article I, § 8.
Procedure	Rules are provided by the Uniform Code of Military Justice (UCMJ), chapter 47, title 10, and the Rules for Courts-Martial (R.C.M.) and the Military Rules of Evidence (Mil. R. Evid.), issued by the President pursuant to art. 36, UCMJ. 10 U.S.C. § 836.	Rules are issued by the Secretary of Defense pursuant to the M.O. No other rules apply (presumably excluding the UCMJ). § 1. The President has declared it "impracticable" to employ procedures used in federal court, pursuant to 10 U.S.C. § 836.	The President may prescribe rules of evidence and procedure for trial by a military commission pursuant to art. 36, UCMJ. The President may further delegate authority to prescribe such rules to the Secretary of Defense. Proposed 10 U.S.C. § 935a(i).	The Secretary of Defense, in consultation with the Secretary of State and the Attorney General, prescribes rules of evidence and procedure. § 5(c).	The Secretary of Defense prescribes rules of evidence and procedure. § 13(a)(2).
Jurisdiction over Persons	Members of the armed forces, cadets, midshipmen, reservists while on inactive-duty training, members of the National Guard or Air National Guard when in federal service, prisoners of war in custody of the armed forces, civilian employees accompanying the armed forces in time of declared war, and certain others, including "persons within an area leased by or otherwise reserved or acquired for the use of the United States." 10 U.S.C. § 802; United States v.	Individual subject to M.O., determined by President to be: 1. a non-citizen, and 2. a member of Al Qaeda or person who has engaged in acts related to terrorism against the United States, or who has harbored one or more such individuals and is referred to the commission by the Appointing Authority. § 3(A).	Any person, not a citizen of the United States (accused of certain offenses). Proposed 10 U.S.C. § 935a(b).	An individual, not a United States person, lawful permanent resident, or POW, who is accused of knowingly planning, authorizing, committing, aiding, or abetting one or more terrorist acts against the United States; or is accused of being part of or supporting forces engaged in armed conflict against the United States. § 2(b).	Unprivileged combatants, defined as persons who have been determined by a Combatant Status Review Tribunal to be "enemy combatants" or who are determined to be persons not entitled to POW status and to have taken up arms against the United States or to have conspired with, assisted, or solicited others to take up arms, or to have assisted or conspired with a group

	General Courts Martial	Military Commission Order No. 1 (M.C.O.)	Military Commissions Act of 2005 H.R. 3044	Guantanamo Detainees Procedures Act of 2005 H.R. 3038	Unprivileged Combatant Act of 2006 S. 3614
	Averette, 17 USCMA 363 (1968) (holding "in time of war" to mean only wars declared by Congress. Individuals who are subject to military tribunal jurisdiction under the law of war may also be tried by general court martial. 10 U.S.C. § 818.				or individual "hostile to the United States. §§ 2(11) and 4.
Jurisdiction over Offenses	Any offenses made punishable by the UCMJ; offenses subject to trial by military tribunal under the law of war. 10 U.S.C. § 818.	Offenses in violation of the laws of war and all other offenses triable by military commission. § 3(B). M.C.I. No. 2 clarifies that terrorism and related crimes are "crimes triable by military commission."	Offenses against the law of war or any offense defined in United States law when such offense is committed in furtherance of international terrorism as defined in 18 U.S.C. § 2331. Proposed 10 U.S.C. § 935a(b).	Violations of the law of war, international laws of armed conflict, and crimes against humanity targeted against United States persons or residents. § 5(b)	Criminal prosecutions for international terrorism offenses as defined under chap. 113B of title 18, U.S. Code; violations of the laws of war committed by unprivileged combatants, and other offenses traditionally triable by military commissions or pursuant to M.C.I. No. 2. § 4.
Composition	A military judge and not less than five members. R.C.M. 501.	From three to seven members, as determined by the Appointing Authority. § 4(A)(2).	From three to seven members; in a cases where the death penalty is possible, the commission must have seven members. Proposed 10 U.S.C. § 935a(c)	Procedural rules must require that the tribunal be comprised of a military judge and not less than five members. § 6(a)(20).	At least three military officers, at least one of whom is a military judge. § 6.

Source: Congressional Research Service.

Table 2. Comparison of Procedural Safeguards

	General Courts-Martial	Military Commission Order No. 1 (M.C.O.)	Military Commissions Act of 2005 H.R. 3044	Guantanamo Detainees Procedures Act of 2005 H.R. 3038	Unprivileged Combatant Act of 2006 S. 3614
Presumption of Innocence	If the defendant fails to enter a proper plea, a plea of not guilty will be entered. R.C.M. 910(b). Members of court martial must be instructed that the "accused must be presumed to be innocent until the accused's guilt is established by legal and competent evidence beyond a reasonable doubt." R.C.M. 920(e). The accused shall be properly attired in uniform with grade insignia and any decorations to which entitled. Physical restraint shall not be imposed unless prescribed by the military judge. R.C.M. 804.	The accused shall be presumed innocent until proven guilty. § 5(B). Commission members must base their vote for a finding of guilty on evidence admitted at trial. §§ 5(C); 6(F). The presiding officer must determine the voluntary and informed nature of any plea agreement submitted by the accused and approved by the Appointing Authority before admitting it as stipulation into evidence. § 6(A)(4).	Procedural rules are required to provide that the accused must be presumed innocent until proven guilty on each element of an offense. Proposed 10 U.S.C. § 935a(i)(2).	Procedural rules are required to provide that the accused be presumed innocent until proven guilty, and not be found guilty except upon proof beyond a reasonable doubt. § 6(a)(14).	Presumption of innocence is not expressly mentioned, although only those persons may be tried who have been designated "enemy combatants" or who are determined by a classification tribunal to have taken up arms against the United States or to have conspired with, assisted, or solicited others to take up arms, or to have assisted or conspired with a group or individual "hostile to the United States."§ 2(11).
Right to Remain Silent	Coerced confessions or confessions made without statutory equivalent of Miranda warning are not admissible as evidence. Persons subject to the UCMJ are prohibited from compelling any individual to make a confession 10 U.S.C. § 831. The prosecutor must notify the defense of any incriminating statements made	Not provided. Neither the M.O. nor M.C.O. requires a warning or bars the use of statements made during military interrogation, or any coerced statement, from military commission proceedings. Art. 31(a), UCMJ (10 U.S.C. § 831) bars persons subject to it from compelling any individual to make a	Procedural rules must provide that evidence obtained through the use of torture will not be admitted in evidence at trial by a military commission. Proposed 10 U.S.C. § 935a(i)(5-7). Presumably, art. 31 UCMJ would also apply, insofar as it prohibits service	Procedural rules must provide that the accused not be compelled to confess guilt. § 6(a)(15). Presumably, art. 31 UCMJ would also apply, insofar as it prohibits service members from compelling testimony, but not as to its	Not addressed, although art. 31 UCMJ would presumably apply to prohibit coerced confessions. 10 U.S.C. § 831.

	General Courts-Martial	Military Commission Order No. 1 (M.C.O.)	Military Commissions Act of 2005 H.R. 3044	Guantanamo Detainees Procedures Act of 2005 H.R. 3038	Unprivileged Combatant Act of 2006 S. 3614
	by the accused that are relevant to the case prior to the arraignment. Motions to suppress such statements must be made prior to pleading. Mil. R. Evid. 304.	confession, but there does not appear to be a remedy in case of violation. No person subject to the UCMJ may compel any person to give evidence before any military tribunal if the evidence is not material to the issue and may tend to degrade him. 10 U.S.C. § 831.	members from compelling testimony, but not as to its exclusionary rule. 10 U.S.C. § 831.	exclusionary rule. 10 U.S.C. § 831. Rules must also afford the accused "all necessary means of defense before and after the trial." § 6(a)(11).	
Freedom from Unreasonable Searches & Seizures	"Evidence obtained as a result of an unlawful search or seizure ... is inadmissible against the accused ..." unless certain exceptions apply. Mil. R. Evid. 311. "Authorization to search" may be oral or written, and may be issued by a military judge or an officer in command of the area to be searched, or if the area is not under military control, with authority over persons subject to military law or the law of war. It must be based on probable cause. Mil. R. Evid. 315. Interception of wire and oral communications within the United States requires judicial application in accordance with 18 U.S.C. §§ 2516 *et seq.* Mil. R. Evid. 317. A search conducted by foreign officials is unlawful only if the	Not provided; no exclusionary rule appears to be available. However, monitored conversations between the detainee and defense counsel may not be communicated to persons involved in prosecuting the accused or used at trial M.C.O. No. 3. No provisions for determining probable cause or issuance of search warrants are included. Insofar as searches and seizures take place outside of the United States against non-U.S. persons, the Fourth Amendment may not apply. United States v. Verdugo Urquidez, 494 U.S. 259 (1990).	Not provided.	Not provided.	Not provided.

	General Courts-Martial	Military Commission Order No. 1 (M.C.O.)	Military Commissions Act of 2005 H.R. 3044	Guantanamo Detainees Procedures Act of 2005 H.R. 3038	Unprivileged Combatant Act of 2006 S. 3614
	accused is subject to "gross and brutal treatment." Mil. R. Evid. 311(c).				
Assistance of Effective Counsel	The right to an attorney attaches during the investigation phase under art. 32, UCMJ. 10 U.S.C. § 832. The defendant has a right to military counsel at government expense. The defendant may choose counsel, if that attorney is reasonably available, and may hire a civilian attorney in addition to military counsel. 10 U.S.C. § 838. Appointed counsel must be certified as qualified and may not be someone who has taken any part in the investigation or prosecution, unless explicitly requested by the defendant. 10 U.S.C. § 827. The attorney-client privilege is honored. Mil. R. Evid. 502.	M.C.O. 1 provides that the accused must be represented "at all relevant times" (presumably, once charges are approved until findings are final — but not for individuals who are detained but not charged) by detailed defense counsel. § 4(C)(4).The accused is assigned a military judge advocate to serve as counsel, but may request to replace or augment the detailed counsel with a specific officer, if that person is available. § 4(C)(3)(a). The accused may also hire civilian attorney who is a U.S. citizen, is admitted to the bar in any state, district, or possession, has a SECRET clearance (or higher, if necessary for a particular case), and agrees to comply with all applicable rules. The civilian attorney does not replace the detailed counsel, and is not guaranteed access to classified evidence or	Procedural rules are required to provide that the accused be entitled to "assistance of counsel at all stages of proceedings" and to "adequate time and facilities available for the preparation of his defense." The accused would also have the right to represent himself , subject to the discretion of the presiding officer. Proposed 10 U.S.C. § 935a(i)(8). Trial and defense counsel would be detailed on the same basis as such counsel are detailed for a general court-martial under 10 U.S.C. § 827 (UCMJ art. 27), which delegates to the "Secretaries involved" the authority to make regulations concerning the appointment of counsel. Presumably, the rules for military commissions could	Procedural rules must ensure that the accused has a right to be represented by counsel. § 6(a)(6).	The defendant has the right to be represented by counsel, who must be a U.S. citizen admitted to a bar without any disciplinary history and who is admitted to practice before a commission under rules to be determined by the Secretary of Defense. A defendant who is unable to obtain counsel is entitled to have counsel appointed and to be represented by such counsel at every stage of the proceeding subsequent to indictment. § 12(a). Counsel are not allowed to confer with colleagues who do not have the appropriate clearance, which includes at least access to information classified 'secret.' § 15(b). Prospective counsel who are seeking a security counsel are entitled to timely consideration for same. §

	General Courts-Martial	Military Commission Order No. 1 (M.C.O.)	Military Commissions Act of 2005 H.R. 3044	Guantanamo Detainees Procedures Act of 2005 H.R. 3038	Unprivileged Combatant Act of 2006 S. 3614
		closed hearings. § 4(C)(3)(b). Defense Counsel may present evidence at trial and cross-examine witnesses for the prosecution. § 5(I). The Appointing Authority must order such resources be provided to the defense as he deems necessary for a "full and fair trial." § 5(H). Communications between defense counsel and the accused are subject to monitoring by the government. Although information obtained through such monitoring may not be used as evidence against the accused, M.C.I. No. 3, the monitoring could have a chilling effect on attorney-client conversations, possibly hampering the ability of defense counsel to provide effective representation.	differ from those for courtsmartial. The right of the accused to select reasonably available counsel, found in 10 U.S.C. § 838, would not be incorporated. Proposed 10 U.S.C. § 935a(e). Procedural rules would be required to provide that detailed defense counsel may not be excluded from any trial proceeding or any portion thereof. Proposed 10 U.S.C. § 935a(i)(12).		15(c).
Right to Indictment and Presentment	The right to indictment by grand jury is explicitly excluded in "cases arising in the land or naval forces." U.S. Constitution, Amendment V. Whenever an offense is alleged, the commander is	Probably not applicable to military commissions, provided the accused is an enemy belligerent. *See Ex parte* Quirin, 317 U.S. 1 (1942). The Office of the Chief Prosecutor prepares	Procedural rules are required to provide that the accused is informed of the charges against him in a language he understands as soon as practicable prior to	Procedural rules are required to provide a preliminary proceeding within 30 days of detention, which may be continued for an additional 30 days for	Not expressly addressed, although the entitlement to appointed counsel does not attach until after indictment. § 12(a).

	General Courts-Martial	Military Commission Order No. 1 (M.C.O.)	Military Commissions Act of 2005 H.R. 3044	Guantanamo Detainees Procedures Act of 2005 H.R. 3038	Unprivileged Combatant Act of 2006 S. 3614
	responsible for initiating a preliminary inquiry under art. 32, UCMJ, and deciding how to dispose of the offense. 10 U.S.C. § 832; R.C.M. 303-06. The accused must be advised of the charges brought against him and has the right to an attorney during the investigation and hearing proceedings. 10 U.S.C. § 832.	charges for referral by the Appointing Authority. § 4(B). There is no requirement for an impartial investigation prior to a referral of charges. The Commission may adjust a charged offense in a manner that does not change the nature or increase the seriousness of the charge. § 6(F).	trial. Proposed 10 U.S.C. § 935a(i)(3). There is no requirement for a preliminary inquiry.	good cause shown, to determine whether there is jurisdiction under over the person and the offenses charged. § 6(a)(18).	
Right to Written Statement of Charges	Charges and specifications must be signed under oath and made known to the accused as soon as practicable. 10 U.S.C. § 830.	Copies of approved charges are provided to the accused and Defense Counsel in English and another language the accused understands, if appropriate. § 5(A).	No express requirement that charges be written.	No express requirement that charges be written.	
Right to be Present at Trial	The presence of the accused is required during arraignment, at the plea, and at every stage of the courtmartial unless the accused waives the right by voluntarily absenting him or herself from the proceedings after the arraignment or by persisting in conduct that justifies the trial judge in ordering the removal of the accused from the proceedings. R.C.M. 801.	The accused may be present at every stage of trial before the Commission unless the presiding officer excludes the accused because of disruptive conduct or for security reasons or "any other reason necessary for the conduct of a full and fair trial." §§ 4(A)(5)(b); 5(K); 6B(3).	The procedural rules are required to provide that the accused has the "right to be present at each stage of the proceedings, unless he engages in conduct that the presiding officer determines to be disruptive, or the presiding officer determines that exclusion of the accused is necessary to protect national security interests of the	The procedural rules are required to provide that the accused has the opportunity to be present at trial. § 6(a)(5). Rules must also provide that the proceedings be made simultaneously intelligible for participants not conversant in the English language by translation or interpretation. § 6(a)(3).	The defendant may be excluded from portions of the trial in order to protect classified information or to ensure the security of witnesses or to permit witnesses to testify freely. § 12(c).

	General Courts-Martial	Military Commission Order No. 1 (M.C.O.)	Military Commissions Act of 2005 H.R. 3044	Guantanamo Detainees Procedures Act of 2005 H.R. 3038	Unprivileged Combatant Act of 2006 S. 3614
			United States." Proposed 10 U.S.C. § 935a(i)(12).		
Prohibition against Ex Post Facto Laws or Punishments	Courts-martial will not enforce an ex post facto law, including increasing amount of pay to be forfeited for specific crimes. U.S. v. Gorki, 47 M.J. 370 (1997).	Not provided, but may be implicit in restrictions on jurisdiction over offenses. *See* § 3(B). M.C.I. No. 2 § 3(A) provides that "no offense is cognizable in a trial by military commission if that offense did not exist prior to the conduct in question."	Not expressly provided, but may be implicit in jurisdictional limitation to "offenses against the law of war or any offense defined in United States law when such offense is committed in furtherance of international terrorism."	Procedural rules are to prohibit conviction for an alleged offense not based upon an act, offense, or omission that was not an offense under law when it was committed, and to provide that the penalty for an offense not be greater than it was when the offense was committed. § 6(a)(12-13).	Not provided.
Protection against Double Jeopardy	Double jeopardy clause applies. *See* Wade v. Hunter, 336 US 684, 688-89 (1949). Art. 44, UCMJ prohibits double jeopardy, provides for jeopardy to attach after introduction of evidence. 10 U.S.C. § 844. General court-martial proceeding is considered to be a federal trial for double jeopardy purposes. Double jeopardy does not result from charges brought in state or foreign courts, although court-martial in such cases is disfavored. U. S. v. Stokes, 12 M.J. 229 (C.M.A. 1982). Once military	The accused may not be tried again by any Commission for a charge once a Commission's finding becomes final. (Jeopardy appears to attach when the finding becomes final, at least with respect to subsequent U.S. military commissions.) § 5(P). However, although a finding of Not Guilty by the Commission may not be changed to Guilty, either the reviewing panel, the Appointing Authority, the Secretary of Defense, or the President may return the	Procedural rules are required to prohibit the trial of an accused "a second time for the same offense," presumably including cases where the accused has been tried for the offense in another jurisdiction, although it could be read to prohibit only second trials by military commission. Proposed 10 U.S.C. § 935a(i)(13). The Secretary of Defense does not have the	Not expressly provided. The Secretary of Defense is not required to review verdicts of not guilty. § 6(e).	Not expressly provided. It appears that an innocent verdict may be appealed by the government. § 5.

	General Courts-Martial	Military Commission Order No. 1 (M.C.O.)	Military Commissions Act of 2005 H.R. 3044	Guantanamo Detainees Procedures Act of 2005 H.R. 3038	Unprivileged Combatant Act of 2006 S. 3614
	authorities have turned service member over to civil authorities for trial, military may have waived jurisdiction for that crime, although it may be possible to charge the individual for another crime arising from the same conduct. *See* 54 AM. JUR. 2D, Military and Civil Defense §§ 227- 28. The government may only appeal orders or rulings that do not amount to a finding of not guilty. 10 U.S.C. § 862. The judge advocate only reviews cases in which there has been a finding of guilty. 10 U.S.C. § 864.	case for "further proceedings" prior to the findings' becoming final. If a finding of Not Guilty is vacated and retried, double jeopardy may be implicated. The order does not specify whether a person already tried by any other court or tribunal may be tried by a military commission under the M.O. The M.O. reserves for the President the authority to direct the Secretary of Defense to transfer an individual subject to the M.O. to another governmental authority, which is not precluded by the order from prosecuting the individual. This subsection could be read to authorize prosecution by federal authorities after the individual was subject to trial by military commission. M.O. § 7(e).	discretion to disapprove a finding of "not guilty," and consequently, such verdicts would not be subject to appellate review. Proposed 10 U.S.C. § 935a(k).		
Speedy & Public Trial	In general, accused must be brought to trial within 120 days of the preferral of charges or the imposition of restraint, whichever date is earliest. R.C.M. 707(a). Charges must be referred	The Commission is required to proceed expeditiously, "preventing any unnecessary interference or delay." § 6(B)(2). Failure to meet a specified deadline does not	The presiding officer would be responsible for ensuring an expeditious trial. Proposed 10 U.S.C. § 935a(d). Procedural rules are required to	Procedural rules would be required to provide that the proceeding and disposition be expeditious. § 6(a)(9).Procedural rules are required to provide	Once commission proceedings begin, the presiding officer is responsible for ensuring an expeditious trial, ensuring that accomodation of counsel

	General Courts-Martial	Military Commission Order No. 1 (M.C.O.)	Military Commissions Act of 2005 H.R. 3044	Guantanamo Detainees Procedures Act of 2005 H.R. 3038	Unprivileged Combatant Act of 2006 S. 3614
	within eight days of arrest or confinement, unless it is not practicable to do so. 10 U.S.C. § 835. The right to a public trial applies in courts-martial but is not absolute. R.C.M. 806. The military trial judge may exclude the public from portions of a proceeding for the purpose of protecting classified information if the prosecution demonstrates an overriding need to do so and the closure is no broader than necessary. United States v. Grunden, 2 M.J. 116 (CMA 1977).	create a right to relief. § 10. The rules do not prohibit detention without charge, or require charges to be brought within a specific time period. Proceedings "should be open to the maximum extent possible," but the Appointing Authority has broad discretion to close hearings, and may exclude the public or accredited press from open proceedings.§ 6(B)(3).	provide for the right to a public trial, "unless the appointing authority or presiding officer determines that a closed trial, or any portion thereof, is necessary to the national security of the United States." Proposed 10 U.S.C. § 935a(i)(4).	a preliminary proceeding within 30 days of detention. § 6(a)(18). Rules must also provide that the trial be open and public, including public availability of the transcripts of the trial and the pronouncement of judgment, consistent with the need to protect participants and the need to protect sensitive government information, the publication of which is certified to pose a risk of identifiable harm to the prosecution of military objectives; significant, identifiable harm to intelligence sources or methods; or substantial risk that such evidence could be used for planning future terrorist attacks.§ 6(a)(16); § 6(c-d).	is never permitted to delay proceedings. § 6(a)(1)(E)(III). Commissions are to be open to the public unless the government requests a closed hearing to avoid disclosure of classified information. § 12(c). The presiding officer has the authority to close hearings for any reason necessary for the conduct of a full and fair trial. § 6(a)(1)(E)(I).
Burden & Standard of Proof	Members of court martial must be instructed that the burden of proof to establish guilt is upon the government and that any reasonable doubt must be resolved in favor of	Commission members may vote for a finding of guilty only if convinced beyond a reasonable doubt, based on evidence admitted at trial, that the accused is guilty.	Procedural rules must provide that "the burden of proof shall be upon the prosecution to prove each element of an offense beyond a	Procedural rules must provide that the accused be "presumed innocent until proven guilty," and "not be found guilty except	A guilty verdict must be supported by a finding of guilt beyond a reasonable doubt by all three members of the commission. § 13(a)(1).

	General Courts-Martial	Military Commission Order No. 1 (M.C.O.)	Military Commissions Act of 2005 H.R. 3044	Guantanamo Detainees Procedures Act of 2005 H.R. 3038	Unprivileged Combatant Act of 2006 S. 3614
	the defendant. R.C.M. 920(e).	§§ 5(C); 6(F). The burden of proof of guilt is on the prosecution, § 5(C); however, M.C.I. No. 2 states that element of wrongfulness of an offense is to be inferred absent evidence to the contrary. M.C.I. No. 2 § 4(B).	reasonable doubt." Proposed 10 U.S.C. § 935a(i)(2).	upon proof beyond a reasonable doubt." § 6(a)(14). Under the rules, the tribunal would be required to apply "reasonable rules of evidence designed to ensure admission only of reliable information or material with probative value." § 6(a)(10).	
Privilege Against Self-Incrimination	No person subject to the UCMJ may compel any person to answer incriminating questions. 10 U.S.C. § 831(a). Defendant may not be compelled to give testimony that is immaterial or potentially degrading. 10 U.S.C. § 831(c). No adverse inference is to be drawn from a defendant's refusal to answer any questions or testify at courtmartial. Mil. R. Evid. 301(f). Witnesses may not be compelled to give testimony that may be incriminating unless granted immunity for that testimony by a general court-martial convening authority, as authorized by the Attorney General, if required.18 U.S.C. § 6002; R.C.M. 704.	The accused is not required to testify, and the commission may draw no adverse inference from a refusal to testify. § 5(F). However, there is no rule against the use of coerced statements as evidence. There is no specific provision for immunity of witnesses to prevent their testimony from being used against them in any subsequent legal proceeding, however, under 18 U.S.C. §§ 6001 *et seq.*, a witness required by a military tribunal to give incriminating testimony is immune from prosecution in any criminal case, other than for perjury, giving false statements, or	Procedural rules must provide that the accused may not be compelled to testify or present evidence against himself, that no adverse inference will be drawn against him for declining to testify. Proposed 10 U.S.C. § 935a(i)(5-7). Presumably, art. 31 UCMJ would also apply, insofar as it prohibits service members from compelling testimony, but not as to its exclusionary rule. 10 U.S.C. § 831. Immunity for witnesses would presumably be provided for in 18	Procedural rules must provide that the accused "not be compelled to confess guilt or testify against himself." § 6(a)(15). There is no express requirement for a rule prohibiting adverse inferences against an accused for not testifying. Presumably, art. 31 UCMJ would also apply, insofar as it prohibits service members from compelling testimony, but not as to its exclusionary rule. 10 U.S.C. § 831. Immunity for witnesses would presumably be provided for in 18	Not provided.

	General Courts-Martial	Military Commission Order No. 1 (M.C.O.)	Military Commissions Act of 2005 H.R. 3044	Guantanamo Detainees Procedures Act of 2005 H.R. 3038	Unprivileged Combatant Act of 2006 S. 3614
		otherwise failing to comply with the order. 18 U.S.C. §§6002; 6004.	U.S.C. §§ 6001 *et seq.*	U.S.C. §§ 6001 *et seq.*	
Right to Examine or Have Examined Adverse Witnesses	Hearsay rules apply as in federal court. Mil. R. Evid. 801 *et seq*. A duly authenticated deposition, or video or audio-taped testimony, may be used in lieu of a live witness only if the witness is beyond 100 miles from the place or trial, the witness is unavailable due to death, health reasons, military necessity, nonamenability to process, or other reasonable cause, or the whereabouts of the witness is unknown. In capital cases, sworn depositions may not be used in lieu of witness, unless court-martial is treated as non-capital or it is introduced by the defense. 10 U.S.C. § 849. The military judge may allow the government to use a summary of classified information, unless the use of the classified information itself is necessary to afford the accused a fair trial. Mil. R. Evid. 505.	Defense Counsel may crossexamine the Prosecution's witnesses who appear before the Commission. § 5(I). However, the Commission may also permit witnesses to testify by telephone or other means not requiring the presence of the witness at trial, in which case crossexamination may be impossible. § 6(D)(2). In the case of closed proceedings or classified evidence, only the detailed defense counsel may be permitted to participate. Hearsay evidence is admissible as long as the Commission determines it would have probative value to a reasonable person. § 6(D)(1). The Commission may consider testimony from prior trials as well as sworn and unsworn written statements, apparently without regard to the availability of the declarant, in apparent contradiction with 10 U.S.C. § 849. §	Procedural rules are required to provide the accused the right to present evidence and to cross-examine each witness and to have access to all evidence that trial counsel intends to offer at trial. Proposed 10 U.S.C. § 935a(i)(9-11). There is no express provision for the use of evidence where a witness is unavailable (hearsay), however, UCMJ art. 49 expressly applies to military commissions as it does for general courts-martial. 10 U.S.C. § 849. There is no provision for preventing access to classified evidence to be used against the accused, although the accused may be prohibited from attending classified proceedings. Proposed 10 U.S.C. §935a(i)(12).	Procedural rules are required to provide the accused access to all of the evidence supporting each alleged offense be given to the accused, unless such information is certified by the head of the appropriate agency to pose a risk of identifiable harm to the prosecution of military objectives; significant, identifiable harm to intelligence sources or methods; or substantial risk that such evidence could be used for planning future terrorist attacks. § 6(a)(4); § 6(b-c). Rules must also provide the accused the opportunity to respond to the evidence supporting each alleged offense; to obtain exculpatory evidence from the prosecution; and to present exculpatory evidence. § 6(a)(7). Rules must further provide the	The prosecution is required to provide the defense counsel with access to evidence it intends to introduce at trial as well as exculpatory evidence that is or should be known to the government. § 12(b).

	General Courts-Martial	Military Commission Order No. 1 (M.C.O.)	Military Commissions Act of 2005 H.R. 3044	Guantanamo Detainees Procedures Act of 2005 H.R. 3038	Unprivileged Combatant Act of 2006 S. 3614
		6(D)(3).		accused the opportunity to confront and cross-examine adverse witnesses and to offer witnesses. § 6(a)(8). There is no express provision for the use of evidence where a witness is unavailable (hearsay), but such evidence might qualify as admissible under the "reasonable rules of evidence designed to ensure admission only of reliable information or material with probative value." § 6(a)(10).	
Right to Compulsory Process to Obtain Witnesses	Defendants before courtmartial have the right to compel appearance of witnesses necessary to their defense. R.C.M. 703. Process to compel witnesses in court-martial cases is to be similar to the process used in federal courts.10 U.S.C. § 846.	The accused may obtain witnesses and documents "to the extent necessary and reasonably available as determined by the Presiding Officer." § 5(H). The Commission has the power to summon witnesses as requested by the Defense. § 6(A)(5). The power to issue subpoenas is exercised by the Chief Prosecutor; the Chief Defense Counsel has no such authority. M.C.I. Nos. 3-4.	Procedural rules are required to provide the accused the equal opportunity to obtain witnesses and other evidence. Proposed 10 U.S.C. § 935a(i)(10). The authority of military commissions to subpoena witnesses not subject to the UCMJ is not clearly stated in the UCMJ, but those witnesses who are "duly subpoenaed" and refuse	Rules must provide the accused the opportunity to offer witnesses, but it is unclear whether there is any authority to compel witnesses to appear. § 6(a)(8).	The prosecution is required to provide the defense counsel with access to exculpatory evidence that is or should be known to the government. § 12(b).

	General Courts-Martial	Military Commission Order No. 1 (M.C.O.)	Military Commissions Act of 2005 H.R. 3044	Guantanamo Detainees Procedures Act of 2005 H.R. 3038	Unprivileged Combatant Act of 2006 S. 3614
			to appear or testified are subject to trial in federal court. 10 U.S.C. § 847.		
Right to Trial by Impartial Judge	A qualified military judge is detailed to preside over the court-martial. The convening authority may not prepare or review any report concerning the performance or effectiveness of the military judge. 10 U.S.C. § 826. Article 37, UCMJ, prohibits unlawful influence of courtsmartial through admonishment, censure, or reprimand of its members by the convening authority or commanding officer, or any unlawful attempt by a person subject to the UCMJ to coerce or influence the action of a court-martial or convening authority. 10 U.S.C. § 837. Military defendants have the opportunity to challenge the military judge for cause. 10 U.S.C. § 41.	The presiding officer is appointed directly by the Appointing Authority, which decides all interlocutory issues. There do not appear to be any special procedural safeguards to ensure impartiality, but challenges for cause have been permitted. § 4(A)(4). The presiding judge, who decides issues of admissibility of evidence, also votes as part of the commission on the finding of guilt or innocence. Article 37, UCMJ, provides that no person subject to the UCMJ "may attempt to coerce or, by any unauthorized means, influence the action of a court-martial *or any other military tribunal* or any member thereof, in reaching the findings or sentence in any case, or the action of any convening, approving, or reviewing authority with respect to his	Not expressly provided. Article 37, UCMJ, prohibits any unlawful attempt by a person subject to the UCMJ to coerce or influence the action of any military tribunal. 10 U.S.C. § 837.	Procedural rules must require that the tribunal be "independent and impartial." § 6(a)(1).	The Secretary of Defense appoints military judges to serve on panels and to carry out other duties under the Act, presumably including serving on status determination tribunals. § 6(a)(1)(A). Article 37, UCMJ, which prohibits any unlawful attempt by a person subject to the UCMJ to coerce or influence the action of any military tribunal, would presumably apply. 10 U.S.C. § 837.

	General Courts-Martial	Military Commission Order No. 1 (M.C.O.)	Military Commissions Act of 2005 H.R. 3044	Guantanamo Detainees Procedures Act of 2005 H.R. 3038	Unprivileged Combatant Act of 2006 S. 3614
		judicial acts." 10 U.S.C. § 837. M.C.I. No. 9 clarifies that Art. 37 applies with respect to members of the review panel. M.C.I. No. 9 § 4(F).			
Right to Trial By Impartial Jury	A military accused has no Sixth Amendment right to a trial by petit jury. *Ex Parte* Quirin, 317 U.S. 1, 39-40 (1942) (*dicta*). However, "Congress has provided for trial by members at a court-martial." United States v. Witham, 47 MJ 297, 301 (1997); 10 U.S.C. § 825. The Sixth Amendment requirement that the jury be impartial applies to courtmartial members and covers not only the selection of individual jurors, but also their conduct during the trial proceedings and the subsequent deliberations. United States v. Lambert, 55 M.J. 293 (2001). Military defendants have the opportunity to exercise peremptory challenge and challenge panel members for cause. 10 U.S.C. § 41. The military judge does not take part in the deliberations of the panel, and cannot preside over cases in which he has taken	Military tribunals probably do not require a jury trial.. *See Ex Parte* Quirin, 317 U.S. 1, 39-40 (1942) (*dicta*). The commission members are appointed directly by the Appointing Authority. While the Commission is bound to proceed impartially, there do not appear to be any special procedural safeguards designed to ensure their impartiality. However, defendants have successfully challenged members for cause. § 6(B).	Military commissions are to have three to seven commissioned officers to serve as members, but safeguards concerning their impartiality are not expressly addressed. Proposed 10 U.S.C. § 935a(c).	Procedural rules must require that the tribunal be "independent and impartial." § 6(a)(1).	Each commission is to have three military officers, with a military judge serving as presiding officer, as well as one or two alternate members. § 6. The role of non-presiding panel members is not set forth in detail, nor are safeguards to address impartiality.

	General Courts-Martial	Military Commission Order No. 1 (M.C.O.)	Military Commissions Act of 2005 H.R. 3044	Guantanamo Detainees Procedures Act of 2005 H.R. 3038	Unprivileged Combatant Act of 2006 S. 3614
	part in any investigation or acted as accuser or counsel. 10 U.S.C. § 26. The absence of a right to trial by jury precludes criminal trial of civilians by courtmartial. Reid v. Covert, 354 U.S. 1 (1957); Kinsella v. United States *ex rel.* Singleton, 361 U.S. 234 (1960).				
Right to Appeal to Independent Reviewing Authority	The appropriate Court of Criminal Appeals for the military service involved automatically reviews all convictions that result in sentences of sufficient severity, unless the defendant waives such review. 10 U.S.C. § 622 The defendant may seek discretionary review by the Court of Appeals for the Armed Forces (CAAF), 10 U.S.C. § 867, and, upon losing an appeal on the merits at the CAAF, may seek review from the Supreme Court on a writ of certiorari. 28 U.S.C. § 1259. The writ of habeas corpus provides the primary means by which those sentenced by military court, having exhausted military appeals, can challenge a conviction or sentence in a civilian court. The scope of	A review panel appointed by the Secretary of Defense reviews the record of the trial in a closed conference, disregarding any procedural variances that would not materially affect the outcome of the trial, and recommends its disposition to the Secretary of Defense. Although the Defense Counsel has the duty of representing the interests of the accused during any review process, the review panel need not consider written submissions from the Defense, nor does there appear to be an opportunity to rebut the submissions of the prosecution. If the majority of the review panel forms a "definite and firm conviction that a material error of law	A person found guilty by military commission and sentenced to death or imprisonment for more than five years would have a right to a review of that finding and sentence, with respect to issues of law, by the CAAF, and may appeal an adverse ruling there to the Supreme Court on a writ of certiorari. Proposed 10 U.S.C.§ 935a(k).	The procedural rules must, "at a minimum, allow for review of the proceedings of the tribunals, and the convictions and sentences of such tribunals, by the [CAAF]." The Supreme Court would have jurisdiction to grant certiorari in such cases. § 6(e)(2-3). The bill would not explicitly alter the jurisdiction of the CAAF. 10 U.S.C. § 867. The procedural rules must provide that the right to habeas corpus may not be infringed. § 6(e)(19).	The U.S. Court of Military Appeals would have jurisdiction to hear appeals of final decisions, with Supreme Court review available by certiorari. § 5. (What was formerly called the U.S. Court of Military Appeals is now known as the Court of Appeals for the Armed Forces).

	General Courts-Martial	Military Commission Order No. 1 (M.C.O.)	Military Commissions Act of 2005 H.R. 3044	Guantanamo Detainees Procedures Act of 2005 H.R. 3038	Unprivileged Combatant Act of 2006 S. 3614
	matters that a court will address is more narrow than in challenges of federal or state convictions. Burns v. Wilson, 346 U.S. 137 (1953).	occurred," it may return the case to the Appointing Authority for further proceedings. § 6(H)(4). The review panel recommendation does not appear to be binding. The Secretary of Defense may serve as Appointing Authority and as the final reviewing authority, as designated by the President. Although the M.O specifies that the individual is not privileged to seek any remedy in any U.S. court or state court, the court of any foreign nation, or any international tribunal, M.O. § 7(b), Congress established jurisdiction in the Court of Appeals for the D.C. Circuit to hear challenges to final decisions of military commissions. Detainee Treatment Act of 2005.			
Protection against Excessive Penalties	Death may only be adjudged for certain crimes where the defendant is found guilty by unanimous vote of courtmartial members present at the time of the vote. Prior to arraignment, the trial counsel must give the defense written	The death sentence may be imposed only on the unanimous vote of a sevenmember panel. § 6(F). The commission may only impose a sentence that is appropriate to the offense for which there was a	Three quarters of members present for deliberation must concur in order to issue a finding of guilty, except in the case the death penalty, in which case the concurrence of	The UCMJ requirements for the imposition of the death penalty apply in any case in which a tribunal is requested to adjudge the death penalty. § 6(b).	Not addressed.

	General Courts-Martial	Military Commission Order No. 1 (M.C.O.)	Military Commissions Act of 2005 H.R. 3044	Guantanamo Detainees Procedures Act of 2005 H.R. 3038	Unprivileged Combatant Act of 2006 S. 3614
	notice of aggravating factors the prosecution intends to prove. R.C.M. 1004. A conviction of spying during time of war under article 106, UCMJ, carries a mandatory death penalty. 10 U.S.C. § 906. Cruel and unusual punishment, including flogging, or branding or otherwise branding the body is prohibited against persons subject to the UCMJ. 10 U.S.C. § 855. The convicted person may appeal a sentence, and the sentence may be mitigated or commuted, but not increased, by the judge advocate reviewing the case. 10 U.S.C. §§ 864, 866, 867.	finding of guilty, including death, imprisonment, fine or restitution, or "other such lawful punishment or condition of punishment as the commission shall determine to be proper." § 6(G). If the Secretary of Defense has the authority to conduct the final review of a conviction and sentence, he may mitigate, commute, defer, or suspend, but not increase, the sentence. However, he may disapprove the findings and return them for further action by the military commission. § 6(H).	all seven members present is required. Proposed 10 U.S.C. § 935a(c). The death sentence would be available only if the accused has been found guilty of spying or an offense causing the death of one or more persons, where such offense was committed after the accused attained the age of eighteen years. A sentence of death would require approval by the President. Proposed 10 U.S.C. § 935a(h).		

Source: Congressional Research Service.

REFERENCES

[1] Rasul v. Bush, 124 S. Ct. 2686 (2004). For a summary of Rasul and related cases, see CRS Report RS21884, The Supreme Court and Detainees in the War on Terrorism: Summary and Analysis of Recent Decisions; CRS Report RS22466, Hamdan v. Rumsfeld: Military Commissions in the 'Global War on Terrorism,' by Jennifer K. Elsea.

[2] Detention, Treatment, and Trial of Certain Non-Citizens in the War Against Terrorism §1(a), 66 Fed. Reg. 57,833 (Nov. 16, 2001) (hereinafter "M.O.").

[3] P.L. 109-148, §1005(e)(1) amends 28 U.S.C. § 2441 to provide that "no court ... shall have jurisdiction to hear or consider ... an application for ... habeas corpus filed by ... an alien detained ... at Guantanamo Bay." However, it creates new, albeit limited, jurisdiction in the D.C. Cir. to hear challenges of "any final decision of a Combatant Status Review Tribunal that an alien is properly detained as an enemy combatant" as well as reviews of "final decisions of military commissions," which are discretionary unless the sentence is greater than ten years or involves the death penalty. DTA § 1005(e)(2-3).

[4] Hamdan v. Rumsfeld, 548 U.S. __ (2006), rev'g 415 F.3d 33 (D.C. Cir. 2005). The Court found that the DTA does not apply to Hamdan's petition, which was an appeal of an interlocutory ruling rather than the final decision of a military commission, but did not resolve whether it affects other pending cases that fall under the DTA's provisions regarding final review of Combatant Status Review Tribunals. Slip op. at 19, and n.14.

[5] 10 U.S.C. § 801 et seq.

[6] See CRS Report RL31191, Terrorism and the Law of War: Trying Terrorists as War Criminals before Military Commissions (providing a general background of U.S. history of military commissions), by Jennifer Elsea.

[7] See 10 U.S.C. § 818; 18 U.S.C. §2441.

[8] See U.S. Army Field Manual (FM) 27-10, The Law of Land Warfare, section 505(e) [hereinafter "FM 27-10"].

[9] See WILLIAM WINTHROP, MILITARY LAW AND PRECEDENTS 841-42 (2d ed. 1920)(noting that "in the absence of any statute or regulation," the same principles and procedures commonly govern, though possibly more "liberally construed and applied"); David Glazier, Note, Kangaroo Court or Competent Tribunal?: Judging the 21st Century Military Commission, 89 VA. L. REV. 2005 (2003).

[10] See Letter from Timothy H. Edgar, ACLU Legislative Counsel, Military Commission Order No. 1, March 21, 2002 (April 16, 2002), available at [http://www.aclu.org/National Security/NationalSecurity.cfm?ID=10150 and c=111] (last visited July 21, 2006); American College of Trial Lawyers, Report on Military Commissions for the Trial of Terrorists, March 2003 [hereinafter "ACTL"], available at [http://www.actl.com/AM/Template.cfm ?Section=All_Publications and Template=/CM/ContentDisplay.cfm and ContentFileID=63] (last visited July 21, 2006); ACTL, Supplemental Report on Military Commissions for the Trial of Terrorists, Oct. 2005, online at [http://www.actl.com/AM/Template.cfm?Section=Home and template=/CM/ContentDisplay.cfm and ContentID=2152] (last visited July 21, 2006).

[11] The president of the National Association of Criminal Defense Lawyers (NACDL) announced that NACDL "cannot advise its members to act as civilian counsel" because it deems the rules too restrictive to allow for zealous and professional representation on their part. See Lawrence Goldman, Guantanamo: Little Hope for Zealous Advocacy, NACDL CHAMPION, July 2003, at 4, available at [http://www.nacdl.org/public.nsf/ Champion Articles/A0307p04?OpenDocument] (last visited July 21, 2006).

[12] The Administration has not explicitly used this authority; instead, it says the prisoners are being held as "enemy combatants" pursuant to the law of war.

[13] See Bruce Zagaris, U.S. Defense Department Issues Order on Military Commissions, 18 No. 5 INT'L ENFORCEMENT L. REP 215 (2002) (citing comments by DoD chief counsel William J. Haynes II to a New York Times reporter).

[14] See Neil A. Lewis, Two Prosecutors Faulted Trials For Detainees, NEW YORK TIMES, August 1, 2005, at A1.

[15] Department of Defense ("DoD") documents related to military commissions are available online at [http://www.defenselink.mil/news/commissions.html] (last visited July 24, 2006).

[16] Reprinted at 41 I.L.M. 725 (2002). The most recent version was issued Aug. 31, 2005.

[17] See Press Release, Department of Defense, Secretary Rumsfeld Approves Changes to Improve Military Commission Procedures (Aug. 31, 2005), available at [http://www.defenselink.mil/releases/2005/nr20050831-4608.html] (last visited July 21, 2006).

[18] See Press Release, Department of Defense, President Determines Enemy Combatants Subject to His Military Order (July 3, 2003), available at [http://www.defenselink.mil/ releases/2003/nr20030703-0173.html] (last visited July 21, 2006). According to the Defense Department, that determination is effectively "a grant of [military] jurisdiction over the person." See John Mintz, 6 Could Be Facing Military Tribunals, WASH. POST, July 4, 2003, at A1. In 2004, nine additional detainees were determined to be eligible. See Press Release, Department of Defense, Presidential Military Order Applied to Nine more Combatants (July 7, 2004), available at [http://www.defenselink.mil/releases/ 2004/nr20040707-0987.html] (last visited July 21, 2006). In November 2005, five more detainees were charged. See Press Release, Department of Defense, Military Commission Charges Approved (November 7, 2005), available at [http://www.defenselink.mil/releases/2005/nr20051107-5078.html] (last visited July 21, 2006).

[19] See John Mintz and Glenn Frankel, 2 Britons, Australian Among Six Facing Trial, WASH. POST, July 5, 2003, at A13.

[20] See Press Releases, Department of Defense, Statement on British Detainee Meetings and Statement on Australian Detainee Meetings (July 23, 2003), available at [http://www.defenselink.mil/news/Aug2004/ commissions_releases.html] (last visited July 21, 2006).

[21] See Press Release, Department of Defense, U.S. and Australia Announce Agreements on Guantanamo Detainees (Nov. 25, 2003), available at [http://www.defenselink.mil/ releases/2003/nr20031125-0702.html] (last visited July 21, 2006).

[22] See Ed Johnson, British Guantanamo Detainees to Be Freed, AP, Jan. 11, 2005.

[23] See Press Release, Department of Defense, Guantanamo Detainee Charged (June 10, 2004), available at [http://www.defenselink.mil/releases/2004/nr20040610-0893.html]

(last visited July 21, 2006). Justice Stevens found for a plurality in the Hamdan case that "conspiracy" is not an "offense triable by military commission" within the meaning of the UCMJ.

[24] Press Release, Department of Defense, Two Guantanamo Detainees Charged (Feb. 24, 2004), available at [http://www.defenselink.mil/releases/2004/nr20040224-0363.html] (last visited July 21, 2006). The two defendants are charged with "willfully and knowingly joining an enterprise of persons who shared a common criminal purpose and conspired with Osama bin Laden and others to commit the following offenses: attacking civilians; attacking civilian objects; murder by an unprivileged belligerent; destruction of property by an unprivileged belligerent; and terrorism." One of the detainees filed for a writ of prohibition and writ of mandamus with the U.S. Court of Appeals for the Armed Forces (CAAF) in an effort to halt the military commission proceedings, but the CAAF dismissed the petition without prejudice in January, 2005. Al Qosi v. Altenburg, 60 M.J. 461(2005).

[25] Press Release, Department of Defense, Additional Military Commission Charges Referred (July 14, 2004), available at [http://www.defenselink.mil/releases/2004/nr20040714-1030.html] (last visited July 21, 2006).

[26] 344 F.Supp.2d 152 (D. D.C. 2004), rev'd 415 F.3d 33 (D.C. Cir. 2005), cert. granted 2005 U.S. LEXIS 8222 (Nov. 7, 2005).

[27] 10 U.S.C. §§ 801 et seq.

[28] There are four Conventions, the most relevant of which is The Geneva Convention Relative to the Treatment of Prisoners of War, August 12, 1949, 6 U.S.T. 3317 (hereinafter "GPW").

[29] 344 F.Supp.2d at 161.

[30] GPW art. 102.

[31] 344 F.Supp.2d at 158-59.

[32] 10 U.S.C. § 836 (procedures for military commissions may not be "contrary to or inconsistent with" the UCMJ).

[33] 344 F.Supp.2d at 166.

[34] See Brief for Appellants, Hamdan v. Rumsfeld, No. 04-5393 (D.C. Cir.).

[35] Rumsfeld v. Hamdan, 415 F.3d 33, 39-40 (D.C. Cir. July 15, 2005).

[36] Id. at 19.

[37] Authorization for Use of Military Force ("the AUMF"), P.L. 107-40, 115 Stat. 224 (2001).

[38] Hamdan, 415 F.3d at 37.

[39] Johnson v. Eisentrager, 339 U.S. 763 (1950) (holding that the federal courts did not have jurisdiction to hear a petition on behalf of German citizens who had been convicted by U.S. military commissions in China because the writ of habeas corpus was not available to "enemy alien[s], who at no relevant time and in no stage of [their] captivity [have] been within [the court's] jurisdiction"). The Supreme Court, in Rasul v. Bush, declined to apply Eisentrager to deny Guantánamo detainees the right to petition for habeas corpus. See Rasul at 2698 (finding authority for federal court jurisdiction in 28 U.S.C. § 2241, which grants courts the authority to hear applications for habeas corpus "within their respective jurisdictions," by any person who claims to be held "in custody in violation of the Constitution or laws or treaties of the United States").

[40] 339 U.S. at 789 n.14.

[41] P.L. 109-148, §1005(e)(1) provides that "no court ... shall have jurisdiction to hear or consider ... an application for ... habeas corpus filed by ... an alien detained ... at Guantanamo Bay." The provision was not yet law when the appellate court decided against the petitioner, Hamdan v. Rumsfeld, 415 F.3d 33 (D.C. Cir. 2005), rev'd 548 U.S. __ (2006). At issue was whether this provision applies to pending cases. The Court found that the provision does not apply to Hamdan's petition, but did not resolve whether it affects other cases that fall under the DTA's provisions regarding final review of Combatant Status Review Tribunals. Slip op. at 19, and n.14.

[42] Id. at 7. To resolve the question, the majority employed canons of statutory interpretation supplemented by legislative history, avoiding the question of whether the withdrawal of the Court's jurisdiction would constitute a suspension of the Writ of Habeas Corpus, or whether it would amount to impermissible "court-stripping." Justice Scalia, joined by Justices Alito and Thomas in his dissent, interpreted the DTA as a revocation of jurisdiction.

[43] 10 U.S.C. § 821 ("The provisions of [the UCMJ] conferring jurisdiction upon courts-martial do not deprive military commissions, provost courts, or other military tribunals of concurrent jurisdiction with respect to offenders or offenses that by statute or by the law of war may be tried by military commissions, provost courts, or other military tribunals."). The Hamdan majority concluded that "compliance with the law of war is the condition upon which the authority set forth in Article 21 is granted." Hamdan, slip op. at 63.

[44] Hamdan, slip op. at 63-65.

[45] GPW art. 3 § 1(d). The identical provision is included in each of the four Geneva Conventions and applies to any "conflict not of an international character." The majority declined to accept the President's interpretation of Common Article 3 as inapplicable to the conflict with al Qaeda and interpreted the phrase "in contradistinction to a conflict between nations," which the Geneva Conventions designate a "conflict of international character." Hamdan, slip op. at 67.

[46] Id. at 70 (plurality opinion); Id. (Kennedy, J., concurring) at 10. Justice Stevens, joined by Justices Ginsburg, Breyer, and Souter, further based their conclusion on the basis that M.C.O. No. 1 did not meet all criteria of art. 75 of Protocol I to the Geneva Conventions of 1949, adopted in 1977 (Protocol I). While the United States is not party to Protocol I, the plurality noted that many authorities regard it as customary international law.

[47] Hamdan, slip op. at 27 (citing Congress's powers to "declare War ... and make Rules concerning Captures on Land and Water," Art. I, §8, cl. 11, to "raise and support Armies," id., cl. 12, to "define and punish ... Offences against the Law of Nations," id., cl. 10, and "To make Rules for the Government and Regulation of the land and naval Forces," id., cl. 14.).

[48] P.L. 107-40, 115 Stat. 224 (2001).

[49] Hamdan, slip op. at 30.

[50] The government took the position that the "contrary to or consistent with" language applies only with respect to parts of the UCMJ that make specific reference to military commissions.

[51] The term "military tribunal" in the UCMJ should be interpreted to cover all forms of military courts, encompassing courts-martial as well as military commissions.

[52] Hamdan, slip op. at 59.

[53] Id at 61. Regarding the defendant's right to be present during trial, the Court stated, "[w]hether or not that departure technically is 'contrary to or inconsistent with' the terms of the UCMJ, 10 U. S. C. §836(a), the jettisoning of so basic a right cannot lightly be excused as 'practicable.'"

[54] M.C.I. No. 1 at § 4.C.

[55] M.C.I. No. 1 lists 10 U.S.C. § 898 as a reference. That law, Article 98, UCMJ, Noncompliance with procedural rules, provides: Any person subject to this chapter who - (1) is responsible for unnecessary delay in the disposition of any case of a person accused of an offense under this chapter; or (2) knowingly and intentionally fails to enforce or comply with any provision of this chapter regulating the proceedings before, during, or after trial of an accused; shall be punished as a court-martial may direct

[56] P.L. 107-40, 115 Stat. 224 (2001) (authorizing military force against those who "planned, authorized, committed, [or] aided" the Sept. 11 attacks or who "harbored such ... persons").

[57] M.O. § 1(e) (finding such tribunals necessary to protect the United States and for effective conduct of military operations).

[58] 10 U.S.C. § 821.

[59] 10 U.S.C. §§ 904 and 906, respectively. The circumstances under which civilians accused of aiding the enemy may be tried by military tribunal have not been decided, but a court interpreting the article may limit its application to conduct committed in territory under martial law or military government, within a zone of military operations or area of invasion, or within areas subject to military jurisdiction. See FM 27-10, supra note 8, at para. 79(b)(noting that treason and espionage laws are available for incidents occurring outside of these areas, but are triable in civil courts). Spying is not technically a violation of the law of war, however, but violates domestic law and traditionally may be tried by military commission. See id. at para. 77 (explaining that spies are not punished as "violators of the law of war, but to render that method of obtaining information as dangerous, difficult, and ineffective as possible").

[60] See, e.g., United States v. Schultz, 4 C.M.R. 104, 114 (1952)(listing as crimes punishable under the law of war, in occupied territory as murder, manslaughter, robbery, rape, larceny, arson, maiming, assaults, burglary, and forgery).

[61] See WINTHROP, supra note 9, at 836. See NATIONAL INSTITUTE OF MILITARY JUSTICE, ANNOTATED GUIDE: PROCEDURES FOR TRIALS BU MILITARY COMMISSIONS OF CERTAIN NON-UNITED STATES CITIZENS IN THE WAR AGAINST TERRORISM 10-11 (hereinafter "NIMJ")(noting that civilians in occupied Germany after World War II were sometimes tried by military commission for ordinary crimes unrelated to the laws of war). Military trials of civilians for crimes unrelated to the law of war on U.S. territory under martial law are permissible only when the courts are not functioning. See Duncan v. Kahanamoku, 327 U.S. 304 (1945).

[62] See id. (citing Ex parte Milligan, 71 U.S. (4 Wall.) 2 (1866)). Winthrop notes that the limitations as to place, time, and subjects were not always strictly followed, mentioning a Civil War case in which seven persons who had conspired to seize a U.S. merchant vessel at Panama were captured and transported to San Francisco for trial by military commission. Id. at 837 (citing the pre-Milligan case of T.E. Hogg).

[63] Hamdan, slip op. at 33-34.

[64] See Leila Nadya Sadat, Terrorism and the Rule of Law, 3 WASH. U. GLOBAL STUD. L. REV. 135 (2004)(arguing that no armed conflict exists with respect to terrorists, making the law of war inapplicable to them).

[65] The Geneva Convention Relative to the Treatment of Prisoners of War [hereinafter "GPW"] art. 102 states: A prisoner of war can be validly sentenced only if the sentence has been pronounced by the same courts according to the same procedure as in the case of members of the armed forces of the Detaining Power, and if, furthermore, the provisions of the present Chapter have been observed. 6 U.S.T. 3317. The Supreme Court finding to the contrary in In re Yamashita, 327 U.S. 1 (1946), is likely superceded by the 1949 Geneva Convention. For more information about the treatment of prisoners of war, see CRS Report RL31367, Treatment of "Battlefield Detainees" in the War on Terrorism.

[66] GPW art. 3 § 1(d). The identical provision is included in each of the four Geneva Conventions and applies to any "conflict not of an international character." The Hamdan majority declined to accept the President's interpretation of Common Article 3 as inapplicable to the conflict with al Qaeda and interpreted the phrase "in contradistinction to a conflict between nations," which the Geneva Conventions designate a "conflict of international character". Hamdan, slip op. at 67. The Court did not expressly decide whether the Global War on Terror (GWOT) is international or non-international for the purposes of the Geneva Convention, but merely that it is one or the other.

[67] See NATIONAL INSTITUTE OF MILITARY JUSTICE, MILITARY COMMISSION INSTRUCTIONS SOURCEBOOK 95 (2003) [hereinafter "SOURCEBOOK"]. DoD has not made public an exact account of who provided comments to the instruction, but some of them are published in the Sourcebook.

[68] See M.C.I. No. 2 § 3(A) ("No offense is cognizable in a trial by military commission if that offense did not exist prior to the conduct in question.").

[69] Crimes against the law of war listed in M.C.I. No. 2 are: 1) Willful Killing of Protected Persons; 2) Attacking Civilians; 3) Attacking Civilian Objects; 4) Attacking Protected Property; 5) Pillaging; 6) Denying Quarter; 7) Taking Hostages; 8) Employing Poison or Analogous Weapons; 9) Using Protected Persons as Shields; 10) Using Protected Property as Shields; 11) Torture; 12) Causing Serious Injury; 13) Mutilation or Maiming; 14) Use of Treachery or Perfidy; 15) Improper Use of Flag of Truce; 16) Improper Use of Protective Emblems; 17) Degrading Treatment of a Dead Body; and 18) Rape.

[70] Crimes "triable by military commissions" include 1) Hijacking or Hazarding a Vessel or Aircraft; 2) Terrorism; 3) Murder by an Unprivileged Belligerent; 4) Destruction of Property by an Unprivileged Belligerent; 5) Aiding the Enemy; 6) Spying; 7) Perjury or False Testimony; and 8) Obstruction of Justice Related to Military Commissions. Listed as "other forms of liability and related offenses" are: 1) Aiding or Abetting. 2) Solicitation; 3) Command/Superior Responsibility - Perpetrating; 4) Command/Superior Responsibility -Misprision; 5) Accessory After the Fact; 6) Conspiracy; and 7) Attempt.

[71] Ordinarily, the charge of "aiding the enemy" would require the accused have allegiance to the party whose enemy he has aided. DoD added a comment to this charge explaining that the wrongfulness requirement may necessitate that "in the case of a

lawful belligerent, the accused owe allegiance or some duty to the United States or an ally or coalition partner..." such as "citizenship, resident alien status, or a contractual relationship with [any of these countries]." M.C.I. No.2 §6(A)(5)(b)(3). It is unclear what is meant by limiting the requirement to "a lawful belligerent." It could be read to make those persons considered the "enemy" also subject to trial for "aiding the enemy,"as is the case with Australian detainee David Hicks. See United States v. Hicks, Charge Sheet, available online at [http://www.defenselink.mil/news/Jun2004/d20040610cs.pdf] (last visited July 21, 2006).

[72] 18 U.S.C. § 2331 et seq. defines and punishes terrorism, providing exclusive jurisdiction to federal courts. See id. at 35 (letter from National Association of Criminal Defense Lawyers (NACDL) noting that Congress has defined war crimes in 18 U.S.C. § 2441 with reference to specific treaties).

[73] 327 U.S. at 17 ("Obviously charges of violations of the law of war triable before a military tribunal need not be stated with the precision of a common law indictment.").

[74] M.C.I. No. 2 § 6(18). One of the elements of the crime of terrorism is that the "accused did not enjoy combatant immunity or an object of the attack was not a military objective." Another element required that "the killing or destruction was an attack or part of an attack designed to intimidate or coerce a civilian population, to influence the policy of a government by intimidation or coercion, or to affect the conduct of a government." The final version of the M.C.I. omits the reference to "affect[ing] the conduct of a government."

[75] M.C.I. No. 2 § 6(19).

[76] Under M.C.I. No. 2, the lack of combatant immunity is considered an element of some of the crimes rather than a defense, so the prosecutor has the burden of proving its absence.

[77] Whether the prisoners at Guantánamo Bay should be considered lawful combatants with combatant immunity is an issue of some international concern. See generally CRS Report RL31367, Treatment of 'Battlefield Detainees' in the War on Terrorism. DoD's original draft included the requirement that a lawful combatant be part of the "armed forces of a legitimate party to an armed conflict." The Lawyers' Committee for Human Rights (now known as Human Rights First or "HRF") and Human Rights Watch ("HRW") urged DoD to revise the definition in line with the Geneva Convention. See SOURCEBOOK, supra note 67, at 50-51 and 59. The revised version leaves ambiguous who might be a "lawful combatant."

[78] M.C.I. No. 2 § 4(B). The American Civil Liberties Union (ACLU) objected to this provision in its comments on the DoD draft, remarking that it "not only places the ordinary burden on the accused to going forward with evidence that establishes affirmative defense, but it also appears to place an unprecedented burden on the accused to overcome the presumption that the defenses do not apply." See SOURCEBOOK, supra note 67, at 69.

[79] See WINTHROP, supra note 9, at 773 (the law of war "prescribes the rights and obligations of belligerents, or ... define[s] the status and relations not only of enemies — whether or not in arms — but also of persons under military government or martial law and persons simply resident or being upon the theatre of war, and which authorizes their trial and punishment when offenders"); id at 836 (military commissions have valid

jurisdiction only in theater of war or territory under martial law or military government).

[80] It may be argued that no war has a specific deadline and that all conflicts are in a sense indefinite. In traditional armed conflicts, however, it has been relatively easy to identify when hostilities have ended; for example, upon the surrender or annihilation of one party, an annexation of territory under dispute, an armistice or peace treaty, or when one party to the conflict unilaterally withdraws its forces. See GERHARD VON GLAHN, LAW AMONG NATIONS 722-730 (6th ed. 1992).

[81] See Human Rights First, Trial Under Military Order, A Guide to the Final Rules for Military Commissions (revised May 2006)[hereinafter "HRF"], available at [http://www.humanrightsfirst.org/us_law/PDF/detainees/trials_under_order0604.pdf]] (last visited July 21, 2006); Sadat, supra note 64, at 146 (noting possibly advantageous domestic aspects of treating terrorist attacks as war crimes, but identifying possible pitfalls of creating a new international legal regime).

[82] M.C.I. No. 2 § 5(C).

[83] Id.

[84] See SOURCEBOOK, supra note 67, at 38-39 (NACDL comments); id. at 51 (Human Rights Watch (HRW) comments); id. at 59-60 (LCHR). However, M.C.I. No. 9 lists among possible "material errors of law" for which the Reviewing Panel might return a finding for further procedures, "a conviction of a charge that fails to state an offense that by statute or the law of war may be tried by military commission. ..." M.C.I. No. 9 § 4(C)(2)(b).

[85] See id. at 38 (NACDL comments).

[86] See id. at 98 (commentary of Eugene R. Fidell and Michael F. Noone).

[87] M.C.O. No. 1 § 4(A)(3).

[88] See 10 U.S.C. § 603, listed as reference (e) of M.C.O. No. 1.

[89] M.C.O. No. 1 § 4(A)(4). See NIMJ, supra note 61, at 17 (commenting that the lack of a military judge to preside over the proceedings is a significant departure from the UCMJ). A judge advocate is a military officer of the Judge Advocate General's Corps of the Army or Navy (a military lawyer). A military judge is a judge advocate who is certified as qualified by the JAG Corps of his or her service to serve in a role similar to civilian judges.

[90] See M.C.O. No. 1 § 3(C) (asserting jurisdiction over participants in commission proceedings "as necessary to preserve the integrity and order of the proceedings").

[91] See 10 U.S.C. § 848.

[92] See 10 U.S.C. § 847. It is unclear how witnesses are "duly subpoenaed;" 10 U.S.C. § 846 empowers the president of the court-martial to compel witnesses to appear and testify and to compel production of evidence, but this statutory authority does not explicitly apply to military commissions. The subpoena power extends to "any part of the United States, or the Territories, Commonwealth and possessions."

[93] M.C.I. No. 6.

[94] Id. § 3(A)(7).

[95] Cf United States v. Wiesen, 56 M.J. 172 (2001), aff'd on reconsideration, 57 M.J. 48 (2002)(noting that command relationships among participants in court-martial proceeding may give rise to "implied bias").

[96] Hamdan, slip op. at 11-16 (Kennedy, J. concurring).

[97] See 10 U.S.C. § 836 (providing military commission rules "may not be contrary to or inconsistent with [the UCMJ]"). But see In re Yamashita, 327 U.S. 1, 19-20 (1946)(finding Congress did not intend the language "military commission" in Article 38 of the Articles of War, the precursor to UCMJ Art. 36, to mean military commissions trying enemy combatants). On the other hand, President Bush explicitly invoked UCMJ art. 36 as statutory authority for the M.O., and included a finding, "consistent with section 836 of title 10, United States Code, that it is not practicable to apply in military commissions under this order the principles of law and the rules of evidence generally recognized in the trial of criminal cases in the United States district courts." M.O. § 1(g). However, the Supreme Court rejected the finding as unsupported by the record and read the "uniformity" clause of UCMJ art. 36 as requiring that military commissions must follow rules as close as possible to those that apply in courts-martial.

[98] M.C.O. No. 1 § 1.

[99] Id. § 10.

[100] Id.; M.C.I. No. 1 § 6 (Non-Creation of Right).

[101] M.C.O. No. 1 § 5(A).

[102] Id. §§ 5(B-C); 6(F).

[103] Id. §§ 4(A)(5)(a); 5(K); 6B(3).

[104] Id. §§ 5(B) and 6(B).

[105] M.C.O. No. 1 § 6(D)(5).

[106] See DoD Press Release, DoD Announces Media Coverage Opportunities for Military Commissions (Feb. 11, 2004), available at [http://www.defenselink.mil/advisories/2004/ pa20040211-0205.html] (last visited July 24, 2006).

[107] See Toni Locy, Human Rights Groups Denied Seats at Tribunals, USA TODAY, Feb. 24, 2004, at A3.

[108] M.C.O. No. 1 at § 6(B)(3)("Open proceedings may include, at the discretion of the Appointing Authority, attendance by the public and accredited press, and public release of transcripts at the appropriate time."). In courts-martial, "public" is defined to include members of the military as well as civilian communities. R.C.M. 806.

[109] M.C.I. No. 3 § 5(C) (Prosecutor's Office); M.C.I. No. 4 § 5(C) (Defense counsel, including members of civilian defense counsel pool).

[110] See Globe Newspaper Co. v. Super. Ct., 457 U.S. 596, 602 (1982)(newspaper had standing to challenge court order closing portions of criminal trial).

[111] United States v. Hershey, 20 M.J. 433 (C.M.A.1985), cert. denied, 474 U.S. 1062 (1986); United States v. Grunden, 2 M.J. 116 (C.M.A.1977). The press has standing to challenge closure of military justice proceedings. ABC, Inc. v. Powell, 47 M.J. 363, 365 (1997).

[112] See Press-Enterprise Co. v. Superior Court of California, 464 U.S. 501 (1984).

[113] Pell v. Procunier, 417 U.S. 817, 822-24 (1974).

[114] See Juan R. Torruella, On the Slippery Slopes of Afghanistan: Military Commissions and the Exercise of Presidential Power, 4 U. PA. J. CONST. L. 648, 718 (2002) (noting that proceedings, if held at the Guantánamo Bay Naval Station, may be de facto closed due to the physical isolation of the facility).

[115] Cf. Detroit Free Press v. Ashcroft, 303 F.3d 681 (6th Cir.2002), (finding closure of immigration hearings based on relation to events of Sept. 11 unconstitutional

infringement on the First Amendment right to free press). But see North Jersey Media Group, Inc. v. Ashcroft, 308 F.3d 198 (3d Cir. 2002) cert denied 538 U.S. 1056 (2003)(no presumption of openness for immigration hearings).

[116] In practice, some of the detainees have been assigned counsel upon their designation as subject to the President's M.O.

[117] M.C.O. No. 1 § 4(C). M.C.I. No. 4 § 3(D) lists criteria for the "availability" of selected detailed counsel.

[118] But see Faretta v. California , 422 U.S. 806 (1975) (Const. Amend. VI guarantees the right to self-representation).

[119] M.C.I. No. 4 § 3(C).

[120] See HRF, supra note 81, at 2-3; Vanessa Blum, Tribunals Put Defense Bar in Bind, LEGAL TIMES, July 14, 2003, at 1 (reporting that only 10 civilian attorneys had applied to join the pool of civilian defense lawyers).

[121] See SOURCEBOOK, supra note 67, at 136-37.

[122] M.C.I. No. 5, Annex B, "Affidavit and Agreement by Civilian Defense Counsel," at § II(E)(1). The communications are subject to restrictions on classified or "protected" information. Id.

[123] See DoD Press Release, supra note 21.

[124] Originally, civilian attorneys were required to pay the costs associated with obtaining a clearance. M.C.I. No. 5 §3(A)(2)(d)(ii). DoD has waived the administrative costs for processing applications for TOP SECRET clearances in cases that would require the higher level of security clearance. See DoD Press Release No. 084-04 , New Military Commission Orders, Annex Issued (Feb. 6, 2004), available at [http://www.defenselink.mil/releases/ 2004/nr20040206-0331.html] (Last visited July 24, 2006).

[125] M.C.O. No. 1 § 4(C)(3)(b).

[126] Id.; see Edgar, supra note 10 (emphasizing that national security may be invoked to close portions of a trial irrespective of whether classified information is involved).

[127] See M.C.O. No. 3, "Special Administrative Measures for Certain Communications Subject to Monitoring." The required affidavit and agreement annexed to M.C.I. No. 3 was modified to eliminate the following language: I understand that my communications with my client, even if traditionally covered by the attorney-client privilege, may be subject to monitoring or review by government officials, using any available means, for security and intelligence purposes. I understand that any such monitoring will only take place in limited circumstances when approved by proper authority, and that any evidence or information derived from such communications will not be used in proceedings against the Accused who made or received the relevant communication.

[128] M.C.I. No. 5, Annex B § II(J).

[129] M.C.O. No 1 § 4(C)(1); see Torruella, supra note 114, at 719 (noting that the civilian criminal defense system has no equivalent to this system, in which the accused has no apparent choice over the supervision of the defense efforts).

[130] M.C.O. No 1 § 4(A)(5)(c).

[131] Id. § 4(A)(5)(b).

[132] See NACDL Ethics Advisory Committee Opinion 03-04 (August 2003), available at [http://www.nacdl.org] (Last visited July 24, 2006); Participation in Secret Military

Terror Trials Unethical, U.S. Lawyers Say, AP Aug. 2, 2003 (quoting incoming NACDL president Barry Scheck).

[133] See U.S. May Ease Tribunal Rules, NEWSDAY, Aug. 14, 2003, at A18.

[134] See NIMJ Statement on Civilian Attorney Participation as Defense Counsel in Military Commissions, July 13, 2003, available at [http://www.nimj.com/documents/NIMJ_Civ_Atty_Participation_Statement(1).pdf] (last visited July 24, 2006).

[135] Id. § 5(E).

[136] See R.C.M. 701(a)(6); NIMJ, supra note 61, at 31-32.

[137] M.C.O. No. 1 § 5(H). Civilian defense counsel must agree not to submit any claims for reimbursement from the government for any costs related to the defense. M.C.I. No. 5 Annex B.

[138] M.C.I. No. 4 § 5.

[139] Id. § 6(D)(5)(b). Some observers note that protected information could include exculpatory evidence as well as incriminating evidence, which could implicate 6th Amendment rights and rights under the Geneva Convention, if applicable. See HRF, supra note 81, at 3.

[140] Id.

[141] Id. § 6(D)(5)(d).

[142] Id. § 6(D)(2)(d).

[143] See 10 U.S.C. §§ 849 -50. UCMJ art. 49 states: (d) A duly authenticated deposition taken upon reasonable notice to the other parties, so far as otherwise admissible under the rules of evidence, may be read in evidence or, in the case of audiotape, videotape, or similar material, may be played in evidence before any military court or commission in any case not capital, or in any proceeding before a court of inquiry or military board, if it appears — (1) that the witness resides or is beyond the State, Territory, Commonwealth, or District of Columbia in which the court, commission, or board is ordered to sit, or beyond 100 miles from the place of trial or hearing; (2) that the witness by reason of death, age, sickness, bodily infirmity, imprisonment, military necessity, nonamenability to process, or other reasonable cause, is unable or refuses to appear and testify in person at the place of trial or hearing; or (3) that the present whereabouts of the witness is unknown. (e) Subject to subsection (d), testimony by deposition may be presented by the defense in capital cases. (f) Subject to subsection (d), a deposition may be read in evidence or, in the case of audiotape, videotape, or similar material, may be played in evidence in any case in which the death penalty is authorized but is not mandatory, whenever the convening authority directs that the case be treated as not capital, and in such a case a sentence of death may not be adjudged by the court-martial.

[144] See In re Yamashita, 327 U.S. 1, 19 (1946) (declining to apply art. 25 of the Articles of War, which is substantially the same as current UCMJ art. 49, to trial by military commission of an enemy combatant). The Yamashita Court concluded that Congress intended the procedural safeguards in the Articles of War to apply only to persons "subject to military law" under article 2. But see id. at 61-72 (Rutledge, J. dissenting)(arguing the plain language of the statute does not support that interpretation).

[145] Hamdan v. Rumsfeld, 344 F.Supp.2d 152, 167-68 (D.D.C. 2004).

[146] Id. at 168.

[147] 10 U.S.C.§ 839.

[148] M.C.O. No. 1 § 6(D)(1).

[149] Mil. R. Evid. 402.

[150] Mil. R. Evid. 403.

[151] See Torruella, supra note 114, at 715; ACTL, supra note 10, at 11.

[152] See NIMJ, supra note 61, at 37 (citing United States v. Rosato, 32 M.J. 93, 96 (C.M.A. 1991)).

[153] The method of execution used by the Army to carry out a death sentence by military commission is lethal injection. See U.S. Army Correctional System: Procedures for Military Executions, AR 190-55 (1999). It is unclear whether DoD will follow these regulations with respect to sentences issued by these military commissions, but it appears unlikely that any such sentences would be carried out at Ft. Leavenworth, in accordance with AR 190-55.

[154] M.C.I. No. 7 § 3(A).

[155] M.C.O. No. 1 § 6(F).

[156] 10 U.S.C. § 851.

[157] See Laurence H. Tribe, Trial by Fury, THE NEW REPUBLIC, Dec. 10, 2001.

[158] See Press Release, Military Commission Review Panel Members to be Designated and Instruction Issued (Dec. 30, 2003), available at [http://www.defenselink.mil/releases/2003/nr20031230-0822.html] (last visited July 24, 2006). 10 U.S.C. § 603 permits the President, during war or national emergency, to appoint any qualified person as a military officer in the grade of major general or below.

[159] The convening authority of a general court-martial is required to consider all matters presented by the accused. 10 U.S.C. § 860.

[160] M.C.I. No. 9 § 4(C).

[161] 10 U.S.C. § 8037 (listing among duties of Air Force Judge Advocate General to "receive, revise, and have recorded the proceedings of ... military commissions"); 10 U.S.C. § 3037 (similar duty ascribed to Army Judge Advocate General).

[162] 10 U.S.C. § 859.

[163] M.C.I. No. 9 § 4(C)(2)(a).

[164] M.C.I. No. 9 § 4(C)(1)(b).

[165] M.O. at § 7(b).

[166] See Alberto R. Gonzales, Martial Justice, Full and Fair, NEW YORK TIMES (op-ed), Nov. 30, 2001 (stating that the original M.O. was not intended to preclude habeas corpus review). Rasul v. Bush clarified that the detainees at Guantanamo Bay have access to federal courts, but the extent to which the findings of military commissions will be reviewable remains unclear. 124 S. Ct. 2686 (2004).

[167] M.C.O. No. 1 § 5(P). The finding is final when "the President or, if designated by the President, the Secretary of Defense makes a final decision thereon pursuant to Section 4(c)(8) of the President's Military Order and in accordance with Section 6(H)(6) of [M.C.O. No. 1]." Id. § 6(H)(2).

[168] 10 U.S.C. § 844. Federal courts and U.S. military courts are considered to serve under the same sovereign for purposes of double (or former) jeopardy.

[169] In regular courts-martial, the record of a proceeding is "authenticated," or certified as to its accuracy, by the military judge who presided over the proceeding. R.C.M. 1104.

None of the military orders or instructions establishing procedures for military commissions explains what is meant by "authenticated finding."

[170] M.C.O. No. 1 § 6(H)(2).

[171] The UCMJ does not permit rehearing on a charge for which the accused is found on the facts to be not guilty.

[172] See NIMJ, supra note 61, at 39.

[173] See M.C.O. No. 1 § 6(A)(1).

[174] M.O. § 7(e).

[175] P.L. 107-56 § 412 (requiring aliens detained as suspected terrorists must be charged with a crime, subjected to removal proceedings under the Immigration and Naturalization Act, or released with seven days).

[176] See 10 U.S.C. § 836 (delegating authority to the President).

[177] See M.C.O. No. 1 §. 1.

[178] See In re Yamashita, 327 U.S. 1, 8 (1946); Ex parte Vallandigham, 68 (1 Wall.) 243 (1863).

[179] 18 U.S.C. § 2331 defines "international terrorism" to mean activities that — (A) involve violent acts or acts dangerous to human life that are a violation of the criminal laws of the United States or of any State, or that would be a criminal violation if committed within the jurisdiction of the United States or of any State; (B) appear to be intended — (i) to intimidate or coerce a civilian population; (ii) to influence the policy of a government by intimidation or coercion; or (iii) to affect the conduct of a government by mass destruction, assassination, or kidnapping; and (C) occur primarily outside the territorial jurisdiction of the United States, or transcend national boundaries in terms of the means by which they are accomplished, the persons they appear intended to intimidate or coerce, or the locale in which their perpetrators operate or seek asylum.

[180] See, e.g., Wong Wing v. United States, 163 U.S. 228 (1896)(aliens are entitled to due process of law).

In: Law and Law Enforcement Issues
Editor: Gerald M. Kessler, pp. 163-196
ISBN: 978-1-60456-044-2

Chapter 6

EXTRADITION BETWEEN THE UNITED STATES AND GREAT BRITAIN: THE 2003 TREATY*

Charles Doyle

ABSTRACT

Federal court denial of British extradition requests in the cases of four fugitives from Northern Ireland led to the Supplementary Extradition Treaty. The Treaty proved controversial, and before the Senate would give its consent, it insisted upon modifications, some quite unusual. Those modifications have been eliminated in a newly negotiated treaty to which the Senate has recently given its advice and consent and which incorporates features often more characteristic of contemporary extradition treaties with other countries.

There was initial criticism of the new Treaty's

- exemptions to the political offense bar to extradition;
- elimination of judicial inquiry into politically motivated extradition request;
- treatment of probable cause;
- clause relating to extradition for crimes committed overseas;
- dropping the statute of limitations defense;
- discretionary authority for provisional arrest and detention;
- language relating to the seizure of assets;
- exceptions to the rule of speciality (permitting prosecution for crimes other than those for which extradition was granted); and retroactive application.

The Treaty also contains articles relating to capital punishment, waiver of extradition, extradition involving third countries, double jeopardy, the elimination of nationality as a bar to extradition, translations, and deferred prosecution.

The Senate conditioned its approval of the Treaty upon an understanding, two declarations and three provisos which relate to the Treaty's treatment of the exception for politically motivated requests and the role of the courts, its changes in the double jeopardy clause, assurances that the Treaty is not designed to accomplish the extradition

* Excerpted from CRS Report RL32096, dated October 10, 2006.

of fugitives from Northern Ireland covered by the Belfast/Good Friday Agreement, and reporting requirements concerning the disposition of requests under the Treaty.

INTRODUCTION

"One of the most divisive and contentious issues the committee has faced...." So the Senate Foreign Relations Committee described its consideration and subsequent approval of the 1985 Supplementary Treaty to the 1972 extradition treaty between Great Britain and the United States, S.Ex.Rept. 99-17, at 6 (1986).[1] The Supplementary Treaty limits the political offense bar to extradition; it authorizes judicial inquiry into the motives behind an extradition request; and it allows an individual sought by the British to be heard by the court on the issues of probable cause and dual criminality. On March 31, 2003, Attorney General John Ashcroft and United Kingdom Home Secretary David Blunkett announced the signing of a new extradition treaty that reopened the matter.[2] The Senate gave its advice and consent to the 2003 Treaty on September 29, 2006, subject to an understanding, two declarations, and three provisos, 152 *Cong. Rec.* S10766-767 (daily ed. Sept. 29, 2006).[3]

The understanding, declarations and provisos confirm that (1) federal courts will retain the authority to bar extradition when a request fails to meet the demands of 2003 Treaty; (2) the 2003 Treaty does not obligate the United States to take any action proscribed by the Constitution; (3) the parties have disclaimed any interest in prosecuting offenses committed in Northern Ireland prior to and addressed in the Belfast/Good Friday Agreement. It also urges the Secretary of State to consider carefully any requests for the extradition of a fugitive who was previous acquitted, and after the Treaty becomes effective it requires annual reports from the Secretary on the number and disposition of extradition requests under the Treaty.

BACKGROUND

Extradition is the process by which one country formally surrenders a person to another country for criminal prosecution or punishment.[4] Ordinarily, extradition is governed by a treaty which operates in the nature of a contract and by implementing statutory provisions.[5] The United States has extradition treaties in force with most of the countries of the world and under most circumstances will extradite an individual to another country only pursuant to a treaty of extradition.[6]

Supplementary Treaty

The 2003 Treaty is the latest in a long line of extradition pacts with Great Britain.[7] The difficulties that led to the Supplementary Treaty arose from judicial application of the "political offense exception" found in the 1977 Treaty.[8] The federal courts in this country had held that the political offense exception found in most of our extradition treaties precluded extradition on the basis of criminal charges growing out of conduct "committed in the course of and incidental to a violent political disturbance, such as a war, revolution or rebellion."[9] Shortly after the 1977 Treaty became effective, federal courts denied extradition requests on the basis of the political offense exception in four instances growing out of the unrest in Northern Ireland.[10] The two countries responded by negotiating a Supplementary Treaty, S.Treaty Doc. 99-8 (1985).[11] As transmitted to the Senate, the Supplementary Treaty curtailed the political offense exception, and also eased the statute of limitations bar, extended the permissible duration of provisional arrest pending the formal submission of evidence sufficient to support an extradition request, and made its changes retroactively applicable, S.Treaty Doc. 99-8 (1985).

Exemptions to the political offense exception were the most controversial aspect of the treaty offered to the Senate. The Administration argued that the political offense exception should not be available for crimes of violence committed in a nation open to nonviolent resolution of political differences, and that contrary to critics' suggestions the treaty posed no threat to civil liberties.[12] Critics, on the other hand, argued that the repudiated political offense exception reflected a long-held reluctance to deny refuge to the opponents of repressive governments,[13] lest we be forced to extradite the overseas equivalents of the farmers and other minutemen at Lexington and Concord.[14] In addition, some suggested that adjustments in the political offense exception might best be addressed uniformly in statute rather than on an ad hoc treaty by treaty basis;[15] while others questioned the wisdom of endorsing some aspects of criminal justice system in Northern Ireland.[16]

Apart from the political offense question, opponents also protested that the Supplementary Treaty as transmitted eliminated the statute of limitations defense to any British request and made its alternations retroactively applicable.[17] The Administration pointed out that the treatment of retroactivity and the lapse of time issues were standard features of "our newer treaties."[18]

After consulting with the Administration and the British Government, the Senate produced a compromise. First, the Supplementary Treaty that entered into force after Senate amendment limits the political offense exception to permit the extradition of terrorists in most cases.[19] Second, in such purported terrorist extradition cases, it creates a defense to extradition where the fugitive can establish that extradition has been sought or would result in his trial or punishment because of his race, religion, nationality or political opinions. And it establishes a procedure for appellate review in such cases.[20] Third, it makes it clear that the federal courts may deny extradition in the absence of probable cause and in response to evidence presented by the individual sought.[21] Finally, it drops the proposed revision of the statute of limitations clause, so that extradition must be denied if prosecution would be barred under the laws of either country.[22]

Since the Supplementary Treaty

Of the four men whose extradition cases served as a catalyst for the Supplementary Treaty, Desmond Mackin returned to Ireland;[23] William Quinn was extradited;[24] and Peter McMullen was deported,[25] as was Joseph Doherty.[26] Others appear to have found little refuge in the Supplementary Treaty.[27] Commentary on the Supplementary Treaty and on the cases that followed has been mixed, often depending upon whether the author's focus was terrorism,[28] intervention in foreign civil conflicts,[29] or inquiry into foreign judicial systems.[30] Finally, the conditions in Northern Ireland that rested at the heart of the extradition controversy seem to have improved somewhat. Under the Belfast/Good Friday Agreement violence subsided, and those held under the Diplock and similar procedures have been released.[31]

While they lack the more individualist attributes of the Supplementary Treaty, the extradition treaties with other nations transmitted to the Senate since then have generally featured a more modest series of exemptions to the political offense bar. Most would permit extradition for a political offense that involves a crime of violence against a head of state or his family, or a crime covered by a treaty obligation to extradite, or attempt or conspiracy to commit either of these types of crimes.[32] A few, however, do contain exemptions to the political offense ban reminiscent of the Supplementary Treaty.[33]

Initial Objections to 2003 Treaty

At least one early critic of the 2003 Treaty contended that it:

1. Eliminates the political offense for any offense allegedly involving violence or weapons, including any solicitation, conspiracy or attempt to commit such crimes;
2. Transfers responsibility for determining whether the extradition request is politically-motivated from the courts to the executive;
3. Allows for extradition even if no U.S. federal law is violated;
4. Eliminates any statute of limitations;
5. Eliminates the need for any showing by the United Kingdom of facts sufficient to show the person requested is guilty of the crime charged — mere unsupported allegations are sufficient;
6. Allows for "provisional arrest" and detention for 60 days upon request by the United Kingdom;
7. Allows for seizure of assets by the United Kingdom;
8. Allows for extradition for one offense, and then subsequent prosecution in the UK for an unrelated offense (thus eliminating the time-honored "rule of speciality"); and
9. Applies retroactively, for offenses allegedly committed even before the ratification of the treaty. Boyle, *supra* n.2.

The understanding, declarations, and provisos that accompany the Senate's approval of the 2003 Treaty seem to reflect its concerns over some of these objections.

Exemptions to the Political Offense Exception

Eliminates the political offense for any offense allegedly involving violence or weapons, including any solicitation, conspiracy or attempt to commit such crimes

It does and more. There is likely to be little consensus over whether this is objectionable. It is the issue that dominated debate over the Supplementary Treaty. There is little disagreement over the origins or original rationale of the exception. As one court has explained:

> The political offense exception is premised on a number of justifications. First, its historical development suggests that it is grounded on the belief that individuals have a "right to resort to political activism to foster political change." This justification is consistent with the modern consensus that political crimes have greater legitimacy than common crimes. Second, the exception reflects a concern that individuals — particularly unsuccessful rebels — should not be returned to countries where they may be subjected to unfair trial and punishments because of their political opinions. Third, the exception comports with the notion that governments — and certainly their non-political branches — should not intervene in the internal political struggles of other nations. *Quinn v. Robinson*, 783 F.2d 776, 792-93 (9th Cir. 1986).

The difficulty comes in defining the exception's proper scope. Should it protect fleeing insurgents from prosecution and punishment for acts of violence they committed against the military forces of the government they sought to overthrow? Absent a treaty bar, United States courts have held that it should apply to crimes committed incidental to and in furtherance of rebellion or similar political disturbance, *Id.* at 797-78. Reliance upon the exception led to the exemptions to the exception found in the proposed Supplementary Treaty. The Senate accepted a somewhat reduced list of exemptions to the political offense exception in exchange for expanded judicial authority to verify probable cause and the bona fides of a request.

The 2003 Treaty undoes the Senate changes in the Supplementary Treaty and enlarges its list of exemptions from the political offense exception (noted in the italics below):

1. Extradition shall not be granted if the offense for which extradition is requested is a political offense.
2. For the purposes of this Treaty, the following offenses shall not be considered political offenses:
    a. an offense for which both Parties have the obligation pursuant to a multilateral international agreement to extradite the person sought or to submit the case to their competent authorities for decision as to prosecution;
    b. *a murder or other violent crime against the person of a Head of State or one of the Parties, or of a member of the Head of State's family*;
    c. murder, manslaughter, malicious wounding, or inflicting grievous bodily harm;
    d. an offense involving kidnaping, abduction, or any form of unlawful detention, including the taking of a hostage;
    e. *placing or* using, or *threatening the placement or use of*, an explosive, incendiary, *or destructive device or firearm* capable of endangering life, of causing grievous bodily harm, *or of causing substantial property damage*;
    f. *possession of an explosive, incendiary, or destructive device capable of endangering life, or causing grievous bodily harm, or of causing substantial property damage*;

g. an attempt or *a conspiracy* to commit, participation in the commission of, *aiding or abetting, counseling or procuring the commission of, or being an accessory before or after the fact to* any of the foregoing offenses. *2003 Treaty*, Art.4(1),(2)(emphasis added).

The new head of state exemption is a standard feature of our recent treaties, even those with comparatively modest exemptions. At first blush, it seems unlikely to arise with any great frequency. Its actual reach, nevertheless, may increase slightly depending upon the Parties' understandings of the meaning of "family" and the new breadth of subparagraph 4(2)(g) relating to accessories. It might, for example, embrace anyone who harbored or otherwise afterwards assisted those who assassinated Lord Mountbatten, assuming the underlying offense were found to be a political offense.[34]

Several of the enlargements — those dealing with possession, conspiracy, property damage, expanding voluntary manslaughter to include involuntary, and reaching unlawful detention (serious or otherwise) — repeal specific Senate amendments to the Supplementary Treaty as originally transmitted to the Senate.[35] The inclusion of threats, firearms, possession of explosives, property damage (independent of bodily injury), and accessories after the fact appears to carry the provision well beyond the coverage of even the more ambitious of such provisions in our other recent extradition treaties. Its sweep is made all the more dramatic by removal of the judicial safety valve found in the Supplementary Treaty's "improper motives" Article.

The Senate responded with the explicit understanding that as part of the extradition process normally conducted under the laws of the United States, "a United States judge makes determinations regarding the application of the political offense exception."[36] The understanding is reenforced by the second declaration confirming the role of the courts in the extradition process and by the provisos indicating that the 2003 Treaty is not designed to permit the prosecution of fugitives from Northern Ireland for offenses committed prior to the Good Friday Agreement.[37]

The Courts, Improper Motives, and Probable Cause

Transfers responsibility for determining whether the extradition request is politically-motivated from the courts to the executive

It does. Again whether this is objectionable may depend upon perspective. Born of a concern for fairness, the features of the Supplementary Treaty are nonetheless unique. Of course, the question — of whether the crime upon which an extradition request rests is political crime — is closely related to the question of whether an extradition request is grounded in improper political motives. The 2003 Treaty strikes or at least extensively prunes perhaps the most individualistic features of the existing treaty — the treatment of improperly motivated requests and the specifics concerning the existence of probable cause. Article 3 of the Supplementary Treaty establishes a judicial procedure replete with appellate rights to bar extradition based on trumped-up charges or improperly motivated requests.[38]

The Senate Foreign Relations Committee which added Article 3 to the Supplementary Treaty explained its extraordinary dimensions:

> Article 3, part (a) contains two distinct concepts, First, it authorizes a court to deny extradition based upon a persuasive factual showing that the requesting party has trumped-up charges against a dissident in order to obtain his extradition for trial or punishment. Second, it authorizes a court to deny extradition if the person sought for extradition can establish by a preponderance of the evidence that he would be prejudiced at this trial, or punished, detained or restricted in his personal liberty because of his race, religion, nationality or political opinions.
>
> Article 3(a) adapts language found in Article 5 of the European Convention on the Suppression of terrorism to which the United Kingdom is a party....
>
> During the June 12 business meeting the following colloquy with respect to article 3(a) took place: Senator Kerry. Mr. Chairman, as part of that report language I would ask you if it is your understanding and intention ... that an individual, as part of showing that he would ... if surrendered be prejudiced at his trial or punished, detained or restricted in his personal liberty by reason of his race, religion, nationality or political opinion, would that individual be able to challenge the fairness of the judicial system to which he would be returned and thereby raise a right of inquiry into the fairness of that system?
>
> The Chairman. Yes.
>
> ***
>
> Article 3(b) applies only to the United States. It does two things. First, it limits the scope of article 3(a) in U.S. extradition proceedings to offenses listed in Article 1 of the Supplementary Treaty, In other words, if an individual is wanted for extradition to the United Kingdom for fraud, drug smuggling or some other offense not listed in article 1, that individual may not involve article 3(a) before a Federal magistrate or judge. Article 3(b) also gives either party to the extradition proceeding the right to appeal a finding under article 3(a). S.Ex.Rept. 99-17, at 4-5 (1986).

The 2003 Treaty's pruning of the improper motivation clause leaves only political motives suspect and expressly removes the issue from the courts.[39] More broadly drafted clauses — proscribing racial, religious or other improperly motivated extradition requests — are not uncommon elsewhere.[40] The 2003 Treaty's repeal of the judicial authority to inquiry into extradition motivation, however, comports with treatment of the issue diplomatically[41] and judicially.[42] Moreover as noted above, the understandings, declarations and provisos, upon which the Senate insisted, emphasize that whether a particular extradition request satisfies treaty requirements remains an initial judicial determination and disclaim any intent to reopen the Good Friday Agreement.

> Eliminates the need for any showing by the United Kingdom of facts sufficient to show the person requested is guilty of the crime charged — mere unsupported allegations are sufficient

The Supplementary Treaty's probable cause article reenforces the benefits of article 3.[43] Again the Senate Executive Report is instructive:

> The committee has made a second major change in the Supplementary Treaty as submitted. It has included, as article 2 of the amended treaty, a restatement of the procedures that have traditionally governed the consideration of an extradition request in U.S. courts. This article reaffirms that the magistrate or Federal judge is to permit the individual to present evidence in connection with the request. It insures that no individual

is to be extradited without a fair hearing. It is designed to lay to rest any assumption that extradition under this Supplementary Treaty will be automatic or that Federal magistrates and judges will not carefully evaluate the evidence presented in support of extradition. Id. at 5-6.

While the 2003 Treaty strikes (1) the Supplementary Treaty language insuring an individual the right to contest the existence of probable cause to justify extradition, and (2) the original treaty language on the weight of evidence required for extradition,[44] it does insist that the documentation accompanying a request include "such information as would provide a reasonable basis to believe that the person sought committed the offense for which extradition is requested," *2003 Treaty*, Art.8(3)(c).

Extraterritorial Crimes

Allows for extradition even if no U.S. federal law is violated

It does, but in a less dramatic manner than the objection might imply. As a general rule, the 2003 Treaty, like its predecessor, limits extradition to misconduct outlawed in both countries. The exception is found in cases of extraterritoriality. The existing treaty obligates the Parties to extradite with respect to crimes committed within the jurisdiction of the requesting country, *1977 Treaty*, Art.I. Historically, the United States has construed this language to mean offenses committed within the territory of the requesting country.[45] As the United States began to assert its criminal extraterritorial jurisdiction more regularly, it began to negotiate extradition treaties that either permitted or required extradition to the United States with respect to crimes committed outside this country.

Our present treaty favors the historical model ("Each Contracting Party undertakes to extradite to the other ... any person found in its territory who has been accused or convicted of any offense ... committed within the jurisdiction of the other Party," *1977 Treaty*, Art.I). The 2003 Treaty requires extradition in extraterritorial cases where the law of the two countries would apply comparably; but permits extradition in other cases:

> If the offense has been committed outside the territory of the Requesting State, extradition shall be granted in accordance with the provisions of the Treaty if the laws in the Requested State provide for the punishment of such conduct committed outside the territory in similar circumstances. If the laws of the Requested State do not provide for the punishment of such conduct committed outside of its territory in similar circumstances, the executive authority of the Requested State, in its discretion, may grant extradition provided that all other requirements of this Treaty are met. *2003 Treaty*, Art. 2(4).

Thus, the United States would be permitted to honor a British extradition request for an individual charged with a violation of British law on the basis of conduct committed entirely within this country (even if the conduct were completely lawful under our laws). And it would be required to honor a request based upon conduct here but in violation of a British version of a statute like 18 U.S.C. 2339B (providing material support to terrorist organizations) or 18 U.S.C. 956 (conspiracy to commit various acts of violence or property damage overseas).

Statute of Limitations

Eliminates any statute of limitations

It does, as do several of our more recent extradition treaties. The vast majority of the extradition treaties to which the United States is a party contain a statute of limitations bar of some kind. In some instances the bar is triggered by the law of the requesting country; in some by the law of the requested country; and in others by the law in either country.[46] The rationale is presumably the same as in other contexts: that at least in some instances it is unfair to require individuals to defend themselves against stale charges after memories have faded, evidence has disappeared, and witnesses have died.[47]

Our existing treaty with the United Kingdom bars extradition if trial would be barred by the lapse of time under the laws of either country.[48] The Supplementary Treaty submitted to the Senate contained an amendment which would have limited this clause to instances barred by the laws of the requesting country. The change was thought to benefit the United Kingdom in terrorism cases which were not subject to a statute of limitations.[49] The Senate dropped the amendment from the Supplementary Treaty, S.Ex.Rept. 99-17, at 6 (1986).

Since then, a number of the treaties submitted to the Senate continue to contain a statute of limitations clause,[50] but perhaps an equal number of others either silently omit the clause[51] or include a clause specifically declaring that the expiration of a period of limitation is no bar to extradition.[52] The 2003 Treaty eliminates the passage of time as a defense altogether regardless of the nature of the crime, "The decision by the Requested State whether to grant the request for extradition shall be made without regard to any statute of limitations in either State," *2003 Treaty*, Art.6.

Provisional Arrest

Allows for "provisional arrest" and detention for 60 days upon request by the United Kingdom

It does, but so does the existing treaty.[53] Provisional arrest refers to the authority to arrest the individual sought for extradition before receiving the full documentation required to initiate extradition proceedings. The 2003 Treaty is more precise than the existing treaty in its description of the information that must accompany a request for provisional arrest. The 2003 Treaty also affords the Parties great flexibility as to the permissible recipients of requests and documentation, but the most substantial change seems to be that under the existing treaty the individual must be released after 60 days if the necessary documentation has not arrived while under the 2003 Treaty release is discretionary.[54]

Evidence and Forfeitable Property

Allows for seizure of assets by the United Kingdom

Crime-related assets are subject to seizure under the laws of the United Kingdom and of the United States under various circumstances, some of which implement or supplement our treaty obligations. The existing treaty permits the transfer of evidence and assets from one country to the another.[55] Facially, the 2003 Treaty's treatment of forfeitable property differs from its predecessor in two respects. It describes the property subject to confiscation more broadly and it omits any reference to the rights of claimants:

> To the extent permitted under its law, the Requested State may seize and surrender to the Requesting State all items in whatever form, and assets, including proceeds, that are connected with the offense in respect of which extradition is granted. The items and assets mentioned in this Article may be surrendered even when the extradition cannot be effected due to the death, disappearance, or escape of the person sought. *2003 Treaty*, Art. 16(1).

The existing treaty provision is limited to proceeds rather than items "connected with the offense," and only extends to items in the actual possession of the individual to be extradited. The changes reflect a greater federal emphasis on forfeiture as a law enforcement tool than was the case when the existing treaty was negotiated. Federal law now authorizes confiscation of property derived from, or in some instances used to facilitate, any number of federal crimes including terrorism,[56] organized crime,[57] drug trafficking,[58] and other profit generating crimes.[59] When they are involved in financial transactions in this country, it permits the confiscation of the proceeds from drug trafficking, crimes of violence, fraud, public corruption or smuggling in violation of the laws of other countries.[60]

Federal law also provides for federal court orders freezing property located in this country but subject to confiscation under foreign forfeiture laws comparable to our own,[61] and for enforcement of foreign forfeiture orders by federal courts under some circumstances.[62] Moreover, it vests the Attorney General with the power to share the proceedings from federal confiscations with foreign countries pursuant to an international agreement to do so.[63] The innocent claimant protections of these statutes[64] would seem to mitigate any adverse consequences attributable to the omission of any reference to the rights of claimants in the 2003 Treaty.

Rule of Specialty

Allows for extradition for one offense, and then subsequent prosecution in the UK for an unrelated offense (thus eliminating the time-honored "rule of speciality")

The 2003 Treaty continues the rule in effect, but allows the United States to consent to deviation by the Great Britain and vice versa. The rule of specialty permits individuals to be tried and/or punished only for the crimes for which they are extradited.[65] The rule is designed to ensure that an individual is not tried or punished for a crime for which he would not have been extradited.[66] And the elimination of the rule might be particularly unfair where the individual sought has waived extradition.

For purposes of American law, the rule is a matter of statutory construction,[67] and consequently can be overcome by a provision in a later treaty.[68] Most recent treaties permit the requested country to consent to trial or punishment for offenses other than those for which the individual was extradited.[69] Even without a specific treaty clause, federal courts have held that the requested country may consent to trial or punishment for offenses other than those for which extradition was granted.[70]

Federal courts are divided, however, over the question of whether an individual may successfully raise the rule on behalf of the country of refuge.[71]

Our existing treaty with Great Britain codifies the rule and has no consent exception.[72] The 2003 Treaty preserves the rule but contains an explicit consent exception: "A person extradited under this Treaty may not be detained, tried, or punished in the Requesting State except for ... (c) any offense for which the executive authority of the Requested State waives the rule of specialty and thereby consents to the person's detention, trial, or prosecution...." *2003 Treaty*, Art.18(1).

Retroactivity

> Applies retroactively, for offenses allegedly committed even before the ratification of the treaty

It does;[73] most extradition treaties do.[74] The significance of the clause in the 2003 Treaty may be what it does not do. The Supplementary Treaty endorses the general rule but makes it applicable to earlier offenses only if the offense was proscribed by the laws of both countries at the time of its commission.[75] The 2003 Treaty clause has no such reservation. The omission may be significant when read in conjunction with the extraterritorial clause to permit extradition for earlier misconduct committed outside the territory of the requesting country under circumstances where the misconduct is not proscribed by the laws of the country of refuge.

Other Treaty Clauses

The 2003 Treaty has other clauses, some of them a departure from our earlier benefits and obligations.

Extradition to Third Countries or Entities

As in the case with our existing treaty with Great Britain, the specialty ban on prosecution of additional crimes often includes a ban on re-extradition to a third country, *1977 Treaty*, Art.XII. Beginning in the 106th Congress, several extradition treaties submitted to the Senate bar re-extradition to international tribunals without consent.[76] This may have been done at our behest with an eye to the International Criminal Court; or at the behest of our treaty partners with an eye to our statutory provisions relating to the Yugoslav and Rwandan tribunals, 18 U.S.C. 3181 note; or both; or for some other reason.

In any event, the 2003 Treaty may yield the same result through its more cryptic reference to "onward extradition" — "A person extradited under this Treaty may not be the subject of onward extradition or surrender for any offense committed prior to extradition to the Requesting State unless the Requested State consents," *2003 Treaty*, Art. 18(2). At this juncture it is not completely clear what the Parties understand "onward extradition" to mean.[77]

In the case of multiple extradition requests, the 2003 Treaty maintains essentially the same standards for dealing with requests from a third country that elects to submit a contemporaneous request to the country of refuge rather than submitting a subsequent request to the country to whom extradition has been granted:

> If the Requested State receives requests form two or more States for the extradition of the same person, either for the same offense or for different offenses, the executive authority of the Requested State shall consider all relevant factors, including but not limited to: (a) whether the requests were made pursuant to a treaty; (b) the place where each offense was committed; (c) the gravity of the offenses; (d) the possibility of any subsequent extradition between the respective Requesting States; and (e) the chronological order in which the requests were received from the respective Requesting States. *2003 Treaty*, Art. 15.

The only real difference is that the existing treaty specifically mentions the nationality of the individual sought as a factor to be considered, *1977 Treaty*, Art.X, while the Parties may count nationality among the unmentioned "relevant factors" that the 2003 Treaty considers in play. It may be, however, that the Parties have rejected nationality as a relevant extradition factor under any circumstances. After all, elsewhere in the 2003 Treaty they have denied themselves the right to refuse to extradite on the basis of nationality, Art. 3, and have removed the identification of the nationality of the person sought from the information that must be provided with an extradition request, Art.8(2).

Double Jeopardy

Ordinarily, an individual cannot be extradited on the basis of conduct for which he has already been tried.[78] Implementation of this principle takes several forms in our various extradition treaties. Our existing treaty with Great Britain bars extradition if prosecution would be precluded in the country of refuge by virtue of any earlier trial there, or in the requesting country, or in a third country.[79] Thus, the United States may not extradite an individual tried here for the same misconduct. The United States may, however, honor requests where the individual has previously been tried in Great Britain or in a third country, because double jeopardy in the United States only proscribes trial by the same sovereign.[80] The 2003 Treaty prohibits extradition where the individual has been tried in the country of refuge, and allows a country of refuge to deny a request for an individual tried in a third country, *2003 Treaty*, Art.5. A Senate proviso addresses the question of extradition following acquittal in the requesting country:

> The Senate notes that, as in other recent United States extradition treaties, the Treaty does not address the situation where the fugitive is sought for trial on an offense for which he had previously been acquitted in the Requesting State. The Senate further notes that a United Kingdom domestic law may allow for the retrial in the United Kingdom, in certain limited circumstances, of an individual who has previously been tried and acquitted in that country. In this regard, the Senate understands that under U.S. law and practice a person sought for extradition can present a claim to the Secretary of State that an aspect of foreign law that may permit retrial may result in an unfairness that the Secretary could conclude warrants denial of the extradition request. The Senate urges the Secretary of State to review carefully any such claims made involving a request for extradition that implicates this provision of United Kingdom domestic law.[81]

Nationality

Some nations prefer not to extradite their own citizens and have insisted that their extradition treaties preserve their right to decline requests to extradite their own nationals.[82] The United States opposes his view.[83] Our existing treaty with Great Britain does not address the issue directly, *1977 Treaty*, and as a consequence the United States may not decline to extradite an American to Great Britain solely on the grounds of citizenship.[84] Like several of our more recent extradition agreements with common law countries,[85] the 2003 Treaty makes this result explicit, "Extradition shall not be refused based on the nationality of the person sought," *2003 Treaty*, Art.3.

Waiver

Neither federal law nor most early treaties provide any obvious mechanism under which an individual might waive extradition proceedings in this country.[86] This can work to the inconvenience of both countries involved in cases where the delay is of no real benefit to the individual sought. The present treaty does not address the issue, but like most modern treaties,[87] the 2003 Treaty has a waiver clause: "If the person sought waives extradition and agrees to be surrendered to the Requesting State, the requested State may surrender the person as expeditiously as possible without further proceedings," *2003 Treaty*, Art.17.

Translations

Our extradition agreements with English-speaking countries do not ordinarily include a translation clause. The 2003 Treaty requires documentation in English, *2003 Treaty*, Art.11, with the cost of any translation to be borne by the requesting country as is ordinarily the case in our extradition relations with non-English-speaking countries.[88]

Deferred Prosecution or Punishment

Our existing treaty with Great Britain requires deferral of an extradition request for an individual being tried or serving a sentence in the requested country for another offense, *1977 Treaty*, Art. VI. The *2003 Treaty* affords the requested country greater flexibility; it may defer the extradition request, the trial, or service of the sentence.[89] In the case of the United States, one commentator has suggested that because of constraints on stale prosecutions, the United States may be willing to postpone service of sentence but is not likely to surrender an individual pending trial unless it is willing to abandon the prospect of future prosecution.[90]

Transit

Although the present treaty is silent on the matter, most modern extradition treaties to which the United States is a party contain a transit clause that allows each country to effectuate its extradition relations with third nations by transporting individuals across each other's territory.[91] The 2003 Treaty clause grants federal and British authorities discretionary authority to approve transfers through their respective countries,[92] with exceptions for transportation through a Party's air space and procedures in the case of unscheduled aircraft landings.[93]

Capital Crimes

The existing extradition treaty makes special provision for capital cases, Art.IV. The 2003 Treaty makes essentially the same accommodation: "When the offense for which extradition is sought is punishable by death under the laws in the Requesting State and is not punishable by death under the laws in the Requested State, the executive authority in the Requested State may refuse extradition unless the Requesting State provides an assurance that the death penalty will not be imposed or, if imposed, will not be carried out," *2003 Treaty*, Art.7.

APPENDIX[94]
RESOLUTION OF ADVICE AND CONSENT TO RATIFICATION

Resolved (two-thirds of the Senators present concurring therein)

Section 1. Senate Advice and Consent Subject to Understanding, Declarations, and Provisos

The Senate advises and consents to the ratification of the Extradition Treaty between the United States of America and the United Kingdom of Great Britain and Northern Ireland, and related exchanges of letters, signed at Washington on March 31, 2003 (hereinafter in this resolution referred to as the "Treaty") (Treaty Doc. 108-23), subject to the understanding in section 2, the declarations in section 3, and the provisos in section 4.

Section 2. Understanding

The advice and consent of the Senate under section 1 is subject to the following understanding: Under United States law, a United States judge makes a certification of extraditability of a fugitive to the Secretary of State. In the process of making such certification, a United States judge also makes determinations regarding the application of the political offense exception. Accordingly, the United States of America understands that the statement in paragraphs 3 and 4 of Article 4 that "in the United States, the executive branch is the competent authority for the purposes of this Article" applies only to those specific paragraphs of Article 4, and does not alter or affect the role of the United States judiciary in making certifications of extraditability or determinations of the application of the political offense exception.

Section 3. Declarations

The advice and consent of the Senate under section 1 is subject to the following declarations: (1) Nothing in the Treaty requires or authorizes legislation or other action by the United States of America that is prohibited by the Constitution of the United States.

(2) The Treaty shall be implemented by the United States in accordance with the Constitution of the United States and relevant federal law, including the requirement of a judicial determination of extraditability that is set forth in Title 18 of the United States Code.

Section 4. Provisos

The advice and consent of the Senate under section 1 is subject to the following provisos: (1)(A) The Senate is aware that concerns have been expressed that the purpose of the Treaty is to seek the extradition of individuals involved in offenses relating to the conflict in Northern Ireland prior to the Belfast Agreement of April 10, 1998. The Senate understands that the purpose of the Treaty is to strengthen law enforcement cooperation between the United States and the United Kingdom by modernizing the extradition process for all serious offenses and that the Treaty is not intended to reopen issues addressed in the Belfast Agreement, or to impede any further efforts to resolve the conflict in Northern Ireland. (B) Accordingly, the Senate notes with approval — (i) the statement of the United Kingdom Secretary of State for Northern Ireland, made on September 29, 2000, that the United Kingdom does not intend to seek the extradition of individuals who appear to qualify for early release under the Belfast Agreement; (ii) the letter from the United Kingdom Home Secretary to the United States Attorney General in March 2006, emphasizing that the "new treaty does not change this position in any way," and making clear that the United Kingdom "want[s] to address the anomalous position of those suspected but not yet convicted of terrorism-related offences committed before the Belfast Agreement"; and (iii) that these policies were reconfirmed in an exchange of letters between the United Kingdom Secretary of State for Northern Ireland and the United States Attorney General in September 2006. (2) The Senate notes that, as in other recent United States extradition treaties, the Treaty does not address the situation where the fugitive is sought for trial on an offense for which he had previously been acquitted in the Requesting State. The Senate further notes that a United Kingdom domestic law may allow for the retrial in the United Kingdom, in certain limited circumstances, of an individual who has previously been tried and acquitted in that country. In this regard, the Senate understands that under U.S. law and practice a person sought for extradition can present a claim to the Secretary of State that an aspect of foreign law that may permit retrial may result in an unfairness that the Secretary could conclude warrants denial of the extradition request. The Senate urges the Secretary of State to review carefully any such claims made involving a request for extradition that implicates this provision of United Kingdom domestic law. (3) Not later than one year after entry into force of the Treaty, and annually thereafter for a period of four additional years, the Secretary of State shall submit to the Committee on Foreign Relations of the Senate a report setting forth the following information with respect to the implementation of the Treaty in the previous twelve months: (A) the number of persons arrested in the United States pursuant to requests from the United Kingdom under the Treaty, including the number of persons subject to provisional arrest; and a summary description of the alleged conduct for which the United Kingdom is seeking extradition; (B) the number of extradition requests granted; and the number of extradition requests denied, including whether the request was denied as a result of a judicial decision or a decision of the Secretary of State; (C) the number of instances the person sought for extradition made a claim to the Secretary of State of political motivation, unjustifiable delay, or retrial after acquittal and whether such extradition requests were denied or granted; and (D) the number of instances the Secretary granted a request under Article 18(1)(c).

APPENDIX

HOME OFFICE,
London SW1P 4DF, March 31, 2006.

ALBERTO GONZALES,
Attorney General, U.S. Department of Justice, Washington, DC.

DEAR AL: At our meeting on 6 March I said that I would write to clarify the UK Government's position relating to the extradition of individuals wanted or convicted of terrorist offences associated with the Troubles in Northern Ireland who are currently in the United States.

In September 2000 the Government decided that it was no longer proportionate or in the public interest to seek the extradition of individuals convicted of terrorist offences committed prior to 10th April 1998, the date of the Belfast Agreement. The new treaty does not change this position in any way. We have also made it clear that we want to address the anomalous position of those suspected but not yet convicted of terrorism-related offences committed before then. Had these individuals been convicted at the time of their offences they would, by now, have been able to apply for early release and so find themselves in a similar position to those already covered by the Agreement. Unfortunately, the legislation that would have resolved this anomaly had to be withdrawn due to a lack of cross-party support. However, the British Government remains keen to make progress on this and I can assure you that when the new treaty was being negotiated, there was no intention on our part to make it easier to target these people, whose position we accept to be anomalous.

CHARLES CLARKE,
Home Secretary.
NORTHERN IRELAND OFFICE,
Belfast BT4 3TT, September 4, 2006.

ALBERTO GONZALES,
Attorney General, U.S. Department of Justice, Washington, DC.

DEAR ATTORNEY GENERAL: I am writing to reiterate the UK Government's position relating to the extradition of individuals from the United States in relation to terrorist offences committed during the Troubles in Northern Ireland. In September 2000, the Government decided that it was no longer proportionate or in the public interest to seek the extradition of individuals convicted of terrorist offences prior to 10th April 1998, "who appear to qualify for early release under the Good Friday Agreement scheme, and who would, on making a successful application to the Sentence Review Commissioners, have little if any of their original prison sentence to serve." I attach a copy of the statement made by the then Secretary of State for Northern Ireland when this decision was announced. I know that the former Home Secretary reiterated this when he wrote to you in March this year. I can confirm, on behalf of the UK Government, that this remains the case. We have also made it clear that we want to address the anomalous position of those suspected but not yet convicted of terrorism-related offences committed before the Belfast Agreement. Had these individuals been convicted at the time of their offences they would, by now, have been able to apply for early release and so find themselves in a similar position to those already covered by the Agreement. The UK Government introduced legislation to resolve this anomaly last year. Unfortunately, that legislation had to be withdrawn due to a lack of cross-party support. However, the UK Government continues to accept that the position of these people is anomalous and I can assure you, as the former Home Secretary did in March, that when the new treaty was being negotiated there was no intention on our part to make it easier to target them. I attach a short note which explains in more detail the provisions of the early release scheme and the position of various groups of people. It remains a matter of great importance to the UK Government that the extradition treaty should be ratified by the United States, so that its benefits can be fully realised. This is not because of any agenda related to Northern Ireland, but because of the improvements that the updated treaty will bring to the extradition process in general in both countries. My colleague, John Reid, the Home Secretary, has seen this letter and agrees fully with its contents.

I am copying this letter to Senator Lugar. Both you and he are welcome to share it with other members of the Senate if that would be helpful.

The Rt. Hon. PETER HAIN MP, *Secretary of State for Northern Ireland.*
Enclosures.

US-UK Extradition Treaty — Northern Ireland Issues

Political Background

The political and security situation in Northern Ireland has been transformed following the 1998 Good Friday Agreement. A huge amount of progress has been made since then, including the historic statement from the Provisional IRA in July 2005, in which they made clear that their armed campaign was over. The focus in Northern Ireland today is on restoring devolved Government and continuing to build a prosperous and peaceful society.

Good Friday Agreement and Early Release Scheme

As part of the Good Friday Agreement (GFA), individuals convicted of terrorist-related offences committed before 1998 were able to apply for early release after serving only two years of their sentences. Over 400 prisoners have been released on license under this scheme. The license requires that individuals do not become re-engaged in terrorism or serious crime. Those released include many members of the Provisional IRA, which has maintained a ceasefire during this time. The Early Release Scheme was a very difficult part of the Good Friday Agreement for many people to accept, but it demonstrated the UK Government's commitment to moving forward with the peace process. The Early Release Scheme is part of UK law and remains in force. Any individuals who are convicted of qualifying, pre-1998 offences in the future, including any individuals extradited to the UK, will be able to apply for the scheme.

Individuals Convicted of Pre-GFA Offences

In 2000, the UK Government announced that it would no longer pursue the extradition of individuals convicted of pre-1998 offences who had escaped from prison and who would, if they returned to Northern Ireland and successfully applied for early release, have little if any of their time left to serve. That remains the position.

Individuals Suspected of Pre-GFA Offences ("on the Runs")

Whilst the Early Release Scheme addressed the situation of individuals who had been convicted of past offences, there remained an anomaly in relation to individuals suspected of past offences, who had gone "on the run" before they were tried. The British Government accepts that these individuals are in an anomalous position since, if they had been convicted before 1998 they could have been released by now under the terms of the Good Friday Agreement. In 2003, the British Government therefore published proposals for a scheme which would have allowed suspects "on the run" to be tried in their absence and to return to Northern Ireland without arrest or imprisonment. Following the IRA's statement that its armed campaign was over in July 2005, legislation was introduced to implement that commitment. Agreement could not be reached on that legislation during its passage through Parliament and it was withdrawn in January 2006. The British Government is currently reflecting on the way forward. However, as the 2003 proposals and the subsequent legislation demonstrate, the British Government is committed to addressing these cases in a way which resolves the anomaly.

In the absence of any change in the law, decisions on whether to seek the extradition of suspects "on the run" for pre-1998 offences are still taken by the prosecuting authorities, in line with the legal obligations on them, as part of the normal criminal justice process. But, as the UK Government's decision in 2000 not to pursue the extradition of convicted fugitives (including in the United States) who would qualify for early release under the GFA illustrates, there is no "political" agenda to pursue the extradition and trial of these people. And any suspects who were extradited and subsequently convicted would be able to apply for early release after two years, under the terms of the Good Friday Agreement.

Other Individuals

Anyone convicted of an offence unconnected with terrorism, or an offence committed after the Good Friday Agreement, will not be eligible for the Early Release Scheme. The UK law enforcement authorities continue to seek the extradition of such individuals in line with UK law.

Outstanding Warrants

When Home Office Minister Baroness Scotland visited the US, she explained that there were currently no outstanding warrants for the extradition of individuals from the US to Northern Ireland.

SECRETARY OF STATE, NORTHERN IRELAND OFFICE,
September 29, 2000.

Statement by Peter Mandelson on Extradition of Convicted Fugitives

On 28 July, all remaining prisoners eligible under the early release scheme who had completed 2 years of their sentences were released as envisaged in the Good Friday Agreement. The completion of these remaining releases has implications for a number of people who were sentenced to imprisonment for offences committed before the Good Friday Agreement, but who failed to complete these sentences. In most cases those concerned escaped from custody and fled to other countries up to 20 years ago. In many cases, extradition proceedings were initiated and in some of these the government is now being pressed by Court authorities to clarify its position. Whether to pursue an extradition request depends on the public interest at stake, including the remaining sentence which the fugitive would stand to serve if he or she were returned. It is clearly anomalous to pursue the extradition of people who appear to qualify for early release under the Good Friday Agreement scheme, and who would, on making a successful application to the Sentence Review Commissioners, have little if any of their original prison sentence to serve. In view of this and the time that has elapsed, I do not believe that it would now be proportionate or in the public interest to continue to pursue such cases. If these individuals wish to benefit from the early release scheme, they will be able to return to Northern Ireland and make an application to the Sentence Review Commissioners. If this is granted, normal licence conditions, including liability to recall to prison, will apply. The decision has no implications for the prosecution of other offences where sufficient evidence exists. It is not an amnesty. As with the rest of the early release programme, I do not under-estimate the hurt this decision may cause the victims of those whose extradition will no longer be pursued, and the onus it places on all of us to ensure that the Good Friday Agreement does result in a permanent peace in which there are no more victims.

OFFICE OF THE ATTORNEY GENERAL, DEPARTMENT OF JUSTICE,
Washington, DC, September 5, 2006.

The Rt. Hon. PETER HAIN,
Secretary of State for Northern Ireland, Northern Ireland Office, London SW1P 4PN.

DEAR SECRETARY HAIN: I am writing in response to your recent letter regarding the 2003 United States-United Kingdom extradition treaty. I appreciate your reconfirmation of the position of the Government of the United Kingdom (originally taken in September 2000) that it is "no longer proportionate or in the public interest to seek the extradition of individuals convicted of terrorist offences prior to 10th April 1998, 'who appear to qualify for early release under the Good Friday Agreement scheme, and who would, on making a successful application to the Sentence Review Commissioners, have little if any of their original prison sentence to serve.'" Additionally, you have reconfirmed that it was not the intention of your Government, in negotiating this Treaty, to make it easier for the UK to seek extradition of individuals suspected of committing terrorist offenses in Northern Ireland prior to April 10, 1998. Please accept this letter as my acknowledgement of your Government's official position and our mutual understanding of these matters. I believe that we share the view that the 2003 Treaty is critical to our mutual security in this age of global terrorism and transnational crime. Accordingly, the Bush Administration has made it a priority to seek the Senate's advice and consent to ratification of this Treaty. To that end, I will ask the Senate Foreign Relations Committee to include your letter, and this reply, in the official record of the Committee's consideration of the Treaty.

Sincerely,
Alberto R. Gonzales,
Attorney General.

REFERENCES

[1] Supplementary Treaty Between the United States of America and the United Kingdom of Great Britain and Northern Ireland, T.I.A.S. 12050, 1556 U.N.T.S. 369 (eff. Dec. 23, 1986) (Supplementary Treaty).

[2] Department of Justice Press Release dated Mar. 31, 2003, available on May 6, 2004 at [http://www.usdoj.gov/opa/pr/2003/March/03_ag_196.htm]; see also, S. Treaty Doc. 108-23 (2004). Early on a group of Irish-Americans objected to its provisions, Boyle, A Threat to Irish-Americans: The New U.S./U.K. Extradition Treaty, available on May 6, 2004 at [http://www.irishfreedomcommittee.net].

[3] See also, S.Ex.Rept. 109-91. The text of the resolution of approval and related documents from the report are appended.

[4] See generally, Extradition To and From the United States: Overview of the Law and Recent Treaties, CRS Rept. 98-958 (2003); Abbell, EXTRADITION TO AND FROM THE UNITED STATES (2002)(Abbell); Bassiouni, INTERNATIONAL EXTRADITION: UNITED STATES LAW AND PRACTICE (4th ed. 2002)(Bassiouni); 1 RESTATEMENT (THIRD) OF

THE FOREIGN RELATIONS LAW OF THE UNITED STATES, Subch.7B (1986 and 2003 Supp.)(RESTATEMENT). Interstate rendition, the surrender of a person by one of the states of the United States to another and sometimes also referred to as extradition, is beyond the scope of this report.

[5] In the case of the United States, 18 U.S.C. 3181-3196.

[6] 18 U.S.C. 3181, 3184. A somewhat dated list appears following in 18 U.S.C. 3181; see also, United States Department of State: Treaties in Force — January 1, 2003 (2003). In the absence of a treaty, the United States may only honor extradition requests under two circumstances: (1) when foreign nationals accused or convicted of committing crimes of violence against Americans overseas are sought, 18 U.S.C. 3181(b), or (2) in response to extradition requests from the international tribunals for Yugoslavia and Rwanda, P.L. 104-132, §443, 110 Stat. 1280 (1996), 18 U.S.C. 3181 note.

[7] In fact, the extradition provision of Jay's Treaty with Great Britain was our first extradition treaty, 8 Stat. 116, 129 (1794).

[8] "Extradition shall not be granted if . . . (c)(i) the offense for which extradition is requested is regarded by the requested Party as one of a political character; or (ii) the person sought proves that the request for his extradition has in fact been made with a view to try or punish him for an offense of a political character," Extradition Treaty Between the Government of the United States of America and the Government of the United Kingdom of Great Britain and Norther Ireland, Art.V(1), 28 U.S.T. 227, 230 (1977) (1977 Treaty). The 1977 Treaty, with the modifications found in the Supplementary Treaty, is still in effect.

[9] Eain v. Wilkes, 641 F.2d 504, 518 (7th Cir. 1981); Escobedo v. United States, 623 F.2d 1098, 1104 (5th Cir.1980); Sindona v. Grant, 619 F.2d 167, 173 (2d Cir. 1980); cf., Ornelas v. Ruiz, 161 U.S. 502, 511-12 (1896)("Can it be said that the commissioner had no choice on the evidence but to hold, in view of the character of the foray, the mode of attack, the persons killed or captured, and the kind of property taken or destroyed, that this was a movement in aid of a political revolt, an insurrection or a civil war, and that acts which contained all the characteristics of crimes under the ordinary law were exempt from extradition because of the political intentions of those who committed them? In our opinion this inquiry must be answered in the negative").

[10] In re McMullen, Magistrate No. 3-78-1099 MG (N.D.Cal. May 11, 1979), printed in, 132 Cong.Rec. 16585 (1986); In re Mackin, 80 Cr.Misc. 1 (S.D.N.Y. Aug. 13, 1981), appeal dism'd, pets. for mand. and hab.corp. den'd, 668 F.2d 122 (2d Cir. 1981); Quinn v. Robinson, No. C-82-668 RDA (N.D.Cal. 1983), rev'd, 783 F.2d 776 (9th Cir. 1986); In re Doherty, 599 F.Supp. 270 (S.D.N.Y. 1984).

[11] 132 Cong.Rec. 16586 (1986)(remarks of Sen. Lugar)("it was because of these cases that on June 25, 1985, the United States and the United Kingdom signed the Supplementary Extradition. Its purpose is to reverse the three cases where extradition was denied and put an end to this development in the law"); see generally, United States and United Kingdom Supplementary Extradition Treaty: Hearings Before the Senate Comm. on Foreign Relations, 99th Cong., 1st Sess. (1985)(Hearings); id. at 4 (testimony of Department of State Legal Adviser Abraham D. Sofaer)(". . .United States courts have refused to extradite to the United Kingdom four members of the Provisional Irish Republican Army [PIRA] who are accused, or convicted of violent terrorist crimes. In each case, extradition was denied because the terrorist crimes were committed as part of

a political struggle. These decisions direct a blow to the rule of law. . ."); id. at 7-8 (testimony of Dep.Att'y Gen. D. Lowell Jensen)("In recent years, there have been four cases involving request by the United Kingdom for the extradition of Irish Republican Army members charged or convicted of terrorist crimes. . . . In each of the four cases described, the fugitive claimed that the unsettled political situation in Northern Ireland constituted a war, revolution, or rebellion and that his offenses qualified for treatment as political offenses. The U.S. courts have accepted this argument in all but one case. . . . The British Government has concurred in our view that it is unacceptable that a criminal may commit a heinous offense which shocks the sensibilities of all decent people, flee the country which he has terrorized, and find safe haven in another country by labeling his crime a political offense").

[12] E.g., Hearings at 3-5 (testimony of State Department Legal Adviser Abraham D. Sofaer) ("The political offense doctrine is an exception to the general principle of extradition. This exception arose in the 18th century, as revolutionaries struggled for freedom against despotic regimes. When revolutionaries fled to the fledgling democracies of Western Europe, those governments sheltered them from political persecution. They refused to extradite fugitives whom requesting states sought to punish for engaging political activities. . . . In recent years, the exception has resulted in refusals of U.S. courts to extradite persons suspected or convicted of committing heinous crimes that are not, by their nature, political acts.... This supplementary treaty ... narrows the political offense exception as applied to United Kingdom requests to pure political and nonviolent crimes. It reflects the basic principle that terrorist violence should not be tolerated against stable democracies in which the political process is available to redress legitimate grievances and in which the judicial system provides fair treatment. Moreover, by using a bilateral treaty to implement this principle, we would not alter our extradition laws across the board. Instead, we are abler to decide whether to limit the exception on a nation-by-nation basis.... [T]he United Kingdom is also an ideal nation with whom to begin this process from the moral and political point of view. It is our longest and closest ally ... [and] one of the most open political systems in the world.... Some opponents have condemned this supplementary treaty as an assault upon civil liberties. They claim it will destroy the political offense exception, will facilitate repression of dissent, and will abolish judicial review of extradition decisions. These criticisms are unfounded. The treaty does not eliminate the political offense exception, but only removes from its scope certain specified violent crimes.... Moreover, the exception will continue in full force with respect to all nations other than the United Kingdom, and will never be revised with respect to repressive regimes").

[13] E.g., Hearings at 99 (statement of Professor Christopher H. Pyle) ("The political crimes defense has been part of Anglo-American extradition practice since the American Civil War, when Britain refused to surrender gunmen for the Southern cause who had sought refuge in Canada. It is a standard provision of nearly 90 treaties of extradition that the United States has concluded with other nations, and is common to the extradition treaties of most western nations. The defense has survived for more than a century, despite periodic bouts with political assassinations, kidnappings, and bombings, for two reasons. First, western nations have found it prudent not to commit themselves, by treaty, to use their legal systems to help other nations suppress any and all rebellions. Second, they have not wanted to be complicit in victors' justice, particularly where that

complicity would outrage sympathetic nationality groups within their own borders"); id. at 51 (statement of Rep. Biaggi).

[14] E.g., S.Ex.Rep.No,. 99-17, at 12 (additional views of Sen. Helms)("If this treaty had been in effect in 1776 ... this language would have labeled the boys who fought at Lexington and Concord as terrorists. There is no question that the British authorities in 1776 would have considered the guerilla operations of the Americans to be murder and assault ... there is no doubt whatsoever that such a treaty would have required us to extradite the patriots who fired the shot heard 'round the world to swing on a British gallows"); cf., id. at 491 (statement of Professor Keara M. O'Dempsey)("In the first ten Congresses of the United States, a total of 56 senators would probably have been extraditable under a treaty such as this, for they 'maliciously wounded and killed' British soldiers and possessed firearms with the intent 'to endanger life'").

[15] E.g., Hearings at 71 (testimony of Rep. Hughes) ("The principal effect of the supplementary treaty would be the derogation of over 100 years of American extradition practice and case law by virtually destroying the so-called political offense exception to extradition law.... Moreover, the legal adviser to the State Department admitted ... that the United Kingdom is 'an ideal nation from a moral and political point of view' to begin a process of exempting 'stable democracies' with fair legal systems from the restrictions of the political crimes defense. I strongly oppose this treaty-by-treaty stratagem, which I believe would effectively preempt the legislative process. As a result, our extradition laws will not be consistently applied, but will depend upon the status of the requesting nation as a friend or ally"); id. at 407-9 (statement of Rep. Rodino).

[16] E.g., Hearings at 143 (testimony of Rep. Hamilton Fish, Jr.) ("I ask that you take a long look at the presumption underlying this treaty; namely, that the judicial process in Northern Ireland provides fair treatment. The Emergency Powers Act now in effect in Northern Ireland was originally instituted by the British for the same reasons given for the institution of the treaty: As a response to the terrorism and violence in Northern Ireland. But it has become an instrument of oppression against fair and moral political opposition. The heritage of law, a precious gift of England to so many English-speaking judicial systems throughout the world, has apparently been set aside by Great Britain in Northern Ireland. . . . I visited the north of Ireland. I was appalled . . . and offended at the abuses that I saw in the legal system. In the Diplock courts, there were wide powers of arrest, detention, search and seizure. The right to a trial by jury had been abolished as cases were heard by a single judge; accused persons often faced physical and psychological coercion; and a person charged with an offense had no right to bail and could be detained indefinitely. In the last few years, there have been mass trials of up to 75 defendants at a time, in which one or more supergrasses, or informants, figured prominently. In these cases, the work of one informant, protected by Government immunity was enough to convict without further evidence. In the United States, this would amount, Mr. Chairman, to a loss of constitutional rights under the 1st, 4th, 5th, 6th, 8th and 14th amendments. I ask, can we willingly be a party to the enforcement of these laws under these conditions"); id. at 65-6 (statement of Sen. DeConcini).

[17] E.g., Hearings at 52 (statement of Rep. Biaggi) ("Sam O'Reilly lives in upstate New York. He is 89 years old. In 1916 he fought against the British in the so-called Easter Rebellion. If this treaty were passed Great Britain could extradite Sam O'Reilly to face

charges relating to his activities almost 70 years ago"). Other commentators asked whether these features might raise ex post facto or bill of attainder issues, id. at 305 (statement of Professor M. Cherif Bassiouni); id. at 528 (statement of Professor Francis A. Boyle).

[18] Hearings at 8 (statement of Dep.Att'y Gen. D. Lowell Jensen).

[19] "For the purposes of the Extradition Treaty, none of the following shall be regarded as an offense of a political character: (a) an offense for which both Contracting Parties have the obligation pursuant to a multilateral international agreement to extradite the person sought or to submit his case to their competent authorities for decision as to prosecution; (b) murder, voluntary manslaughter, and assault causing grievous bodily harm; (c) kidnaping, abduction, or serious unlawful detention, including taking a hostage; (d) an offense involving the use of a bomb, grenade, rocket, firearm, letter or parcel bomb, or any incendiary device if this use endangers any person; and (e) an attempt to commit any of the foregoing offenses or participation as an accomplice of a person who commits or attempts to commit such an offense," Supplementary Treaty, Art. 1. The agreements mentioned in (a) above appear to include the: Hague Convention for the Suppression of Unlawful Seizure of Aircraft, 22 U.S.T. 1641 (eff. Oct. 14, 1977); Montreal Convention for the Suppression of Unlawful Acts Against the Safety of Civil Aviation, 24 U.S.T. 564 (eff. Jan. 26, 1973); United Nations Convention Against Illicit Traffick in Narcotic Drugs and Psychotropic Substances, S.Treaty Doc. 101-4 (eff. Nov. 11, 1990); Protocol Amending the Single Convention on Narcotic Drugs, 1961, 26 U.S.T. 1439 (eff. Aug. 8, 1975); Convention on the Prevention and Punishment of Crimes Against Internationally Protected Persons, 28 U.S.T. 1975 (eff. Feb. 20, 1977); International Convention Against the Taking of Hostages, T.I.A.S. 11081 (eff. Jan. 6, 1985); Convention on the Physical Protection of Nuclear Material, T.I.A.S. 11080 (Feb. 8, 1987); Convention Against Torture and Other Cruel, Inhuman,or Degrading Treatment or Punishment, S.Treaty Doc. 100-20 (eff. Nov. 20, 1994); Protocol for the Suppression of Unlawful Acts of Violence at Airports Serving International Civil Aviation, S.Treaty Doc. 100-19 (eff. Nov. 18, 1994); Convention for the Suppression of Unlawful Acts Against the Safety of Maritime Navigation, S.Treaty Doc. 101-1 (eff. Mar. 6, 1995); Convention on Combating Bribery of Foreign Public Officials in International Business Transactions, S.Treaty Doc. 105-43 (eff. Feb. 15, 1997). Here and elsewhere treaties are referred to by their Senate Treaty Document number if an official citation is unavailable. The text of Senate Treaty Documents beginning with the 104th Congress are available at [http://www.gpoaccess.gov].

[20] "(a) Notwithstanding any other provision of this Supplementary Treaty, extradition shall not occur if the person sought establishes to the satisfaction of the competent judicial authority by a preponderance of the evidence that the request for extradition has in fact been made with a view to try or punish him on account of his race, religion, nationality, or political opinions, or that he would, if surrendered, be prejudiced at his trial or punished, detained or restricted in his personal liberty by reason of his race, religion, nationality or political opinions. "(b) In the United States, the competent judicial authority shall only consider the defense to extradition set forth in paragraph (a) for offenses listed in Article 1 of this Supplementary Treaty. A finding under paragraph (a) shall be immediately appealable by either party to the United States district court, or court of appeals, as appropriate. The appeal shall receive expedited consideration at

every stage. The time for filing a notice of appeal shall be 30 days from the date of the filing of the decision. In all other respects, the applicable provisions of the Federal Rules of Appellate Procedure or Civil Procedure, as appropriate, shall govern the appeals process," Supplementary Treaty, Art.3.

[21] "Nothing in this Supplementary Treaty shall be interpreted as imposing the obligation to extradite if the judicial authority of the requested Party determines that the evidence of criminality presented is not sufficient to sustain the charge under the provisions of the treaty. The evidence of criminality must be such as, according to the law of the requested Party, would justify committal for trial if the offense had been committed in the territory of the requested Party. "In determining whether an individual is extraditable from the United States, the judicial authority of the United States shall permit the individual sought to present evidence on the questions of whether: (1) there is probable cause; (2) a defense to extradition specified in the Extradition Treaty or this Supplementary Treaty, and within the jurisdiction of the courts, exists; and (3) the act upon which the request for extradition is based would constitute an offense punishable under the laws of the United States. "Probable cause means whether there is sufficient evidence to warrant a man of reasonable caution in the belief that: (1) the person arrested or summoned to appear is the person sought; (2) in the case of a person accused of having committed a crime, an offense has been committed by the accused; and (3) in the case of a person alleged to have been convicted of an offense, a certificate of conviction or other evidence of conviction or criminality exists," Supplementary Treaty, Art.2.

[22] The treaty offered to the Senate would have permitted extradition as long as the laws of the requesting nation did not bar prosecution because of the lapse of time (S.Treaty Doc. 99-8, at 2) — a change thought disadvantageous to fugitives in this country, Hearings at 312-13 (statement of Professor Charles Rice).

[23] Marshall, Extradited American Gets Life Sentence in IRA Killing, LOS ANGELES TIMES 7 (Feb. 17, 1988).

[24] Id.

[25] Extradition and the Conflict in Norther Ireland: The Past, the Present and Future of an Intractable Problem, 25 HASTINGS INTERNATIONAL AND COMPARATIVE LAW REVIEW 169, 182 n.104 (2002). McMullen's initially successful contention, that the Supplementary Treaty applied to him would constitute a bill of attainder, ultimately failed, In re Extradition of McMullen, 769 F.Supp. 1278 (S.D.N.Y. 1991), aff'd, 953 F.2d 761 (2d Cir. 1992), aff'd in part and rev'd in part en banc, 989 F.2d 603 (2d Cir. 1993).

[26] 138 Cong.Rec. 2639 (1992) (remarks of Rep.Gilman); see also, Kelly, The Empire Strikes Back: The Taking of Joe Doherty, 61 FORDHAM LAW REVIEW 317 (1992); 138 Cong.Rec. 1421, 4027, 23160 (1992)(remarks of Sen. Specter, Rep. Neal, and Rep. Engel, respectively); INS v. Doherty, 502 U.S. 314 (1992).

[27] See e.g., In re Extradition of Howard, 791 F.Supp. 31 (D.Mass. 1992), aff'd, 996 F.2d 1320, 1332 (1st Cir. 1993) (magistrate did not err in concluding that a black murder suspect had failure to show that he would be prejudiced on account of his race if extradited); In re Extradition of Smyth, 61 F.3d 711, 713 (9th Cir. 1995)(escaped prisoner failed to establish that he would be discriminatorily punished); In re Extradition of Artt, 972 F.Supp.1253 (N.D.Cal. 1997), rev'd, 158 F.3d 462 (9th Cir.

1998), op. withdrawn, 183 F.3d 944 (9th Cir. 1999)(requests for extradition were withdrawn following the Belfast/Good Friday Agreement under which the contemporaries of those sought had been released), reinstated, 248 F.3d 1197 (9th Cir. 2001).

[28] Hannay, An Analysis of the U.S.-U.K. Supplementary Extradition Treaty, 21 INTERNATIONAL LAWYER 925, 937 (1987)("The Supplementary Treaty's restriction of the political offense exception represents a substantial improvement in the ability of the United States and the United Kingdom to fight the rising tide of international political violence and is a good model for similar treaties with other democracies"); Sofaer, The Political Offense Exception and Terrorism, 15 DENVER JOURNAL OF INTERNATIONAL LAW and POLICY 125 (1986); Lubet, Taking the Terror Out of Political Terrorism: The Supplementary Treaty of Extradition Between the United States and the United Kingdom, 19 CONNECTICUT LAW REVIEW 862, 892-93 (1987).

[29] Bassiouni, The "Political Offense Exception" Revisited: Extradition Between the U.S. and U.K. — A Choice Between Friendly Cooperation Among Allies and Sound Law and Policy, 15 DENVER JOURNAL OF INTERNATIONAL LAW and POLICY 255 (1987)("The Supplementary Treaty reverses a historical trend in the U.S.... Such a reversal ... means only that the U.S. has taken sides in an internal political conflict, which it had carefully avoided doing in the past. A policy of neutrality toward foreign internal civil strife is wisest in light of the many ongoing civil conflicts occurring all over the world"); Extradition and the Conflict in Northern Ireland: The Past, Present and Future of an Intractable Problem, 25 HASTINGS INTERNATIONAL AND COMPARATIVE LAW REVIEW 169, 197 (2002)("The Northern Ireland peace process has created a landscape where the Supplementary Treaty is no longer necessary or desirable as a means of effecting extradition.... Elimination of the Supplementary Treaty ... eliminate many of the problems identified above that can flow from using a treaty-by-treaty approach to extradition, such as eliminating the appearance of U.S. involvement in the U.K.'s policies in Northern Ireland").

[30] Foreign Courts on Trial: Why U.S. Courts Should Avoid Applying the Inquiry Provision of the Supplementary U.S.-U.K. Extradition Treaty, 25 STANFORD JOURNAL OF INTERNATIONAL LAW 257, 288 (1988)("If application of the traditional political offense exception strained relations between the United States and United Kingdom, the result of a judicial determination that the United Kingdom's request was made in bad faith or that its court system is unfair will have even more disastrous consequences on U.S. foreign policy"); but see, Revolutionaries Beware: The Erosion of the Political Offense Exception Under the 1986 United States-United Kingdom Supplementary Extradition Treaty, 136 UNIVERSITY OF PENNSYLVANIA LAW REVIEW 1515, 1545 (1988)("The problem with this new treaty is that, although it remedies certain problems that existed under the old regime, it still does not resolve adequately the problem of how to deal fairly with alleged political offenders. Article 1, for example, sweeps too broadly in its denial of the political offense exception to those who commit acts of political violence. It ignores the possibility that there may be some circumstances under which a person committing such act deserves protection").

[31] Reconciliation of the Penitent: Sectarian Violence, Prisoner Release, and Justice Under the Good Friday Peace Accord, 26 JOURNAL OF LEGISLATION 163, 175-75 (2002); The Legality of the Pardoning of Paramilitaries Under the Early Release Provisions of

Northern Ireland's Good Friday Agreement, 34 CORNELL INTERNATIONAL LAW JOURNAL 227 (2001); Bell, Dealing With the Past in Northern Ireland, 26 FORDHAM INTERNATIONAL LAW JOURNAL 1095, 1111-115 (2003).

[32] "1. Extradition shall not be granted if the offense for which extradition is requested is a political offense. "2. For the purposes of this Treaty, the following offenses shall not be considered to be political offenses: (a) a murder or other willful crime against the person of a Head of State of one of the Contracting States, or of a member of the Head of State's family; (b) an offense for which both Contracting States have the obligation pursuant to a multilateral international agreement to extradite the person sought or to submit the case to their competent authorities for decision as to prosecution; and (c) a conspiracy or attempt to commit any of the foregoing offenses, or aiding or abetting a person who commits or attempts to commit such offenses. "3. Notwithstanding the terms of paragraph 2 of this Article, extradition shall not be granted if the executive authority of the Requested State determines that the request was politically motivated,"Extradition Treaty with Belize, Art.4 (1)-(3) (S.Treaty Doc. 106-38); see also, Extradition Treaty with the Bahamas, Art.3 (1)-(3) (S.Treaty Doc. 102-17); Extradition Treaty with Jordan, Art.4 (1)-(3) (S.Treaty Doc. 104-3); Extradition Treaty with the Philippines, Art.3 (1)-(3) (S.Treaty Doc. 104-16); Extradition Treaty with Bolivia, Art.5 (1) (S.Treaty Doc. 104-22); Extradition Treaty with Malaysia, Art.4 (1)-(3) (S.Treaty Doc. 104-26); Extradition Treaty with Cyprus, Art.4 (1)-(3) (S.Treaty Doc. 105-16); Extradition Treaty with Argentina, Art.4 (1)-(3) (S.Treaty Doc. 105-18); Extradition Treaty with Antigua and Barbuda, Art.4 (1)-(3) (S.Treaty Doc. 105-19); Extradition Treaty with Dominica, Art.4 (1)-(3) (S.Treaty Doc. 105-19); Extradition Treaty with Grenada, Art.4 (1)(3) (S.Treaty Doc. 105-19); Extradition Treaty with St. Lucia, Art.4 (1)-(3) (S.Treaty Doc. 105-19); Extradition Treaty with St. Kitts and Nevis, Art.4 (1)-(3) (S.Treaty Doc. 105-19); Extradition Treaty with St. Vincent and the Grenadines, Art.4 (1)-(3) (S.Treaty Doc. 105-19); Extradition Treaty with Barbados, Art.4 (1)-(3) (S.Treaty Doc. 105-20); Extradition Treaty with Trinidad and Tobago, Art.4 (1)-(3) (S.Treaty Doc. 105-21); Extradition Treaty with Korea, Art.4 (1)-(3) (S.Treaty Doc. 106-2); Extradition Treaty with Austria, Art.4 (1)(3) (and murder)(S.Treaty Doc. 105-50); Extradition Treaty with Paraguay, Art.4 (1)-(3) (S.Treaty Doc. 106-4). Four others list treaty obligations under specific treaties rather than providing a general provision as in Art.4, subpara.2(b) of the Treaty with Belize: Extradition Treaty with France, Art.4 (1)-(4) (S.Treaty Doc. 105-13); Extradition Treaty with India, Art.4 (1)-(3) (S.Treaty Doc. 105-30); Extradition Treaty with Sri Lanka, Art.4 (1)-(3) (S.Treaty Doc. 106-34); Extradition Treaty with Peru, Art.4 (1)-(3) (S.Treaty Doc. 107-6). The Extradition Treaty with Switzerland, Art.3 (S.Treaty Doc. 104-9) has no exceptions to the political offense bar.

[33] "1. Extradition shall not be granted if the offense for which extradition is requested is a political offense. "2. for the purposes of this Treaty, the following offenses shall not be considered to be political offenses: (a) a murder or other willful crime against the person of a Head of State of one of the Contracting States, or of a member of the Head of State's family; (b) an offense for which both Contracting States have the obligation pursuant to a multilateral international agreement to extradite the person sought or to submit the case to their competent authorities for decision as to prosecution; (c) murder, manslaughter, malicious wounding or inflicting grievous bodily harm; (d) an offense

involving kidnaping, abduction, or any form of unlawful detention, including the taking of a hostage; (e) placing or using an explosive, incendiary or destructive device or substance capable of endangering life or causing grievous bodily harm; (f) an attempt to commit, or participation or complicity in the commission of, any of the foregoing offenses; and (g) an "association of wrongdoers" as provided by the laws of Luxembourg, or a "conspiracy" as provided by the laws of the United States, to commit any of the foregoing offenses. "3. Notwithstanding the terms of paragraph 2 of this Article, extradition shall not be granted if the executive authority of the Requested State determines that the request was politically motivated," Extradition Treaty with Luxembourg, Art.4(1)-(3) (S.Treaty Doc. 105-10); see also, Supplementary Extradition Treaty with Germany, Art.4 (1)-(3) (S.Treaty Doc. 100-6); Second Supplementary Extradition Treaty with Spain, Art.4, (1)-(3) (S.Treaty Doc. 102-24); Extradition Treaty with Hungary, Art.4, (1)-(3) (S.Treaty Doc. 104-5); Supplementary Extradition Treaty with Belgium, Art.2, (S.Treaty Doc. 104-8); Extradition Treaty with Poland, Art.4, (1)-(3) (S.Treaty Doc. 105-14); Extradition Treaty with South Africa, Art.4, (1)-(3) (S.Treaty Doc. 106-24); Extradition Treaty with Lithuania, Art.4, (1)(3) (S.Treaty Doc. 107-4).

[34] Lord Mountbatten, the Queen's cousin, was killed in a bomb blast aboard his yacht while sailing off the coast of Ireland. The man convicted of his murder was released pursuant to the Good Friday Agreement, On This Day: August 27, BBC NEWS, available at http:\news.bbc.co.uk.

[35] S.Ex.Rept.99-17 (1986)("The essence of the committee's compromise is found in what are now Articles 1 and 3 of the Supplementary Treaty. Article 1 narrows the list of offenses which a court may treat as political offenses. However, references in the original Supplementary Treaty to property damage, possession, intent, and conspiracy were deleted; manslaughter was qualified by 'voluntary', and unlawful detention was qualified by 'serious'").

[36] "The advice and consent of the Senate under section 1 is subject to the following understanding: Under United States law, a United States judge makes a certification of extraditability of a fugitive to the Secretary of State. In the process of making such certification, a United States judge also makes determinations regarding the application of the political offense exception. Accordingly, the United States of America understands that the statement in paragraphs 3 [relating to political motivation] and 4 [relating to military offenses] of Article 4 that "in the United States, the executive branch is the competent authority for the purposes of this Article" applies only to those specific paragraphs of Article 4, and does not alter or affect the role of the United States judiciary in making certifications of extraditability or determinations of the application of the political offense exception."

[37] 152 Cong. Rec. S10767 (daily ed. Sept. 29, 2006); S. Ex. Rept. 109-19, at 8-10 (2006).

[38] "(a) Notwithstanding any other provision of this Supplementary Treaty, extradition shall not occur if the person sought establishes to the satisfaction of the competent judicial authority by a preponderance of the evidence that the request for extradition has in fact been made with a view to try or punish him on account of his race, religion, nationality, or political opinions, or that he would, if surrendered, be prejudiced at his trial or punished, detained or restricted in his personal liberty by reason of his race, religion, nationality or political opinions. "(b) In the United States, the competent

judicial authority shall only consider the defense to extradition set forth in paragraph (a) for offenses listed in Article 1 of this Supplementary Treaty. A finding under paragraph (a) shall be immediately appealable by either party to the United States district court, or court of appeals, as appropriate. The appeal shall receive expedited consideration at every stage. The time for filing a notice of appeal shall be 30 days from the date of the filing of the decision. In all other respects, the applicable provisions of the Federal Rules of Appellate Procedure or Civil Procedure, as appropriate, shall govern the appeals process," Supplementary Treaty, Art.3.

[39] "Notwithstanding the terms of paragraph 2 of this Article, extradition shall not be granted if the competent authority of the Requested State determines that the request was politically motivated. In the United States, the executive branch is the competent authority for the purpose of this Article," Art.4(3). It likewise withdraws authority to pass on the military offense defense from the courts, "The competent authority of the Requested State may refuse extradition for offenses under military law that are not offenses under ordinary criminal law. In the United States, the executive branch is the competent authority for the purpose of this Article," Art.4(4).

[40] See e.g., Jamaican Extradition Treaty, Art.3(2), S.Treaty Doc. 98-18 (eff. July 7, 1991); French Extradition Treaty, Art.4(4), S.Treaty Doc. 105-13 (eff. Feb.1, 2002).

[41] Abbell, at 4-60 to 4-61 ("[W]ere it not for the substantial role played by the Senate Foreign Relations Committee in revising the supplementary extradition treaty between the United States and the United Kingdom, in the course of which it delegated responsibility to the courts to decide matters of this nature that would otherwise fall within the Rule of Non-Inquiry, there would be no question that the determination of a requesting country's motives in requesting extradition from the United States would continue to be a matter within the exclusive purview of the Executive.... Nevertheless, except with respect to the application of the supplementary extradition treaty with the United Kingdom itself, the federal courts have continued to apply, if not strengthen, the Rule of Non-Inquiry in this and other areas. Moreover, most United States extradition treaties negotiated subsequent to 1986 expressly leave the determination of the requesting country's motive for requesting extradition to the executive authority of the requested country, or do not specify the manner in which the requested country is to make this determination").

[42] Hannay, Analysis of the U.S.-U.K. Supplementary Treaty, 21 INTERNATIONAL LAWYER 925, 926 (1987)("Under present case law in the United States, it is within the jurisdiction of the courts to decide whether the crime for which extradition has been requested is a political offense. By contrast, the Secretary of State has sole discretion to determine whether an extradition request should be denied because it is a subterfuge, and accordingly, courts traditionally have declined to consider whether the requesting country's motives in seeking extradition are political").

[43] "Nothing in this Supplementary Treaty shall be interpreted as imposing the obligation to extradite if the judicial authority of the requested Party determines that the evidence of criminality presented is not sufficient to sustain the charge under the provisions of the treaty. The evidence of criminality must be such as, according to the law of the requested Party, would justify committal for trial if the offense had been committed in the territory of the requested Party. "In determining whether an individual is extraditable from the United States, the judicial authority of the United States shall

permit the individual sought to present evidence on the questions of whether: (1) there is probable cause; (2) a defense to extradition specified in the Extradition Treaty or this Supplementary Treaty, and within the jurisdiction of the courts, exists; and (3) the act upon which the request for extradition is based would constitute an offense punishable under the laws of the United States. "Probable cause means whether there is sufficient evidence to warrant a man of reasonable caution in the belief that: (1) the person arrested or summoned to appear is the person sought; (2) in the case of a person accused of having committed a crime, an offense has been committed by the accused; and (3) in the case of a person alleged to have been convicted of an offense, a certificate of conviction or other evidence of conviction or criminality exists," Supplementary Treaty, Art.2.

[44] "Extradition shall be granted only if the evidence be found sufficient according to the law of the requested Party either to justify the committal for trial of the person sought if the offense of which he is accused had been committed in the territory of the requested Party or to prove that he is the identical person convicted by the courts of the requesting Party," 1977 Treaty, Art. IX(1).

[45] Abbell, at §3-2(5), citing inter alia, 14 Op.Att'y Gen. 281 (1873).

[46] Abbell, at §3-2(18).

[47] See, Stogner v. California, 123 S.Ct. 2446, 2452 (2003).

[48] "Extradition shall not be granted if . . . (b) the prosecution for the offense for which extradition is requested has become barred by lapse of time according to the law of the requesting or requested Party," 1977 Treaty, Art. 5(1)(b).

[49] Hearings, at 312-13 (statement of Professor Charles Rice). Under American law, there is generally no statute of limitations for murder, e.g., 18 U.S.C. 3281, or for certain federal terrorist crimes, 18 U.S.C. 3286(b). The general period of limitation for other federal crimes is five years, 18 U.S.C. 3282.

[50] E.g., Extradition Treaty with Peru, Art.IV(1)(b), S.Treaty Doc.107-6 (2002); Extradition Treaty with South Africa, Art. 8, S.Treaty Doc. 106-24 (2000); Extradition Treaty with Luxembourg, Art.2(6), S.Treaty Doc. 105-10 (1997).

[51] E.g., Extradition Treaty with Paraguay, S.Treaty Doc. 106-4 (1999); Extradition Treaty with Zimbabwe, S.Treaty Doc. 105-33 (1998); Extradition Treaty with the Philippines, S.Treaty Doc. 104-16 (1995).

[52] E.g., Extradition Treaty with Lithuania, Art.6, S.Treaty Doc. 107-4 (2002); Extradition Treaty with Belize, Art.8, S.Treaty Doc. 106-38 (2000); Extradition Treaty with Argentina, Art. 7, S.Treaty Doc. 105-18 (1997).

[53] "(1) In urgent cases the person sought may, in accordance with the law of the requested Party, be provisionally arrested on application through the diplomatic channel by the competent authorities of the requesting Party. The application shall contain an indication of intention to request the extradition of the person sought and a statement of the existence of a warrant of arrest or a conviction against that person, and, if available, a description of the person sought, and such further information, if any, as would be necessary to justify the issue of a warrant of arrest had the offense been committed, or the person sought been convicted, in the territory of the requested Party. "(2) A person arrested upon such an application shall be set at liberty upon the expiration of sixty days from the date of his arrest if a request for his extradition shall not have been received. This provision shall not prevent the institution of further proceedings for the extradition

of the person sought if a request is subsequently received," 1977 Treaty, Art. VIII (emphasis added). The Supplementary Treaty extended the permissible period of detention from 45 to 60 days.

[54] "1. In an urgent situation, the Requesting State may request the provisional arrested of the person sought pending presentation of the request for extradition. A request for provisional arrest may be transmitted through the diplomatic channel or directly between the United States Department of Justice and such competent authority as the United Kingdom may designate for the purpose of this Article. "2. The application for provisional arrest shall contain: a description of the person sought; (b) the location of the person sought; (c)a brief statement of the facts including, if possible, the date and location of the offense; (d) a description of the law(s) violated; (e) a statement of the existence of a warrant or order of arrest or a finding of guilt or judgment of conviction against the person sought; and (f) a statement that the supporting documents for the person sought will follow within the time specified in this Treaty. "3. The Requesting State shall be notified without delay of the disposition of its request for provisional arrest and the reasons for any inability to proceed with the request. "4. A person who is provisionally arrested may be discharged from custody upon the expiration of sixty (60) days from the date of provisional arrest pursuant to this Treaty if the executive authority of the Requested State has not received the formal request for extradition and the documents supporting the extradition request as required in Article 8. For this purpose, receipt of the formal request for extradition and supporting documents by the Embassy of the Requested State in the Requesting State shall constitute receipt by the executive authority of the Requested State. "5. The fact that the person has been discharged from custody pursuant to paragraph 4 of this article shall not prejudice the subsequent re-arrest and extradition of that person if the extradition request and supporting documents are delivered at a later date, 2003 Treaty, Art. 12 (emphasis added).

[55] "When a request for extradition is granted, the requested Party shall, so far as its laws allows and subject to such conditions as it may impose having regard to the rights of other claimants, furnish the requesting Party with all sums of money and other articles . . .(b) which may have been acquired by the person sought as a result of the offense and are in his possession," Art. XIII.

[56] 18 U.S.C. 981(a)(1)(G).

[57] 18 U.S.C. 1963.

[58] 21 U.S.C. 881, 853.

[59] 18 U.S.C. 981, 982.

[60] 18 U.S.C. 1956(a),(c)(7)(B); 1957(a),(f)(3); 981(a)(1); 982(a)(1).

[61] 18 U.S.C. 981(b)(4).

[62] 28 U.S.C. 2467.

[63] 18 U.S.C. 981(i)(1).

[64] 18 U.S.C. 983(d), 1963(l); 21 U.S.C. 853(n); 28 U.S.C. 2467(b)(1)(C).

[65] United States v. Antonakeas, 255 F.3d 714, (9th Cir. 2001), citing, United States v. Rauscher, 119 U.S. 407, 409-10 (1886) and United States v. Alvarez-Machain, 504 U.S. 655, 659-60 (1992); Gallo-Chamorro v. United States, 233 F.3d 1298, 1305 (11th Cir. 2000).

[66] RESTATEMENT, §477, Comment b.

[67] United States v. Rauscher, 119 U.S. at 423, 433; cf., United States v. Alvarez-Machain, 504 U.S. at 659-60. Abbell, at §3-2(11).

[68] Abbell, at 3-3, citing, Valentine v. United States ex rel. Neidecker, 299 U.S. 5, 10 (1936) and Charlton v. Kelly, 229 U.S. 447, 463 (1913), respectively ("In analyzing any possible inconsistencies between the federal extradition statutes and United States extradition treaties, it should be borne in mind that: (1) to the extent that provisions of extradition treaties are self-executing, they have the equivalent status of legislation; [and] (2) a later treaty supersedes an earlier statute to the extent they are inconsistent. . .").

[69] Abbell, at 3-33.

[70] United States v. Tse, 135 F.3d 200, 206 (1st Cir. 1998); United States v. Andonian, 29 F.3d 1432, 1435 (9th Cir. 1994); United States v. Diwan, 864 F.2d 715, 721 (11th Cir. 1989).

[71] Compare, United States v. Puentes, 50 F.3d 1567, 1572 (11th Cir. 1995); United States v. Levy, 905 F.2d 326, 328 (10th Cir. 1990); United States v. Thirion, 813 F.2d 146, 151 (8th Cir. 1987); United States v. Najohn, 785 F.2d 1420, 1422 (9th Cir. 1986); with, United States v. Kaufman, 874 F.2d 242, 243 (5th Cir. 1989); Demjanjuk v. Petrovsky, 776 F.2d 571, 583-84 (6th Cir. 1985).

[72] "A person extradited shall not be detained or proceeded against in the territory of the requesting Party for any offense other than an extraditable offense established by the facts in respect to which his extradition has been granted, or on account of any other matters, nor be extradited by that Party to a third State. . . ." 1977 Treaty, Art. XII.

[73] "This Treaty shall apply to offenses committed before as well as after the date it enters into force," 2003 Treaty, Art.22(1).

[74] E.g., Extradition Treaty with Lithuania, Art. 21, S.Treaty Doc. 107-4 (2002); Extradition Treaty with Sri Lanka, Art.21, S.Treaty Doc. 106-34 (2000); Extradition Treaty with Korea, Art.20, S.Treaty Doc. 106-2 (1999).

[75] "This Supplementary Treaty shall apply to any offense committed before or after this Supplementary Treaty enters into force, provided that this Supplementary Treaty shall not apply to an offense committed before this Supplementary Treaty enters into force which was not an offense under the laws of both Contracting Parties at the time of its commission," Supplementary Treaty, Art.5.

[76] E.g., Extradition Treaty with Lithuania, Art.16(2), S.Treaty Doc.107-4 (2002)("A person extradited under this Treaty may not be extradited to a third State or extradited or surrendered to an international tribunal for an offense committed prior to extradition unless the Requested State consents"); see also, Extradition Treaty with Sri Lanka, Art.16(2), S.Treaty Doc. 106-34 (2000); Extradition Treaty with South Africa, Art.18, S.Treaty Doc. 106-24 (2000).

[77] An exchange of notes has made it clear, however, that the ban on onward extradition at least "applies to preclude in accordance with that provision the onward surrender to the International Criminal Court (ICC) of a person extradited from the United States," S. Treaty Doc. at 17, 19.

[78] RESTATEMENT §476, Comment c.

[79] "Extradition shall not be granted if: (a) the person sought would, if proceeded against in the territory of the requested Party for the offense for which his extradition is requested, be entitled to be discharged on the grounds of a previous acquittal or conviction in the

territory of the requesting or requested Party or of a third State," 1977 Treaty, Art.V(1)(a).

[80] Abbell at §3-2(22), citing, Abbate v. United States, 359 U.S. 187 (1959).

[81] 152 Cong. Rec. S10767 (daily ed. Sept. 29, 2006); S.Ex.Rept. 109-19, at 9 (2006).

[82] Bassiouni, 682-84; RESTATEMENT §475, Comment f.

[83] There may be some dispute as to the vintage of our policy, compare, Abbell §2-2(18)("it has consistently been the policy of the United States that all nations should extradite their own nationals"); with, Bassiouni at 684 ("The official policy of the United States in treaty negotiations has been, until lately, to prevent when possible the surrender of nationals, but this is no longer the case").

[84] Charlton v. Kelly, 229 U.S. 447, 466-76 (1913); Abbell, 3-23 to 3-24.

[85] E.g., Extradition Treaty with Belize, Art.3, S.Treaty Doc.106-38 (2000); Extradition Treaty with South Africa, Art. 3, S.Treaty Doc. 106-24 (2000); Extradition Treaty with Grenada, Art.3, S.Treaty Doc. 105-19(1997).

[86] Abbell, at §3-3(8).

[87] E.g., Extradition Treaty with Korea, Art. 16, S.Treaty Doc. 106-2 (1999); Extradition Treaty with Luxembourg, Art. 18, S.Treaty Doc.105-10 (1997); Extradition Treaty with Jamaica, Art. XV, S.Treaty Doc. 98-18 (1984).

[88] 2003 Treaty, Art. 20(2); see e.g., Extradition Treaty with Argentina, Arts.9, 19(2), S.Treaty Doc. 105-18 (1997) ("All documents submitted by the Requesting State pursuant to this Treaty shall be accompanied by a translation into the language of the Requested State. . . . The Requesting State shall bear the expenses relating to the translation of documents. . ."); Extradition Treaty with Korea, Arts. 8(6), 18(2), S.Treaty Doc.106-2 (1999); Extradition Treaty with Austria, Arts. 12, 22(2), S.Treaty Doc. 105-50 (1998).

[89] "1. If the extradition request is granted for a person who is being proceeded against or is serving a sentence in the Requested State, the Requested State may temporarily surrender the person sought to the Requesting State for the purpose of prosecution. If the Requested States requests, the Requesting State shall keep the person so surrendered in custody and shall return that person to the Requested State after the conclusion of the proceedings against that person, in accordance with conditions to be determined by mutual agreement of the States. "2. The Requested State may postpone the extradition proceedings against a person who is being prosecuted or who is serving a sentence in that State. The postponement may continue until the prosecution of the person sought has been concluded or until such person has served any sentence imposed," 2003 Treaty, Art.14.

[90] "In view of the United States confrontation and speedy trial requirements in criminal cases, it is unlikely that the United States would, except in exceptional circumstances, temporarily surrender a requested person whom it wished to prosecute for an offense other than that for which his extradition has been requested because temporary surrender might preclude subsequent prosecution in the United States. . . . [T]he United States can be expected frequently to exercise its prerogative to temporarily surrender persons serving sentences for different offenses in the United States," Abbell at 3-30 to 3-31.

[91] E.g., Extradition Treaty with France, Art. 21, S.Treaty Doc. 105-13 (1997); Extradition Treaty with Bolivia, Art. XV, S.Treaty Doc. 104-22 (1995); Extradition Treaty with Costa Rica, Art. 19, S.Treaty Doc. 98-17 (1984).

[92] "Either State may authorize transportation through its territory of a person surrendered to the other State by a third State or from the other State to a third State. A request for transit shall contain a description of the person being transported and brief statement of the facts of the case. A person in transit shall be detained in custody during the period of transit," 2003 Treaty, Art. 19(1).

[93] "Authorization is not required when air transportation is used by one State and no landing is scheduled on the territory of the other State. If an unscheduled landing does occur, the state in which the unscheduled landing occurs may require a request for transit pursuant to paragraph 1 of this Article, and it may detain the person until the request for transit is received and the transit is effected, as long as the request is received within 96 hours of the unscheduled landing," 2003 Treaty, Art. 19(2)

[94] The bold emphasis found in the correspondence, which follows the resolution of approval below, appears in the original, see S.Ex.Rept. 109-19, at 12-3 (2006).

In: Law and Law Enforcement Issues
Editor: Gerald M. Kessler, pp. 197-212

ISBN: 978-1-60456-044-2

Chapter 7

SHARING LAW ENFORCEMENT AND INTELLIGENCE INFORMATION: THE CONGRESSIONAL ROLE*

Richard A. Best Jr.

ABSTRACT

Almost all assessments of the attacks of September 11, 2001, have concluded that U.S. intelligence and law enforcement agencies had failed to share information that might have provided advance warning of the plot. This realization led Congress to approve provisions in the USA PATRIOT Act (P.L. 107-56) and subsequent legislation that removed barriers to information sharing between intelligence and law enforcement agencies, and mandated exchanges of information relating to terrorist threats. Most experts agreed that statutory changes, albeit difficult to enact, were essential to change the approaches taken by executive branch agencies.

The barriers that existed prior to September 2001 had a long history based on a determination to prevent government spying on U.S. persons. This had led to the establishment of high statutory barriers to the sharing of law enforcement and intelligence information. The statutes laid the foundation of the so-called "wall" between intelligence and law enforcement that was buttressed by regulations, Justice Department policies, and guidance from the judicial branch.

Despite the widespread acceptance of a barrier between law enforcement and intelligence, by the early 1990s it had become apparent to some that the two communities could mutually support efforts to combat international criminal activities including narcotics smuggling. Later in the decade dangerous threats to the U.S. posed by international terrorists came into sharper focus. Nevertheless, efforts to adjust laws, regulations, and practices did not succeed, drawing strong opposition from civil libertarians. Only the tragedy of the 9/11 attacks overcame earlier concerns and led Congress and the executive branch to remove most statutory barriers to information sharing.

Laws and regulations have changed significantly since September 2001 and an Information Sharing Executive (ISE) has been established within the Office of the Director of National Intelligence to design and implement information sharing procedures. It is clear, however, that sustaining the exchange of law enforcement and

---

* Excerpted from CRS Report RL33873, dated February 13, 2007.

intelligence information remains a challenge. In particular, there is continued concern about sharing of information that might in some way jeopardize the rights of free speech or association of U.S. persons. This opposition has contributed to the difficulty Congress has had in addressing legislation in this area and can be expected to continue. Some argue that, given the extent of legislation enacted in recent years, extensive oversight of information sharing efforts may be an appropriate way to ensure that the balance between ensuring domestic security and protecting civil liberties can be maintained.

Introduction

The failure of the U.S. Intelligence Community to provide better warning of the September 11, 2001, attacks has been widely attributed to the existence of "walls" between intelligence and law enforcement agencies. The walls arguably kept analysts from talking to each other and from sharing pieces of information that, if they had been viewed in close relationship, might have yielded a coherent picture of the emerging plot. This theory cannot of course be fully proven — the overall plot might not have been discerned even if the best analysts had had access to all available information in every agency. Nevertheless, the fact that available data had not in fact been shared focused public and congressional attention on the real or perceived walls that inhibited the exchange of information among agencies.

A consensus emerged that the walls should be torn down. In December 2002, the Joint Inquiry into Intelligence Community Activities Before and After the Terrorist Attacks of September 11, 2001, established by the two congressional intelligence committees, made a factual finding that the "important point is that the Intelligence Community, for a variety of reasons, did not bring together and fully appreciate a range of information that could have greatly enhanced its chances of uncovering and preventing Usama Bin Ladin's plan to attack the United States on September 11, 2001."[1] The Inquiry also made a systemic finding that:

> Within the Intelligence Community, agencies did not adequately share relevant counterterrorism information, prior to September 11. This breakdown in communications was the result of a number of factors, including differences in the agencies' missions, legal authorities and cultures. Information was not sufficiently shared, not only between different Intelligence Community agencies, but also within individual agencies, and between the intelligence and law enforcement agencies.[2]

Similar conclusions were reached in July2004 by the 9/11 Commission (the National Commission on Terrorist Attacks Upon the United States) carefully documented the failures of pre-9/11 information sharing among agencies and within different offices of the Justice Department and recommended a number of initiatives to encourage unity of effort in sharing information.[3]

The Legacy of FISA

The failure to share information prior to 9/11 had not occurred by happenstance. Law enforcement and intelligence information was not routinely shared and collectors and analysts were walled off from one another through a complex arrangement of constitutional principles, statutes, policies, and practices. These regulations had their origin in longstanding divisions of labor that reached back far into pre-World War II practices and in the provision of the National Security Act of 1947 requiring that the Central Intelligence Agency (CIA) "have no police, subpoena, or law enforcement powers or internal security functions."[4] The regulations were significantly strengthened in the 1970s when, in reaction to domestic intelligence gathering activities during the Vietnam War era, Congress undertook extensive investigations of intelligence activities and enacted legislation regulating domestic surveillance activities. Ultimately, in response to recommendations derived from this investigation, in 1978 Congress passed and President Jimmy Carter signed the Foreign Intelligence Surveillance Act (FISA), P.L. 95-511.[5] FISA provides a statutory framework for electronic surveillance in foreign intelligence investigations while electronic surveillance in criminal investigations continues to be governed by Title III of the Omnibus Crime Control Act of 1968 (usually referred to as Title III).[6]

The implementation of FISA came to have an important influence on the relationship between law enforcement and intelligence.

FISA required that "the purpose" of domestic electronic surveillance (or a physical search) had to be the gathering of foreign intelligence information.[7] FISA permitted the dissemination to the law enforcement community of information relating to criminal activity incidentally acquired during a FISA electronic surveillance or physical search. When such dissemination was challenged by defense attorneys as running afoul of the Fourth Amendment,[8] a number of federal courts of appeals had upheld the government's contention in several cases that the "primary purpose" of an electronic surveillance or physical search had been the collection of foreign intelligence information. Thus, this use of FISA was held to be not inconsistent with Fourth Amendment requirements for criminal cases.[9]

Before 9/11 a considerable body of government practice and Justice Department policy increasingly reflected an understanding that adhering to the primary purpose standard effectively precluded Fourth Amendment challenges. The concern was to avoid letting aggressive criminal investigators obtain FISA court orders when they were interested in obtaining evidence of criminal activities. There was a pervasive concern within the Justice Department that a court in a criminal trial would suppress information obtained through a FISA investigation on the grounds that it was primarily being used, not to collect foreign intelligence, but to gather criminal evidence or even that FISA itself would be overturned. In practice, information collected by intelligence agencies (including the parts of the Federal Bureau of Investigation (FBI) dealing with counterterrorism and counterintelligence) was kept apart from information collected for the use of prosecutors.

RECOGNIZING THE NEED TO SHARE INFORMATION

FISA's requirements appear not to have posed major problems until the mid1990s,[10] but law enforcement and intelligence agencies tended to function in separate worlds. Concern about these divisions did exist and there had been major initiatives largely as a result of concerns about the development of barriers between law enforcement and intelligence agencies in the aftermath of the controversy surrounding the illegal activities of the Banca

Nazionale del Lavoro (BNL) and the Bank of Credit and Commerce International (BCCI) in the early 1990s. The controversy involved complex banking fraud and other criminal activities undertaken by the two foreign banks. Congressional investigators developed information that the CIA had obtained information indicating suspicious activities by the two banks that had not been passed to prosecutors in large measure because channels of communications had not been established between intelligence and law enforcement agencies. The Senate Intelligence Committee investigators concluded that:

> The fundamental policy governing the relationship between law enforcement and intelligence needs to be addressed by the Attorney General and the DCI [Director of Central Intelligence], in conjunction with the congressional oversight committees. Confusion is apparent on both sides as to what the proper role (and authority) of intelligence agencies is in circumstances like those presented in the BNL case.[11]

The reaction to the BNL/BCCI affairs reflected a shift away from emphasis on a strict separation of law enforcement and intelligence efforts to an appreciation by Congress of the need for closer cooperation. As a result of congressional concerns, the DCI and the Attorney General directed that a review of the intelligence-law enforcement relationship be conducted. The review, undertaken by a group of senior executive branch officials known as the Joint Task Force on Intelligence and Law Enforcement, submitted a report in August 1994. The Task Force described the failure by intelligence and law enforcement agencies to make use of all available information on the activities of the two foreign banks. It called for a number of bureaucratic mechanisms to ensure greater information exchanges in the future, but argued that no statutory changes were called for:

> What is required is not new legislation radically altering the relationship [between intelligence and law enforcement agencies], but rather a different approach to the existing relationship — one that is more interactive on a number of fronts, yet maintains the important distinctions between these two communities based on law, culture, and mission.[12]

The Joint Task Force Report led to the establishment of a series of interagency coordinative mechanisms — the Intelligence-Law Enforcement Policy Board, the Joint Intelligence-Law Enforcement Working Group (JICLE) — at various levels to encourage information exchanges and resolve difficulties.[13] Although the Task Force provided a perceptive analysis of the difficulties that then existed and officials assigned to the resultant interagency bodies worked diligently at overcoming obstacles, progress was limited.[14]

By the 1990s, the threat of new forms of international terrorism was becoming apparent. Middle Eastern terrorists were operating against U.S. forces overseas and, occasionally, within the U.S. (as in the 1993 World Trade Center attacks). Observers believed that both intelligence and law enforcement agencies were collecting relevant information on international terrorism. Members of Congress began to seek administrative and statutory changes that could facilitate information sharing in this area.

Pursuant to P.L. 105-277, a supplemental appropriations act passed in 1998, the National Commission on Terrorism, headed by former Ambassador L. Paul Bremer, was established to review the laws, regulations, directives, policies and practices for preventing and punishing international terrorism. The Bremer Commission's June 2000 report highlighted concerns about the inadequate sharing of terrorism-related information. It recommended the elimination of barriers to the aggressive collection of information on terrorists and suggested that the FBI suffered from bureaucratic and cultural obstacles to gathering terrorism information. It found that the "Department of Justice applies the statute governing electronic surveillance and physical searches of international terrorists in a cumbersome and overly cautious manner."[15] Although it noted that the FISA application process had been recently streamlined, it recommended that the Justice Department's Office of Intelligence Policy Review (OIPR) should not require the inclusion of information in excess of that which was actually mandated by FISA. It also recommended that OIPR be substantially expanded and that it be directed to cooperate with the FBI.[16]

The Commission further concluded:

> Law enforcement agencies are traditionally reluctant to share information outside of their circles so as not to jeopardize any potential prosecution. The FBI does promptly share information warning about specific terrorist threats with the CIA and other agencies. But the FBI is far less likely to disseminate terrorist information that may not relate to an immediate threat even though this could be of immense long-term or cumulative value to the intelligence community. . . . Moreover, certain laws limit the sharing of law enforcement information, such as grand jury or criminal wiretap information, with the intelligence community. These laws are subject to different interpretations, so that in some cases it is unclear whether the restrictions apply."[17]

The Commission did not indicate a need for immediate statutory changes, but recommended that the "Attorney General should clarify what information can be shared and direct maximum dissemination of terrorist-related information to policymakers and intelligence analysts consistent with the law."[18]

INITIAL EFFORTS TO LEGISLATE

Members of Congress did propose various approaches to address the lack of information sharing. S. 2089 as introduced in February 2000 by Senator Specter, would have required that the Attorney General prescribe in regulations the circumstances under which information acquired pursuant to FISA "shall be disclosed for law enforcement purposes." The bill would also have required two reports addressing issues of information sharing. First, it would have tasked the Director of the FBI to submit a report on "the feasibility of establishing within the Bureau a comprehensive intelligence reporting function having the responsibility for disseminating among the elements of the intelligence community information collected and assembled by the Bureau on international terrorism and other national security matters." Secondly, the bill would have required the President to submit a report on the legal authorities that govern the sharing of criminal wiretap information with intelligence agencies and with recommendations to improve the capability of the Justice Department to share "foreign intelligence information or counterintelligence information with elements of the United States intelligence community on matters such as counterterrorism."

In its report on the bill, the Senate Intelligence Committee argued:

> For the intelligence mission of the United States to be successful, there must be a cooperative and concerted effort among intelligence agencies. Any information collected by one agency under foreign intelligence authorities that could assist another agency in executing its lawful mission should be shared fully and promptly....
>
> The Committee has been briefed on the recent efforts by the Federal Bureau of Investigation and the Central Intelligence Agency to enhance their ability to share valuable information collected under FISA orders. The Committee commends these efforts and expects them to continue and to be broadened to include all areas of the foreign intelligence mission.[19]

As reported to the Senate in July 2000, S. 2089 was modified to include only a request for reports from the Attorney General on mechanisms for determinations of disclosure of FISA-derived information for law enforcement purposes and on actions taken by the Department of Justice (DOJ) to coordinate the dissemination of intelligence information within DOJ.

Congressional concern about the growing threat of terrorism was also demonstrated in S. 3205, introduced in October 2000 and known as the Kyl-Feinstein Counterterrorism Act of 2000, which was based directly on recommendations of the Bremer Commission that had been released in August. The bill took notice of the attack on the U.S.S. *Cole*, which had occurred on October 12, 2000, and aimed to discourage financial support of terrorist organizations. This bill also addressed information sharing issues; section 9 would have required a report on the feasibility of assigning the FBI responsibility for disseminating among the elements of the Intelligence Community information collected and assembled by the FBI on international terrorism and other national security matters. Section 10 of the bill would have required a report on the legal authorities that govern the sharing of criminal wiretap information with various law enforcement agencies and intelligence agencies and "recommendations, if any," for legislative language that would improve the Justice Department's capabilities to share information on matters such as counterterrorism with intelligence agencies "with elements of the United States intelligence community on matters such as counterterrorism."

Consideration of the legislation reflected many of the same privacy and civil liberties concerns that had influenced existing procedures in the Justice Department. Criticisms of the approach taken by the legislation were voiced by some civil libertarians. One group opposed the sharing of information obtained by electronic surveillance conducted under Title III authorities with intelligence agencies. Such an effort, it was argued, "breaches the well-established and constitutionally vital line between law enforcement and intelligence activities."[20] Concern was also expressed about the potential use of such information by the CIA and other intelligence agencies: "The secretive data gathering, storage and retention practices of the intelligence agencies are appropriate only when conducted overseas for national defense and foreign policy purposes and only when directed against people who are not U.S. citizens or permanent residents."[21] Further concern was directed at the potential use of information gathered under counterintelligence authorities (presumably FISA) in criminal proceedings:

> Since the period of ... the Church committee, it has been recognized that the rights of Americans are better protected (and the FBI may be more effective) when international

> terrorism and national security investigations are conducted under the rules for criminal investigations.[22]

Such views reflected a continuing distrust of intelligence agencies and a fear that past practices might be revived. In floor debate, Senator Leahy noted that initial drafts of S. 3205 had posed "serious constitutional problems and risks to important civil liberties we hold dear." After modifications, however, "no longer does the bill require a change in the wiretap statute allowing the permissive disclosure of information obtained in a Title III wiretap to the intelligence agencies."[23]

The Clinton Administration Justice Department took a different approach, arguing that then-current statutes and regulations provided law enforcement agencies with "authority under current law to share Title III information regarding terrorism with intelligence agencies when the information is of over-riding importance to the national security." Any change "must accommodate legal constraints such as Criminal Rule 6(e) and the need to protect equities relating to ongoing criminal investigations."[24] Accordingly, the Justice Department specifically opposed the provision in the bill that would permit the sharing of foreign intelligence or counterintelligence information collected under Title III by investigative or law enforcement officer with intelligence agencies.[25]

The Kyl-Feinstein bill would not have changed statutory language, but only asked for reports on the issue of information. Even so, according to Senator Leahy, the initial proposal to mandate such changes "prompted a firestorm of controversy from civil liberties and human rights organizations, as well as the Department of Justice."[26] Even though the House took no action on this bill, passage of the legislation by the Senate reflected concerns at the end of 2000 regarding the possible need to adjust information sharing mechanisms, coupled with a determination to move cautiously before implementing changes that could affect civil liberties. Ultimately, the legislation was adopted by the Senate on November 14, 2000, but it was not sent to the House before the adjournment of the 106th Congress.

The FY2001 Intelligence Authorization Act, P.L. 106-567, signed on December 27, 2000, reflected the concerns that had inspired both S. 2089 and S. 3205. It included a requirement for a report from the Attorney General on "the authorities and procedures utilized by the Department of Justice for determining whether or not to disclose information acquired under the Foreign Intelligence Surveillance Act of 1978 (50 U.S.C. 1801 et seq.) for law enforcement purposes."[27] This Act also formalized procedures for authorizing FISA surveillance, expanded grounds for establishing probable cause, established new procedures for physical searches within FISA, and specified mechanisms to facilitate the use of intelligence in counterintelligence investigations. It provided increased funding for OIPR subsequent to the submission of a report indicating efforts taken to streamline and improve the FISA application process. It included a provision (in section 606) derived from S. 2089 requiring a report from the Attorney General on actions taken to "coordinate the dissemination of intelligence information within the appropriate components of the [Justice] Department and the formulation of policy on national security issues." It did not, however, address the question of making information from law enforcement sources available to the Intelligence Community.

Clearly, the problems created by the existence of the "wall" had not been unrecognized prior to 9/11. The Justice Department's opposition in 2000 to legislative proposals to remove barriers has been noted. On the other hand, some argue that the primary factor in preventing statutory changes was, as one observer has claimed, that "in most instances both the Department of Justice and The White House turned down the requests because it was firmly believed by senior members of the Executive Branch that the United States Congress would not allow the IC [Intelligence Community] to have broader surveillance powers."[28] This view would be expressed by former Attorney General William Barr in testimony to the 9/11 Commission:

> For three decades leading up to 9/11, Congress was at the fore of a steady campaign to curtail the Bureau's domestic intelligence activities and impose on all its activities the standards and process of the criminal justice system. These concerns made it extremely difficult for the Bureau to pursue domestic security matters outside the strictures of the criminal justice process. Prohibitions on sharing grand jury information with intelligence agencies and with using intelligence information in criminal investigations created a 'wall of separation.'[29]

It is clear in retrospect that there were those in both the Executive Branch and Congress who realized the need to lower barriers to sharing law enforcement and intelligence information, but their views did not, prior to 9/11, reflect a consensus in either branch. Those opposed to greater information sharing did so in large measure because of their awareness of the past history of domestic surveillance and a distrust of intelligence organizations. The result was a number of very tentative steps that, in the event, proved wholly inadequate to task of gathering information about al Qaeda's plot. The FY2001 Intelligence Authorization Act included some minimalist provisions, but the wall was left in place. Neither the Clinton Administration or the Bush Administration, in the first eight months of 2001, sought to amend the relevant laws.[30] The problem was recognized but proposed solutions faced strong opposition.

AFTER 9/11, CONGRESS TEARS DOWN THE WALL

The attacks of September 11, 2001, destroyed the World Trade Center and a portion of the Pentagon; they also demolished the wall between U.S. law enforcement and intelligence. After 9/11, it was almost immediately accepted that counterterrorism would have to involve all parts of the U.S. Government, including law enforcement agencies and the Intelligence Community. It was agreed that the counterterrorism effort must be based on sharing information from whatever source. The problem for both Congress and the executive branch was to establish appropriate mechanisms for information sharing with adequate safeguards for using the information in future criminal trials.

Congress immediately set about to consider the most appropriate legislative response that could be quickly enacted. Former Attorney General John Ashcroft writes, "The 9/11 attacks occurred on a Tuesday. By Saturday, we had a full-blown legislative proposal. Part of the reasons we were able to move so quickly was that a number of the provisions had been proposed to Congress in 1996, and Congress had rejected them."[31] Attention focused on various proposals and recommendations of commissions that had looked at international terrorism and related issues and to earlier legislative proposals that had not been adopted.[32] A wide number of proposals came together as the USA PATRIOT Act (P.L. 107-56) that would be debated in the final weeks of September and early October 2001.[33] The USA PATRIOT Act changed the requirement that "the purpose" of a FISA surveillance be to collect foreign intelligence information, to require that collecting such information be "a significant purpose" of FISA electronic surveillance or physical search. This provided latitude to use FISA authority for electronic surveillance or physical searches where the primary purpose was criminal investigation, as long as a significant foreign intelligence purpose was also present.

The USA PATRIOT Act also addressed concerns about sharing intelligence and law enforcement information. Although a discussion of all the complex provisions that were included in the USA PATRIOT Act lies beyond the scope of this Report,[34] several provisions address the sharing of law enforcement and intelligence information. Section 203 of the Act removed some of the restrictions on federal government attorneys sharing grand jury information. Subsection 203(a) authorized federal government attorneys to share matters occurring before the grand jury involving foreign intelligence, counterintelligence, or foreign intelligence information with a federal law enforcement, intelligence, protective, immigration, national defense, or national security official to assist that official in the performance of his or her duties. Subsection (a) authorized the sharing of grand jury information "when the matters involve foreign intelligence or counterintelligence."[35]

Subsection 203(b) permitted investigative and law enforcement officers and Government attorneys to share information acquired under or derived from the interception of a wire, oral, or electronic communication under Title III with any other federal law enforcement, intelligence, protective, immigration, national defense or national security official for use in his or her official duties to the extent that the contents of that communication include foreign intelligence or counterintelligence information.

Subsection (c) provides authority for the Attorney General to establish implementing procedures.

Subsection 203(d) permitted the disclosure of foreign intelligence, counterintelligence, or foreign intelligence information obtained as part of a federal criminal investigation, notwithstanding any other provision of law, to any federal law enforcement, intelligence, protective, immigrations, national defense, or national security official in order to assist that official in carrying out his or her official duties, subject to any limitations on the unauthorized disclosure of that information.

Section 504 permitted federal officers conducting electronic surveillance or physical searches under FISA to consult with federal law enforcement officers or state or local law enforcement personnel to coordinate against actual or potential attacks or other grave hostile acts of a foreign power or its agent; sabotage or international terrorism by a foreign power or its agent, or clandestine intelligence activities by an intelligence service or network of a foreign power or its agent.

Section 905 requires the Attorney General or heads of other Federal agencies with law enforcement responsibilities to disclose expeditiously to the DCI (later replaced by the Director of National Intelligence (DNI)), under relevant guidelines, foreign intelligence acquired in the course of a criminal investigation. Exceptions could be made where the disclosure of such foreign intelligence would jeopardize an ongoing law enforcement investigation or impair other significant law enforcement interests. In addition, Section 905 required the Attorney General, in consultation with the DCI (now the DNI), to develop procedures to give the Director timely notice of the Attorney General's decision to begin or decline to begin a criminal investigation based on information from an element of the intelligence community regarding possible criminal activity of a foreign intelligence source or potential source.[36]

The provisions included in the USA PATRIOT Act and DOJ's effort to implement them were far-reaching and to some extent were not welcomed by the FISA Court. In particular, the FISA Court in *In re all Matters Submitted to the Foreign Intelligence Court* found that proposed 2002 procedures issued by the Attorney General "eliminate[d] the bright line in the 1995 procedures prohibiting direction and control by prosecutors on which the Court has relied to moderate the broad acquisition[,] retention, and dissemination of FISA information in overlapping intelligence and criminal investigations."[37] The FISA Court thus attempted to "reinstate the bright line used in the 1995 procedures, on which the Court has relied."[38]

Concerned that its proposed procedures were rejected, the Justice Department appealed the Foreign Intelligence Surveillance Court's granting of a request modified in accordance with its earlier ruling in *In re All Matters Submitted to the Foreign Intelligence Surveillance Court*. The appeal went to the Foreign Intelligence Surveillance Court of Review and was the first appeal to that court. In a sweeping decision, the Court of Review overruled the limitations imposed by the FISA Court, along with a considerable amount of customary FISA practice. The Court of Review expressed concern that the FISA Court had overstepped its role by prescribing the internal procedures for handling surveillances within the Justice Department. The Court of Review maintained that the FISA Court "determined an investigation became primarily criminal when the Criminal Division played a lead role. This approach has led, over time, to the quite intrusive organizational and personnel tasking the FISA [C]ourt adopted. Putting aside the impropriety of an Article III court imposing such organizational strictures ... [the wall] was unstable because it generates dangerous confusion and creates perverse organizational incentives."[39] The Court of Review thereby gave the final blow to the legal structure supporting the wall between law enforcement and intelligence information.

Implementation of the information-sharing provisions of the USA PATRIOT Act and other legislation is underway. The Homeland Security Act of 2002 (P.L. 107-296) and the Intelligence Reform and Terrorism Prevention Act of 2004 (P.L. 108-458) required that procedures be established under which federal agencies can share intelligence and law enforcement information about international terrorism. The Intelligence Reform Act mandated the creation of an Information Sharing Environment (ISE) that combines policies, procedures, and technologies to link information collections and users. In November 2006 the Administration released a lengthy implementation plan for the ISE. The plan sets forth procedures for sharing information among agencies at federal, state, and local levels and seeks to promote a culture of information sharing. It also provides procedures for protecting information privacy and civil liberties.[40] Congress may choose to review the implementation of the ISE during coming months.

Conclusion

A fundamental issue that faces both Congress and the U.S. public remains the need to balance the advantages to be gained by sharing information from all sources with the possibility that the availability of data accumulations could be used to undermine lawful political or religious activities. An unstable balance between these two separate goals — often portrayed as competing — greatly complicated the counterterrorism and counterintelligence effort prior to 9/11. The fact that public opinion appeared deeply ambivalent made procedural changes difficult and contributed to the luxuriant growth of complex regulations adopted by DOJ and endorsed by the FISA Court. After 9/11, public opinion shifted dramatically, resulting in the rapid passage of the USA PATRIOT Act and other legislation. The need to encourage the sharing of information and the connection of dots is now unquestioned, but there are lingering concerns about the risks that widespread information sharing may jeopardize civil liberties. Congress will undoubtedly seek to determine whether the new statutes, regulations, and procedures that have been adopted will prove both effective and sensitive to individual rights.

The importance of sharing intelligence and law enforcement information is not limited to issues relating to international terrorism but extends to banking fraud, narcotics smuggling, and a variety of international concerns. Narcotics smuggling, for instance, can be addressed by encouraging other countries to halt the cultivation of opium poppies or coca, as well as by law enforcement in the U.S. Terrorism, of course, is uniquely threatening and in combating terrorists more vigorous non-law enforcement approaches are considered more legitimate than is the case with drug smugglers or embezzlers. What is advantageous in all cases is assembling the full range of information about the activity and subjecting it to rigorous analysis.

There is, however, the possibility that the current consensus may unravel. The political controversy surrounding NSA's electronic surveillance efforts and other data mining programs may come to focus on the sharing of information that some argue was not lawfully obtained, and this concern could lead to efforts to restrict information sharing across the boards. There is also a possibility that the use of information obtained by surveillance in accordance with FISA might ultimately not be allowed in court cases out of concern that the Fourth Amendment has been bypassed.[41] Despite the widespread acceptance of the need for information sharing, concerns that sharing information could lead to governmental abuses persists across the political spectrum. These concerns are tenaciously held, and have in the past made legislating very controversial. There is no reason to believe that they will not resurface should the threat from international terrorism seem less menacing.

The potential threat to civil liberties does not, of course, represent the full extent of the issues raised by increased information sharing. Sharing sensitive information inevitably raises the danger that intelligence sources and methods may be compromised either accidentally or purposefully. For intelligence professionals, in particular, the danger to valuable sources that may have taken years to develop is a fundamental concern. Moreover, when a human source is compromised there is not only a danger to a particular individual, but also a potential loss of confidence in U.S. intelligence agencies by other actual or potential sources.

The role of Congress in dealing with information sharing issues is especially important. There are delicate questions of liberty and security involved and a sensitive balance is crucial. Air Force General Michael V. Hayden, who now serves as CIA Director, in the past argued that Members of Congress are in close touch with their constituents and "What I really need you to do is talk to your constituents and find out where the American people want that line between security and liberty to be."[42] Congress also can provide the ongoing oversight to ensure that the sorts of abuses that occurred in the 1960s and 1970s do not recur. Ultimately, an information sharing policy that is largely consistent with public opinion and is held to account by rigorous oversight should enhance the chances that the dots can be connected without jeopardizing the rights of Americans. Observers see a danger, however, that gridlock in both the Executive and Legislative Branches might inhibit the government's ability to find effective and sensible ways to acquire and analyze information on new threats to the national security.

REFERENCES

[1] U.S. Congress, 107th Congress, Senate, Select Committee on Intelligence, and House of Representatives, Permanent Select Committee on Intelligence, *Joint Inquiry into Intelligence Community Activities Before and After the Terrorist Attacks of September 11, 2001*, Report, S.Rept. 107-351, H.Rept. 107-792 [Hereafter: *Joint Inquiry Report]*, December 2002, p. 33.

[2] Ibid., p. xvii. Intelligence agencies focus on concerns outside U.S. territory (and are sometimes known as "foreign intelligence" agencies). They include the Central Intelligence Agency (CIA), the National Security Agency (NSA), the Defense Intelligence Agency (DIA), the National Reconnaissance Office (NRO), the National Geospatial-Intelligence Agency (NGA), the Bureau of Intelligence and Research of the State Department, the intelligence components of the military services and the Department of Homeland Security. Law enforcement agencies include the Federal Bureau of Investigation (FBI), the Drug Enforcement Administration, the Secret Service, and the Customs Service. The FBI is considered both a foreign intelligence agency and a law enforcement agency; this is also the case with the Coast Guard.

[3] U.S., National Commission on Terrorist Attacks upon the United States, *The 9/11 Commission Report* (Washington: Government Printing Office, 2004); see pp. 416-419.

[4] 50 U.S.C. 403-3(d)(1); on FISA generally, see CRS Report RL30465, The Foreign Intelligence Surveillance Act: An Overview of the Statutory Framework and Recent Judicial Decisions, by Elizabeth B. Bazan.

[5] In 1994 FISA was modified to include physical searches (section 807 of the Intelligence Authorization Act for FY1995, P.L. 103-359).

[6] Title III prohibits all interception of wire or electronic communications unless that interception falls within one of the exceptions to Title III; electronic surveillance under FISA is one of the exceptions (18 U.S.C. 2511(2)(f). It is to be noted that "foreign intelligence" may not involve actual or potential violations of U.S. laws, *e.g.* intelligence could be acquired, in the U.S., regarding a plot involving parties outside the U.S. that would not involve activities prohibited by U.S. law. Such intelligence could be of great interest to national policymakers but there would be no justification for relying on Title III surveillance authorities in trying to obtain it. As will be noted below, there is, however, a significant potential for overlap when intelligence provides evidence of activities that are illegal under U.S. law.

[7] 50 U.S.C. 1804(a)(7)(B), 50 U.S.C. 1823(a)(7)(B). Sec. 218 of the USA PATRIOT Act (P.L. 107-56) had amended these sections to replace "the purpose" with "a significant purpose."

[8] The Fourth Amendment to the Constitution states: "The right of the people to be secure in their persons, houses, papers, and effects, against unreasonable searches and seizures, shall not be violated, and no Warrants shall issue, but upon probable cause, supported by Oath or affirmation, and particularly describing the place to be searched, and the persons or things to be seized."

[9] A detailed assessment of the various judicial views and rulings on this question lies beyond the scope of this Report; see, however, David S. Kris, "The Rise and Fall of the FISA Wall," *Stanford Law and Policy Review*, Spring 2006, pp. 487-529.

[10] See Diane Carraway Piette and Jesselyn Radack, "Piercing the 'Historical Mists': the People and Events Behind the Passage of FISA and the Creation of the 'Wall,'" *Stanford Law and Policy Review*, Spring 2006, p. 461.

[11] U.S. Congress, 103d Congress, 1st session, Senate, Select Committee on Intelligence, *The Intelligence Community's Involvement in the Banca Nazionale del Lavoro (BNL) Affair*, S. Prt. 103-12, February 1993, p. 27.

[12] U.S., Joint Task Force on Intelligence and Law Enforcement, *Report to the Attorney General and Director of Central Intelligence*, August, 1994, p. 4. The absence of a need for legislation was also the position of the then-DCI James Woolsey: "Rather, we can accomplish our goal of enhanced cooperation through a series of initiatives — such as joint training of law enforcement and intelligence officers." Address by R. James Woolsey, Director of Central Intelligence, before the American Bar Association, Washington, DC, April 29, 1994. In 2001, however, Woolsey would write in regard to the 1993 World Trade Center bombing, "No one other than the prosecutors, the Clinton Justice Department, and the FBI had access to the materials surrounding the case until they were presented in court, because they were virtually all obtained by a federal grand jury and hence kept not only from the public but from the rest of the government under the extreme secrecy requirements of Rule 6(e) of the Federal Rules of Criminal Procedure." R. James Woolsey, "Blood Baath: the Iraq Connection," *New Republic*, September 24, 2001, p. 21. Rule 6(e) established requirements for the secrecy of grand jury proceedings.

[13] See CRS Report RL30252, Intelligence and Law Enforcement: Countering Transnational Threats to the U.S., by Richard A. Best Jr.

[14] A key factor appears to have been the potential that litigation over important espionage cases could jeopardize existing practices; see, for instance, the testimony of John Gannon, former head of the National Intelligence Council and other senior government positions, to the Senate Judiciary Committee, May 2, 2006; Gannon claimed that the "early post-war determination to share information and push the 'wall' on information sharing between intelligence and law enforcement was set back by the sensational Ames, Nicholson, and Hanson espionage cases."

[15] U.S., National Commission on Terrorism, *Countering the Changing Threat of International Terrorism*, June 2000, p. 10.

[16] Ibid., p. 12.

[17] Ibid., pp. 15-16.

[18] Ibid, p.16.

[19] U.S. Congress, 106th Congress, 2d session, Senate, Select Committee on Intelligence, *The Counterintelligence Reform Act of 2000*, S.Rept. 106-352, July 20, 2000, p. 6.

[20] Letter from Laura W. Murphy, Director, American Civil Liberties Union, Washington National Office, James X. Dempsey, Senior Staff Counsel, Center for Democracy and Technology, and Kate Martin, Executive Director, Center for National Security Studies, reprinted in *Congressional Record*, October 26, 2000, p. S11118.

[21] Ibid.

[22] Ibid., p. S11119.

[23] *Congressional Record*, November 14, 2000, p. S11540. Almost a year later during consideration of the USA PATRIOT Act, Senator Leahy would note that the Justice Department had opposed the original Kyl legislation because it might have opened sensitive materials to the discovery process and it raised issues about sharing information about U.S. persons. *Congressional Record*, October 25, 2001, p. S11001.

[24] Letter from Robert Raben, Assistant Attorney General, Department of Justice, reprinted in *Congressional Record*, October 26, 2000, pp. S11119. The letter did not elaborate on how Rule 6(e) and the need to protect equities could be balanced against the need to share information. Apparently, precise details of a planned assassination plot would meet the "overriding importance" standard, but Raben gave no recognition that intelligence agencies should have access to ambiguous data that might yield evidence of a plot only when combined with other information; in other words, dots that are innocuous in themselves but which, when connected to other information, reveal a dangerous threat.

[25] Ibid., p. S11119.

[26] *Congressional Record*, November 14, 2000, p. S11540; Leahy himself, however, had earlier that year indicated support for legislation that would promote information sharing and consultation between intelligence agencies in regard to counterintelligence. "In an area of such national importance, it is critical that our law enforcement and intelligence agencies work together as efficiently and cooperatively as possible." Prepared Statement of Hon. Patrick Leahy printed in U.S. Congress, 106th Congress, 2d session, Senate, Committee on the Judiciary, Subcommittee on Administrative Oversight and the Courts, *Counterintelligence Reform Act of 2000,* S.Hrg. 106-993, March 7, 2000, p. 12.

[27] Section 604(b), P.L. 106-567.

[28] Robert M. Blitzer (a former FBI official), "Domestic Intelligence Challenges in the 21st Century," (Arlington, VA: Lexington Institute, 2002), p. 10; available at [http://www.lexingtoninstitute.org/docs/497.pdf].

[29] Statement of William P. Barr to the 9/11 Commission, December 8, 2003; available at [http://www.9-11commission.gov/hearings/hearing6/witness_barr.htm].

[30] The incoming Bush Administration was reviewing procedures relating to the wall, but as late as August 2001, Larry D. Thompson, the Deputy Attorney General, reiterated that departmental guidelines regarding the wall were still in effect; Larry D. Thompson Memorandum to Criminal Division, Office of Intelligence Policy and Review, and FBI, August 6, 2001 available at [http://www.cnss.org/9.11commissionintelligence.htm]; see also, John Ashcroft, *Never Again: Securing America and Restoring Justice* (New York: Center Street, 2006), p. 147; Thomas H. Kean and Lee H. Hamilton, *Without Precedent: the Inside Story of the 9/11 Commission* (New York: Knopf, 2006), p. 195.

[31] Ashcroft, *Never Again*, p. 154.

[32] One skeptical observer noted that the "great majority of the new surveillance provisions had been discussed within the executive branch or Congress in previous years and had not been adopted. After the September 11 attacks, professional staff in the agencies simply went into their files and pulled out provisions they had been advocating previously. In the super-charged climate of the fall of 2001 many of these provisions received remarkablylittle scrutiny or debate." Peter P. Swire, "The System of Foreign Intelligence Surveillance Law," *George Washington Law Review*, August 2004, p. 1349.

[33] Unitingand Strengthening America by Providing Appropriate Tools Required to Intercept and Obstruct Terrorism (USA PATRIOT Act) Act of 2001 (P.L. 107-56; signed October 26, 2001). The legislation was adopted by a 357-66 vote in the House and a 98-1 vote in the Senate.

[34] See CRS Report RL31377, *The USA PATRIOT Act: A Legal Analysis*, by Charles Doyle.

[35] Section 203(a)(1) provides that any Federal official to whom such information is made available may use it only in the conduct of that person's official duties. Further: "Within a reasonable time after such disclosure, an attorney for the government shall file under seal a notice with the court stating the fact that such information was disclosed and the departments, agencies, or entities to which the disclosure was made."

[36] The Act provided that some, but not all, of its provisions would expire (or "sunset") at the end of 2005, giving Congress the opportunity to assess their effects in the intervening months. Subsections 203(b) and 203(d) (but not (a) and (c)) were among those that were scheduled to sunset; section 905 was not scheduled to sunset. As noted by Charles Doyle, CRS Report RL32186, *USA PATRIOT Act Sunset Provisions That Were to Expire on December 31, 2005*, these provisions are similar to and may duplicate other statutory provisions in the USA PATRIOT Act and other legislation that were not scheduled to sunset; the legal issue regarding the extent to which these provisions are in fact duplicative lies beyond the scope of this Report. In any event, P.L.109-177, signed on March 9, 2006, made subsections 203(b), 203(d) and 905 permanent. See also CRS Report RL33332, *USA PATRIOT Improvement and Reauthorization Act of 2005: A Legal Analysis*, by Brian T. Yeh and Charles Doyle.

[37] In re all matters submitted to the Foreign Intelligence Surveillance Court, 218 F. Supp.2d, pp. 621-622 (May 17, 2002).

[38] Ibid., p. 625.

[39] In re Sealed Case, 310 F.3d, p. 743 (November 18, 2002).

[40] The implementation plan is available at [http://www.ise.gov/docs/ISE-impplan200611.pdf]. For additional background see U.S. Government Accountability Office, *Information Sharing: the Federal Government Needs to Establish Policies and Processes for Sharing Terrorism-Related and Sensitive but Unclassified Information*, GAO-06-385, March 17, 2006. Many of the initiatives in regard to the ISE have been widely criticized; see Ellen Nakashima, "Civil Libertarians Protest Privacy Policy; New Guidelines Do Little to Protect Established Rights, White House Board Told," *Washington Post*, Dec. 6, 2006, p. A11.

[41] This possibility was even alluded to by the November 2002 Foreign Intelligence Court of Review that maintained that "...a FISA order may not be a 'warrant' contemplated by the Fourth Amendment. The government does not actually claim that it is, instead

noting only that there is authority for the proposition that a FISA order is a warrant in the constitutional sense." The Court of Review added: "We do not decide the issue but note that to the extent a FISA order comes close to meeting Title III, that certainly bears on its reasonableness under the Fourth Amendment." In re: Sealed Case, 310 F.3d, p. 742.

[42] Testimony of Lt. Gen. Michael V. Hayden, USAF, U.S. Congress, 107th Congress, Senate, Select Committee on Intelligence, and House of Representatives, Permanent Select Committee on Intelligence, *Joint Inquiry into Intelligence Community Activities Before and After the Terrorist Attacks of September 11, 2001*, Hearings, Vol. II, October 1, 3, 8 and 17, 2002, S.Hrg. 107-1086, pp.801-802.

In: Law and Law Enforcement Issues
Editor: Gerald M. Kessler, pp. 213-226

ISBN: 978-1-60456-044-2

Chapter 8

THE WHISTLEBLOWER PROTECTION ACT: AN OVERVIEW*

L. Paige Whitaker

ABSTRACT

This article discusses the federal statutory protections contained within the Whistleblower Protection Act (WPA) for federal employees who engage in "whistleblowing," that is, making a disclosure evidencing illegal or improper government activities. The protections of the WPA apply to most federal executive branch employees and become applicable where a "personnel action" is taken "because of" a "protected disclosure" made by a "covered employee." Generally, whistleblower protections may be raised within four forums or proceedings: (1) employee appeals to the Merit Systems Protection Board of an agency's adverse action against an employee, known as "Chapter 77" appeals; (2) actions instituted by the Office of Special Counsel; (3) individually maintained rights of action before the Merit Systems Protection Board (known as an individual right of action, or IRA); and (4) grievances brought by the employee under negotiated grievance procedures.

On March 9, 2007, the House Committee on Oversight and Government Reform reported H.R. 985 (110th Cong.) H.Rept. 110-42, the Whistleblower Protection Enhancement Act of 2007, which would amend the WPA by providing protections for certain national security, government contractor, and science-based agency whistleblowers, and by enhancing the existing whistleblower protections for all federal employees.

INTRODUCTION AND BACKGROUND

The Whistleblower Protection Act (WPA) provides statutory protections for federal employees who engage in "whistleblowing," that is, making a disclosure evidencing illegal or improper government activities. The protections of the WPA apply to most federal executive

* Excerpted from CRS Report RL33918, March 12, 2007.

branch employees and become applicable when a "personnel action" is taken "because of" a "protected disclosure" made by a "covered employee." Generally, whistleblower protections may be raised within four forums or proceedings: (1) employee appeals to the Merit Systems Protection Board of an agency's adverse action against an employee, known as "Chapter 77" appeals; (2) actions instituted by the Office of Special Counsel; (3) individually maintained rights of action before the Merit Systems Protection Board (known as an individual right of action, or IRA); and (4) grievances brought by the employee under negotiated grievance procedures.

When Congress first enacted the Whistleblower Protection Act (WPA) in 1989, it stated that the intent of the legislation was to:

> strengthen and improve protection for the rights of Federal employees, to prevent reprisals, and to help eliminate wrongdoing within the Government by — (1) mandating that employees should not suffer adverse consequences as a result of prohibited personnel practices; and (2) establishing ... that while disciplining those who commit prohibited personnel practices may be used as a means by which to help accomplish that goal, the protection of individuals who are the subject of prohibited personnel practices remains the paramount consideration.[1]

The operative statutory protections of the WPA are embodied in its definition of "prohibited personnel practices":

> § 2302. Prohibited Personnel Practices
>
> (b) Any employee who has authority to take, direct others to take, recommend, or approve any personnel action, shall not, with respect to such authority — ...
>
> (8) take or fail to take, or threaten to take or fail to take, a personnel action with respect to any employee or applicant for employment because of —
>
> (A) any disclosure of information by an employee or applicant which the employee or applicant reasonably believes evidences — (i) a violation of any law, rule, or regulation, or (ii) gross mismanagement, a gross waste of funds, an abuse of authority, or a substantial and specific danger to public health or safety, if such disclosure is not specifically prohibited by law and if such information is not specifically required by Executive Order to be kept secret in the interest of national defense or the conduct of foreign affairs; or
>
> (B) any disclosure to the Special Counsel, or to the Inspector General of an agency or another employee designated by the head of the agency to receive such disclosures, of information which the employee or applicant reasonably believes evidences — (i) a violation of any law, rule, or regulation, or (ii) gross mismanagement, a gross waste of funds, an abuse of authority, or a substantial and specific danger to public health or safety.[2]

Essential Elements Triggering Application of the Whistleblower Protection Act (WPA)

In order to trigger the protections of the WPA, a case must contain the following elements: a *personnel action* that was taken *because of a protected disclosure* made by a *covered employee*.[3]

Covered Employees

Although anyone may disclose whistleblowing information to the Special Counsel for referral to the appropriate agency, the Special Counsel may order an investigation and require a report from the head of the agency only if the information is received from a "covered employee." In addition, with few exceptions, prohibited personnel practices apply only to covered employees. Hence, as a threshold matter, it is important to note which federal employees are statutorily covered.

Generally, current employees, former employees, or applicants for employment to positions in the executive branch of government in both the competitive and the excepted service, as well as positions in the Senior Executive Service, are considered covered employees.[4] However, those positions that are excepted from the competitive service because of their "confidential, policy-determining, policy-making, or policy-advocating character,"[5] and any positions exempted by the President based on a determination that it is necessary and warranted by conditions of good administration,[6] are not protected by the whistleblower statute. Moreover, the statute does not apply to federal workers employed by the Postal Service or the Postal Rate Commission,[7] the Government Accountability Office, the Federal Bureau of Investigation, the Central Intelligence Agency, the Defense Intelligence Agency, the National Imagery and Mapping Agency,[8] the National Security Agency, and any other executive entity that the President determines primarily conducts foreign intelligence or counter-intelligence activities.[9]

Protected Disclosures

"[A]ny disclosure of information" that a covered employee "reasonably believes" evidences "a violation of any law, rule, or regulation" or evidences "gross mismanagement, a gross waste of funds, an abuse of authority, or a substantial and specific danger to public health or safety" is protected on the condition that the disclosure is not prohibited by law nor required to be kept secret by Executive Order.[10] Moreover, "any disclosure" made to the Special Counsel or to the Inspector General of an agency or another employee designated by the head of the agency to receive such disclosures, which the employee "reasonably believes" evidences "a violation of any law, rule, or regulation," or evidences "gross mismanagement, a gross waste of funds, an abuse of authority, or a substantial and specific danger to public health or safety" is also protected.[11] Agency heads are required to inform their employees of these protections.[12]

Any Disclosure of Information

The WPA expressly provides that "any disclosure of information" is protected. With enactment of the WPA, Congress amended its statutory predecessor, the Civil Service Reform Act (CSRA).[13] In so doing, it changed the phrase "a disclosure" to "any disclosure," emphasizing the point that the courts, the OSC, and the MSPB should not erect barriers to disclosures that will limit the necessary flow of information from employees with information of government wrongdoing.[14] In the Committee Report accompanying the WPA legislation, the Senate specifically criticized a 1986 decision by the U.S. Court of Appeals for the Federal Circuit, *Fiorello v. Department of Justice*,[15] where an employee's disclosures were found not to be protected because the employee's "primary motivation" was not for the public good, but rather was for personal reasons.[16] The court reached this conclusion despite a lack of any indication in the Civil Service Reform Act that employee motives were relevant to deciding whether a disclosure is protected.[17]

Following enactment of the WPA in 1989, case law did not reflect the statutory expansion of "a disclosure" to "any disclosure." This lack of responsiveness by the courts and the MSPB was one factor prompting Congress in 1994 to amend the whistleblower statute. As the House report accompanying the 1994 amendments notes:

> Perhaps the most troubling precedents involve the Board's inability to understand that "any" means "any." The WPA protects "any" disclosure evidencing a reasonable belief of specified misconduct, a cornerstone to which the MSPB remains blind. The only restrictions are for classified information or material the release of which is specifically prohibited by statute. Employees must disclose that type of information through confidential channels to maintain protection; otherwise there are no exceptions.[18]

Reasonable Belief

For a disclosure to be protected, an employee must have a "reasonable belief" that the information is true. This is substantially a good faith requirement. In theory, the actual veracity of any disclosure does not affect whether a disclosure is protected.[19] In addition, for those disclosures enumerated under section 2302(b)(8)(A) that do not have to be kept confidential, the statute does not specify to whom the disclosures must be made in order to qualify as protected.[20]

Subject Matter of Disclosure

The statutory language of the whistleblower protections requires the disclosure to (a) evidence (i) a violation of any law, rule, or regulation, or (ii) gross mismanagement, a gross waste of funds, an abuse of authority, or a substantial and specific danger to public health or safety; and (b) not be prohibited by law or Executive Order, except when the disclosure is made to the Special Counsel or to the Inspector General of an agency or another employee designated by the head of the agency to receive such disclosures.[21]

The WPA limits evidence of mismanagement to only "gross" mismanagement. As explained in the accompanying Senate report,

> While the Committee is concerned about improving the protection of whistleblowers, it is also concerned about the exhaustive administrative and judicial remedies provided under S. 508 that could be used by employees who have made disclosures of trivial matters. CSRA specifically established a de minimis standard for disclosures affecting the waste of funds by defining such disclosures as protected only if they involved "a gross waste of funds." Under S. 508, the Committee establishes a similar de minimis standard for disclosures of mismanagement by protecting them only if they involve "gross mismanagement."[22]

Moreover, whistleblowing disclosures that are made public must not contain information the disclosure of which is prohibited by law or which is prohibited by an Executive Order in the interest of national defense or the conduct of foreign affairs.[23] Disclosures that are otherwise "protected" disclosures may be made, however, regardless of statutory Executive

Order secrecy requirements, to the Special Counsel or to an Inspector General of an agency or to an employee designated by the agency head to receive disclosures.[24]

Disclosures to Members of Congress

The WPA expressly provides that the statute is "not to be construed to authorize ... the taking of any personnel action against an employee who discloses information to the Congress."[25] With this provision of the law, Congress sought to protect its right to receive even "confidential" information from federal employees, without employee fear of reprisals:

> The provision is intended to make clear that by placing limitations on the kinds of information any employee may publicly disclose without suffering reprisal, there is not intent to limit the information an employee may provide to Congress or to authorize reprisal against an employee for providing information to Congress. For example, 18 U.S.C. 1905 prohibits public disclosure of information involving trade secrets. That statute does not apply to transmittal of such information by an agency to Congress. Section 2302(b)(8) of this act would not protect an employee against reprisal for public disclosure of such statutorily protected information, but it is not to be inferred that an employee is similarly un-protected if such disclosure is made to the appropriate unit of the Congress. Neither title I nor any other provision of the act should be construed as limiting in any way the rights of employees to communicate with or testify before Congress.[26]

Personnel Actions

The WPA protects employees from reprisals in the form of an agency taking or failing to take a "personnel action." This encompasses a broad range of actions by an agency having a negative or adverse impact on the employee. The statute specifically defines the term "personnel action" to include 11 areas of agency activity:

> (2) For the purpose of this section —
>
> (A) "personnel action" means —
>
> (i) an appointment;
> (ii) a promotion;
> (iii) an action under chapter 75 of this title or other disciplinary or corrective action;
> (iv) a detail, transfer, or reassignment;
> (v) a reinstatement;
> (vi) a restoration;
> (vii) a reemployment;
> (viii) a performance evaluation under chapter 43 of this title;
> (ix) a decision concerning pay, benefits, or awards, or concerning education or training if the education or training may reasonably be expected to lead to an appointment, promotion, performance evaluation, or other action described in this subparagraph;
> (x) a decision to order psychiatric testing or examination; and
> (xi) any other significant change in duties, responsibilities, or working conditions; with respect to an employee in, or applicant for, a covered position in an agency, and in the case of an alleged prohibited personnel practice described in subsection (b)(8), an employee or applicant for

> employment in a Government corporation as defined in section 9101 of title 31.[27]

The final category, (xi), of covered personnel actions was intended to embrace significant actions or changes that, in relation to an employee's overall duties, responsibilities, or working conditions, are inconsistent with his or her professional qualifications, training, grade, or rank. The conference report accompanying WPA provided a detailed discussion of the types of actions that may fall within or be excluded from the final category of personnel actions:

> To be covered under this provision a personnel action must be significant, but it need not be expected to result in a reduction in pay or grade. It must also be inconsistent with an employee's salary or grade level. Thus, for example, if an individual is currently employed and assigned duties or responsibilities consistent with the individual's professional training or qualifications for the job, it would constitute a personnel action if the individual were detailed, transferred, or reassigned so that the employee's new overall duties or responsibilities were inconsistent with the individual's professional training or qualifications. Or, if an individual holding decisionmaking responsibilities or supervisory authority found that such responsibilities or authority were reduced so that the employee's responsibilities were inconsistent with his or her salary or grade level, such an action could constitute a personnel action within the meaning of this subsection. This is not intended to interfere with management's authority to assign individuals in accordance with available work, the priorities of the agency, and the needs of the agency for individuals with particular skills or to establish supervisory relationships. Moreover, it is the overall nature of the individual's responsibilities and duties that is the critical factor. The mere fact that a particular aspect of an individual's job assignment has been changed would not constitute a personnel action, without some showing that there has been a significant impact as described above on the overall nature or quality of his responsibilities or duties.[28]

Nexus between a Protected Disclosure and a Personnel Action

The WPA changed the CSRA's definition of prohibited reprisals against whistleblowers in such a manner that personnel actions taken "because of" protected conduct are prohibited, rather than personnel actions taken "as a reprisal for" protected conduct, as the original statute provided. The amendment was made because the phrase, "as a reprisal for" had been interpreted to require a showing of an improper, retaliatory motive on the part of the acting official.[29] Indeed, two disciplinary action cases decided prior to the enactment of the WPA, *Starrett v. Special Counsel[30]* and *Harvey v. M.S.P.B.*,[31] required employees to show proof of the acting official's state of mind. These cases stand for the proposition that reprisal will not be found even if an agency's actions against an employee were based on factors arising from protected whistleblowing activities, so long as the agency officials were motivated by valid management reasons and not by any intent to "punish" the employee.[32] With the definition of "because of," Congress intended that a showing of the official's state of mind is no longer required. As stated in the Senate report accompanying the WPA legislation, "[r]egardless of the official's motives, personnel actions against employees should quite simply not be based on protected activities such as whistleblowing."[33] The WPA also expanded the CSRA definition of prohibited reprisal against whistleblowers to include "threats to take or fail to take" a personnel action against a whistleblower.[34]

Other Protected Activities

The WPA also expressly protects employees from prohibited personnel practices taken because they engaged in activities that are often related to whistleblowing, including testifying for others or lawfully assisting others exercise any appeal, complaint, or grievance right;[35] cooperating with or disclosing information to an Inspector General or Special Counsel;[36] or for refusing to obey an order that would violate the law.[37] In addition, employees are also protected from prohibited personnel practices taken because they exercised any appeal, complaint, or grievance right granted by any law, rule, or regulation.[38]

Forums Where Whistleblower Protections May Be Raised

There are four general forums or proceedings where whistleblower protections may be raised: (A) in employee appeals to the Merit Systems Protection Board (MSPB) of an agency's adverse action against the employee, known as "Chapter 77" appeals;[39] (B) in actions instituted by the Office of Special Counsel (OSC);[40] (C) in individual rights of action;[41] and (D) in grievances brought by the employee under negotiated grievance procedures.[42] As a result of the 1994 WPA amendments, an aggrieved employee affected by a prohibited personnel action is precluded from choosing more than one of the above remedies.[43]

"Chapter 77" Appeals

The MSPB is authorized to hear and rule on appeals by employees regarding agency actions affecting the employee and which are appealable to the Board by law, rule, or regulation.[44] Types of agency actions against employees that are appealable to the MSPB and in which an employee may raise the defense of reprisal for whistleblowing as a "prohibited personnel practice" include adverse actions against the employee for "such cause as will promote the efficiency of the service" (generally referred to as conduct-based adverse actions),[45] and performance-based adverse actions against employees for "unacceptable performance."[46] In such appeals, an agency's decision and action will not be upheld if the employee "shows that the decision was based on any prohibited personnel practice described in section 2302(b) of this title."[47] If the MSPB finds that an employee or applicant for employment has prevailed in an appeal, the employee or applicant may be provided with interim relief, pending the outcome of any petition of review.[48] Moreover, the Special Counsel may not intervene in a "Chapter 77" appeal without the consent of the individual bringing the appeal.[49]

Actions by the Office of Special Counsel (OSC)

The WPA established the OSC as an agency independent from the MSPB.[50] Its primary responsibilities, however, have remained essentially the same as set forth in its statutory predecessor, the CSRA. With the goal of protecting employees, former employees, and applicants for employment from prohibited personnel practices, the OSC has the duty to receive allegations of prohibited personnel practices and to investigate such allegations,[51] as well as to conduct an investigation of possible prohibited personnel practices on its own initiative, absent any allegation.[52]

The Special Counsel has several avenues available through which to pursue allegations, complaints, and evidences of reprisals for whistleblowing activities, including (1) requiring agency investigations and agency reports concerning actions the agency is planning to take to rectify those matters referred;[53] (2) seeking an order for "corrective action" by the agency before the MSPB;[54] (3) seeking "disciplinary action" against officers and employees who have committed prohibited personnel practices;[55] (4) intervening in any proceedings before the MSPB, except that in cases where an individual has brought an individual right of action (IRA) under Section 1221 or a Chapter 77 appeal, the OSC must first obtain the individual's consent;[56] and (5) seeking a stay from the MSPB for any personnel action pending an investigation.[57]

Investigations[58]

Within 240 days of receipt of a complaint, the OSC must make a determination as to whether there are reasonable grounds to believe that a prohibited personnel practice has occurred, exists, or is to be taken.[59] If a positive determination is made and the information was sent to the Special Counsel by an employee, former employee, applicant for employment, or an employee who obtained the information acting within the scope of employment,[60] the Special Counsel must transmit the information to the appropriate agency head and require that the agency head conduct an investigation and submit a written report.[61] The identity of the complaining employee may not be disclosed without such individual's consent, unless the Special Counsel determines that disclosure is necessary to avoid imminent danger to health and safety or an imminent criminal violation.[62] The Special Counsel then reviews the reports as to their completeness and the reasonableness of the findings[63] and submits the reports to Congress, the President, the Comptroller General,[64] and the complainant.[65]

If the Special Counsel does not make a positive determination, however, he or she may only transmit the information to the agency head with the consent of the individual.[66] Further, if the Special Counsel receives the information from some source other than the ones described above, he or she *may* transmit the information to the appropriate agency head who shall inform the Special Counsel of any action taken.[67] In any case evidencing a criminal violation, however, all information is referred to the Attorney General and no report is transmitted to the complainant.[68]

Throughout its investigation, the OSC must give notice of the status of the investigation to the individual who brought the allegation. The 1994 WPA amendments changed the period of this notification from 90 to 60 days.[69] In addition, no later than 10 days before the termination of an investigation, a written status report including the proposed findings and legal conclusions must be made to the individual who made the allegation of wrongdoing.[70]

Corrective Actions

If in any investigation the Special Counsel determines that there are "reasonable grounds to believe" a prohibited personnel practice exists or has occurred, the Special Counsel must report findings and recommendations, and may include recommendations for corrective action, to the MSPB, the agency involved, the Office of Personnel Management and, optionally, to the President.[71] If the agency does not act to correct the prohibited personnel practice, the Special Counsel may petition the MSPB for corrective action.[72] The MSPB, before rendering its decision, is required to provide an opportunity for oral or written comments by the Special Counsel, the agency involved and the Office of Personnel Management, and for written comments by any individual who alleges to be the victim of the prohibited personnel practices.[73]

The WPA made it easier for a complainant to prove retaliation for whistleblowing in a corrective action before the MSPB. The Special Counsel need onlyprove by a preponderance of the evidence that the disclosure was a "contributing factor" in the personnel action, instead of a "significant factor."[74] In addition, once the MSPB renders a final order or decision of corrective action, complainants have the right to judicial review in the U.S. Court of Appeals for the Federal Circuit.[75]

In what is probably the most significant change from its statutory predecessor, the CSRA, the WPA increased the standard by which an agency must prove its affirmative defense that it would have taken the personnel action even if the employee had not engaged in protected conduct. Once the complainant's *prima facie* case of reprisal has been established by showing that the whistleblowing was a contributing factor in the personnel action, the government is required to demonstrate by "clear and convincing evidence" that it would have taken the same personnel action even in the absent of such disclosure.[76] Under the CSRA, the government's standard of proof was a "preponderance of the evidence." "Clear and convincing evidence," although a lesser standard than the criminal standard of "beyond a reasonable doubt," is greater than "preponderance of the evidence."

Disciplinary Actions

Proceedings for disciplinary action against an officer or employee who commits a prohibited personnel practice may be instituted by the Special Counsel by filing a written complaint with the MSPB.[77] After proceedings before the MSPB or an administrative law judge,[78] if violations are found, the MSPB may impose any of various disciplinary actions, including removal, reduction in grade, debarment from federal employment for a period not to exceed five years, suspension, reprimand, or an assessment of civil fines up to $1,000.[79] In addition, the agency involved may be held responsible for reasonable attorney's fees.[80] In the case of presidentially appointed and Senate confirmed employees in "confidential, policy-making, policy-determining, or policy-advocating" positions, the complaint and the statement of facts, along with any response from the employee, are to be presented to the President for disposition in lieu of the presentation to the Board.[81] The OSC may recommend, to the appropriate federal agency head, disciplinary action against members of the uniformed services or contractor personnel who have engaged in a prohibited personnel practice against a federal employee.[82]

Intervention

As a matter of right, the Special Counsel may intervene or otherwise participate in any proceedings before the MSPB, except that in cases where an individual has brought an individual right of action (IRA) under Section 1221 or a Chapter 77 appeal, the OSC must first obtain the individual's consent.[83]

Stays

Upon application by the OSC, a member of the MSPB may "stay" or postpone, for 45 days, pending an investigation, a personnel action that the Special Counsel has reasonable grounds to believe constitutes a prohibited personnel practice, unless the member determines that a stay would not be appropriate under the circumstances.[84] If no MSPB member acts within three days of the OSC application, the stay becomes effective.[85] After the employing agency has had an opportunity to comment on the appropriateness of extending a stay, the MSPB may extend it.[86] A stay may be terminated by the MSPB at any time, except that a stay may not be terminated by the MSPB on its own motion or on the motion of an agency, unless notice and opportunity for oral or written comments are first provided to the Special Counsel and the individual on whose behalf the stay was ordered; or on a motion of the Special Counsel, unless notice and opportunity for oral or written comments are first provided to the individual on whose behalf the stay was ordered.[87]

Individual Right of Action (IRA)

The WPA provides that an employee, former employee, or applicant for employment has the independent right to seek review of whistleblower reprisal cases by the MSPB 60 days after the OSC closes an investigation or 120 days after filing a complaint with the OSC.[88] As a result of the IRA statutory provisions, a greater number of employees, including probationers, temporaries, and excepted service, have a method of appeal to the MSPB for whistleblower reprisals that was not previously available under the CSRA.[89] In addition, retired employees are not barred from instituting this type of appeal.[90] If the employee is the prevailing party before the MSPB, based on the finding of a prohibited personnel practice, or if the employee is the prevailing party in an appeal to the MSPB, regardless of the basis of the decision, the WPA provides several remedies. These may include placing the individual, as nearly as possible, in the position the individual would have been in had the prohibited personnel practice not occurred, awarding back pay and related benefits, recompensing medical costs incurred, travel expenses, or any other reasonable and foreseeable consequential charges.[91] In all cases, corrective action includes awarding attorneys' fees.[92] As a result of the 1994 WPA amendments, the MSPB findings can be based on circumstantial evidence.[93] Moreover, the Special Counsel may not intervene in an individual right of action without the consent of the individual bringing the appeal.[94]

Negotiated Grievance Procedures

Beyond the statutory provisions of the WPA, the fourth general forum where the defense or claim of reprisal for whistleblowing activities may be raised is a grievance proceeding initiated by an employee pursuant to a grievance procedure that was negotiated through collective bargaining between the employee's agency and the employee union representing employees of the agency.[95] The federal statutory provisions for grievance procedures note that certain actions that may be pursued either in a grievance proceeding or by other statutory means, such as discrimination complaints referenced under 5 U.S.C. § 2302(b)(1) or appeals of adverse actions for "conduct" or "performance,"[96] may only be pursued in one forum or the other, but not through both.[97]

Selection of the negotiated procedure does not, however, prejudice the right of an aggrieved employee to request that the MSPB review the final decision in the case of any personnel action that could have been appealed to the Board; or, where applicable, to request that the Equal Employment Opportunity Commission (EEOC) review a final decision in any other matter involving a complaint of discrimination of the type prohibited by any law administered by the EEOC.[98]

SUMMARY OF THE WHISTLEBLOWER PROTECTION ENHANCEMENT ACT OF 2007 (H.R. 985, 110TH CONGRESS)

On February 12, 2007, Representatives Waxman, Platts, Van Hollen, and T. Davis introduced H.R. 985 (110th Cong.), the Whistleblower Protection Enhancement Act of 2007, which on March 9, the House Committee on Oversight and Government Reform reported with amendments (H.Rept. 110-42), and placed on the legislative calendar.

H.R. 985 would amend the WPA to extend whistleblower protections to federal employees who specialize in national security issues. While current law expressly exempts employees of certain agencies relating to national security, Section 10 of the bill extends whistleblower protections to employees of the Federal Bureau of Investigation, the Central Intelligence Agency, the Defense Intelligence Agency, the National Geospatial-Intelligence Agency, the National Security Agency, and the National Reconnaissance Office and "any other Executive agency, or element or unit thereof, determined by the President ... to have as its principal function the conduct of foreign intelligence or counterintelligence activities." Likewise, Section 11 of the bill would extend whistleblower protections to employees of companies with government contracts.

Current law defines "disclosures" covered by the WPA to include information evidencing an abuse of authority. Section 13 of the bill would extend WPA protections to employees of science-based agencies by providing that "abuse of authority" includes "any action that compromises the validity or accuracy of federally funded research and analysis" and "the dissemination of false or misleading scientific, medical, or technical information."

Section 3 of the bill would clarify that "any" disclosure regarding waste, fraud, or abuse means that the WPA applies to such disclosures "without restriction as to time, place, form, motive, context, or prior disclosure" and includes formal and informal communication. Section 4 of the bill would provide that an employee covered by the WPA can rebut the presumption that a federal official performed his or her duties in accordance with the law by providing substantial evidence to the contrary. In addition, Section 9 of the bill would provide that such covered employees may bring an action for *de novo* review in the appropriate U.S.

district court if the Merit Systems Protection Board (MSPB) does not take action on their claims within 180 days.

REFERENCES

[1] 5 U.S.C. § 1201 nt.
[2] 5 U.S.C. § 2302(b)(8).
[3] Id.
[4] 5 U.S.C. § 2302(a)(2)(B).
[5] 5 U.S.C. § 2302(a)(2)(B)(i).
[6] 5 U.S.C. § 2302(a)(2)(B)(ii).
[7] 5 U.S.C. § 2105(e).
[8] The Central Imagery Office was exempted from coverage with the passage of the 1994 WPA amendments. The agency was renamed the "National Imagery and Mapping Agency" with the passage of the National Defense Authorization Act for Fiscal Year 1997. P.L. 104 201, § 1122(b)(1).
[9] 5 U.S.C. § 2302(a)(2)(C).
[10] 5 U.S.C. § 2302(b)(8)(A).
[11] 5 U.S.C. § 2302(b)(8)(B).
[12] 5 U.S.C. § 2302(c).
[13] Civil Service Reform Act of 1978, P.L. 95-454, 92 Stat. 1114.
[14] S.Rept. 100-413 (1988) at 13.
[15] 795 F.2d 1544 (Fed. Cir. 1986).
[16] S.Rept. 100-413 (1988) at 13.
[17] Id.
[18] H.Rept. 103-769 (1994) at 18.
[19] S.Rept. 100-413 (1988) at 12.
[20] Id.
[21] 2 U.S.C. §2302(b)(8)(A).
[22] S.Rept. 100-413, *supra* at 12.
[23] 5 U.S.C. § 2302(b)(8).
[24] Id.
[25] 5 U.S.C. § 2302(b). *See also* 5 U.S.C. § 7211, providing that an employee is guaranteed the right to freely petition or furnish information to Congress, a Member of Congress, a committee, or a Member thereof.
[26] H.Rept. 95-1717 (Conference Report) (1978), *reprinted in* 1978 U.S. CODE CONG. and AD. NEWS 2861.
[27] 5 U.S.C. § 2302(a)(2)(A).
[28] H.Rept. 95-1717 (Conference Report)(1978) at 128, 129-130, *reprinted in* 1978 U.S. CODE CONG. and AD. NEWS 2861.
[29] S.Rept. 100-13 (1988).
[30] 792 F.2d 1246 (4th Cir. 1986).
[31] 802 F.2d 537 (D.C. Cir. 1986).
[32] S.Rept. 100-413 (1988) at 15.

[33] *Id.* at 16.
[34] Id.
[35] 5 U.S.C. § 2302(b)(9)(B).
[36] 5 U.S.C. § 2302(b)(9)(C).
[37] 5 U.S.C. § 2302(b)(9)(D).
[38] 5 U.S.C. § 2302(b)(9)(A).
[39] 5 U.S.C. § 7701.
[40] 5 U.S.C. §§ 1211-1215.
[41] 5 U.S.C. § 1221.
[42] 5 U.S.C. § 7121.
[43] *See 5* U.S.C. § 7121(g)(2).
[44] 5 U.S.C. § 7701, 5 U.S.C. § 1205.
[45] 5 U.S.C. § 7513(a). *See* 5 U.S.C. § 7513(d) as to appealability under § 7701.
[46] 5 U.S.C. § 4303(a). *See* 5 U.S.C. § 4303(e) as to appealability to the MSPB under § 7701.
[47] 5 U.S.C. § 7701(c)(2)(B).
[48] 5 U.S.C. § 7701(b)(2)(A).
[49] 5 U.S.C. § 1212(c)(2).
[50] 5 U.S.C. § 1211(a). This section established the Office of Special Counsel (OSC), and provided that it will be headed by the Special Counsel and have a judicially noted official seal. The Senate report states that although the MSPB and the OSC had "separated themselves administratively in 1984," the whistleblower legislation "completes this process by establishing the OSC as an independent agency." S.Rept. 100-413 at 18. Moreover, the statute provides that the Special Counsel, appointed by the President, with the advice and consent of the Senate, may only be removed from office for "inefficiency, neglect of duty, or malfeasance in office." 5 U.S.C. § 1211(b).
[51] 5 U.S.C. § 1212(a)(2).
[52] 5 U.S.C. § 1214(a)(5).
[53] 5 U.S.C. § 1213(c).
[54] 5 U.S.C. § 1214(b)(2).
[55] 5 U.S.C. § 1215(b).
[56] 5 U.S.C. § 1212(c).
[57] 5 U.S.C. § 1212(b)(1).
[58] In addition to investigating whether prohibited personnel actions have been taken because of protected whistleblowing disclosures, the WPA also charges the OSC with investigating whether there is a "substantial likelihood" that whistleblowing disclosures evidence
violations of a law, rule or regulation. *See* 5 U.S.C. §1213(b).
[59] 5 U.S.C. § 1214(b)(2)(A)(i).
[60] 5 U.S.C. § 1213(c)(2).
[61] 5 U.S.C. § 1213(c)(1).
[62] 5 U.S.C. § 1213(h).
[63] 5 U.S.C. § 1213(e)(2).
[64] 5 U.S.C. § 1213(e)(3).
[65] 5 U.S.C. § 1213(e)(1).
[66] 5 U.S.C. § 1213(g)(2).

[67] 5 U.S.C. § 1213(g)(1).
[68] 5 U.S.C. § 1213(f).
[69] 5 U.S.C. § 1214(a)(1)(C)(ii).
[70] 5 U.S.C. § 1214(a)(1)(D).
[71] 5 U.S.C. § 1214(b)(2)(B).
[72] 5 U.S.C. § 1214(b)(2)(C).
[73] 5 U.S.C. § 1214(b)(3).
[74] 5 U.S.C. §1214(b)(4)(i).
[75] 5 U.S.C. § 1214(c).
[76] 5 U.S.C. § 1214(b)(4)(B).
[77] 5 U.S.C. § 1215(a)(1).
[78] 5 U.S.C. § 1215(a)(2)(C).
[79] 5 U.S.C. § 1215(a)(3).
[80] 5 U.S.C. § 1204(m)(1).
[81] 5 U.S.C. § 1215(b).
[82] 5 U.S.C. §1215(c)(1).
[83] 5 U.S.C. § 1212(c).
[84] 5 U.S.C. § 1214(b)(1)(A)(i),(ii).
[85] 5 U.S.C. § 1214(b)(1)(A)(iii).
[86] 5 U.S.C. § 1214(b)(1)(B),(C).
[87] 5 U.S.C. § 1214(b)(1)(D).
[88] 5 U.S.C. § 1221(a).
[89] *See* 5 U.S.C. § 7701.
[90] 5 U.S.C. § 1221(j).
[91] 5 U.S.C. § 1221(g)(1)(A)(i),(ii).
[92] 5 U.S.C. § 1221(g)(1)(B).
[93] 5 U.S.C. § 1221(e)(1).
[94] 5 U.S.C. § 1212(c)(2).
[95] 5 U.S.C. § 7121.
[96] 5 U.S.C. §§ 4303 and 7512.
[97] 5 U.S.C. § 7121(d),(e).
[98] 5 U.S.C. § 7121(d).

In: Law and Law Enforcement Issues
Editor: Gerald M. Kessler, pp. 227-241

ISBN: 978-1-60456-044-2

Chapter 9

NOMINATIONS TO ARTICLE III LOWER COURTS BY PRESIDENT GEORGE W. BUSH DURING THE 110TH CONGRESS*

Denis Steven Rutkus, Kevin M. Scott and Maureen Bearden

ABSTRACT

This article tracks nominations made by President George W. Bush to judgeships on the U.S. courts of appeals, the U.S. district courts, and the U.S. Court of International Trade — the lower courts on which, pursuant to Article III of the Constitution, judges serve "during good Behaviour." It lists and keeps count of all nominations made to these courts during the 110th Congress, including pertinent actions taken by the Senate Judiciary Committee and the full Senate. It also tracks the number of judicial vacancies on the courts (including vacancies classified by the federal judiciary as "judicial emergencies"), the number of nominations pending to fill the vacancies, and the names of the pending nominees. Last, the report presents the total number of persons nominated by President Bush to each category of lower Article III court during his entire presidency (breaking down each total to show the number confirmed, pending, returned and not re-nominated, and withdrawn).

As of April 9, 2007:

- President Bush had nominated eight individuals to judgeships on the U.S. courts of appeals during the 110th Congress, with the Senate having confirmed two of them.
- President Bush had nominated 36 individuals to U.S. district court judgeships during the 110th Congress, with the Senate having confirmed 13 of them.
- There were 14 judicial vacancies on the U.S. courts of appeals, with six nominations pending to fill these vacancies.
- There were 33 U.S. district court vacancies, with 21 nominations pending to fill these judgeships, and an additional two nominations pending to fill future district court vacancies.

---

* Excerpted from CRS Report RL33953, dated April 9, 2007.

- No vacancies had occurred on the U.S. Court of International Trade during the 110th Congress (and thus no nominations have been made to the court during the Congress).
- During his entire presidency (from January 20, 2001 to the present), President Bush had made 315 nominations to Article III lower court judgeships. Of the 315 total, 271 had received Senate confirmation, 29 were pending in the 110th Congress, nine had been returned to the President in a previous Congress and not resubmitted, and six had been withdrawn by the President.

INTRODUCTION

In recent years, Congress has expressed increasing interest in the nomination and confirmation process for lower federal court judges.[1] To provide Congress with a current overview of this process, this article tracks the status of certain lower court nominations made by President George W. Bush during the 110th Congress. The report deals primarily with nominations to lower Article III courts (those courts on which judges serve "during good Behaviour"), while also accounting for infrequent nominations to the small number of territorial district judgeships, which have fixed-term appointments.[2]

The Article III Lower Courts

Article III, Section 1 of the Constitution provides, in part, that the "judicial Power of the United States shall be vested in one supreme Court, and in such inferior Courts as the Congress may from time to time ordain and establish." It further provides that justices on the Supreme Court and judges on lower courts established by Congress under Article III have what effectively has come to mean life tenure, holding their office "during good Behaviour."[3] By contrast, judges in various federal courts established by Congress under Article I of the Constitution are appointed for fixed terms.[4] Along with the Supreme Court, the courts that constitute the Article III courts in the federal judicial system are the U.S. courts of appeals, the U.S. district courts, and the U.S. Court of International Trade. The following are thumbnail descriptions of each of the lower Article III courts:

The U.S. Courts of Appeals

These courts take appeals from federal trial court decisions and are empowered to review the decisions of many administrative agencies. Cases presented to these courts are generally considered by judges sitting in three-member panels. Altogether, 179 permanent appellate court judgeships are authorized by law. Courts within the courts of appeals system are often called "circuit courts," because they are divided into 12 geographic circuits and an additional nationwide circuit, the Federal Circuit, which has specialized subject matter jurisdiction. In this article, nominations to U.S. courts of appeals judgeships are referred to as "circuit court nominations."

The U.S. District Courts

These are the trial courts of general federal jurisdiction. Each state has at least one district court, while some states have as many as four. There are 674 district court judgeships authorized by law, including those for the District of Columbia and the Commonwealth of Puerto Rico.[5]

The U.S. Court of International Trade

This court has original and exclusive jurisdiction over civil actions against the United States, its agencies and officers, and certain civil actions brought by the United States arising out of import transactions and federal statutes affecting international trade. The court is composed of nine judges, no more than five of whom may belong to one political party.

Congress also has established district courts in the territories of Guam, the U.S. Virgin Islands, and the Northern Mariana Islands. Like the U.S. district courts, the territorial courts are trial courts of general federal jurisdiction, while also having jurisdiction over many local matters that, within the 50 states, are handled in state courts. Because they are trial courts of general federal jurisdiction, whose rulings may be appealed to a U.S. court of appeals,[6] the territorial courts can be viewed as a category of court falling within the federal district court system.[7] Territorial courts, however, are not Article III courts, and judicial appointees to these courts serve 10year terms, with one judgeship each in Guam and the Northern Mariana Islands, and two in the Virgin Islands.

Judicial Nomination Data Tracked

This article lists and keeps count of all nominations made to the above-discussed courts during the 110th Congress, including certain actions taken on these nominations by the Senate Judiciary Committee and the full Senate. The report also provides statistics for all of the nominations that President Bush has made to these courts during his entire presidency, starting with the 107th Congress in January 2001 and carrying through to the present. (Thus far in the 110th Congress, no nominations have been made either to the Court of International Trade or to the territorial district courts, although President Bush made, and the Senate confirmed, nominations to these courts during previous Congresses.)

In the following pages, President Bush's nominations to the lower Article III courts are listed or counted in tables 1 through 6. Some of these tables, where noted, also keep track of nominations made to the territorial courts. Appendix 1 provides a brief textual overview of the principal steps in the process for appointing lower court judges.

JUDICIAL NOMINATION TABLES FOR THE 110TH CONGRESS

Table 1 is a judicial vacancy table. For each type of Article III lower court — circuit, district, and Court of International Trade — it shows the number of judgeships vacant as of the date listed, as well as the number of nominations pending to fill those judgeships. Table 1 also displays the number of nominations pending to fill "future vacancies," which occur when judges in active service announce their retirement to occur on a date that has not yet been reached or when a judge in active service indicates a plan to retire or take senior status upon the confirmation of a successor.

In addition, table 1 shows how many of these vacancies are classified by the federal judiciary as "judicial emergencies." For the courts of appeals, a judicial emergency is any vacancy in a circuit where there are more than 700 adjusted filings per panel, or any vacancy in a circuit that has existed for more than 18 months and where adjusted filings are between 500 to 700 per panel. For a district court, a judicial emergency is any vacancy in a district where weighted filings exceed 600 per judgeship, or any vacancy in existence more than 18 months where weighted filings are between 430 and 600 per judgeship, or any court with more than one authorized judgeship and only one active judge.

Table 1. Vacancies in Article III Lower Court Judgeships (as of April 9, 2007)

Court	Vacancies	Nominations Pending		Judicial Emergencies	
		For Existing Vacancies	For Future Vacancies	Number	Nominees Pending
U.S. Courts of Appeals	14	6	0	11	5
U.S. District Courts	33	21	2	9	6
U.S. Court of International Trade	0	0	0	0	0
Total	47	27	2	20	11

Source: CRS analysis of data provided by the Administrative Office for the United States Courts, available at [http://www.uscourts.gov/judicialvac.html].

Table 2, which lists pending nominations, presents all Article III lower court nominations made during the 110th Congress and pending as of the date listed. The table shows the date each nomination was received by the Senate, the date of any hearing on the nomination before the Judiciary Committee, and the date of any vote by the committee to report the nomination to the Senate. The table also indicates which nominations in the list are renominations — persons nominated to the same judgeship either earlier in the 110th Congress or in a previous Congress.

Tables 3 and 4 list all nominations to the circuit courts of appeals and to the district courts, respectively, made by President Bush during the 110th Congress, as of the date listed, and any actions taken on the nominations.[8] The nominations are listed in chronological order according to the date on which each was received by the Senate. The tables show how far along each nomination has progressed in the appointment process, with separate columns indicating the date on which any of the following occurred:

- the Judiciary Committee held a hearing on the nomination,
- the committee voted to report or take other action on the nomination, or
- the Senate voted for confirmation or some other final action.

Table 2. Pending Nominations to the U.S. Courts of Appeals, District Courts, and Court of International Trade in the 110th Congress (as of April 9, 2007)

No.	Name of Nominee	Court	Date Received by Senate	Hearing	Committee Action
	Circuit Courts of Appeals				
1	Keisler, Peter D.[a]	D.C.	1/9/07	[b]	
2	Livingston, Debra A.[a]	Second	1/9/07		
3	Southwick, Leslie	Fifth	1/9/07		
4	Kethledge, Raymond M.[a]	Sixth	3/19/07		
5	Murphy, Stephen J., III [a]	Sixth	3/19/07		
6	Elrod, Jennifer W.	Fifth	3/29/07		
	District Courts				
1	Donohue, Mary O.[a]	N.NY	1/9/07		
2	Farr, Thomas Alvin [a]	E.NC	1/9/07		
3	Kapala, Frederick J.[a]	N.IL	1/9/07	3/13/07	
4	Mauskopf, Rosslyn R.[a]	E.NY	1/9/07		
5	O'Grady, Liam [a]	E.VA	1/9/07		
6	Osteen, William L., Jr.[a]	M.NC	1/9/07		
7	Ozerden, Halil S.[a]	S.MS	1/9/07	3/13/07	
8	Reidinger, Martin K.[a]	W.NC	1/9/07		
9	Rogan, James E.[a]	C.CA	1/9/07		
10	Schroeder, Thomas D.[a]	M.NC	1/9/07		
11	Settle, Benjamin H.[a]	W.WA	1/9/07	3/13/07	
12	Van Bokkelen, Joseph S.	N.IN	1/9/07		
13	DeGiusti, Timothy D.	W.OK	2/15/07		
14	Sullivan, Richard	S.NY	2/15/07		
15	Aycock, Sharion	N.MS	3/19/07		
16	Dugas, David R.	M.LA	3/19/07		
17	Hall, James R.	S.GA	3/19/07		
18	Honaker, Richard H.	WY	3/19/07		
19	Jones, Richard A.	W.WA	3/19/07		
20	Jonker, Robert J.[a]	W.MI	3/19/07	[b]	
21	Maloney, Paul L.[a]	W.MI	3/19/07	[b]	
22	Neff, Janet T.	W.MI	3/19/07	[b]	
23	Sammartino, Janis L.	S.CA	3/19/07		
	Court of International Trade				
	(There are no pending nominations to the Court of International Trade)				

Source: CRS Judicial Nominations Database

[a] Renomination of an individual first nominated in the 109th Congress (2005-2006).

[b] The individual received a hearing in the 109th Congress on a nomination to the same position.

Table 3. President George W. Bush's Nominations to the U.S. Circuit Courts of Appeals During the 110th Congress (January 3, 2007 - April 9, 2007)

					Date					Days Elapsed,
No.	Name of Nominee	State	Court	Nomination Received	Hearing	Committee Action	Final Action	Disposition	Votea	First Nomination to Final Action
1	Hardiman, Thomas M.b	PA	Third	1/9/07	d	3/8/07	3/15/07	Confirmed	95-0	183
2	Keisler, Peter D.b	MD	D.C.	1/9/07	d					
3	Livingston, Debra A.b	NY	Second	1/9/07						
4	Smith, N. Randy b	ID	Ninth	1/9/07	d		1/16/07	Withdrawn	—	—
5	Southwick, Leslie	MS	Fifth	1/9/07						
6	Smith, N. Randy b, c	ID	Ninth	1/16/07	d	2/8/07	2/15/07	Confirmed	94-0	426
7	Kethledge, Raymond M.b	MI	Sixth	3/19/07						
8	Murphy, Stephen J., III b	MI	Sixth	3/19/07						
9	Elrod, Jennifer W.	TX	Fifth	3/29/07						

Source: CRS Judicial Nominations Database

a. A numerical tally indicates a roll call vote on confirmation (the yeas followed by the nays). "Voice" indicates that the nomination was confirmed by voice vote.

b. Renomination of an individual first nominated in the 109th Congress (2005-2006).

c. Smith was withdrawn as a nominee for a seat vacated by Stephen Trott and resubmitted, the same day, for a seat vacated by Thomas Nelson.

d. The individual received a hearing in the 109th Congress on a nomination to the same position. For additional information, see Appendices 1 and 4 in CRS Report RL31868, *U.S. Circuit and District Court Nominations by President George W. Bush During the 107th 109th Congresses*, by Denis Steven Rutkus, Kevin M. Scott, and Maureen Bearden.

Table 4. President George W. Bush's Nominations to the U.S. District Courts During the 110th Congress (January 3, 2007 - April 9, 2007)

			Date						
No.	Name of Nominee	Court	Nomination Received	Hearing	Committee Action	Final Action	Disposition	Votea	Days Elapsed, First Nomination to Final Action
1	Bailey, John P.b	N.WV	1/9/07	2/6/07	3/1/07	3/15/07	Confirmed	Voice	260
2	Baker, Valerie L.b	C.CA	1/9/07	c	1/25/07	2/1/07	Confirmed	Voice	273
3	Bryant, Vanessa L.b	CT	1/9/07	c	3/8/07	3/28/07	Confirmed	Voice	427
4	Donohue, Mary O.b	N.NY	1/9/07						
5	Farr, Thomas Alvinb	E.NC	1/9/07						
6	Fischer, Nora B.b	W.PA	1/9/07	c	2/8/07	2/14/07	Confirmed	97-0	216
7	Frizzell, Gregory K.b	N.OK	1/9/07	c	1/25/07	2/1/07	Confirmed	99-0	239
8	Gutierrez, Philip S.b	C.CA	1/9/07	c	1/25/07	1/30/07	Confirmed	97-0	281
9	Howard, Marcia M.b	M.FL	1/9/07	c	2/8/07	2/15/07	Confirmed	93-0	253
10	Jarvey, John A.b	S.IA	1/9/07	c	2/8/07	3/8/07	Confirmed	95-0	253
11	Kapala, Frederick J.b	N.IL	1/9/07	3/13/07					
12	Lioi, Sara E.b	N.OH	1/9/07	c	2/8/07	3/8/07	Confirmed	Voice	238
13	Mauskopf, Rosslyn R.b	E.NY	1/9/07						
14	O'Grady, Liamb	E.VA	1/9/07						

Table 4. (Continued).

			Date						Days Elapsed, First Nomination to Final Action
No.	Name of Nominee	Court	Nomination Received	Hearing	Committee Action	Final Action	Disposition	Votea	
15	O'Neill, Lawrence J.b	E.CA	1/9/07	c	1/25/07	2/1/07	Confirmed	97-0	183
16	Osteen, William L., Jr.b	M.NC	1/9/07						
17	Ozerden, Halil S.b	S.MS	1/9/07	3/13/07					
18	Reidinger, Martin K.b	W.NC	1/9/07						
19	Rogan, James E.b	C.CA	1/9/07						
20	Schroeder, Thomas D.b	M.NC	1/9/07						
21	Settle, Benjamin H.b	W.WA	1/9/07	3/13/07					
22	Van Bokkelen, Joseph S.	N.IN	1/9/07						
23	Wood, Lisa G.b	S.GA	1/9/07	c	1/25/07	1/30/07	Confirmed	97-0	232
24	Wright, Otis D., IIb	C.CA	1/9/07	2/6/07	3/1/07	3/15/07	Confirmed	Voice	191
25	Wu, George H.b	C.CA	1/9/07	2/6/07	3/1/07	3/27/07	Confirmed	95-0	203
26	DeGiusti, Timothy D.	W.OK	2/15/07						

Table 4. (Continued).

			Date						
No.	Name of Nominee	Court	Nomination Received	Hearing	Committee Action	Final Action	Disposition	Votea	Days Elapsed, First Nomination to Final Action
27	Sullivan, Richard	S.NY	2/15/07						
28	Aycock, Sharion	N.MS	3/19/07						
29	Dugas, David R.	M.LA	3/19/07						
30	Hall, James R.	S.GA	3/19/07						
31	Honaker, Richard H.	WY	3/19/07						
32	Jones, Richard A.	W.WA	3/19/07						
33	Jonker, Robert J.b	W.MI	3/19/07	c					
34	Maloney, Paul L.b	W.MI	3/19/07	c					
35	Neff, Janet T.b	W.MI	3/19/07	c					
36	Sammartino, Janis L.	S.CA	3/19/07						

Source: CRS Judicial Nominations Database

a. A numerical tally indicates a roll call vote on confirmation (the yeas followed by the nays). "Voice" indicates that the nomination was confirmed by voice vote.

b. Renomination of an individual first nominated in the 109th Congress (2005-2006).

c. The individual received a hearing in the 109th

Congress on a nomination to the same position. For additional information, see Appendices 5 and 8 in CRS Report RL31868, *U.S. Circuit and District Court Nominations by President George W. Bush During the 107th-109th Congresses*, by Denis Steven Rutkus, Kevin M. Scott, and Maureen Bearden.

Table 5. President George W. Bush's Nominations to the Court of International Trade During the 110th Congress (January 3, 2007- April 9, 2007)

	Name of Nominee				Date				Days Elapsed,
No.			State	Court	Nomination Received	Hearing	Committee Action	Final Action	First Nomination to Final Action
		Thus far, during the 110th Congress, there have been no nominations to this court.							

Source: CRS Judicial Nominations Database

When final action has occurred on a nomination, the nature of the action is indicated in another column, under the heading "Disposition." (For each nomination, one of four kinds of disposition is possible — confirmation by the Senate, return of the nomination to the President, withdrawal by the President, and rejection by the Senate. During George W. Bush's presidency, however, the Senate has never voted to reject a judicial nomination.) An additional column, for nominations receiving a Senate confirmation vote, indicates whether the vote was by roll call (by supplying the roll call tally) or by voice vote.

A final column in tables 3 and 4 presents time-span information for nominations having received final action in the 110th Congress. Specifically, for each such nomination, the column measures the number of days that elapsed between a nominee's first nomination to a particular judgeship and the final action on this (the most recent) nomination. In some cases, a nominee has been nominated only once by President Bush for a judgeship, and the time span measured for such a nominee in the final column in tables 3 and 4 is the number of days that elapsed between the date during the 110th Congress that the nomination was received in the Senate and the date it received final action. However, in other cases, a judicial nominee in the 110th Congress has been nominated more than once, with one or more nominations of that person having been made in an earlier Congress. For such a nominee, the final column in tables 3 and 4 measures the number of days that elapsed between the nominee's first nomination in the earlier Congress and the date that the nominee's nomination in the 110th Congress received final action.[9]

Table 3 shows that, thus far in the 110th Congress, President Bush has nominated eight individuals to circuit court judgeships, two of whom have been confirmed by the Senate. Table 4 shows that, thus far in the 110th Congress, the President has nominated 36 individuals to district court judgeships, 13 of whom have been confirmed.

Table 5, for the present, is an empty table, which exists to account for any future nominations that President Bush might make to the U.S. Court of International Trade. (Thus far during the 110th Congress, no nominations have been made to this court.) The table is of the same format as tables 3 and 4. Accordingly, in the event any nominations are made to the court, the table will list actions on the nominations by the Judiciary Committee and the Senate, any other final action taken, and number of days elapsed between the date of nomination and date of final action.

Table 6. President George W. Bush's Nominees to Article III Lower Courts: A Numerical Breakdown According to Status of Their Most Recent Nomination (January 20, 2001 - April 9, 2007)

Court	Confirmed	Pending	Returned, Not Renominated	Withdrawn	Total
Courts of Appeals	53	6	8	3	70
District Courtsa	216	23	1	3	243
Court of International Trade	2	0	0	0	2
Total	271	29	9	6	315

Source: CRS Judicial Nominations Database.

a. Does not include three confirmed nominations to the territorial district courts, whose judges are appointed to renewable 10-year terms. There are no nominees to the territorial district courts in the 110th Congress whose nominations are pending, were returned and have not been renominated, or were withdrawn.

Table 6 presents the total number of persons nominated by President Bush to each category of lower Article III court during his entire presidency. The table also breaks down each numerical total, showing, as of the date listed, the number of nominees whose most recent nominations were: (1) confirmed; (2) pending in the Senate; (3) returned to the President, at the end of a Congress or at the start of a Senate recess of more than 30 days, and not re-submitted; or (4) withdrawn by the President. This table accounts only for the number of persons who were nominees to a particular judgeship during George W. Bush's presidency. The table does not count resubmitted nominations made when President Bush renominated individuals to the same judgeship.[10]

APPENDIX I. THE APPOINTMENT PROCESS FOR NOMINATIONS TO ARTICLE III JUDGESHIPS

Under the Constitution of the United States, the President and the Senate share the responsibility for filling vacancies in the federal judiciary.[11] While it is the President who nominates persons to fill federal judgeships, the appointment of each nominee also requires Senate confirmation. Although not mentioned in the Constitution, the Senate Judiciary Committee also plays an important role midway in the process — after the President selects, but before the Senate as a whole considers, the nominee. It is the Judiciary Committee in the Senate that has committee jurisdiction over most federal judicial nominations — namely, those to the Supreme Court, the courts of appeals, the district courts (including the territorial district courts), the U.S. Court of International Trade, and the U.S. Court of Federal Claims.[12]

The need for the President to make a nomination to an Article III court judgeship arises when a vacancy occurs on the court, due to the death, retirement, or resignation of a judge (or when a judge announces the intention to retire or resign).[13] In considering judicial candidates for possible nomination, the President frequently receives recommendations from U.S. Senators. By longstanding custom, dating back to the mid-1800s, Senators of the President's party have provided Presidents such advice, recommending candidates for judgeships situated in their states or linked by tradition to their states.[14] Also by custom, Senators not of the President's party play a consultative role and may convey to the President their views about candidates under consideration for judgeships in their states.[15] The judgeships for which a Senator ordinarily recommends nominees, or is consulted, are those in the U.S. district court or courts which geographically fall within the Senator's state and the

U.S. court of appeals circuit of which the Senator's state is a geographic part — provided the circuit judgeship historically has been associated with the Senator's state.[16]

After selecting someone to fill a judicial vacancy, the President formally submits a nomination in writing to the Senate.[17] Usually on the same day it is received by the Senate, the nomination is referred to the Judiciary Committee. The committee's first formal public step is to hold a hearing on a nomination. The committee subsequently meets again to vote on whether to report the nomination to the full Senate. A committee vote to report (even a vote to report with an unfavorable recommendation) sends the nomination forward to be considered by the Senate as a whole, while a vote against reporting (historically, a very rare occurrence) prevents the nomination from going forward, and in effect defeats the nomination in committee. The final step in the appointment process occurs when the Senate votes to confirm or disapprove the nomination. A vote to confirm requires a simple majority of Senators present and voting. If the Senate votes in the negative on whether to confirm, the nomination is defeated, and a resolution of disapproval is forwarded to the President.

As with nominations in general, judicial nominations sometimes fail to advance through each procedural step in the appointment process. After referral to committee, a nomination might not receive a hearing or, after receiving a hearing, might not receive a committee vote on whether it should be reported. Even if favorably reported by committee, a nomination might not receive a vote by the Senate on whether to confirm. The majority leader might not schedule a vote, or some Senators might oppose taking such a vote and a "super-majority" of three-fifths of the full membership of the Senate would be needed to invoke cloture on the nomination.[18] If a nomination fails to receive a Senate vote on confirmation, it ultimately will be either withdrawn by the President or returned to the President by the Secretary of the Senate upon a Senate adjournment or recess of more than 30 days.[19] The Senate may, by unanimous consent, carry nominations over a recess of more than 30 days.

REFERENCES

[1] See, for example, Nancy Scherer, Scoring Points: Politicians, Activists, and the Lower Federal Court Appointment Process (Stanford, CA: Stanford University Press, 2005); Lee Epstein and Jefferey A. Segal, Advice and Consent: The Politics of Judicial Appointments (New York: Oxford University Press, 2005); Sheldon Goldman, "Judicial Confirmation Wars: Ideology and the Battle for the Federal Courts," University of Richmond Law Review, vol. 39, March 2005, pp. 871-908; Stephen B. Burbank, "Politics, Privilege and Power: The Senate's Role in the Appointment of Federal Judges," Judicature, vol. 86, Jul.-Aug. 2002, pp. 24-27; and Elliot E. Slotnick, "A Historical Perspective on Federal Judicial Selection," Judicature, vol. 86, Jul.-Aug. 2002, pp. 13-16.

[2] For a detailed narrative and statistical analysis of President George W. Bush's lower court nominations during the first six years of his presidency, see CRS Report RL31868, U.S. Circuit and District Court Nominations by President George W. Bush During the 107th 109th Congresses, by Denis Steven Rutkus, Kevin M. Scott, and Maureen Bearden.

[3] Pursuant to this constitutional language, Article III judges may hold office for as long as they live or until they voluntarily leave office. A President has no power to remove them from office. Article III judges may be removed by Congress only through the process of impeachment by the House and conviction by the Senate

[4] Citing the power to do so in Article I of the Constitution, Congress, in separate statutes, has created four courts of specialized subject matter jurisdiction — the U.S. Court of Federal Claims, the U.S. Tax Court, the U.S. Court of Appeals for Veterans Claims, and the Court of Appeals for the Armed Forces — and has authorized 15-year judicial tenure in these courts.

[5] The 674 total consists of 663 permanently authorized judgeships and 11 "temporary" judgeships (which, pursuant to statute, temporarily increase the number of judgeships

for specified judicial districts. These districts revert back to the permanently authorized number of judgeships at a future time fixed by the statute — typically, when, after a specified number of years, a judgeship in the district is vacated).

[6] Decisions of the U.S. District Courts for the District of Guam and the District of the Northern Mariana Islands are appealed to the Ninth Circuit Court of Appeals. Decisions of the U.S. District Court for the District of Virgin Islands are appealed to the Third Circuit Court of Appeals.

[7] For instance, the federal judiciary subsumes territorial courts under the heading of "District Courts" in various places on its website, at [http://www.uscourts.gov]. In one link on the website, entitled "Authorized Judgeships," accessed via [http://www.uscourts.gov/ judicialvac.html], the judiciary lists the number of authorized judgeships, respectively, on the Supreme Court, the circuit courts, the district courts, and the Court of International Trade. The link, under the heading of "District Courts," provides an "Article III" subheading (with 674 judgeships) and a "Territorial Court" sub-heading (with 4 judgeships), and, in an adjacent column, 678 is shown to be total number of judgeships for the "District Courts" heading.

[8] In the event any nominations are made to the territorial district courts, they will be listed in table 4, and treated as falling within the category of district court nominations, even though, as discussed above, they are not Article III court nominations. Thus far during the 110th Congress, no nominations have been made to the territorial courts.

[9] In the event a person were nominated for the first time to a judgeship during the 110th Congress, only to be re-nominated during the 110th Congress, the final column in tables 3 and 4 would show, in the row for the nominee's last nomination, the time elapsed between date of first nomination and date of final action on the last nomination.

[10] Some of President Bush's nominees were nominated to a circuit or district judgeship more than once within a Congress, or nominated to the judgeship in more than one Congress. For a listing of these nominees, as well as other Presidents' nominees to the circuit and district courts whose nominations were resubmitted from 1977 through 2006, See CRS Report RL33839, Returns and Resubmissions of Nominees to the U.S. Courts of Appeals and District Courts, 1977-2006, by Kevin M. Scott.

[11] Article II, Section 2, clause 2 of the Constitution provides that the President "shall nominate, and by and with the Advice and Consent of the Senate, shall appoint ... Judges of the supreme Court, and all other Officers of the United States, whose Appointments are not herein otherwise provided for, and which shall be established by Law...."

[12] Nominations to the Court of Appeals for the Armed Forces fall within the jurisdiction of the Senate Armed Services Committee; nominations to the U.S. Tax Court fall within the Jurisdiction of the Senate Finance Committee; and nominations to the Court of Appeals for Veterans Claims fall within the jurisdiction of the Senate Veterans' Affairs Committee.

[13] A vacancy also would occur if a judge were removed by Congress through the impeachment process, but historically such occurrences have been extremely rare. Specifically, in our nation's history, "there have been 15 impeachment trials in the Senate, 11 against judges. Seven trials have resulted in convictions, all against judges." CRS Report RL32935, Congressional Oversight of Judges and Justices, by Elizabeth B. Bazan and Morton Rosenberg.

[14] A scholar on the Senate's role in judicial appointments, writing in 1953, described the "well-established custom, which has prevailed since about 1840," wherein U.S. district judges "are normally selected by senators from the state in which the district is situated, provided they belong to the same party as the President." By contrast, the President was said to have "a much freer hand in the selection of judges to the circuit courts of appeals, whose districts cover several states ...." Joseph P. Harris, The Advice and Consent of the Senate (Berkeley, CA: University of California Press, 1953; reprint, New York: Greenwood Press, 1968), p. 314, (page citations are to the reprint edition). See also, for more recent discussion of the continuing role played by Senators in recommending judicial candidates, Sheldon Goldman, Picking Federal Judges: Lower Court Selection from Roosevelt Through Reagan (New Haven, CT: Yale University Press, 1997) (in each presidency chapter, under the heading "Senators and Selection").

[15] See CRS Report RL32013, The History of the Blue Slip in the Senate Committee on the Judiciary, 1917-Present, by Mitchel A. Sollenberger. See also Elliot E. Slotnick, "A Historical Perspective on Federal Judicial Selection,"Judicature, vol. 86, July-Aug. 2002, where, at p.13, the author observes that the blue slip procedure of the Senate Judiciary Committee "has worked to ensure that home state senators of both parties, whether or not they are of the president's party, have some say when judges are being nominated from their state."

[16] A President is generally believed inclined to avoid selecting a judicial nominee opposed by a home-state Senator of the President's party — given the custom of "senatorial courtesy," wherein the Senate, as a collegial body, customarily supports Senators in disputes with the President over judicial appointments in their state. Two scholars have written that, as a result of this custom, Senators of the President's party "who object to a district judgeship in their home state have a virtual veto over the nomination." Robert A. Carp and Ronald Stidham, Judicial Process in America, 3d ed. (Washington: CQ Press, 1996), p. 247.

[17] For a detailed examination of the procedures followed by Senate committees and the full Senate in considering nominations in general, see CRS Report RL31980, Senate Consideration of Presidential Nominations: Committee and Floor Procedure, by Elizabeth Rybicki. For a diagrammatic overview of procedures followed by the Senate Judiciary Committee and the full Senate in considering district and circuit court nominations, see CRS Report RS21735, U.S. District and Circuit Court Nominations: A Diagram of Customary Procedures, by Mitchel A. Sollenberger.

[18] See CRS Report RL32878, Cloture Attempts on Nominations, by Richard S. Beth and Betsy Palmer.

[19] Rule XXXI, paragraph 6, Standing Rules of the Senate, provides, in part, that "if the Senate shall adjourn or take a recess for more than thirty days, all nominations pending and not finally acted upon at the time of taking such adjournment or recess shall be returned by the Secretary to the President and shall not again be considered unless they shall again be made to the Senate by the President."

In: Law and Law Enforcement Issues
Editor: Gerald M. Kessler, pp. 243-252
ISBN: 978-1-60456-044-2

Chapter 10

U.S. ATTORNEYS WHO HAVE SERVED LESS THAN FULL FOUR-YEAR TERMS, 1981-2006*

Kevin M. Scott

ABSTRACT

United States attorneys, who prosecute violations of federal law and defend the federal government in civil suits, are nominated by the President and confirmed by the Senate, and, once confirmed, serve four-year terms. The President may terminate the appointment of a U.S. attorney at any time. Recent controversy over the termination of seven U.S. attorneys, and the method by which the interim appointments were made to replace them, has focused attention on reasons for departure of U.S. attorneys.

This article provides data on U.S. attorneys who did not complete their full four-year term after confirmation by the Senate and whose terms did not carry over a change in presidential administration. The data collected employ records of presidential appointment and Senate confirmation of U.S. attorneys, and rely on secondary sources to provide information on reasons U.S. attorneys left office before completion of their four-year terms.

At least 54 U.S. attorneys appointed by the President and confirmed by the Senate left office before completion of a four-year term between 1981 and 2006 (not counting those whose tenure was interrupted by a change in presidential administration). Of those 54, 17 left to become Article III federal judges, one left to become a federal magistrate judge, six left to serve in other positions in the executive branch, four sought elective office, two left to serve in state government, one died, and 15 left to enter or return to private practice.

Of the remaining eight U.S. attorneys who left before completing a four-year term without a change in presidential administration, two were apparently dismissed by the President, and three apparently resigned after news reports indicated they had engaged in questionable personal actions. No information was available on the three remaining U.S. attorneys who resigned.

Interim U.S. attorneys are appointed by the Attorney General and serve until the President nominates, and the Senate confirms, a successor. Legislation has been

---

* Excerpted from CRS Report RL33889, dated February 22, 2007.

introduced in the 110th Congress (H.R. 580; S. 214) to revert the system of appointment of interim U.S. attorneys to the system in place from 1986 to 2006. Under that system, the appointment of an interim U.S. attorney by the Attorney General expired after 120 days. After that appointment expired, district courts could appoint interim U.S. attorneys who could serve until the President nominated, and the Senate confirmed, a permanent replacement.

Introduction

The primary responsibilities of United States attorneys are twofold: the prosecution of violations of federal criminal and civil law, and defense of the United States in civil actions brought against the federal government in the districts to which they are assigned.[1] By law, U.S. attorneys are appointed by the President with the advice and consent of the Senate for terms of four years.[2] There are 93 U.S. attorneys, generally one for each of the 94 U.S. district courts (Guam and the Northern Mariana Islands district courts share one U.S. attorney.)

Appointment of U.S. Attorneys

Presidential nominations to the position of U.S. attorney are referred to the Senate Judiciary Committee; if the Judiciary Committee reports the nomination, then the nomination may be considered by the entire Senate. If the Judiciary Committee does not report the nomination before the end of a Congress, the nomination is returned to the President, who may resubmit the nomination. As is the case with nominations for Article III federal judgeships and U.S. marshals, nominations to the position of U.S. attorney are the subject of "blue slips," where Senators who represent the state that includes the district to which an individual is nominated are invited to offer their approval or disapproval of the nominee. If a home state Senator returns a negative blue slip or fails to return a positive blue slip, the chair of the Senate Judiciary Committee, by tradition and in deference to the Senator, may decline to schedule a hearing or other committee action on the nomination.[3]

Interim U.S. Attorneys

Once confirmed by the Senate, U.S attorneys can have their appointments terminated at any time by the President.[4] Upon completion of a four-year term, and in the absence of a successor, "a United States attorney shall continue to perform the duties of his office until his successor is appointed and qualifies."[5] If the U.S. attorney resigns or has his or her appointment terminated by the President, an interim U.S. attorney may be appointed by the Attorney General to fill the position until the President nominates, and the Senate confirms, a replacement to the position. As discussed below, legislation has been introduced in the House of Representatives and the Senate in the 110th Congress to alter the mechanism by which interim U.S. attorneys are appointed and how long interim appointees may serve. The two legislative proposals take as their starting point earlier mechanisms for appointing interim U.S. attorneys.

Statutory Changes

In the past 21 years, there have been two changes in how vacant U.S. attorney positions may be filled on an interim basis, pending nomination and Senate confirmation of a permanent successor. In 1966, Congress enacted 28 U.S.C. 541,[6] which governs the appointment of U.S. attorneys. The language for filling vacancies with interim U.S. attorneys enacted at that time reflected existing language.[7] That language read as follows:

> The district court for a district in which the office of United States attorney is vacant may appoint a United States attorney to serve until the vacancy is filled. The order of appointment by the court shall be filed with the clerk of the court.[8]

In 1986, Congress amended the language to allow for the district court to continue to make an interim appointment, but first allowed the Attorney General to make an interim appointment of no more than 120 days. The revised language read as follows:

a. Except as provided in subsection (b), the Attorney General may appoint a United States attorney for the district in which the office of United States attorney is vacant.
b. The Attorney General shall not appoint as United States attorney a person to whose appointment by the President to that office the Senate refused to give advice and consent.
c. A person appointed as United States attorney under this section may serve until the earlier of —
   (1) the qualification of a United States attorney for such district appointed by the President under section 541 of this title; or
   (2) the expiration of 120 days after appointment by the Attorney General under this section.
d. If an appointment expires under subsection (c)(2), the district court for such district may appoint a United States attorney to serve until the vacancy is filled. The order of appointment by the court shall be filed with the clerk of the court.[9]

In 2006, as part of the reauthorization of the USA PATRIOT Act, the method for filling vacancies was again altered, allowing the Attorney General to fill a vacancy indefinitely, not for just 120 days. The current language reads as follows:

a. Except as provided in subsection (b), the Attorney General may appoint a United States attorney for the district in which the office of United States attorney is vacant.
b. The Attorney General shall not appoint as United States attorney a person to whose appointment by the President to that office the Senate refused to give advice and consent.
c. A person appointed as United States attorney under this section may serve until the qualification of a United States Attorney for such district appointed by the President under section 541 of this title.[10]

As a result of the 2006 law, district courts now play no role in appointing interim U.S. attorneys to fill vacancies. Supporters of the 2006 law have argued that district courts occasionally failed to appoint individuals put forward by the Department of Justice to interim U.S. attorney positions,[11] and that allowing federal judges to appoint interim U.S. attorneys raises separation-of-powers concerns.[12] Critics of the 2006 law have claimed that the new law allows U.S. attorneys to be dismissed for "political reasons"[13] and that interim replacements for terminated U.S. attorneys may serve indefinitely without presidential nomination or Senate confirmation to four-year terms.[14]

IDENTIFICATION OF U.S. ATTORNEYS SERVING LESS THAN FOUR YEARS

The recent dismissal of seven U.S. attorneys has raised interest in patterns in departures of U.S. attorneys not related to completion of a four-year term or a change in presidential administration. The dismissal has also renewed focus on how interim

U.S. attorneys are appointed, with several Members of Congress asserting that the 2006 change was "slipped into"[15] the reauthorization of the USA PATRIOT Act. CRS attempted to ascertain how often, prior to 2007, U.S. attorneys left office before completing their four-year terms without a change in presidential administration.

Methodology

In order to determine how many U.S. attorneys had served less than four years with tenure uninterrupted by a change in presidential administration, CRS began by contacting the Executive Office for United States Attorneys (EOUSA), which serves as the liaison between U.S. attorneys and the Department of Justice. CRS first contacted the EOUSA January 24, 2007, to seek records on the appointment and termination dates for U.S. attorneys. As of February 20, 2007, EOUSA had not provided the requested data. CRS also contacted the Office of Personnel Management (OPM), which maintains the Central Personnel Data File (CPDF). CRS spoke with a representative in OPM's Congressional Liaison Office and was told that the database could not produce the information needed. The OPM representative referred CRS to the Department of Justice.

Absent direct information on starting and termination dates of U.S. attorneys, as well as reasons for their termination, CRS collected data on presidential nomination and Senate confirmation of U.S. attorneys during the 97th (1981-1982) through 109th (2005-2006) Congresses. The Legislative Information System (LIS)[16] provides a searchable database of all nominations submitted to the Senate for consideration, which allowed CRS to build records of succession for Senate-confirmed occupants of the 93 U.S. attorney positions. Using the LIS database, CRS identified each U.S. attorney who was nominated to the position less than four years after his or her predecessor was confirmed to the same position. Nomination of a successor less than four years after the confirmation of a predecessor suggests that the predecessor had served less than four years in the office.[17] Excluded from these calculations were U.S. attorneys appointed after a change in presidential administration; U.S.

attorneys have typically been removed from office by a new President so that the new President could appoint his own U.S. attorneys.[18]

Two examples may prove illustrative. In 1991, President George H.W. Bush nominated, and the Senate confirmed, Maurice Ellsworth to the position of U.S. Attorney for the District of Idaho. In September 1993, President Clinton appointed, and the Senate confirmed, Betty Richardson to the same position. Although Maurice Ellsworth served less than four years, CRS did not conduct further analysis of this incomplete term because different Presidents made the initial and new appointments. By contrast, President George W. Bush appointed (and the Senate confirmed) Michael Mosman to the position of U.S. Attorney for the District of Oregon in 2001. President George W. Bush then appointed (and the Senate confirmed) Karin Immergut to the same position in 2003. Given that Michael Mosman left office before the completion of his four-year term, and his replacement was appointed by the same President, CRS attempted to ascertain the reason for his departure.

Using this methodology, CRS identified 54 instances from 1981 through 2006 in which the tenure of a U.S. attorney fell short of the four-year term specified by statute (see the appendix). This approach likely underestimates the number of U.S. attorneys who departed office before completion of their four-year terms. A U.S. attorney would not have been included in the appendix if the individual resigned (of his or her own initiative or at the President's request) before completing a four-year term, was replaced by someone appointed by a district court or the Attorney General, and the President did not make a nomination to replace the individual until after four years from the start of the resigned U.S. attorney's term. If, for example, a U.S. attorney confirmed in 1993 resigned in 1996, but a nomination to replace that individual was not made until 1998, the data collection method utilized by CRS would not have captured the individual who resigned in 1996.

Once CRS identified all U.S. attorneys who met these criteria, CRS used secondary sources, including Martindale Hubbell Lawyer Locator,[19] Nexis news searches,[20] and the LIS nominations database[21] to ascertain the dates and the reasons that the identified U.S. attorneys left office.[22]

FINDINGS

The appendix identifies 54 U.S. attorneys who were appointed between 1981 and 2006, left office before completing their four-year terms, and whose terms did not extend beyond one President's tenure in office. The entries in the appendix are sorted in ascending order of confirmation date. In each case, CRS has annotated the results of secondary source searches regarding the approximate date of departure and the reason for departure from the position. Seventeen of the 54 U.S. attorneys left office early to take positions as Article III federal judges. For each of those individuals, the appendix provides the month that the individual was confirmed to the federal judgeship as the departure date from the position of U.S. attorney. One additional U.S. attorney, Paul Michael Warner, left in January 2006, before the completion of his second term, to become a U.S. magistrate judge. Six U.S. attorneys left their posts early to take other positions in the executive branch; all but one of those (Jim J. Marquez, who left in February 1984 to become General Counsel to the Department of Transportation) took positions elsewhere in the Department of Justice. Four other individuals appear to have left office to seek elective office; two more left to serve in state government. One U.S. attorney died while in office. All of the above categories account for 31 of the 54 U.S. attorneys listed in the appendix.

Of the remaining 23 U.S. attorneys, the secondary sources indicate that 15 left to enter or return to private practice. Included in this category are individuals who explicitly indicated (in news reports or elsewhere) that their intent was to take a position with a law firm or as house counsel for a business. Of the remaining eight individuals, two were apparently dismissed by the President. Those two were:

- William Kennedy, U.S. Attorney for the Southern District of California. Kennedy, appointed by President Reagan, was reportedly dismissed in 1982 "for charging that the Justice Department, at the request of the Central Intelligence Agency, was blocking his attempt to prosecute Mr. [Miguel] Nassar [Haro], because he had been a key CIA informant on Mexican and Central American affairs."[23]
- J. William Petro, U.S. Attorney for the Northern District of Ohio. Petro, appointed by President Reagan, was reportedly dismissed in 1984 because the Department of Justice was "investigating allegations that Mr. Petro disclosed information about an indictment pending from an undercover operation and that the information reached a subject of the investigation."[24] Petro was later convicted on the charges.[25]

For the remaining six U.S. attorneys, the only information available was that they had resigned from office. News reports suggested that, in at least three of those cases, their resignations were the result of questionable conduct. Briefly, those three cases were as follows:

- Larry Colleton, U.S. Attorney for the Middle District of Florida. Colleton, appointed by President Clinton, according to news reports, "had been U.S. attorney for Florida's middle district for only five months on May 6 [1994] when he was videotaped grabbing Jacksonville television reporter Richard Rose by the throat. The newsman had been trying to question him about recent decisions in his office."[26] He resigned in July 1994.
- Kendall Coffey, U.S. Attorney for the Southern District of Florida. Coffey, appointed by President Clinton, resigned on May 12, 1996, according to news reports, "amid accusations that he bit a topless dancer on the arm during a visit to an adult club after losing a big drug case."[27]
- Frank L. McNamara, Jr., U.S. Attorney for the District of Massachusetts. McNamara, appointed by President Reagan, reportedly resigned on January 30, 1989, because he had "been the focus of heated dispute since the Justice Department announced in November [1988] that he was the target of an internal probe."[28] That probe sought to identify "whether he had lied to federal officials when he accused his predecessor as U.S. attorney, William F. Weld, of smoking marijuana. McNamara also admitted experimenting with the drug."[29] The same news story reported that had McNamara not resigned of his own accord, he would have been suspended by Attorney General Richard Thornburgh.[30]

For the remaining three individuals, CRS was unable to locate additional information on the reasons for their resignations. In one of these cases, Humberto Garcia, the tenure was nearly four full years (from March 2003 to January 2007).

LEGISLATION IN THE 110TH CONGRESS

Companion legislation has been introduced in the House and the Senate to change the method of appointing interim U.S. attorneys. Both the House bill, H.R. 580, sponsored by Representative Berman, and the Senate bill, S. 214, sponsored by Senator Feinstein, as amended, would allow the Attorney General to make an interim appointment that would expire after 120 days. After 120 days, the district court would be empowered to appoint an interim U.S. attorney whose tenure would last until the President nominates, and the Senate confirms, a successor. These proposals would return the method for appointing interim U.S. attorneys to the system used between 1986 and 2006.

S. 214 contains an additional provision not currently in H.R. 580 that would terminate the appointments of any existing interim U.S. attorneys 120 days after the legislation is enacted (or a successor is confirmed by the Senate, whichever comes earlier.) Under S. 214, vacancies created by the expiration of the term of an interim U.S. attorney would be filled by the district court. A hearing was held on S. 214 on February 6, 2007, and the bill, as amended, was approved by the Senate Judiciary Committee on February 8, 2007. The chairman reported the bill, as amended, on February 12, 2007. H.R. 580 was referred to the Commercial and Administrative Law Subcommittee of the House Judiciary Committee on February 2, 2007.

APPENDIX. U.S. ATTORNEYS WHO LEFT OFFICE AFTER SERVING LESS THAN FULL FOUR-YEAR TERMS DURING THE TENURE OF ONE PRESIDENT (1981-2006)

District	U.S. Attorney	Nomination Date	Confirmation Date	Departure Date	Departure Reason
N.OK	Francis Anthony Keating II	05/14/81	06/10/81	1983	Sought Elective Office
W.OK	David L. Russell	05/14/81	06/10/81	12/81	Federal Judge
S.IN	Sarah Evans Barker	06/25/81	07/15/81	03/84	Federal Judge
W.TX	Edward C. Prado	06/16/81	07/15/81	03/84	Federal Judge
NH	W. Stephen Thayer III	07/29/81	09/16/81	1984	State Government
N.IL	Dan K. Webb	09/22/81	10/21/81	02/01/85	Private Sector
ID	Guy Gordon Hurlbutt	09/17/81	10/29/81	1984	Private Sector
S.CA	William H. Kennedy	09/17/81	11/10/81	04/05/82	Dismissed

Appendix. (Continued).

District	U.S. Attorney	Nomination Date	Confirmation Date	Departure Date	Departure Reason
CT	Alan H. Nevas	10/07/81	11/18/81	10/85	Federal Judge
KS	Jim J. Marquez	09/17/81	11/24/81	02/84	Executive Branch
DC	Stanley S. Harris	11/04/81	12/16/81	11/83	Federal Judge
NV	Lamond Robert Mills	12/04/81	02/08/82	1985	Private Sector
C.CA	Stephen S. Trott	12/09/81	02/08/82	07/83	Executive Branch
N.OH	J. William Petro	12/11/81	03/04/82	10/02/84	Dismissed
E.OK	Gary Loy Richardson	03/29/82	04/21/82	1984	Private Sector
E.NY	Raymond J. Dearie	07/28/82	08/20/82	03/86	Federal Judge
N.FL	William Thomas Dillard III	12/14/82	02/23/83	1986	Private Sector
S.IN	John D. Tinder	06/04/84	06/15/84	08/87	Federal Judge
M.GA	Joe D. Whitley	03/17/86	04/23/86	1987	Executive Branch
E.WI	Joseph P. Stadtmueller	05/14/86	06/06/86	05/87	Federal Judge
N.FL	K. Michael Moore	04/23/87	05/19/87	05/19/87	Executive Branch
W.OK	William S. Price	04/23/87	07/01/87	1989	Sought Elective Office
MA	Frank L. McNamara, Jr.	04/02/87	11/05/87	01/30/89	Resigned
NJ	Samuel A. Alito, Jr.	08/03/87	12/08/87	04/90	Federal Judge
W.WI	Patrick J. Fiedler	11/19/87	02/25/88	01/91	State Government
SC	E. Bart Daniel	05/16/89	06/22/89	1992	Private Sector
UT	Dee V. Benson	05/31/89	06/22/89	09/91	Federal Judge
W.OK	Vicki Lynn Miles-LaGrange	07/29/93	09/21/93	11/94	Federal Judge
N.AL	Claude Harris Jr.	09/07/93	09/30/93	10/02/94	Died
S.OH	Edmund A. Sargus, Jr.	09/07/93	09/30/93	08/96	Federal Judge
SC	Joseph Preston Strom, Jr.	08/06/93	09/30/93	1996	Private Sector
S.FL	Kendall Brindley Coffey	10/13/93	11/20/93	05/17/96	Resigned
M.FL	Larry Herbert Colleton	11/19/93	02/10/94	07/94	Resigned
M.GA	James Lamar Wiggins	11/19/93	02/10/94	1996	Sought Elective Office

Appendix. (Continued).

District	U.S. Attorney	Nomination Date	Confirmation Date	Departure Date	Departure Reason
N.GA	Kent Barron Alexander	01/26/94	03/25/94	1997	Private Sector
W.KY	Stephen Beville Pence	08/03/01	09/14/01	2003	Sought Elective Office
DC	Roscoe Conklin Howard, Jr.	08/02/01	09/14/01	05/28/04	Resigned
S.IA	Steven M. Colloton	09/05/01	10/12/01	09/03	Federal Judge
OR	Michael W. Mosman	08/01/01	10/12/01	09/03	Federal Judge
W.NC	Robert L. Conrad Jr.	08/03/01	10/23/01	2004	Private Sector
MD	Thomas M. DiBiagio	09/05/01	10/23/01	2005	Resigned
E.MO	Raymond. W. Gruender	08/02/01	10/23/01	05/04	Federal Judge
W.AR	Thomas C. Gean	08/02/01	10/23/01	06/07/04	Private Sector
N.GA	William S. Duffey, Jr.	09/05/01	11/06/01	06/04	Federal Judge
E.MI	Jeffrey Gilbert Collins	09/05/01	11/06/01	08/22/04	Private Sector
S.GA	Richard S. Thompson	10/25/01	11/30/01	2004	Private Sector
W.NY	Michael A. Battle	11/15/01	01/25/02	06/05	Executive Branch
S.NY	James B. Comey	03/04/02	04/12/02	12/09/03	Executive Branch
N.TX	Jane J. Boyle	12/20/01	04/12/02	06/04	Federal Judge
S.IL	Miriam F. Miquelon	05/23/02	07/29/02	09/01/03	Private Sector
S.FL	Marcos D. Jimenez	04/15/02	07/29/02	05/20/05	Private Sector
W.WI	J.B. Van Hollen	05/15/02	08/01/02	01/31/05	Private Sector
PR	Humberto S. Garcia	11/19/02	03/07/03	01/07	Resigned
UT	Paul Michael Warner	07/14/03	08/01/03	01/06	Magistrate Judge

Source: Nomination and Confirmation data from Legislative Information System (LIS), at [http://www.congress.gov/nomis]. CRS obtained information for departure dates and departure reasons from secondary sources.

References

[1] 28 USC § 547.
[2] 28 USC § 541 (a).

[3] See CRS Report RL32013, The History of the Blue Slip in the Senate Committee on the Judiciary, 1917-Present, by Mitchel A. Sollenberger.
[4] 28 USC § 541 (c).
[5] 28 USC § 541 (b).
[6] P.L. 89-554, § 4(c), Sept. 6, 1966, 80 Stat. 617.
[7] Before 1966, 28 USC § 506 (62 Stat. 909) used the same language as enacted in P.L. 89 554.
[8] P.L. 89-554, § 4(c), Sept. 6, 1966, 80 Stat. 618. This language, and all amending language, refers to 28 USC § 546.
[9] P.L. 99-646, § 69, Nov. 10, 1986, 100 Stat. 3616.
[10] P.L. 109-177, § 502, Mar. 9, 2006, 120 Stat. 246.
[11] Marcia Coyle, "In Wake of Seven Firings, Branches Clash Over Interim U.S. Attorney Nominees," *National Law Journal*, Feb. 13, 2007.
[12] Ibid.
[13] Sen. Charles Schumer, "Unanimous-Consent Request — S. 214," remarks in the Senate, *Congressional Record*, daily edition, vol. 153 (Feb. 15, 2007), p. S1995.
[14] Sen. Dianne Feinstein, "Unanimous-Consent Request — S. 214," remarks in the Senate, *Congressional Record*, daily edition, vol. 153 (Feb. 15, 2007), p. S1995.
[15] Ibid.
[16] [http://www.congress.gov/nomis]. LIS only provides this data in electronic format for the 1981-2006 time period.
[17] The President may nominate a successor before the term of a U.S. Attorney expires, anticipating the incumbent's departure at the end of his or her term. Of the 54 cases identified and listed in the appendix, CRS found no instances where the U.S. Attorney served a full four-year term.
[18] Dan Eggen, "U.S. Attorney Firings Set Stage for Congressional Battle," *Washington Post*, Feb. 4, 2007, p. A07.
[19] [http://lawyers.martindale.com/marhub].
[20] [http://www.nexis.com/research].
[21] [http://www.congress.gov/nomis/].
[22] Heather Negley and Maureen Bearden, CRS Information Research Specialists, performed these searches.
[23] "Mexican Security Official Held on Auto Theft Charge," *Christian Science Monitor*, Apr. 26, 1982, p. 2 (Midwestern Edition).
[24] Leslie Maitland Weber, "U.S. Attorney in Cleveland Is Discharged by President," *New York Times*, Oct. 3, 1984, p. A16.
[25] "Conviction Clouding Future for Ohio Republican," *New York Times*, Mar. 10, 1985, p. A23.
[26] Anne Groer, "Colleton Resigns as U.S. Attorney, Gets Another Post," *Orlando Sentinel*, July 30, 1994, p. A1.
[27] Associated Press, "U.S. Attorney Resigns Amid Turmoil," *Tulsa World*, May 18, 1996, p. A13.
[28] Elizabeth Neuffer and Stephen Kurkjian, "McNamara Resigns as US Attorney; Prosecutor Cites Swirl of Controversy," *Boston Globe*, Jan. 31, 1989, p. 1.
[29] Ibid.
[30] Ibid.

In: Law and Law Enforcement Issues
Editor: Gerald M. Kessler, pp. 253-375

ISBN: 978-1-60456-044-2

Chapter 11

AWARDS OF ATTORNEYS' FEES BY FEDERAL COURTS AND FEDERAL AGENCIES*

Henry Cohen

ABSTRACT

In the United States, the general rule, which derives from common law, is that each side in a legal proceeding pays for its own attorney. There are many exceptions, however, in which federal courts, and occasionally federal agencies, may order the losing party to pay the attorneys' fees of the prevailing party. The major common law exception authorizes federal courts (not agencies) to order a losing party that acts in bad faith to pay the prevailing party's fees.

There are also roughly two hundred statutory exceptions, which were generally enacted to encourage private litigation to implement public policy. Awards of attorneys' fees are often designed to help to equalize contests between private individual plaintiffs and corporate or governmental defendants. Thus, attorneys' fees provisions are most often found in civil rights, environmental protection, and consumer protection statutes.

In addition, the Equal Access to Justice Act (EAJA) makes the United States liable for attorneys' fees of up to $125 per hour in many court cases and administrative proceedings that it loses (and some that it wins) and fails to prove that its position was substantially justified. EAJA does not apply in tax cases, but a similar statute, 26 U.S.C. § 7430, does.

Most Supreme Court decisions involving attorneys' fees have interpreted civil rights statutes, and this article focuses on these statutes. It also discusses awards of costs other than attorneys' fees in federal courts, how courts compute the amount of attorneys' fees to be awarded, statutory limitations on attorneys' fees, and other subjects. In addition, it sets forth the language of all federal attorneys' fees provisions, and includes a bibliography of congressional committee reports and hearings concerning attorneys' fees.

In 1997, Congress enacted a statute allowing awards of attorneys' fees to some prevailing criminal defendants.

---

* Excerpted from CRS Report 94-970 A, dated dated January 24, 2006.

I. Introduction: The American Rule and Its Exceptions

"In the United States, the prevailing litigant is ordinarily not entitled to collect a reasonable attorneys' fee from the loser." *Alyeska Pipeline Service Co. v. Wilderness Society*, 421 U.S. 240, 247 (1975). This is known as the "American rule" (as opposed to the English rule, which routinely permits fee-shifting) and derives from court-made law. It has, however, numerous statutory exceptions (listed at the back of this chapter) some, if not most, of which Congress enacted in order to encourage private litigation to implement public policy. *Id.* at 263. Under these exceptions, a federal court (and sometimes a federal agency) may order the losing party to a lawsuit to pay the winning party's attorneys' fees. Although "attorney's fees generally are not a recoverable cost of litigation 'absent explicit congressional authorization,' ... [t]he absence of specific reference to attorney's fees is not dispositive if the statute otherwise evinces an intent to provide for such fees."[1]

Fee-shifting has been proposed, not only to encourage lawsuits, but to discourage them, especially tort suits. The English "loser pays" rule was included in tort reform legislation proposed by the Bush Administration in 1992, and in "The Common Sense Legal Reforms Act," which is part of the "Contract With America" proposed by the Republican House Members in 1994.[2]

The American rule has two major common law exceptions (instances when federal courts may award attorneys' fees without statutory authorization): the common benefit doctrine and the bad faith doctrine.[3] These derive from the historic authority of the courts "to do equity in a particular situation."[4] This authority has been called the "supervisory" or "inherent" power of the federal courts.[5]

Federal courts may use this inherent power even in diversity cases, which are cases arising under state law that are brought in federal court pursuant to 28 U.S.C. § 1332 when the parties are citizens of different states and the amount in controversy exceeds $50,000. *Chambers v. NASCO, Inc.*, 501 U.S. 32 (1991). In *Alyeska*, the Court had written that, "in the ordinary diversity case where the state law does not run counter to a valid federal statute or rule of court, and usually it will not, state law denying the right to attorney's fees or giving right thereto, which reflects a substantial policy of the state, should be followed." 421 U.S. at 259 n.31. In *Chambers*, the Court explained that this limitation "applies only to fee-shifting rules that embody a substantive policy, such as a statute which permits a prevailing party in certain classes of litigation to recover fees." 501 U.S. at 52. A substantive policy of the state is not "implicated by the assessment of attorney's fees as a sanction for bad-faith conduct before the court which involved disobedience of the court's orders and the attempt to defraud the court itself." *Id.* at 52-53.

II. Common Law Exceptions to the American Rule

Common law exceptions to the American rule are "unquestionably assertions of inherent power in the courts to allow attorneys' fees in particular situations, unless forbidden by Congress." *Alyeska*, 421 U.S. at 259. The two major exceptions are cases in which a party at its own expense creates a fund or achieves a substantial benefit in which others share, and cases in which a party acts in bad faith. A former third exception, cases in which a plaintiff acts as a "private attorney general" in effectuating important public policy, was eliminated by the Supreme Court in *Alyeska*.

Common Benefit Doctrine

"In the absence of a statutory prohibition, the federal courts have authority to award attorneys' fees from a fund to a party who, having a common interest with other persons, maintains a suit for the common benefit and at his own expense, resulting in the creation or preservation of a fund, in which all those having the common interest share." Annotation, 8 L.Ed.2d 894, 905 (1963). This exception to the American rule does not shift the cost of attorneys' fees to the losing party, but rather to those who benefit from the suit. The doctrine was originally conceived in *Trustees v. Greenough*, 105 U.S. 527 (1881), a case against trustees of ten or eleven million acres of land who had collusively sold hundreds of thousands of those acres at nominal prices. One beneficiary, after eleven years of litigation at his own expense, recaptured the assets and presented a claim for reimbursement of attorneys' fees. The Supreme Court approved the award, writing that "if the complainant is not a trustee, he has at least acted the part of a trustee in relation to the common interest." *Id.* at 532.

In *Mills v. Electric Auto-Lite Co.*, 396 U.S. 375, 392 (1970), the Supreme Court held that under the common benefit doctrine there is no requirement "that the suit actually bring money into the court as a prerequisite to the court's power to order reimbursement of expenses." *Mills* was a stockholders' derivative suit, a type of case which, the Court noted, may bring substantial non-pecuniary benefits.

Boeing Co. v. Van Gemert, 444 U.S. 472 (1980), was a successful class action in which over $3 million in damages were awarded. Some class members collected their shares of the damages, but others did not. The district court, invoking the common benefit doctrine, ordered that the plaintiffs' attorneys be awarded their fees from the total amount of the judgment, concluding that it was equitable for all class members — claiming and non-claiming alike — to bear a *pro rata* share of the costs of producing the judgment in their favor. The defendant objected to use of the unclaimed money for this purpose, arguing that the ultimate disposition of the unclaimed money had not been decided. But the Supreme Court affirmed the award of attorneys' fees, holding:

> The common-fund doctrine, as applied in this case, is entirely consistent with the American rule against taxing the losing party with the victor's attorney's fees. . . . Boeing presently has no interest in any part of the fund. Any right that Boeing may establish to the return of the money eventually claimed is contingent on the failure of the absentee class members to exercise their present rights of possession. Although Boeing itself cannot be obliged to pay fees awarded to the class lawyers, its latent claim against unclaimed money in the judgment fund may not defeat each class member's equitable obligation to share the expenses of litigation.

Id. at 481-482.

Bad Faith Exception

In *Hall v. Cole*, 412 U.S. 1, 5 (1973), the Supreme Court wrote:

> [I]t is unquestioned that a federal court may award counsel fees to a successful party when his opponent has acted 'in bad faith, vexatiously, wantonly, or for oppressive reasons. . . .' In this class of cases, the underlying rationale of 'fee shifting' is, of course, punitive, and the essential element in triggering the award of fees is therefore the existence of 'bad faith' on the part of the unsuccessful litigant.

A fee award under the bad faith exception requires subjective bad faith —"some proof of malice entirely apart from inferences arising from the possible frivolous character of a particular claim." *Copeland v. Martinez*, 603 F.2d 981, 991 (D.C. Cir. 1979), *cert. denied*, 444 U.S. 1044 (1980).

In *Hall v. Cole*, the Supreme Court wrote: "It is clear . . . that 'bad faith' may be found, not only in the actions that led to the lawsuit, but in the conduct of the litigation." 412 U.S. at 15. Subsequently, as another court wrote: "Federal courts have applied [the bad faith] exception both when bad faith occurred in connection with the litigation and when it was an aspect of the conduct that gave rise to the lawsuit."[6] However, some courts have refused to apply the bad faith exception to a party's underlying claim, noting that the Supreme Court's statement in *Hall v. Cole* had concerned the common benefit exception, not the bad faith exception.[7]

An attorney, as well as a party, who acts in bad faith may be ordered to pay the attorneys' fees of the opposing party. In *Roadway Express, Inc. v. Piper*, 447 U.S. 752, 765-767 (1980), the Supreme Court held:

> [I]n narrowly defined circumstances federal courts have inherent power to assess attorney's fees against counsel. . . . The power of a court over members of its bar is at least as great as its authority over litigants. If a court may tax counsel fees against a party who litigated in bad faith, it certainly may assess those expenses against counsel who willfully abuse judicial processes. . . . Like other sanctions, attorney's fees certainly should not be assessed lightly or without fair notice and an opportunity for a hearing on the record. But in a proper case, such sanctions are within a court's powers.

In *Durrett v. Jenkins Brickyard, Inc.*, 678 F.2d 911, 919 (11th Cir. 1982), the court held "that the Court in *Roadway Express* intended to authorize the assessment of attorney's fees against counsel who either willfully disobeyed a court order or acted in bad faith, vexatiously, wantonly, or for oppressive reasons."

In *Roadway Express*, the Supreme Court also noted that, under Federal Rule of Civil Procedure 37(b), "[b]oth parties and counsel may be held personally liable for expenses, 'including attorney's fees,' caused by the failure to comply with discovery orders." 447 U.S. at 763. The Court also found that only excess costs, not attorneys' fees, could be assessed under 28 U.S.C. § 1927, which provided that any attorney "who so multiplies the proceedings in any case so as to increase costs unreasonably and vexatiously may be required by the courts to satisfy personally such excess costs." However, the section soon after was amended by Public Law 96-349, § 3, to permit awards of attorneys' fees as well as excess costs against counsel.[8]

Private Attorney General Doctrine

The private attorney general doctrine provides that a plaintiff "should be awarded attorneys' fees when he has effectuated a strong Congressional policy which has benefited a large class of people, and where further the necessity and financial burden of private enforcement are such as to make the award essential."[9] Many of the statutory exceptions to the American rule are based on this concept. In *Newman v. Piggie Park Enterprises, Inc.*, 390 U.S. 400, 402 (1968), the Supreme Court, discussing one such exception, wrote:

> If successful plaintiffs were routinely forced to bear their own attorneys' fees, few aggrieved parties would be in a position to advance the public interest by invoking the injunctive power of the federal courts. Congress therefore enacted the provision for counsel fees . . . to encourage individuals injured by racial discrimination to seek judicial relief under Title II [42 U.S.C. § 2000a-3(b)].

Prior to the Supreme Court's decision in *Alyeska*, some lower federal courts had awarded attorneys' fees under the private attorney general doctrine in suits brought under statutes that had no fee-shifting provisions, thereby creating another court-made exception to the American rule. *Alyeska* at 270 n.46. In *Alyeska*, however, the Court held:

> [C]ongressional utilization of the private attorney general concept can in no sense be construed as a grant of authority to the Judiciary to jettison the traditional rule against non-statutory allowances to the prevailing party and to award attorneys' fees whenever the court deems the public policy furthered by a particular statute important enough to warrant the award.

421 U.S. at 263.

The primary reasons the Court gave for its decision were the difficulty "for the courts without legislative guidance to consider some statutes important and some unimportant" and the fact that "the rational application of the private-attorney-general rule would immediately collide with the express provision of 28 U.S.C. § 2412," which at the time prohibited fee awards against the United States, except when specifically permitted by statute. *Id.* at 263-266.

Congress' immediate response to *Alyeska* was enactment of the Civil Rights Attorney's Fees Awards Act of 1976, 42 U.S.C. § 1988(b), which is discussed at page 33.[10] Congress has since enacted many more statutes that authorize awards of attorneys' fees in specific situations, but it has not reversed *Alyeska* to grant courts the power to award attorneys fees to private attorneys general in cases brought under statutes that do not provide for fee-shifting.

III. The Equal Access to Justice Act

Awards of attorneys' fees against the United States were barred at common law not only because of the American rule, but also because of the doctrine of sovereign immunity, under which the United States may not be sued, nor its funds expended, without its consent. "Congress alone has the power to waive or qualify that immunity,"[11] and it did so, with respect to awards of attorneys' fees, with the Equal Access to Justice Act (EAJA) in 1980.

Prior to enactment of EAJA, the common law exceptions to the American rule were inapplicable against the United States.[12] Even statutory exceptions to the American rule were inapplicable against the United States unless they specifically authorized fee awards against the United States.

EAJA allows awards of attorneys' fees against the United States in two broad situations. The first, codified at 28 U.S.C. § 2412(b), makes the United States liable for the prevailing party's attorneys' fees to the same extent that any other party would be under the common law and statutory exceptions to the American rule, including the statutory exceptions that do not specifically authorize fee awards against the United States. This provision, unlike the rest of EAJA, contains no limitations on the assets or number of employees of parties eligible to recover fees, and no maximum hourly rate for fee awards.

The second broad situation in which EAJA authorizes fee awards against the United States is codified at 5 U.S.C. § 504 and 28 U.S.C. § 2412(d). These sections provide that, in specified agency adjudications[13] and in all civil actions (except tort actions and tax cases)[14] brought by or against the United States, the United States shall be liable for the attorneys' fees of prevailing parties, unless it proves that its position was substantially justified or that special circumstances make an award unjust.[15]

This second portion of EAJA contains two limitations on fee awards that are not found in § 2412(b).[16] First, it prescribes a fee cap unless the court or agency determines that a special factor justifies a higher fee. (Most fee statutes authorize awards of "reasonable" fees, with the court determining the amount.) The cap was originally $75 per hour, but Public Law 104-121, §§ 231-233, increased it to $125 per hour for cases commenced on or after the date of its enactment, which was March 29, 1996. Second, this portion of EAJA does not allow (with two exceptions) fees to be awarded to individuals whose net worth exceeds $2 million, or to businesses or organizations, including units of local government, with a net worth exceeding $7 million or more than 500 employees.[17] This portion of EAJA sunset, by the terms of the original Act, on October 1, 1984. In 1985, EAJA was reenacted, retroactive to October 1, 1984, and made permanent.

Public Law 104-121, in addition to raising the cap under EAJA to $125 per hour, added the following provision to 28 U.S.C. § 2412(d), and a corresponding one to 5 U.S.C. § 504 applicable to adversary adjudications:

> If, in a civil action brought by the United States or a proceeding for judicial review of an adversary adjudication described in section 504(a)(4) of title 5, the demand by the United States [other than a recitation of the maximum statutory penalty] is substantially in excess of the judgment finally obtained by the United States and is unreasonable when compared with such judgment, under the facts and circumstances of the case, the court shall award to the party the fees and other expenses related to defending against the excessive demand, unless the party has committed a willful violation of law or otherwise acted in bad faith, or special circumstances make an award unjust. Fees and expenses awarded under this paragraph shall be paid only as a consequence of appropriations provided in advance.

This provision thus authorizes fee awards in favor of *losing* parties and in that respect is unique in the law of attorneys' fees.

In *Pierce v. Underwood*, 487 U.S. 552 (1988), the Supreme Court decided three issues concerning EAJA: (1) the applicable standard of appellate review, (2) the meaning of "substantially justified," and (3) the "special factors" that allow a court to award more than $75 per hour.

1. Standard of Review

Pierce v. Underwood addressed the standard that a federal court of appeals applies in reviewing a decision of a federal district court under EAJA. Either party may appeal a district court's decision under EAJA, and, as the Supreme Court explained:

> For purposes of standard of review, decisions by judges are traditionally divided into three categories, denominated questions of law (reviewable de novo), questions of fact (reviewable for clear error), and matters of discretion (reviewable for "abuse of discretion").

487 U.S. at 558.

The Supreme Court found that EAJA did not provide a clear prescription as to the appropriate standard of review (unlike, for example, 42 U.S.C. § 1988(b), which provides that "the court, in its discretion, may allow the prevailing party . . . a reasonable attorney's fee"). The Court, therefore, for a variety of reasons, held that the "abuse of discretion" standard was most appropriate for appeals of EAJA court decisions.

Awards of attorneys' fees under EAJA at the agency level may be appealed to a court only by the prevailing party, not by the United States. The statute, at 5 U.S.C. § 504(c)(2), provides:

> The court's determination on any appeal heard under this paragraph shall be based solely on the factual record made before the agency. The court may modify the determination of fees and other expenses only if the court finds that the failure to make an award of fees and other expenses, or the calculation of the amount of the award, was unsupported by substantial evidence.

Prior to the 1985 amendments to EAJA, this provision stated that the court could modify an agency decision only if it found "an abuse of discretion." It was intended that the new standard — "unsupported by substantial evidence" — permit "a broader scope of review . . . consistent with the normal scope of judicial review of agency actions."[18]

2. "Substantially Justified"[19]

The United States may avoid liability for attorneys' fees under EAJA by proving that its position "was substantially justified or that special circumstances make an award unjust." 5 U.S.C. § 504(a)(1), 28 U.S.C. § 2412(d). The legislative history of the original EAJA stated that "[t]he test of whether the Government position is substantially justified is essentially one of reasonableness in law and fact."[20] Twelve of the thirteen federal circuits subsequently interpreted "substantially justified" to mean reasonable. *See*, *Pierce v. Underwood*, 487 U.S. at 565-566. The U.S. Court of Appeals for the District of Columbia was the exception. It reasoned:

> The Senate Judiciary Committee considered and rejected an amendment to the bill that would have changed the pertinent language from "substantially justified" to "reasonably justified." S.Rept. 253 [96th Cong., 1st Sess.] at 8. That refusal suggests that the test should, in fact, be slightly more stringent than "one of reasonableness."[21]

According to this view, the government's position may be reasonable, yet fail to be substantially justified, making it easier to recover fees under the substantially justified standard than under a reasonableness standard. The 1985 amendments to EAJA did not alter the text of the substantially justified language, but an accompanying committee report expressed support for the D.C. Circuit's interpretation:

> Several courts have held correctly that "substantial justification" means more than merely reasonable. Because in 1980 Congress rejected a standard of "reasonably justified" in favor of "substantially justified," the test must be more than just reasonableness.[22]

The Supreme Court in *Pierce v. Underwood* held that substantially justified means reasonable. The Court found that a "more than mere reasonableness" test would be "out of accord with prior usage" and "unadministerable." "Between the test of reasonableness," the Court wrote, "and a test such as 'clearly and convincingly justified' . . . there is simply no accepted stopping-place, no ledge that can hold the anchor for steady and consistent judicial behavior." 487 U.S. at 568. The Court found that the 1985 committee report was not controlling because it was neither "(1) an authoritative interpretation of what the 1980 statute meant, or (2) an authoritative expression of what the 1985 Congress intended." *Id.* at 566.

3. Exceeding $75 (Now $125) Per Hour

EAJA provides that fees "shall be based upon prevailing market rates for the kind and quality of the services furnished," but "shall not be awarded in excess of $75 [$125 for cases commenced on or after March 29, 1996] per hour unless the court determines that an increase in the cost of living or a special factor, such as the limited availability of qualified attorneys for the proceedings involved, justifies a higher fee." 28 U.S.C. § 2412(d)(2)(A)(ii). (The same cap applies in agency proceedings; *see*, 5 U.S.C. § 504(b)(1)(A)). The Court in *Pierce v. Underwood* held:

> If "the limited availability of qualified attorneys for the proceedings involved" meant merely that lawyers skilled and experienced enough to try the case are in short supply, it would effectively eliminate the $75 cap — since the "prevailing market rates for the kind and quality of the services furnished" are obviously *determined* by the relative supply and quality of services. . . . We think it refers to attorneys having some distinctive knowledge or specialized skill needful for the litigation in question — as opposed to an extraordinary level of the general lawyerly knowledge and ability useful in all litigation. Examples of the former would be an identifiable practice specialty such as patent law, or knowledge of foreign law or language.

487 U.S. at 571-572.

As for other "special factors," the Court wrote:

> For the same reason of the need to preserve the intended effectiveness of the $75 cap, we think the other "special factors" envisioned by the exception must be such as are not of broad and general application. We need not specify what they might be . . . .

Id. at 573.

The Court, however, specified some items which are not special factors for purposes of exceeding the $75 per hour cap: "the novelty and difficulty of issues," "the undesirability of the case," "the work and ability of counsel," "the results obtained," "customary fees and awards in other cases," and "the contingent nature of the fee." All these "are factors applicable to a broad spectrum of litigation; they are little more than routine reasons why market rates are what they are." Id.

In Commissioner, Immigration and Naturalization Service v. Jean, 496 U.S. 154 (1990), the Supreme Court held that, under EAJA, a prevailing party may recover attorneys' fees for services rendered in seeking a fee award without regard to whether the position of the United States was substantially justified. If the prevailing party is entitled to fees in the main action, then he is automatically entitled to fees for the time spent seeking fees. To hold otherwise could "spawn a 'Kafkaesque judicial nightmare' of infinite litigation for the last round of litigation over fees." Id. at 163.[23]

In Scarborough v. Principi, 541 U.S. 401 (2004), the Supreme Court addressed EAJA's requirement that fee applications be filed "within thirty days of final judgment in the action," and "allege that the position of the United States was not substantially justified." 28 U.S.C. § 2412(d)(1)(B). The Court held that, when a fee application is filed within 30 days, but fails to allege that the position of the United States was not substantially justified, the application may be amended to remedy the oversight, even after the 30 days have elapsed.

IV. THE DUAL STANDARD: PREVAILING PLAINTIFFS AND PREVAILING DEFENDANTS

Most federal fee-shifting provisions authorize courts to award fees if "the fee claimant was the 'prevailing party,' the 'substantially prevailing party,' or 'successful.'" *Ruckelshaus v. Sierra Club*, 463 U.S. 680, 684 (1983). Although most of these statutes on their face do not distinguish between prevailing plaintiffs and prevailing defendants, the Supreme Court has held that Congress intended that under the civil rights statutes a dual standard should be applied in determining the appropriateness of fee awards to prevailing plaintiffs and prevailing defendants.[24]

In *Newman v. Piggie Park Enterprises, Inc.*, 390 U.S. 400 (1968), the Court considered 42 U.S.C. § 2000a-3(b), the provision in Title II of the Civil Rights Act of 1964 that provides for discretionary fee awards to prevailing parties. Noting that a plaintiff who is successful in a Title II suit vindicates "a policy that Congress considered of the highest priority" — enjoining racial discrimination — the Court held that under Title II a successful plaintiff "should ordinarily recover an attorney's fee unless special circumstances would render an award unjust." *Id.* at 402.

In *Albemarle Paper Co. v. Moody*, 422 U.S. 405 (1975), the Court held that the *Piggie Park* standard of awarding attorneys' fees to a successful plaintiff is equally applicable under Title VII of the Civil Rights Act, 42 U.S.C. § 2000e-5(k).

In *Christiansburg Garment Co. v. Equal Employment Opportunity Commission*, 434 U.S. 412, 417 (1978), the Court was faced with the question "what standard should inform a district court's discretion in deciding whether to award attorney's fees to a successful *defendant* in a Title VII action?" The Court noted that the statute on its face provided "no indication whatever of the circumstances under which either a plaintiff *or* defendant should be entitled to attorney's fees," and found that there are "strong equitable considerations" counseling a dual standard in determining the appropriateness of fee awards in the two situations. *Id.* at 418. Although prevailing plaintiffs should ordinarily recover attorneys' fees unless special circumstances would render an award unjust, prevailing defendants should recover fees only upon a finding that a plaintiff's action was "frivolous, unreasonable, or without foundation," although a finding that the action was brought in subjective bad faith is not necessary. *Id.* at 421. (A finding of subjective bad faith entitles either prevailing plaintiffs or defendants to a fee award under the common law exception to the American rule.)

The reason for the dual standard "is that while Congress wanted to clear the way for suits to be brought under the Act, it also wanted to protect defendants from burdensome litigation having no legal or factual basis." *Id.* at 420. Awarding fees to prevailing plaintiffs in the ordinary case will encourage suits to vindicate the public interest, but awarding fees to defendants in the ordinary case might have a chilling effect on the institution of such suits. Awarding fees to defendants in frivolous cases, however, may discourage such suits.[25]

In *Hughes v. Rowe*, 449 U.S. 5, 14 (1980), the Supreme Court discussed the applicability of the *Christiansburg* standard for awards of attorneys' fees to prevailing defendants under the Civil Rights Attorney's Fees Awards Act of 1976, 42 U.S.C. § 1988(b):

> Although arguably a different standard might be applied in a civil rights action under 42 U.S.C. § 1983, we can perceive no reason for applying a less stringent standard. The plaintiff's action must be meritless in the sense that it is groundless or without foundation. The fact that a plaintiff may ultimately lose his case is not in itself a sufficient justification for the assessment of fees.

With respect to awards under § 1988(b) to prevailing plaintiffs, the court of appeals in *Brown v. Culpepper*, 559 F.2d 274, 278 (5th Cir. 1977), wrote:

> In Title II and Title VII [of the Civil Rights Act of 1964] cases the Fifth Circuit has held that the defendant's conduct, be it negligent or intentional, in good faith or bad, is irrelevant to an award of attorneys' fees [citations omitted]. We now hold that, consistent with congressional intent, the same standard should apply to section 1988.

In *Independent Federation of Flight Attendants v. Zipes*, 491 U.S. 754, 755, 761 (1989), the Supreme Court held that, under Title VII of the Civil Rights Act of 1964, a court may "award attorney's fees against intervenors who have not been found to have violated the Civil Rights Act or any other federal law . . . only where the intervenors' action was frivolous, unreasonable, or without foundation."

The dual standard has also been held applicable to the attorneys' fees provisions in federal environmental statutes[26] and under the Truth in Lending Act.[27] However, it apparently is "more difficult for an environmental plaintiff than a civil rights plaintiff to recover an attorney fee."[28]

The Supreme Court has held that the dual standard does not apply under the attorneys' fees provision of the Copyright Act, 17 U.S.C. § 505, which, like those of the civil rights statutes, does not distinguish on its face between plaintiffs and defendants. In *Fantasy, Inc. v. Fogerty*, 510 U.S. 717, 527 (1994), the Court held that, in contrast with the civil rights statutes, under the Copyright Act, "defendants who seek to advance a variety of meritorious copyright defenses should be encouraged to litigate them to the same extent that plaintiffs are encouraged to litigate meritorious claims of infringement." The Court rejected both the dual standard and "the British Rule for automatic recovery of attorney's fees by the prevailing party. Prevailing plaintiffs and prevailing defendants are to be treated alike, but attorney's fees are to be awarded to prevailing parties only as a matter of the court's discretion." *Id.* at 534.

V. The Concept of Prevailing Party

The phrase "prevailing party" is not limited to a victor only after entry of a final judgment following a full trial on the merits. "The fact that respondent prevailed through a settlement rather than through litigation does not weaken her claim to fees." *Maher v. Gagne*, 448 U.S. 122, 129 (1980). Permitting fee awards upon favorable settlements encourages prevailing parties to settle, thereby lessening docket congestion, and it prevents losing parties from escaping liability for fees merely by conceding cases before final judgment.

The simplest means of providing for an award is through a stipulation in the settlement that a particular party has prevailed and that a specified amount constitutes reasonable attorneys' fees. It has been held that, in settled cases in which courts are called upon to determine entitlement to attorneys' fees, judges should engage in "a close scrutiny of the totality of circumstances surrounding the settlement, focusing particularly on the necessity for bringing the action and whether the party is the successful party with respect to the central issue." Use of this standard will prevent fee awards in "nuisance settlements."[29]

In *Buckhannon Board and Care Home, Inc. v. West Virginia Department of Health and Human Resources*, the Supreme Court held that a party is not a "prevailing party" under federal fee-shifting statutes if it "has failed to secure a judgment on the merits or a court-ordered consent decree, but has nonetheless achieved the desired result because the lawsuit brought about a voluntary change in the defendant's conduct."[30] Prior to this decision, most federal courts of appeals had recognized the "catalyst theory" and awarded fees in such circumstances.

In cases that are litigated to conclusion, a party may be deemed to have prevailed for purposes of a fee award prior to the losing party's having exhausted its final appeal. However, a party that prevails at the trial level will ultimately be entitled to a fee award only if it finally prevails on appeal.[31] A party awarded fees upon prevailing at the trial level apparently may be precluded from collecting them pending appeal; Federal Rule of Civil Procedure 62 (28 U.S.C. App. Rule 62) provides for a stay of proceedings to enforce a judgment pending appeal. If a party that prevails at the trial level should collect a fee award and subsequently lose the case on appeal, it apparently would be obligated to return the money.

A party may also be deemed to have prevailed even before final disposition at the trial level. In *Bradley v. Richmond School Board*, 416 U.S. 696, 723 (1974), the Supreme Court wrote:

> To delay a fee award until the entire litigation is concluded would work a substantial hardship on plaintiffs and their counsel, and discourage the institution of actions . . . . A district court must have the discretion to award fees and costs incident to the final disposition of interim matters.

At what stage of the litigation may a party be entitled to an interim award? In *Bradley* the Court would:

> say only that the entry of any order that determines substantial rights of the parties may be an appropriate occasion upon which to consider the propriety of an award of counsel fees . . . .

Id. at 723 n.28.

In Bradley, the statute under which fees were awarded, 20 U.S.C. § 1617 (since repealed), permitted awards only "[u]pon entry of a final order by a court of the United States." The Court, in allowing an interim award under this statute, noted that "many final orders may issue in the course of litigation." Id. at 723. In the case of a statute or common law rule that permits fee awards to prevailing parties but does not expressly make entry of a final order a prerequisite for such awards, fee awards may be appropriate at some stage of the litigation prior to entry of an interim final order.

Some courts have required recipients of interim awards to post bonds to insure recovery of the awards and interest should the recipients ultimately lose.[32]

In Hanrahan v. Hampton, 446 U.S. 754 (1980), a district court had directed verdicts for the defendants, but the court of appeals had reversed and ordered a new trial. The court of appeals had also ordered the defendants, under the Civil Rights Attorney's Fees Awards Act of 1976, 42 U.S.C. § 1988(b), to pay the attorneys' fees incurred by the plaintiffs during the course of their appeal. The Supreme Court reversed the award of attorneys' fees on the ground that the plaintiffs were not "prevailing" parties as required by the statute as a condition for a fee award. The Court concluded that, under § 1988(b), although "a person may in some circumstances be a 'prevailing party' without having obtained a favorable 'final judgment following a full trial on the merits,'" a party must have "established his entitlement to some relief on the merits of his claims, either in the trial court or on appeal." Being granted the right to a new trial was not a victory on the merits; nor were any favorable procedural or evidentiary rulings victories on the merits, even though they may affect the disposition on the merits.[33]

In Hewitt v. Helms, 482 U.S. 755 (1987), the Supreme Court held that, under § 1988(b), a plaintiff was not entitled to a fee award where "[t]he most that he obtained was an interlocutory ruling [by a court of appeals] that his complaint should not have been dismissed for failure to state a constitutional claim." The court of appeals had "explicitly left it to the District Court 'to determine the appropriateness and availability of the requested relief,' 655 F.2d, at 503; the Court of Appeals granted no relief of its own, declaratory or otherwise." Id. at 760.

In Rhodes v. Stewart, 488 U.S. 1, 4 (1988) (per curiam), the Supreme Court held that a declaratory judgment, like any other judgment, "will constitute relief, for purposes of § 1988(b), if, and only if, it affects the behavior of the defendant towards the plaintiff. In this case, there was no such result." In this case, two prisoners had sued prison officials for refusing to allow them to subscribe to a magazine. They won declaratory relief, but only after one had died and the other had been released from prison.

In Ruckelshaus v. Sierra Club, 463 U.S 680, 694 (1983), the Supreme Court held that § 307(f) of the Clean Air Act, 42 U.S.C. § 7607(f), authorizes awards of attorneys' fees only to plaintiffs who have "some degree of success on the merits."

This statute, as well as other federal environmental laws, provides: "In any judicial proceeding under this section, the court may award costs of litigation (including reasonable attorney and expert witness fees) whenever it determines that such an award is appropriate." On their face, these statutes allow fee awards even to parties who do not prevail, and, in the case under consideration, the court of appeals had awarded fees to such a party, holding that it was "appropriate" for it to receive fees for its contributions to the goals of the Clean Air Act.

The Supreme Court acknowledged that the legislative history of the act stated that it was not intended that fee awards "should be restricted to cases in which the party seeking fees was the 'prevailing party.'" 463 U.S. at 687. The Court noted, however, that, prior to enactment of § 307(f), some courts had interpreted the phrase "prevailing party" in various fee-shifting statutes as limited to a party who prevailed "essentially" on "central issues." Id. at 688. When Congress said that awards under § 307(f) should not be restricted to prevailing parties, it meant, the Court held, merely to eliminate these restrictive readings of the phrase "prevailing party." Specifically, Congress meant only "to expand the class of parties eligible for fee awards from prevailing parties to partially prevailing parties — parties achieving some success, even if not major success" (emphasis supplied by Court). Id.[34]

In Hensley v. Eckerhart, 461 U.S. 424, 433 (1983), the Supreme Court noted that "plaintiffs may be considered 'prevailing parties' for attorney's fees purposes if they succeed on any significant issue in litigation which achieves some of the benefit the parties sought in bringing suit." However, if the plaintiffs achieve only some of the benefit, then they will not necessarily be entitled to a full award of attorneys' fees. The Court addressed the issue of whether, under 42 U.S.C. § 1988(b), "a partially prevailing plaintiff may recover an attorney's fee for legal services on unsuccessful claims." Id. at 426. The Court held:

> Where the plaintiff has failed to prevail on a claim that is distinct in all respects from his successful claims, the hours spent on the unsuccessful claim should be excluded in considering the amount of a reasonable fee. Where a lawsuit consists of related claims, a plaintiff who has won substantial relief should not have his attorney's fee reduced simply because the district court did not adopt each contention raised. But where the plaintiff achieved only limited success, the district court should award only that amount of fees that is reasonable in relation to the results obtained.

Id. at 440.

As for how to determine the amount of fees that is reasonable when the plaintiff achieves only limited success, the Court wrote:

> There is no precise rule or formula for making these determinations. The district court may attempt to identify specific hours that should be eliminated, or it may simply

reduce the award to account for the limited success. The court necessarily has discretion in making this equitable judgment.

Id. at 436-437.

In Texas State Teachers Association v. Garland Independent School District, 489 U.S. 782 (1989), the Supreme Court held that, under 42 U.S.C. § 1988(b), although a party must prevail on a "significant" issue in order to be eligible for a fee award, it need not prevail on the "central" issue in the litigation. "[T]he degree of the plaintiff's success in relation to the other goals of the lawsuit is a factor critical to the determination of the size of a reasonable fee, not to eligibility for a fee award at all." Id. at 790 (emphasis in original).

In Farrar v. Hobby, 506 U.S. 103 (1992), the Supreme Court held that, under 42 U.S.C. § 1988(b), a plaintiff who is awarded only nominal damages — in this case one dollar when he had sought $17 million — is a prevailing party for attorneys' fees purposes. Nevertheless, "[w]hen a plaintiff recovers only nominal damages because of his failure to prove an essential element of his claim for monetary relief . . . , the only reasonable fee is usually no fee at all." Id. at 115. In this case, the plaintiff had established "the violation of his right to procedural due process but cannot prove actual injury." Id. at 112. Consequently, although he was a "prevailing party," he was entitled to no award of attorneys' fees.

Can a person receive an award of attorneys' fees for representing himself? In Kay v. Ehrler, 499 U.S. 432, 435 (1991), the Supreme Court noted that there is no disagreement "that a pro se litigant who is not a lawyer is not entitled to attorney's fees" under 42 U.S.C. § 1988(b). The question before the Court however was whether a pro se litigant who is an attorney is entitled to fees under § 1988(b). The Court found no answer in the statute or in its legislative history. It ruled against the attorney in an effort to create an incentive for attorneys not to represent themselves, because an attorney who represents himself "is deprived of the judgment of an independent third party." Id. at 437. It concluded that its decision would serve "[t]he statutory policy of furthering the successful prosecution of meritorious claims." Id. at 438. Kay v. Ehrler has been applied to other fee-shifting statutes, including the Equal Access to Justice Act, the Freedom of Information Act, the Individuals with Disabilities Education Act, the Fair Debt Collection Practices Act, and Title VII of the Civil Rights Act of 1964.[35]

VI. Awards of Attorneys' Fees Incurred in Administrative Proceedings

Title VII of the Civil Rights Act of 1964, 42 U.S.C. § 2000e-5(k), provides, in pertinent part:

> In any action or proceeding under this subchapter the court, in its discretion, may allow the prevailing party . . . a reasonable attorney's fee as part of the costs.

In *New York Gaslight Club v. Carey*, 447 U.S. 54 (1980), the plaintiff sought relief for an alleged violation of Title VII of the Civil Rights Act of 1964, and filed a state administrative proceeding, as required by the act, and a federal court suit. She won the state proceeding and agreed to a dismissal of the federal court suit, except for her request for attorneys' fees. The Supreme Court upheld her right to an award by the court of attorneys' fees incurred at the administrative level. The Court noted "Congress's use of the broadly inclusive disjunctive phrase 'action or proceeding'" (*id.* at 61) and added that it found nothing to indicate that "proceeding" was intended to apply only to federal agency proceedings. In dicta, the Court added that, for purposes of a fee award, it did not matter whether the plaintiff had lost at the administrative level and prevailed in court on the merits, or had prevailed at the administrative level and sued in court solely to recover attorneys' fees incurred at the administrative level. The Court wrote:

> It would be anomalous to award fees to the complainant who is unsuccessful or only partially successful in obtaining state or local remedies, but to deny an award to the complainant who is successful in fulfilling Congress' plan that federal policies be vindicated at the state or local level.

Id. at 66.

Title VII's attorneys' fees provision has been a model for others. One of the statutes modeled on it was the Civil Rights Attorney's Fees Awards Act of 1976, 42 U.S.C. § 1988(b). It provides:

> In any action or proceeding to enforce a provision of sections 1981, 1981a, 1982, 1983, 1985, and 1986 of this title, title IX of Public Law 92-318, the Religious Freedom Restoration Act of 1993, title VI of the Civil Rights Act of 1964, or section 40302 of the Violence Against Women Act of 1994, the court, in its discretion, may allow the prevailing party, other than the United States, a reasonable attorney's fee as part of the costs.

In *Webb v. County Board of Education of Dyer County, Tennessee*, 471 U.S. 234 (1985), the plaintiff lost an administrative hearing authorized by state law but subsequently prevailed in a federal court suit under 42 U.S.C. § 1983. He then filed a motion for an award under § 1988(b) of attorneys' fees incurred in both the hearing and the suit. The Supreme Court faced the same question it had in faced in *Gaslight* — the recoverability of fees incurred at the administrative level — but this time with respect to fee awards under 42 U.S.C. § 1988(b) in cases brought under 42 U.S.C. § 1983. Even though § 1988(b) contains the same "action or proceeding" language as Title VII, the Court held that § 1988(b) does not authorize awards of fees in § 1983 administrative proceedings. The basis for the different results in *Gaslight* and *Webb* was that under Title VII administrative proceedings are mandatory, but under § 1983 they are not, and it is only mandatory proceedings that are brought to "enforce" a federal civil rights statute. Because the plaintiff could have gone "straight to court to assert" his § 1983 claim, the Court found that:

> the school board proceedings in this case simply do not have the same integral function under § 1983 that state administrative proceedings have under Title VII. . . . Administrative proceedings . . . created by state law simply are not any part of the proceedings to enforce § 1983.

471 U.S. at 241.

The Court did not explicitly address whether the word "proceeding" in § 1988(b) had any reference in the context of a § 1983 "action or proceeding," but it did allow that attorneys' fees incurred in an administrative proceeding could be awarded in a § 1983 action to the extent "that any discrete portion of the work product from the administrative proceeding was work that was both useful and of a type ordinarily necessary to advance the civil rights litigation. . . ." *Id.* at 242.

The most recent Supreme Court decision to address the issue of awards of attorneys' fees incurred at the administrative level was *North Carolina Department of Transportation v. Crest Street Community Council, Inc.*, 479 U.S. 6 (1986). The plaintiffs in this case had prevailed in a federal administrative proceeding under Title VI of the Civil Rights Act of 1964, and sought to recover fees under § 1988(b) in an independent action in federal court. It might have been expected that the Supreme Court would decide whether § 1988(b) authorized an award of attorneys' fees incurred at the administrative level on the basis of whether an administrative proceeding under Title VI was mandatory, and therefore was a proceeding to enforce Title VI. However, the Court did not reach this issue because it rejected a fee award on a different ground: that an action solely to recover a fee award is not an action to enforce Title VI. The Court wrote:

> The plain language of § 1988 suggests the answer to the question of whether attorney's fees may be awarded in an independent action which is not to enforce any of the civil rights laws listed in § 1988. The section states that *in the action or proceeding to enforce* the civil rights laws listed — 42 U.S.C. §§ 1981, 1982, 1983, 1985, 1986, Title IX, or Title VI — *the court* may award attorney's fees. The case before us is not, and was never, an action to enforce any of these laws. On its face, § 1988 does not authorize a court to award attorney's fees except in an action to enforce the listed civil rights laws. The legislative history of § 1988 supports the plain import of the statutory language.

Id. at 12.

This means that, under all the statutes listed in § 1988(b), a party who prevails at the administrative level may not bring a court action solely to recover a fee award. A party who loses an administrative proceeding, however, and prevails on the merits in court, may recover attorneys' fees incurred at both the administrative and court levels. He may recover fees incurred in an administrative proceeding in either of two situations: if the proceeding was one to enforce the statute (i.e., was mandatory), or if a "discrete portion of the work product from the administrative proceedings . . . was both useful and of a type ordinarily necessary to advance the civil rights litigation. . . ." Id. at 15, quoting Webb, 471 U.S. at 243.

The Court in Crest Street acknowledged that in Gaslight it had said that it would be "anomalous" to distinguish in this way between a party who sues in court solely to recover fees (after having prevailed at the administrative level) and one who sues also on the merits. In Crest Street, however, the Court referred to this comment in Gaslight as "dicta" (id. at 13), presumably because the plaintiff in Gaslight had filed a court action not solely to recover fees. The Court in Crest Street added:

> Moreover, we now believe that the paradoxical nature of this result may have been exaggerated. There are many types of behavior that may lead others to comply with civil rights laws. For example, an employee, after talking to his lawyer, may choose to discuss hiring or promotion practices with an employer, and as a result of this discussion the employer may alter those practices to comply more fully with employment discrimination laws. In some sense it may be considered anomalous that this employee's initiative would not be awarded with attorney's fees. But an award of attorney's fees under § 1988

depends not only on the results obtained, but also on what actions were needed to achieve those results. It is entirely reasonable to limit the award of attorney's fees to those parties who, in order to obtain relief, found it necessary to file a complaint in court.

Id. at 14.

The dissent in Crest Street, apart from disagreeing with the majority's interpretation of the language and the legislative history of § 1988(b), argued that the effect of the decision would be to burden federal courts by causing parties who are not required to exhaust administrative remedies to "immediately file suit in federal court to protect any possible claim for attorney's fees should they subsequently prevail." Id. at 21. In Gaslight, in fact, the Court had acknowledged "that if fees were authorized only when the complainant found an independent reason for suing in federal court under Title VII, such a ground almost always could be found." 447 U.S. at 66 n.6. Thus, Crest Street may have little practical import for Title VII.

It may also be argued that the reasoning of Crest Street does not even apply to Title VII. Although § 1988(b) was modeled on the attorneys' fees provision of Title VII, there is a difference in their language that may be relevant. Section 1988(b) provides that a court may award attorneys' fees in any action or proceeding "to enforce" various civil rights statutes. Title VII, by contrast, says that a court may award fees in any action or proceeding "under this title" (as enacted) or "under this subchapter" (as codified), in either case referring to Title VII itself. Arguably, a suit solely to recover fees incurred in an administrative proceeding under Title VII is an action or proceeding under Title VII, even though a suit solely to recover fees incurred in an administrative proceeding under Title VI is not an action or proceeding to enforce Title VI. However, this may be an overly literal reading in that when the attorneys' fees provision in Title VII refers to an action or proceeding "under" Title VII, it may not have been intended that it refer to itself, but rather only to the rest of Title VII.[36]

The Supreme Court, in Gaslight, of course, has already interpreted this language and concluded that it "encompasses a suit solely to obtain an award of attorney's fees for legal work done in state and local proceedings." Yet in Crest Street the Court labeled as "dicta" its statement in Gaslight that to hold otherwise would be anomalous. It appears uncertain whether the Court would reach the result it reached in Gaslight in a Title VII case in which a court action was never filed on the merits.[37]

Awards of Attorneys' Fees by Administrative Agencies

An issue that has never reached the Supreme Court is whether administrative agencies themselves may award attorneys' fees under any of the civil rights statutes. Title VII's attorneys' fees provision and the statutes modeled on it authorize only "the court" to award fees, but, to the extent that a court may award fees incurred at the agency level, the question has arisen whether an agency itself may do so in order to save the parties and a federal court from litigation solely on a fee claim.[38] Of course, only if a court may award fees incurred at the administrative level will the question arise whether the agency itself may award such fees. There are two circumstances in which a court clearly may not award fees incurred at the administrative level: the circumstances of *Crest Street* and of *Webb*.

Crest Street prohibits courts from awarding fees in suits solely to recover fees, at least in suits under § 1988(b), so it seems clear that agencies may not award fees under § 1988. Assuming that the reasoning of *Crest Street* does not apply to some statutes, such as Title VII, *Webb* still would preclude courts from awarding fees incurred in non-mandatory administrative proceedings under such statutes, except to the extent that such fees cover "any discrete portion of the work product . . . that was both useful and of a type ordinarily necessary to advance the civil rights litigation." However, Title VII provides for mandatory administrative proceedings, so the question arises under Title VII whether an agency itself may award fees and thereby save the prevailing party from going to court.

The court of appeals in *Crest Street* had held that a party who prevailed in an administrative proceeding under Title VI could bring a court action under § 1988(b) solely to recover fees. The court of appeals in *Crest Street*, in addition, citing the fact that § 1988(b) on its face authorizes only "the court" to award fees, said in dicta that "it follows that plaintiffs *must* apply to a court for their fees." 769 F.2d at 1033 (emphasis in original). However, in *Smith v. Califano*, 446 F. Supp. 530 (D.D.C. 1978), the court held that an agency could award fees in a Title VII proceeding. It wrote:

> Title VII is a statute in which Congress already has specifically provided for an award of attorneys' fees. Although the expression of that exception [to the American Rule] is contained in the remedial authority of the courts, the rights protected by the courts are the very same rights the agencies are to protect. Thus, finding authority for the agency also to award counsel fees to one who prevails at the administrative level would not create a "far-reaching" exception to the Rule. Rather, it would make the existing exception applicable regardless of the stage at which that federal right is protected.

Id. at 532-533.

In addition, the court noted:

> [A]lthough Title VII does not expressly state that an agency may award attorneys' fees, it does state that [in proceedings brought by federal employees] the agency is to enforce the Act "through appropriate remedies . . . as will effectuate the policies of this section. . . ." 42 U.S.C. § 2000e-16(b) (Supp. V 1975). Because the "make-whole" concept is one of those policies, this provision can be read to permit the agency to award attorneys' fees, thereby making whole one who appears before it.

Id. at 533.

This decision was followed in two other Title VII cases.[39] However, two other cases in the same district came to the contrary conclusion, holding that a party who prevails at the agency level under Title VII must go to court to recover his fees.[40] In 1980, the EEOC issued a regulation (amended in 1987) providing that it or other federal agencies may award attorneys' fees to federal employees under Title VII. 29 C.F.R. § 1613.271(d). No reported case appears to have challenged the EEOC's authority to promulgate this regulation.

An argument may be made, however, that, if the reasoning of *Crest Street* applies to Title VII, then the legality of these regulations would be placed in doubt. For, if the reasoning of *Crest Street* applies, which means that courts may not award attorneys' fees incurred by parties who prevail at the administrative level, then the only basis for an agency to award fees would be the "appropriate remedies" provision. It is not clear, however, that *Smith v. Califano* would have reached the same result in the absence of the statute's authorizing courts to award fees. If, under *Crest Street*, courts cannot award fees to parties who prevail in administrative proceedings under Title VII, then to allow agencies to award fees apparently would constitute a "far-reaching" exception to the American rule. Before an agency may order a litigant to bear his adversary's expenses, "it must be granted clear statutory power by Congress."[41] The power to employ "appropriate remedies" might not be sufficient.

Two lower court cases have addressed the question of the recoverability of fees in administrative proceedings under the Rehabilitation Act. In *Department of Education v. Katherine D.*, 531 F. Supp. 517, 531 (D. Hawaii 1982), *rev'd on other grounds*, 727 F.2d 809 (9th Cir. 1983), *cert. denied*, 471 U.S. 1117 (1985), the district court held that it could award attorneys' fees for services rendered in connection with both judicial and administrative proceedings under § 504 of the act. In *Watson v. United States Veterans Administration*, 88 F.R.D. 267 (C.D. Cal. 1980), a district court held that the agency itself could award fees under § 501 of the act. The court, citing *Smith v. Califano*, held that construing § 501 "to authorize the agency to award attorney's fees is more in keeping with the purpose of the statute and the intent of Congress than the contrary interpretation." 88 F.R.D. at 269. The court noted that the "'appropriate remedies' concept" is "incorporated in the Rehabilitation Act from Title VII." *Id.* at 268.[42] Notwithstanding this decision, if the reasoning of *Crest Street* precludes courts from awarding fees in suits solely to recover attorneys' fees incurred in administrative proceedings under the Rehabilitation Act, then it apparently would also preclude agencies from awarding fees. However, in 1987, the EEOC amended the regulation cited above (29 C.F.R. § 1613.271(d)) to authorize federal agencies to award attorneys' fees in proceedings under § 501 or § 505 of the Rehabilitation Act.

VII. Awards of Attorneys' Fees in Civil Rights Cases

All federal civil rights laws permit awards of attorneys' fees and the major litigation concerning fee awards has occurred under these laws. Some aspects of these laws have already been discussed: the dual standard they have been construed to include, the meaning of the term "prevailing" they contain, and the extent to which they permit awards of fees incurred in administrative proceedings. This section of the report quotes or summarizes each attorney's fee provision applicable to a civil rights law, and discusses significant court decisions not covered in the discussions of the aspects of these laws just mentioned.

Civil Rights Act of 1964, Title II — Public Accommodations

Title II prohibits discrimination and segregation on the basis of race, color, religion, or national origin in places of public accommodation such as hotels, restaurants, gasoline stations, theaters, and other places of exhibition or entertainment, if their operations affect commerce or if their acts of discrimination or segregation are supported by state action. 42 U.S.C. § 2000a. Title II's attorneys' fees provision, 42 U.S.C. § 2000a-3(b), states:

> the court, in its discretion, may allow the prevailing party, other than the United States, a reasonable attorney's fee as part of the costs, and the United States shall be liable for costs the same as a private person.[43]

In addition, the court may appoint an attorney for a complainant. 42 U.S.C. § 2000a-3(a).

Civil Rights Act of 1964, Title III — Public Facilities

Title III gives the Attorney General the authority to bring a civil action on behalf of any person unable to initiate and maintain appropriate legal proceedings who claims:

> that he is being deprived of or threatened with the loss of his right to equal protection of the laws, on account of his race, color, religion, or national origin, by being denied equal utilization of any public facility which is owned, operated, or managed by or on behalf of any State or subdivision thereof, other than a public school or public college, as defined in section 2000c of this title . . . .

42 U.S.C. § 2000b(a).

In any action under Title III "the United States shall be liable for costs, including a reasonable attorney's fee, the same as a private person." 42 U.S.C. § 2000b-1.

Civil Rights Act of 1964, Title VII — Equal Employment Opportunities

Title VII prohibits discrimination by employers, employment agencies, and labor organizations on the basis of race, color, religion, sex, or national origin. Before an individual may bring a civil action in federal court under Title VII, he must file a charge with the Equal Employment Opportunity Commission (EEOC), which will attempt to resolve the complaint.[44] However, if the individual alleges discrimination in a state or locality that prohibits it, then federal proceedings must be deferred until relief through state or local proceedings has been sought. 42 U.S.C. § 2000e-5(c). If the matter does end up in federal court, the court may appoint an attorney for the complainant. 42 U.S.C. § 2000e-5(f)(1). Relief may include injunctions and "such affirmative action as may be appropriate, which may include, but is not limited to, reinstatement or hiring of employees, with or without back pay . . . ." 42 U.S.C. § 2000e-5(g).[45]

Title VII's attorneys' fees provision, 42 U.S.C. § 2000e-5(k), provides:

> In any action or proceeding under this subchapter the court, in its discretion, may allow the prevailing party, other than the Commission or the United States, a reasonable attorney's fee (including expert fees) as part of the costs, and the Commission and the United States shall be liable for costs the same as a private person.[46]

Title VII's attorneys' fees provision on its face bars awards in favor of the EEOC or the United States. In 1964, when the provision was enacted, Title VII did not apply to federal workers, so the United States at the time could be only a plaintiff in a Title VII suit. The 1972 amendments that made it possible for the United States to be a defendant under the act did not amend the attorneys' fees provision, and, in *Copeland v. Martinez*, 603 F.2d 981 (D.C. Cir. 1979), *cert. denied*, 444 U.S. 1044 (1980), the issue arose whether an employee who sues the United States may be held liable for attorneys' fees. In this case the employee was found to have sued in bad faith, so the court did not have to decide whether Title VII affirmatively authorizes fee awards to the federal government as defendant. The court held only "that § 706(k) does not preclude a court from awarding the United States its attorneys' fees [under the common law exception] when it has been sued in bad faith." *Id.* at 987.

Of course, as discussed above, even if the United States is entitled to fees as a prevailing defendant under Title VII in the absence of bad faith on the part of the plaintiff, it may recover only upon a finding that the plaintiff's suit was "frivolous, unreasonable, or without foundation." Prevailing plaintiffs (other than the United States), in contrast, may recover fees "in all but very unusual circumstances." *Albemarle Paper Co. v. Moody*, 422 U.S. 405, 415 (1975).

Courts have held that in Title VII suits attorneys' fees may be awarded against state governments (*Fitzpatrick v. Bitzer*, 427 U.S. 445, 456 (1976)), and in favor of state governments (*Kutska v. California State College*, 564 F.2d 108 (3d Cir. 1977)).

Fair Housing Act

The Fair Housing Act, Title VIII of the Civil Rights Act of 1968, as amended by the Fair Housing Amendments Act of 1988, Public Law 100-430, prohibits discrimination on the basis of race, color, religion, sex, handicap, familial status (having children), or national origin in the sale or rental of housing, the financing of housing, or the provision of brokerage services. 42 U.S.C. §§ 3404-3606. An aggrieved person may bring a civil action, in which the prevailing party, other than the United States, may recover reasonable attorneys' fees and costs, with the United States liable for such fees and costs to the same extent as a private person. 42 U.S.C. § 3613(c).[47] Presumably, the dual standard that applies to the fee-shifting provisions of other federal civil rights statutes will apply here. The court may appoint an attorney for the plaintiff. 42 U.S.C. § 3613(b).

In addition, the Secretary of Housing and Urban Development may bring an administrative proceeding, and the Attorney General may bring a civil action, against a violator. In either case, the prevailing party, other than the United States, may recover a reasonable attorney's fee and costs, except that the United States shall be liable for fees and costs only to the extent provided by the Equal Access to Justice Act. 42 U.S.C. §§ 3612(p), 3614(d).

Fair Labor Standards Act

The Fair Labor Standards Act, among other things, prohibits employers from discriminating on the basis of sex in the amount of wages paid employees for equal work, and it prohibits labor organizations from causing employers to so discriminate. 29 U.S.C. § 206(d). Section 216(b) of Title 29 provides that in actions to enforce such provision, the court:

shall, in addition to any judgment awarded to the plaintiff or plaintiffs, allow a reasonable attorney's fee to be paid by the defendant, and costs of the action.

Age Discrimination in Employment Act of 1967

The Age Discrimination in Employment Act of 1967 (ADEA), 29 U.S.C. §§ 621 *et seq.*, prohibits, with certain exceptions, employers, employment agencies, and labor organizations from discriminating on the basis of age against individuals who are at least 40 years old. Section 7(b) of the act, 29 U.S.C. § 626(b), incorporates the attorneys' fees provision of the Fair Labor Standards Act, 29 U.S.C. § 216(b).[48]

In 1974, a section was added to the ADEA to protect federal employees from age discrimination. 29 U.S.C. § 633a. However, this section provides that other provisions of the ADEA shall not apply in the case of federal employees (29 U.S.C. § 633a(f)), and the section makes no reference to attorneys' fees. Consequently, it is unsettled whether they may be awarded to federal employees who prevail at the administrative or the judicial level.[49]

The Civil Service Reform Act of 1978 provides for awards of attorneys' fees "in accordance with the standards prescribed under § 706(k) of the Civil Rights Act of 1964 (42 U.S.C. 2000e(k)" to a federal "employee or applicant for employment" who is discriminated against "on the basis of age, as prohibited under §§ 12 and 15 of the Age Discrimination in Employment Act of 1976 (29 U.S.C. 631, 633a)." 5 U.S.C. §§ 7701(g)(2), 2302(b)(1)(B). However, these provisions of the Civil Service Reform Act authorize only the Merit Systems Protection Board (MSPB), not the EEOC, to award attorneys' fees, and federal employees who wish to file age discrimination complaints at the administrative level ordinarily must do so before the EEOC. The MSPB becomes involved in age discrimination complaints when it hears appeals of "mixed case" complaints, which are discrimination complaints that an employee or job applicant raises as an affirmative defense to an adverse action. 29 C.F.R. § 1613.402.

Equal Credit Opportunity Act

The Equal Credit Opportunity Act, 15 U.S.C. §§ 1691 *et seq.*, makes it unlawful for any person, business, or governmental agency that regularly extends credit to discriminate against any credit applicant:

> (1) on the basis of race, color, religion, national origin, sex or marital status, or age (provided the applicant has the capacity to contract); (2) because all or part of the applicant's income derives from any public assistance program; or (3) because the applicant has in good faith exercised any right under the Consumer Credit Protection Act.

Section 1691e(d) provides that in any successful action to enforce the act, "the costs of the action, together with a reasonable attorney's fee as determined by the court, shall be added to any damages awarded. . . ."

Voting Rights Act of 1965

The Voting Rights Act's attorneys' fees provision, 42 U.S.C. § 1973*l*(e), provides:

> In any action or proceeding to enforce the voting guarantee of the fourteenth or fifteenth amendment, the court, in its discretion, may allow the prevailing party, other than the United States, a reasonable attorney's fee as part of the costs.[50]

The Voting Accessibility for the Elderly and Handicapped Act, 42 U.S.C. § 1973ee-4(c), provides:

> Notwithstanding any other provision of law, no award of attorney fees may be made with respect to an action under this section, except in any action brought to enforce the original judgment of the court.

Civil Service Reform Act of 1978

The Civil Service Reform Act of 1978, 5 U.S.C. § 5596(b)(1)(A)(ii), provides:

> An employee of an agency who . . . is found . . . to have been affected by an unjustified or unwarranted personnel action . . . is entitled, on correction of the personnel action, to receive . . . reasonable attorney fees related to the personnel action which, with respect to any decision relating to an unfair labor practice or grievance processed under a procedure negotiated in accordance with chapter 71 of this title, or under chapter 11 of title I of the Foreign Service Act of 1980, shall be awarded in accordance with standards established under section 7701(g) of this title.

Section 7701(g) provides:

1. Except as provided in paragraph (2) of this subsection, the [Merit Systems Protection] Board, or an administrative law judge or other employee of the Board designated to hear a case, may require payment by the agency involved of reasonable attorney fees . . . if warranted in the interest of justice . . . .
2. If an employee or applicant for employment is the prevailing party and the decision is based on a finding of discrimination prohibited under section 2302(b) of this title, the payment of attorney fees shall be in accordance with the standards prescribed under section 706(k) of the Civil Rights Act of 1964 (42 U.S.C. 2000e-5(k)).

Section 2302(b) provides:

> Any employee who has authority to take, direct others to take, recommend, or approve any personnel action, shall not, with respect to such authority — (1) discriminate for or against any employee or applicant for employment —

a. on the basis of race, color, religion, sex, or national origin, as prohibited under section 717 of the Civil Rights Act of 1964 (42 U.S.C. 2000e-16);
b. on the basis of age, as prohibited under sections 12 and 15 of the Age Discrimination in Employment Act of 1967 (29 U.S.C. 631, 633a);
c. on the basis of sex, as prohibited by section 6(d) of the Fair Labor Standards Act of 1938 (29 U.S.C. 206(d));
d. on the basis of handicapping conditions, as prohibited under section 501 of the Rehabilitation Act of 1973 (29 U.S.C. 791); or
e. on the basis of marital status or political affiliation as prohibited under any law, rule, or regulation.

Thus, in the ordinary case, fees may be awarded if "warranted in the interest of justice," but in civil rights cases the standards of 42 U.S.C. § 2000e-5(k) are incorporated, which apparently means that a prevailing plaintiff should recover fees "in all but very unusual circumstances." *Albemarle Paper Co. v. Moody*, 422 U.S. 405, 415 (1975).[51]

Age Discrimination Act of 1975

The Age Discrimination Act of 1975, 42 U.S.C. §§ 6101 *et seq.*, prohibits age discrimination in programs or activities receiving federal, financial assistance. Public Law 95-478, § 401, amended 42 U.S.C. § 6104(e) to provide that "the court shall award the costs of suit, including a reasonable attorney's fee, to the prevailing plaintiff."

Civil Rights of Institutionalized Persons Act

Section 3 of the Civil Rights of Institutionalized Persons Act, 42 U.S.C. § 1997a, provides that the Attorney General may institute a civil action against any state or political subdivision of a state or employee thereof whom he has reasonable cause to believe is engaging in a pattern or practice of subjecting persons residing in or confined to an institution (which includes, among other things, mental institutions, prisons, and nursing homes) to egregious or flagrant conditions which deprive such persons of any rights, privileges, or immunities conferred by the Constitution or laws of the United States. In any such action, "the court may allow the prevailing party, other than the United States, a reasonable attorney's fee against the United States as part of the costs." 42 U.S.C. § 1997a(b).

Section 5 of the act, 42 U.S.C. § 1997c, provides that the Attorney General may intervene in any private action commenced in any federal court seeking relief from a pattern or practice of egregious or flagrant conditions which deprive persons in institutions of any rights, privileges, or immunities secured by the Constitution or laws of the United States. (This section does not appear to create a new private right of action; rather, it contemplates actions under existing law, such as 42 U.S.C. § 1983.) Section 5(d) reads:

> In any action in which the United States joins as an intervenor under this section, the court may allow the prevailing party, other than the United States, a reasonable attorney's

fee against the United States as part of the costs. Nothing in this subsection precludes the award of attorney's fees available under any other provisions of the United States Code.

The conference report that accompanied this law explains:

> In both the initiation and intervention sections, the Act makes clear the liability of the United States to opposing parties for attorneys' fees whenever it loses. The award is discretionary with the court, and it is intended that the present standards used by courts under the civil rights laws will apply. However, it is not intended that recovery be allowed from the United States, as a plaintiff, by another plaintiff or plaintiff-intervenor. The award is to be made to an opposing party who prevails.[52]

Thus, in actions instituted by or intervened in by the Attorney General, fees may be awarded against the United States only to prevailing defendants, and only if the suit was, in the words of *Christiansburg, supra*, 434 U.S. at 421, "frivolous, unreasonable, or without foundation." Prevailing plaintiffs, other than the United States, apparently may recover attorneys' fees against defendants if awards are authorized under a statute such as the Civil Rights Attorney's Fees Awards Act of 1976 or the common law bad faith exception to the American rule.

In 1996, the Prison Litigation Reform Act, Public Law 104-134, § 803, amended § 7 of the Civil Rights of Institutionalized Persons Act, 42 U.S.C. § 1997e, to provide that no prisoner may bring an action with respect to prison conditions, under 42 U.S.C. § 1983 or any other federal law, "until such administrative remedies as are available are exhausted." It also limited the right to recover attorneys' fees under the Civil Rights Attorney's Fees Awards Act of 1976, 42 U.S.C. § 1988(b), as detailed below in the discussion of that statute.

Rehabilitation Act of 1973

Section 501 of the Rehabilitation Act of 1973 provides protection from employment discrimination on the basis of handicap by federal executive branch agencies. 29 U.S.C. § 791. Section 504, as amended in 1978, prohibits discrimination solely by reason of handicap under programs receiving federal financial assistance or under programs conducted by executive agencies or by the Postal Service. 29 U.S.C. § 794. Section 505, which was added in 1978, provides that specified remedies, procedures, and rights set forth in Title VII of the Civil Rights Act of 1964 shall be available with respect to complaints under § 501, and the remedies, procedures, and rights set forth in Title VI of the Civil Rights Act of 1964 shall be available with respect to complaints under § 504. Section 505 also provides that, in any "action or proceeding" under the Rehabilitation Act, "the court, in its discretion, may allow the prevailing party, other than the United States, a reasonable attorney's fee as part of the costs." 29 U.S.C. § 794a.

Individuals with Disabilities Education Act

An attorneys' fees provision was added to the Education of the Handicapped Act by the Handicapped Children's Protection Act of 1986, Public Law 99-372, 20 U.S.C. § 1415(e)(4).

This statute was enacted to overturn *Smith v. Robinson*, 468 U.S. 992 (1984), which precluded fee awards under the EHA. The plaintiffs in *Smith v. Robinson* had sued on behalf of a handicapped child who allegedly had been deprived of his right to a free special education. They had sued under state law and under three federal statutes: EHA, § 504 of the Rehabilitation Act of 1973 (29 U.S.C. § 794), and 42 U.S.C. § 1983. The EHA guarantees the right to a free appropriate public education in states that receive grants under the statute; the Rehabilitation Act prohibits discrimination on the basis of handicap in any program or activity that receives federal financial assistance; and § 1983 permits suits against state or local officials if, under color of state law, they deprive someone of a federal constitutional or statutory right.

The EHA prior to the 1986 Act did not authorize awards of attorneys' fees, but the Rehabilitation Act did, and 42 U.S.C. § 1988(b) permits fee awards in § 1983 cases. The plaintiffs in *Smith v. Robinson*, after prevailing on the merits of their case, asked the court to award fees pursuant to either the Rehabilitation Act or § 1988(b). The Supreme Court held that they were not entitled to relief under the Rehabilitation Act or § 1983, and therefore were not entitled to a fee award under either statute. Although these statutes on their face appear to apply to cases of handicapped children who are denied their right to a free appropriate public education, the Court found that, in cases in which these statutes do not provide rights greater than those available under the EHA, Congress intended the EHA to be the exclusive remedy.

Congress, therefore, added 20 U.S.C. § 1415(i)(3)(B) to the EHA, which, as amended, provides:

> In any action or proceeding brought under this section, the court, in its discretion, may award reasonable attorneys' fees as part of the costs....

Administrative proceedings are mandatory under the EHA, and the legislative history makes clear that courts may award fees incurred at the administrative and the judicial levels, including when a party prevails at the administrative level and brings a court action solely to recover fees. Therefore, the Supreme Court's decisions in neither *Webb* nor *Crest Street* appear to preclude a court from awarding attorneys' fees incurred at the administrative level. The attorneys' fees provision prohibits bonuses and multipliers (discussed below under "Determining a Reasonable Attorneys' Fee"), and contains a section based on Rule 68 of the Federal Rules of Civil Procedure (discussed below under "Rule 68 of the Federal Rules of Civil Procedure").[53]

Americans with Disabilities Act of 1990

The ADA, 42 U.S.C. §§ 12101 *et seq*., provides protection against discrimination on the basis of disability in employment, public services, public accommodations, and telecommunications. It supplements the Rehabilitation Act of 1973 by extending such protection, to varying degrees, to Congress and the legislative branch agencies, to the states,[54] and to the private sector. Section 505 of the ADA, 42 U.S.C. § 12205, provides:

> In any action or administrative proceeding commenced pursuant to this Act, the court or agency, in its discretion, may allow the prevailing party, other than the United States, a

reasonable attorney's fee, including litigation expenses, and costs, and the United States shall be liable for the foregoing the same as a private individual.

Civil Rights Attorney's Fees Awards Act of 1976

The Civil Rights Attorney's Fees Awards Act of 1976, 42 U.S.C. § 1988(b), provides:

> In any action or proceeding to enforce a provision of sections 1981, 1981a, 1982, 1983, 1985, and 1986 of this title, title IX of Public Law 92-318, the Religious Freedom Restoration Act of 1993, the Religious Land Use and Institutionalized Persons Act of 2000, title VI of the Civil Rights Act of 1964, or section 40302 of the Violence Against Women Act of 1994, the court, in its discretion, may allow the prevailing party, other than the United States, a reasonable attorney's fee as part of the costs, except that in any action brought against a judicial officer for an act or omission taken in such officer's judicial capacity such officer shall not be held liable for any costs, including attorney's fees, unless such action was clearly in excess of such officer's jurisdiction.[55]

In 1996, the Prison Litigation Reform Act, Public Law 104-134, § 803, amended § 7 of the Civil Rights of Institutionalized Persons Act, 42 U.S.C. § 1997e(d), to provide:

(1) In any action brought by a prisoner . . . fees shall not be awarded [under § 1988(b)], except to the extent that —
 (A) the fee was directly and reasonably incurred in proving an actual violation of the plaintiff's rights protected by a statute pursuant to which a fee may be awarded under [§ 1988(b)]; and
 (B) (B)(i) the amount of the fee is proportionately related to the court ordered relief for the violation; or (ii) the fee was directly and reasonably incurred in enforcing the relief ordered for the violation.

(2) Whenever a monetary judgment is awarded in an action described in paragraph (1), a portion of the judgment (not to exceed 25 percent) shall be applied to satisfy the amount of attorney's fees awarded against the defendant. If the award of attorney's fees is not greater than 150 percent of the judgment, the excess shall be paid by the defendant.

(3) No award of attorney's fees in an action described in paragraph (1) shall be based on an hourly rate greater than 150 percent of the hourly rate established under section 3006A of title 18, United States Code, for payment of court-appointed counsel.

(4) Nothing in this subsection shall prohibit a prisoner from entering into an agreement to pay an attorney's fee in an amount greater than the amount authorized under this subsection . . . .

In *Martin v. Hadix*, 527 U.S. 343 (1999), the Supreme Court held that 42 U.S.C. § 1997e(d)(3) "limits attorney's fees with respect to postjudgment monitoring services performed after the PLRA's [Prison Litigation Reform Act's] effective date but it does not so limit fees for postjudgment monitoring performed before the effective date." In *Johnson v. Daley*, 339 F.3d 582 (7th Cir. 2003), the Seventh Circuit upheld the constitutionality of the Prison Litigation Reform Act's discrimination against prisoners as compared with other plaintiffs, and cited other circuits that had reached the same result.

The eleven statutes under which § 1988(b) authorizes fee awards are now examined in the order listed in § 1988(b).

42 U.S.C. § 1981

This section provides:

> All persons within the jurisdiction of the United States shall have the same right in every State and Territory to make and enforce contracts, to sue, be parties, give evidence, and to the full and equal benefit of all laws and proceedings for the security of persons and property as is enjoyed by white citizens, and shall be subject to like punishment, pains, penalties, taxes, licenses, and exactions of every kind, and to no other.

42 U.S.C. § 1981a

This section, enacted by the Civil Rights Act of 1991, Public Law 102-166, § 102, provides for punitive damages in actions for unlawful intentional employment discrimination under specified statutes.

42 U.S.C. § 1982

This section provides:

> All citizens of the United States shall have the same right, in every State and Territory, as is enjoyed by white citizens thereof to inherit, purchase, lease, sell, hold, and convey real and personal property.

42 U.S.C. § 1983

This section provides:

> Every person who, under color of any statute, ordinance, regulation, custom, or usage, of any State or Territory, subjects, or causes to be subjected, any citizen of the United States or other person within the jurisdiction thereof to the deprivation of any rights, privileges, or immunities secured by the Constitution, and laws, shall be liable to the party injured in an action at law, suit in equity, or other proper proceeding for redress, except that in any action brought against a judicial officer for an act or omission taken in such officer's judicial capacity, injunctive relief shall not be granted unless a declaratory decree was violated or declaratory relief was unavailable. For the purposes of this section, any Act of Congress applicable exclusively to the District of Columbia shall be considered to be a statute of the District of Columbia.[56]

Section 1983 permits suits against state and local officials, as individuals, if, under color of state law, they deprive someone of a federally protected right. The Supreme Court has held that a state is not a "person" subject to suit under § 1983.

Will v. Michigan Department of State Police, 491 U.S. 58 (1989). Furthermore, a suit for damages against a state official acting in his or her official capacity "is no different from a suit against the State itself." *Id.* at 71.

However, "a State official in his or her official capacity, when sued for injunctive relief, would be a person under § 1983 because 'official-capacity actions for prospective relief are not treated as actions against the State.'" *Id.* at 71 n.10. In such suits, attorneys' fees may be awarded against a state under § 1988(b), but not against the state official personally, except under the common law bad faith standard. *Hutto v. Finney*, 437 U.S. 678, 692 n.19, 693, 700 (1978) (discussed in detail in section IX of this report).

State officials may be sued in their individual capacities for damages under § 1983. *Hafer v. Melo*, 502 U.S. 21 (1991). In such suits, a state official may be held liable for attorneys' fees even in the absence of bad faith. However, the state will not be liable for fees. *Kentucky v. Graham*, 473 U.S. 159 (1985).

Section 1983 permits suits against local governments, provided that the deprivation of rights was based on official policy and not merely *respondeat superior* (the common law liability of employers for acts of employees). *Monell v. Department of Social Services of the City of New York*, 436 U.S. 658 (1978). If a local official is sued under § 1983 in his official capacity, the public entity is liable, "provided, of course, the public entity received notice and an opportunity to respond." *Brandon v. Holt*, 469 U.S. 464, 471-472 (1985).

Maine v. Thiboutot, 448 U.S. 1 (1980), was a case brought under § 1983 in a state court challenging the state's method of computing benefits under a federally-funded public assistance program. The state argued that § 1983 does not provide for suits brought to enforce purely statutory, non-constitutional claims, but the Supreme Court held that "the phrase 'and laws,' as used in § 1983, means what it says." *Id.* at 4. In other words, according to this case, suits may be brought under § 1983 to enforce statutory as well as constitutional claims — even statutory claims unrelated to civil rights and even claims arising under statutes that do not themselves contain an express or implied private right of action. And, the Court held, under §1988(b), state as well as federal courts may award attorneys' fees in § 1983 suits.[57]

In *Dennis v. Higgins*, 498 U.S. 439 (1991), the Supreme Court held that suits against state officials for violation of the Commerce Clause (Art. I, § 8, cl. 3) may be brought under § 1983. The Court found that the Commerce Clause confers a right "to engage in interstate trade free from restrictive state regulation" (*id.* at 448), and that this right is protected by § 1983.

There may be another limitation upon awards of attorneys' fees under § 1988(b) in § 1983 cases. In *Maher v. Gagne*, 448 U.S. 122 (1980), which the Supreme Court decided the same day as *Thiboutot*, the Court left open the question whether the Eleventh Amendment prohibits federal courts from awarding fees in wholly-statutory, non-civil rights cases. The impact of the Eleventh Amendment on fee awards against the states is considered in section IX of this article, but brief mention of it will be made here in order to explain more fully the holdings of *Maine v. Thiboutot* and *Maher v. Gagne*.

The Eleventh Amendment generally prohibits suits for damages in federal court against a state. Notwithstanding the Eleventh Amendment, however, a state may be sued for damages in federal court for violations of laws enacted to enforce the Fourteenth Amendment. Section 1983, and civil rights laws generally, were enacted to enforce the Fourteenth Amendment. *Maine v. Thiboutot*, however, held that § 1983 permits assertion of claims arising under both civil rights and non-civil rights laws. This raises the question whether claims arising under non-civil rights laws should be considered as having been brought under a law enacted to enforce the Fourteenth Amendment merely because the laws under which they arise may be enforced through the use of § 1983. The Court did not have to answer this question in *Maine v. Thiboutot* because that case was brought in state court, where the Eleventh Amendment does not apply.

Maher v. Gagne the Court also avoided the question, but for a different reason. This case was brought in federal court, and, like *Maine v. Thiboutot*, it charged a state with having violated a non-civil rights law. However, the plaintiff in *Maher v. Gagne* also raised a constitutional claim, and that was decisive. Prior to trial, the case was settled favorably for the plaintiff, without the constitutional issue's being reached. The state argued that the Eleventh Amendment prohibited a fee award because the case involved a purely statutory, non-civil rights claim. The Court held, however, that, under § 1988(b), a federal court, notwithstanding the Eleventh Amendment, may award attorneys' "fees in a case in which the plaintiff prevails on a wholly statutory, non-civil rights claim pendent to a substantial constitutional claim or in one in which both a statutory and a substantial constitutional claim are settled favorably to the plaintiff without adjudication." *Id.* at 132. Because of the constitutional claim (which was held to be substantial), the Court found "there is no need to reach the question whether a federal court could award attorney's fees against a State based on a statutory, non-civil-rights claim." *Id.* at 130.[58]

42 U.S.C. § 1985

This section has three subsections. Subsection (a) gives to "any person" a right to be free from a conspiracy "to prevent, by force, intimidation, or threat" the acceptance of a federal office "or from discharging any duties thereof." Subsection (b) gives any person who is a party or a witness, or a grand or petit juror, in any court of the United States a right to be free from a conspiracy to obstruct justice. Subsection (c) protects persons from deprivations "of equal protection of the laws, or of equal privileges and immunities under the laws."

42 U.S.C. § 1986

This section provides that any person who has knowledge that any of the wrongs mentioned in 42 U.S.C. § 1985 are about to be committed, and has the power to prevent or aid in preventing the commission of such wrongs, who neglects or refuses so to do, shall be liable to the party injured for all damages caused by the wrongful act which such person by reasonable diligence could have prevented.

Title IX of Public Law 92-318

This statute, codified at 20 U.S.C. §§ 1681 *et seq.*, prohibits discrimination on the basis of sex, blindness, or severe visual impairment under any educational program or activity receiving federal assistance. In *Cannon v. University of Chicago*, 441 U.S. 667 (1979), the Supreme Court held that Title IX contains an implied private right of action. In *Franklin v. Gwinnett County Public Schools*, 503 U.S. 60 (1992), the Court added that this right includes the remedy of monetary damages.

Religious Freedom Restoration Act of 1993

This statute (Public Law 103-141, 42 U.S.C. §§ 2000bb *et seq.*), was enacted in response to *Employment Division, Oregon Department of Human Resources v. Smith*, 494 U.S. 872 (1990), in which the Supreme Court held that religiously neutral laws (in this case a law proscribing the use of peyote) usually may be applied without regard to any burden they place on the exercise of religion. In other words, the First Amendment's guarantee of the free exercise of religion ordinarily mandates no religious exemptions from otherwise valid laws. The Religious Freedom Restoration Act provides statutory protection in lieu of constitutional protection. It prohibits government at all levels from substantially burdening a person's exercise of religion unless the government demonstrates that the burden is in furtherance of a compelling governmental interest and is the least restrictive means of furthering that interest. The act contains an express private right of action.[59]

The Religious Land Use and Institutionalized Persons Act of 2000

This statute (Public Law 106-274, 42 U.S.C. §§ 2000cc *et seq.*) provides that "[n]o [state or local] government shall impose or implement a land use regulation in a manner that imposes a substantial burden on the religious exercise of a person, including a religious assembly or institution, unless the government demonstrates that imposition of the burden on that person, assembly, or institution — (A) is in furtherance of a compelling governmental interest; and (B) is the least restrictive means of furthering that compelling governmental interest." This prohibition applies if the burden is imposed in a program or activity that receives federal financial assistance, affects interstate commerce, or is imposed through a process that permits the government to make individualized assessments of the proposed uses for the property involved.

The statute also provides that "[n]o [state or local] government shall impose a substantial burden on the religious exercise of a person residing in or confined to an institution, as defined in section 2 of the Civil Rights of Institutionalized Persons Act (42 U.S.C. 1997) . . . unless the government demonstrates that imposition of the burden on that person — (1) is in furtherance of a compelling governmental interest; and (2) is the least restrictive means of furthering that compelling governmental interest." This prohibition applies if the burden is imposed in a program or activity that receives federal financial assistance or affects interstate commerce.

The statute also provides that "[n]o [state or local] government shall impose or implement a land use regulation in a manner that treats a religious assembly or institution on less than equal terms with a nonreligious assembly or institution," or "that discriminates against any assembly or institution on the basis of religion or religious denomination."

Civil Rights Act of 1964, Title VI — Federally Assisted Programs

This statute, codified at 42 U.S.C. §§ 2000d *et seq.*, provides:

> No person in the United States shall, on the ground of race, color, or national origin, be excluded from participation in, be denied the benefits of, or be subjected to discrimination under any program or activity receiving Federal financial assistance.

In *Guardians Association v. Civil Service Commission of the City of New York*, 463 U.S. 582 (1983), a majority of the Justices indicated that Title VI contains a private right of action.

Violence Against Women Act of 1994

Section 40302 of this act provides that "[a] person . . . who commits a crime of violence motivated by gender . . . shall be liable to the party injured, in an action for the recovery of compensatory and punitive damages, injunctive and declaratory relief, and such other relief as a court may deem appropriate."[60]

VIII. Awards of Attorneys' Fees in Tax Cases

Section 7430 of the Internal Revenue Code, 26 U.S.C. § 7430, authorizes the Internal Revenue Service and federal courts to award attorneys' fees of up to $125 an hour in tax cases in which the United States fails to establish that its position in the proceedings was substantially justified. In this respect, § 7430 is similar to EAJA, discussed at page 6, *supra*. In other respects, however, it is different, and the law governing awards of attorneys' fees in tax cases has undergone multiple changes since Congress first authorized fee-shifting in tax cases in 1976.

Awards of attorneys' fees in tax cases were first permitted by the Civil Rights Attorney's Fees Awards Act of 1976, 42 U.S.C. § 1988(b), which authorized federal courts to award attorneys' fees to a prevailing party, other than the United States, "in any civil action or proceeding, by or on behalf of the United States of America, to enforce, or charging a violation of, a provision of the United States Internal Revenue Code." This provision, commonly known as the "Allen amendment," had little effect because of its limitation to tax cases brought "by or on behalf of the United States." Although in several circumstances the United States may bring suit under the Internal Revenue Code, in the vast majority of tax cases the taxpayer is the plaintiff. See *Key Buick Company v. Commissioner of Internal Revenue*, 613 F.2d 1306 (5th Cir. 1980). Even in those cases that are brought by or on behalf of the United States in which the taxpayer is the defendant, a prevailing defendant is entitled to fees under § 1988(b) only upon a finding that the action is "meritless in the sense that it is groundless or without foundation." *Hughes v. Rowe*, 449 U.S. 5, 14 (1980).

The Equal Access to Justice Act (EAJA), which took effect October 1, 1981, amended § 1988(b) to remove its authorization for awards of attorneys' fees in tax cases. EAJA instead itself authorized federal courts to award attorneys' fees against the United States in tax cases, except those brought in Tax Court. This exception had not been explicit in the act, but a committee report indicated that the courts empowered by the act to award attorneys' fees "are those defined in section 451 of title 28," and the Tax Court is not among them.[61] Apart from this, awards of attorneys' fees in tax cases could be awarded under the same conditions as other awards against the United States under the EAJA: a prevailing plaintiff whose net worth was within the prescribed limits was entitled to an award up to $75 per hour (or more if a special factor justified a higher fee) unless the United States proved that its position was substantially justified or that special circumstances made an award unjust.

Next, § 292 of the Tax Equity and Fiscal Responsibility Act of 1982 (TEFRA), Public Law 97-248, made the EAJA inapplicable to tax cases and enacted § 7430 of the Internal Revenue Code. Section 7430 authorized fee awards in federal courts, including Tax Court, placed a cap of $25,000 on fee awards, and authorized awards only if the taxpayer proved that the position of the United States was "unreasonable." It contained no limits on hourly rates or the net worth of eligible plaintiffs. Section 7430 sunset, but was reenacted with amendments by § 1551 of the Tax Reform Act of 1986, Public Law 99-514. Then, in 1988, Public Law 100-647, §6239, amended § 7430 to apply in administrative, as well as court, proceedings.

The 1986 Act, while not placing tax cases back within the EAJA, amended § 7430 to make it more like the EAJA. Section 7430, as amended in 1988 and 1996, provides that, in any administrative or court proceeding brought by or against the United States, in connection with the determination, collection, or refund of any tax, interest, or penalty under the Internal Revenue Code, the prevailing party, other than the United States or a creditor of the taxpayer, may be awarded litigation costs, including reasonable attorneys' fees. Section 7430 contains the same limitations as the EAJA on the net worth of eligible plaintiffs (see § 7430(c)(4)(A)(ii), as renumbered by Public Law 104-168, § 701(a)), and it originally contained the same $75 cap on hourly rates. However, in 1996, Public Law 104-121 raised EAJA's rate to $125, and Public Law 104-168, § 702, raised § 7430's to $110, with cost of living increases after 1996. In 1998, Public Law 105-206, § 3101, raised § 7430's cap to $125, without amending the language authorizing cost of living increases after 1996.

As under the EAJA, a party is not eligible for a fee award "if the United States establishes that the position of the United States in the proceeding was substantially justified." 26 U.S.C. § 7430(c)(4)(B)(i). (Prior to enactment of this provision by Public Law 104-168, § 701(b), the burden of proof as to this issue was on the taxpayer.) Unlike the EAJA, § 7430 does not allow the government to avoid a fee award where "special circumstances make an award unjust."

Section 6673(a) of the Internal Revenue Code, 26 U.S.C. § 6673(a), as amended by Public Law 101-239, § 7731(a), allows the Tax Court to impose upon a taxpayer a penalty of up to $25,000 if it finds that —

> (A) proceedings before it have been instituted or maintained by the taxpayer primarily for delay, (B) the taxpayer's position in such proceedings is frivolous or groundless, or (C) the taxpayer unreasonably failed to pursue available administrative remedies.

Section 6673(a) also allows the Tax Court to require any attorney who unreasonably and vexatiously multiplies the proceedings in any case to pay personally the excess costs, expenses, and attorneys' fees reasonably incurred because of such conduct. If the attorney is appearing on behalf of the IRS, then the United States must pay the amount awarded.

Section 6673(b) allows the court to impose upon a taxpayer a penalty of up to $10,000 "[w]henever it appears to the court that the taxpayer's position in proceedings . . . under section 7433 is frivolous or groundless. . . ." Section 7433 authorizes taxpayers to sue the United States in federal district court if an Internal Revenue Service officer or employee "recklessly or intentionally disregards" any provision of the Internal Revenue Code. Under § 7433, a prevailing taxpayer may recover up to $100,000 of "(1) actual, direct economic damages sustained as a proximate result of the reckless or intentional actions of the officer or employee, and (2) the costs of the action." Awards of attorneys' fees are already provided for by § 7430.

IX. Awards of Attorneys' Fees Against the States

Article III, § 2, of the United States Constitution provides that the judicial power of the United States (i.e., federal court jurisdiction) shall extend to controversies between a state and citizens of another state. The Eleventh Amendment modifies this section by providing that the judicial power of the United States shall not be construed to extend to any suit against a state by citizens of another state or of a foreign state. In *Hans v. Louisiana*, 134 U.S. 1 (1890), the Supreme Court construed the Eleventh Amendment to prohibit a citizen from suing even his own state in federal court.[62] In *Alden v. Maine*, 527 U.S. 706 (1999), the Supreme Court held that the Eleventh Amendment prevents Congress from authorizing private suits against a state, even in its own courts, without the state's consent. Notwithstanding the Eleventh Amendment, a state may consent to suit by its citizens or citizens of other states. *Missouri v. Fiske*, 290 U.S. 18, 24 (1933).

In *Ex parte Young*, 209 U.S. 123 (1908), the Supreme Court held that federal courts may enjoin state officials as individuals from enforcing state laws that violate the United States

Constitution.[63] The Court reasoned that an official who attempts such action "comes into conflict with the superior authority of that Constitution, and he is in that case stripped of his official or representative character and is subject in his person to the consequences of his individual conduct." *Id.* at 159-160. One commentator noted:

> The idea that the court restrained the individual rather than the state was, of course, pure fiction, since the state could not act other than through its officials. But through this fiction the Court apparently sought to guarantee the nation's authority to limit state action.[64]

In *Edelman v. Jordan*, 415 U.S. 651 (1974), the Supreme Court explicitly limited the types of relief that may be granted under the theory of *Ex parte Young*. The plaintiffs in *Edelman* had sued state officials, alleging that the officials were administering a welfare program in a manner inconsistent with various federal regulations. The district court found for the plaintiffs and ordered the state officials to comply with federal regulations in the future and to disburse all benefits wrongfully withheld in the past. The court of appeals affirmed. The Supreme Court affirmed the prospective portion of the district court's order, but reversed the retroactive portion of the order, holding that because the award "must inevitably come from the general revenues of the State of Illinois," it "resembles far more closely the monetary award against the State itself . . . than it does the prospective injunctive relief awarded in *Ex parte Young*." *Id.* at 665. The Court acknowledged that "the difference between the type of relief barred by the Eleventh Amendment and that permitted under *Ex parte Young* will not in many instances be that between day and night." *Id.* at 667. This is evidenced by the fact that the prospective portion of the district court's order, as well as the retroactive portion, necessarily required the payment of state funds, but this the Court termed a permissible "ancillary effect" of the prospective order.[65]

In *Fitzpatrick v. Bitzer*, 427 U.S. 445, 456 (1976), the Supreme Court lessened the importance of its ruling in *Edelman* by holding that the Eleventh Amendment is "necessarily limited by the enforcement provisions of § 5 of the Fourteenth Amendment." In *Fitzpatrick* the plaintiffs had sued a state official under Title VII of the Civil Rights Act of 1964, which was enacted under § 5 of the Fourteenth Amendment and which includes a fee-shifting provision. Like the plaintiffs in *Edelman*, the plaintiffs in *Fitzpatrick* had sought prospective injunctive relief and retroactive benefits; in addition, in *Fitzpatrick* they had sought attorneys' fees. The district court awarded only the prospective relief, holding that the other relief was barred by *Edelman*. The court of appeals agreed that *Edelman* barred an award of retroactive benefits, but held that an award of attorneys' fees was a permissible ancillary benefit.

The Supreme Court did not decide whether an award of attorneys' fees constituted an impermissible retroactive benefit or a permissible ancillary benefit. Instead, it reversed the denial of retroactive benefits, holding that neither they nor an award of attorneys' fees were barred in situations in which Congress, under § 5 of the Fourteenth Amendment, had provided for suits against states or state officials. The Supreme Court held, in other words, that the constitutional power of Congress to enforce "by appropriate legislation" the Fourteenth Amendment was intended to supersede the Eleventh Amendment and allow congressionally authorized suits (and awards of attorneys' fees) against both states and state officials.

In *Atascadero State Hospital v. Scanlon*, 473 U.S. 234, 242 (1985), the Supreme Court held "that Congress may abrogate the States' constitutionally secured immunity from suit in federal court only by making its intention unmistakably clear in the language of the statute." Subsequently, Congress made explicit that states are not immune under the Eleventh Amendment from suits in federal court under any "Federal statute prohibiting discrimination by recipients of Federal financial assistance." 42 U.S.C. § 2000d-7.[66]

In *Pennsylvania v. Union Gas Co.*, 491 U.S. 1 (1989), the Supreme Court held that Congress also has the authority to override states' Eleventh Amendment immunity when legislating pursuant to the Commerce Clause. However, in *Seminole Tribe of Florida v. Florida*, 517 U.S. 44, 72 (1996), the Supreme Court overruled *Pennsylvania v. Union Gas Co.*, writing: "Even when the Constitution vests in Congress complete lawmaking authority over a particular area, the Eleventh Amendment prevents congressional authorization of suits by private parties against unconsenting States." The Court noted, however, that "an individual may [still] obtain injunctive relief under *Ex parte Young* in order to remedy a state officer's ongoing violation of federal law." *Id.* at 72 n.16.

In *Alden v. Maine*, 527 U.S. 706, 712 (1999), the Supreme Court held "that the powers delegated to Congress under Article I of the United States Constitution do not include the power to subject nonconsenting States to private suits for damages in state courts." This decision continues to allow the federal government to sue the states in federal or state courts, and continues to allow private suits for damages in state courts under statutes enacted pursuant to the Fourteenth Amendment.[67]

In *Hutto v. Finney*, 437 U.S. 678 (1978), the Supreme Court affirmed two awards of attorneys' fees against the State of Arkansas: a $20,000 award by a federal district court and a $2,500 award for services on appeal by the Court of Appeals for the Eighth Circuit. The district court based its award on the bad faith exception to the American rule. The court of appeals affirmed this award on the basis of the Civil Rights Attorney's Fees Awards Act of 1976, 42 U.S.C. § 1988(b), which had been enacted while the appeal was pending, although the court of appeals noted that the award would have been justified under the bad faith exception. 548 F.2d 740, 742 n.6.

Because § 1988(b) is a statute enacted pursuant to § 5 of the Fourteenth Amendment, and *Fitzpatrick* held that the Eleventh Amendment does not apply to such statutes, the Supreme Court apparently could have affirmed the district court fee award in *Hutto* on the basis of § 1988(b) merely by finding that § 1988(b) permitted awards of attorneys' fees against the states. The Court chose, however, to affirm on the basis of the bad faith exception. As the bad faith exception is a common law rule, not enacted pursuant to a statute that abrogates Eleventh Amendment immunity, the Court had to address the Eleventh Amendment question. It held that the district court award served the same purpose as a remedial fine imposed for civil contempt and did not constitute a retroactive monetary award, and therefore was not barred by the Eleventh Amendment under *Edelman*.

In *Missouri v. Jenkins*, 491 U.S. 274, 280 (1989), the Supreme Court made clear that the "holding of *Hutto* . . . was not just that Congress had spoken sufficiently clearly to overcome Eleventh Amendment immunity in enacting § 1988, but rather that the Eleventh Amendment did not apply to an award of attorney's fees ancillary to a grant of prospective relief." The holding of *Missouri* was that the Eleventh Amendment also does not apply to the calculation of the amount of a fee award and therefore does not prohibit enhancement of a fee award against a state to compensate for delay in payment.

The $2,500 court of appeals award in *Hutto* was made solely pursuant to § 1988(b), and in affirming this award the Court held that Congress intended § 1988(b) to permit awards of attorneys' fees against the states. The Court based this conclusion on the legislative history of § 1988(b) and on the fact that § 1988(b) provides for fee awards "as part of the costs," and "[c]osts have traditionally been awarded without regard for the States' Eleventh Amendment immunity." *Id.* at 695. The Court also held that fees could be awarded against the state even though the state had not been named as a defendant. "Congress recognized that suits brought against individual officers for injunctive relief are for all practical purposes suits against the state itself." *Id.* at 700.

Thus, in a suit for injunctive relief, the state, not the state official, may be held liable for fees under § 1988(b). However, in a suit for injunctive relief, a state official may be assessed fees under the common law bad faith standard, which was not affected by § 1988(b). *Id.* at 692 n.19, 693, 700.

In addition, in *Kentucky v. Graham*, 473 U.S. 159 (1985), the Supreme Court indicated that state officials who are not, like judges (discussed below), immune from damages liability, may be sued in their personal capacities for damages under § 1983, and in such cases may be liable for fees even in the absence of bad faith. In such cases, however, the state will not be liable for fees.

The holding in *Hutto v. Finney* that § 1988(b) permits fee awards against the states took on added importance in 1980, when the Supreme Court expanded the reach of § 1988(b) in *Maine v. Thiboutot* and *Maher v. Gagne*, both of which were discussed in detail in section VI of this article. Briefly, *Maine v. Thiboutot* permitted state courts to award fees in any action against a state for violation of any federal law (although subsequent cases discussed above narrowed this holding), and *Maher v. Gagne* permitted federal courts to do the same, provided there is a substantial claim raised under the Constitution or a statute enacted under § 5 of the Fourteenth Amendment. The Court left open the question whether the Eleventh Amendment allows federal courts to award fees in wholly statutory non-civil rights cases.[68]

Awards of Attorneys' Fees Against State Judges

In *Supreme Court of Virginia v. Consumers Union of the United States*, 446 U.S. 719 (1980), and in *Pulliam v. Allen*, 466 U.S. 522 (1984), the issue arose whether state judges, sued in their official capacities under 42 U.S.C. § 1983, enjoy any immunity from awards of attorneys' fees that other state officials lack. The answer, the Court found, depended upon whether the judges were sued for damages or injunctive relief, and whether the conduct concerning which they were sued had been performed in their legislative, enforcement, or adjudicative capacity. In 1996, Public Law 104-317, § 309, modified the law announced in *Pulliam*.

In *Consumers Union*, the Virginia court's restrictions on lawyer advertising were found to violate the First Amendment's guarantee of freedom of speech. The Supreme Court held that in propounding the advertising prohibitions the Virginia court had acted in a legislative capacity, and that in such capacity it enjoys common law immunity from damages liability and from declaratory and injunctive relief, and thus from awards of attorneys' fees. However, the Court noted, although *Consumers Union* had alleged only that the Virginia court had promulgated the advertising prohibitions, the Virginia court, in addition to its legislative function, has adjudicative and enforcement authority in attorney disciplinary cases.

In their adjudicative and enforcement capacities, judges enjoy absolute immunity from damages liability. However, in both these capacities, they are subject to suits for injunctive relief, and, under § 1988(b), to awards of attorneys' fees. (*Consumers Union* held this with respect to courts' enforcement authority, and *Pulliam* held it with respect to their adjudicatory authority.) In *Pulliam*, the Court wrote:

> Petitioner insists that judicial immunity bars a fee award because attorney's fees are the functional equivalent of monetary damages and monetary damages indisputably are prohibited by judicial immunity. She reasons that the chilling effect of a damages award is not less chilling when the award is denominated attorney's fees. There is, perhaps, some logic to petitioner's reasoning. The weakness in it is that it is for Congress, not this Court, to determine whether and to what extent to abrogate the judiciary's common-law immunity. *See Pierson v. Ray*, 386 U.S., at 554. Congress has made clear in § 1988 its intent that attorney's fees be available in any action to enforce a provision of § 1983.

466 U.S. at 543.

It should be emphasized that, under *Pulliam*, the state and not the judge ordinarily will be liable for attorneys' fees. As noted above, in *Hutto*, the Supreme Court held that, in injunctive suits, the state must pay fees awarded under § 1988(b); state officials may be held personally liable for fees only under the common law bad faith standard.

In 1996, Public Law 104-317, § 309(b), amended 42 U.S.C. § 1988(b) to make judicial officers immune from awards of costs, including attorneys' fees, for any "act or omission taken in such officer's judicial capacity . . . unless such action was clearly in excess of such officer's jurisdiction." Section 309(a) prescribed the same rule for federal judicial officers who are subject to *Bivens* actions.[69] Section 309(c) amended 42 U.S.C. § 1983 to prohibit injunctive relief against a state judicial officer "unless a declaratory decree was violated or declaratory relief was unavailable."

X. AWARDS OF COSTS IN FEDERAL COURTS

Federal Rule of Civil Procedure 54(d), 28 U.S.C. App. Rule 54(d), defines the power of federal courts to allow costs to prevailing parties. It states:

> Except when express provision therefor is made in a statute of the United States or in these rules, costs shall be allowed as of course to the prevailing party unless the court otherwise directs; but costs against the United States, its officers, and agencies shall be imposed only to the extent permitted by law. . . .

"Costs" that may be awarded are those items enumerated in 28 U.S.C. § 1920, which do not include attorneys' fees. Section 1920 provides that federal courts may tax as costs" (order the losing party to pay) the following:

1. Fees of the clerk and marshal;
2. Fees of the court reporter for all or any part of the stenographic transcript necessarily obtained for use in the case;
3. Fees and disbursements for printing and witnesses;
4. Fees for exemplification and copies of papers necessarily obtained for use in the case;
5. Docket fees under section 1923 of this title;
6. Compensation of court appointed experts, compensation of interpreters, and salaries, fees, expenses, and costs of special interpretation services under section 1828 of this Title.

In *Crawford Fitting Co. v. J.T. Gibbons, Inc.*, 482 U.S. 437, 438 (1987), the Supreme Court "addressed the power of federal courts to require a losing party to pay the compensation of the winner's expert witnesses." The Court held that "a federal court is bound by the limits of [28 U.S.C.] § 1821, absent contract or explicit statutory authority to the contrary." *Id.* at 439. Section 1821, the cited statute, provides that witnesses in federal courts "shall be paid an attendance fee of $40 per day for each day's attendance." Thus, if no contract or expert witness fee-shifting statute provides otherwise, a fee award to an expert witness may not exceed $40 per day; the only exception is "when the witness is court-appointed." *Id.* at 442.[70]

The Court based its opinion on its reading of 28 U.S.C. § 1821 together with 28 U.S.C. § 1920 and Federal Rule of Civil Procedure 54(d). It rejected the view that

> § 1920 does not preclude taxation of costs above and beyond the items listed, and more particularly, amounts in excess of the § 1821 fee. Thus, the discretion granted by Rule 54(d) is a separate source of power to tax as costs expenses not enumerated in § 1920. We think, however, that no reasonable reading of these provisions together can lead to this conclusion, for petitioners' view renders § 1920 superfluous. If Rule 54(d) grants courts discretion to tax whatever costs may seem appropriate, then § 1920, which enumerates the costs that may be taxed, serves no role whatsoever. We think the better view is that § 1920 defines the term "costs" as used in Rule 54(d). Section 1920 enumerates expenses that a federal court may tax as a cost under the discretionary authority found in Rule 54(d).

Id. at 441-442.

In *West Virginia University Hospitals, Inc. v. Casey*, 499 U.S. 83, 87 (1991), the Supreme Court held that "the term 'attorney's fee' in § 1988" does not provide "the 'explicit statutory authority' required by *Crawford Fitting*" for the shifting of expert fees.[71] The Civil Rights Act of 1991, Public Law 102-166, §113, authorized courts to include expert fees as part of the attorney's fee under 42 U.S.C. § 1981 and 1981a, and under Title VII of the Civil Rights Act of 1964, 42 U.S.C. § 2000e-5(k). 42 U.S.C. § 1988(c).[72]

Awards of Costs for and Against the United States

At common law, the United States could recover costs "as if they were a private individual." *Pine River Logging Co. v. United States*, 186 U.S. 279, 296 (1902). No statute has changed this. Costs against the United States, however, at common law were barred by sovereign immunity, absent express statutory consent. *Id.* The provision of Rule 54(d) that "costs against the United States, its officers, and agencies shall be imposed only to the extent permitted by law," "is merely declaratory and effected no change in principle." *Reconstruction Finance Corp. v. J.G. Menihan Corp.*, 312 U.S. 81, 83 (1941).

Costs were made allowable against the United States in 1966 by 28 U.S.C. § 2412(a), which provides:

> Except as otherwise specifically provided by statute, a judgment for costs, as enumerated in section 1920 of this title but not including the fees and expenses of attorneys may be awarded to the prevailing party in any civil action brought by or against the United States . . . .

A Senate report said that the 1966 change was enacted to correct the —

> disparity of treatment between private litigants and the United States concerning the allowance of court costs. . . . As things now stand, only in rare cases can costs be awarded against the United States in the event that it is the losing party. On the other hand when it sues on a claim and wins, it can collect full costs.[73]

Whether this disparity has been entirely eliminated appears questionable, because Rule 54(d), which allows costs against parties other than the United States, provides that costs "shall be allowed as of course," whereas § 2412, which allows costs against the United States, provides only that costs "may be awarded."

XI. Determining a Reasonable Attorneys' Fee

The amount of attorneys' fees to be awarded pursuant to a statutory or common law exception to the American rule "should, as a general rule, be fixed in the first instance by the District Court, after hearing evidence as to the extent and nature of the services rendered." *Perkins v. Standard Oil of California*, 399 U.S. 222, 223 (1970).

The evidence presented to the district court must be relatively specific:

> It is not necessary to know the exact number of minutes spent nor the precise activity to which each hour was devoted nor the specific attainment of each attorney. But without some fairly definite information as to the hours devoted to various general activities, *e.g.*, pretrial discovery, settlement negotiations, and the hours spent by various classes of attorneys, *e.g.*, senior partners, junior partners, associates, the court cannot know the nature of the services for which compensation is sought.

Lindy Bros. Builders, Inc. v. American Radiator and Standard Sanitary Corp., 487 F.2d 161, 167 (3d Cir. 1973).

In Pennsylvania v. Delaware Valley Citizens' Council for Clean Air (Delaware Valley I), 478 U.S. 546, 562-566 (1986), the Supreme Court explained "the proper measure for determining the 'reasonableness' of a particular fee award":

> One method, first employed by the Fifth Circuit in *Johnson v. Georgia Highway Express, Inc.*, 488 F.2d 714 (1974), involved consideration of 12 factors. *Johnson* was widely followed by other courts, and was cited with approval by both the House and the Senate when [42 U.S.C.] § 1988 was enacted . . . .[74] Setting attorney's fees by reference to a series of sometimes subjective factors placed unlimited discretion in trial judges and produced disparate results.
>
> For this reason, the Third Circuit developed another method of calculating "reasonable" attorney's fees. This method, known as the "lodestar" approach, involved two steps. First, the court was to calculate the "lodestar," determined by multiplying the hours spent on a case by a reasonable hourly rate of compensation for each attorney involved. *Lindy Bros. Builders, Inc. v. American Radiator and Standard Sanitary Corp.*, 487 F. 2d 161, 167 (CA3 1973) (*Lindy I*).
>
> Second, using the lodestar figure as a starting point, the court could then make adjustments to this figure, in light of "(1) the contingent nature of the case, reflecting the likelihood that hours were invested and expenses incurred without assurance of compensation; and (2) the quality of the work performed as evidenced by the work observed, the complexity of the issues and the recovery obtained." . . .
>
> We first addressed the question of the proper manner in which to determine a "reasonable" attorney's fee in *Hensley v. Eckerhart*, 461 U.S. 424 (1983). We there adopted a hybrid approach that shared elements of both the *Johnson* and the lodestar method of calculation. "The most useful starting point for determining the amount of a reasonable fee is the number of hours reasonably expended on the litigation multiplied by a reasonable hourly rate. . . ." To this extent, the method endorsed in *Hensley* follows the Third Circuit's description of the first step of the lodestar approach. Moreover, we went on to state: "The product of reasonable hours times a reasonable rate does not end the inquiry. There remain other considerations that may lead the district court to adjust the fee upward or downward. . . . We then took a more expansive view of what those "other considerations" might be, however, noting that "[t]he district court also may consider [the] factors identified in *Johnson v. Georgia Highway Express, Inc.*, 488 F. 2d 714, 717-719 (CA5 1974), though it should note that many of these factors usually are subsumed within the initial calculation of hours reasonably expended at a reasonable hourly rate." *Id.*, at 434, n. 9 (citation omitted).
>
> We further refined our views in *Blum v. Stenson*, 465 U.S. 886 (1984). . . . *Blum* also limited the factors which a district court may consider in determining whether to make adjustments to the lodestar amount. Expanding on our earlier finding in *Hensley* that many of the *Johnson* factors "are subsumed within the initial calculation" of the lodestar, we specifically held in *Blum* that the "novelty [and] complexity of the issues," "the special skill and experience of counsel," the "quality of representation," and the "results obtained" from the litigation are presumably fully reflected in the lodestar amount and thus cannot serve as independent bases for increasing the basic fee award. 465 U.S., at 898-900. Although upward adjustments of the lodestar figure are still permissible, *id.*, at 901, such modifications are proper only in certain "rare" and "exceptional" cases, supported by both "specific evidence" on the record and detailed findings by the lower courts.[75]
>
> In short, the lodestar figure includes most, if not all of the relevant factors comprising a "reasonable" attorney's fee, and it is unnecessary to enhance the fee for superior performance in order to serve the statutory purpose of enabling plaintiffs to secure legal assistance.[76]

In *Delaware Valley I*, the Court indicated that to be entitled to an upward adjustment, a prevailing party must show that it would have been unable "to obtain counsel without any promise of reward for extraordinary performance." It must present "specific evidence as to what made the results it obtained . . . so 'outstanding.'" It must show "that the lodestar figure . . . was far below awards made in similar cases where the court found equally superior quality of performance." Finally, to adjust a fee upward, a court must make "detailed findings as to why the lodestar amount was unreasonable, and in particular as to why the quality of representation was not reflected in the number of hours times the reasonable hourly rate." 478 U.S. at 567-568. The Court left open "the question of upward adjustment . . . based on the likelihood of success, or to put it another way, the risk of loss." *Id.* at 568. By "risk of loss" the Court apparently meant an attorney's risk of losing and not being paid at all because he had agreed to represent his client on a contingency basis, being paid out of the winnings or not at all.

The Court answered this question in a second opinion in the same case. *Pennsylvania v. Delaware Valley Citizens' Council for Clean Air (Delaware Valley II)*, 483 U.S. 711 (1987), which was a 4-1-4 decision. Justice O'Connor concurred in parts of each plurality, which makes her opinion pivotal in determining what a majority of the Court decided in the case. Five justices (Justice O'Connor and the four who joined Justice Blackmun's dissent) decided that upward adjustments generally are appropriate in contingency fee cases. However, five justices (Justice O'Connor and the four who joined Justice White's plurality), decided that, even if "typical fee-shifting statutes are construed to permit supplementing the lodestar in appropriate cases by paying counsel for assuming the risk of nonpayment . . . it was error to do so in this case." 483 U.S. at 728.

Subsequently, however, in *Burlington v. Dague*, 505 U.S. 557, 567 (1992), the Court, "[a]dopting the position set forth in Justice White's opinion in *Delaware Valley II*," held "that enhancement for contingency is not permitted under the fee-shifting statutes at issue." Those statutes were § 7002(e) of the Solid Waste Disposal Act, 42 U.S.C. § 6972(e), and § 505(d) of the Clean Water Act, 33 U.S.C. § 1365(d). However, the Court noted that the relevant language of these statutes "is similar to that of many other federal fee-shifting statutes . . . ; our case law construing what is a 'reasonable' fee applies uniformly to all of them." *Id.* at 562. The Court's primary reason for its decision in *Burlington* was "that an enhancement for contingency would likely duplicate in substantial part factors already subsumed in the lodestar."*Id.*

In *Blum v. Stenson*, 465 U.S. 886, 895 (1984), the Supreme Court held that "'reasonable fees' are to be calculated under [42 U.S.C.] § 1988 according to the prevailing market rates in the relevant community, regardless of whether the plaintiff is represented by private or nonprofit counsel."[77] The Court rejected the position that awards be calculated according to the cost of providing legal services, which for legal aid groups that pay low salaries is usually less than the prevailing market rates.[78]

The Handicapped Children's Protection Act of 1986, Public Law 99-372, which added an attorneys' fees provision to the Education of the Handicapped Act, adopted this feature of *Blum v. Stenson*, but at the same time prohibited upward adjustments entirely. The statute, 20 U.S.C. § 1415(e)(4)(C), provides:

> For purposes of this subsection, fees awarded under this subsection shall be based on rates prevailing in the community in which the action or proceeding arose for the kind and quality of services furnished. No bonus or multiplier may be used in calculating fees awarded under this subsection.

In *Laffey v. Northwest Airlines, Inc.*, 746 F.2d 4 (D.C. Cir. 1984), *cert. denied*, 472 U.S. 1021 (1985), the court of appeals held that, for purposes of computing awards of attorneys' fees in civil rights cases, although a nonprofit legal organization is entitled under *Blum v. Stenson* to the prevailing market rate, a "for-profit" law firm that ordinarily charges less than the prevailing market rate — a "'quasi' public interest law firm," as the court called it in footnote 69 — is entitled "in almost every case" only to its "established billing rates." *Id.* at 24. In *Save Our Cumberland Mountains, Inc. v. Hodel*, 857 F.2d 1516, 1520 (D.C. Cir. 1988) (en banc), the full court of appeals overruled *Laffey*, on the ground that its "anomalous" result was not intended by Congress. "Henceforth," the court wrote, "the prevailing market rate method heretofore used in awarding fees to traditional for-profit firms and public interest firms and public interest legal service organizations shall apply as well to those attorneys who practice privately and for profit but at reduced rates reflecting non-economic goals." *Id.* at 1524.

In *City of Riverside v. Rivera*, 477 U.S. 561, 564 (1986), the Supreme Court held that, under 42 U.S.C. § 1988(b), an award of attorneys' fees is not "per se 'unreasonable' within the meaning of the statute if it exceeds the amount of damages recovered by the plaintiff in the underlying civil rights action." The Court wrote:

> Unlike most private tort litigants, a civil rights plaintiff seeks to vindicate important civil and constitutional rights that cannot be valued solely in monetary terms. . . . And, Congress has determined that "the public as a whole has an interest in the vindication of the rights conferred by the statutes enumerated in § 1988, over and above the value of a civil rights remedy to a particular plaintiff. . . ."

Id. at 574.

Nevertheless, in *Farrar v. Hobby*, 506 U.S. 103, 115 (1992), the Supreme Court held that, under 42 U.S.C. § 1988(b), "[w]hen a plaintiff recovers only nominal damages because of his failure to prove an essential element of his claim for monetary relief . . . , the only reasonable fee is usually no fee at all." The Court held that a plaintiff who is awarded only nominal damages — in this case one dollar when he had sought $17 million — is a prevailing party for attorneys' fees purposes, as he had established "the violation of his right to procedural due process." *Id.* at 112. However, because he could not prove actual injury, he was not entitled to a fee award.

What if a prevailing party is entitled to an award of "reasonable" fees from his opponent and has also agreed to pay his lawyer a contingent fee? Under 42 U.S.C. § 1988(b), if the "reasonable" fee is higher, then, the Supreme Court held in *Blanchard v. Bergeron*, 489 U.S. 87 (1989), the defendant must pay the higher fee. If the contingent fee is higher, then, the Supreme Court held in *Venegas v. Mitchell*, 495 U.S. 82 (1990), the defendant is liable only for the "reasonable" fee, but the plaintiff must still pay his lawyer the higher contingent fee. The Court emphasized in *Venegas* that "Section 1988 makes the prevailing *party* eligible for a discretionary award of attorney's fees." *Id.* at 87 (emphasis supplied by the Court). It would seem to follow that, in the *Blanchard* situation, where the "reasonable" fee is higher, the prevailing party may keep the difference between the "reasonable" fee paid by the defendant and the amount owed under the contingent fee agreement. This inference is supported by the Court's statement in *Venegas* that it "rejected the argument that the entitlement to a § 1988 award belongs to the attorney rather than the plaintiff." *Id.* at 89. Yet, in *Blanchard*, the Court wrote:

> Respondent cautions us that refusing to limit recovery to the amount of the contingency agreement will result in a "windfall" to *attorneys* who accept § 1983 actions. Yet the very nature of recovery under § 1988 is designed to prevent any such "windfall." Fee awards are to be reasonable . . . .

489 U.S. at 96 (emphasis added).[79]

In *Missouri v. Jenkins*, 491 U.S. 274 (1989), in addition to deciding the Eleventh Amendment question discussed in section IX of this article, the Supreme Court held that, under § 1988(b), the time of paralegals and law clerks should be considered in determining the amount of a fee award.

Finally, there is the question of how to compute fee awards against the United States. Under the Equal Access to Justice Act and under the Internal Revenue Code, awards ordinarily are limited to $125 per hour. Apart from this, fee awards against the United States are calculated the same way as fee awards against other parties. *Copeland v. Marshall*, 641 F.2d 880 (D.C. Cir. 1980) (*en banc*). The full court of appeals in this case reversed an earlier opinion by a three judge panel of the court. 594 F.2d 244 (D.C. Cir. 1978). The panel had held that the *Johnson* guidelines:

> are applicable generally to Title VII cases against a federal agency, but that special caution must be shown by the trial court in scrutinizing the claims of attorneys for fees against a federal agency in such litigation. Special caution is required because of the incentive which the defendant's "deep pocket" offers to attorneys to inflate their billing charges and to claim far more as reimbursement than would be sought or could reasonably be recovered from most private parties.

Id. at 250. To exercise that caution, the court wrote:

> the trial court should give consideration to abandoning the traditional claimed hourly-fee starting point for its calculations in favor of a principle of reimbursement to a firm for its costs, plus a reasonable and controllable margin for profit.

Id. at 251.

This "cost-plus" formula would have lowered fee awards in Title VII cases against the federal government, and consequently had been called "a serious blow to the whole public interest law movement." (N.Y. Times, Nov. 14, 1978, at A25). The three judge panel, however, on June 29, 1979, denied a rehearing and issued an unreported opinion clarifying its decision.

The full court of appeals reversed, writing that it did "not think that the amount of the fee should depend on the identity of the losing party." 641 F.2d at 894. It noted that Title VII provides that the "United States shall be liable for costs the same as a private person," and that the incentive supplied by fee awards to refrain from discrimination should not be less for the government than it is for private employers. Id. at 895. Furthermore, the court feared "that the proposed 'cost-plus' method of calculating fees would indeed become the inquiry of 'massive proportions' that we strive to avoid." Id. at 896. In sum, the court believed that in

Title VII cases, against the government or otherwise, attorneys should be compensated "for the market value of the services rendered." Id. at 900.

XII. RULE 68 OF THE FEDERAL RULES OF CIVIL PROCEDURE

Rule 68 of the Federal Rules of Civil Procedure, 28 U.S.C. App. Rule 68, creates an exception to the general rule in federal courts that a prevailing party is entitled to collect its court costs from the losing party. "The plain purpose of Rule 68 is to encourage settlement and avoid litigation." *Marek v. Chesny*, 473 U.S. 1, 5 (1985). Rule 68 provides that if, at any time more than 10 days before a trial begins, a party defending against a claim offers a settlement including costs then accrued,[80] and the offeree fails to accept the offer within 10 days, then, if the offeree wins the lawsuit, but the judgment he obtains "is not more favorable than the offer, the offeree must pay the costs incurred after the making of the offer."[81] In other words, the plaintiff forfeits his right under Rule 54(d) to recover costs incurred after such time. In addition, the plaintiff must pay the defendant's costs incurred after such time.[82]

In *Marek v. Chesny*, the Supreme Court addressed the interaction of Rule 68 and the Civil Rights Attorney's Fees Awards Act of 1976, 42 U.S.C. § 1988(b). Section 1988(b) authorizes the award of "a reasonable attorney's fee as part of the costs" in suits brought under 42 U.S.C. § 1983, and several other civil rights statutes. The Court held that, if a lawsuit is brought under a statute, such as § 1988(b), that provides for awards of attorneys' fees as *part* of the costs, then the term "costs" in Rule 68 includes attorneys' fees. The Court viewed this as the "'plain meaning' interpretation of the interplay between Rule 68 and § 1988." *Id.* at 9.[83]

Though, under *Marek v. Chesney*, a prevailing civil rights plaintiff who has rejected a settlement offer for as much as he won must pay the defendant's post-offer costs, he never has to pay the defendant's post-offer attorneys' fees. This is because a civil rights defendant may not be awarded attorneys' fees unless he prevails, and unless the court determines that the plaintiff's action was "frivolous, unreasonable, or without foundation." Neither of these would be the case if the plaintiff prevailed.[84]

This decision in *Marek v. Chesney* means that Rule 68 creates an exception not only to Rule 54(d), but also to all statutes that authorize awards of attorneys' fees to prevailing parties as part of the costs. Under *Marek v. Chesny*, a prevailing plaintiff otherwise entitled to recover attorneys' fees under one of these statutes is not entitled to recover attorneys' fees incurred after an offer to settle was made if the prevailing plaintiff rejected the offer and then won no more than had been offered.

The dissent in *Marek v. Chesny* pointed out that this means that "Rule 68 will operate to *include* the potential loss of otherwise-recoverable attorney's fees as an incentive to settlement in litigation under" the following statutes (of which the dissent listed 63): those that refer "to the awarding of 'attorney's fees *as part of* the costs,' to 'costs *including* attorney's fees,' and to 'attorney's fees and *other* litigation costs.'" *Id.* at 23. Rule 68 will *not* include the potential loss of attorneys' fees in statutes (of which the dissent listed 49) that refer "to the awarding of 'costs *and* a reasonable attorney's fee,' of 'costs *together* with a reasonable attorney's fee,' or simply of 'attorney's fees' without reference to costs." *Id.* In addition, as the dissent pointed out: "A number of statutes authorize the award of 'costs and expenses, including attorney's fees.' It is altogether uncertain how such statutes [of which the dissent listed 7] should be categorized under the Court's 'plain language' approach to Rule 68." *Id.* at 44. In short, the dissent believed that *Marek v. Chesny* sanctions "a senseless patchwork of fee-shifting that flies in the face of the fundamental purpose of the Federal Rules — the provision of uniform and consistent procedure in federal courts." *Id.* at 24.

If Congress wishes to restore uniformity with respect to the effect of Rule 68 on awards of attorneys' fees, then it could amend Rule 68 to define "costs" as used in Rule 68 either to include or to exclude attorneys' fees in suits brought under statutes authorizing awards of attorneys' fees. If it defines "costs" to include attorneys' fees, then attorneys' fees incurred after an offer would not be recoverable by plaintiffs who reject a settlement offer and then fail to win more than they had been offered. If it defines "costs" to exclude attorneys' fees, then such parties would lose their opportunity under Rule 54(d) to be awarded costs incurred after an offer, but would retain their entitlement to an award of attorneys' fees.

Alternatively, Congress could amend individual attorneys' fees statutes to provide that attorneys' fees may be awarded either as part of the costs or in addition to costs. It will also have to make this decision with respect to attorneys' fees statutes it enacts in the future.[85] In the Handicapped Children's Protection Act of 1986, Public Law 99-372, which was enacted after *Marek v. Chesny*, Congress adopted a compromise approach to settlement offers. It included a provision modeled on Rule 68 that bars recovery of attorneys' fees and costs of plaintiffs who reject settlement offers, and applies to administrative proceedings as well as to civil actions under the Individuals with Disabilities Education Act (formerly the Education of the Handicapped Act; see ch. VII of this chapter). However, it allows a prevailing plaintiff who would otherwise forfeit costs and attorneys' fees to recover them nevertheless if he had been substantially justified in rejecting a settlement offer. 20 U.S.C. § 1415(e)(4)(D). The conference report that accompanied the legislation stated: "Substantial justification for rejection would include relevant pending court decisions which could have an impact on the case in question."[86]

XIII. Negotiated Fee Waivers

In *Evans v. Jeff D.*, 475 U.S. 717 (1986), the Supreme Court upheld the legality of negotiated waivers of attorneys' fees. *Evans* was a class action brought under 42 U.S.C. § 1983 seeking injunctive relief concerning the conditions of mentally and emotionally handicapped children institutionalized by the State of Idaho. One week before trial, the defendant offered the plaintiffs virtually all the injunctive relief they had sought — on condition that the plaintiffs waive their claim to fees and costs under 42 U.S.C. § 1988(b). The plaintiff's lawyer "determined that his ethical obligation to his clients mandated acceptance of the proposal" (*Id.* at 722),[87] but he requested the district court to approve the settlement except for the provision on costs and attorneys' fees. (Class action settlements must be approved by the court under Rule 23 of the Federal Rules of Civil Procedure.) The district court upheld the fee waiver, but the court of appeals reversed on the ground that § 1988(b) "normally requires an award of fees to prevailing plaintiffs in civil rights actions, including those who have prevailed through settlement. The court added that '[w]hen attorney's fees are negotiated as part of a class action settlement, a conflict of interest frequently exists between the class lawyers' interest in compensation and the class members' interest in relief.'" *Id.* at 725. If negotiated fee waivers are permitted, then a defendant can exploit a plaintiff's lawyer's ethical obligation to his client to force him to waive fees that Congress arguably intended him to recover.

The Supreme Court rejected this view, holding that "[t]he statute and its legislative history nowhere suggest that Congress intended to forbid *all* waivers of attorney's fees . . . ." *Id.* at 731. The Court added that "there are many . . . civil rights actions in which potential liability for attorney's fees may overshadow the potential cost of relief on the merits and darken prospects for settlement if fees cannot be negotiated." *Id.* at 735.

In response to these two points of the majority, the dissent argued first, that, although there is no evidence that Congress intended to ban all fee waivers, "[t]here is no evidence that Congress gave the question of fee waivers any thought at all" (*id.* at 743-744), and second, that "a *judicial* policy favoring settlements cannot possibly take precedence over . . . express *congressional* policy" favoring "incentives for lawyers to devote time to civil rights cases" (*id.* at 760-761). The dissent concluded:

> Although today's decision will undoubtedly impair the effectiveness of the private enforcement scheme Congress established for civil rights legislation, I do not believe that it will bring about the total disappearance of "private attorneys general." It is to be hoped that Congress will repair this Court's mistake. In the meantime, other avenues of relief are available. . . . Indeed, several Bar Associations have already declared it unethical for defense counsel to seek fee waivers. . . . In addition, it may be that civil rights attorneys can obtain agreements from their clients not to waive attorney's fees.

Id. at 765-766.[88]

XIV. Statutory Limitations on Attorneys' Fees

Some federal statutes and regulations limit the amount attorneys may charge their clients for representing them before various federal agencies. These provisions have different types of limitations. For example, 42 U.S.C. § 406(a) limits contingent fees in agency proceedings under Title II of the Social Security Act to the lesser of 25 percent of past-due old-age, survivor, or disability benefits that are awarded, or $4,000; and 42 U.S.C. § 406(b) limits contingent fees in court proceedings under the same statute to 25 percent, with no dollar maximum.[89] Contingent fees in cases before the Department of Veterans Affairs are limited by 38 U.S.C. § 5904(d) to 20 percent of past-due benefits awarded; 15 U.S.C. §§ 79g(d)(4) and 79j(b)(2)) provide that the amount of compensation paid under the Public Utility Holding Company Act of 1935 is subject to approval of the Securities and Exchange Commission; and 42 U.S.C. § 1383(d)(2) provides that the Secretary of Health and Human Services shall by rule and regulation prescribe maximum fees in Supplemental Security Income cases.[90]

Some of these attorneys' fees limitations are controversial because, although they may protect claimants from having to pay to their attorneys a large portion of any amount awarded, they may also so limit fees as to deter lawyers from handling cases, thus in effect denying claimants legal representation. The Supreme Court, however, held that the former $10 ceiling in Veterans' Administration cases is not unconstitutional for this reason. *Walters v. National Association of Radiation Survivors*, 473 U.S. 305 (1985). The Court noted Congress's desire "that the system should be as informal and non-adversarial as possible." *Id.* at 323-324. The Court did not, however, preclude the possibility that the $10 limitation could be unconstitutional as applied in a particular case. *See, id.* at 336 (O'Connor, J., concurring).

In *United States Department of Labor v. Triplett*, 494 U.S. 715 (1990), the Supreme Court upheld the fee limitations of the Black Lung Benefits Act, 30 U.S.C. § 932(a), which are incorporated from the Longshore and Harbor Workers' Compensation Act, 33 U.S.C. § 928. These limitations prohibit an attorney from receiving a fee unless approved by the appropriate agency or court. In addition, "[t]he Department's regulations invalidate all contractual arrangements for fees . . . and the Department will not approve a fee if the claimant is unsuccessful." *Id.* at 718. The Court concluded that there was no evidence adequate to "establish *either* that black lung claimants are unable to retain qualified counsel *or* that the cause of such inability is the attorney's fee system administered by the Department." *Id.* at 726 (emphasis in original). Therefore, there was "no basis for concluding that that system deprives claimants of property without due process of law." *Id.*

The American Bar Association's Special Committee on Federal Limitations on Attorneys' Fees recommended in August, 1980 that Congress enact legislation establishing uniform principles for the regulation of attorneys' fees in proceedings conducted before federal administrative agencies, and that such legislation prohibit arbitrary maximum fees and provide for reasonable fees.

XV. Funding of Participants in Federal Agency Proceedings

Federal agencies, like federal courts, may not, absent statutory authority, order one party to a proceeding to pay the attorneys' fees of another. Even the common law exceptions to the American rule are unavailable to federal agencies, as those exceptions stem from the inherent power of federal courts to do equity. *Turner v. Federal Communications Commission*, 514 F.2d 1354 (D.C. Cir. 1975). In addition, courts of appeals for two circuits have held that, absent statutory authority, an agency may not pay the attorneys' fees of participants in its proceedings. *Greene County Planning Board v. Federal Power Commission*, 559 F.2d 1227 (2d Cir. 1976), *rev'd on rehearing en banc*, 559 F.2d at 1237, *cert. denied*, 434 U.S. 1086 (1978); *Pacific Legal Foundation v. Goyan*, 664 F.2d 1221 (4th Cir. 1981).[91]

Three federal agencies have explicit statutory authority to provide compensation for reasonable attorneys' fees, expert witness fees, and other costs of participating in their proceedings: the Environmental Protection Agency, which has such authority for rulemaking proceedings under the Toxic Substances Control Act (15 U.S.C. § 2605(c)(4)), the Federal Energy Regulatory Commission, which has such authority for all proceedings before it (16 U.S.C. § 825q-1(b)(2)), and the Department of State, which has such authority for all proceedings, advisory committees, and delegations (22 U.S.C. § 2692).[92] In addition, the Consumer Product Safety Commission may contribute to any person's cost with respect to participation with the Commission in the development of a consumer product safety standard (15 U.S.C. § 2056(c)).

Notwithstanding these statutes, Congress has refused to allow EPA or FERC to compensate participants in their proceedings. Public Law 103-327 (1994), § 510, which appropriated funds for EPA, provides:

> None of the funds in this Act shall be used to pay the expenses of, or otherwise compensate, non-Federal parties intervening in regulatory or adjudicatory proceedings. Nothing herein affects the authority of the Consumer Product Safety Commission pursuant to section 7 of the Consumer Product Safety Act (15 U.S.C. 2056 et seq.).

Public Law 102-377 (1992), § 502, which appropriated funds for FERC, provides:

> "None of the funds in this Act or subsequent Energy and Water Development Appropriations Acts shall be used to pay the expenses of, or otherwise compensate, parties intervening in regulatory or adjudicatory proceedings funded in such Acts."[93]

At one time, several federal agencies without explicit statutory authority to fund intervenors did so under what they viewed as their general statutory powers, and had the support of the Comptroller General in so doing. The latter, in a decision (B-92288), wrote:

> [I]f the NRC in the exercise of its administrative discretion, determines that it cannot make the required determination unless it extends financial assistance to certain interested parties who require it, and whose participation is essential to dispose of the matter before it, we would not object to the use of appropriated funds for this purpose.[94]

The courts, however, decided the *Greene County* and *Pacific Legal Foundation* cases cited above, and Congress eliminated most intervenor funding by prohibiting it in appropriations measures, such as those cited above.

XVI. Some Arguments for and Against the American Rule

One line of arguments for and against the American rule centers around the philosophical question of whose expense an attorney should be. "In support of the American rule, it has been argued that since litigation is at best uncertain, one should not be penalized for merely defending or prosecuting a lawsuit. . . ." *Fleischmann v. Maier Brewing Co.*, 386 U.S. 714, 718 (1967). "[T]he expenses of litigation are . . . not the 'natural and proximate consequences of the wrongful act' . . . but are remote, future and contingent." *St. Peter's Church v. Beach*, 26 Conn. 355, 366 (1857). On the other hand, it has been noted that an injured person will not be made whole if he has to bear the expense of a lawyer. "[A] person who is successful in litigation is a part loser because he has to pay his own expenses and counsel fees, except a few minor items that are taxable as costs." *Rodulfa v. United States*, 295 F. Supp. 28 (D.D.C. 1969), *appeal dismissed*, 461 F.2d 1240 (D.C. Cir. 1972), *cert. denied*, 409 U.S. 949 (1972). "On what principle of justice can a plaintiff wrongfully rundown on a public highway recover his doctor's but not his lawyer's bill?" Judicial Council of Massachusetts, *First Report*, 11 Massachusetts Law Quarterly 1, 64 (1925).

Another line of arguments centers around the question of whether keeping or abandoning the American rule will more effectively further the public policy of encouraging meritorious claims and deterring non-meritorious ones. "Current practice tends to deter prosecution of even clearly meritorious claims by litigants who could at best recover less than the often high expenses of counsel. . . . And what is true for plaintiffs also holds true for defendants: the cost of defending against an unjust small claim may easily exceed the cost of simply paying what is demanded. The result is distasteful, for it ranks legal rights by dollar value. . . ." *Court Awarded Attorney's Fees and Equal Access to the Courts*, 122 University of Pennsylvania Law Review 636, 650 (1974).

Requiring the loser to pay the winner's attorneys' fees might encourage litigation of some meritorious claims and discourage litigation of some non-meritorious ones. On the other hand, the uncertainty of litigation might also lead to the opposite results. "[T]he poor might be unjustly discouraged from instituting actions to vindicate their rights if the penalty for losing included the fees of their opponents' counsel." *Fleischmann, supra*. In addition, non-meritorious claims might be encouraged by the prospect of avoiding the expense of a lawyer. However, it has also been argued in support of requiring losers to pay winners' lawyers' fees that, while conceding the uncertainty of litigation, it should be assumed that courts will more often than not arrive at a correct result. Otherwise, courts might as well be dispensed with entirely, as it would be cheaper and less time consuming simply to flip a coin.

In support of the American rule it has also been argued that "the time, expense, and difficulties of proof inherent in litigating the question of what constitutes reasonable attorney's fees would pose substantial burdens for judicial administration." *Fleischmann, supra*. Since this comment was made, however, Congress has enacted many fee-shifting statutes that require courts to determine what constitutes a reasonable fee.

It has also been argued that abandonment of the American rule might have serious consequences for developing areas of the law, since potential litigants might be loath to espouse novel legal theories for fear of incurring additional expenses if they do not prevail.

Finally, since the prospect of an award of attorneys' fees might at times encourage suits and at other times deter them, the crowding of court calendars has been cited as an argument both for and against the American rule.

XVII. Awards of Attorneys' Fees to Prevailing Criminal Defendants

Until the enactment of Public Law 105-119 (known as the "Hyde Amendment") in 1997, no federal statutory or common law exceptions to the American rule authorized fee-shifting from the losing to the winning party in federal criminal cases.[95] Of course, the Supreme Court has held that the Constitution requires the government to provide for the legal representation of indigent criminal defendants.[96] Congress does so with respect to persons accused of federal crimes in the Criminal Justice Act, 18 U.S.C. § 3006A.

Public Law 105-119, § 617, codified at 18 U.S.C. § 3006A note, provides, in pertinent part:

> the [federal] court, in any criminal case (other than a case in which the defendant is represented by assigned counsel paid for by the public) . . . may award to a prevailing party, other than the United States, a reasonable attorney's fee and other litigation expenses, where the court finds that the position of the United States was vexatious, frivolous, or in bad faith, unless the court finds that special circumstances make an award unjust. Such awards shall be granted pursuant to the procedures and limitations (but not the burden of proof) provided for an award under section 2412 of title 28, United States Code. . . .

Section 2412 is the Equal Access to Justice Act, and the procedures and limitations referred to have been held to be those mentioned in § 2412(d), including the $125 per hour cap, and the ineligibility for fee awards of prevailing parties whose assets exceed the amounts specified.[97] (These are spelled out at above under "The Equal Access to Justice Act.") The burden of proof under EAJA is on the United States to prove that its position was substantially justified; the burden of proof under Public Law 105-119 is on the prevailing defendant to prove that the position of the United States was vexatious, frivolous, or in bad faith. "[A] determination that a prosecution was 'vexatious' for the purposes of the Hyde Amendment requires both a showing that the criminal case was objectively deficient, in that it lacked either legal merit or factual foundation, and a showing that the government's conduct, when viewed objectively, manifests maliciousness or an intent to harass or annoy."[98]

Public Law 105-119 does not define "prevailing party," so the courts may have to determine whether it includes, for example, a defendant against whom charges are dropped prior to trial, a defendant who is convicted of a lesser charge than the one brought, or a defendant whose conviction is reversed on appeal. One court has held that a defendant was "not a 'prevailing party' because he was not acquitted or otherwise exonerated. Defendant voluntarily settled his case with the advice of counsel by signing the Diversion Agreement, under which Defendant acknowledged paying the 'capping' fee, paid restitution, performed community service and submitted to 'probation-like reporting.'"[99] Another court rejected "the Government's call for a bright-line rule that a dismissal without prejudice can never render a defendant a prevailing party under the statute."[100] It also held that the EAJA requirement "of a 'final judgment' is incorporated into the Hyde Amendment. Using this term, the Court further finds that, under the facts present here, both the dismissals with and without prejudice are final judgments under the Hyde Amendment. If the Court were to accept the Government's position that a dismissal without prejudice is never a 'final judgment' under the Hyde Amendment, then Mr. Gardner's only alternative would be to wait to request attorneys' fees until the statute of limitations on each of the charges had expired. This result is inconsistent with both logic and the purpose behind the statute, which is to deter vexatious governmental conduct."[101]

FEDERAL STATUTES THAT AUTHORIZE AWARDS OF ATTORNEYS' FEES

Ethics in Government Act of 1978

2 U.S.C. § 288i(d) (See Also, 28 U.S.C. § 593(F))

"The Senate may by resolution authorize the reimbursement of any Member, officer, or employee of the Senate who is not represented by the [Senate Legal] Counsel for fees and costs, including attorneys' fees, reasonably incurred in obtaining representation. Such reimbursement shall be from funds appropriated to the contingent fund of the Senate."

Federal Contested Elections Act

2 U.S.C. § 396

"The committee [on House Administration of the House of Representatives] may allow any party reimbursement from the contingent fund of the House of Representatives of his reasonable expenses of the contested election case, including reasonable attorneys fees. . . ."

Government Employee Rights Act of 1991

2 U.S.C. § 1220(E)

"If the individual referred to in subsection (a) is the prevailing party in a proceeding under this section, attorney's fees maybe allowed by the court in accordance with the standards prescribed under section 706(k) of the Civil Rights Act of 1964 (42 U.S.C. 2000e-5(k))."

Congressional Accountability Act of 1995

2 U.S.C. § 1361(A)

"If a covered employee, with respect to any claim under this chapter, or a qualified person with a disability, with respect to any claim under section 1331 of this title, is a prevailing party in any proceeding under section 1405, 1406, 1407, or 1408 of this title, the hearing officer, Board, or court, as the case may be, may award attorney's fees, expert fees, and any other costs as would be appropriate if awarded under section 2005e-5(k) of Title 42."

Presidential and Executive Office Accountability Act

3 U.S.C. § 435(A) (See Also, 28 U.S.C. § 3905(A))

"If a covered employee, with respect to any claim under this chapter, or a qualified person with a disability, with respect to any claim under section 421 [making sections of the Americans with Disabilities Act of 1990 applicable to the White House and specified other executive facilities], is a prevailing party in any proceeding under section 453(1), the administrative agency may award attorney's fees, expert fees, and other costs as would be appropriate if awarded under section 706(k) of the Civil Rights Act of 1964."

Equal Access to Justice Act

5 U.S.C. § 504(A)(1) (See Also, 28 U.S.C. § 2412)

"An agency that conducts an adversary adjudication shall award, to the prevailing party other than the United States, fees and other expenses incurred by that party in connection with that proceeding, unless the adjudicative officer of the agency finds that the position of the agency was substantially justified or that special circumstances make an award unjust."

Freedom of Information Act

5 U.S.C. § 552(A)(4)(E)

"The court may assess against the United States reasonable attorney fees and other litigation costs reasonably incurred in any case under this paragraph in which the complainant has substantially prevailed."

Privacy Act

5 U.S.C. § 552a(G)(2)(B)

"The court may assess against the United States reasonable attorney fees and other litigation costs reasonably incurred in any case under this paragraph in which the complainant has substantially prevailed."

5 U.S.C. § 552a(G)(3)(B)

"The court may assess against the United States reasonable attorney fees and other litigation costs reasonably incurred in any case under this paragraph in which the complainant has substantially prevailed."

5 U.S.C. § 552a(G)(4)

"In any suit brought under the provisions of subsection (g)(1)(C) or (D) of this section in which the court determines that the agency acted in a manner which was intentional or willful, the United States shall be liable to the individual in an amount equal to the sum of . . . the costs of the action together with reasonable attorney fees as determined by the court."

Government in the Sunshine Act

5 U.S.C. § 552b(I)

"The court may assess against any party reasonable attorney fees and other litigation costs reasonably incurred by any other party who substantially prevails in any action brought in accordance with the provisions of subsection (g) or (h) of this section, except that costs may be assessed against the plaintiff only where the court finds that the suit was initiated by the plaintiff primarily for frivolous or dilatory purposes. In the case of assessment of costs against an agency, the costs may be assessed by the court against the United States."

Whistleblower Protection Act of 1989 5 U.S.C. § 1204(M)(1)

"[T]he Board, or an administrative law judge or other employee of the Board designated to hear a case arising under section 1215, may require payment by the agency involved of reasonable attorney fees incurred by an employee or applicant for employment if the employee or applicant is the prevailing party and the Board, administrative law judge, or other employee (as the case may be) determines that payment by the agency is warranted in the interest of justice, including any case in which a prohibited personnel practice was engaged in by the agency or any case in which the agency's action was clearly without merit."

5 U.S.C. § 1204(M)(2)

"If an employee or applicant for employment is the prevailing party of a case arising under section 1215 and the decision is based on a finding of discrimination prohibited under section 2302(b)(1) of this title, the payment of attorney fees shall be in accordance with the standards prescribed under section 706(k) of the Civil Rights Act of 1964 (42 U.S.C. 2000e-5(k))."

5 U.S.C. § 1214(G)

"If the Board orders corrective action under this section, such corrective action may include . . . (2) reimbursement for attorney's fees . . . ."

5 U.S.C. § 1221(G)(1)(B)

"Corrective action shall include attorney's fees and costs . . . ."

5 U.S.C. § 1221(G)(2)

"If an employee, former employee, or applicant for employment is the prevailing party before the Merit Systems Protection Board, and the decision is based on a finding of a prohibited personnel practice, the agency involved shall be liable to the employee, former employee, or applicant for reasonable attorney's fees and any other reasonable costs incurred."

5 U.S.C. § 1221(G)(3)

"If an employee, former employee, or applicant for employment is the prevailing party in an appeal from the Merit Systems Protection Board, the agency involved shall be liable to the employee, former employee, or applicant for reasonable attorney's fees and any other reasonable costs incurred, regardless of the basis of the decision."

Federal Erroneous Retirement Coverage Corrections Act

5 U.S.C. § 8331 Note (Public Law 106-265, § 2208(A)(2))

"The Director of the Office of Personnel Management may . . . (2) provide for the reimbursement of necessary and reasonable expenses incurred by an individual with respect to settlement of a claim for losses resulting from a retirement coverage error, including attorney's fees, court costs, and other actual expenses . . . ."

Civil Service Reform Act of 1978

5 U.S.C. § 5596(B)(1)

"An employee of an agency who . . . is found . . . to have been affected by an unjustified or unwarranted personnel action which has resulted in the withdrawal or reduction of all or a part of the pay, allowances, or differentials of the employee —(A) is entitled, on correction of the personnel action, to receive . . . (ii) reasonable attorney fees related to the personnel action which . . . shall be awarded in accordance with standards established under section 7701(g) of this title."

5 U.S.C. § 7701(G)

"(1) Except as provided in paragraph (2) of this subsection, the Board . . . may require payment by the agency involved of reasonable attorney fees incurred by the employee or applicant for employment if the employee or applicant for employment is the prevailing party and the Board . . . determines that payment by the agency is warranted in the interest of justice. . . ."

"(2) If an employee or applicant for employment is the prevailing party and the decision is based on a finding of discrimination prohibited under section 2302(b)(1) of this title, the payment of attorney fees shall be in accordance with the standards prescribed under section 706k of the Civil Rights Act of 1964 (42 U.S.C. 2000e-5(k))."

Commodity Exchange Act

7 U.S.C. § 18(C)

"In case a complaint is made by a nonresident of the United States, the complainant shall be required, before any formal action is taken on his complaint, to furnish a bond in double the amount of the claim conditioned upon the payment of costs, including a reasonable attorney's fee for the respondent if the respondent shall prevail . . . ."

7 U.S.C. § 18(D)

"If the petitioner finally prevails, he shall be allowed a reasonable attorney's fee, to be taxed and collected as a part of the costs of the suit."

7 U.S.C. § 18(E)

"If the appellee prevails, he shall be allowed a reasonable attorney's fee to be taxed and collected as a part of his costs."

Packers and Stockyards Act

7 U.S.C. § 210(F)

"If the petitioner finally prevails, he shall be allowed a reasonable attorney's fee to be taxed and collected as a part of the costs of the suit."

Perishable Agricultural Commodities Act

7 U.S.C. § 499f(E)

"In case a complaint is made by a nonresident of the United States . . . the complainant shall be required . . . to furnish a bond . . . conditioned upon the payment of costs, including a reasonable attorney's fee for respondent if the respondent shall prevail . . . ."

7 U.S.C. § 499g(B)

"If the petitioner finally prevails, he shall be allowed a reasonable attorney's fee, to be taxed and collected as a part of the costs of the suit."

7 U.S.C. § 499g(C)

"Either party adversely affected by the entry of a reparation order by the Secretary may . . . appeal therefrom . . . . Such appeal shall not be effective unless . . . the appellant also files with the clerk a bond . . . conditioned upon the payment of the judgment entered by the court, plus interest and costs, including a reasonable attorney's fee for the appellee, if the appellee shall prevail. . . . [I]f appellee prevails he shall be allowed a reasonable attorney's fee to be taxed and collected as a part of his costs."

Federal Crop Insurance Act

7 U.S.C. § 1507(C)

"The Board shall provide such agents and brokers with indemnification, including costs and reasonable attorney fees, from the Corporation for errors or omissions on the part of the Corporation or its contractors for which the agent or broker is sued or held liable, except to the extent the agent or broker has caused the error or omission."

7 U.S.C. § 1508(J)(3)

"The Corporation shall provide approved insurance providers with indemnification, including costs and reasonable attorney fees incurred by the approved insurance provider, due to errors or omissions on the part of the Corporation."

Animal Welfare Act

7 U.S.C. § 2157(D)

"It shall be unlawful for any member of an Institutional Animal Committee to release any confidential information of the research facility. . . . Any person, including any research facility, injured in its business or property by reason of a violation of this section may recover all actual and consequential damages sustained by such person and the cost of the suit including a reasonable attorney's fee."

Agricultural Unfair Trade Practices

7 U.S.C. § 2305(A)

"In any action commenced pursuant hereto, the court, in its discretion, may allow the prevailing party a reasonable attorney's fee as part of the costs."

7 U.S.C. § 2305(C)

"In any action commenced pursuant to this subsection, the court may allow the prevailing party a reasonable attorney's fee as a part of the costs."

Plant Variety Act

7 U.S.C. § 2565

"The court in exceptional cases may award reasonable attorney fees to the prevailing party."

7 U.S.C. § 2570(B)

"Such remedies include . . . attorney fees under section 2565 of this title."

Immigration and Nationality Act

8 U.S.C. § 1324b(H)

"In any complaint respecting an unfair immigration-related employment practice, an administrative law judge, in the judge's discretion, may allow a prevailing party, other than the United States, a reasonable attorney's fee, if the losing party's argument is without reasonable foundation in law and fact."

8 U.S.C. § 1324b(J)(4)

"In any judicial proceeding under subsection (i) of this section or this subsection, the court, in its discretion, may allow a prevailing party , other than the United States, a reasonable attorney's fee as part of the costs but only if the losing party's argument is without reasonable foundation in law and fact."

Gonzales Act

10 U.S.C. § 1089(F)(2)

"With respect to the Secretary of Defense and the Armed Forces Retirement Home Board, the authority provided by paragraph (1) also includes the authority to provide for reasonable attorney's fees for persons described in subsection (a), as determined necessary pursuant to regulations prescribed by the head of the agency concerned." (The persons in question are medical personnel who are sued for malpractice where a suit against the federal government under the Federal Tort Claims Act is the exclusive remedy.)

Whistleblower Protections for Contractor Employees of Department of Defense, Coast Guard, and National Aeronautics and Space Administration

10 U.S.C. § 2409(C)(1)

"If the head of an agency determines that a contractor has subjected a person to a reprisal prohibited by subsection (a), the head of the agency may . . . (C) Order the contractor to pay the complainant an amount equal to the aggregate of all costs and expenses (including attorneys' fees and expert witnesses' fees) that were reasonably incurred . . . ."

Bankruptcy Act (as Amended by P.L. 109-8 (2005))

11 U.S.C. § 110(I)(1)

"[I]f a bankruptcy petition preparer ["a person, other than an attorney"] violates this section or commits any act that the court finds to be fraudulent, unfair, or deceptive . . . , the court shall order the bankruptcy petition preparer to pay to the debtor . . . (C) reasonable attorneys' fees and costs in moving for damages under this subsection."

11 U.S.C. § 110(I)(2)

"If the trustee or creditor moves for damages on behalf of the debtor under this subsection, the bankruptcy petition preparer shall be ordered to pay the movant the additional amount of $1,000 plus reasonable attorneys' fees and costs incurred."

11 U.S.C. § 110(J)(4)

"The court shall award to a debtor, trustee, or creditor that brings a successful action under this subsection reasonable attorneys fees and costs of the action, to be paid by the bankruptcy petition preparer."

11 U.S.C. § 111(G)(2)

"A nonprofit budget and credit counseling agency that willfully or negligently fails to comply with any requirement under this title with respect to a debtor shall be liable for . . . any court costs or reasonable attorneys' fees . . . ."

11 U.S.C. § 303(I)

"[T]he court may grant judgment — (1) against the petitioners and in favor of the debtor for — (B) a reasonable attorney's fee . . . ."

11 U.S.C. § 330(A)(1)

"[T]he court may award to a trustee, a consumer privacy ombudsman appointed under section 332, an examiner, an ombudsman appointed under section 333, or a professional person employed under section 327 or 1103 — (A) reasonable compensation for actual, necessary services rendered by the trustee, examiner, ombudsman, professional person, or attorney and by any paraprofessional person employed by such person."

11 U.S.C. § 362(H)

"[A]n individual injured by any willful violation of a stay provided by this section shall recover actual damages, including costs and attorneys' fees, and, in appropriate circumstances, punitive damages."

11 U.S.C. § 363(N)

"The trustee may . . . recover any costs, attorneys' fees or expenses incurred in avoiding such sale or recovering such amount."

11 U.S.C. § 503(B)

"After notice and a hearing, there shall be allowed administrative expenses . . . including — (4) reasonable compensation for professional services rendered by an attorney . . . ."

11 U.S.C. § 506(B)

"To the extent that an allowed secured claim is secured by property the value of which, after any recovery under subsection (c) of this section, is greater than the amount of such claim, there shall be allowed to the holder of such claim, interest upon such claim, and any reasonable fees, costs, or charges provided for under the agreement or State statute under which such claim arose." Some courts have interpreted this provision to allow attorneys' fees.

11 U.S.C. § 523(D)

"[T]he court shall grant judgment in favor of the debtor for the costs of, and a reasonable attorney's fee for, the proceeding if the court finds that the position of the creditor was not substantially justified, except that the court shall not award such costs and fees if special circumstances would make the award unjust."

11 U.S.C. § 526(C)(2)

"Any debt relief agency shall be liable to an assisted person . . . for reasonable attorneys' fees and costs . . . ."

11 U.S.C. § 526(C)(3)(C)

"[I]n the case of any successful action under subparagraphs (A) or (B), [the State] shall be awarded the costs of the action and reasonable attorneys' fees as determined by the court."

11 U.S.C. § 707(B)(4)(A)

"The court . . . may order the attorney for the debtor to reimburse the trustee for all reasonable costs in prosecuting a motion filed under section 707(b), including reasonable attorneys' fees . . . ."

11 U.S.C. § 707(B)(5)(A)

"[T]he court . . . may award a debtor all reasonable costs (including reasonable attorneys' fees) in contesting a motion filed by a party in interest . . . ."

Federal Home Loan Bank Act 12 U.S.C. § 1441a(C)(11)(B)

"The parties specified in the preceding sentence shall be entitled to reasonable attorney fees upon prevailing in any such judicial action."

Home Owners' Loan Act 12 U.S.C. § 1464(D)(1)(B)(Vii)

"Any court having jurisdiction of any proceeding instituted under this section by a savings association, or a director or officer thereof, may allow to any such party reasonable expenses and attorneys' fees. Such expenses and fees shall be paid by the savings association."

12 U.S.C. § 1464(Q)(3)

"Any person injured by a violation of paragraph (1) may bring an action . . . and shall be entitled to recover three times the amount of the damages sustained, and the cost of the suit, including a reasonable attorney's fee."

Housing Act of 1959

12 U.S.C. § 1701q-1(F)

"The monetary judgment may, in the court's discretion, include the attorneys fees and other expenses incurred by the United States in connection with the action."

National Housing Act

12 U.S.C. § 1715k(H)(6)

"In cases of defaults on loans insured under this subsection . . . the Secretary . . . may acquire the loan and any security therefor upon . . . reimbursement for such collection costs, court costs, and attorney fees as may be approved by the Secretary."

12 U.S.C. § 1723i(E) (Action to Collect Civil Money Penalty)

"The monetary judgment may, in the discretion of the court, include any attorneys fees and other expenses incurred by the United States in connection with the action."

12 U.S.C. § 1735f-14(E) (Action to Collect Civil Money Penalty)

"The monetary judgment may, in the court's discretion, include the attorneys fees and other expenses incurred by the United States in connection with the action."

12 U.S.C. § 1735f-15(F) (Action to Collect Civil Money Penalty)

"The monetary judgment may, in the court's discretion, include the attorneys fees and other expenses incurred by the United States in connection with the action."

Federal Credit Union Act

12 U.S.C. § 1786(P)

"Any court having jurisdiction of any proceeding instituted under this section by any credit union or a director, officer, or committee member thereof, may allow to any party such reasonable expenses and attorneys' fees as it deems just and proper, and such expenses and fees shall be paid by the credit union or from its assets."

Federal Deposit Insurance Act

12 U.S.C. § 1818(N)

"Any court having jurisdiction of any proceeding instituted under this section by an insured bank or director or officer thereof, may allow to any such party such reasonable expenses and attorneys' fees as it deems just and proper; and such expenses and fees shall be paid by the bank or from its assets."

Bank Holding Company Act

12 U.S.C. § 1844(F)

"Any court having jurisdiction of any proceeding instituted under this subsection may allow to any such party such reasonable expenses and attorneys' fees as it deems just and proper."

Bank Tying Act

12 U.S.C. § 1975

"Any person who is injured in his business or property by reason of anything forbidden in section 1972 of this title . . . shall be entitled to recover. . . a reasonable attorney's fee."

Farm Credit Amendments Act of 1985

12 U.S.C. § 2273

"Any court having jurisdiction of any proceeding instituted under this part by a System institution or a director or officer thereof, may allow to any such party such reasonable expenses and attorneys' fees as it deems just and proper; and such expenses and fees shall be paid by the System institution or from its assets."

Real Estate Settlement Procedures Act

12 U.S.C. § 2605(F)

"Whoever fails to comply with any provision of this section shall be liable to the borrower for each such failure in the following amounts: . . . (3) Costs. — In addition to the amounts under paragraph (1) or (2), in the case of any successful action under this section, the costs of the action, together with any attorneys fees incurred in connection with such action as the court may determine to be reasonable under the circumstances."

12 U.S.C. § 2607(D)(5)

"In any private action brought pursuant to this subsection, the court may award to the prevailing party the court costs of the action together with reasonable attorneys fees."

International Banking Act of 1978

12 U.S.C. § 3108(B)(5)

"Any court having jurisdiction of any proceeding instituted under this subsection may allow any party to such proceeding such reasonable expenses and attorneys' fees as the court deems just and proper."

Right to Financial Privacy Act of 1978

12 U.S.C. § 3417(A)

"Any agency or department of the United States or financial institution obtaining or disclosing financial records or information obtained therein in violation of this chapter is liable to the customer to whom such records relate . . . (4) in the case of any successful action to enforce liability under this section, the costs of the action together with reasonable attorney's fees as determined by the court."

12 U.S.C. § 3418

"In the event of any successful action [for injunctive relief], costs together with reasonable attorney's fees as determined by the court may be recovered."

Expedited Funds Availability Act

12 U.S.C. § 4010(A)

"[A]ny depository institution which fails to comply with any requirement imposed under this title . . . is liable . . . (3) in the case of any successful action to enforce the foregoing liability, [for] the costs of the action, together with a reasonable attorney's fee as determined by the court."

Financial Institutions Anti-Fraud Enforcement Act of 1990

12 U.S.C. § 4246 (See Also, 18 U.S.C. § 3059A(E)(2))

"When the United States, through private counsel retained under this subchapter, prevails in any civil action, the court, in its discretion, may allow the United States reasonable attorney's fees and other expenses of litigation as part of the costs."

Truth in Savings Act

12 U.S.C. § 4310(A)(3)

"[A]ny depository institution which fails to comply with any requirement imposed under this subtitle . . . is liable . . . in an amount equal to the sum of . . . (3) in the case of any successful action to enforce any liability under paragraph (1) or (2), the costs of the action, together with a reasonable attorney's fee as determined by the court."

Homeowners Protection Act of 1998

12 U.S.C. § 4907

"Any servicer, mortgagee, or mortgage insurer that violates a provision of this Act shall be liable to each mortgagor to whom the violation relates for . . . (4) reasonable attorney fees, as determined by the court."

Check Clearing for the 21st Century Act or Check 21 Act 12 U.S.C. § 5005(B)

"The amount of the indemnity under subsection (a) shall be the amount of any loss (including costs and reasonable attorney's fees and other expenses of representation) proximately caused by a breach of a warranty provided under section 5. . . . In the absence of a breach of warranty provided under section 5, the amount of the indemnity under subsection (a) shall be . . . interest and expenses (including costs and reasonable attorney's fees and other expenses of representation)."

12 U.S.C. § 5009(A)(1)

"[A]ny person who, in connection with a substitute check, breaches any warranty under this Act or fails to comply with any requirement imposed by, or regulation prescribed pursuant to, this Act . . . shall be liable [for] ... interest and expenses (including costs and reasonable attorney's fees and other expenses of representation) related to the substitute check."

Clayton Act 15 U.S.C. § 15(A)

"[A]ny person who shall be injured in his business or property by reason of anything forbidden in the antitrust laws may sue therefor . . . and shall recover threefold the damages sustained by him, and the cost of suit, including a reasonable attorney's fee."

15 U.S.C. § 15(B)(1)

"[A]ny person who is a foreign state may not recover under subsection (a) of this section an amount in excess of the actual damages sustained by it, and the cost of suit, including a reasonable attorney's fee."

15 U.S.C. § 15c(A)(2)

"The court shall award the State as monetary relief threefold the total damage sustained as described in paragraph (1) of this subsection, and the cost of suit, including a reasonable attorney's fee."

15 U.S.C. § 15c(D)(2)

"[T]he court may, in its discretion, award a reasonable attorney's fee to a prevailing defendant upon a finding that the State attorney general has acted in bad faith, vexatiously, wantonly, or for oppressive reasons."

15 U.S.C. § 26

"In any action under this section in which the plaintiff substantially prevails the court shall award the cost of suit, including a reasonable attorney's fee, to such plaintiff."

15 U.S.C. § 35(A)

"No damages, interest on damages, costs, or attorney's fees may be recovered under section 15, 15a, or 15c of this title from any local government, or official or employee thereof acting in an official capacity."

15 U.S.C. § 36(A)

"No damages, interest on damages, costs or attorney's fees may be recovered under section 15, 15a, or 15c of this title in any claim against a person based on any official action directed by a local government, or official or employee thereof acting in an official capacity."

Unfair Competition Act

15 U.S.C. § 72

"Any person injured in his business or property by reason of any violation of, or combination or conspiracy to violate, this section, may sue therefor . . . and shall recover . . . a reasonable attorney's fee."

Securities Act of 1933

15 U.S.C. § 77k(E)

"In any suit under this or any other section of this subchapter the court may, in its discretion, require an undertaking for the payment of the costs of such suit, including reasonable attorney's fees . . . ."

15 U.S.C. § 77z-1(A)(6) (See Also, § 77z-1(A)(7)(C), (C)(3))

"Total attorney's fees and expenses awarded by the court to counsel for the plaintiff class shall not exceed a reasonable percentage of the amount of any damages and prejudgment interest actually paid to the class."

Trust Indenture Act

15 U.S.C. § 77ooo(E)

"The indenture to be qualified may contain provisions to the effect that all parties thereto, including the indenture security holders, agree that the court may in its discretion . . . assess reasonable costs, including reasonable attorneys' fees, against any party litigant . . . ."

15 U.S.C. § 77www(A)

"[T]he court may, in its discretion . . . assess reasonable costs, including reasonable attorneys' fees, against either party litigant . . . ."

Securities Exchange Act of 1934

15 U.S.C. § 78i(E)

"In any such suit the court may, in its discretion, require an undertaking for the payment of the costs of such suit, and assess reasonable costs, including reasonable attorneys' fees, against either party litigant."

15 U.S.C. § 78r(A)

"In any such suit the court may, in its discretion, require an undertaking for the payment of the costs of such suit, and assess reasonable costs, including reasonable attorneys' fees, against either party litigant."

15 U.S.C. § 78u(H)(8)

"In the case of an unsuccessful action under paragraph (7), the court shall award the costs of the action and attorney's fees to the Commission if the presiding judge or magistrate finds that the customer's claims were made in bad faith."

Securities Investor Protection Act

15 U.S.C. § 78eee(B)(5)(A)

"The court shall grant reasonable compensation for services rendered and reimbursement for proper costs and expenses incurred . . . by a trustee, and by the attorney for such trustee, in connection with a liquidation proceeding."

Jewelers' Liability Act

15 U.S.C. § 298(B)

"Any competitor, customer, or competitor of a customer . . . may sue . . . and shall recover . . . a reasonable attorney's fee."

15 U.S.C. § 298(C)

"Any duly organized and existing jewelry trade association shall be entitled to injunctive relief . . . and if successful shall recover the cost of suit, including a reasonable attorney's fee."

15 U.S.C. § 298(D)

"Any defendant against whom a civil action is brought under the provisions of sections 294 to 300 of this title shall be entitled to recover the cost of defending the suit, including a reasonable attorney's fee, in the event such action is terminated without a finding by the court that such defendant is or has been in violation of sections 294 to 300 of this title."

Lanham (Trademark) Act

15 U.S.C. § 1116(D)(11)

"Any person who suffers damage by reason of a wrongful seizure under this subsection has a cause of action against the applicant for the order under which the seizure was made, and shall be entitled . . . unless the court finds extenuating circumstances, to recover a reasonable attorney's fee."

15 U.S.C. § 1117(A)

"The court in exceptional cases may award reasonable attorney fees to the prevailing party."

15 U.S.C. § 1117(B)

"In assessing damages under subsection (a) of this section, the court shall, unless the court finds extenuating circumstances, enter judgment for three times such profits or damages, whichever is greater, together with a reasonable attorney's fee. . . ."

15 U.S.C. § 1122

"Such remedies include . . . costs and attorney's fees under section 35 [15 U.S.C. § 1117]."

Truth in Lending Act

15 U.S.C. § 1640(A)

"[A]ny creditor who fails to comply with any requirement imposed under this part, including any requirement under section 1635 of this title, or part D or E of this subchapter [the Fair Credit Billing Act or the Consumer Leasing Act] with respect to any person is liable

[for] . . . the costs of the action, together with a reasonable attorney's fee as determined by the court."

Fair Credit Billing Act

15 U.S.C. §§ 1666-1666j

See, 15 U.S.C. § 1640(a)

Consumer Leasing Act

15 U.S.C. § 1667b(A) (See Also, 15 U.S.C. § 1640(A))

"In all actions, the lessor shall pay the lessee's reasonable attorney's fees."

Credit Repair Organization Act, 15 U.S.C. § 1679g(A)

"Any person who fails to comply with any provision of this title with respect to any other person shall be liable in an amount equal to . . . (3) . . . . In the case of any successful action to enforce any liability under paragraph (1) or (2), the costs of the action, together with a reasonable attorneys' fee."

Fair Credit Reporting Act

15 U.S.C. § 1681n(C)

"Upon a finding by the court that an unsuccessful pleading, motion, or other paper filed in connection with an action under this section was filed in bad faith or for purposes of harassment, the court shall award to the prevailing party attorney's fees reasonable in relation to the work expended in responding to the pleading, motion, or other paper."

15 U.S.C. § 1681o(B)

"On a finding by the court that an unsuccessful pleading, motion, or other paper filed in connection with an action under this section was filed in bad faith or for purposes of harassment, the court shall award to the prevailing party attorney's fees reasonable in relation to the work expended in responding to the pleading, motion, or other paper."

15 U.S.C. § 1681s(C)(1)

"In addition to such other remedies as are provided under State law, if the chief law enforcement officer of a State, or an official or agency designated by the State, has reason to believe that any person has violated or is violating this title, the State . . . (C) in the case of any successful action under subparagraph (A) or (B), shall be awarded the costs of the action and reasonable attorney fees as determined by the court."

15 U.S.C. § 1681u(I)

"Any agency or department of the United States obtaining or disclosing any consumer reports, records, or information contained therein in violation of this section is liable to the consumer to whom such consumer reports, records, or information relate in an amount equal to the sum of . . . (4) in the case of any successful action to enforce liability under this subsection, the costs of the action, together with reasonable attorney fees, as determined by the court."

Equal Credit Opportunity Act

15 U.S.C. § 1691e(D)

"In the case of any successful action under subsection (a), (b), or (c), the costs of the action, together with a reasonable attorney's fee as determined by the court, shall be added to any damages awarded by the court under such subsection."

Fair Debt Collection Practices Act

15 U.S.C. § 1692k(A)

"[A]ny debt collector who fails to comply with any provision of this title with respect to any person is liable [for] . . . a reasonable attorney's fee as determined by the court. On a finding by the court that an action under this section was brought in bad faith and for the purpose of harassment, the court may award to the defendant attorney's fees reasonable in relation to the work expended and costs."

Electronic Fund Transfer Act

15 U.S.C. § 1693m(A)

"[A]ny person who fails to comply with any provision of this title with respect to any consumer . . . is liable [for] . . . a reasonable attorney's fee as determined by the court."

15 U.S.C. § 1693m(F)

"On a finding by the court that an unsuccessful action under this section was brought in bad faith or for purposes of harassment, the court shall award the defendant attorney's fees reasonable in relation to the work expended and costs."

Interstate Land Sales Full Disclosure Act

15 U.S.C. § 1709(C)

"The amount recoverable in a suit authorized by this section may include . . . reasonable amounts for attorneys' fees."

15 U.S.C. § 1717a(D)

"The monetary judgment may, in the discretion of the court, include any attorneys fees and other expenses incurred by the United States in connection with the action."

Consumer Product Safety Act

15 U.S.C. § 2060(C)

"A court may in the interest of justice include in such relief an award of the costs of the suit, including reasonable attorneys' fees (determined in accordance with subsection (f) of this section) and reasonable expert witnesses' fees. Attorneys' fees may be awarded against the United States (or any agency or official of the United States) without regard to section 2412 of title 28 or any other provision of law."

15 U.S.C. § 2060(F)

"For purposes of this section and sections 2072(a) and 2073 of this title, a reasonable attorney's fee is a fee (1) which is based upon (A) the actual time expended by an attorney in providing advice and other legal services in connection with representing a person in an action brought under this section, and (B) such reasonable expenses as may be incurred by the attorney in the provision of such services, and (2) which is computed at the rate prevailing for the provision of similar services with respect to actions brought in the court which is awarding such fee."

15 U.S.C. § 2072(A)

"Any person who shall sustain injury by reason of any knowing (including willful) violation of a consumer product safety rule . . . may, if the court determines it to be in the interest of justice, recover the costs of suit, including reasonable attorneys' fees (determined in accordance with section 2060(f) of this title) and reasonable expert witnesses' fees . . . ."

15 U.S.C. § 2073

"In any action under this section the court may in the interest of justice award the costs of suit, including reasonable attorneys' fees (determined in accordance with section 2060(f) of this title) and reasonable expert witnesses' fees."

Hobby Protection Act

15 U.S.C. § 2102

"In any such action, the court may award the costs of the suit, including reasonable attorneys' fees."

Magnuson-Moss Warranty Act

15 U.S.C. § 2310(D)(2)

"If a consumer finally prevails in any action brought under paragraph (1) of this subsection, he may be allowed by the court to recover as part of the judgment a sum equal to the aggregate amount of cost and expenses (including attorneys' fees based on actual time expended) . . . unless the court in its discretion shall determine that such an award of attorneys' fees would be inappropriate."

Toxic Substances Control Act

15 U.S.C. § 2618(D)

"The decision of the court in an action commenced under subsection (a), or of the Supreme Court of the United States on review of such a decision, may include an award of costs of suit and reasonable fees for attorneys and expert witnesses if the court determines that such an award is appropriate."

15 U.S.C. § 2619(C)(2)

"The court in issuing any final order in any action brought pursuant to subparagraph (a) may award costs of suit and reasonable fees for attorneys and expert witnesses if the court determines that such an award is appropriate. Any court, in issuing its decision in an action brought to review such an order, may award costs of suit and reasonable fees for attorneys if the court determines that such an award is appropriate."

15 U.S.C. § 2620(B)(4)(C)

"The court in issuing any final order in any action brought pursuant to subparagraph (A) may award costs of suit and reasonable fees for attorneys and expert witnesses if the court determines that such an award is appropriate. Any court, in issuing its decision in an action brought to review such an order, may award costs of suit and reasonable fees for attorneys if the court determines that such an award is appropriate."

15 U.S.C. § 2622(B)(2)(B)

"If such an order issued, the Secretary, at the request of the complainant, shall assess against the person against whom the order is issued a sum equal to the aggregate amount of all costs and expenses (including attorney's fees) reasonably incurred, as determined by the Secretary. . . ."

Petroleum Marketing Practices Act

15 U.S.C. § 2805(D)(1)

"If the franchisee prevails in any action under subsection (a), such franchisee shall be entitled . . . to reasonable attorney and expert witness fees to be paid by the franchisor, unless the court determines that only nominal damages are to be awarded to such franchisee, in which case the court, in its discretion, need not direct that such fees be paid by the franchisor."

15 U.S.C. § 2805(D)(3)

"If any action under subsection (a), the court may, in its discretion, direct that reasonable attorney and expert witness fees be paid by the franchisee if the court finds that such action is frivolous."

Condominium and Cooperative Abuse Relief Act of 1980

15 U.S.C. § 3608(D)

"Such relief may include, but shall not be limited to rescission, reformation, restitution, the award of damages and reasonable attorney fees and court costs. A defendant may recover reasonable attorneys' fees if the court determines that the cause of action filed by the plaintiff is frivolous, malicious, or lacking in substantial merit."

15 U.S.C. § 3611(D)

"The amount recoverable under this section may include interest paid, reasonable attorneys' fees, independent engineer and appraisers' fees, and court costs. A defendant may recover reasonable attorneys' fees if the court determines that the cause of action filed by the plaintiff is frivolous, malicious, or lacking in substantial merit."

Export Trading Company Act of 1982

15 U.S.C. § 4016(B)(1)

"Any person who has been injured as a result of conduct engaged in under a certificate of review may bring a civil action for injunctive relief, actual damages, the loss of interest on actual damages, and the cost of suit (including a reasonable attorney's fee) for failure to comply with the standards of section 303(a) [15 U.S.C. § 4013(a)]."

15 U.S.C. § 4016(B)(4)

"In any action brought under paragraph (1), if the court finds that the conduct does comply with the standards of section 303(a) [15 U.S.C. § 4013(a)], the court shall award to the person against whom the claim is brought the cost of suit attributable to defending the claim (including a reasonable attorney's fee)."

National Cooperative Research Act of 1984

15 U.S.C. § 4303(A)

"Notwithstanding section 4 of the Clayton Act (15 U.S.C. 15) and in lieu of the relief specified in such section, any person who is entitled to recovery on a claim under such section shall recover . . . the cost of suit attributable to such claim, including a reasonable attorney's fee pursuant to section 5 of this Act [15 U.S.C. § 4304] . . . ."

15 U.S.C. § 4303(B)

"Notwithstanding section 4C of the Clayton Act (15 U.S.C. 15c), and in lieu of the relief specified in such section, any State that is entitled to monetary relief on a claim under such section shall recover . . . the cost of suit attributable to such claim, including a reasonable attorney's fee pursuant to section 4C of the Clayton Act . . . ."

15 U.S.C. § 4303(C)

"Notwithstanding any provision of any State law providing damages for conduct similar to that forbidden by the antitrust laws, any person who is entitled to recover on a claim under such provision shall not recover in excess of . . . the cost of suit attributable to such claim, including a reasonable attorney's fee pursuant to section 5 of this Act [15 U.S.C. § 4304] . . ."

15 U.S.C. § 4304(A)

"Notwithstanding sections 4 and 16 of the Clayton Act [15 U.S.C. §§ 15 and 26], in any claim under the antitrust laws, or any State law similar to the antitrust laws, based on the conducting of a joint venture, the court shall, at the conclusion of the action — (1) award to a substantially prevailing claimant the cost of suit attributable to such claim, including a reasonable attorney's fee, or (2) award to a substantially prevailing party defending against any such claim the cost of suit attributable to such claim, including a reasonable attorney's fee, if the claim, or the claimant's conduct during the litigation of the claim, was frivolous, unreasonable, without foundation, or in bad faith."

15 U.S.C. § 4304(B)

"The award made under subsection (a) may be offset in whole or in part by an award in favor of any other party for any part of the cost of suit, including a reasonable attorney's fee, attributable to conduct during the litigation by any prevailing party that the court finds to be frivolous, unreasonable, without foundation, or in bad faith."

Telemarketing and Consumer Fraud Abuse and Prevention Act 15 U.S.C. § 6104(D)

"The court, in issuing any final order in any action brought under subsection (a), may award costs of suit and reasonable fees for attorneys and expert witnesses to the prevailing party."

CAN-SPAM Act of 2003 (P.L. 108-187) 15 U.S.C. § 7706(F)(4)

"In the case of any successful action under paragraph (1), the court, in its discretion, may award the costs of the action and reasonable attorney fees to the State."

15 U.S.C. § 7706(G)(4)

"In any action brought pursuant to paragraph (1), the court may, in its discreation, requiring an undertaking for the payment of the costs of such action, and assess reasonable costs, including reasonable attorneys' fees, against any party."

National Historic Preservation Act

16 U.S.C. § 470w-4

"In any civil action brought in any United States district court by any interested person to enforce the provisions of sections 470 to 470a, 470b, and 470c to 470w-6 of this title, if such person substantially prevails in such action, the court may award attorneys' fees, expert witness fees, and other costs of participating in such action, as the court deems reasonable."

Endangered Species Act

16 U.S.C. § 1540(G)(4)

"The court, in issuing any final order in any suit brought pursuant to paragraph (1) of this subsection, may award costs of litigation (including reasonable attorney and expert witness fees) to any party, whenever the court determines such award is appropriate."

Public Utility Regulatory Policies Act of 1978

16 U.S.C. § 2632(A)

"[S]uch utility shall be liable to compensate such consumer (pursuant to paragraph (2)) for reasonable attorneys' fees, expert witness fees, and other reasonable costs incurred."

Alaska National Interest Lands Conservation Act

16 U.S.C. § 3117(A) (See Also, 43 U.S.C. § 1631(C)(3))

"Local residents and other persons and organizations who are prevailing parties in an action filed pursuant to this section shall be awarded their costs and attorney's fees."

Federal Cave Resources Protection Act of 1988

16 U.S.C. § 4307(C)

"If any person fails to pay an assessment of a civil penalty . . . the Attorney General shall bring a civil action in an appropriate United States district court to recover the amount of the penalty assessed (plus costs, attorney's fees, and interest . . .)."

Copyright Act

17 U.S.C. § 505

"In any civil action under this title, the court in its discretion may allow the recovery of full costs by or against any party other than the United States or an officer thereof. Except as otherwise provided by this title, the court may also award a reasonable attorney's fee to the prevailing party as part of the costs."

17 U.S.C. § 511(B)

"Such remedies include . . . costs and attorney's fees under section 505. . . ."

17 U.S.C. § 512(K)

"As used in this section, the term 'monetary relief' means damages, costs, attorneys' fees, and any other form of monetary payment."

17 U.S.C. § 911(F)

"In any civil action arising under this chapter, the court in its discretion may allow the recovery of full costs, including reasonable attorneys' fees, to the prevailing party."

17 U.S.C. § 911(G)(2)

"Such remedies include . . . costs and attorney's fees under subsection (f)."

17 U.S.C. § 1009(C)

"In an action under subsection (a), the court . . . (4) in its discretion may award a reasonable attorney's fee to the prevailing party."

17 U.S.C. § 1203(B)(5)

"In an action brought under subsection (a), the court . . . in its discretion may award reasonable attorney's fees to the prevailing party."

17 U.S.C. § 1322(B)

"A seller or distributor who suffers damage . . . may recover such relief as may be appropriate, including . . . reasonable attorney's fees."

17 U.S.C. § 1323(D)

"In an action for infringement under this chapter, the court may award reasonable attorney's fees to the prevailing party."

17 U.S.C. § 1325

"That amount shall be to compensate the defendant and shall be charged against the plaintiff and paid to the defendant, in addition to such costs and attorney's fees of the defendant as may be assessed by the court."

Firearm Owners' Protection Act 18 U.S.C. § 924(D)(2)(A)

"In any action or proceeding for the return of firearms or ammunition seized under the provisions of this chapter, the court shall allow the prevailing party, other than the United States, a reasonable attorney's fee, and the United States shall be liable therefor."

18 U.S.C. § 924(D)(2)(B)

"In any other action or proceeding under the provisions of this chapter, the court, when it finds that such action was without foundation, or was initiated vexatiously, frivolously, or in bad faith, shall allow the prevailing party, other than the United States, a reasonable attorney's fee, and the United States shall be liable therefor."

18 U.S.C. § 924(D)(2)(D)

"The United States shall be liable for attorneys' fees under this paragraph only to the extent provided in advance by appropriation Acts."

Brady Handgun Violence Prevention Act

18 U.S.C. § 925a

"In any action under this section, the court, in its discretion, may allow the prevailing party a reasonable attorney's fee as part of the costs."

Civil Asset Forfeiture Reform Act of 2000

18 U.S.C. § 983(B)(2)(B)(Ii)

"The court shall enter a judgment in favor of the Legal Services Corporation for reasonable attorney fees and costs submitted pursuant to clause (i) and treat such judgment as payable under section 2465 of title 28, United States Code, regardless of the outcome of the case."

18 U.S.C. § 983(B)(3)

"The court shall set the compensation for representation under this subsection, which shall be equivalent to that provided for court-appointed representation under section 3006A of this title."

Major Fraud Act of 1988

18 U.S.C. § 1031(H)

"Any individual who . . . is . . . discriminated against in the terms or conditions of employment by an employer because of lawful acts done by the employee on behalf of the employee or others in furtherance of a prosecution under this section . . . may, in a civil action, obtain all relief necessary to make such individual whole. Such relief shall include . . . compensation for any special damages sustained as a result of the discrimination, including litigation costs and reasonable attorney's fees."

Organized Crime Control Act of 1970

18 U.S.C. § 1964(C)

"Any person injured in his business or property by reason of a violation of section 1962 of this chapter may . . . sue and shall recover . . . a reasonable attorney's fee. . . ."

Protect Act (P.L. 108-21, § 510 (2003))

18 U.S.C. § 2252A(F)

"Any person aggrieved by reason of the conduct prohibited under subsection (a) or (b) [of 18 U.S.C. § 2252A] or section 1466A may commence a civil action for . . . (A) temporary, preliminary, or permanent injunctive relief; (B) compensatory and punitive damages; and (C) the costs of the civil action and reasonable fees for attorneys and expert witnesses."

Child Abuse Victims' Rights Act of 1986

18 U.S.C. § 2255(A)

"Any minor who is a victim of a violation of section 2241(c)(, 2242, 2243, 2251, 2251A, 2252, 2252A, 2260, 2421, 2422, or 2423 of this title and who suffers personal injury as a result of such violation may sue in any appropriate United States District Court and shall recover the actual damages such minor sustains and the cost of the suit, including a reasonable attorney's fee."

Safe Streets for Women Act of 1994 18 U.S.C. § 2259(B)(3)(E)

"[T]he court shall order restitution for any offense under this chapter. . . . The order of restitution under this section shall direct that . . . the defendant pay to the victim . . . the full amount of the victim's losses as determined by the court . . . . [including] attorneys' fees, as well as other costs incurred . . . ."

Safe Homes for Women Act of 1994

18 U.S.C. § 2264(B)(3)(E)

"[T]he court shall order restitution for any offense under this chapter. . . . The order of restitution under this section shall direct that . . . the defendant pay to the victim . . . the full amount of the victim's losses as determined by the court . . . . [including] attorneys' fees plus any costs incurred in obtaining a civil protective order . . . ."

Anti-Counterfeiting Amendments Act of 2004, P.L. 108-482, § 102

18 U.S.C. § 2318(F) "(1) . . .

Any copyright owner who is injured, or is threatened with injury, by a violation of subsection (a) may bring a civil action in an appropriate United States district court. ... In any action brought under paragraph (1), the court . . . may award to the injured party — (i) reasonable attorney fees and costs."

Antiterrorism Act of 1990

18 U.S.C. § 2333(A)

"Any national of the United States injured in his or her person, property, or business by reason of an act of international terrorism, or his or her estate, survivors, or heirs, may sue therefor in any appropriate district court of the United States and shall recover threefold the damages he or she sustains and the cost of the suit, including attorney's fees."

Wire Interception Act

18 U.S.C. § 2520(B)(3)

"In any action under this section, appropriate relief includes . . . a reasonable attorney's fee and other litigation costs reasonably incurred."

Electronic Communications Privacy Act of 1986 18 U.S.C. § 2707(B)(3)

"In a civil action under this section, appropriate relief includes . . . a reasonable attorney's fee and other litigation costs reasonably incurred."

18 U.S.C. § 2707(C)

"In the case of a successful action to enforce liability under this section, the court may assess the costs of the action, together with reasonable attorney fees determined by the court."

Video Privacy Protection Act of 1988 18 U.S.C. § 2710(C)(2)(C)

"The court may award . . . reasonable attorneys' fees and other litigation costs reasonably incurred."

Driver's Privacy Protection Act of 1994

18 U.S.C. § 2724(B)(3)

"The court may award . . . reasonable attorneys' fees and other litigation costs reasonably incurred."

Criminal Defendants

18 U.S.C. § 3006A Note

"[T]he [federal] court, in any criminal case (other than a case in which the defendant is represented by assigned counsel paid for by the public) . . . may award to a prevailing party, other than the United States, a reasonable attorney's fee and other litigation expenses, where the court finds that the position of the United States was vexatious, frivolous, or in bad faith, unless the court finds that special circumstances make an award unjust. Such awards shall be granted pursuant to the procedures and limitations (but not the burden of proof) provided for an award under section 2412 of title 28, United States Code. . . ."

Financial Institutions Anti-Fraud Enforcement Act of 1990

18 U.S.C. § 3059A(E)(2) (See Also, 12 U.S.C. § 4246)

"(1) A person who . . . is . . . discriminated against in the terms or conditions of employment by an employer because of lawful acts done by the person on behalf of the person or others in furtherance of a prosecution under any of the sections referred to in subsection (a) . . . may, in a civil action, obtain all relief necessary to make the person whole. (2) Relief under paragraph (1) shall include . . . compensation for any special damages sustained as a result of the discrimination, including litigation costs and reasonable attorney's fees."

Authentication of Foreign Documents

18 U.S.C. § 3495(A)

"Every foreign counsel selected pursuant to a commission issued on application of the United States . . . shall be paid by the United States, such compensation . . . as [the consular officer] may allow."

Witness Security Reform Act of 1984

18 U.S.C. 3524(D)(6)

"The United States shall be required by the court to pay litigation costs, including reasonable attorneys' fees, incurred by a parent who prevails in enforcing a custody or visitation order; but shall retain the right to recover such costs from the protected person."

Juvenile Delinquency

18 U.S.C. § 5034

"In cases where the juvenile and his parents, guardian, or custodian are financially able to obtain adequate representation but have not retained counsel, the magistrate may assign counsel and order the payment of reasonable attorney's fees or may direct the juvenile, his parents, guardian, or custodian to retain private counsel within a specified period of time."

Higher Education Act of 1965

20 U.S.C. § 1078(C)(6)(B)(I)

"'administrative costs of collection of loans' means . . . attorney's fees. . . ."

20 U.S.C. § 1095a(8)

"The court shall award attorneys' fees to a prevailing employee . . . ."

Individuals with Disabilities Education Act

20 U.S.C. § 1415(I)(3)

"In any action or proceeding brought under this section, the court, in its discretion, may award reasonable attorneys' fees as part of the costs . . . ."

Discrimination Based on Sex or Blindness (Title IX of Public Law 92-318) 20 U.S.C. §§ 1681 Et Seq.

See, 42 U.S.C. § 1988(b).

Foreign Service Act of 1980

22 U.S.C. § 4137(B)

"If the Board finds that the grievance is meritorious, the Board shall have the authority to direct the Department — (5) to pay reasonable attorney fees to the grievant to the same extent and in the same manner as such fees may be required by the Merit Systems Protection Board under section 7701(g) of Title 5."

Cuban Liberty and Democratic Solidarity (LIBERTAD) Act of 1996 22 U.S.C. § 6082(A)(1)(A)(Ii)

"[A]ny person that . . . traffics in property which was confiscated by the Cuban Government on or after January 1, 1959, shall be liable to any United States national who owns the claim of such property for . . . court costs and reasonable attorneys' fees."

Indian Arts and Crafts Act of 1990

25 U.S.C. § 305e(B)

"In addition to the relief specified in subsection (a), the court may award punitive damages and the costs of suit and a reasonable attorney's fee."

Indian Self-Determination and Education Assistance Act

25 U.S.C. § 450m-1(C)

"The Equal Access to Justice Act [5 U.S.C. § 504, 28 U.S.C. § 2412] shall apply to administrative appeals . . . by tribal organizations regarding self-determination contracts."

Navajo and Hopi Indian Relocation Amendments Act of 1980

25 U.S.C. § 640d-27(A)

"In any litigation or court action between or among the Hopi Tribe, the Navajo Tribe and the United States or any of its officials, departments, agencies, or instrumentalities, arising out of the interpretation or implementation of this subchapter, as amended, the Secretary shall pay, subject to the availability of appropriations, attorney's fees, costs and expenses as determined by the Secretary to be reasonable."

25 U.S.C. § 640d-27(B)

"Upon the entry of a final judgment in any such litigation or court action, the court shall award reasonable attorney's fees, costs and expenses to the party, other than the United States or its officials, departments, agencies, or instrumentalities, which prevails or substantially prevails, where it finds that any opposing party has unreasonably initiated or contested such litigation. Any party to whom such an award has been made shall reimburse the United States out of such award to the extent that it has received payments pursuant to subsection (a) of this section."

American Indian Agricultural Resource Management Act

25 U.S.C. § 3713(A)(1)(C)

"[T]he Secretary [of the Interior] shall issue regulations that . . . establish civil penalties for the commission of trespass on Indian agricultural lands, which provide for . . . court costs, and attorney fees."

Internal Revenue Code

26 U.S.C. § 6110(F)(4)(A)

"Any person who has exhausted the administrative remedies prescribed pursuant to paragraph (2) with respect to a request for disclosure may file a petition in the United States Tax Court or a complaint in the United States District Court for the District of Columbia . . . . [T]he provisions of subparagraphs (C), (D), (E), (F), and (G) of section 552(a)(4) of title 5, United States Code, shall apply to any proceeding under this paragraph." (Subparagraph (E) is the attorneys' fees provision of the Freedom of Information Act.)

26 U.S.C. § 6110(I)(2)

"In any suit brought under the provisions of paragraph (1)(A) . . . or in any suit brought under subparagraph (1)(B) . . . the United States shall be liable [for] the costs of the action together with reasonable attorney's fees as determined by the Court."

26 U.S.C. § 6673(A)(1)

"Whenever it appears to the Tax Court that — (A) proceedings before it have been instituted or maintained by the taxpayer primarily for delay, (B) that the taxpayer's position in such proceedings is frivolous or groundless, or (C) that the taxpayer unreasonably failed to pursue available administrative remedies, the Tax Court, in its decision, may require the taxpayer to pay to the United States a penalty not in excess of $25,000."

26 U.S.C. § 6673(A)(2)

"Whenever it appears to the Tax Court that any attorney or other person admitted to practice before the Tax Court has multiplied the proceedings in any case unreasonably and vexatiously, the Tax Court may require — (A) that such attorney or other person pay personally the excess costs, expenses, and attorney's fees reasonably incurred because of such conduct, or (B) if such attorney is appearing on behalf of the Commissioner of Internal Revenue, that the United States pay such excess costs, expenses, and attorneys' fees in the same manner as such an award by a district court."

26 U.S.C. § 6673(B)(1)

"Whenever it appears to the court that the taxpayer's position in the proceedings before the court instituted or maintained by such taxpayer under section 7433 is frivolous or groundless the court may require the taxpayer to pay to the United States a penalty not in excess of $10,000."

26 U.S.C. § 7430(A)

"In any administrative or court proceeding which is brought by or against the United States in connection with the determination, collection, or refund of any tax, interest, or penalty under this title, the prevailing party [other than the United States or any creditor of the taxpayer involved] may [unless the United States establishes that the position of the United States in the proceeding was substantially justified] be awarded a judgment or a settlement for — (1) reasonable administrative costs incurred in connection with such administrative proceeding within the Internal Revenue Service, and (2) for reasonable litigation costs incurred in connection with such court proceeding."

26 U.S.C. § 7431(C)(3)

"[I]n the case of a plaintiff which is described in section 7430(c)(4)(A)(ii), reasonable attorneys fees, except that if the defendant is the United States, reasonable attorneys fees may be awarded only if the plaintiff is the prevailing party . . . ."

26 U.S.C. § 7434(B)

"In any action brought under subsection (a), upon a finding of liability on the part of the defendant, the defendant shall be liable to the plaintiff in an amount equal to greater of $5,000 or the sum of — (1) any actual damages . . . (2) the costs of the action, and (3) in the court's discretion, reasonable attorneys fees."

26 U.S.C. § 9501(D) (See Also, 30 U.S.C. § 932(A))

"Amounts in the Black Lung Disability Trust Fund shall be available, as provided by appropriations Acts, for . . . (7) the reimbursement of operators and insurers for amounts paid by such operators and insurers (other than amounts paid as penalties, interest, or attorney fees) at any time in satisfaction (in whole or in part of any claim denied . . . before March 1, 1978. . . ."

Judicial Discipline and Removal Reform Act of 1990

28 U.S.C. § 372(C)(16)

"Upon the request of a judge or magistrate whose conduct is the subject of a complaint under this subsection, the judicial council may, if the complaint has been finally dismissed under paragraph 6(C), recommend that the Director of the Administrative Office of the United States Courts award reimbursement, from funds appropriated to the Federal judiciary, for those reasonable expenses, including attorneys' fees, incurred by that judge or magistrate during the investigation which would not have been incurred but for the requirements of this subsection."

Independent Counsel Reauthorization Act of 1987 28 U.S.C. § 593(F)(1) (See Also, 5 U.S.C. § 288i(D))

"Upon the request of an individual who is the subject of an investigation conducted by an independent counsel pursuant to this chapter, the division of the court may, if no indictment is brought against such individual pursuant to that investigation, award reimbursement for those reasonable attorney's fees incurred by that individual . . . ."

Judicial Improvements and Access to Justice Act

28 U.S.C. § 655(E)

"In any trial de novo demanded under subsection (a) in which arbitration was done by consent of the parties, a district court may assess costs, as provided in section 1920 of this title, and reasonable attorney fees against the party demanding the trial de novo if — (1) such party fails to obtain a judgment, exclusive of interest and costs, in the court which is substantially more favorable to such party than the arbitration award, and (2) the court determines that the party's conduct in seeking a trail de novo was in bad faith."

Tucker Act

28 U.S.C. §§ 1346(A), 1491

See, 42 U.S.C. § 4654

Removal of Cases From State Court

28 U.S.C. § 1447(c) "An order remanding the case [back to state court, if the federal court lacks jurisdiction] may require payment of just costs and actual expenses, including attorney fees, incurred as a result of the removal." In *Martin v. Franklin Capital Corp.*, No. 04-1140 (U.S. Dec. 7, 2005), the Supreme Court held that, "[a]bsent unusual circumstances, courts may award attorney's fees under § 1447(c) only where the removing party lacked an objectively reasonable basis for seeking removal."

U.S. Court of Federal Claims — Patent and Copyright Cases

28 U.S.C. § 1498(A)

"Reasonable and entire compensation shall include the owner's reasonable costs, including reasonable fees for expert witnesses and attorneys, in pursuing the action if the owner is an independent inventor, a nonprofit organization, or an entity that had no more than 500 employees at any time during the 5-year period preceding the use or manufacture of the patented invention by or for the United States. Notwithstanding the preceding sentences, unless the action has been pending for more than 10 years from the time of filing to the time that the owner applies for such costs and fees, reasonable and entire compensation shall not include such costs and fees if the court finds that the position of the United States was substantially justified or that special circumstances make an award unjust."

Parental Kidnapping Prevention Act of 1980

28 U.S.C. § 1738A Note

"In furtherance of the purposes of section 1738A of title 28 . . . State courts are encouraged to . . . award to the person entitled to custody or visitation . . . attorneys' fees . .."

Jury System Improvements Act of 1978

28 U.S.C. § 1875(D)(2)

"In any action or proceeding under this section, the court may award a prevailing employee who brings such action by retained counsel a reasonable attorney's fee as part of the costs. The court may tax a defendant employer, as costs payable to the court, the attorney fees and expenses incurred on behalf of a prevailing employee, where such costs were expended pursuant to paragraph (1) of this subsection. The court may award a prevailing employer a reasonable attorney's fee as part of the costs only if the court determines that the action is frivolous, vexatious, or brought in bad faith."

Fees and Costs

28 U.S.C. § 1912

"Where a judgment is affirmed by the Supreme Court or a court of appeals, the court in its discretion may adjudge to the prevailing party just damages for his delay, and single or double costs." This provision has been interpreted to permit awards of attorneys' fees. *See*, 50 ALR Fed 652, 67 ALR Fed 319.

28 U.S.C. § 1927

"Any attorney or other person admitted to conduct cases in any court of the United States or any Territory thereof who so multiplies the proceedings in any case unreasonably and vexatiously may be required by the court to satisfy personally the excess costs, expenses, and attorneys' fees reasonably incurred because of such conduct."

Equal Access to Justice Act

28 U.S.C. § 2412 (See Also, 5 U.S.C. § 504)

"(a)(1) Except as otherwise specifically provided by statute, a judgment for costs, as enumerated in section 1920 of this title, but not including the fees and expenses of attorneys, may be awarded to the prevailing party in any action brought by or against the United States . . . ."

"(b) Unless expressly prohibited by statute, a court may award reasonable fees and expenses of attorneys, in addition to the costs which may be awarded pursuant to subsection (a), to the prevailing party in any civil action brought by or against the United States . . . . The United States shall be liable for such fees and expenses to the same extent that any other party would be liable under the common law or under the terms of any statute which specifically provides for such an award."

"(d)(1)(A) Except as otherwise specifically provided by statute, a court shall award to a prevailing party other than the United States fees and other expenses, in addition to any costs awarded pursuant to subsection (a), incurred by that party in any civil action (other than cases sounding in tort), including proceedings for judicial review of agency action, brought by or against the United States . . . unless the court finds that the position of the United States was substantially justified or that special circumstances make an award unjust."

"(d)(3) In awarding fees and other expenses under this subsection to a prevailing party in any action for judicial review of an adversary adjudication, as defined in subsection (b)(1)(C) of section 504 of title 5, United States Code, or an adversary adjudication subject to the Contract Disputes Act of 1978, the court shall include in that award fees and other expenses to the same extent authorized under subsection (a) of such section, unless the court finds that during such adversary adjudication the position of the United States was substantially justified, or that special circumstances make an award unjust."

"(e) The provisions of this section shall not apply to any costs, fees, and other expenses in connection with any proceedings to which section 7430 of the Internal Revenue Code of 1986 applies . . . ."

Civil Asset Forfeiture Reform Act of 2000

28 U.S.C. § 2465(B)(1)

"Except as provided in paragraph (2), in any civil proceeding to forfeit property under any provision of Federal law in which the claimant substantially prevails, the United States shall be liable for — (A) reasonable attorney fees and other litigation costs reasonably incurred by the claimant."

28 U.S.C. § 2465(B)(2)(C)

"If there are multiple claims to the same property, the United States shall not be liable for costs and attorneys fees associated with any such claim if the United States . . . (iii) does not cause the claimant to incur additional, reasonable costs or fees . . . ."

28 U.S.C. § 2465(B)(2)(D)

"If the court enters judgment in part for the claimant and in part for the Government, the court shall reduce the award of costs and attorney fees accordingly."

Federal Debt Collection Procedures Act of 1990

28 U.S.C. § 3205(C)(6)

"The court may award a reasonable attorney's fee to the United States and against the garnishee if the writ is not answered within the time specified therein . . . ."

Presidential and Executive Office Accountability Act (See Also, 3 U.S.C. § 435)

28 U.S.C. § 3905(A)

"If a covered employee, with respect to any claim under chapter 5 of title 3, or a qualified person with a disability, with respect to any claim under section 421 of title 3, is a prevailing party in any proceeding under section 1296 or section 1346(g), the court may award attorney's fees, expert fees, and other costs as would be appropriate if awarded under section 706(k) of the Civil Rights Act of 1964."

Assumption of Contractual Obligations Related to Transfers of Rights in Motion Pictures

28 U.S.C. § 4001(G)

"[T]he court in its discretion may allow recovery of full costs by or against any party and may also award a reasonable attorney's fees to the prevailing party as part of the costs."

Federal Rules of Civil Procedure 28 U.S.C. App. Rule 11(C)(2)

"[T]he sanction may consist of, or include . . . an order directing payment to the movant of some or all of the reasonable attorneys' fees and other expenses incurred as a direct result of the violation."

28 U.S.C. App. Rule 16(F)

"[T]he judge shall require the party or the attorney representing the party or both to pay the reasonable expenses incurred because of any noncompliance with this rule, including attorney's fees, unless the judge finds that the noncompliance was substantially justified or that other circumstances make an award of expenses unjust."

28 U.S.C. App. Rule 26(G)(3)

"If without substantial justification a certification is made in violation of the rule, the court, upon motion or upon its own initiative, shall impose upon the person who made the certification, the party on whose behalf the disclosure, request, response, or objection is made, or both, an appropriate sanction, which may include an order to pay the amount of the reasonable expenses incurred because of the violation, including a reasonable attorney's fee."

28 U.S.C. App. Rule 30(G)(1)

"If the party giving notice of a deposition fails to attend and proceed there with and another party attends in person or by attorney pursuant to the notice, the court may order the party giving notice to pay to such other party the reasonable expenses incurred by that party and that party's attorney in attending, including reasonable attorney's fees."

28 U.S.C. App. Rule 30(G)(2)

"If the party giving the notice of the taking of the deposition of a witness fails to serve a subpoena on him and the witness because of such failure does not attend, and if another party attends in person or by attorney because that party expects the deposition of that witness to be taken, the court may order the party giving the notice to pay to such other party the reasonable expenses incurred by that party and that party's attorney in attending, including reasonable attorney's fees."

28 U.S.C. App. Rule 37(A)(4)

"(A) If the motion is granted or if the disclosure or requested discovery is provided after the motion was filed, the court shall, after affording an opportunity to be heard require the party or deponent whose conduct necessitated the motion or the party or attorney advising such conduct or both of them to pay to the moving party the reasonable expenses incurred in making the motion, including attorney's fees, unless the court finds . . . ."

"(B) If the motion is denied, the court may enter any protective order authorized under Rule 26(c) and shall, after affording an opportunity to be heard, require the moving party or the attorney filing the motion or both of them to pay to the party or deponent who opposed the motion the reasonable expenses incurred in opposing the motion, including attorney's fees, unless the court finds . . . ."

28 U.S.C. App. Rule 37(B)(2)

"In lieu of any of the foregoing orders or in addition thereto, the court shall require the party failing to obey the order or the attorney advising that party or both to pay the reasonable expenses, including attorney's fees, caused by the failure, unless the court finds . . . ."

28 U.S.C. App. Rule 37(C)(1)

"In addition to requiring payment of reasonable expenses, including attorney's fees, caused by the failure, these sanctions may include . . . ."

28 U.S.C. App. Rule 37(C)(2)

"If a party fails to admit the genuineness of any document or the truth of any matter as requested under Rule 36, and if the party requesting the admissions thereafter proves the genuineness of the document or the truth of the matter, the requesting party may apply to the court for an order requiring the other party to pay the reasonable expenses incurred in making the proof, including reasonable attorney's fees . . . ."

28 U.S.C. App. Rule 37(D)

"In lieu of any order or in addition thereto, the court shall require the party failing to act or the attorney advising that party or both to pay the reasonable expenses, including attorney's fees, caused by the failure, unless the court finds that the failure was substantially justified or that other circumstances make an award of expenses unjust."

28 U.S.C. App. Rule 37(G)

"If a party or a party's attorney fails to participate in good faith in the development and submission of a discovery plan by agreement as required by Rule 26(f), the court may, after opportunity for hearing, require such party or attorney to pay to any other party the reasonable expenses, including attorney's fees, caused by the failure."

28 U.S.C. App. Rule 56(G)

"[T]he court shall forthwith order the party . . . to pay to the other party the amount of the reasonable expenses which the filing of the affidavits caused him to incur, including reasonable attorney's fees . . . ."

28 U.S.C. App. Rule 68

If, more than ten days before trial begins, a party defending a claim makes a settlement offer which is rejected by the offeree, and, "[i]f the judgment finally obtained by the offeree is not more favorable than the offer, the offeree must pay the costs incurred after the making of the offer." In *Marek v. Chesny*, 473 U.S. 1 (1985), the Supreme Court held that "costs" includes attorneys' fees in actions brought under statutes that allow attorneys' fees as part of the costs.

Federal Rules of Appellate Procedure

28 U.S.C. App. Rule 38

"If a court of appeals determines that an appeal is frivolous, it may, after a separately filed motion or notice from the court and reasonable opportunity to respond, award just damages and single or double costs to the appellee." This provision has been interpreted to permit awards of attorneys' fees. *See*, 50 ALR Fed 652, 67 ALR Fed 319.

Norris-Laguardia Act 29 U.S.C. § 107(E)

"No temporary restraining order or temporary injunction shall be issued except on condition that complainant shall first file an undertaking with adequate security in an amount to be fixed by the court sufficient to recompense those enjoined for any loss, expense, or damage caused by the improvident or erroneous issuance of such order or injunction, including all reasonable costs (together with a reasonable attorney's fee) . . . ."

Fair Labor Standards Act

29 U.S.C. § 216(B)

"The court in such action shall, in addition to any judgment awarded to the plaintiff or plaintiffs, allow a reasonable attorney's fee to be paid by the defendant, and costs of the action."

Labor-Management Reporting and Disclosure Act of 1959

29 U.S.C. § 431(C)

"The court in such action may, in its discretion, in addition to any judgment awarded to the plaintiff or plaintiffs, allow a reasonable attorney's fee to be paid by the defendant, and costs of the action."

29 U.S.C. § 501(B)

"The trial judge may allot a reasonable part of the recovery in any action under this subsection to pay the fees of counsel prosecuting the suit . . . ."

Age Discrimination in Employment Act of 1967

29 U.S.C. § 626(B)

This section incorporates the attorneys' fees provision of the Fair Labor Standards Act, 29 U.S.C. § 216(b).

Rehabilitation Act of 1973

29 U.S.C. § 794a(B)

"In any action or proceeding to enforce or charge a violation of a provision of this title, the court, in its discretion, may allow the prevailing party, other than the United States, a reasonable attorney's fee as part of the costs."

Employee Retirement Income Security Act

29 U.S.C. § 1132(G)

"In any action under this subchapter by a participant, beneficiary, or fiduciary, the court in its discretion may allow a reasonable attorney's fee and costs of the action to either party."

29 U.S.C. § 1305(B)(1)

"Each fund established under this section shall be credited with the appropriate portion of . . . (F) attorney's fees awarded to the corporation. . . ."

29 U.S.C. § 1370(E)

"(1) General Rule. — In any action brought under this section, the court in its discretion may award all or a portion of the costs and expenses incurred in connection with such action, including reasonable attorney's fees, to any party who prevails or substantially prevails in such action."

"(2) Exemption for Plans. — Notwithstanding the preceding provisions of this subsection, no plan shall be required in any action to pay any costs and expenses (including attorney's fees)."

29 U.S.C. § 1401(A)(2)

"The arbitrator may also award reasonable attorney's fees."

29 U.S.C. § 1451(E)

"In any action under this section, the court may award all or a portion of the costs and expenses incurred in connection with such action, including reasonable attorney's fees, to the prevailing party."

Employee Polygraph Protection Act of 1988

29 U.S.C. § 2005(C)(3)

"The court, in its discretion, may allow the prevailing party (other than the United States) reasonable costs, including attorney's fees."

Worker Adjustment and Retraining Notification Act

29 U.S.C. § 2104(A)(6)

"In any such suit, the court, in its discretion, may allow the prevailing party a reasonable attorney's fee as part of the costs."

Family and Medical Leave Act of 1993

29 U.S.C. § 2617(A)(3)

"The court in such an action shall, in addition to any judgment awarded to the plaintiff, allow a reasonable attorney's fee, reasonable expert witness fees, and other costs of the action to be paid by the defendant."

Federal Coal Mine Health and Safety Act of 1969

30 U.S.C. § 815(C)(3)

"Whenever any order is issued sustaining the complainant's charges under this subsection, a sum equal to the aggregate amount of all costs and expenses (including attorney's fees) . . . shall be assessed against the person committing such violation."

30 U.S.C. § 932(A) — Black Lung Benefits Act

(*see also*, 26 U.S.C. § 9501(d)(7)) This subsection incorporates 33 U.S.C. § 928(a) and (b).

30 U.S.C. § 938(C)

"Whenever an order is issued under this subsection granting relief to a miner at the request of such miner, a sum equal to the aggregate amount of all costs and expenses (including attorney's fees) . . . shall be assessed against the person committing the violation."

Surface Mining Control and Reclamation Act

30 U.S.C. § 1270(D)

"The court, in issuing any final order in any action brought pursuant to subsection (a) of this section, may award costs of litigation (including attorney and expert witness fees) to any party, whenever the court determines such award is appropriate."

30 U.S.C. § 1270(F)

"Any person who is injured in his person or property through the violation by any operator of any rule, regulation, order, or permit issued pursuant to this chapter may bring an action for damages (including reasonable attorney and expert witness fees). . . ."

30 U.S.C. § 1275(E)

"Whenever an order is issued under this section, or as a result of any administrative proceeding under this chapter, at the request of any person, a sum equal to the aggregate amount of all costs and expenses (including attorney fees) . . . may be assessed against either party. . . ."

30 U.S.C. § 1293(C)

"Whenever an order is issued under this section to abate any violation, at the request of the applicant a sum equal to the aggregate amount of all costs and expenses (including attorneys' fees) . . . shall be assessed against the persons committing the violation."

Deep Seabed Hard Mineral Resources Act

30 U.S.C. § 1427(C)

"The court, in issuing any final order in any action brought under subsection (a) of this section, may award costs of litigation, including reasonable attorney and expert witness fees, to any party whenever the court determines that such an award is appropriate."

General Accounting Office Act of 1980

31 U.S.C. § 755(B)

"If an officer, employee, applicant for employment, or employee of the Architect of the Capitol, the Botanic Garden, or the Senate Restaurants is the prevailing party in a proceeding under this section, and the decision is based on a finding of discrimination prohibited under section 732(f) of this title or section 312(e)(2) of the Architect of the Capitol Human Resources Act, attorney's fees may be allowed by the court in accordance with the standards prescribed under section 706(k) of the Civil Rights Act of 1964 [42 U.S.C. § 2000e-5(k)]."

Federal Acquisition Streamlining Act of 1994

31 U.S.C. § 3554(C)(1)

"If the Comptroller General determines that a solicitation for a contract or a proposed award or the award of a contract does not comply with a statute or regulation, the Comptroller General may recommend that the Federal agency conducting the procurement pay to an appropriate interested party the costs of — (A) filing and pursuing the protest, including reasonable attorneys' fees and consultant and expert witness fees . . . ."

31 U.S.C. § 3554(C)(2)

"No party . . . may be paid, pursuant to a recommendation made under the authority of paragraph (1) — (A) costs for consultant and expert witness fees that exceed the highest rate of compensation for expert witnesses paid by the Federal Government; or (B) costs for attorneys' fees that exceed $150 per hour unless the agency determines, based on the recommendation of the Comptroller General on a case by case basis, that an increase in the cost of living or a special factor, such as the limited availability of qualified attorneys for the proceedings involved, justifies a higher fee."

Debt Collection Improvement Act of 1996 31 U.S.C. § 3720D(E)(2)

"The court shall award attorneys' fees to a prevailing employee . . ."

31 U.S.C. § 3720D(F)(1)(B)

"The employer of an individual . . . shall be liable for any amount that the employer fails to withhold from wages due an employee following receipt by such employer of notice of the withholding order, plus attorneys' fees, costs, and, in the court's discretion, punitive damages."

False Claims Act

31 U.S.C. § 3730(D)(1)

"Any such person shall also receive an amount for reasonable expenses which the court finds to have been necessarily incurred, plus reasonable attorneys' fees and costs. All such expenses, fees, and costs shall be awarded against the defendant."

31 U.S.C. § 3730(D)(2)

"Such person shall also receive an amount for reasonable expenses which the court finds to have been necessarily incurred, plus reasonable attorneys' fees and costs. All such expenses, fees, and costs shall be awarded against the defendant."

31 U.S.C. § 3730(D)(4)

"[T]he court may award to the defendant its reasonable attorneys' fees and expenses if the defendant prevails in the action and the court finds that the claim of the person bringing the action was clearly frivolous, clearly vexatious, or brought primarily for purposes of harassment."

31 U.S.C. § 3730(G)

"In civil actions brought under this section by the United States, the provisions of section 2412(d) of title 28 shall apply."

31 U.S.C. § 3730(H)

"Such relief shall include . . . litigation costs and reasonable attorneys' fees."

Local Partnership Act

31 U.S.C. § 6716(C)

"In an action under this section, the court . . . to enforce compliance with section 6711(a) or (b), may allow a prevailing party (except the United States Government) a reasonable attorney's fee."

Longshore and Harbor Workers' Compensation Act

33 U.S.C. § 928(A)

"[T]here shall be awarded, in addition to the award of compensation, in a compensation order, a reasonable attorney's fee against the employer or carrier in an amount approved by the deputy commissioner, the Board, or court, as the case may be . . . ."

33 U.S.C. § 928(B)

"[A] reasonable attorney's fee based solely upon the difference between the amount awarded and the amount tendered or paid shall be awarded in addition to the amount of compensation. . . . If the claimant is successful in review proceedings before the Board or court in any such case an award may be made in favor of the claimant and against the employer or carrier for a reasonable attorney's fee for claimant's counsel . . . ."

33 U.S.C. § 933(E)(1)

"The employer shall retain an amount equal to — (A) the expenses incurred by him in respect to such proceedings or compromise (including a reasonable attorney's fee) as determined by the deputy commissioner or Board . . . ."

Water Pollution Prevention and Control Act

33 U.S.C. § 1319(G)(9)

"Any person who fails to pay on a timely basis the amount of an assessment of a civil penalty as described in the first sentence of this paragraph shall be required to pay, in addition to such amount and interest, attorneys fees and costs for collection proceedings . . . ."

33 U.S.C. § 1321(B)(6)(H)

"Any person who fails to pay on a timely basis the amount of an assessment of a civil penalty as described in the first sentence of this subparagraph shall be required to pay, in addition to such amount and interest, attorneys fees and costs for collection proceedings . . . ."

33 U.S.C. § 1365(D)

"The court, in issuing any final order in any action brought pursuant to this section, may award costs of litigation (including reasonable attorney and expert witness fees) to any prevailing or substantially prevailing party, whenever the court determines such award is appropriate."

33 U.S.C. § 1367(C)

"[A] sum equal to the aggregate amount of all costs and expenses (including the attorney's fees), as determined by the Secretary of Labor . . . shall be assessed against the person committing such violation."

33 U.S.C. § 1369(B)(3)

"In any judicial proceeding under this subsection, the court may award costs of litigation (including reasonable attorney and expert witness fees) to any prevailing or substantially prevailing party whenever it determines that such award is appropriate."

Marine Protection, Research, and Sanctuaries Act

33 U.S.C. § 1415(G)(4)

"The court, in issuing any final order in any suit brought pursuant to paragraph (1) of this subsection may award costs of litigation (including reasonable attorney and expert witness fees) to any party, whenever the court determines such award is appropriate."

Deepwater Ports Act

33 U.S.C. § 1515(D)

"The court, in issuing any final order in any action brought pursuant to subsection (a) of this section, may award costs of litigation (including reasonable attorney and expert witness fees) to any party, whenever the court determines such award is appropriate."

Act to Prevent Pollution from Ships

33 U.S.C. § 1910(D)

"The court, in issuing any final order in any action brought pursuant to this section, may award costs of litigation (including reasonable attorney and expert witness fees) to any party including the Federal Government."

Oil Pollution Act of 1990

33 U.S.C. § 2715(C)

"At the request of the Secretary, the Attorney General shall commence an action on behalf of the Fund to recover any compensation paid by the Fund to any claimant pursuant to this chapter, and all costs incurred by the Fund by reason of the claim, including . . . attorney's fees."

Patent Infringement

35 U.S.C. § 271(E)(4)

"The remedies prescribed by subparagraphs (A), (B), and (C) are the only remedies which may be granted by a court for an act of infringement described in paragraph (2), except that a court may award attorney fees under section 285."

35 U.S.C. § 285

"The court in exceptional cases may award reasonable attorney fees to the prevailing party."

35 U.S.C. § 296(B)

"Such remedies include . . . attorney fees under [35 U.S.C.] section 285 . . . ."

Amateur Sports Act of 1978 (Use of Olympic Symbols)

36 U.S.C. § 380(A)

This provision incorporates the attorneys' fees provision of the Trademark Act, 15 U.S.C. § 1117. *See*, *International Olympic Committee v. San Francisco Arts and Athletics*, 781 F.2d 733 (9th Cir. 1986), *rehearing denied*, 789 F.2d 1319 (9th Cir. 1986), *aff'd* (not on an attorneys' fees issue), 483 U.S. 522 (1987).

Uniformed Services Employment and Reemployment Rights Act of 1994 38 U.S.C. § 4323(C)(2)(B)

"In any action or proceeding to enforce a provision of this chapter by a person under subsection (a)(2) who obtained private counsel for such action or proceeding, the court may award any such person who prevails in such action or proceeding reasonable attorney fees, expert witness fees, and other litigation expenses."

Federal Acquisition Streamlining Act of 1994

41 U.S.C. § 265(C)(1)

"If the head of an executive agency determines that a contractor has subjected a person to a reprisal prohibited by subsection (a), the head of the executive agency may . . . (C) Order the contractor to pay the complainant an amount equal to the aggregate amount of all costs and expenses (including attorneys' fees and expert witnesses' fees) that were reasonably incurred . . . ."

Contract Disputes Act of 1978

41 U.S.C. §§ 601 Et Seq.

See, 28 U.S.C. § 2412(d)(3)

Public Readiness and Emergency Preparedness Act, P.L. 109-148 (2005), Division C (Limits on Liability for Pandemic Flu and Medical Biodefense Countermeasures)

42 U.S.C. § 247d-6d

"Whenever a district court of the United States determines that there has been a violation of Rule 11 of the Federal Rules of Civil Procedure in an action under subsection (d), the court shall impose upon the attorney, law firm, or parties that have violated Rule 11 or are responsible for the violation, an appropriate sanction, which may include an order to pay the other party or parties for the reasonable expenses incurred as a direct result of the filing of the pleading, motion, or other paper that is the subject of the violation, including a reasonable attorney's fee. Such sanction shall be sufficient to deter repetition of such conduct or comparable conduct by others similarly situated, and to compensate the party or parties injured by such conduct."

Safe Drinking Water Act

42 U.S.C. § 300h-2(C)(7)

"If any person fails to pay an assessment of a civil penalty . . . the Administrator may request the Attorney General to bring a civil action in an appropriate district court to recover the amount assessed (plus costs, attorneys' fees, and interest . . .)."

42 U.S.C. § 300j-8(D)

"The court, in issuing any final order in any action brought under subsection (a) of this section, may award costs of litigation (including reasonable attorney and expert witness fees) to any party whenever the court determines such an award is appropriate."

42 U.S.C. § 300j-9(I)(2)(B)(Ii)

"If such an order is issued, the Secretary, at the request of the complainant, shall assess against the person against whom the order is issued a sum equal to the aggregate amount of all costs and expenses (including attorneys' fees) reasonably incurred . . . ."

National Childhood Vaccine Injury Act of 1986 42 U.S.C. § 300aa-15(B)

"Compensation awarded under the [National Vaccine Injury Compensation] Program . . . may also include an amount, not to exceed a combined total of $30,000, for —(1) lost earnings . . . (2) pain and suffering . . . , and (3) reasonable attorneys' fees and costs (as provided in subsection (e) of this section."

42 U.S.C. § 300aa-15(E)

"(1) In awarding compensation on a petition filed under section 300aa-11 of this title the special master or court shall also award as part of such compensation an amount to cover — (A) reasonable attorneys' fees, and (B) other costs, incurred in any proceeding on such petition. If the judgment of the United States Court of Federal Claims on such a petition does not award compensation, the special master or court may award an amount of compensation to cover petitioner's reasonable attorneys' fees and other costs incurred in any proceeding on such petition if the special master or court determines that the petition was brought in good faith and there was a reasonable basis for the claim for which the petition was brought."

"(2) If the petitioner, before the effective date of this subpart, filed a civil action for damages for any vaccine-related injury or death for which compensation may be awarded under the Program, and petitioned under section 300aa-11(a)(5) of this title to have such action dismissed and to file a petition for compensation under the Program, in awarding compensation on such petition the special master or court may include an amount of compensation limited to the costs and expenses incurred by the petitioner and the attorney of the petitioner before the effective date of this subpart in preparing, filing, and prosecuting such civil action (including the reasonable value of the attorney's time if the civil action was filed under contingent fee arrangements)."

42 U.S.C. § 300aa-31(C)

"The court, in issuing any final order in any action under this section, may award costs of litigation (including reasonable attorney and expert witness fees) to any plaintiff who substantially prevails on one or more significant issues in the action."

Social Security Act

42 U.S.C. § 669a(C)

"In any action brought under paragraph (1), upon a finding of liability on the part of the defendant, the defendant shall be liable to the plaintiff in an amount equal to the sum of . . . (B) the costs (including attorney's fees) of the action."

42 U.S.C. § 673(A)(6)(A)

"For purposes of paragraph (1)(B)(i), the term 'non-recurring adoption expenses' means reasonable and necessary adoption fees, court costs, attorney fees, and other expenses which are directly related to the legal adoption of a child with special needs and which are not incurred in violation of State or Federal law."

42 U.S.C. § 1320a-8(B)(4)(G)

"The official conducting a hearing under this section may sanction a person, including any party or attorney . . . . Such sanction may include . . . ordering the party or attorney to pay the attorneys' fees and other costs caused by the failure or misconduct . . . ."

United States Housing Act of 1937

42 U.S.C. § 1437d(Q)(7)

"Appropriate relief that may be awarded by such district courts shall include reasonable attorney's fees and other litigation costs."

Civil Money Penalties Against Section 8 Owners

42 U.S.C. § 1437z-1(E)(1)(B)

"Any monetary judgment awarded in an action brought under this paragraph may, in the discretion of the court, include the attorney's fees and other expenses incurred by the United States in connection with the action."

Homeownership and Opportunity through HOPE Act

42 U.S.C. § 1437aaa-4(H) (See Also, 42 U.S.C. §§ 12875, 12895)

"The parties specified in the preceding sentence shall be entitled to reasonable attorney fees upon prevailing in any such judicial action."

Housing Act of 1949

42 U.S.C. § 1490s(B)(5)(A)

"The monetary judgment may, in the court's discretion, include the attorney's fees and other expenses incurred by the United States in connection with the action."

Voting Rights Act of 1965

42 U.S.C. § 19731(E)

"In any action or proceeding to enforce the voting guarantees of the fourteenth or fifteenth amendment, the court, in its discretion, may allow the prevailing party, other than the United States, a reasonable attorney's fee as part of the costs."

Voting Accessibility for the Elderly and Handicapped Act

42 U.S.C. § 1973ee-4(C)

"Notwithstanding any other provision of law, no award of attorney fees may be made with respect to an action under this section, except in any action brought to enforce the original judgment of the court."

National Voter Registration Act of 1993

42 U.S.C. § 1973gg-9(C)

"In a civil action under this section, the court may allow the prevailing party (other than the United States) reasonable attorney fees, including litigation expenses, and costs."

Civil Rights Attorney's Fees Awards Act of 1976

42 U.S.C. § 1988(B)

"In any action or proceeding to enforce a provision of sections 1981, 1981a, 1982, 1983, 1985, and 1986 of this title, title IX of Public Law 92-318, the Religious Freedom Restoration Act of 1993, the Religious Land Use and Institutionalized Persons Act of 2000, title VI of the Civil Rights Act of 1964, or section 40302 of the Violence Against Women Act of 1994, the court, in its discretion, may allow the prevailing party, other than the United States, a reasonable attorney's fee as part of the costs, except that in any action brought against a judicial officer for an act or omission taken in such officer's judicial capacity such officer shall not be held liable for any costs, including attorney's fees, unless such action was clearly in excess of such officer's jurisdiction."

Civil Rights Act of 1991

42 U.S.C. § 1988(C)

"In awarding an attorney's fee under subsection (b) of this section in any action or proceeding to enforce a provision of section 1981 or 1981a of this title, the court, in its discretion, may include expert fees as part of the attorney's fee."

Civil Rights of Institutionalized Persons Act

42 U.S.C. § 1997a(B)

"In any action commenced under this section, the court may allow the prevailing party, other than the United States, a reasonable attorney's fee against the United States as part of the costs."

42 U.S.C. § 1997c(D)

"In any action in which the United States joins as an intervenor under this section, the court may allow the prevailing party, other than the United States, a reasonable attorney's fee against the United States as part of the costs. . . ."

42 U.S.C. § 1997e(D)

"In an action brought by a prisoner who is confined to any jail, prison, or other correctional facility, in which attorney's fees are authorized under section 1988 of this title, such fees shall not be awarded, except to the extent that . . . ."

Civil Rights Act of 1964, Title II

42 U.S.C. § 2000a-3(B)

"In any action commenced pursuant to this subchapter, the court, in its discretion, may allow the prevailing party, other than the United States, a reasonable attorney's fee as part of the costs, and the United States shall be liable for costs the same as a private party."

Civil Rights Act of 1964, Title III

42 U.S.C. § 2000b-1

"In any action or proceeding under this subchapter the United States shall be liable for costs, including a reasonable attorney's fee, the same as a private party."

Civil Rights Act of 1964, Title VII

42 U.S.C. § 2000e-5(G)(2)(B)

"On a claim in which an individual proves a violation under section 703(m) [42 U.S.C. § 2000e-2(m)] and a respondent demonstrates that the respondent would have taken the same action in the absence of the impermissible motivating factor, the court — (i) may grant declaratory relief, injunctive relief (except as provided in clause (ii)), and attorney's fees and costs demonstrated to be directly attributable only to the pursuit of the claim under section 703(m) . . . ."

42 U.S.C. § 2000e-5(K)

"In any action or proceeding under this subchapter the court, in its discretion, may allow the prevailing party, other than the [Equal Employment Opportunity] Commission or the United States, a reasonable attorney's fee (including expert fees) as part of the costs, and the Commission and the United States shall be liable for costs the same as a private person."

Privacy Protection Act of 1980

42 U.S.C. § 2000aa-6(F)

"A person having a cause of action under this section shall be entitled to recover . . . such reasonable attorneys' fees and other litigation costs reasonably incurred as the court, in its discretion, may award . . . ."

Atomic Energy Act of 1954

42 U.S.C. § 2184

"If, in any action against such patent licensee, the court shall determine that the defendant is exercising such license, the measure of damages shall be the royalty fee determined pursuant to section 2187(c) of this title, together with such costs, interest and reasonable attorney's fees as may be fixed by the court. . . . If any such patent licensee shall fail to pay such royalty fee, the patentee may bring an action in any court of competent jurisdiction for such royalty fee, together with such costs, interest and reasonable attorney's fees as may be fixed by the court."

Legal Services Corporation Act

42 U.S.C. § 2996e(F)

"If an action is commenced by the Corporation or by a recipient and a final order is entered in favor of the defendant and against the Corporation or a recipient's plaintiff, the court shall, upon motion by the defendant and upon a finding by the court that the action was commenced or pursued for the sole purpose of harassment of the defendant or that the Corporation or a recipient's plaintiff maliciously abused legal process, enter an order (which shall be appealable before being made final) awarding reasonable costs and legal fees incurred by the defendant in defense of the action, except when in contravention of a State law, a rule or court, or a statute of general applicability. Any such costs and fees shall be directly paid by the Corporation."

Department of Housing and Urban Development Act

42 U.S.C. § 3537a(C)(5)

"The monetary judgment may, in the court's discretion, include the attorneys' fees and other expenses incurred by the United States in connection with the action."

42 U.S.C. § 3544(C)(3)

"Appropriate relief that may be ordered by such district courts shall include reasonable attorney's fees and other litigation costs."

42 U.S.C. § 3545(I)

"The monetary judgment may, in the court's discretion, include the attorneys' fees and other expenses incurred by the United States in connection with the action."

Fair Housing Act

42 U.S.C. § 3612(P)

"In any administrative proceeding brought under this section, or any court proceeding arising therefrom, or any civil action under section 812 [42 U.S.C. § 3612], the administrative law judge or the court, as the case may be, in its discretion, may allow the prevailing party, other than the United States, a reasonable attorney's fee and costs. The United States shall be liable for such fees and costs to the extent provided by section 504 of title 5, United States Code, or by section 2412 of title 28, United States Code."

42 U.S.C. § 3613(C)(2)

"In a civil action under subsection (a), the court, in its discretion, may allow the prevailing party, other than the United States, a reasonable attorney's fee and costs. The United States shall be liable for such fees and costs to the same extent as a private person."

42 U.S.C. § 3614(D)(2)

"In a civil action [by the Attorney General] under this section, the court, in its discretion, may allow the prevailing party, other than the United States, a reasonable attorney's fee and costs. The United States shall be liable for such fees and costs to the extent provided by section 2412 of title 28, United States Code."

Omnibus Crime Control and Safe Streets Act of 1968

42 U.S.C. § 3789d(C)(4)(B)

"In any civil action brought by a private person to enforce compliance with any provision of this subsection, the court may grant to a prevailing plaintiff reasonable attorney fees, unless the court determines that the lawsuit is frivolous, vexatious, brought for harassment purposes, or brought principally for the purpose of gaining attorney fees."

National Flood Insurance Act of 1968

42 U.S.C. § 4081(C)

"The Director of the Federal Emergency Management Agency . . . shall provide any such agent or broker with indemnification, including court costs and reasonable attorney fees, arising out of and caused by an error or omission on the part of the Federal Emergency Management Agency and its contractors."

Uniform Relocation Assistance and Real Property Acquisition Policies Act 42 U.S.C. § 4654

"(a) The Federal court . . . shall award . . . such a sum as will in the opinion of the court reimburse such owner for his reasonable costs, disbursements, and expenses, including reasonable attorney, appraisal, and engineering fees, actually incurred because of the condemnation proceedings, if . . . ."

"(c) The court rendering a judgment for the plaintiff in a proceeding brought under section 1346(a)(2) or 1491 of Title 28, awarding compensation for the taking of property by a Federal agency, or the Attorney General effecting a settlement of any such proceeding, shall determine and award or allow to such plaintiff . . . reasonable attorney, appraisal, and engineering fees, actually incurred because of such proceeding."

Noise Control Act of 1972

42 U.S.C. § 4911(D)

"The court, in issuing any final order in any action brought pursuant to subsection (a) of this section, may award costs of litigation (including reasonable attorney and expert witness fees) to any party, whenever the court determines such an award is appropriate."

National Manufactured Housing Construction and Safety Standards Act

42 U.S.C. § 5412(B)

"[T]he person bringing the action shall also be entitled to recover any damage sustained by him, as well as all court costs plus reasonable attorneys' fees."

Energy Reorganization Act of 1974

42 U.S.C. § 5851(B)(2)(B)

"If an order is issued under this paragraph, the Secretary, at the request of the complainant shall assess against the person against whom the order is issued a sum equal to the aggregate amount of all costs and expenses (including attorneys' and expert witness fees) reasonably incurred . . . ."

42 U.S.C. § 5851(E)(2)

"The court, in issuing any final order under this subsection, may award costs of litigation (including reasonable attorney and expert witness fees) to any party whenever the court determines such award is appropriate."

Age Discrimination Act of 1975

42 U.S.C. § 6104(E)(1)

"Such interested person may elect, by a demand for relief in his complaint, to recover reasonable attorney's fees, in which case the court shall award the costs of the suit, including a reasonable attorney's fee, to the prevailing plaintiff."

National Oil Heat Research Alliance Act of 2000

42 U.S.C. § 6201 Note (P.L. 106-469, § 712(E))

"(1) Meritorious Case — In a case in Federal court in which the court grants a public utility injunctive relief under subsection (d), the public utility shall be entitled to recover an attorney's fee from the Alliance and any qualified State association undertaking the consumer education activity with respect to which a complaint under this section is made.

(2) Nonmeritorious Case — In any case under subsection (d) in which the court determines a complaint under subsection (b) to be frivolous and without merit, the prevailing party shall be entitled to recover an attorney's fee.

Energy Policy and Conservation Act

42 U.S.C. § 6305(D)

"The court, in issuing any final order in any action brought pursuant to subsection (a) of this section, may award costs of litigation (including reasonable attorney and expert witness fees) to any party, whenever the court determines such award is appropriate."

Solid Waste Disposal Act

42 U.S.C. § 6971(C)

"[A] sum equal to the aggregate amount of all costs and expenses (including attorney's fees) . . . shall be assessed against the person committing such violation."

42 U.S.C. § 6972(E)

"The court, in issuing any final order in any action brought pursuant to this section or section 7006 [42 U.S.C. § 6976], may award costs of litigation (including reasonable attorney and expert witness fees) to the prevailing or substantially prevailing party, whenever the court determines that such award is appropriate."

Clean Air Act

42 U.S.C. § 7413(B)

"In the case of any action brought by the Administrator under this subsection, the court may award costs of litigation (including reasonable attorney and expert witness fees) to the party or parties against whom such action was brought in any case where the court finds that such action was unreasonable."

42 U.S.C. § 7524(C)(6)

"Any person who fails to pay on a timely basis the amount of an assessment of a civil penalty as described in the first sentence of this paragraph shall be required to pay, in addition to that amount and interest, the United States' enforcement expenses, including attorneys fees and costs for collection proceedings . . . ."

42 U.S.C. § 7604(D)

"The court, in issuing any final order in any action brought pursuant to subsection (a) of this section, may award costs of litigation (including reasonable attorney and expert witness fees) to any party, whenever the court determines such award is appropriate."

42 U.S.C. § 7607(F)

"In any judicial proceeding under this section, the court may award costs of litigation (including reasonable attorney and expert witness fees) whenever it determines that such award is appropriate."

42 U.S.C. § 7622(B)(2)(B)

"If an order is issued under this paragraph, the Secretary, at the request of the complainant, shall assess against the person against whom the order is issued a sum equal to the aggregate amount of costs and expenses (including attorneys' and expert witness fees) reasonably incurred . . . ."

42 U.S.C. § 7622(E)(2)

"The court, in issuing any final order under this subsection, may award costs of litigation (including reasonable attorney and expert witness fees) to any party whenever the court determines such award is appropriate."

Power Plant and Industrial Fuel Use Act

42 U.S.C. § 8435(D)

"The court, in issuing any final order in any action brought under subsection (a) of this section, may award costs of litigation (including reasonable attorney and expert witness fees) to any party, whenever the court determines such award is appropriate."

Ocean Thermal Energy Conservation Act of 1980

42 U.S.C. § 9124(D)

"The court, in issuing any final order in any action brought pursuant to subsection (a) of this section, may award costs of litigation (including reasonable attorney and expert witness fees) to any party whenever the court determines that such an award is appropriate."

Comprehensive Environmental Response, Compensation, and Liability Act

42 U.S.C. § 9606(B)(2)(E)

"Reimbursement awarded by a court under subparagraph (C) or (D) may include appropriate costs, fees, and other expenses in accordance with subsections (a) and (d) of section 2412 of title 28 of the United States Code."

42 U.S.C. § 9610(C)

"Whenever an order is issued under this section to abate such violation, at the request of the applicant a sum equal to the aggregate amount of all costs and expenses (including the attorney's fees) . . . shall be assessed against the person committing such violation."

42 U.S.C. § 9612(C)(3)

"Upon the request of the President, the Attorney General shall commence an action on behalf of the [Hazardous Substance Response] Fund to recover any compensation paid by the Fund to any claimant pursuant to this subchapter, and, without regard to any limitation of liability, all interest, administrative and adjudicative costs, and attorney's fees incurred by the Fund by reason of the claim. . . ."

42 U.S.C. § 9622(H)(3)

"If any person fails to pay a claim that has been settled under this subsection, the department or agency head shall request the Attorney General to bring a civil action in an appropriate district court to recover the amount of such claim plus costs, attorneys' fees, and interest from the date of the settlement."

42 U.S.C. § 9659(F)

"The court, in issuing any final order in any action brought pursuant to this section, may award costs of litigation (including reasonable attorney and expert witness fees) to the prevailing or the substantially prevailing party whenever the court determines such an award is appropriate."

42 U.S.C. § 11046(F)

"The court, in issuing any final order in any action brought pursuant to this section, may award costs of litigation (including reasonable attorney and expert witness fees) to the prevailing or the substantially prevailing party whenever the court determines such an award is appropriate."

Health Care Quality Improvement Act of 1986

42 U.S.C. § 11113

"[T]he court shall award to a substantially prevailing party defending against any such claim the cost of the suit attributable to such claim, including a reasonable attorney's fee, if the claim, or the claimant's conduct during the litigation of the claim, was frivolous, unreasonable, without foundation, or in bad faith. . . ."

International Child Abduction Remedies Act

42 U.S.C. § 11607(B)(3)

"Any court ordering the return of a child pursuant to an action brought under section 11603 of this title shall order the respondent to pay necessary expenses incurred by or on behalf of the petitioner, including court costs, legal fees . . . unless the respondent establishes that such order would be clearly inappropriate."

Americans with Disabilities Act

42 U.S.C. § 12205

"In any action or administrative proceeding commenced pursuant to this Act, the court or agency, in its discretion, may allow the prevailing party, other than the United States, a reasonable attorney's fee, including litigation expenses, and costs, and the United States shall be liable for the foregoing the same as a private individual."

National and Community Service Act of 1990

42 U.S.C. § 12636(F)(4)((D)(Ii)

"If a participant, labor organization, or other interested individual described in paragraph (1) prevails under a binding arbitration proceeding, the State or local applicant described in paragraph (1) that is a party to such grievance shall pay the total cost of such proceeding and the attorneys' fees of such participant, labor organization, or individual, as the case may be."

Homeownership and Opportunity through HOPE Act 42 U.S.C. § 12875(E) (See Also, 42 U.S.C. § 1437aaa-4(H))

"The parties specified in the preceding sentence shall be entitled to reasonable attorney fees upon prevailing in any such judicial action."

42 U.S.C. § 12895(D)

"The parties specified in the preceding sentence shall be entitled to reasonable attorney fees upon prevailing in any such judicial action."

Outer Continental Shelf Lands Act

43 U.S.C. § 1349(A)(5) (See Also, 43 U.S.C. § 1845(E))

"A court, in issuing any final order in any action brought pursuant to subsection (a)(1) or subsection (c) of this section, may award costs of litigation, including reasonable attorney and expert witness fees, to any party, whenever such court determines such award is appropriate."

43 U.S.C. § 1349(B)(2)

"Any resident of the United States who is injured in any manner through the failure of any operator to comply with any rule, regulation, order, or permit issued pursuant to this Act may bring an action for damages (including reasonable attorney fee and expert witness fees). . . ."

Alaska Native Claims Settlement Act

43 U.S.C. § 1619(B)

"A claim for attorney and consultant fees and out-of-pocket expenses may be submitted to the Chief Commissioner of the United States Court of Claims for services rendered before December 18, 1971 to any Native tribe. . . ."

Alaska National Interest Lands Conservation Act

43 U.S.C. § 1631(C)(3) (See Also, 16 U.S.C. § 3117(A))

"If title to land conveyed to a Native Corporation pursuant to the Alaska Native Claims Settlement Act or this Act which underlies a lake, river, or stream is challenged in a court of competent jurisdiction and such court determines that such land is owned by the Native Corporation, the Native Corporation shall be awarded a money judgment against the plaintiffs in an amount equal to its costs and attorney's fees, including costs and attorney's fees incurred on appeal."

Outer Continental Shelf Lands Act

43 U.S.C. § 1845(E) (See Also, 43 U.S.C. § 1349)

"If the decision of the Secretary under subsection (d) of this section is in favor of the commercial fisherman filing the claim, the Secretary, as a part of the amount awarded, shall include reasonable claim preparation fees and reasonable attorney's fees, if any, incurred by the claimant in pursuing the claim."

Railway Labor Act

45 U.S.C. § 153(P)

"If the petitioner shall finally prevail he shall be allowed a reasonable attorney's fee to be taxed and collected as part of the costs of the suit."

Commercial Instruments and Maritime Liens

46 U.S.C. § 31304(B)

"If the plaintiff prevails, the court shall award costs and attorney fees to the plaintiff."

46 U.S.C. § 31325(D)(3)

"If the plaintiff prevails, the court may award costs and attorney fees to the plaintiff."

Merchant Marine Act of 1936

46 U.S.C. App. § 1227

"Any person who shall be injured in his business or property by reason of anything forbidden by this section may sue therefor . . . and shall recover threefold the damages by him sustained, and the cost of suit, including a reasonable attorney's fee."

Shipping Act of 1984

46 U.S.C. App. § 1710(H)(2)

"A defendant that prevails in a suit under this paragraph shall be allowed reasonable attorney's fees to be assessed and collected as part of the costs of the suit."

Communications Act of 1934

47 U.S.C. § 206

"[S]uch common carrier shall be liable to the person or persons injured thereby for . . . a reasonable counsel or attorney's fee. . . ."

Satellite Home Viewer Improvement Act of 1999

47 U.S.C. § 325(E)(8)(B)(Iii)

"If the Commission determines that a satellite carrier has retransmitted the television broadcast station to at least one person in the local market of such station and has failed to meet its burden of proving one of the defenses under paragraph (4) with respect to such retransmission, the Commission shall be required to . . . issue an order, within 45 days after the filing of the complaint, containing . . . an award to the complainant of that complainant's costs and reasonable attorney's fees."

47 U.S.C. § 407

"If the petitioner shall finally prevail, he shall be allowed a reasonable attorney fee to be fixed by the court."

Cable Communications Policy Act of 1984

47 U.S.C. § 553(C)(2)

"The court may . . . direct the recovery of full costs, including awarding reasonable attorneys' fees to an aggrieved party who prevails."

47 U.S.C. § 605(E)(3)(B)

"The court may . . . direct the recovery of full costs, including awarding reasonable attorneys' fees to an aggrieved party who prevails."

Alien Owners of Land

48 U.S.C. § 1506

"[S]uch suit shall be dismissed on payment of costs and a reasonable attorney fee to be fixed by the court."

ICC Termination Act of 1995 49 U.S.C. § 11704(D)(3)

"The district court shall award a reasonable attorney's fee as a part of the damages for which a rail carrier if found liable under this subsection. The district court shall tax and collect that fee as a part of the costs of the action."

49 U.S.C. § 11707(B)

"The court shall award a reasonable attorney's fee to the plaintiff in a judgment against the defendant rail carrier under subsection (a) of this section. The court shall tax and collect that fee as a part of the costs of the action."

49 U.S.C. § 14704(E)

"The district court shall award a reasonable attorney's fee under this section. The district court shall tax and collect that fee as a part of the costs of the action."

49 U.S.C. § 14707(C)

"In a civil action under subsection (a), the court may determine the amount of and award a reasonable attorney's fee to the prevailing party. That fee is in addition to costs allowable under the Federal Rules of Civil Procedure."

49 U.S.C. § 14708(D)

"In any court action to resolve a dispute between a shipper of household goods and a carrier providing transportation or service subject to jurisdiction under subchapter I or III of chapter 135 concerning the transportation of household goods by such carrier, the shipper shall be awarded reasonable attorney's fees if . . . ."

49 U.S.C. § 14708(E)

"In any court action to resolve a dispute between a shipper of household goods and a carrier providing transportation, or service subject to jurisdiction under subchapter I or III of chapter 135 concerning the transportation of household goods by such carrier, such carrier may be awarded reasonable attorney's fees by the court only if the shipper brought such action in bad faith . . . ."

49 U.S.C. § 15904(D)(2)

"The district court shall award a reasonable attorney's fee as part of the damages for which a carrier is found liable under this subsection. The district court shall tax and collect that fee as a part of the costs of the action."

Transportation

49 U.S.C. § 30116(C) (Motor Vehicle Safety)

"The action may be brought . . . to recover damages, court costs, and a reasonable attorney's fee."

49 U.S.C. § 31105(B)(3)(B) (Commercial Motor Vehicle Safety)

"[T]he Secretary may assess against the person against whom the order is issued the costs (including attorney's fees) reasonably incurred by the complainant in bringing the complaint."

49 U.S.C. § 32508 (Bumper Standards)

"The court shall award costs and a reasonable attorney's fee to the owner when a judgment is entered for the owner."

49 U.S.C. § 32710(B) (Odometers)

"The court shall award costs and a reasonable attorney's fee to the person when a judgment is entered for that person."

49 U.S.C. § 42121(B)(3)(C) (Whistleblower Protection)

"If the Secretary of Labor finds that a complaint under paragraph (1) is frivolous or has been brought in bad faith, the Secretary of Labor may award to the prevailing employer a reasonable attorney's fee not exceeding $ 1,000."

49 U.S.C. § 42121(B)(6)(B)

"The court, in issuing any final order under this paragraph, may award costs of litigation (including reasonable attorney and expert witness fees) to any party whenever the court determines such award is appropriate."

49 U.S.C. § 60121(B) (Pipelines)

"The court may award costs, reasonable expert witness fees, and a reasonable attorney's fee to a prevailing plaintiff in an action under this section. The court may award costs to a prevailing defendant when the action is unreasonable, frivolous, or meritless."

49 U.S.C. § 80114(A) (Lost, Stolen, and Destroyed Negotiable Bills)

"The court may order payment of reasonable costs and attorney's fees to the carrier."

Foreign Intelligence Surveillance Act of 1978

50 U.S.C. § 1810

"An aggrieved person . . . shall be entitled to recover . . . reasonable attorney's fees . . . ."

50 U.S.C. § 1828

"An aggrieved person . . . whose premises, property, information, or material has been subjected to a physical search within the United States, or about whom information obtained by such a physical search has been disclosed or used in violation of section 307 shall have a cause of action against any person who committed such violation and shall be entitled to recover — (1) actual damages . . . ; (2) punitive damages; and (3) reasonable attorney's fees and other investigative and litigation costs reasonably incurred."

Bibliography of Congressional Publications

Committee Prints and Reports

On the Civil Rights Attorney's Fees Awards Act of 1976

House: Committee on the Judiciary. Civil Rights Attorney's Fees Awards Act of 1976; report to accompany H.R. 15460. Report No. 94-1558. 3 p. (94th Cong., 2d Sess.)

Senate: Committee on the Judiciary. Civil Rights Attorney's Fees Awards Act of 1976; report to accompany S. 2278. Report No. 94-1011. 7 p. (94th Cong., 2d Sess.)

Senate: Committee on the Judiciary. Subcommittee on Constitutional Rights. Civil Rights Attorney's Fees Awards Act of 1976; Source Book: Legislative History, Texts, and Other Documents. Committee Print. 313 p. (94th Cong., 2d Sess.)

On the Equal Access to Justice Act

House: Conference Report. Small Business Assistance and Reimbursement for Certain Fees; report to accompany H.R. 5612. Report No. 96-1434. 29 p.(96th Cong., 2d Sess.)

House: Committee on the Judiciary. Equal Access to Justice Act; report to accompany S. 265. Report No. 96-1418. 30 p. (96th Cong., 2d Sess.)

House: Committee on Small Business. Small Business Equal Access to Justice Act; report to accompany H.R. 6429. Report No. 96-1005, Part 1. 29 p. (96th Cong., lst Sess.)

Senate: Committee on the Judiciary. Equal Access to Justice Act; report to accompany S. 265. Report No. 96-253. 28 p. (96th Cong., lst Sess.)

Senate: Committee on the Judiciary. Department of Justice Authorization Act, Fiscal Year 1981; report to accompany S. 2377 (incorporates S. 265).

Report No. 96-786. 34 p. (96th Cong., 2d Sess.)

House: Committee on the Judiciary. Equal Access to Justice Act Amendments; report to accompany H.R. 5479. Report No. 98-992. 26 p. (98th Cong., 2d Sess.)

Senate: Committee on the Judiciary. Equal Access to Justice Act; report to accompany S. 919. Report No. 98-586. 39 p. (98th Cong., 2d Sess.)

House: Committee on the Judiciary. Equal Access to Justice Act Amendments; report to accompany H.R. 2378. Report No. 99-120. 30 p.; Part 2. 7 p. (99th Cong., lst Sess.)

On Awards of Attorneys' Fees in Tax Cases

House: Committee on Ways and Means. Subcommittee on Select Revenue Measures. Description of Laws and Bills Relating to Awards of Attorney's Fees in Tax Cases (Public Law 96-481, H.R. 1095, H.R. 2555, and H.R. 3262). Joint Committee Print. 10 p. (97th Cong., lst Sess.)

Senate: Committee on Finance. Subcommittee on Oversight of the Internal Revenue Service. Description of S. 1444 Relating to Awards of Attorney's Fees in Tax Cases. Joint Committee Print. 4 p. (95th Cong., lst Sess.)

On the Handicapped Children's Protection Act of 1985

House: Committee on Education and Labor. Handicapped Children's Protection Act of 1985; report to accompany H.R. 1523. Report No. 99-296. 18 p. (99th Cong., lst Sess.)

Senate: Committee on Labor and Human Resources. Handicapped Children's Protection Act of 1985; report to accompany S. 415. Report No. 99-112.18 p. (99th Cong., lst Sess.)

House: Conference Report. Handicapped Children's Protection Act of 1986; report to accompany S. 415. Report No. 99-687. 8 p. (99th Cong., 2d Sess.)

On Funding of Participants in Agency Proceedings

House: Committee on the Judiciary. Regulation Reform Act of 1980; report together with supplemental and dissenting views to accompany H.R. 3263. Report No. 96-1393. (96th Cong., 2d Sess.)

Senate: Committee on Commerce. Agency Comments on the Payment of Reasonable Fees for Public Participation in Agency Proceedings. Committee Print. 75 p. (95th Cong., lst Sess.)

Senate: Committee on Governmental Affairs. Study of Federal Regulation, Vol. III. Public Participation in Regulatory Agency Proceedings. Document No. 95-71. 162 p. (95th Cong., lst Sess.)

Senate: Committee on the Judiciary. Participation in Government Proceedings Act of 1976; report together with minority views to accompany S. 2715. Report No. 94-863. 52 p. (94th Cong., 2d Sess.)

Senate: Committee on Governmental Affairs and Committee on the Judiciary. Reform of Federal Regulation; report together with additional views to accompany S. 262. Report No. 96-1018, Part 1. (96th Cong., 2d Sess.)

On Attorneys' Fees Limitations

House: Committee on Veterans' Affairs. Legislative History of the Ten Dollar Attorney Fee Limitation in Claims for Veterans' Benefits. House Committee Print No. 8. 16 p. (100th Cong., 1st Sess.)

On Attorney Accountability Act of 1995

House: Committee on the Judiciary. Attorney Accountability Act of 1995. House Report 104-62. 34 p. (104th Cong., 1st Sess.)

Committee Hearings

House: Committee on Education and Labor. Subcommittee on Select Education.

Handicapped Children's Protection Act. Hearings on H.R. 1523. 67 p. Mar. 12, 1985 (99th Cong., lst Sess.)

House: Committee on the Judiciary. Subcommittee on Administrative Law and Governmental Relations. Public Participation in Agency Proceedings.

Hearings on H.R. 3361 and related bills. 728 p. Mar. 30, 31; Apr. 1, 27 and 28, 1977 (95th Cong., lst Sess.)

House: Committee on the Judiciary. Subcommittee on Administrative Law and Governmental Relations. Waiver to Obtain Attorney Fee Reimbursement [to Anne Burford]. 55 p. Mar. 20, 1986 (99th Cong., 2d Sess.)

House: Committee on the Judiciary. Subcommittee on Courts and Intellectual Property. Attorney Accountability. 294 p. Feb. 6 and 10, 1995 (104th Cong., lst Sess.)

House: Committee on the Judiciary. Subcommittee on Courts, Civil Liberties, and the Administration of Justice. Awarding of Attorneys' Fees. 426 p. Oct. 6, 8, and Dec. 3, 1975 (94th Cong., lst Sess.)

House: Committee on the Judiciary. Subcommittee on Courts, Civil Liberties, and the Administration of Justice. The Awarding of Attorneys' Fees in Federal Courts. 337 p. Nov. 16 and 17, 1977; Apr. 26 and 27, 1978 (95th Cong., lst and 2d Sess.)

House: Committee on the Judiciary. Subcommittee on Courts, Civil Liberties and the Administration of Justice. Awards of Attorneys' Fees Against the Federal Government. Hearings on S. 265. 629 p. May 20 and June 24, 1980 (96th Cong., 2d Sess.)

House: Committee on the Judiciary. Subcommittee on Courts, Civil Liberties, and the Administration of Justice. Implementation of the Equal Access to Justice Act. 302 p. Mar. 18 and Apr. 1, 1982 (97th Cong., 2d Sess.)

House: Committee on the Judiciary. Subcommittee on Courts, Civil Liberties, and the Administration of Justice. Equal Access to Justice Act Amendments.

Hearings on H.R. 5059. 413 p. Mar. 14, 1984 (98th Cong., 2d Sess.)

House: Committee on the Judiciary. Subcommittee on Courts, Civil Liberties, and the Administration of Justice. Equal Access to Justice Act Amendments.

Hearings on H.R. 2223. 122 p. Apr. 30, 1985 (99th Cong., lst Sess.)

House: Committee on the Judiciary. Subcommittee on Courts, Civil Liberties, and the Administration of Justice. Rules Enabling Act of 1985 [Rule 68 of the Federal Rules of Civil Procedure]. Hearings on H.R. 2633 and H.R. 3550. 342 p. June 6, 1985 (99th Cong., lst Sess.)

House: Committee on the Judiciary. Subcommittee on Intellectual Property and Judicial Administration. Judicial Immunity Legislation. Hearings on H.R. 3206 and H.R. 671. 141 p. October 3, 1991 (102d Cong., lst Sess.)

House: Committee on Small Business. Subcommittee on SBA and SBIC Authority and General Small Business Problems. Judicial Access/Court Costs — H.R. 5103 and H.R. 6429. 335 p. Apr. 17, 23, and May 1, 1980 (96th Cong., 2d Sess.)

House: Committee on Ways and Means. Subcommittee on Select Revenue Measures. Payment of Attorneys' Fees in Tax Litigation. Hearings on H.R. 4584 and Similar Bills. 111 p. Oct. 6, 1980 (96th Cong., 2d Sess.)

House: Committee on Ways and Means. Subcommittee on Select Revenue Measures. Payment of Attorneys' Fees in Tax Litigation. 100 p. Sept. 28, 1981 (97th Cong., lst Sess.)

House: Committee on Ways and Means. Subcommittee on Social Security. Attorneys' Fees in Social Security Disability Cases. 299 p. May 13, 1987 (100th Cong., 1st Sess.)

House: Committee on Ways and Means. Subcommittee on Social Security. Processing of Attorney Fees by the Social Security Administration. 93 p. June 14, 2000 (106th Cong., 2d Sess.)

House: Committee on Ways and Means. Subcommittee on Select Revenue Measures. Award of Attorney's Fees in Tax Cases. 75 p. Apr. 25, 1985 (99th Cong., lst Sess.)

Senate: Committee on Finance. Subcommittee on Oversight of the Internal Revenue Service. Taxpayer Protection and Reimbursement Act. Hearings on S. 1444. 192 p. July 19, 1979 (96th Cong., lst Sess.)

Senate: Committee on Finance. Subcommittee on Oversight of the Internal Revenue Service. Recovery of Attorney's Fees in Tax Cases. Hearings on S. 752 and S. 1673. 173 p. Oct. 19, 1981 (97th Cong., lst Sess.)

Senate: Committee on the Judiciary. Subcommittee on Administrative Practice and Procedure. Public Participation in Federal Agency Proceedings. Hearings on S. 2715. 905 p. Jan. 30 and Feb. 6, 1976 (94th Cong., 2d Sess.)

Senate: Committee on the Judiciary. Subcommittee on Administrative Practice and Procedure. Public Participation in Federal Agency Proceedings Act of 1977. Hearings on S. 270. Part 1: 745 p. Feb. 3, 11, and May 9, 1977. Part 2: 425 p. June 14 and 21, 1977 (95th Cong., lst Sess.)

Senate: Committee on the Judiciary. Subcommittee on Agency Administration. Equal Access to Justice Act. 264 p. December 9, 1982 (97th Cong., 2d Sess.)

Senate: Committee on the Judiciary. Subcommittee on the Constitution. HUD Attorney's Fees. Hearings on S. 571. 117 p. Apr. 10, 1978 (95th Cong., 2d Sess.)

Senate: Committee on the Judiciary. Subcommittee on the Constitution. Attorney's Fees Awards. Hearings on S. 585. 127 p. Mar. 1, 1982 (97th Cong., 2d Sess.)

Senate: Committee on the Judiciary. Subcommittee on the Constitution. The Legal Fee Equity Act. Hearings on S. 2802. 758 p. Sept. 11, 1984 (98th Cong., 2d Sess.)

Senate: Committee on the Judiciary. Subcommittee on the Constitution. Legal Fees Equity Act. Hearings on S. 1580, S. 1794, and S. 1795. 522 p. Oct. 8 and 29, 1985 (99th Cong., lst Sess.)

Senate: Committee on the Judiciary. Subcommittee on Courts and Administrative Practice. A Judicial Immunity. Hearings on S. 1482, S. 1512, and S. 1515. 291 p. Feb. 26, 1988 (100th Cong., 2d Sess.)

Senate: Committee on the Judiciary. Subcommittee on Improvements in Judicial Machinery. Equal Access to Courts. Hearings on S. 2354. 103 p. Mar. 13, 1978 (95th Cong., 2d Sess.)

Senate: Committee on the Judiciary. Subcommittee on Improvements in Judicial Machinery. Equal Access to Justice Act of 1979. Hearings on S. 265. 197 p. Apr. 19-21, 1979 (96th Cong., lst Sess.)

Senate: Committee on the Judiciary. Subcommittee on Representation of Citizen Interests. The Effect of Legal Fees on the Adequacy of Representation. 1778 p. Sept. 19 and 20; Oct. 1, 2, 4, and 5, 1973 (93d Cong., lst Sess.)

Senate: Committee on Labor and Human Resources. Subcommittee on the Handicapped. Handicapped Children's Protection Act of 1985. Hearings on S. 415. 115 p. May 16, 1986 (99th Cong., lst Sess.)

House and Senate: Joint Hearing before the Committees on Veterans' Affairs. Issues Arising In Connection with NARS v. Turnage. 424 p. Mar. 17, 1987 (100th Cong., 1st Sess.)

REFERENCES

[1] Key Tronic Corp. v. United States, 511 U.S. 809, 814-815 (1994) (holding that the phrase "any other necessary costs of response incurred by any other person" in § 107 of the Comprehensive Environmental Response, Compensation, and Liability Act, 42 U.S.C. § 9607, does not include attorneys' fees).

[2] See, CRS Report 92-237, Attorneys' Fees: The Bush Administration Proposal to Adopt the English Rule by Henry Cohen (archived, available from author). CRS Report 95-27, Common Sense Legal Reforms Act of 1995: Title I — Civil Justice Reform (Attorneys' Fees, Products Liability, Etc.), by Henry Cohen (archived, available from author). The Attorney Accountability Act of 1995, H.R. 988, 104th Cong., which grew out of the Common Sense Legal Reforms Act of 1995 (which was part of the House Republicans' "Contract With America"), passed the House. It would have required, among other things, the payment of attorneys' fees in connection with rejected settlement offers in diversity cases.

[3] The Supreme Court has noted a third exception: "a court may assess attorney's fees as a sanction for the 'willful disobedience of a court order.'" Chambers v. NASCO, Inc., 501 U.S. 32, 45 (1991). However, this may be viewed as falling within the bad faith doctrine.

[4] Sprague v. Ticonic National Bank, 307 U.S. 161, 166 (1939).

[5] *See*, United States v. Horn, 29 F.3d 754, 759 (1st Cir. 1994) (sovereign immunity precludes use of supervisory power to order the United States to pay the fees and costs incurred by criminal defendants in litigating prosecutorial misconduct issue; *but see*,

Public Law 105-119 (1997), discussed below in Ch. XVII). Although the Supreme Court noted in *Chambers*, *supra* note 3, "that the exercise of the inherent power of lower federal courts can be limited by statute or rule, for '[t]hese courts were created by act of Congress'" (501 U.S. at 47; the Supreme Court was created by the Constitution, Art. III, § 1), the court of appeals in *Horn* wrote: "It is not yet settled whether some residuum of the courts' supervisory power is so integral to the judicial function that it may not be regulated by Congress (or, alternatively, may only be regulated up to a certain point)." 29 F.3d at 760 n.5.

[6] Nepera Chemical, Inc. v. Sea-Land Service, 794 F.2d 688, 701 (D.C. Cir. 1986).

[7] *See*, e.g., Sanchez v. Rowe, 870 F.2d 291, 295 (5th Cir. 1989) ("We hold that the requisite bad faith may be found in a party's conduct in response to a substantive claim, whether before or after the action is filed, but it may not be based on a party's conduct forming the basis for that substantive claim" (emphasis in original)). In *Shimman v. International Union of Operating Engineers*, 744 F.2d 1226, 1231 (6th Cir. 1984) (en banc), *cert. denied*, 469 U.S. 1215 (1985), the court wrote: "To allow an award of attorneys' fees based on bad faith in the act underlying the substantive claim would not be consistent with the rationale behind the American Rule regarding attorneys' fees. . . . Attorneys' fees incurred while curing the original wrong are not compensable because they represent the cost of maintaining open access to an equitable system of justice." Attorneys' fees incurred as the result of bad faith in the conduct of the litigation, however, are compensable because such bad faith constitutes a new wrong imposed upon the aggrieved party.

[8] Cases under 28 U.S.C. § 1927 are discussed at 12 ALR Fed 910. Other cases concerning the bad faith exception to the American rule are discussed at 31 ALR Fed 833.

[9] La Raza Unida v. Volpe, 57 F.R.D. 94, 98 (N.D. Cal. 1972), *aff'd*, 488 F.2d 559 (9th Cir. 1973), *cert. denied*, 417 U.S. 968 (1974).

[10] When enacted in 1976, this statute was codified as the last sentence of 42 U.S.C. § 1988. In 1991, Public Law 102-166, § 113(a), made it a separate subsection. For simplicity, it is referred to throughout this report (except in quotations) as § 1988(b), even when discussing court decisions between 1976 and 1991, when it was the last sentence of § 1988.

[11] United States v. Chemical Foundation, Inc., 272 U.S. 1, 20 (1926).

[12] *See*, e.g., National Association of Regional Medical Health Programs, Inc. v. Mathews, 551 F.2d 340 (D.C. Cir. 1977), *cert. denied*, 431 U.S. 954 (1977) (common benefit exception); Gibson v. Davis, 587 F.2d 280 (6th Cir. 1978), *cert. denied*, 441 U.S. 905 (1979) (bad faith exception).

[13] The type of agency adjudication in which fees may be awarded is an "adversary adjudication," which is defined at 5 U.S.C. § 504(b)(1)(C). In *Ardestani v. Immigration and Naturalization Service*, 502 U.S. 129 (1991), the Supreme Court held that administrative deportation proceedings are not adversary adjudications. In *Sullivan v. Hudson*, 490 U.S. 877, 891 (1989), the Supreme Court held "that for purposes of the EAJA Social Security benefit proceedings are not 'adversarial' within the meaning of § 504(b)(1)(C) either initially or on remand from a court." However, "where a court orders a remand to the Secretary [of Health and Human Services] in a benefits litigation and retains continuing jurisdiction over the case pending a decision from the Secretary

which will determine the claimant's entitlement to benefits, the proceedings on remand are an integral part of the 'civil action' for judicial review and thus attorney's fees for representation on remand are available [under 28 U.S.C. § 2412(d)(1)(A)] subject to the other limitations in the EAJA." *Id.* at 892. *See*, 96 ALR Fed 336. Social Security cases also raise complications in applying EAJA's requirement that the prevailing party submit a fee application "within thirty days of the final judgment in the action" (28 U.S.C. § 2412(d)(1)(B)) or "within thirty days of a final disposition in the adversary adjudication" (5 U.S.C. § 504(a)(2)). *See*, Melkonyan v. Sullivan, 501 U.S. 89 (1991); Shalala v. Schaefer, 509 U.S. 292 (1993).

[14] EAJA applies in all Article III courts (*see*, 28 U.S.C. § 2412(c)), and explicitly applies in two Article I courts: the Court of Federal Claims and the United States Court of Veterans Appeals (28 U.S.C. § 2412(d)(2)(F)). As for other Article I courts, it does not apply in Tax Court (Bowen v. Commissioner, 706 F.2d 1087 (11th Cir. 1983)); as for tax cases, see ch. VIII of this article). In addition, "[t]he circuits are divided about whether bankruptcy courts are 'courts of the United States' and therefore have authority under EAJA or [26 U.S.C.] section 7430." *In re* Cascade Roads, Inc., 34 F.3d 756, 767 n.12 (9th Cir. 1994). *See*, Charles R. Haywood, *The Power of Bankruptcy Courts to Shift Fees under the Equal Access to Justice Act*, 61 University of Chicago Law Review 985 (1994). Tort cases against the United States are brought under the Federal Tort Claims Act (FTCA), 28 U.S.C. §§ 1346(b), 2671-2680. The FTCA requires that, prior to filing suit, a claimant must first present his claim to the federal agency out of whose activities his claim arose. If the claim is settled before suit is filed, the claimant's attorney may receive up to 20 percent of the settlement; if it is not, the claimant's attorney may receive up to 25 percent of a court award or settlement. 28 U.S.C. § 2678. *See*, 86 ALR Fed 866. Fee awards against the United States are not authorized by the FTCA or by 28 U.S.C. § 2412(d). They presumably may be awarded under the common law bad faith doctrine made applicable against the United States by 28 U.S.C. § 2412(b). In *Sanchez v. Rowe*, 870 F.2d 291, 295 (5th Cir. 1989), the court found a lack of the requisite bad faith and therefore did "not reach the issue whether an award of attorneys fees would . . . be barred by the FTCA prohibition against punitive damages [28 U.S.C. § 2674]." Subsequently, however, in *Molzof v. United States*, 502 U.S. 301, 312 (1992), the Supreme Court, in a different context, held "that § 2674 bars the recovery only of what are *legally* considered 'punitive damages' under traditional commonlaw principles." (Emphasis in original.)

[15] EAJA does not specify which party has the burden of proof as to whether the position of the United States was substantially justified or special circumstances make an award unjust. However, the conference report to the original EAJA states: "After a prevailing party has submitted an application for an award, the burden of proving that a fee award should not be made rests with the Government." H.Rept. 96-1434, at 22. In addition, in *Scarborough v. Principi*, 541 U.S. 401 (2004), the Supreme Court noted that "the Government may defeat this entitlement [to a fee award] by showing that its position in the underlying litigation 'was substantially justified.'" The "position" of the United States which the government must prove to have been substantially justified in order to avoid a fee award includes both the conduct of the government in the proceeding itself and the action of the government that gave rise to the proceeding. 5 U.S.C. § 504(b)(1)(E); 28 U.S.C. § 2412(d)(2)(D).

[16] These limitations are incorporated into Public Law 105-119 (1997), which authorizes awards of attorneys' fees to prevailing criminal defendants, and is discussed in ch. XVII of this report.

[17] The two exceptions are tax-exempt organizations and agricultural cooperatives; they may recover fees regardless of their net worth but apparently may not recover fees if they have more than 500 employees. *See*, 5 U.S.C. § 504(b)(1)(B); 28 U.S.C. § 2412(d)(2)(B); Unification Church v. Immigration and Naturalization Service, 762 F.2d 1077 (D.C. Cir. 1985).

[18] H.Rept. 99-120, 99th Cong., 1st Sess. 16 (1985), *reprinted in* 1985 U.S.C.C.A.N. 132, 145.

[19] Cases construing this term as used in EAJA are collected at 69 ALR Fed 130.

[20] H.Rept. 96-1434, 96th Cong., 2d Sess. 22 (1980), *reprinted in* 1980 U.S.C.C.A.N. 5003, 5011.

[21] Spencer v. National Labor Relations Board, 712 F.2d 539, 558 (D.C. Cir. 1983), *cert. denied*, 466 U.S. 936 (1984).

[22] H.Rept. 99-120, 99th Cong., 1st Sess. 9 (1985), *reprinted in* 1985 U.S.C.C.A.N. 132, 138.

[23] Annotations concerning EAJA include 69 ALR Fed 130, 96 ALR Fed. 275, 96 ALR Fed 336, 105 ALR Fed 110, 106 ALR Fed 191, 107 ALR Fed 827, and 113 ALR Fed 267.

[24] Cases that interpret an attorneys' fees provision of one civil rights statute generally apply to the attorneys' fees provisions of all civil rights statutes, as they are all generally modeled on the fee-shifting provisions of the Civil Rights Act of 1964. The Supreme Court has noted "that fee-shifting statutes' similar language is a 'strong indication' that they are to be interpreted alike." Independent Federation of Flight Attendants v. Zipes, 491 U.S. 754, 758 n.2 (1989).

[25] In *Durrett v. Jenkins Brickyard, Inc.*, 678 F.2d 911 (llth Cir. 1982), the court held that a Title VII plaintiff is not relieved from liability for attorneys' fees by the fact that his attorney was primarily responsible for the fact that his lawsuit was frivolous, unreasonable, or without foundation. The court wrote: In virtually all actions without legal basis, and in many without factual basis, it will be the plaintiff's attorney who should first recognize the insufficiency of the case. . . . If plaintiffs in such cases were permitted to escape liability under § 706 [42 U.S.C. § 2000e-5(k)], the salutary effect of that provision would be diluted. . . . [I]n many cases . . . in which the plaintiff's counsel may appear to be primarily culpable, the plaintiff may find relief from the effect of our rule in the form of a malpractice action. *Id.* at 916.

[26] Consolidated Edison Co. v. Realty Investment Associates, 524 F. Supp. 150 (S.D.N.Y. 1981).

[27] Postow v. OBA Federal S and L Ass'n, 627 F.2d 1370, 1387-1388 (D.C. Cir. 1980) (rejecting an equal protection challenge by citing *Christiansburg* "in concluding that the interest in such private enforcement constitutes a rational basis for a legislative distinction to be drawn between attorneys' fee awards to successful plaintiffs but not successful defendants").

[28] Mary Frances Derfner and Arthur D. Wolf, 1 COURT AWARDED ATTORNEY FEES, 8.02[2], pp. 8-9 (Matthew Bender, 1997) (attributing this fact to the Supreme Court's decision in *Ruckelshaus*, discussed in section V.)

[29] Parker v. Matthews, 411 F. Supp. 1059, 1064 (D.D.C. 1976), *aff'd sub nom.* Parker v. Califano, 561 F.2d 320 (D.C. Cir. 1977).

[30] 532 U.S. 598, 600 (2001).

[31] *See*, Poelker v. Doe, 432 U.S. 519, 521 n.2 (1977). Fee awards may include amounts incurred in litigation over the fee award. *See*, 16 ALR Fed 643, § 10. However, in *Jensen v. City of San Jose*, 806 F.2d 899 (9th Cir. 1986) (en banc), the defendant prevailed on the merits and was awarded fees. On appeal, the fee award (but not the decision on the merits) was overturned, and the plaintiff was held ineligible to recover attorneys' fees incurred in overturning the fee award.

[32] Nicodemus v. Chrysler Corp. — Toledo Machining Plant, 445 F. Supp. 559 (N.D. Ohio 1977), *rev'd on other grounds*, 596 F.2d 152 (6th Cir. 1979); Howard v. Phelps, 443 F. Supp. 374 (E.D. La. 1978).

[33] The Court's holding in *Hanrahan* apparently applies to cases brought under Title II and Title VII of the Civil Rights Act of 1964, 42 U.S.C. §§ 2000a-3(b) and 2000e-5(k), and § 402 of the Voting Rights Act Amendments of 1975, 42 U.S.C. § 1973l(e), because, as the Court noted, § 1988(b) was patterned on these statutes. 446 U.S. at 758 n.4. Under Title VII, a party who prevails on an interlocutory appeal apparently is entitled to attorneys' fees at least "when an interlocutory appeal results in a final resolution of a separable dispute." Grubbs v. Butz, 548 F.2d 973, 975 n.5 (D.C. Cir. 1976). *See also*, Smith v. University of North Carolina, 632 F.2d 316 (4th Cir. 1980); Van Hoomissen v. Xerox Corp., 503 F.2d 1131 (9th Cir. 1974).

[34] Public Law 104-121 (1996), as quoted above, amended the Equal Access to Justice Act was amended to authorize fees to losing parties in some instances. In footnote 1 of its opinion in *Ruckelshaus*, the Court wrote: "Sixteen federal statutes and § 304(d) of the Clear Air Act contain provisions for awards of attorney's fees identical to § 307(f)." It then listed 13 of them. The others are the Solid Waste Disposal Act, 42 U.S.C. § 6792(e), and two sections of the Toxic Substances Control Act (TOSCA), 15 U.S.C. §§ 2619(c)(2) and 2620(b)(4)(C). (The Court did list a third section of TOSCA, 15 U.S.C. § 2618(d)). The Court then wrote: "As explained below [it did not explain below], the interpretation of 'appropriate' in § 307(f) controls construction of the term in these statutes." The interpretation of these other statutes had not been at issue in the case.

[35] Gregory Paul Barbee, *Attorney's Fee Awards to Pro Se Litigants After* Kay v. Ehrler: *No Fees. It's Simple. But is it Absolute?*, 69 Southern California Law Review 1795, 1817 (1996).

[36] In *Slade for Estate of Slade v. U.S. Postal Service*, 952 F.2d 357, 361 (10th Cir. 1991), the court wrote: Here, Plaintiff's claim for attorney's fees was brought pursuant to § 2000e-5(k), which provides for attorney's fees to the prevailing party "[i]n any action or proceeding under this subchapter [2000e]." The applicable statute here does not require that the federal court proceeding be brought to enforce [emphasis supplied by the court] the laws set forth in § 2000e. Therefore, *Crest Street* is not dispositive of the issue of jurisdiction in this case. (By "jurisdiction," the court meant subject matter jurisdiction to hear a claim solely for attorneys' fees.)

[37] In *Jones v. American State Bank*, 857 F.2d 494 (8th Cir. 1988), the court of appeals affirmed a fee award under Title VII in a suit brought solely to recover fees incurred in a state administrative proceeding.

[38] In a situation in which a party who prevails at the agency level may bring a court action solely to recover fees, the litigating arm of the agency of course may agree to a settlement with respect to a fee award, thereby avoiding litigation of the issue and the incurring of additional fees. The question raised here is whether the adjudicating arm of the agency may award fees over the objections of the litigating arm.

[39] Patton v. Andrus, 459 F. Supp. 1189 (D.D.C. 1978); and Williams v. Boorstin, 451 F. Supp. 1117 (D.D.C. 1978), *rev'd on other grounds*, 663 F.2d 109 (D.C. Cir. 1980), *cert. denied*, 451 U.S. 985 (1981).

[40] Noble v. Claytor, 448 F. Supp. 1242 (D.D.C. 1978); Taylor v. Claytor, 15 EPD § 7854 (D.D.C. 1977).

[41] Turner v. Federal Communications Commission, 514 F.2d 1354 (D.C. Cir. 1975).

[42] The concept is mentioned in § 505(a)(1), 29 U.S.C § 794a(1), which makes available to persons aggrieved by a violation of § 501 "[t]he remedies, procedures, and rights set forth in" Title VII.

[43] Cases under this provision are collected at 16 ALR Fed 621.

[44] Prior to 1979, federal employees filed discrimination charges with the Civil Service Commission (CSC). Pursuant to Reorganization Plan No. 1 of 1978, the function of the CSC in this regard was transferred to the EEOC by Executive Order 12106 (44 Fed. Reg. 1053 (1979)). (Reorganization Plan No. 2 of 1978 abolished the CSC.)

[45] Title VII has been held not to include compensatory damages; consequently, a teacher who retired before bringing suit based on discriminatory working conditions could not be a "prevailing party" eligible to recover attorneys' fees, although she had proved discrimination. Harrington v. Vandalia-Butler Board of Education, 585 F.2d 192 (6th Cir. 1978).

[46] Cases under this provision are collected at 16 ALR Fed 643 and 77 ALR Fed 272.

[47] Cases under this provision are collected at 38 ALR Fed 164.

[48] *See*, 24 ALR Fed 808, 862 on this point; *see*, 99 ALR Fed 30 on fee awards under the ADEA generally.

[49] *See*, e.g., Lewis v. Federal Prison Industries, Inc., 953 F.2d 1277 (11th Cir. 1992); Palmer v. General Services Administration, 787 F.2d 300 (8th Cir. 1986).

[50] Cases under this provision are collected at 68 ALR Fed 206.

[51] See, Annotation, Attorneys' Fees Under Back Pay Act (5 USCS § 5596), 122 ALR Fed 465.

[52] H.Rept. 96-897, 96th Cong., 2d Sess. 12-13 (1980), *reprinted in* 1980 U.S.C.C.A.N. 832, 837.

[53] For additional information, see, CRS Report RS22055, The Individuals with Disabilities Education Act (IDEA): Attorneys' Fees Provisions in P.L. 108-446, by Nancy Lee Jones.

[54] Eleventh Amendment immunity (discussed in ch. IX of this report) is explicitly waived by § 502 of the ADA, 42 U.S.C. § 12202. In *Tennessee v. Lane*, No. 02-1667 (May 17, 2004), the Supreme Court held that Title II of the ADA, which makes the ADA applicable to the states, constitutes a valid exercise of Congress' authority under section 5 of the Fourteenth Amendment insofar as it requires the states to provide access to their courts.

[55] As for the citation of this statute, *see*, note 10, *supra*. Cases under § 1988(b) are collected at 43 ALR Fed 243, 69 ALR Fed 712, and 118 ALR Fed 1. The exception for

judicial officers was added by Public Law 104-317, § 309(b) (discussed in ch. IX of this report).

[56] The exception for judicial officers was added by Public Law 104-317, § 309(c).

[57] Subsequently, the Supreme Court limited the scope of *Thiboutot*, finding exceptions to the rule that § 1983 provides a cause of action for violations of federal statutes as well as the Constitution. *See*, e.g., Livadas v. Bradshaw, 512 U.S. 107, 132 (1994); Suter v. Artist M., 503 U.S. 347, 355 (1992); Wilder v. Virginia Hospital Association, 496 U.S. 498, 508 (1990); Middlesex County Sewerage Authority v. National Sea Clammers Association, 453 U.S. 1, 20 (1981); Pennhurst State School and Hospital v. Halderman, 451 U.S. 1, 15 (1981).

[58] *See*, note 67, *infra*.

[59] *See*, CRS Report 97-795, *The Religious Freedom Restoration Act: Its Rise, Fall, and Current Status*, by David M. Ackerman. In *City of Boerne v. Flores*, 521 U.S. 507 (1997), the Supreme Court declared RFRA unconstitutional as applied to the states, on the ground that Congress had exceeded its power under § 5 of the Fourteenth Amendment in applying it to the states.

[60] Section 40302 is part of the Civil Rights Remedies for Gender-Motivated Violence Act, which is Subtitle C of the Violence Against Women Act of 1994, which is part of Title IV of the Violent Crime Control and Law Enforcement Act of 1994, Public Law 103-322.

[61] H.Rept. 96-1418, 96th Cong., 2d Sess. 17 (1980), *reprinted in* 1980 U.S.C.C.A.N. 4984, 4996.

[62] Dissenting in *Dellmuth v. Muth*, 491 U.S. 223, 233 (1989), Justices Brennan, Marshall, Blackmun, and Stevens expressed the view that *Hans v. Louisiana* should be overruled.

[63] In subsequent cases, the Court has indicated that federal courts may also enjoin state officials from enforcing state laws that violate federal laws or regulations. *See*, e.g., *Edelman v. Jordan*, discussed in the text below.

[64] *Attorneys' Fees and the Eleventh Amendment*, 88 Harvard Law Review 1875, 1879 (1975).

[65] In *Pennhurst State School and Hospital v. Halderman*, 465 U.S. 89, 106, 121 (1984), the Supreme Court held "that *Young* and *Edelman* are inapplicable in a suit against state officials on the basis of state law. . . . [T]his principle applies as well to state-law claims brought into federal court under pendent jurisdiction." In other words, the Eleventh Amendment prohibits a state-law claim against state officials from being brought in federal court, even if it is joined with a federal-law claim. This has caused some state courts to refuse to "hear claims under 42 U.S.C. § 1983 (1982) that seek an award of attorney's fees under the Civil Rights Attorney's Fees Awards Act of 1976 (section 1988)." Wilbur, *Concurrent Jurisdiction and Attorney's Fees: The Obligation of State Courts to Hear Section 1983 Claims*, 134 University of Pennsylvania Law Review 1207 (1986).

[66] In *Dellmuth v. Muth*, 491 U.S. 223, 232 (1989), the Court held that the Education of the Handicapped Act, did "not evince an unmistakably clear intention to abrogate the States' constitutionally secured immunity from suit [in federal court]." This decision apparently applied only to suits alleging violations that occurred before 42 U.S.C. § 2000d-7 took effect in 1986. *See*, *id.* at 228-229. Yet, in 1990, Public Law 101-476, § 103, amended the Education of the Handicapped Act to provide, effective Oct. 30,

1990: "A State shall not be immune under the eleventh amendment to the Constitution of the United States from suit in Federal court for a violation of this Act." 20 U.S.C. § 1403. A committee report states that this was intended to overturn *Dellmuth v. Muth.* H.Rept. 101-544, 101st Cong., 2d Sess. 12; *reprinted in* 1990 U.S.C.C.A.N. 1723, 1734.

[67] In *Kimel v. Florida Board of Regents*, 528 U.S. 62 (2000), the Court held that the Age Discrimination in Employment Act, though a valid exercise of Congress's commerce power, could not be applied to the states unless Congress also had the power to enact it under § 5 of the Fourteenth Amendment, which Congress does not.

[68] Although the Supreme Court has not explicitly decided the question, the fact that it held in *Seminole Tribe*, *supra*, that Congress may not override the Eleventh Amendment when legislating pursuant to the Commerce Clause suggests that § 1988(b) does not apply to § 1983 claims that do not arise under the Fourteenth Amendment.

[69] *See*, S.Rep. No. 104-366, 104th Cong., 2d Sess. 37 (1996).

[70] At the time of *Crawford Fitting*, witness fees were set at $30; Public Law 101-650, § 314, raised them to $40.

[71] The Court listed "34 statutes in 10 different titles of the U.S. Code [that] explicitly shift attorney's fees *and* [emphasis supplied by the Court] expert witness fees." 499 U.S. at 89.

[72] See, CRS Report 91-818, Attorneys' Fees and Expert Witness Fees Under the Civil Rights Act of 1991, by Henry Cohen (archived, available from author).

[73] S.Rep. No. 1329, 89th Cong., 2d Sess. (1966); *reprinted in* 1966 U.S.C.C.A.N. 2527, 2528.

[74] Footnote 7 of the Court's opinion states: "The 12 factors are: (1) the time and labor required; (2) the novelty and difficulty of the question; (3) the skill requisite to perform the legal service properly; (4) the preclusion of other employment by the attorney due to acceptance of the case; (5) the customary fee; (6) whether the fee is fixed or contingent; (7) time limitations imposed by the client or the circumstances; (8) the amount involved and the results obtained; (9) the experience, reputation, and ability of attorney; (10) the "undesirability" of the case; (11) the nature and length of the professional relationship with the client; and (12) awards in similar cases. 488 F.2d, at 717-719. These factors were taken from the American Bar Association Code of Professional Responsibility, Disciplinary Rule 2-106 (1980)." They are now embodied in the American Bar Association Model Rules of Professional Conduct, Rule 1.5 (1983).

[75] Upward adjustments are also called "bonuses." The Supreme Court has stated that it thinks the characterization "upward adjustments" is "fairer." Blum v. Stenson, 465 U.S. at 896 n.12. Upward adjustments may be made "by way of multipliers or enhancement of the lodestar." *Delaware Valley I*, 478 U.S. at 568.

[76] The dissent thought that the Court had "improperly heightened the showing required to the point where it may be virtually impossible for a plaintiff to meet." 478 U.S. at 569.

[77] In *Blum v. Stenson*, the Court also contrasted calculation of fee awards under the common fund doctrine (see ch. II of this article) and under § 1988. Under the former "a reasonable fee is based on a percentage of the fund bestowed on the class," while "a reasonable fee under § 1988 reflects the amount of attorney time reasonably expended on the litigation." 465 U.S. at 900 n.16. Risk multipliers are also more permissible in common fund cases. *See*, e.g., Florin v. Nationsbank of Georgia, 34 F.3d 560 (7th Cir.

1994); *In re* Washington Public Power Supply System Securities Litigation, 19 F.3d 1291 (9th Cir. 1994); Swedish Hospital Corp. v. Shalala, 1 F.3d 1261 (D.C. Cir. 1993); Camden I Condominium Association v. Dunkle, 946 F.2d 768 (11th Cir. 1991); Skelton v. General Motors Corp., 860 F.2d 250 (7th Cir. 1988).

[78] Funds received from the Legal Services Corporation may not be used to provide legal assistance with respect to fee-generating cases, with some exceptions. 42 U.S.C. § 2996f(b)(1). A "fee-generating" case includes any case that "reasonably may be expected to result in a fee for legal services from an award to a client, from public funds, or from the opposing party." 45 C.F.R. § 1609.2. In addition, Public Law 104-134, § 504 (110 Stat. 1321-55 (1996)), provides: "None of the funds appropriated in this Act to the Legal Services Corporation may be used to provide financial assistance to any person or entity . . . (13) that claims (or whose employee claims), or collects and retains, attorneys' fees pursuant to any Federal or State law permitting or requiring the awarding of such fees." This provision was carried forward into subsequent appropriations acts. See, e.g., P.L. 105-119, § 502 (1997); P.L. 106-553, App. B, 114 Stat. 2762A-101 (2000); P.L. 108-7, 117 Stat.97 (2003).

[79] *See*, Annotation, *Effect of Contingent Fee Contract on Fee Award Authorized by Federal Statute*, 76 ALR Fed 347. The Equal Access to Justice Act provides that § 206(b) of the Social Security Act, 42 U.S.C. § 406(b)(1), which limits contingent fees to 25 percent of past-due old-age, survivor, or disability benefits that a court awards, shall not prevent an award under EAJA, but the claimant's attorney must refund to the claimant the amount of the smaller fee. Public Law 99-80, § 3 (1985), 28 U.S.C. § 2412 note. Similarly, EAJA provides that the 38 U.S.C. § 5904(d), which limits contingent fees to 20 percent of past-due veterans benefits that a court awards, shall not prevent an award under EAJA, but the claimant's attorney must refund to the claimant the amount of the smaller fee. Public Law 102-572, § 506(c), 28 U S.C. § 2412 note.

[80] An offer under Rule 68 need not "separately recite the amount that the defendant is offering in settlement of the substantive claim and the amount he is offering to cover accrued costs . . . ; if the offer does not state that costs are included and an amount for costs is not specified, the court will be obliged by the terms of the Rule to include in its judgment an additional amount . . . to cover the costs." Marek v. Chesny, 473 U.S. 1, 5-6 (1985).

[81] Rule 68 also provides that the fact that an offer is not accepted does not preclude a subsequent offer, and that, if a party is adjudged liable for a claim, but the amount of liability remains to be determined, the party adjudged liable may then offer to settle, and the offer shall have the same effect as an offer made before trial.

[82] Crossman v. Marcoccio, 806 F.2d 329, 332 (5th Cir. 1986), *cert. denied*, 481 U.S. 1029 (1987) ("every court addressing the issue thus far has held that Rule 68 obligates plaintiffs to pay defendants' post-offer costs after rejecting an offer more favorable than the judgment eventually obtained").

[83] If a statute provides for awards of attorneys' fees, but not as part of the costs, and a settlement offer made under Rule 68 does not specifically either include or exclude attorneys' fees, then a plaintiff who accepts the offer may still file a motion for attorneys' fees. *See*, Minnick v. Dollar Financial Group, Inc., 2002 U.S. Dist. LEXIS 9115, 2002 WL 1023101, 52 Fed.R.Serv.3d 1347 (May 20, 2002), and cases cited therein.

[84] Crossman v. Marcoccio, 806 F.2d 329, 333-334 (5th Cir. 1986), *cert. denied*, 481 U.S. 1029 (1987); O'Brien v. City of Greers Ferry, 873 F.2d 1115 (8th Cir. 1989); EEOC v. Bailey Ford, Inc., 26 F.3d 570 (5th Cir. 1994); Le v. University of Pennsylvania, 321 F.3d 403 (3d Cir. 2003). In a copyright case, however, a court allowed a defendant, under Rule 68, to recover its post-offer attorneys' fees. Jordan v. Time, Inc., 111 F.3d 102 (11th Cir. 1997).

[85] The Civil Rights Act of 1990, S. 2104, 101st Congress, which was vetoed by President Bush, would have amended Title VII of the Civil Rights Act of 1964, 42 U.S.C. § 2000e-5(k), to authorize "a reasonable attorney's fee . . . and costs," instead of "a reasonable attorney's fee as part of the costs," as it now reads.

[86] H.Rept. 99-687, 99th Cong., 2d Sess. 6 (1986), *reprinted in* 1986 U.S.C.C.A.N. 1807, 1809.

[87] The Supreme Court wrote: "it is argued that an attorney is required to evaluate a settlement offer on the basis of his client's interest, without considering his own interest in obtaining a fee; upon recommending settlement, he must abide by the client's decision whether or not to accept the offer." *Id.* at 728 n.14. The Court stated that the plaintiffs' lawyer's decision in this case "to recommend acceptance was consistent with the highest standards of our profession." *Id.* at 728.

[88] The majority and the dissent agreed that § 1988(b) "should not be interpreted to prohibit simultaneous negotiations of a defendant's liability on the merits and his liability for his opponent's attorney's fees." *Id.* at 738 n.30. The dissent, however, would have permitted the parties to negotiate "reasonable" fees, not waivers. *Id.* at 764-765.

[89] This statute provides that the court may allow "a reasonable fee . . . not in excess of 25 percent of the total of past-due benefits." In *Gisbrecht v. Barnhart*, 535 U.S. 789, 808 (2002), the Supreme Court held that a court should not determine the reasonableness of a fee by the lodestar method that is used in fee-shifting statutes, but should "approach fee determinations by looking first to the contingent-fee agreement, then testing it for reasonableness." *See also* note 78, *supra*.

[90] For a list of examples of federal statutes that limit attorneys' fees, see, Robert L. Rossi, ATTORNEYS' FEES (3d ed.) § 2.10, n.1 (West Group, 2001). Among recent examples not listed in Rossi are Public Law 104-201, § 657(i) (1996) (compensation for prisoners of war in Vietnam); Public Law 105-369 (1998) (Ricky Ray Hemophilia Relief Fund Act of 1998); Public Law 106-245, § 3 (2000) (Radiation Exposure Compensation Act); Public Law 106-246, § 104(j) (2000) (Cerro Grande Fire Assistance Act); Public Law 106-398, § 3648 (2000) (Energy Employees Occupational Illness Compensation Program of 2000).

[91] See, Annotation, Authority of Federal Agency to Spend Public Funds to Reimburse Expenses of Qualified Participants in its Proceedings, 62 ALR Fed 849.

[92] The Federal Trade Commission formerly had such authority for all its rulemaking proceedings. P.L. 93-637 (1975), § 202(a); formerly codified at 15 U.S.C. § 57a(h); repealed by P.L. 103-312 (1994), § 3.

[93] Congress apparently has placed no similar restriction on the Department of State, but an attorney at the Department of State informed us that it has not used its authority to fund intervenors in recent years and may never have done so.

[94] In a subsequent letter (B-180224), the Comptroller General indicated that the above decision applied to several other agencies. This letter appears in a committee print of the Senate Committee on Commerce entitled Agency Comments on the Payment of Reasonable Fees for Public Participation in Agency Proceedings, 95th Cong., lst Sess. (1977). *See also*, B-139703 and 56 C.G. 111 (1976).

[95] *See*, United States v. Horn, 29 F.3d 754 (1st Cir. 1994); *see also*, K.S. Rosenn, *Compensating the Innocent Accused*, 37 Ohio State L.J. 705 (1976). The Independent Counsel Reauthorization Act of 1987, 28 U.S.C. § 593(f)(1), however, authorizes fee awards to investigated individuals who are not indicted.

[96] Johnson v. Zerbst, 304 U.S. 458 (1938) (federal cases); Gideon v. Wainwright, 372 U.S. 355 (1963) (state cases).

[97] United States v. Knott, 256 F.3d 20 (1st Cir. 2001); United States v. Ranger Electronic Communications, Inc., 210 F.3d 627, 632-633 (6th Cir. 2000).

[98] *Knott, supra* note 97, at 29.

[99] United States v. Campbell, 134 F. Supp.2d 1104, 1108 (C.D. Cal. 2001).

[100] United States v. Gardner, 23 F. Supp.2d 1283, 1291 (N.D. Okla.1998).

[101] *Id.* at 1292.

In: Law and Law Enforcement Issues
Editor: Gerald M. Kessler, pp. 377-385
ISBN: 978-1-60456-044-2

Chapter 12

JUVENILE JUSTICE: RIGHTS DURING THE ADJUDICATORY PROCESS*

Alison M. Smith

ABSTRACT

As more attention is being focused on juvenile offenders, some question whether the justice system is dealing with this population appropriately. Since the late 1960s, the juvenile justice system has undergone significant modifications resulting from U.S. Supreme Court decisions, changes in federal and state law, and the growing belief that juveniles were increasingly involved in more serious and violent crimes. Consequently, at both the federal and states levels, the juvenile justice system has shifted from a mostly rehabilitative system to a more punitive one, with serious ramifications for juvenile offenders. Despite this shift, juveniles are generally not afforded the panoply of rights afforded to adult criminal defendants. The U.S. Constitution requires that juveniles receive many of the features of an adult criminal trial, including notice of charges, right to counsel, privilege against self-incrimination, right to confrontation and cross-examination, proof beyond a reasonable doubt, and double jeopardy. However, in *McKeiver v. Pennsylvania*, the Court held that juveniles do not have a fundamental right to a jury trial during adjudicatory proceedings.

The Sixth Amendment explicitly guarantees the right to an impartial jury trial in criminal prosecutions. In *Duncan v. Louisiana*, the U.S. Supreme Court held that this right is fundamental and guaranteed by the Due Process Clause of the Fourteenth Amendment. However, the Court has since limited its holding in *Duncan* to adult defendants by stating that the right to a jury trial is not constitutionally required for juveniles in juvenile court proceedings. Some argue that because the Court has determined that jury trials are not constitutionally required for juvenile adjudications, courts should not treat or consider juvenile adjudications in subsequent criminal proceedings. In addition, some argue that the use of non-jury juvenile adjudications in subsequent criminal proceedings violates due process guarantees, because juvenile justice and adult criminal proceedings are fundamentally different.

Has the juvenile justice system changed in such a manner that the Supreme Court should revisit the question of jury trials in juvenile adjudications? Are the procedural

---

* Excerpted from CRS Report RL33966, dated April 16, 2007.

safeguards in the juvenile justice system sufficient to ensure their reliable use for sentence enhancement purposes in adult criminal proceedings? To help address these questions, this article provides a brief background on the purpose of the juvenile system and discusses procedural due process protections provided by the Court for juveniles during adjudicatory hearings. It also discusses the Court's emphasis on the jury's role in criminal proceedings.

As attention continues to focus on juvenile offenders, some question the way in which they are treated in the U.S. criminal justice system. Since the late 1960s, the juvenile justice system has undergone significant modifications as a result of United States Supreme Court decisions, changes in federal and state law and the growing perception that juveniles were increasingly involved in more serious and violent crimes.[1] As a result, federal and state juvenile justice systems have focused less on rehabilitation and more on punishment, which may have significant ramifications for juvenile offenders once they reach adulthood. For example, recidivist statutes such as the Armed Career Criminal Act (ACCA)[2] impose mandatory minimums based on prior convictions, including juvenile adjudications.[3] As such, adult criminal defendants are exposed to longer terms of imprisonment based on prior juvenile misconduct. Despite this shift in focus to one more closely resembling the adult criminal justice system, juvenile offenders are not generally afforded the full panoply of rights provided to adult criminal defendants.

Background: The Juvenile Justice System

The establishment of a juvenile court in Cook County, Illinois, in 1899 marked the first statewide implementation of a separate judicial framework whose sole concern was the problems and misconduct of children. The juvenile court was designed to be more than a court for children. The underlying theory behind a separate juvenile court system was that the state has a duty to assume a custodial and protective role over individuals who cannot act in their own best interest.[4] As such, the separate system for juvenile offenders was predicated on the notion of rehabilitation — not punishment, retribution, or incapacitation. Because the juvenile court focused on protection rather than punishment, the juvenile proceeding was conceptualized as a civil proceeding (not a criminal one), with none of the trappings of an adversarial proceeding.[5]

By the mid-20th century, questions arose regarding the fairness and efficacy of the juvenile justice system and its ability to effectively rehabilitate young offenders. Concerns that the differences between the adult and juvenile systems were illusory prompted the need to preserve the legal rights of children adjudicated in the juvenile justice system.[6] As such, state courts began to expand the legal rights of juvenile offenders. The emerging focus on juveniles' rights in the state courts prompted intervention from the U.S. Supreme Court, which had traditionally deferred to the states.

PROCEDURAL DUE PROCESS RIGHTS

Beginning in the mid-1960s, the Court examined the due process rights of minors in four landmark cases: *Kent v. United States*,[7] *In re Gault*,[8] *In re Winship*,[9] and *McKeiver v. Pennsylvania*.[10] Through these cases, the Court left an indelible mark on the juvenile justice system by restricting the discretion of juvenile court judges and enumerating the constitutional rights retained by juveniles during adjudication. These decisions resulted in a hybrid juvenile justice system that renders some of the procedural rights afforded to adult criminal defendants. Some argue that this hybrid system blurs the historical distinction between the juvenile justice and adult criminal systems.

Kent v. United States

The Court first recognized that the U.S. Constitution guaranteed juveniles due process rights in *Kent v. United States*.[11] In *Kent*, the Court reviewed a District of Columbia case in which the petitioner challenged the validity of the juvenile court's decision to waive jurisdiction over him, on the ground that the procedure used by the court in reaching its decision constituted a denial of due process of law. The U.S. Supreme Court held that the waiver of jurisdiction was a "critically important" stage in the juvenile process and must be attended by minimum requirements of due process and fair treatment required by the Fourteenth Amendment.[12] In reaching its decision, the Court expressed concern that the non-criminal nature of the juvenile proceeding was an invitation to "procedural arbitrariness"[13] including broad judicial fact-finding.

In re Gault

In *In re Gault*,[14] the Court held that the informal procedures of juvenile courts amount to a denial of juveniles' fundamental due process rights.[15] Although the Court recognized that juvenile courts were attempting to help juveniles, it reasoned that this worthy purpose failed to justify informal procedure, particularly when a juvenile's liberty was threatened.[16] After a thorough examination of the history of the juvenile court system, the Court reiterated much of the criticism it raised in *Kent*, specifically expressing concern about the juvenile court's informality and the broad discretion of its judges.[17] To ensure that juveniles receive the essentials of fair treatment during an adjudicatory hearing, the Court found that juveniles were entitled to certain due process rights afforded to adult criminal defendants under the U.S. Constitution.[18] These rights include the right to reasonable notice of the charges, the right to counsel, the right to confrontation, and the right against self-incrimination.[19]

In re Winship

In *In re Winship*, the Court continued to expand the rights of juveniles by holding that the state must show proof beyond a reasonable doubt to adjudicate a minor as delinquent for an act that would be a crime if committed by an adult.[20] The state of New York charged Samuel Winship with delinquency for stealing $112 from a woman's pocketbook in a furniture store.[21] Having already established that juvenile proceedings must conform to due process and fair treatment, the Court considered a single issue: whether due process and fair treatment require a state to demonstrate proof beyond a reasonable doubt to hold a juvenile accountable for committing an adult criminal act.[22]

Although a New York juvenile court found Winship to be delinquent under a statute that required the state to show guilt merely by a preponderance of the evidence, the Court reversed, emphasizing that criminal charges have always required a higher burden of persuasion than civil cases.[23] The Court expressly held that the Due Process Clause of the Fourteenth Amendment protects the accused against conviction except upon proof beyond a reasonable doubt of every fact necessary to constitute the crime with which he or she is charged.[24] Finding that juveniles are constitutionally entitled to the reasonable doubt standard, the Court stated, "[t]he same considerations that demand extreme caution in fact-finding to protect the innocent adult apply as well to the innocent child."[25] The Court rejected the state's argument that the delinquency adjudication is a civil proceeding that did not require due process protections, calling this argument the "civil label of convenience."[26]

McKeiver v. Pennsylvania

By 1970, the Supreme Court had ruled that the due process notion of fundamental fairness entitled juveniles to various procedural protections in juvenile court. However, in *McKeiver v. Pennsylvania*,[27] the Court held that juveniles do not have a fundamental right to a jury trial when being adjudicated in the juvenile justice system.[28] *McKeiver* was a consolidation of three similar appeals involving minors adjudicated delinquent in juvenile court by judges who had rejected their requests for a jury to serve as fact-finder at their hearing.[29] The Court narrowed the issue presented to whether the Due Process Clause of the Fourteenth Amendment ensured the right to trial by jury in the adjudicative phase of a juvenile court delinquency proceeding.[30] After reviewing its previous juvenile court jurisprudence, the Court first considered whether the right to a jury was automatically guaranteed to minors by the Sixth and Fourteenth Amendments.[31] Although it had never expressly characterized juvenile court proceedings as criminal prosecutions within the meaning and reach of the Sixth Amendment, the Court reiterated that the juvenile court system reflected many of the adult criminal court's punitive aspects.[32]

However, a plurality of the Court rejected the argument that adjudicatory proceedings were substantively similar to criminal trials,[33] reasoning that a jury trial was only constitutionally required if due process required fact-finding by a jury.[34]

In support of its conclusion that a jury is unnecessary for fair fact-finding, the plurality noted that equity cases, workmen's compensation cases, probate matters, deportation cases, and military trials, among others, had been traditionally decided by judges without juries.[35] In reaching its decision, the Court expressed doubt as to whether imposing such a right would improve the fact-finding ability of juvenile courts. In addition, the Court reasoned that imposing such a right would jeopardize the unique nature of the juvenile system and blur the distinctions between juvenile court and adult criminal court.[36] To do so would make the juvenile system obsolete. The plurality's holding signaled the Court's return to the more paternalistic approach it had rejected in its previous opinions and marked the end of the era of expansion of procedural rights in juvenile adjudications.[37]

RIGHT TO JURY TRIAL REVISITED

Arguably, the absence of a jury trial requirement in adjudicatory proceedings presents a host of questions that may warrant a reexamination of the issue. First, some are likely to argue that the increasingly punitive nature of cases adjudicated in the juvenile justice system calls into question the validity of the Court's reasoning underlying its holding in *McKeiver* that juveniles are not entitled to the right to a jury trial.[38] When the Court decided *McKeiver*, it did so to maintain the civil and rehabilitative nature of the juvenile justice system.[39] At the time of the decision, juvenile adjudication hearings were closed to the public, the system was informal, and the records of the juvenile adjudications were confidential and not relied on in criminal prosecutions.[40] Currently, some juvenile adjudication hearings are open to the public, the system is more formal and adversarial, and juvenile adjudications are frequently used in criminal prosecutions for sentence enhancement.[41] From their perspective, the civil and rehabilitative nature of the juvenile justice system has shifted to a more punitive one which more closely resembles the adult criminal justice system.

Central to the *McKeiver's* holding was the Court's conclusion that juries were not essential to accurate fact-finding. However, this premise may be called into question in light of the Court's reemphasis on the importance of a jury. In a series of cases, the U.S. Supreme Court has recognized and emphasized the important role that juries play in criminal proceedings. In *Duncan v. Louisiana*,[42] the U.S. Supreme Court held that the right to jury trial is fundamental and guaranteed by due process.

In *Williams v. Florida*,[43] the Court reaffirmed that the "purpose of the jury trial ... is to prevent oppression by the Government."[44] The U.S. Supreme Court recognized the superiority of group decision-making over individual judgments in *Ballew v. Georgia*,[45] which defined the constitutional minimum number of jurors that a state must empanel in a criminal prosecution. In *Ballew*, the Court, relying on empirical data, found that a jury composed of less than six members was less likely to foster effective group deliberation and more likely to lead to inaccurate fact-finding and incorrect application of the community's common sense to the facts. In addition, the court concluded that a smaller panel could increase the risk of convicting an innocent person. More recently, the Court has stressed the constitutional necessity of juries, rather than judges, making factual determinations upon which sentences are based.[46] The Court's reasoning in *Ballew* and subsequent cases regarding fact-finding by juries during sentencing may call into question the Court's conclusion in *McKeiver* that a jury would not improve the fact-finding ability and fairness of juvenile courts.[47]

An argument can also be made that the absence of a jury trial in the adjudicatory process could lead to inequities in other criminal proceedings. For example, recidivist statutes such as the Armed Career Criminal Act[48] impose mandatory minimums based on prior convictions, which by definition include juvenile adjudications.[49] As such, adult criminal defendants are subjected to longer terms of imprisonment based on prior juvenile misconduct. Some state and lower federal courts have found that equating juvenile adjudications with a conviction as a predicate offense for the purposes of state recidivism statutes subverts the civil nature of the juvenile adjudication to an extent that makes it fundamentally unfair and, thus, violative of due process.[50] One way to remedy the perceived inequities in using non-jury juvenile adjudication as sentence enhancements, critics of the current system maintain, might be to grant juveniles a right to a jury trial during adjudicatory hearings.

REFERENCES

[1] The focus of this report is on juvenile offenders adjudicated delinquent within the juvenile justice system and not juvenile offenders tried as adults.

[2] 18 U.S.C. § 924(e) requires the imposition of a minimum 15-year term of imprisonment for unlawful possession of a firearm in violation of 18 U.S.C. § 922(g) by an individual with three prior serious drug or violent felony convictions.

[3] 18 U.S.C. § 924(e)(2)(C)(defining the term "conviction" to include prior juvenile adjudications involving a violent felony).

[4] *See, Kent v. United States*, 383 U.S. 541, 555 (1966) (stating that theory of the state's juvenile court act is "rooted in social welfare philosophy rather than in corpus juris.").

[5] For a historical account of the early efforts toward juvenile reform, see Mennel, "Origins of the Juvenile Court: Changing Perspectives on the Legal Rights of Juvenile Delinquent," 18 CRIME AND DELINQ. 68 (1972); See generally, *Ex parte Sharp*, 96 P. 563 (1908).

[6] *See, e.g., Shioutakon v. District of Columbia*, 236 F.2d 666, 669 (D.C. Cir 1956)(recognizing juveniles' right to legal counsel during adjudications in the District of Columbia); *In re Contreras*, 241 P.2d 631,633 (Cal. Dist. Ct. App. 1952)(acknowledging that the claim that a delinquency adjudication is not a criminal conviction is "legal fiction" and that a delinquency adjudication has future implications on a minor's character just as a criminal conviction does); *but see, e.g. In re Holmes*, 109 A.2d 523, 525 (Pa. 1954)(reaffirming that the civil nature of juvenile proceedings justified a denial of constitutional rights guaranteed to adults who were charged with a crime).

[7] 383 U.S. 541 (1966).

[8] 387 U.S. 1 (1967).

[9] 397 U.S. 358 (1970).

[10] 403 U.S. 528 (1971).

[11] 383 U.S. 541 (1966).

[12] *Id.* at 560. Specifically, the Court found that the "essentials of due process and fair treatment" require (1) a hearing on the issue of waiver with legal representation, (2) juvenile court judges to give juveniles' counsel access to records that the judges relied on in making the waiver decision, and (3) juvenile court judges to provide a brief statement of the facts they considered when making the waiver decision. *Id.* at 561-63.

[13] *Id.* at 555.

[14] 387 U.S. 1 (1967). The police took Gerald Gault, age 15, into custody for allegedly making a lewd and obscene phone call to a neighbor. Neither of his parents received

notice that the police had taken Gault into custody. Gault's mother learned that her son was in custody only when she returned home from work and sent her other son to look for him. Gault's brother learned from friends that Gault was in custody. When Gault's mother picked him up at the detention home, an officer told her that there would be a hearing the following day. At the hearing, the accuser was not present, the judge did not swear in anyone, and the court did not make a record of the proceeding. At a subsequent hearing, the judge found Gault to be a juvenile delinquent and committed him to an "industrial school" until the age of 21. Because state law did not allow Gault to appeal the decision, he filed a habeas corpus petition.

[15] *Id.* at 30-31.

[16] *Id.* at 26-27.

[17] *Id.* at 17-18 (calling the juvenile court's constitutional and theoretical bases "debatable" and stating that, in practice, the results are unsatisfactory). Further, the Court asserted that principle and procedure cannot be substituted by a judge's vast discretion to determine what is in the child's best interest.

[18] *Id.* at 20 (stating that due process is a fundamental element of the justice system that limits the state's power over the individual). The Court declined to address other pre-trial procedures relating to juveniles. *Id.* at 12-13.

[19] *Id.* at 31-42.

[20] 397 U.S. 358, 368 (1970).

[21] *Id* at 360 (noting that the charge against Winship would have been larceny if he had been an adult).

[22] *Id.* at 359 n. 1 (declining to consider the due process requirement of any stage other than the adjudicatory phase and declining to consider other constitutional issues).

[23] *Id.* at 361-63 (stating that the reasonable doubt standard has always been assumed to be the requisite standard of proof in criminal cases and that there has been ubiquitous adoption of this standard by the states).

[24] *Id.* at 364 (expressing that the reasonable doubt standard is "indispensable" as a safeguard against convictions resting on factual error and to maintain the community's respect and confidence in the criminal law system).

[25] *Id.* at 365.

[26] *Id.* at 365-66 (rejecting the civil nature argument as untenable after *Gault* and discarding the argument that incorporating due process rights in a juvenile proceeding would necessarily equate a delinquency adjudication with a criminal conviction, destroy the confidentiality of the proceeding, formalize the proceeding, and delay the adjudicatory process).

[27] 403 U.S. 528 (1971).

[28] *Id.* at 545.

[29] *Id.* at 534-38.

[30] *Id.* at 541 (stating that the court would limit its analysis to whether the fundamental fairness standard of due process required juveniles the right to elect a jury in delinquency proceedings).

[31] *Id.* at 540 (stating that the Sixth Amendment guarantees the right to an impartial jury in all criminal prosecutions under federal law, and the Fourteenth Amendment compels states to grant a jury trial in state courts if one is held in federal court).

[32] *Id.* at 541.

[33] Id. at 541-42 (arguing that an adjudication mirrored a criminal trial because the petition charged a violation of the penal code in language similar to an indictment, juveniles were detained in facilities similar to adult prisons prior to their hearings, defense counsel and the prosecution conducted plea bargains, similar motions were heard and decided, the same rules of evidence applied, the public could observe both types of proceedings, and the stigma attached to a delinquency adjudication amounted to a criminal conviction).

[34] *Id.* at 545 (refraining from holding that all rights constitutionally ensured to adult criminal defendants extend to minors, and noting that the *Gault* and *Winship* Courts incorporated the right to notice, counsel, confrontation, cross-examination, and reasonable doubt standard of proof because those rights were considered essential to adequate fact-finding and thereforerequired by due process).

[35] *Id.* at 543 (acknowledging the benefits of a jury but finding that a defendant may be treated as fairly by a judge alone as he or she would be by a jury).

[36] *Id.* at 547. The Court reasoned that the non-criminal juvenile justice system in place provided certain rehabilitative benefits to juveniles. The Court concluded that granting juveniles the right to a jury trial would threaten these rehabilitative benefits to juveniles by creating delay, imposing formality, forcing juvenile courts to be more adversarial, and possibly even resulting in public trials.

[37] Because *McKeiver* held that juveniles are not constitutionally guaranteed the right to a jury, some states have granted this right by statute. Approximately one-third of the states provide juveniles with either a conditional or unconditional right to fact-finding by a jury. See Alaska Stat. § 47.10.070; Mass Gen. Laws Ann. ch. 19, § 55A; Mich. Comp. Laws Ann. § 712A.17(2); Mont. Code Ann. § 41-5-1502; N.M. Stat. Ann. § 32A-2-16; Okla. Stat. Ann. tit. 10, § 7003-3.8; Tex. Fam. Code Ann. § 54.03(c); W. Va. Code Ann. § 49-5-6; Wis. Stat. Ann. § 48.31(2); Wyo. Stat. Ann. § 14-6-223(c)(codifying an unconditional right to fact-finding by jury in juvenile adjudications in the respective states); see also Colo. Rev. Stat. Ann. § 19-2-107; Idaho Code § 20-509; 705 Ill. Comp. Stat. Ann. 405/5-101; Kan. Stat. Ann. § 38-1656; R.I. Gen. Laws § 14-1-47; S.D. Codified Laws § 26-7A-34; S.D. Codified Laws § 15-6-38(a); Va. Code Ann. § 16.1-272 (providing a conditional right to a jury in juvenile adjudications in the respective states).

[38] Barry C. Feld, "The Constitutional Tension Between Apprendi and McKeiver: Sentence Enhancements Based on Delinquency Convictions and the Quality of Justice in Juvenile Courts," 38 *Wake Forest L. Rev.* 1111, 1156-57 (2003).

[39] 403 U.S. at 547.

[40] *Id.* at 1147.

[41] For example, the Armed Career Criminal Act (ACCA) requires imposition of a minimum 15-year term of imprisonment for unlawful possession of a firearm in violation of 18 U.S.C. § 922(g) by an individual with three prior serious drug or violent felony convictions. Congress defined the term "conviction" to include "a finding that a person has committed an act of juvenile delinquency involving a violent felony." 18 U.S.C. § 924(e)(2)(C).

[42] 391 U.S. 145 (1968).

[43] 399 U.S. 78 (1970)(holding that the constitutional guarantee of a jury trial does not require that jury membership be fixed at 12).

[44] 399 U.S. at 100 (stating that "providing an accused with the right to be tried by a jury of his peers gave him an inestimable safeguard against the corrupt or overzealous prosecutor and against the compliant, biased or eccentric judge").

[45] 435 U.S. 223, 232-39 (1978) (stating that "when individual and group decisionmaking were compared [in social scientific studies], it was seen that groups performed better because prejudices of individuals were frequently counterbalanced, and objectivity resulted. Groups ... exhibited ... self-criticism.... Because juries frequently face complex problems laden with value choices, the[se] benefits are important.... In particular, the counterbalancing of various biases is critical to the accurate application of the common sense of the community to the facts of any given case").

[46] See *Jones v. United States*, 526 U.S. 227 (1999)(holding that under the Sixth Amendment's jury trial guarantee, any fact [other than a prior conviction] that increases the maximum penalty for a crime must be charged in an indictment, submitted to a jury, and proven beyond a reasonable doubt); *Apprendi v. New Jersey*, 520 U.S. 466 (2000); *Ring v. Arizona*, 536 U.S. 584 (2002)(holding that an aggravating circumstance that makes a defendant eligible for a death sentence is the functional equivalent of an element of an offense for purposes of the Sixth Amendment right to jury trial and therefore must be found by a jury); *Blakely v. Washington*, 542 U.S. 296 (2004)(finding that the "statutory maximum" for *Apprendi* purposes is the maximum sentence a judge may impose solely on the basis of facts reflected in the jury verdict or admitted by the defendant); *United States v. Booker*, 543 U.S. 220 (2005)(finding that the mandatory nature of the Federal Sentencing Guidelines violates the Sixth Amendment right to jury trial).

[47] 403 U.S. at 543 (finding that a defendant may be treated as fairly by a judge alone as he or she would be by a jury).

[48] 18 U.S.C. § 924(e) requires the imposition of a minimum 15-year term of imprisonment for unlawful possession of a firearm in violation of 18 U.S.C. § 922(g) by an individual with three prior serious drug or violent felony convictions.

[49] 18 U.S.C. § 924(e)(2)(C)(defining the term "conviction" to include prior juvenile adjudications involving a violent felony).

[50] *Id.*; *State v. Chatman*, 2005 WL 901138 (Tenn. Crim. App. 2005) (Apr. 19, 2005); *Pinkston v. State*, 836 Ne 2d 453 (2005); *United States v. Jones*, 332 F.3d 688 (3d Cir. 2003), *cert. denied*, 540 U.S. 1150 (2004); *United States v. Smalley*, 294 F.3d 1030 (8th Cir. 2002), *cert. denied*, 537 U.S. 1114 (2003); *State v. Hitt*, 42 P.3d 732 (Kan. 2002), *cert. denied*, 537 U.S. 1104 (2003). For a discussion of the constitutionality using non-jury juvenile adjudications in subsequent criminal proceedings for sentence enhancement, refer to CRS Report RS22610, *Armed Career Criminal Act (ACCA): Using Prior Juvenile Adjudications for Sentence Enhancements*, by Alison M. Smith.

In: Law and Law Enforcement Issues
Editor: Gerald M. Kessler, pp. 387-392

ISBN: 978-1-60456-044-2

Chapter 13

ARMED CAREER CRIMINAL ACT (ACCA): USING PRIOR JUVENILE ADJUDICATIONS FOR SENTENCE ENHANCEMENTS*

Alison M. Smith

ABSTRACT

With recent U.S. Supreme Court decisions regarding the role of judges and juries in making factual determinations upon which sentences are made, there has been increased congressional interest in federal sentencing. One aspect of federal sentencing includes recidivism statutes that provide longer sentences for repeat offenders. One such statute, the Armed Career Criminal Act (ACCA), requires imposition of a 15-year prison sentence for an individual with prior serious drug or violent felony convictions. Under the ACCA, non-jury juvenile adjudications qualify as prior convictions. The use of these non-jury juvenile adjudications raises several constitutional due process questions and continues to spark debate among courts at the federal and state levels. Opinions vary, in part, because of conflicting interpretations of the U.S. Supreme Court's jury trial jurisprudence stressing the constitutional requirement of juries, rather than judges, making factual determinations upon which sentences are based. This article summarizes the competing views on the constitutionality of the use of non-jury juvenile adjudications in subsequent criminal proceedings.

The Armed Career Criminal Act (ACCA) requires imposition of a minimum 15-year term of imprisonment for unlawful possession of a firearm in violation of 18 U.S.C. § 922(g) by an individual with three prior serious drug or violent felony convictions.[1] The ACCA defines "conviction" to include "a finding that a person has committed an act of juvenile delinquency involving a violent felony."[2] Defendants have begun to challenge, with mixed results, the courts' ability to use non-jury juvenile adjudications as a prior conviction under the ACCA. Opinions vary, in part, because of conflicting interpretations of the U.S. Supreme Court's recent jury trial jurisprudence, as well as the the nature of juvenile court proceedings.

In a series of cases, the U.S. Supreme Court has held that given the Sixth Amendment right to trial by jury, judges cannot impose sentences beyond the prescribed

* Excerpted from CRS Report RS22610, dated February 22, 2007.

statutory maximum unless the facts supporting such an increase are found by a jury beyond a reasonable doubt.[3] In *Jones v. United States*,[4] the Court struck down the federal carjacking statute that enhanced the maximum prison sentence that Nathaniel Jones could receive depending upon the amount of bodily injury that accompanied the carjacking. In *Jones*, it was the sentencing judge, not a jury, who found the victims incurred serious bodily injury and imposed a prison sentence of 25 years. The *Jones* majority held that

> under the Due Process Clause of the Fifth Amendment and the notice and jury trial guarantees of the Sixth Amendment, any fact (other than a prior conviction) that increases the maximum penalty for a crime must be charged in an indictment, submitted to a jury, and proven beyond a reasonable doubt.[5]

Apprendi v. New Jersey (*Apprendi*)[6] reaffirmed *Jones* by holding that "other than the fact of a prior conviction, any fact that increases the penalty for a crime beyond the prescribed statutory maximum must be submitted to a jury, and proved beyond a reasonable doubt."[7] In *Apprendi*, the Court struck down New Jersey's hate crime law, which allowed a judge to increase a sentence to double the statutory maximum if he or she found, by a preponderance of the evidence, that the defendant acted with a purpose to intimidate an individual or group of individuals because of race. In reversing the lower court's decision, the Court declared that the jury trial and notification clauses of the Sixth Amendment and the due process clauses of the Fifth and Fourteenth Amendments embody a principle that insists that, except in the case of recidivists, a judge could not on his own findings sentence a criminal defendant to a term of imprisonment greater than the statutory maximum assigned for which he had been convicted by the jury. The *Apprendi* Court specifically held that its "prior conviction" exception was a narrow one.[8]

PRIOR CONVICTION EXCEPTION UNDER *ALMENDAREZ-TORRES*

The narrow "prior conviction" exception from the general rule that all facts going to punishment must be found by a jury is based on assumptions regarding the reliability and fairness of the procedures available to the defendant at the time his or her prior convictions were entered.[9] The U.S. Supreme Court first addressed sentence enhancement based upon recidivism as a jury trial issue in *Almendarez-Torres v. United States*,[10] where, in a 5-4 decision, it held that a judge, rather than a jury, may decide the fact of a defendant's prior conviction for purposes of determining whether a sentence should be imposed in excess of the statutory maximum.[11] The Court set forth three principal reasons for reaching its conclusion. First, recidivism has been a traditional basis for a sentencing court's increase in an offender's sentence.[12] Second, recidivism should be treated differently from other sentencing enhancement factors because "the introduction of evidence of a defendant's prior crimes risks significant prejudice."[13] Third, although a factor may trigger an increase in the maximum permissive sentence, as opposed to an increase in the mandatory minimum sentence as seen in *McMillan v. Pennsylvania*,[14] that factor should not automatically require a greater burden of proof, as it "does not systematically, or normally, work to the disadvantage of a criminal defendant."[15] As such, the Court held that the factor of recidivism need not be included in the indictment, nor proved beyond a reasonable doubt, even if that factor increases the criminal sentence beyond the prescribed statutory maximum.[16]

There is doubt concerning the continued viability of *Almendarez-Torres*. The four *Almendarez-Torres* dissenters and Justice Thomas have all expressed belief that *Almendarez-Torres* was decided in error. Justice Thomas, the only member of the *Almendarez-Torres* majority to join the *Apprendi* majority, renounced his vote with the majority in *Almendarez-Torres* and declared that the decision was in error.[17] Moreover, the Court's decision in *Shepard v. United States[18]* appears to further question the continued viability of *Almendarez-Torres*. In *Shepard*, the Court addressed whether a sentencing court, acting pursuant to the ACCA, can examine police reports or complaints to determine whether a prior guilty plea to burglary counts as a prior conviction of a "violent felony."[19] In reading the "prior conviction" exception narrowly, the Court concluded that the judicial inquiry under the ACCA, as to whether a guilty plea to burglary is a "violent felony," "is limited to the terms of the charging document, the terms of a plea agreement or transcript of colloquy between judge and defendant in which the factual basis for the plea was confirmed by the defendant, or some comparable judicial record of this information."[20] It would appear that requiring that recidivism in the *Shepard* context be proved beyond a reasonable doubt calls into question the distinction between "traditional sentencing factors"such as recidivism and "elements of the offense." However, it should be noted that *Shepard* was decided on statutory grounds, invoking the doctrine of avoiding constitutional doubt.

Two Interpretations of the Prior Conviction Exception as Applied to Prior Juvenile Adjudications

The scope of the "prior conviction" exception and its applicability to prior juvenile adjudications have been the focus of debate. Following the *Almendarez-Torres* and *Apprendi* decisions, two conflicting views have arisen as to whether a juvenile adjudication constitutes a "prior conviction" for the purpose of enhancing an adult's sentence. The legal issue with using juvenile adjudications as sentence enhancers is not the constitutional validity of the adjudication itself, but instead the constitutional validity of the adjudication's subsequent use in an adult criminal court. Historically, prior juvenile criminality was not used as a sentencing factor because records of juvenile adjudications were confidential and often expunged.[21] The Ninth Circuit was the first to publish an opinion on the matter in *United States v. Tighe*.[22] The defendant pled guilty to bank robbery, being a felon in possession of a firearm, and interstate transportation of a stolen vehicle. The government argued that the defendant's sentence could be enhanced because of a prior adjudication as a juvenile of reckless endangerment, first-degree robbery, and unauthorized use of a motor vehicle.[23] However, the Court found that the juvenile adjudication could not be used for enhancement purposes pursuant to the ACCA because his juvenile adjudication was not tried by a jury trial, thus evidencing "significant constitutional differences between adult convictions and juvenile adjudications."[24] The Court held that "the 'prior conviction' exception to *Apprendi's* general rule must be limited to prior convictions that were themselves obtained through proceedings that included the right to a jury trial and proof beyond a reasonable doubt."[25]

In *United States v. Smalley*,[26] the Eighth Circuit rejected the Ninth Circuit's reasoning in *Tighe*. The court, in employing a broader interpretation than the Ninth Circuit, found that the question of whether juvenile adjudications should be exempt from *Apprendi's* general rule should not turn on the narrow parsing of words, but on an examination of whether juvenile adjudications, like adult convictions, are so reliable that due process of law is not offended by such an exemption.[27] The court reasoned that as juvenile courts apply a "beyond a reasonable doubt" standard, the juvenile bench trial was procedurally adequate to constitute a "prior conviction."[28]

States have also adopted different approaches for allowing the use of juvenile adjudications as sentence enhancers. One approach used by some states (e.g., Indiana and Kansas) allows courts to consider a prior juvenile adjudication as part of a defendant's criminal history.[29] The majority of states that have addressed the constitutionality of such provisions have found that as long as juveniles receive all the process they are constitutionally due in the juvenile system, an adult court can treat a juvenile adjudication as a sentence enhancer.[30]

However, in *State v. Brown*,[31] the Louisiana Supreme Court adopted the minority view and held that courts cannot use a juvenile adjudication to enhance a sentence.[32] The defendant pleaded guilty to one count of robbery, and a jury found him guilty under a separate count of armed robbery. After his conviction, the state charged the defender under its habitual offender law and enhanced his sentence based on a prior juvenile adjudication.[33] He challenged the sentence and argued that the trial court's use of his juvenile adjudication for sentence enhancement violated *Apprendi*. The Louisiana Supreme Court distinguished civil adjudications from criminal convictions, noting that juvenile courts afford juveniles less due process, which results in a proceeding that is more civil in nature than criminal.[34] The court decided that although juvenile adjudications are sufficiently reliable for use in the juvenile court system, the absence of the right to a jury trial makes juvenile adjudications too unreliable for use as an adult sentence enhancer.[35]

The future of the "prior conviction" exception and its applicability to juvenile adjudications remain unclear, as the U.S. Supreme Court has denied petitions for writ of certiorari in the cases that have adopted the majority view and in cases that have adopted the minority view.[36]

References

[1] 18 U.S.C. § 924(e).

[2] 18. U.S.C. § 924(e)(2)(C).

[3] See *Jones v. United States,* 526 U.S. 227 (1999); *Apprendi v. New Jersey,* 520 U.S. 466 (2000); *Ring v. Arizona*, 536 U.S. 584 (2002)(holding that an aggravating circumstance that makes a defendant eligible for a death sentence is the functional equivalent of an element of an offense for purposes of the Sixth Amendment right to jury trial and therefore must be found by a jury); *Blakely v. Washington*, 542 U.S. 296 (2004)(finding that the "statutory maximum" for *Apprendi* purposes is the maximum sentence a judge may impose solely on the basis of facts reflected in the jury verdict or admitted by the defendant); *United States v. Booker*, 543 U.S. 220 (2005)(finding that the mandatory nature of the Federal Sentencing Guidelines violates the Sixth Amendment right to jury).

[4] 526 U.S. 227 (1999).

[5] *Id.* at 243.

[6] 520 U.S. 466 (2000).

[7] *Id.* at 490.

[8] Id.

[9] For example, the defendant received a jury trial or validly waived this right and facts upon which the sentence was based were found beyond reasonable doubt. *See Jones* at 249 (explaining that using the fact of a prior conviction to enhance a sentence is constitutionally distinct from the use of other facts and does not raise the same due process and Sixth Amendment concerns because "a prior conviction must itself have been established through procedures satisfying the fair notice, reasonable doubt, and jury trial guarantees.").

[10] 523 U.S. 224 (1998). In this case, the Court considered a federal statute authorizing a two-year prison term for deportees who returned to the U.S. without permission, but authorizing a prison term of up to 20 years for aliens whose deportation was subsequent to a felony conviction. The question before the Court was whether the statute defined two separate crimes, in which case the prior conviction must be mentioned in the indictment, or simply authorized an enhanced penalty, in which case the prior conviction is not an element that must be charged.

[11] *Id.* at 225-27.

[12] *Id.* at 231.

[13] *Id.* at 235.

[14] 477 U.S. 79 (1986)(upholding Pennsylvania's Mandatory Minimum Sentencing Act, which prescribed a mandatory minimum sentence of five years upon a judge's finding by a preponderance of the evidence that the defendant "visibly possessed a firearm" during the commission of certain enumerated offenses).

[15] *Almendarez-Torres*, 523 U.S. at 244.

[16] *Id.* at 227.

[17] In his concurrence in *Apprendi*, (Id. at 520-21) Justice Thomas wrote: [O]ne of the chief errors of Almendarez-Torres — an error to which I succumbed — was to attempt to discern whether a particular fact is traditionally (or typically) a basis for a sentencing court to increase an offender's sentence. For the reasons I have given, it should be clear that this approach just defines away the real issue. What matters is the way by which a fact enters into the sentence. If a fact is by law the basis for imposing or increasing punishment — for establishing or increasing the prosecution's entitlement — it is an element. (To put the point differently, I am aware of no historical basis for treating as a nonelement a fact that by law sets or increases punishment.) When one considers the question from this perspective, it is evident why the fact of a prior conviction is an element under a recidivism statute. Indeed, cases addressing such statutes provide some of the best discussions of what constitutes an element of a crime. One reason frequently offered for treating recidivism differently, a reason on which we relied in Almendarez-Torres is a concern for prejudicing the jury by informing it of the prior conviction. But this concern, of which earlier courts were well aware, does not make the traditional understanding of what an element is any less applicable to the fact of a prior conviction.

[18] 544 U.S. 13 (2005).

[19] *Id.* The ACCA mandates a 15-year minimum sentence for any person found to have committed certain federal firearms violations if that person has three prior convictions

for "violent felonies." The term "violent felony" includes "burglary," and the Court in *Taylor v. United States* (495 U.S. 575, 598-99 (1990)) held that the ACCA's use of the term "burglary" encompasses only "generic burglary."

[20] *Id.* at 1263.

[21] David S. Tanenhaus, The Evolution of Juvenile Courts in the Early Twentieth Century: Beyond the Myth of Immaculate Construction, in A Century of Juvenile Justice 42, 69-70 (Margaret K. Rosenhem et al., Eds., 2002).

[22] 266 F.3d 1187 (2001).

[23] *Id.* at 1190.

[24] *Id.* at 1192-93.

[25] *Id.* at 1194.

[26] 294 F.3d 1030 (2002).

[27] *Id.* at 1032-1033.

[28] The Third and Eleventh Circuits have heard factually similar cases involving a criminal defendant's sentence enhancement under the ACCA and followed the same rationale as the Eighth Circuit. *United States v. Jones*, 332 F.3d 688 (3d Cir. 2003), *cert. denied*, 540 U.S. 1150 (2004); *United States v. Burge*, 407 F.3d 1183 (11th Cir. 2005). A similar split exists with respect to the use of prior delinquency adjudications for the purpose of a defendant's sentencing guideline criminal history score. Compare, *United States v. Washington*, 462 F/3d 1124 (9th Cir. 2006), with *United States v. Williams*, 410 F.3d 397 (7th Cir. 2007); *United States v. McKoy*, 452 F.3d 234 (3rd Cir. 2006).

[29] See Joseph B. Sanborn, Jr., Striking Out on the First Pitch in Criminal Court, 1 Barry L. Rev. 7, 17 (2000).

[30] *See, e.g., People v. Bowden*, 125 Cal. Rptr. 2d 513, 518 (Cal. Ct. App. 2002); *Ryle v. State*, 819 N.E.2d 119, 123 (Ind. Ct. App. 2004); *State v. Hitt*, 42 P.3d 732, 740 (Kan. 2002), *cert. denied*, 537 U.S. 1104 (2003).

[31] 879 So. 2d 1276 (La. 2004), *cert. denied*, 543 U.S. 826 (2005).

[32] *Id.* at 1280.

[33] *Id.* Louisiana's habitual offender law provides that any person who has previously been convicted of a felony or adjudicated as a juvenile of a serious drug or violent offense will receive an enhanced sentence if convicted of a second felony. *Id.* at 1279.

[34] *Id.* at 1289.

[35] *Id.* at 1290.

[36] *United States v. Jones*, 332 F.3d 688 (3d Cir. 2003), *cert. denied*, 540 U.S. 1150 (2004); *United States v. Smalley*, 294 F.3d 1030 (8th Cir. 2002), *cert. denied*, 537 U.S. 1114 (2003); *State v. Hitt*, 42 P.3d 732 (Kan. 2002), *cert. denied*, 537 U.S. 1104 (2003); *State v. Brown*, 879 So.2d 276 (La. 2004), *cert. denied*, 534 U.S. 826 (2005).

INDEX

#

A

B

C

E

F

G

H

I

J

K

L

M

Q

R

S

T

U

V

W

Y

Z